Second Edition

Social Problems in a Diverse Society

Diana Kendall

BAYLOR UNIVERSITY

ALLYN AND BACON
Boston   London   Toronto   Sydney   Tokyo   Singapore

SERIES EDITOR: Sarah L. Kelbaugh
EDITOR IN CHIEF, SOCIAL SCIENCES: Karen Hanson
EDITORIAL ASSISTANT: Lori Flickinger
MARKETING MANAGER: Jude Hall
EDITORIAL-PRODUCTION ADMINISTRATOR: Annette Joseph
EDITORIAL-PRODUCTION SERVICE: Karen Mason
TEXT DESIGNER/ELECTRONIC COMPOSITION: Karen Mason
COMPOSITION BUYER: Linda Cox
MANUFACTURING BUYER: Megan Cochran
COVER ADMINISTRATOR: Linda Knowles
COVER DESIGNER: Susan Paradise

Between the time website information is gathered and then published, it is not unusual for some sites to have closed. Also, the transcription of URLs can result in unintended typographical errors. The publisher would appreciate being notified of any problems so that they may be corrected in subsequent editions. Thank you.

LIBRARY OF CONGRESS CATALOGING-IN-PUBLICATION DATA
Kendall, Diana Elizabeth.
    Social problems in a diverse society / by Diana Kendall.--2nd ed.
       p.   cm.
    Includes bibliographical references and index.
    ISBN 0–205–32520-3
       1. Social problems.   I. Title.

    HN17.5 .K457   2000
    361.1--dc21
                                                                  00-030581

Printed in the United States of America
10 9 8 7 6 5 4 3 2 1   QWV   05 04 03 02 01 00

PHOTO CREDITS
appear on page 461, which constitutes a continuation of the copyright page.

Contents

Chapter Four
GENDER INEQUALITY   62

Chapter Five
INEQUALITY BASED ON AGE   84

Chapter Six
INEQUALITY BASED ON SEXUAL
ORIENTATION   106

PREFACE

[A social problems course] can provide a mind-opening . . . overview of a field of study, providing a method of perceiving and understanding the social realities we construct, playing a central role in leading students through the cognitive developmental processes that turn unchallenged dualism and other oversimplifications about everyday life into the complex formulations that better represent the social world in which we live.

—*Sociologists Michael Brooks and Kendal Broad describe the social problems course in the* Instructor's Resource Manual on Social Problems *(Brooks and Broad, 1997:1)*

This statement sums up the main reasons why I wrote *Social Problems in a Diverse Society*. Learning about social problems can be a highly rewarding experience. Although we live in difficult and challenging times, the social problems course provides an excellent avenue for developing patterns of critical thinking and for learning how to use sociological concepts and perspectives to analyze specific social concerns ranging from drug addiction and violence to inequalities of race, class, and gender.

My first and foremost goal in writing this book is to make the study of social problems *interesting* and *relevant* for students. To stimulate interest in reading the chapters and participating in class discussions, I have used lived experiences (personal narratives of *real* people) and statements from a wide variety of analysts to show how social problems impinge on people at the individual, group, and societal levels. Moreover, I have applied sociological imagination and relevant sociological concepts and perspectives to all the topics in a systematic manner.

This second edition of *Social Problems in a Diverse Society* continues to focus on the significance of race, class, and gender in understanding social problems in the United States and around the globe. Throughout the text, people—especially people of color and white women—are shown not merely as "victims" of social problems but as individuals who resist discrimination and inequality and seek to bring

about change in families, schools, workplaces, and the larger society. To facilitate the inclusion of previously excluded perspectives, Chapters 2 through 6 examine wealth and poverty, racial and ethnic inequality, gender inequality, and inequalities based on age and sexual orientation. Thereafter, concepts and perspectives related to race, class, and gender are intertwined in the discussion of specific social problems such as education, health care, and the media.

This new edition is balanced in its approach to examining social problems. However, it includes a more comprehensive view of feminist and postmodern perspectives on a vast array of subjects—such as the effect of new technologies and how the media depict social issues—than other social problems textbooks. As a sociologist who specializes in social theory, I was disheartened by the minimal use of sociological theory in most social problems texts. Those that discuss theory typically do so in early chapters but then fail to use these theories as a systematic framework for examining specific social issues in subsequent chapters. Similarly, many texts give the impression that social problems can be solved if people reach a consensus on what should be done, but *Social Problems in a Diverse Society* (Second Edition) emphasizes that how people view a social problem is related to how they believe the problem should be reduced or solved. Consider poverty, for example: People who focus on individual causes of poverty typically believe that individual solutions (such as teaching people the work ethic and reforming welfare) are necessary to reduce the problem, whereas those who focus on structural causes of poverty (such as chronic unemployment and inadequate educational opportunities) typically believe that solutions must come from the larger society. Moreover, what some people see as a *problem*, others see as a *solution* for a problem (e.g., the sex industry as a source of income, or abortion to terminate a problematic pregnancy). A new chapter (Chapter 18) has been added to this edition so that students can more fully explore the question, "Can Social Problems Be Solved?"

Finally, I wrote *Social Problems in a Diverse Society* (Second Edition) in hopes of providing students and instructors with a text that covers all the major social concerns of our day but does not leave them believing that the text—and perhaps the course—was a "depressing litany of social problems that nobody can do anything about anyway," as one of my students stated about a different text. I have written this book in hopes of resolving that student's concern (which no doubt is shared by many other students) because I believe the sociological perspective has much to add to our national and global dialogues on a host of issues such as environmental degradation; domestic and international terrorism; discrimination based on race, class, gender, age, sexual orientation, or other attributes; and problems in education. Welcome to an innovative examination of social problems—one of the most stimulating and engrossing fields of study in sociology!

ORGANIZATION OF THIS TEXT

Social Problems in a Diverse Society (Second Edition) has been organized with the specific plan of introducing disparities in wealth and poverty, race and ethnicity, gender, age, and sexual orientation early on, so that the concepts and perspectives developed in these chapters may be applied throughout the text. Chapter 1 explains the *sociological perspective* and highlights the issue of violence to draw students into an examination of such debates as whether "guns kill people" or "people kill people."

Chapter 2 looks at *wealth and poverty* in the United States and around the world. Students will gain new insights on how some people become wealthy and on problems such as homelessness, low-income and poverty-level neighborhoods, and the relationship between teen pregnancies and school dropout rates. The chapter concludes with a thematic question, "Can class-based inequality be reduced?" This question will be asked throughout the text as new topics are discussed. Chapter 3 integrates the previous discussion of class-based inequalities with an examination of *racial and ethnic inequality*. The chapter ends on the optimistic note that perhaps racial and ethnic relations in the future will be better than they have been in the past as the children of today become the leaders of tomorrow. Chapter 4, *gender inequality*, highlights factors such as mainstream gender socialization and social barriers that contribute to the unequal treatment of women in the workplace and family and at school and other social institutions. Ageism and *inequality based on age* are discussed in Chapter 5, and *inequality based on sexual orientation* is examined in Chapter 6, placing these important topics in a context similar to the studies of prejudice and discrimination rooted in racism and sexism in contemporary societies.

Chapter 7 links previous discussions of race, class, and gender to an analysis of *prostitution, pornography, and the sex industry*. The chapter provides up-to-date information on the globalization of prostitution and gives students insights on how sex workers view themselves, why they engage in this line of work, and why some other people view sex workers as a social problem. In Chapter 8, *alcohol and other drugs* are discussed in depth, and students are provided with information about the so-called date rape drug and the abuse of prescription drugs, over-the-counter drugs, and caffeine. Chapter 9 discusses *crime and criminal justice* and takes an incisive look at sociological explanations of crime.

Beginning with Chapter 10, a look at *health care and its problems*, we examine some of the major social institutions in our society and note aspects of each that constitute a social problem for large numbers of people. Chapter 11 explores *the changing family*, emphasizing diversity in intimate relationships and families and child-related family issues. Chapter 12 presents contemporary *problems in education*, tracing the problems to such issues as what schools are supposed to accomplish, how they are financed, and why higher education is not widely accessible. Chapter 13 focuses on *problems in politics and the global economy* and provides a variety of perspectives on political power and the role of the military-industrial complex in U.S. politics and the economy. Chapter 14, a discussion of *problems in the media,* looks at how the recent concentration in the media industries affects the news and entertainment that people receive. Chapter 15 provides a survey of problems associated with *population and the environmental crisis*, particularly focusing on the causes and consequences of overpopulation and high rates of global migration. Chapter 16, a look at *urban problems*, details the powerful impact of urbanization on both high-income and low-income nations of the world. Chapter 17 discusses *global social problems related to war and terrorism*. After examining such topics as militarism, military technology and war, and domestic and international terrorism, the text concludes on a hopeful note, that large-scale war and terrorism can be averted in the twenty-first century. Chapter 18 asks *"Can social problems be solved?"* and includes a review of the sociological theories used to explain social problems, plus an analysis of attempts at problem solving at the microlevel, mid-range, and macrolevel of society.

NEW TO THIS EDITION

▲ *Chapter One:* The focus of this chapter has been changed so that students may see how sociological theories and research methods can be used to study such pressing social issues as violence in schools. For this edition the Social Problems and Social Policy feature asks, "Do Guns Kill People or Do People Kill People?" and a new boxed feature, Social Problems and Information Technology, examines violence in television programming. A new table, "Changing Perceptions of What Constitutes a Social Problem, 1950–1999," is included.

▲ *Chapter Two:* This chapter contains new statistics on wealth, poverty, and growing income inequality in the United States and other nations. It also shows the relationships among factors such as age, gender, racial and ethnic group, and poverty. The Social Problems and Social Policy

box looks at a new topic, "The End of Welfare as We Know It?"

▲ *Chapter Three:* This revised chapter provides recent information on racial and ethnic inequality and includes an updated discussion of the lack of representation of Latinas/os in television programming. A new Social Problems and Social Policy box, "Social Justice: Beyond Black and White," makes students aware of the experiences of Asian and Pacific Americans.

▲ *Chapter Four:* This chapter is also updated with the latest available information on how gender is linked to inequality in the United States and other nations. The experience of Frances K. Conley, M.D., opens the chapter and highlights problems with sexism.

▲ *Chapter Five:* This discussion of age-based inequality features updated statistics as well as a new Social Problems in the Media box that examines media ageism and reporting on teenagers.

▲ *Chapter Six:* This pathbreaking chapter on inequality based on sexual orientation opens with the thoughts of Dennis Shepard, the father of Matthew Shepard, a college student who was brutally murdered because of his sexual orientation. A new Social Problems in the Media box discusses depictions of gay men and lesbians in television programming and asks how realistic these depictions are.

▲ *Chapter Seven:* In this chapter on prostitution, pornography, and the sex industry, a new boxed feature, Social Problems and Information Technology, examines the Internet and child pornography.

▲ *Chapter Eight:* This chapter contains updated information on alcohol and other drugs and discusses recent efforts by members of Mothers Against Drunk Driving to control alcohol-related traffic deaths.

▲ *Chapter Nine:* This chapter has been combined with the former chapter on violence to provide a more thorough analysis of all forms of crime. An updated crime clock and crime statistics provide students with insights on the current crime problem in the United States and some other nations.

▲ *Chapter Ten:* New data on illness and health care delivery are offered in this chapter, which continues to emphasize the relationship between physical and mental illness and examines how medical services are paid for in our society and others.

▲ *Chapter Eleven:* All the information on today's changing family has been updated, including the map showing births to teenage mothers.

▲ *Chapter Twelve:* This discussion of problems in education contains recent information on the percentage of persons not completing high school by race and "Hispanic origin," which indicates that some progress is being made in years of educational attainment, although a vast gap still remains between the attainment of whites and that of African Americans and Hispanics.

▲ *Chapter Thirteen:* A new vignette on the recent Seattle, Washington, protests during the World Trade Organization meeting opens this chapter on politics and the global economy and shows the intertwining nature of politics and the global economy. Recent data on major campaign contributions to political candidates allow readers to realize that only a small percentage of the U.S. population contributes extraordinarily large amounts to get their candidates elected.

▲ *Chapter Fourteen:* This all-new, cutting-edge chapter on the media gives students the latest information on media concentration and how it affects people worldwide. The chapter analyzes the way in which the media perpetuate stereotypes of race, ethnicity, and gender. It also examines aggression and violence against women in advertisements that appear on television and in print. A new Social Problems in the Media box discusses the virtual media versus the mainstream press, and a new Social Problems in Global Perspective box describes perceived cultural biases in U.S. media coverage of Africa.

▲ *Chapter Fifteen:* This chapter offers a revised box on Social Problems in Global Perspective, examining the challenges and opportunities presented by worldwide migration. An updated Social Problems and Social Policy box, "What to Do with Waste? NIMBY (Not in My Back Yard!)," discusses how New York City has dealt with its garbage problem.

▲ *Chapter Sixteen:* This chapter provides recent information on urban problems and an updated discussion of urban empowerment zones.

▲ *Chapter Seventeen:* This chapter's box, Social Problems in the Media, offers an expanded discussion of the U.S. media's focus on four forms of terrorism.

▲ *Chapter Eighteen:* "Can Social Problems Be Solved?" is a new chapter that provides students with a review of major social theories on social problems, discusses the role of social change in reducing social problems, and analyzes microlevel, mid-range, and macrolevel attempts to solve social problems. It offers many examples of how people attempt to reduce or alleviate social problems at each of these levels.

DISTINCTIVE FEATURES

A number of special features have been designed to incorporate race, class, and gender into our analysis of social problems and to provide students with new insights on the social problems that they hear about on the evening news. The following sections discuss the text's distinctive features.

▲ Lived Experiences throughout Each Chapter

These authentic, first-person accounts are used as vignettes—"real words from real people"—to create interest and show how the problems being discussed affect people as they go about their daily lives. Lived experiences provide opportunities for students to examine social life beyond their own experiences ("to live vicariously," as one student noted) and for instructors to systematically incorporate into lectures and class discussions examples of relevant, contemporary issues that have recently been on the evening news and in newspaper headlines. Some examples of lived experiences include:

▲ Lawrence Otis Graham, a Harvard-educated corporate lawyer and author, describes how much trouble he and many other middle- and upper-middle-class African Americans have catching taxis in cities like New York and working in corporate America. (Chapter 3, "Racial and Ethnic Inequality")

▲ Hazel Wolf, age ninety-five, of Seattle, Washington, discusses her trip to Decatur, Alabama, to visit with a group of elementary students who saw her picture in *USA Today* and wrote letters to her. (Chapter 5, "Inequality Based on Age")

▲ Nadia, a nineteen-year-old prostitute in New York City, explains how she went from being a minister's daughter to working in the sex industry. (Chapter 7, "Prostitution, Pornography, and the Sex Industry")

▲ Cesilee Hyde, age twenty-three, describes the night her car struck and killed a police officer directing traffic at an accident site and how she was subsequently charged with driving under the influence of alcohol. (Chapter 8, "Alcohol and Other Drugs")

▲ Ruben Navarette, Jr., a Harvard graduate, recalls the day when his second-grade teacher divided the class into ability groups and notes how he believes this process has a harmful effect on students, especially Latinos/as, African Americans, and Native Americans who attend racially integrated schools. (Chapter 12, "Problems in Education")

▲ Interesting and Highly Relevant Boxed Features

Four different boxes—Social Problems and Information Technology, Social Problems in the Media, Social Problems and Social Policy, and Social Problems in Global Perspective—highlight current hot topics involving various long-term social problems:

▲ *Social Problems and Information Technology:* "Cracking Down on Internet Child Pornography" (Chapter 7, "Prostitution, Pornography, and the Sex Industry")

▲ *Social Problems in the Media:* "Media Ageism and Reporting on Teenagers" (Chapter 5, "Inequality Based on Age")

▲ *Social Problems and Social Policy:* "The Battle over Marijuana: Medicalization or Legalization?" (Chapter 8, "Alcohol and Other Drugs")

▲ *Social Problems in Global Perspective:* "Challenges and Opportunities Presented by World-wide Migration" (Chapter 15, "Population and the Environmental Crisis")

Built-in Study Features

These pedagogical aids promote students' mastery of sociological concepts and perspectives:

▲ *Chapter Outlines.* A concise outline at the beginning of each chapter gives students an overview of major topics.

▲ *Key Terms.* Major concepts and key terms are defined and highlighted in bold print within the text. Definitions are provided the first time a concept is introduced; they are also available in the Glossary at the back of the text.

▲ *Summary in Question-and-Answer Format.* Each chapter concludes with a concise summary in a convenient question-and-answer format to help students master the key concepts and main ideas in each chapter.

SUPPLEMENTS

▲ *For the Instructor.* A variety of supplements are offered, including an Instructor's Manual and Test Bank, Practice Tests, Computerized Test Bank, and the Allyn and Bacon Interactive Video for Social Problems. Please contact your local Allyn and Bacon representative for more information on any of these items.

▲ *For the Student.* Because I believe a study guide is one of the most important study tools available for students, I prepared a comprehensive Study Guide for *Social Problems in a Diverse Society* (Second Edition). The guide provides the following for each chapter: a chapter summary, learning objectives, a detailed chapter outline, a glossary of key terms, and a practice test comprised of multiple-choice, true-false, matching, and fill-in-the-blank questions.

▲ In addition, a wealth of online resources are now available to adopters of this book, including a *Companion Website with Online Practice Tests* (http://www.abacon.com/kendall) and the *Allyn and Bacon Social Problems Website* (http://www.abacon.com/socprobs). The booklet *Social Problems on the Net* provides a guide to this website, in addition to hundreds of additional resources for studying social problems online.

ONLINE EDITION

An exciting alternative version of this text is also available. *Social Problems in a Diverse Society Online,* in black and white only and without photos, provides the chapters most frequently used in a social problems class. Six chapters have been moved out of the printed textbook and onto the web, making it less expensive and easier to transport, and exploding the chapter content into a full-color, online experience with hotlinks to relevant websites. A comprehensive, password-protected website (http://www.abacon.com/kendallonline) offers these six downloadable chapters, plus additional resources to support the entire book, including more of the popular "Lived Experiences" vignettes, an image gallery, numerous Weblinks, video clips, learning exercises, and more.

ACKNOWLEDGMENTS

I wish to thank personally the many people who have made this second edition a reality. First, I offer my profound thanks to the following reviewers who provided valuable comments and suggestions on how to make this text outstanding. Whenever possible, I have incorporated their suggestions into the text. The reviewers are:

First Edition:
Allan Bramson, Wayne County Community College
Scott Burcham, University of Memphis
Keith Crew, University of Northern Iowa
Mike Hoover, Western Missouri State College
Mary Riege Laner, Arizona State University
Patricia Larson, Cleveland State University
Kathleen Lowney, Valdosta State College
Edward Morse, Tulane University

Charles Norman, Indiana State University
James Payne, St. Edward's University
Anne R. Peterson, Columbus State Community College
Margaret Preble, Thomas Nelson Community College
Dale Spady, Northern Michigan University
John Stratton, University of Iowa

Second Edition:
Susan Cody, Brookdale Community College
William A. Cross, Illinois College
Jennifer A. John, Germanna Community College
James J. Norris, Indiana University, South Bend
Anne R. Peterson, Columbus State Community College

This second edition of *Social Problems in a Diverse Society* has involved the cooperative efforts of many people who have gone above and beyond the call of duty to make the book possible. I wish to thank Sarah Kelbaugh, Series Editor, for her efforts throughout the publishing process. Likewise, the production was supervised by Annette Joseph who made everything run smoothly. The copyediting of Patricia S. Carda is greatly appreciated, and I am extremely grateful to Karen Mason, production editor.

I could not have written this book without the assistance of my husband, Terrence Kendall, who has done so much outstanding advising, editing—and sometimes consoling—on this and other texts I have written that I have declared him to be not only a lawyer but also an "Honorary Sociologist."

To each of you reading this preface, I wish you the best in teaching or studying social problems and hope that you will share with me any comments or suggestions you have about *Social Problems in a Diverse Society* (Second Edition). The text was written with you in mind, and your suggestions (with appropriate attribution) will be included whenever possible in future editions. Let's hope that our enthusiasm for "taking a new look at social problems" will spread to others so that we together may seek to reduce or solve some of the pressing social problems we encounter during our lifetime.

Diana Kendall, Ph.D.

Social Problems
in a Diverse Society

Chapter One

Taking a New Look at Social Problems

I do not want to attend another memorial service. I do not want to put up another memorial plaque. [I want each of you to say to yourselves]: "I am an important member of the Columbine family. I value life. I will make wise choices each and every day of my life." Then I told them, "I want you to . . . look at the person next to you and visualize what it would be like if they weren't here on Monday morning. I want to see all your smiling faces here on Monday morning. [On Monday morning, after the students had a successful and safe prom], one of the students came up to me and said, "I think all our smiling faces are here."

—Principal Frank DeAngelis recalling what he told Columbine High School students in Littleton, Colorado, at a pep rally held four days before two students ambushed their classmates and teachers with gunfire and pipe bombs, taking thirteen lives before fatally shooting themselves
(Rimer, 1999:A1)

All we're doing is what our son asked us to do. Seventy-two hours before my son was slain down like he was some kind of animal . . . out of nowhere Isaiah asked us, "What would you do if someone gunned down all your children? Would you go get guns?" I said, "Is there a reason you ask that?" He said, "Dad, I was just asking a hypothetical." He got real testy. I said: "Son, no, we won't get guns, because we're not vengeful people. If anybody or anything will take one of my children down I will try to beat it down. I will try to strike it down, I'll speak against it the rest of my life."

— Michael Shoels, father of Isaiah, the popular African American youth killed in the Columbine High shootings, explaining why he is speaking out against school violence and has started a nonprofit foundation, called Let's Stomp Out Hate Before It's Too Late, in memory of his son
(Belkin, 1999:63)

Whether it takes place in the central city or in a suburban high school or Kosovo, Sudan, or Chechnya violence leaves shock and anguish behind. *Violence* **is the use of physical force to cause pain, injury, or death to another or damage to property.** Around the world, violence is a major social problem. On an almost daily basis, the Internet and global cable television news channels quickly spread word of the latest bombing, the latest massacre, the latest murder. In the United States today, gunfire is the second-leading cause of death among U.S. youths between the ages of ten and nineteen (U.S. Bureau of the Census, 1998). Only accidents take a higher toll on the lives of young people in this country. Indeed, this country has the highest homicide rate of any high-income nation, and the deaths are concentrated in a particular segment of the population. Statistics show that African American males living in central cities of the United States have less chance of reaching their fortieth birthday than do people in the low-income nations of the world.

In the wake of each new episode of violence, a renewed call for gun control goes out from advocates of restricted access to guns and other weaponry. However, a corresponding cry of alarm arises from the strong antigun control lobby and such organizations as the National Rifle Association (see Box 1.1, "Social Problems and Social Policy").

SOCIAL PROBLEMS
AND SOCIAL POLICY

BOX 1.1

Do Guns Kill People or Do People Kill People?

Not long after the shooting [at Columbine High School], I joined a new, bipartisan organization called SAFE Colorado; the acronym stands for Sane Alternatives to the Firearms Epidemic. Our goal is to obtain reasonable gun legislation. . . . [In July of 1999], a group of us from SAFE went to Washington, D.C., to lobby for gun legislation, including an end to unregulated sales at gun shows. We talked to the president and the vice president, but half of Colorado's congressional delegation turned a deaf ear to us. My lobbying experience has left me disappointed in politicians. They just don't get it—that 13 young people die every day in this country from gun violence. . . . This must stop, and it must stop now.

—*Devon Adams (1999:41), a Columbine High School student, describing how she and others tried to change social policy regarding guns in the aftermath of the 1999 school shooting that devastated many families in her community*

Like thousands of other concerned people, Devon Adams worries about gun-related violence in the United States and believes that it should be possible to bring about change through social policies that control access to guns.

What is social policy and how is it supposed to alleviate such problems as violence in society? Although social scientists may disagree over what an existing social policy *is* or *should be*, many use the term to refer to a written set of ideas and goals that are formally adopted by a relevant decision-making body, for example, a government bureaucracy, a state legislature, or the U.S. Congress. The written statement usually does not set forth the specific means by which a certain goal (for example, an end to gun-related violence) is to be achieved (Marshall, 1998).

According to the sociologist Joel Best (1999:143), we often think of social policy as a means of "declaring war" on a social problem. Social policy discussions on gun-related violence at the state and federal levels have focused on how to win the "war" on guns, and a *Newsweek* (1999b) article on the debate over firearms was titled "The Gun War Comes Home." However, as Best (1999:147) notes, "Warfare presumes that fighting the enemy is a common cause of the entire society; individuals should set aside their doubts and reservations and join in the larger struggle. . . . Declaring war, then, is a call for a united, committed campaign against a social problem."

In the case of gun-related violence, as Devon Adams has discovered, there is a profound lack of societal consensus on the causes of the problem and what should be done about it. Some favor regulation of the gun industry and gun ownership; others believe regulation will not curb random violence perpetrated by frustrated individuals.

Underlying the arguments for and against gun control are these words from the Second Amendment to the Constitution: "A well regulated Militia, being necessary to the security of a free State, the right of the people to keep and bear Arms, shall not be infringed."

Those in favor of legislation to regulate the gun industry and gun ownership argue that the Second Amendment does not guarantee an individual's right to own guns: The right "to keep and bear Arms" applies only to those citizens who do so as part of an official state militia (Lazare, 1999:57). Although most gun-control activists believe that legislation banning all guns will not be passed, they advocate such measures as: (1) requiring background checks on all gun sales and transfers of ownership; (2) enforcing existing federal gun laws; (3) banning assault weapons such as Uzis; (4) licensing all firearms owners and registering all guns (*Newsweek,* 1999a:25).

In contrast, the National Rifle Association (NRA) and others opposed to gun-control legislation argue that such measures violate the individual's constitutional right to own a gun and are an ineffective means of curbing random violence. They note that Hawaii, which has some of the nation's toughest gun laws, recently faced a violent shooting spree by a man who legally owned seventeen weapons (twelve handguns, three rifles, and two shotguns) (Purdum, 1999). Requiring gun owners to possess "smart" guns (guns that have devices that allow only "authorized users" to fire them) and trigger locks (which supposedly prevent children from firing them), they say,

does not prevent people who want to use guns from doing so (Sugarmann, 1999).

What solutions exist for the quandary over gun regulations? Can state legislatures or the U.S. Congress pass effective gun-control legislation that will *actually* reduce or eliminate these forms of violence? Some people believe that arming state militias is no longer an issue, and therefore we should revise the Constitution (Lazare, 1999); others believe that such a wide variety of factors contribute to so-called "shootings-of-the-week" (*Newsweek,* 1999b:23), including high rates of divorce, television and movies, video-games, the Internet, and music (see Box 1.2 on pages 16–17) that gun control may not be the solution.

Best notes that declaring war on a social problem such as gun-related violence is difficult for several reasons. First, social problems are not simple issues: most problems have multiple causes and a variety of possible resolutions. Second, it is difficult to determine what constitutes victory in such a war. Third, it takes a long time to see the outcome of social policies, and efforts to produce change may receive reduced funding or be eliminated before significant changes actually occur. Finally, it is impossible to rally everyone behind a single policy, and thus much time is spent in arguing over how to proceed, how much money to spend, and who or what is the real enemy (Best, 1999).

INTERNET ACTIVITY

Compare the perspectives of activists for and against gun control by analyzing the issues discussed on the following web resources. *Note:* Web addresses often change. Those given here were accurate at the time of publication.

HANDGUN CONTROL, INC.:
    http://www.handguncontrol.org
VIOLENCE POLICY CENTER: http://www.vpc.org
NATIONAL RIFLE ASSOCIATION:
    http://www.nra.org
CITIZENS COMMITTEE FOR THE RIGHT TO KEEP AND BEAR ARMS: http://www.ccrkba.org

Even those of us who do not support the National Rifle Association are rather ambivalent about violence. Although we condemn drive-by shootings and cold-blooded murders, we like to see a good action movie with lots of "blood and guts" or watch contact sports such as football, hockey, and boxing. However we explain this contradictory behavior, violence is a major social problem in this country and around the world.

WHAT IS A SOCIAL PROBLEM?

Although not all sociologists agree on what constitutes a social problem, probably they would all agree with this general definition: A *social problem* is a **social condition (such as poverty) or a pattern of behavior (such as substance abuse) that people believe warrants public concern and collective action to bring about change.** Social conditions or certain patterns of behavior are defined as social problems when they systematically disadvantage or harm a significant number of people or when they are seen as harmful by many of the people who wield power, wealth, and influence in a group or society. To put it another way, social problems are social in their causes, consequences, and sources of possible resolution.

The study of social problems is one area of inquiry within *sociology*—**the academic and scholarly discipline that engages in systematic study of human society and social interactions.** A sociological examination of social problems focuses primarily on issues that affect an entire *society*—**a large number of individuals who share the same geographical territory and are subject to the same political authority and dominant cultural expectations**—and the groups and organizations that make up that society. Because social problems are social in their causes, public perception of what constitutes a social problem can change. Consider, for example, how public perception of what constitutes a social problem has changed over the last fifty years (see Table 1.1).

Sociologists apply theoretical perspectives and use a variety of research methods to examine social problems. Some social problems—such as violence and crime—are commonly viewed as conditions that affect all members of a population. Other social

TABLE 1.1   CHANGING PERCEPTIONS OF WHAT CONSTITUTES A SOCIAL PROBLEM, 1950–1999

Nationwide Gallup polls taken over the last half century reflect dramatic changes in how people view social problems. Notice how responses to the question "What do you think is the most important problem facing the country today?" have changed over the years.

1950		1965		1975	
War	40%	Civil rights	52%	High cost of living	60%
The economy	15%	Vietnam War	22%	Unemployment	20%
Unemployment	10%	Other international		Dissatisfaction with	
Communism	8%	problems	14%	government	7%
		Racial strife	13%	Energy crisis	7%

1990		1999	
Budget deficit	21%	Decline in morality	
Drug abuse	18%	and family values	18%
Poverty, homelessness	7%	Crime, violence	17%
The economy	7%	Education	11%
		Guns, gun control	10%

Source: New York Times, 1999b.

problems—such as racial discrimination and sexual harassment—may be viewed (correctly or incorrectly) as conditions that affect some members of a population more than others. However, all social problems may be harmful to all members in a society whether they realize it or not. Sociological research, for example, has documented the extent to which white racism wastes the energies and resources of people who engage in racist actions as well as those of the targets of the actions (see Feagin and Sikes, 1994; Feagin and Vera, 1995).

Social problems often involve significant discrepancies between the ideals of a society and their actual achievement. For example, the United States was founded on basic democratic principles that

What does this photo show us about the discrepancies that exist between the democratic ideals and the social realities of our society? Does discrimination against subordinate group members take place in other societies as well?

include the right to "Life, Liberty, and the pursuit of Happiness," as set forth in the Declaration of Independence. The rights of individuals are guaranteed by the U.S. Constitution, which also provides the legal basis for remedying injustices. Significant discrepancies exist, however, between the democratic ideal and its achievement. One such discrepancy is *discrimination*—**actions or practices of dominant group members (or their representatives) that have a harmful impact on members of subordinate groups.** Discrimination may be directed along class, racial, gender, and age lines. It also may be directed against subordinate group members whose sexual orientation, religion, nationality, or other attributes or characteristics are devalued by those who discriminate against them. Sometimes, discrimination is acted out in the form of violence. This type of violent act is referred to as a *hate crime*—**a physical attack against a person because of assumptions regarding his or her racial group, ethnicity, religion, disability, sexual orientation, national origin, or ancestry** (Levin and McDevitt, 1993). Currently, about forty states have hate crime laws, but only twenty-one have laws dealing with violence against gays (Barrett, 1999). To date, Congress has resisted creating federal hate crime laws concerning violent acts perpetrated against individuals because of their sexual orientation (Barrett, 1999).

Subjective Awareness and Objective Reality

A subjective awareness that a social problem exists usually emerges before the objective reality of the problem is acknowledged. Subjective awareness tends to be expressed as a feeling of uneasiness or skepticism about something, but the feeling is not founded on any concrete evidence that a problem actually exists. When people fly in airplanes, for example, they may have a subjective awareness that something bad can happen while they are traveling through the air at 30,000 feet in a metal canister. When they see an engine catch fire, they experience, quickly, the objective reality that a major problem—perhaps life-threatening—is at hand.

A subjective awareness that there was potential for violent acts in settings such as schools, day-care centers, business, churches, and other public locations existed prior to the string of killings that occurred in these settings in the late 1990s. As school officials, political leaders, members of the media, and the general public began to see what appeared to be a pattern in these occurrences, gun-related violence began to be seen as a pressing social problem. However, a lack of consensus on the causes, effects, and possible ways to reduce or eliminate the problem continues to hinder most efforts to deal with the problem on a less than superficial (for example, metal detectors) level.

Increasingly, the media play a significant role in making people aware of social problems. For many people, hate crimes became an objective reality with extensive media coverage of the brutal killing of Matthew Shepard, a gay student at the University of Wyoming, and the racially motivated dragging death of James Byrd, Jr., an African American man in Jasper, Texas (Barrett, 1999; Cohen, 1999a). Although television, the Internet, and other forms of media coverage may increase people's awareness of violence, these sources sometimes also sensationalize events.

 Why Study Social Problems?

Studying social problems helps us to understand the social forces that shape our lives on both personal and societal levels. In our daily lives, we rely on common sense—"what everybody knows"—to guide our conduct and make sense out of human behavior. But many commonsense notions about why people behave the way they do, who makes the rules, and why some people break rules and others follow them are *myths*—beliefs that persist even when the actual truth is different. Myths about social problems frequently garner widespread acceptance and sometimes extensive media coverage.

A sociological examination of social problems enables us to move beyond commonsense notions, to gain new insights into ourselves, and to develop an awareness of the connection between our own world and the worlds of other people. According to sociologist Peter Berger (1963:23), a sociological examination allows us to realize that "things are not what they seem." Indeed, most social problems are multifaceted. When we recognize this, we can approach pressing national and global concerns in new ways and make better decisions about those concerns. In taking a global perspective on social problems, we soon realize that the lives of all people are closely intertwined, and that any one nation's problems are part of a larger global problem.

THE SOCIOLOGICAL IMAGINATION AND SOCIAL PROBLEMS

Just like other people, sociologists usually have strong opinions about what is "good" and "bad" in society and what might be done to improve conditions. However, sociologists know their opinions are often subjective. Thus, they use systematic research techniques and report their findings to other social scientists for consideration. In other words, sociologists strive to view social problems *objectively*. Of course, complete objectivity may not be an attainable—or desirable—goal in studying human behavior. Max Weber, an early German sociologist, acknowledged that complete objectivity might be impossible and pointed out that *verstehen* ("understanding" or "insight") was critical to any analysis of social problems. According to Weber, *verstehen* enables individuals to see the world as others see it and to empathize with them. *Verstehen*, in turn, enables us to develop what is called the sociological imagination.

According to sociologist C. Wright Mills, the *sociological imagination* is the ability to see the relationship between individual experiences and the larger society. The sociological imagination enables us to connect the private problems of individuals to public issues. Public issues (or social problems) are matters beyond a person's control that originate at the regional or national level and can be resolved only by collective action. In *The Sociological Imagination* (1959b), Mills used unemployment as an example of how people may erroneously separate personal troubles from public issues in their thinking. The unemployed individual may view his or her unemployment as a personal trouble concerning only the individual, other family members, and friends. However, widespread unemployment resulting from economic changes, corporate decisions (downsizing or relocating a plant abroad), or technological innovations (computers and advanced telecommunications systems displacing workers) is a public issue. The sociological imagination helps us to shift our focus to the larger social context and see how personal troubles may be related to public issues.

Sociologists make connections between personal and public issues in society through microlevel and macrolevel analysis. *Microlevel analysis* focuses on **small-group relations and social interaction among**

individuals. Using microlevel analysis, a sociologist might investigate how fear of unemployment affects workers and their immediate families. In contrast, *macrolevel analysis* **focuses on social processes occurring at the societal level, especially in large-scale organizations and major social institutions such as politics, government, and the economy.** Using macrolevel analysis, a sociologist might examine how the loss of more than 43 million jobs over the past two decades has affected the U.S. economy. As Mills suggested, a systematic study of a social problem such as unemployment gives us a clearer picture of the relationship between macrolevel structures such as the U.S. economy and microlevel social interactions among people in their homes, workplaces, and communities.

SOCIOLOGICAL PERSPECTIVES ON SOCIAL PROBLEMS

To determine how social life is organized, sociologists develop theories and conduct research. A *theory* **is a set of logically related statements that attempt to describe, explain, or predict social events.** Theories are useful for explaining relationships between social concepts or phenomena, such as age and unemployment. They also help us to interpret social reality in a distinct way by giving us a framework for organizing our observations. Sociologists refer to this theoretical framework as a *perspective*—**an overall approach or viewpoint toward some subject.** Three major theoretical perspectives have emerged in sociology: the functionalist perspective, which views society as a basically stable and orderly entity; the conflict perspective, which views society as an arena of competition and conflict; and the interactionist perspective, which focuses on the everyday, routine interactions among individuals. The functionalist and conflict perspectives are based on macrolevel analysis because they focus on social processes occurring at the societal level. The interactionist perspective is based on microlevel analysis because it focuses on small-group relations and social interaction.

 The Functionalist Perspective

The functionalist perspective grew out of the works of early social thinkers such as Auguste Comte (1798–1857), the founder of sociology. Comte compared society to a living organism. Just as muscles, tissues, and organs of the human body perform specific functions that maintain the body as a whole, the various parts of society contribute to its maintenance and preservation. According to the *functionalist perspective*, **society is a stable, orderly system composed of a number of interrelated parts, each of which performs a function that contributes to the overall stability of society** (Parsons, 1951). These interrelated parts are social institutions (such as families, the economy, education, and the government) that a society develops to organize its main concerns and activities so that social needs are met. Each institution performs a unique function, contributing to the overall stability of society and the well-being of individuals (Merton, 1968). For example, the functions of the economy are producing and distributing goods (such as food, clothing, and shelter) and services (such as health care and dry cleaning), whereas the government is responsible for coordinating activities of other institutions, maintaining law and order, dealing with unmet social needs, and handling international relations and warfare.

MANIFEST AND LATENT FUNCTIONS

Though the functions of the economy and the government seem fairly clear-cut, functionalists suggest that not all the functions of social institutions are intended and overtly recognized. In fact, according to the functionalist perspective, social institutions perform two different types of societal functions: manifest and latent. *Manifest functions* are intended and recognized consequences of an activity or social process. A manifest function of education, for example, is to provide students with knowledge, skills, and cultural values. In contrast, *latent functions* are the unintended consequences of an activity or social process that are hidden and remain unacknowledged by participants (Merton, 1968). The latent functions of education include the babysitter function of keeping young people off the street and out of the full-time job market and the matchmaking function whereby schools provide opportunities for students to meet and socialize with potential marriage partners. These functions are latent because schools were not created for babysitting or matchmaking, and most organizational participants do not acknowledge that these activities take place.

DYSFUNCTIONS AND SOCIAL DISORGANIZATION

From the functionalist perspective, social problems arise when social institutions do not fulfill their functions or when dysfunctions occur. *Dysfunctions* are the undesirable consequences of an activity or social process that inhibit a society's ability to adapt or adjust (Merton, 1968). For example, a function of education is to prepare students for jobs, but if schools fail to do so, then students have problems finding jobs, employers have to spend millions of dollars on employee training programs, and consumers have to pay higher prices for goods and services to offset worker training costs. In other words, dysfunctions in education threaten other social institutions, especially families and the economy.

Dysfunctions can occur in society as a whole or in a part of society (a social institution). According to functionalists, dysfunctions in social institutions create social disorganization in the entire society. *Social disorganization* **refers to the conditions in society that undermine the ability of traditional social institutions to govern human behavior.** Early in the twentieth century, sociologists Robert E. Park (1864–1944) and Ernest W. Burgess (1886–1966) developed a social disorganization theory to explain why some areas of Chicago had higher rates of *social deviance*, which they defined as a pattern of rule violation, than other areas had. Social disorganization causes a breakdown in the traditional values and norms that serve as social control mechanisms, which, under normal circumstances, keep people from engaging in nonconforming behavior. *Values* **are collective ideas about what is right or wrong, good or bad, and desirable or undesirable in a specific society** (Williams, 1970). Although values provide ideas about behavior, they do not state explicitly how we should behave. Norms, on the other hand, have specific behavioral expectations. *Norms* **are established rules of behavior or standards of conduct.** French sociologist Emile Durkheim (1858–1917) suggested that social problems arise when people no longer agree on societal values and norms. According to Durkheim, periods of rapid social change produce *anomie*—a loss of shared values and sense of purpose in society. During these periods, social bonds grow weaker, social control is diminished, and people are more likely to engage in nonconforming patterns of behavior such as crime.

Early sociologists examining the relationship between social problems and rapid industrialization and urbanization in Britain, Western Europe, and the United States in the late nineteenth and early twentieth centuries, noted that rapid social change intensifies social disorganization. *Industrialization* **is the process by which societies are transformed from a dependence on agriculture and handmade products to an emphasis on manufacturing and related industries.** At the beginning of the Industrial Revolution, thousands of people migrated from rural communities to large urban centers to find employment in factories and offices. New social problems emerged as a result of industrialization and *urbanization,* **the process by which an increasing proportion of a population lives in cities rather than in rural areas.** During this period of rapid technological and social change, a sharp increase occurred in urban social problems such as poverty, crime, child labor, inadequate housing, unsanitary conditions, overcrowding, and environmental pollution.

APPLYING THE FUNCTIONALIST PERSPECTIVE TO PROBLEMS OF VIOLENCE

Some functionalists believe that violence arises from a condition of anomie, in which many individuals have a feeling of helplessness, normlessness, or alienation. Others believe that violence increases when social institutions such as the family, schools, and religious organizations weaken and the main mechanisms of social control in people's everyday lives are external (i.e., law enforcement agencies and the criminal justice system).

One functionalist explanation of violence, known as the *subculture of violence hypothesis,* **states that violence is part of the normative expectations governing everyday behavior among young males in the lower classes** (Wolfgang and Ferracuti, 1967). Violence is considered a by-product of their culture, which idealizes toughness and even brutality in the name of masculinity. According to criminologists Marvin E. Wolfgang and Franco Ferracuti (1967), violent subcultures (for example, violent juvenile gangs, neo-Nazi skinhead groups, and some organized crime groups) are most likely to develop when young people, particularly males, have few legitimate opportunities available in their segment of society and when subcultural values accept and encourage violent behavior. In this context, young people come to consider aggression or violence a natural response to certain situations.

Still other functionalist explanations of violence focus on how changes in social institutions put some people at greater risk of being victims of violent crime than others. According to the *lifestyle-routine activity approach,* **the patterns and timing of people's daily movements and activities as they go about obtaining such necessities of life as food, shelter, companionship, and entertainment, are the keys to understanding violent personal crimes and other types of crime in our society** (Cohen and Felson, 1979). Among the changes over the past fifty years that have increased violent crime in the United States are more families in which both parents (or the sole parent) working outside the home, more people living by themselves, shopping hours extended into the night, and more people eating outside the home (Parker, 1995). Social structure may also put constraints on behavior, thus making certain people more vulnerable to violent attack (e.g., people who are required to work at night). The lifestyle-routine activity approach suggests that people who willingly put themselves in situations that expose them to the potential for violent crime should modify their behavior or that society should provide greater protection for people whose lifestyle routine leaves them vulnerable to attackers. The lifestyle-routine activity approach is good as far as it goes, but it does not address the issue of violence in the home and other supposedly safe havens in society.

The brutal murder of Matthew Shepard, a gay college student in Wyoming, produced an outcry from many people. Some were concerned that hate crimes against individuals because of race, class, gender, or sexual orientation might go unpunished; others used their own beliefs or moral values to harshly judge categories of people who often are the victims of hate crimes.

How would a functionalist approach the problem of violence? Most functionalists emphasize shared moral values and social bonds. They believe that when rapid social change or other disruptions occur, moral values may erode and problems such as school violence or hate crimes are likely to occur. Functionalists believe that to reduce violence, families, schools, religious organizations and other social institutions should be strengthened so that they can regenerate shared values and morality. Most functionalists also believe that those who engage in violent criminal behavior should be prosecuted to the full extent of the law.

 The Conflict Perspective

The *conflict perspective* **is based on the assumption that groups in society are engaged in a continuous power struggle for control of scarce resources.** Unlike functionalist theorists, who emphasize the degree to which society is held together by a consensus on values, conflict theorists emphasize the degree to which society is characterized by conflict and discrimination. According to some conflict theorists, certain groups of people are privileged while others are disadvantaged through the unjust use of political, economic, or social power. Not all conflict theorists hold the same views about what constitutes the most important form of conflict. We will examine two principal perspectives: the value conflict perspective and the critical-conflict perspective.

THE VALUE CONFLICT PERSPECTIVE
According to value conflict theorists, social problems are conditions that are incompatible with group values. From this perspective, value clashes are ordinary occurrences in families, communities, and the larger society, in which individuals commonly hold many divergent values. Although individuals may share certain core values, they do not share all values or a common culture. Culture refers to the knowledge, language, values, customs, and material objects that are passed from person to person and from one generation to the next in a human group or society.

Discrepancies between ideal and real culture are a source of social problems in all societies. *Ideal culture* refers to the values and beliefs that people claim they hold; *real culture* refers to the values and beliefs that they actually follow. In the United States, for example, members of the National Association for the

Advancement of Colored People (NAACP), La Raza, the Ku Klux Klan, and the White Aryan Resistance all claim to adhere to ideal cultural values of equality, freedom, and liberty; however, these ideal cultural values come into direct conflict with real cultural values when issues of racial-ethnic relations arise. Urban marches and protest rallies held by members of the NAACP and the Ku Klux Klan on Martin Luther King Day, which celebrates the birthday of the African American minister and civil rights activist who was murdered in 1968, are a concrete example of the clash between ideal and real cultural values.

The value conflict perspective has been criticized by critical-conflict theorists, who argue that it overlooks the deeper social problems of inequality and oppression based on class, race, and gender.

CRITICAL-CONFLICT PERSPECTIVE

Unlike the value conflict approach, critical-conflict theorists suggest that social problems arise out of the major contradictions inherent in the way societies are organized. Some critical-conflict perspectives focus on class inequalities in the capitalist economic system; others focus on inequalities based on race/ethnicity or gender.

Most class perspectives on inequality have been strongly influenced by Karl Marx (1818–1883), a German economist and activist, who recognized that the emergence of capitalism had produced dramatic and irreversible changes in social life. **Capitalism is an economic system characterized by private ownership of the means of production, from which personal profits can be derived through market competition and without government intervention.** According to Marx, members of the *capitalist class* (the *bourgeoisie*), who own and control the means of production (e.g., the land, tools, factories, and money for investment), are at the top of a system of social stratification that affords them different lifestyles and life chances from those of the members of the *working class* (the *proletariat*), who must sell their labor power (their potential ability to work) to capitalists. In selling their labor power, members of the working class forfeit control over their work, and the capitalists derive excessive profit from the workers' labor.

Marx believed that capitalism led workers to experience increased levels of impoverishment and alienation—a feeling of powerlessness and estrangement from other people and from oneself (Marx and Engels, 1847, 1971:96). He predicted that the work-

ing class would eventually overthrow the capitalist economic system. Although Marx's prediction has not come about, Erik Olin Wright (1997) and other social scientists have modified and adapted his perspective to apply to contemporary capitalist nations. In today's capitalist nations, according to Wright, ownership of the means of production is only one way in which people gain the ability to exploit others. Two other ways in which individuals gain control are through *control* of property and *control* over other people's labor. In this view, upper-level managers and others in positions of authority gain control over societal resources and other individuals' time, knowledge, and skills in such a manner that members of the upper classes are able to maintain their dominance (Wright, 1997).

Some critical-conflict perspectives focus on racial and gender subordination instead of class-based inequalities. Critical-conflict theorists who emphasize discrimination and inequality based on race or ethnicity note that many social problems are rooted in the continuing exploitation and subordination of people of color by white people. For example, some scholars suggest that Native Americans have the highest rates of poverty in the United States because of extended periods of racial subordination and exploitation throughout this country's history (see Feagin and Feagin, 1999).

Critical-conflict theorists who use a feminist approach focus on *patriarchy*, a system of male dominance in which males are privileged and women are oppressed. According to a feminist approach, male domination in society contributes not only to domestic violence, child abuse, and rape but also to poverty and crimes such as prostitution. Feminist scholars state that gender inequality will not be eliminated in the home, school, and workplace until patriarchy is abolished and women and men are treated equally.

Finally, there are some critical-conflict theorists who note that race, class, and gender are interlocking systems of privilege and oppression that result in social problems. For example, black feminist scholar Patricia Hill Collins (1990) has pointed out that race, class, and gender are simultaneous forces of oppression for women of color, especially African American women. Critical-conflict analysts focusing on these intersections believe that equality can come about only when women across lines of race and class receive equal treatment (Andersen and Collins, 1995; Collins, 1995).

Feminist critical-conflict theorists believe that African American women face a system of interlocking oppression of race, class, and gender.

Throughout this text, we will use critical-conflict theory (rather than value conflict approach) to highlight the power relations that result in social problems.

APPLYING THE CONFLICT PERSPECTIVE TO PROBLEMS OF VIOLENCE

Conflict theorists who focus on class-based inequalities believe that the potential for violence is inherent in capitalist societies. In fact, say these theorists, the wealthy engage in one form of violence, and the poor engage in another. They note that the wealthy often use third parties to protect themselves and their families from bodily harm as well as to secure their property and investments in this country and elsewhere in the world. For example, the wealthy who live in the United States or other high-income nations and own factories (or own stock in factories) in middle- and low-income nations use the governments and police of those nations—third parties—to control workers who threaten to strike. The wealthy also influence U.S. government policy. For instance, they are likely to support U.S. military intervention—and thus violence—in nations such as Kuwait and Haiti where they have large investments at stake.

In contrast, these theorists say, when the poor engage in violence, the violence is typically commit-

ted by the individual and is a reaction to the unjust social and economic conditions he or she experiences daily on the bottom rung of a capitalist society. The economic exploitation of the poor, these theorists note, dramatically affects all aspects of the individual's life, including how the person reacts to daily injustices, stress, and other threatening situations. In violent street crimes, the vast majority of offenders—as well as victims—are poor, unemployed, or working in low-level, low-paying jobs. In fact, most violent street crime is an intraclass phenomenon: Poor and working-class people typically victimize others who are like themselves.

The conflict perspective argues that the criminal justice system is biased in favor of the middle and upper classes. Because it is, its definition of violence depends on where a person's race, class, and gender locate him or her in the system of stratification. In this way, violent crimes are but one part of a larger system of inequality and oppression. Sexism and racism are reinforced by the overarching class structure that benefits the powerful at the expense of the powerless. Exploitation of people of color and the poor creates a sense of hopelessness, frustration, and hostility in them that may boil over into violent acts such as rape or murder. At the same time, it is important to note that violent acts, including murder, occur across all class and racial-ethnic categories in the United States.

The conflict perspective that focuses on feminist issues specifically examines violence against women, for example, rape and most spouse abuse. One feminist perspective suggests that violence against women is a means of reinforcing patriarchy. According to the feminist perspective, in a patriarchal system, the sexual marketplace is characterized by unequal bargaining power, making transactions between men and women potentially coercive in nature. Gender stratification is reinforced by powerful physical, psychological, and social mechanisms of control, including force or the threat of force. Fear of violence forces women to change their ways of living, acting, and dressing and thus deprives them of many basic freedoms (see Gardner, 1995).

The conflict perspective that focuses on racial-ethnic inequalities points out that racism is an important factor in explaining such violent acts as hate crimes. Recently, a number of white supremacists spouting anti-black and anti-Semitic dogma have been convicted of violent crimes against people of color. Some analysts trace contemporary brutality against

African Americans, particularly men, to earlier periods when hanging or dragging was used to punish slave insurrections and to keep African Americans subservient during the Reconstruction and the subsequent years of legal racial segregation in the South (see Feagin and Feagin, 1999).

No matter what approach conflict theorists take, they all agree on one thing: Violence is unlikely to diminish significantly unless inequalities based on class, gender, and race are reduced at the macrolevel in society.

 ## The Interactionist Perspective

Unlike the conflict perspective, which focuses on macrolevel inequalities in society, the interactionist perspective focuses on a microlevel analysis of how people act toward one another and how they make sense of their daily lives. The **interactionist perspective views society as the sum of the interactions of individuals and groups.** Most interactionists study social problems by analyzing how certain behavior comes to be defined as a social problem and how individuals and groups come to engage in activities that a significant number of people and/or a number of significant people view as a major social concern.

German sociologist Georg Simmel (1858–1918), a founder of the interactionist approach, investigated the impact of industrialization and urbanization on people's values and behavior within small social units. Simmel (1950/1902) noted that rapid changes in technology and dramatic urban growth produced new social problems by breaking up the "geometry of social life," which he described as the web of patterned social interactions among the people who constitute a society. According to Simmel, alienation is brought about by a decline in personal and emotional contacts. How people *interpret* the subjective messages that they receive from others and the situations that they encounter in their daily life, greatly influences their behavior and perceptions of what constitutes a social problem.

LABELING THEORY AND THE SOCIAL CONSTRUCTION OF REALITY

While Simmel focused on how people interpret their own situations, other interactionists have examined how people impose their shared meanings on others. According to sociologist Howard Becker

(1963), *moral entrepreneurs* are people who use their own views of right and wrong to establish rules and *label* others as deviant (nonconforming). *Labeling theory,* as this perspective is called, suggests that behavior that deviates from established norms is deviant because it has been labeled as such by others. According to this theory, deviants (nonconformists) are people who have been successfully labeled as such by others. Labeling theory raises questions about why certain individuals and certain types of behavior are labeled as deviant but others are not.

According to some interaction theorists, many social problems can be linked to the *social construction of reality*—the process by which people's perception of reality is shaped largely by the subjective meaning that they give to an experience (Berger and Luckmann, 1967). From this perspective, little shared reality exists beyond that which people socially create. It is, however, this social construction of reality that influences people's beliefs and actions.

Other interactionists suggest that how we initially define a situation affects our future actions. According to sociologist W. I. Thomas (1863–1947), when people define situations as real, the situations become real in their consequences. Elaborating on Thomas's idea, sociologist Robert Merton (1968) has suggested that when people perceive a situation in a certain way and act according to their perceptions, the end result may be a *self-fulfilling prophecy*—**a false definition of the situation that evokes a new behavior that makes the original false conception come true.** For example, a teenager who is labeled a "juvenile delinquent" may accept the label and adopt the full-blown image of a juvenile delinquent as portrayed in television programs and films: wearing gang colors, dropping out of school, and participating in gang violence or other behavior that is labeled as deviant. If the teenager subsequently is arrested, the initial label becomes a self-fulfilling prophecy.

APPLYING INTERACTIONIST PERSPECTIVES TO PROBLEMS OF VIOLENCE

Interactionist explanations of violence begin by noting that human behavior is learned through social interaction. Violence, they state, is a learned response, not an inherent characteristic, in the individual. Some of the most interesting support for this point of view comes from studies done by social psychologist Albert Bandura who studied aggression in children (1973). Showing children a film of a person beating, kicking, and hacking an inflatable doll produced a violent response in the children, who, when they were placed in a room with a similar doll, duplicated the person's behavior and engaged in additional aggressive behavior. Others have noted that people tend to repeat their behavior if they feel rewarded for it. Thus, when people learn that they can get their way by inflicting violence or the threat of violence on others, their aggressive behavior is reinforced.

Interactionists also look at the types of social interactions that commonly lead to violence. According to the *situational approach,* **violence results from a specific interaction process, termed a "situational transaction."** Criminologist David Luckenbill (1977) has identified six stages in the situational transaction between victim and offender. In the first stage, the future victim does something behavioral or verbal that is considered an affront by the other (e.g., a glare or an insult). In the second, the offended individual verifies that the action was directed at him or her personally. In the third, the offended individual decides how to respond to the affront and may issue a verbal or behavioral challenge (e.g., a threat or a raised fist). If the problem escalates at this point, injury or death may occur in this stage; if not, the participants enter into the fourth stage. In this stage, the future victim further escalates the transaction, often prodded on by onlookers siding with one party or the other. In the fifth stage, actual violence occurs when neither party is able to back down without losing face. At this point, one or both parties produce weapons, which may range from guns and knives to bottles, pool cues, or other bludgeoning devices, if they have not already appeared, and the offender kills the victim. The sixth and final stage involves the offender's actions after the crime; some flee the scene, others are detained by onlookers, and still others call the police themselves.

The situational approach is based, first, on the assumption that many victims are active participants in the violence perpetrated against them and, second, on the idea that confrontation does not inevitably lead to violence or death. As Robert Nash Parker (1995) has noted, in the first four stages of the transaction, either the victim or the offender can decide to pursue another course of action.

According to interactionists, reducing violence requires changing those societal values that encourage excessive competition and violence. These changes must occur at the microlevel, which means

agents of socialization must transmit different attitudes and values toward violence. The next generation must learn that it is an individual's right—regardless of gender, race, class, religion, or other attributes or characteristics—to live free from violence and the devastating impact it has on individuals, groups, and the social fabric of society.

SOCIAL RESEARCH METHODS FOR STUDYING SOCIAL PROBLEMS

Sociologists use a variety of research methods to study social problems such as violence. *Research methods* are strategies or techniques for systematically collecting data. Some methods produce quantitative data that can be measured numerically and lend themselves to statistical analysis. For example, the *Uniform Crime Report (UCR),* published annually by the Federal Bureau of Investigation, provides crime statistics that sociologists and others can use to learn more about the nature and extent of violent crime in the United States. Other research methods produce qualitative data that are reported in the form of interpretive descriptions (words) rather than numbers. For example, qualitative data on violence in the United States might provide new insights on how the victims or their families and friends cope in the aftermath of a violent attack such as the recent school shootings.

Sociologists use three major types of research methods: field research, survey research, and secondary analysis of existing data. Although our discussion focuses on each separately, many researchers use a combination of methods to enhance their understanding of social issues.

Field Research

Field research **is the study of social life in its natural setting: observing and interviewing people where they live, work, and play.** When sociologists want firsthand information about a social problem, they often use *participant observation*—field research in which researchers collect systematic observations while participating in the activities of the group they are studying. Field research on social problems can take place in many settings, ranging from schools and neighborhoods to universities, prisons, and large corporations.

Using field research, sociologists have studied gang violence and found that gang members are not all alike. Some do not approve of violence; others engage in violence only to assert authority; still others may engage in violence only when they feel threatened or want to maintain their territory.

Field research is valuable because some kinds of behavior and social problems can be studied best by being there; a more complete understanding can be developed through observations, face-to-face discussions, and participation in events than through other research methods. For example, field research on gang violence led sociologist Martín Sánchez Jankowski (1991) to conclude that violence attributed to gangs is often committed by members who are acting as *individuals* rather than as agents of the organization. According to Jankowski, most gang members do not like violence and fear that they may be injured or killed in violent encounters. As a result, gang members engage in collective violence only to accomplish specific objectives such as asserting authority or punishing violations by their own members who are incompetent or who break the gang's code. Violence against other gangs occurs primarily when gang members feel threatened or need to maintain or expand their operations in a certain area. According to Jankowski, gang members use collective violence to achieve the goals of gang membership (proving their masculinity and toughness, providing excitement, and maintaining their reputation) mainly when they are provoked by others or when they are fearful.

Sociologists using field research must have good interpersonal skills. They must be able to gain and keep the trust of the people they want to observe or interview. They also must be skilled interviewers who can keep systematic notes on their observations and conversations. Above all, they must treat research subjects fairly and ethically. The Code of Ethics of the American Sociological Association provides professional standards for sociologists to follow when conducting social science research.

Survey Research

Survey research is probably the research method most frequently used by social scientists. *Survey research* **is a poll in which researchers ask respondents a series of questions about a specific topic and record their responses.** Survey research is based on the use of a sample of people who are thought to represent the attributes of the larger population from which they are selected. Survey data are collected by using self-administered questionnaires or by interviewers who ask questions of people in person or by mail, telephone, or the Internet.

The Bureau of Justice Statistics conducts survey research every year with its national crime victimization survey (NCVS), which fills in some of the gaps in the *UCR* data. The NCVS interviews 100,000 randomly selected households to identify crime victims, whether the crime has been reported or not. These surveys indicate that the number of crimes committed is substantially higher than the number reported in the *UCR*.

Survey research allows sociologists to study a large population without having to interview everyone in that population. It also yields numerical data that may be compared between groups and over periods of time. However, this type of research does have certain limitations. The use of standardized questions limits the types of information researchers can obtain from respondents. Also, because data can be reported numerically, survey research may be misused to overestimate or underestimate the extent of a specific problem such as violence.

Secondary Analysis of Existing Data

Whereas the NCVS is primary data—data that researchers collected specifically for that study—sociologists often rely on *secondary analysis of existing data*—**a research method in which investigators analyze data that originally were collected by others for some other purpose.** This method is also known as *unobtrusive research* because data can be gathered without the researcher having to interview or observe research subjects. Secondary data include public records such as birth and death records, official reports of organizations or governmental agencies such as the U.S. Bureau of the Census, and information from large databases such as the general social surveys, which are administered by the National Opinion Research Center (see Davis and Robinson, 1988).

Secondary analysis often involves *content analysis*, a systematic examination of cultural artifacts or written documents to extract thematic data and draw conclusions about some aspect of social life. For example, for the National Television Violence Study, researchers at several universities conducted content analyses of violence in television programming. During a nine-month period each year from October 1994 to June 1997, researchers selected a variety of programs, including drama, comedy, movies, music videos, reality programs, and children's shows on twenty-three television channels, thus creating a composite of the content in a week of television viewing. The viewing hours were from 6:00 A.M. until 11:00 P.M., for a total of seventeen hours a day across the seven days of the week (National Television Violence Study, 1998). Some of the findings from this study are discussed in Box 1.2, "Social Problems and Information Technology."

A strength of secondary analysis is its unobtrusive nature and the fact that it can be used when subjects refuse to be interviewed or the researcher does not have the opportunity to observe research subjects firsthand. However, secondary analysis also has inherent problems. Because the data originally were gathered for some other purpose, they may not fit the exact needs of the researcher, and they may be incomplete or inaccurate.

In Sum

Sociologists view social problems from a variety of perspectives. Each perspective involves different assumptions. Functionalists, who emphasize social cohesion and order in society, commonly view social problems as the result of institutional and societal dysfunctions, social disorganization, or cultural lag, among other things. Conflict theorists, who focus on value conflict or on structural inequalities based on class, race, gender, or other socially constructed attributes, suggest that social problems arise either from disputes over divergent values or from exploitative relations in society, such as those between capitalists and workers or between women and men. In contrast, interactionists focus on individuals' interactions and on the social construction of reality. For interactionists, social problems occur when social interaction is disrupted and people are dehumanized, when people are labeled deviant, or when the individual's definition of a situation causes him or her to act in a way that produces a detrimental outcome. Table 1.1 (on page 4) summarizes these perspectives, which we will use throughout the book.

No matter what perspectives sociologists employ, they use research to support their ideas. All research methods have certain strengths and weaknesses, but taken together, they provide us with valuable insights that go beyond commonsense knowledge about social problems and stereotypes of people. Using multiple methods and approaches, sociologists can broaden their knowledge of social problems such as violence in the United States and other nations.

In this chapter, we have looked at violence from these sociological perspectives. Like many other social problems, people do not always agree on the causes of violence. They also do not always agree on what should be done about violence. However, this does not mean that we should simply "give up" and do nothing. Throughout this book, we will explore a variety of pressing social problems, and we will try to think of creative ways that our nation and others may reduce or end these problems. Please join me now in exploring many of the crucial issues of the twenty-first century.

SOCIAL PROBLEMS
AND INFORMATION TECHNOLOGY

BOX 1.2

Studying Violence in Television Programming

As a result of the rise in gun-related violence, members of the media now begin their accounts of the latest incidents with "It happened again." Rob Schickler (1999:2), a columnist for the *Baylor Lariat,* has suggested that there is almost a fill-in-the-blank form for writing the reports: "A gunman armed with a [insert weapon] walked into an [insert building] in [insert city] and opened fire, killing [insert number] and wounding [insert number] others."

Although many of us learn about the latest acts of violent behavior from the media, we are less inclined to think about the amount of violence shown on television. In the interest of discovering how much violence is depicted in television programming overall, researchers at the University of California, Santa Barbara; the University of Texas at Austin; the University of Wisconsin, Madison; and the University of North Carolina, Chapel Hill decided to conduct the National Television Violence Study (NTVS). Between 1994 and 1997, more than 300 researchers videotaped approximately 10,000 hours of television programming, and 1,600 participants took part in five separate experiments (Federman, 1998). The purpose of the study was to investigate how television portrays violence. The researchers explained their approach in this way:

> We examined three different aspects of the program when assessing how violence is portrayed on television. First, we identified each *violent incident,* or interaction between a perpetrator and a victim. Second, we analyzed each *violent scene,* or instance of ongoing, uninterrupted violence. A violent scene, such as a bar fight, often contains several violent incidents between different types of characters. Finally, we analyzed the entire *violent program.* . . . By analyzing violence at all of these levels—the incidence, the scene, and the overall program—we provide rich information about the meaning of violence in television programming (NTVS, 1998:20).

Although their findings are too numerous to discuss in total, here are a few:

- Much of television violence is glamorized, sanitized, and trivialized. Characters seldom show remorse for their actions, and there is no criticism or penalty for the violence at the time that it occurs. Those who are victimized do not show physical harm or pain even though the serious physical aggression they have experienced would be lethal or incapacitating if such actions were to occur in real life (NTVS, 1998:26).
- Across the three years of the study, violence was found in 60 percent of the television programs taped and few of these programs carried antiviolence themes (NTVS, 1998:29).
- In the three-year period of the study, broadcast networks and basic cable stations increased the proportion of programs containing violence during prime time (the three-hour period each night that draws the most viewers) (NTVS, 1998:29).
- "High risk" depictions (those that may encourage aggressive attitudes and behaviors) often involve: (1) "a perpetrator who

is an attractive role model"; (2) "violence that seems justified"; (3) "violence that goes unpunished"; (4) "minimal consequences to the victims"; and (5) "violence that seems realistic to the viewer" (NTVS, 1998:29). According to the study, for young viewers (particularly those under age seven), these factors often come together in cartoons (NTVS, 1998:30).

The typical preschool child who watches cartoons regularly will come into contact with more than 500 high-risk portrayals of violence each year. For preschoolers who watch television for two to three hours a day, there will be, on average, about one high-risk portrayal of violence per hour in cartoons. As a result, a child who watches two hours of cartoons each day will see more than 500 high-risk portrayals that encourage aggression each year (NTVS, 1998:31).

Is violence on television anything to be concerned about? These researchers believe that it is. Does violence on television encourage or discourage the learning of aggression? While researchers acknowledge that such factors as "peer influences, family role models, social and economic status, educational level, and the availability of weapons can significantly alter the likelihood of a particular reaction to viewing violence on television" (Federman, 1998), they feel their study supports other research findings that indicate viewing televised violence contributes to "learning aggressive attitudes and behaviors." Researchers note that the same graphic depiction of violence that elicits aggression in some people brings about fear of victimization by violence in others (Federman, 1998). Finally, they suggest that television violence serves as a form of "desensitization to violence" (NTVS, 1998:7).

Ironically, depictions of violence have also increased on news programs in recent years, as journalists have spent hours covering the string of shootings that have taken place across the nation. In the final analysis, perhaps the mantra "If it bleeds, it leads" applies to both news coverage and popular, prime-time television shows that attract a young—and often impressionable—audience (Turner, 1999).

Will television producers, directors, and advertisers become more aware of this problem and do something about it? The answer to this question may be similar to one given by the NTVS researchers who concluded that the portrayal of violence on television had changed relatively little over the three-year period of their study. If this is true, we can probably expect to see few, if any, changes in the nature and extent of the violence depicted on television in the near future. But, scholars will continue to examine the depiction and document what they believe to be the possible effects of these depictions, particularly on young people.

INTERNET ACTIVITY

Read more about the National Television Violence Study. Then, develop an informal coding system and conduct your own content analysis of the television programs that you like to watch.

An executive summary of the NTVS report can be found at: http://www.ccsp.ucsb.edu/execsum.pdf. For additional information, contact the Center for Communication and Social Policy at University of California, Santa Barbara: http://research.ucsb.edu/cori/ccsp.html

Full reports for the first, second, and third years of the study are available in some college and public libraries or through interlibrary loan. The reports can be purchased from Sage Publications: http://www.sagepub.com.

SUMMARY

➤ *How do sociologists define a social problem?*

According to sociologists, a social problem is a social condition (such as poverty) or a pattern of behavior (such as substance abuse) that people believe warrants public concern and collective action to bring about change.

➤ *How do sociologists view violence?*

Sociologists view violence as a social problem that involves both a subjective awareness and objective reality. We have a subjective awareness that violence can occur in such public settings as schools, day-care centers, businesses, and churches. Our subjective awareness becomes an objective reality when we can measure and experience the effects of violent criminal behavior.

➤ *How do sociologists examine social life?*

Sociologists use both microlevel and macrolevel analyses to examine social life. Microlevel analysis focuses on small-group relations and social interaction among individuals; macrolevel analysis focuses on social processes occurring at the societal level, especially in large-scale organizations and major social institutions.

➤ *How does the functionalist perspective view society and social problems?*

In the functionalist perspective, society is a stable, orderly system composed of interrelated parts, each of which performs a function that contributes to the overall stability of society. According to functionalists, social problems such as violence arise when social institutions do not fulfill the functions that they are supposed to perform or when dysfunctions occur.

➤ *How does the conflict perspective view society and social problems?*

The conflict perspective asserts that groups in society are engaged in a continuous power struggle for control of scarce resources. This perspective views violence as a response to inequalities based on race, class, gender, and other power differentials in society.

➤ *How does the value conflict perspective differ from the critical-conflict perspective?*

According to value conflict theorists, social problems are conditions that are incompatible with group values. From this perspective, value clashes are ordinary occurrences in families, communities, and the larger society, in which people commonly hold many divergent values. In contrast, critical-conflict theorists suggest that social problems arise out of major contradictions inherent in the way societies are organized.

➤ *Why are there so many different approaches in the conflict perspective?*

Different conflict theorists focus on different aspects of power relations and inequality in society. Perspectives based on the works of Karl Marx emphasize class-based inequalities arising from the capitalist economic system. Feminist perspectives focus on patriarchy—a system of male dominance in which males are privileged and women are oppressed. Other perspectives emphasize that race, class, and gender are interlocking systems of privilege and oppression that result in social problems. However, all of these perspectives are based on the assumption that inequality and exploitation, rather than social harmony and stability, characterize contemporary societies.

➤ *How does the interactionist perspective view society and social problems?*

Unlike the functionalist and conflict perspectives that focus on society at the macrolevel, the interactionist perspective views society as the sum of the interactions of individuals and groups. For interactionists, social problems occur when social interaction is disrupted and people are dehumanized, when people are labeled deviant, or when the individual's definition of a situation causes him or her to act in a way that produces a detrimental outcome.

➤ *How do sociological research methods differ?*

In field research sociologists observe and interview people where they live, work, and play. In survey research, sociologists use written questionnaires or structured interviews to ask respondents a series of questions about a specific topic. In secondary analysis of existing data, sociologists analyze data that originally were collected by others for some other purpose.

KEY TERMS

capitalism, p. 10
conflict perspective, p. 9
discrimination, p. 5
field research, p. 13
functionalist perspective, p. 7
hate crime, p. 5
industrialization, p. 8
interactionist perspective, p. 12
lifestyle-routine activity
  approach, p. 9

macrolevel analysis, p. 7
microlevel analysis, pp. 6–7
norms, p. 8
perspective, p. 7
secondary analysis of existing
  data, p. 15
self-fulfilling prophecy, p. 12
situational approach, p. 13
social disorganization, p. 8
social problem, p. 4

society, p. 4
sociological imagination, p. 6
sociology, p. 4
subculture of violence
  hypothesis, p. 8
survey research, p. 14
theory, p. 7
urbanization, p. 8
values, p. 8
violence, p. 2

QUESTIONS FOR CRITICAL THINKING

1. The functionalist perspective focuses on the stability of society. How do acts of violence undermine stability? Can a society survive when high levels of violence exist within its borders? Do you believe that violence can be controlled in the United States?

2. Value conflict theorists suggest that social problems are conditions that are incompatible with group values. How would value conflict theorists view debates over gun control laws?

3. Some critical-conflict theorists believe that social problems arise from the major contradictions inherent in capitalist economies. What part do guns play in a capitalist economy?

4. Using feminist and interactionist perspectives, what kind of argument can you make to explain why males are more frequently involved in acts of physical violence than females? What do your own observations tell you about the relationship between social norms and aggressive/violent behavior?

Chapter Two

Wealth and Poverty
U.S. and Global Economic Inequalities

I'd like to be able to fix the kids' rooms up nice and I haven't been able to. And if I do have the money, it's always something else that comes up. . . . It's so frustrating when you're trying to lead a normal life, but you can't do it. And then I was trying to think, "Well, if I get this in this month. If I can take so much out of this from the savings account. . . ." There was a time where I could have done that, but now I'm down so low that I [don't] have anything. I got paid and that week it was gone. It was all gone. So it was hard. I had to resort to borrowing.

▲ **—Joyce Mills**
Quoted in Rank (1994:53)

In his study of poverty in the United States, sociologist Mark Robert Rank interviewed low-income women to determine their most pressing day-to-day problems. Joyce Mills, who was separated from her husband, told Rank that she was having a hard time taking care of herself and her three children even though she was working full-time in a clerical position and receiving eighty-one dollars a month from the food stamp program.

What kinds of opportunities exist today for families such as Joyce's? For decades, the United States has been described as the "land of opportunity"—the land of the "American Dream." Simply stated, the American Dream is the belief that each generation can have a higher standard of living than that of its parents (Danziger and Gottschalk, 1995). Implicit in the American Dream is the belief that all people—regardless of race, creed, color, national origin, sex, sexual orientation, or religion—should have an equal opportunity for success. But do all the people in this nation and other parts of the world have an equal opportunity for success? How equally divided are national and global resources?

In this chapter, we look at inequality and poverty in the U.S. class system and worldwide. **A *class system* is a system of social inequality based on the ownership and control of resources and on the type of work people do** (Rothman, 1993). A primary characteristic of any class system is social mobility. *Social mobility* refers to the upward or downward movement in the class structure that occurs during a person's lifetime and from one generation to another.

WEALTH AND POVERTY IN GLOBAL PERSPECTIVE

On a global basis, there is a vast disparity in economic resources both across nations and within nations. In any one nation, there are both very wealthy and very poor individuals and families. When sociologists conduct research on these disparities, they frequently analyze secondary data that originally were collected by the World Bank and the United Nations. These data focus on quality-of-life indicators such as wealth; income; life expectancy; health; sanitation; the treatment of women; and education for high-income, middle-income, and low-income nations. *High-income nations are countries with highly industrialized economies; technologically advanced industrial, administrative, and service occupations; and relatively high levels of national and per capita (per person) income.* Examples include Australia, New Zealand, Japan, the European nations, Canada, and the United States. *Middle-income nations are countries undergoing transformation from agrarian to industrial economies.* Columbia, Guatemala, Panama, Poland, and Romania are examples of middle-income nations. These nations still have many people who work the land, and national and per capita incomes remain relatively low. *Low-income nations are primarily agrarian countries that have little industrialization and low levels of national and personal income.* For example, the countries in sub-Saharan Africa have experienced little or no benefit from recent changes in global economic markets (United Nations Development Programme, 1999). Examples of low-income nations include Rwanda, Mozambique, Ethiopia, Nigeria, Cambodia, Vietnam, Afghanistan, Bangladesh, Honduras, and Nicaragua.

Comparisons of high-income and low-income nations reveal a growing gap between the rich and the poor, both within and among nations. Indeed, throughout the world today, the wealthiest and poorest people are living in increasingly separate worlds (Crossette, 1996b). By the late 1990s, the fifth of the world's population living in the highest-income countries had 86 percent of the world's gross domestic product. The gross domestic product (GDP) is all of the goods and services produced *within* a country's economy during a given year (revenue from sources outside the country is not included in the GDP). The

world's GDP, then, is the total of the GDP for each nation. By contrast, the bottom fifth of the world's population had only 1 percent of the world's GDP. Similarly, the highest-income countries contained 82 percent of world export markets, whereas the lowest-income countries had only 1 percent of those markets (United Nations Development Programme, 1999). Perhaps the easiest way to bring these statistics to life is to think in terms of the common telephone line: 74 percent of all the telephone lines in the world are in the highest-income countries; the bottom one-fifth of the world's nations have only 1.5 percent of all the telephone lines.

Disparity in the GDPs of high-income and low-income nations reflects disparity in the life chances of the populations of these nations. *Life chances are the extent to which individuals have access to important societal resources such as food, clothing, shelter, education, and health care.* Poverty, food shortages, hunger, and rapidly growing populations are pressing problems in many middle- and low-income nations. Today, more than 1.3 billion people live in *absolute poverty, a condition that exists when people do not have the means to secure the most basic necessities of life.* Absolute poverty is often life-threatening. People living in absolute poverty may suffer from chronic malnutrition or die from hunger-related diseases. Current estimates suggest that more than 600 million people suffer from chronic malnutrition and more than 40 million people die each year from hunger-related diseases. To put this figure in perspective, the number of people worldwide dying from hunger-related diseases each year is the equivalent of more than 300 jumbo jet crashes a day with no survivors and half the passengers being children (Kidron and Segal, 1995).

Despite the disparity in life chances and the prevalence of absolute poverty, experts project that the populations of middle- and low-income nations will increase by almost 60 percent by the year 2025, while the populations of high-income nations increase by about 11 percent. Because half of the world's population of about 6 billion people already lives in low-income nations (see Map 2.1), this rapid increase in population can only compound existing problems and increase inequality on a global basis.

How do social scientists explain the disparity between wealth and poverty in high-income and low-income nations? According to the "new international

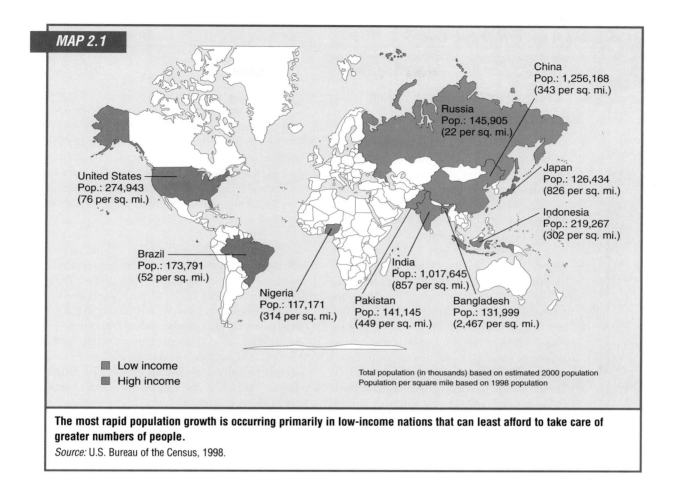

MAP 2.1

China
Pop.: 1,256,168
(343 per sq. mi.)

Russia
Pop.: 145,905
(22 per sq. mi.)

Japan
Pop.: 126,434
(826 per sq. mi.)

United States
Pop.: 274,943
(76 per sq. mi.)

Indonesia
Pop.: 219,267
(302 per sq. mi.)

Brazil
Pop.: 173,791
(52 per sq. mi.)

India
Pop.: 1,017,645
(857 per sq. mi.)

Nigeria
Pop.: 117,171
(314 per sq. mi.)

Pakistan
Pop.: 141,145
(449 per sq. mi.)

Bangladesh
Pop.: 131,999
(2,467 per sq. mi.)

■ Low income
■ High income

Total population (in thousands) based on estimated 2000 population
Population per square mile based on 1998 population

The most rapid population growth is occurring primarily in low-income nations that can least afford to take care of greater numbers of people.
Source: U.S. Bureau of the Census, 1998.

division of labor" perspective, the answer lies in the global organization of manufacturing production (Bluestone and Harrison, 1982). Today, workers in a number of low-income nations primarily produce goods such as clothing, electrical machinery, and consumer electronics for export to the United States and other developed nations (see Box 2.1). Using this global assembly line, transnational corporations find they have an abundant supply of low-cost (primarily female) labor, no corporate taxes, and no labor unions or strikes to interfere with their profits (Petras, 1983). Owners and shareholders of transnational corporations, along with subcontractors and managers in middle- and low-income nations, thus benefit while workers remain in poverty despite long hours in sweatshop conditions.

ANALYZING U.S. CLASS INEQUALITY

Despite the American Dream, one of this country's most persistent social problems is that the United States is a highly stratified society. *Social stratification* **is the hierarchical arrangement of large social groups on the basis of their control over basic resources** (Feagin and Feagin, 1997). Today, the gap between the rich and the poor in this nation is wider than it has been in half a century.

This widening gap, which is linked with global systems of stratification, has a dramatic impact on everyone's life chances and opportunities. Affluent people typically have better life chances than the less affluent because the affluent have greater access to

SOCIAL PROBLEMS

"Cheap Labor" and Global Wealth and Poverty

▲ Jakarta, Indonesia. "I think maybe I could work for a month and still not be able to buy one pair [of Reebok sneakers]"—Tini Heyun Alwi, an assembly line worker at the Dong Joe shoe factory where Reeboks are made. Although Tini works ten-hour shifts six days a week (in a poorly ventilated factory in stifling heat), she earns only 2,600 Indonesian rupiah ($1.28) a day. With overtime, her monthly wages are about $39, less than half of the $110 retail price of a pair of the Reeboks (Goodman, 1996:F1, F6).

▲ San Salvador, El Salvador. When a U.S. journalist asked a woman who works in an assembly plant (located behind cinderblock walls and barbed wire and patrolled by armed guards) whether her three-year-old daughter had enough to eat, the woman replied, "Oh no. We are very poor." Asked whether her daughter drinks milk, the woman answered, "No. We can't afford it. We give her coffee." According to the woman, her daughter's diet is an egg for breakfast and boiled or fried beans for dinner. Meals with meat or vegetables are extremely rare. "My daughter is very thin and also weak, sometimes she falls down," the woman said (Herbert, 1995:A11).

▲ The United States of America. Professional basketball player Michael Jordan earns $20 million a year endorsing Nike sneakers, a sum that is greater than the total annual payroll for the thousands of Indonesian workers who assemble the shoes. When he was asked about recent allegations that Nike exploits its

Indonesian workers, Jordan replied, "I'm not really aware of that. My job with Nike is to endorse the product. Their job is to be up on that" (quoted in Gibbs, 1996:29). According to a spokesperson, Nike owns no plants in Indonesia; it hires Korean- and Taiwanese-owned factories to make its products, which earned profits of more than $397 million in 1995 alone (*Time*, 1996:79).

What do these examples tell us about global wealth and poverty? Over the past three decades, many companies have closed their plants and factories in the United States and set up business in nations where wages are low, environmental and worker safety standards are weak, and local government officials offer assurances that strikes and independent unions will not be tolerated. Today, U.S.-based multinational corporations employ more than 8 million workers in other nations. Many executives believe that the use of cheap labor is a survival strategy that they must use to be competitive in the global marketplace. Although some labor activists and social analysts call for a shutdown of global sweatshops, one analyst has pointed out that a crucial irony exists in the demand to end the exploitation of workers in middle- and low-income nations: Demanding that corporations either shut down plants or pay higher wages could mean that people who currently live in near poverty will have no wages at all in the future (Gibbs, 1996). What do you think will happen when corporations run out of nations where labor is cheap? What part does technology play in the global factory of the twenty-first century?

quality education, safe neighborhoods, high-quality nutrition and health care, police and private security protection, and an extensive array of other goods and services. In contrast, people who have low and poverty-level incomes tend to have limited access to these resources.

How are social classes determined in the United States? Most contemporary research on class has been influenced by either Karl Marx's means of production model or Max Weber's multidimensional model. In Marx's model, class position is determined by people's relationship to the means of production. Chapter 1 described Marx's division of capitalist societies into two classes: the bourgeoisie, or capitalist class, which owns the means of production; and the proletariat, or working class, which sells its labor power to the capitalists to survive. According to Marx, inequality and poverty are inevitable by-products of the exploitation of workers by capitalists (Vanneman and Cannon, 1987:39).

Like Karl Marx, early German sociologist Max Weber (1864–1920) believed that economic factors were important in determining class location and studying social inequality, but he also believed that other factors were important. Weber developed a multidimensional class model that focused on the interplay of wealth, power, and prestige as determinants of people's class position. *Wealth* **is the value of all economic assets, including income, personal property, and income-producing property.** While some people have great wealth and are able to live off their investments, others must work for wages. *Power* **is the ability of people to achieve their goals despite opposition from others.** People who hold positions of power can achieve their goals because they can control other people; on the other hand, people who hold positions that lack power must carry out the wishes of others. *Prestige* **is the respect, esteem, or regard accorded to an individual or group by others.** Individuals who have high levels of prestige tend to receive deferential and respectful treatment from those with lower levels of prestige.

Recent theorists have modified Marx's and Weber's theories of economic inequality. According to the sociologist Erik O. Wright (1997), neither Weber's multidimensional model of wealth, power, and prestige nor Marx's two-class system fully define classes in modern capitalist societies or explain economic inequality. Wright sets forth four criteria for placement in the class structure: (1) ownership of the means of production; (2) purchase of the labor of others (employing others); (3) control of the labor of others (supervising others on the job); and (4) sale of one's own labor (being employed by someone else). Based on these criteria, Wright (1979, 1985) has identified four classes in the U.S. economy: the capitalist class, the managerial class, the small-business class, and the working class.

 ## Wealth versus Income Inequality

Today, more than 250 families have a net worth above $1 billion, and at least 5 million U.S. households (about 5 percent of all households) have a net worth of at least $1 million. The poorest 20 percent of U.S. households, on the other hand, have a net worth close to zero (D'Souza, 1999).

How is the unequal distribution of wealth associated with social problems? According to sociologists Melvin L. Oliver and Thomas M. Shapiro (1995:2), wealth is a particularly important indicator of individual and family access to life chances:

> Wealth signifies the command over financial resources that a family has accumulated over its lifetime along with those resources that have been inherited across generations. Such resources, when combined with income, can create the opportunity to secure the "good life" in whatever form is needed—education, business, training, justice, health, comfort, and so on. Wealth is a special form of money not used to purchase milk and shoes and other life necessities. More often it is used to create opportunities, secure a desired stature and standard of living, or pass class status along to one's children.

Using secondary analysis of existing data and in-depth interviews with African American and white American families, Oliver and Shapiro found that African Americans have accumulated much less wealth than white Americans because whites, especially well-off whites, have had the opportunity to amass assets and pass them on from generation to generation, whereas African Americans have not. According to Oliver and Shapiro, African Americans have experienced the cumulative effects of racial discrimination as evidenced by poor schooling, high unemployment rates, and low wages. As a result, it has been difficult, if not impossible, for multiple generations of African Americans to acquire wealth, which has kept them cemented to the bottom of the U.S. economic hierarchy.

Like wealth, income is extremely unevenly divided in the United States. *Income* **is the economic gain derived from wages, salaries, income transfers (governmental aid such as Temporary Aid to Needy Families [TANF] or ownership of property)** (Beeghley, 1989). The income gap between the richest and

Although most people are aware of the wide disparity in lifestyles and life chances between the rich and the poor, far fewer of us stop to analyze the differences between middle-class and poverty-level living arrangements in the United States. Should social policies be implemented to equalize opportunities for the young people shown in these photos? Why or why not?

poorest U.S. households has been wide for many years (U.S. Bureau of the Census, 1998). The top 20 percent of households earned more than half of the nation's aggregate income in 1996, and the top 5 percent alone received more than 20 percent of aggregate income (see Figure 2.1). As is shown in Figure 2.2, median income for households across racial and ethnic lines has remained relatively constant over the last decade. Although African Americans have made some gains in income in recent years, median income for both African American and Latina/o households remains far behind median income for white households (Rawlings, 1995).

Divisions in the U.S. Class Structure

The United States has a number of class divisions that are characterized by widely diverse lifestyles and life chances. The upper, or capitalist, class, the wealthiest and most powerful class, is made up of investors, heirs, and executives. Some members of the capitalist class derive their income from investments in income-producing property such as media conglomerates, high-rise hotels, apartment buildings, and office parks; others earn their wealth as entrepreneurs, pres-

idents of major corporations, sports or entertainment celebrities, or top-level professionals. For example, the top ten corporate executives in a recent *Forbes* survey of executive compensation had 1995 salaries and bonuses ranging from about $17.4 million to more than $65.5 million. The upper-middle class is composed of professionals (for example, physicians and attorneys), business analysts, owners of small businesses, stockbrokers, and corporate managers. These individuals generally do not own the means of production but have substantial control over production and other workers (Wright, 1979, 1985). The middle class includes white-collar office workers, middle-management personnel, and people in support positions (for example, medical technologists, nurses, and legal and medical secretaries), semiprofessionals, and nonretail salesworkers.

The working class is composed of people who work as semiskilled machine operators in industrial settings and in nonmanual, semiskilled positions (for example, day-care workers, checkout clerks, cashiers, and counter help in fast-food restaurants). The working poor are those who work full-time in unskilled positions such as seasonal or migrant agricultural workers or the lowest-paid service sector workers but still remain at the edge of poverty. In an interview with sociologist Mark Robert Rank, Jack

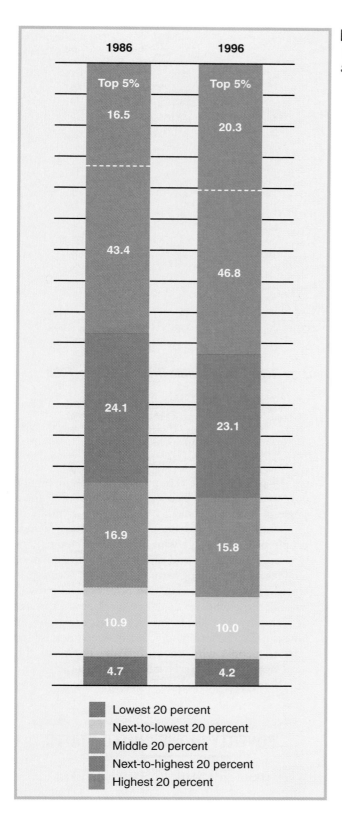

FIGURE 2.1 *Share of Aggregate Income, 1986 and 1996*

Source: U.S. Bureau of the Census, 1998.

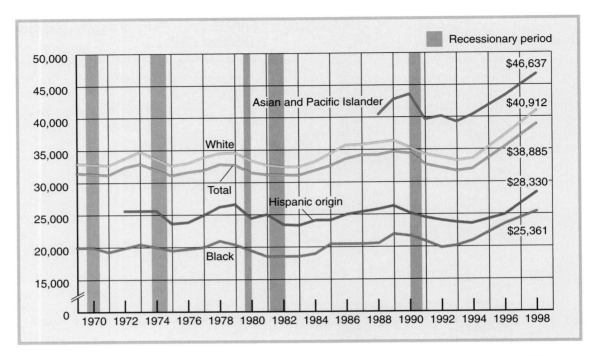

FIGURE 2.2   *Median U.S. Household Income by Race and Hispanic Origin, 1970 to 1998 (median income in 1994 dollars)*

Note: People of Hispanic origin may be of any race. Data for Hispanic-origin households are not available prior to 1972. Data for Asian and Pacific Islander households are not available prior to 1988. Data points represent the midpoints of the respective years.

Source: U.S. Bureau of the Census, 1999a.

Collins, a married father with six children, described the transitory nature of work for the working poor:

> You name it, I've done it. I started out cooking. I've been a janitor. I've been an auto mechanic. I drove a school bus for five years. I drove a semi [truck] coast to coast. I've worked in a foundry. I've worked in a shoe factory. I've worked in other factories, warehouses. I'll do just about anything. . . . The main problem was findin' [a job] with starting pay that's enough to really get by on. (Rank, 1994:43)

Jack Collins and his family may be only one paycheck away from the chronically poor, the bottom division in the U.S. class system.

The chronically poor constitute about 20 percent of the U.S. population but receive only 3.6 percent of the overall U.S. income. People in this category have an average net worth of –$7,075 (i.e., they owe more than they own). In 1998, more than 35 million peo-

ple (14 percent of the U.S. population) fell below the poverty threshold, which ranged from $7,995 for a single-person household to $16,660 for a family of four. Individuals who are chronically poor include people of working age who are unemployed or outside the labor force and children who live in poor families caught in long-term deprivation. Overrepresented among low-income and poverty-level individuals are those who are unable to work because of age or disability and single mothers who are heads of households. The term *underclass* is sometimes used to refer to people who are chronically poor, but this term not only negatively labels poor people, it also puts them outside the mainstream of society.

POVERTY IN THE UNITED STATES

When sociologist Mark Robert Rank asked Denise Turner, an African American mother of four living in poverty, to describe her daily life, Denise Turner replied,

> . . . it can be summarized in one word, and that's survival. That's what we're tryin' to do. We're tryin' to survive. And . . . I talk to a lot of people, and they say, "Well, hey, if you went to Ethiopia, you know, survival would be one thing. And that's . . . eating." But, damn it, I'm not in Ethiopia! You know. So I want a little bit more than just . . . having some food. Having a coupla meals. So, if I can just summarize it, in one word, it would be we're tryin' to survive. We're tryin' to stay together. That's my major concern, keepin' all my family together, my children together. And to survive. (quoted in Rank, 1994:88)

Sociologists refer to the distinction that Denise makes between poverty in Ethiopia and poverty in the United States as the difference between absolute poverty and relative poverty. Absolute poverty exists when people do not have the means to secure the most basic necessities of life (food, clothing, and shelter). *Relative poverty* **exists when people may be able to afford basic necessities such as food, clothing, and shelter but cannot maintain an average standard of living in comparison to that of other members of their society or group** (Ropers, 1991). Denise Turner does not suffer from absolute poverty, but she does experience relative poverty on the basis of what is available to other people in the United States.

The United States has the highest poverty rate of any advanced industrial nation (Rothchild, 1995). The *poverty rate* **is the proportion of the population whose income falls below the government's official poverty line—the level of income below which a family of a given size is considered to be poor.** As is shown in Figure 2.3, the U.S. poverty rate has remained relatively constant over the past several decades, although both the rate and the number of people living in poverty has decreased slightly during the most recent few years. The official poverty line is based on money income and cash government assistance programs such as Social Security payments; however, it does not reflect the value of in-kind benefits such as public housing subsidies, food stamps, Medicare, or Medicaid.

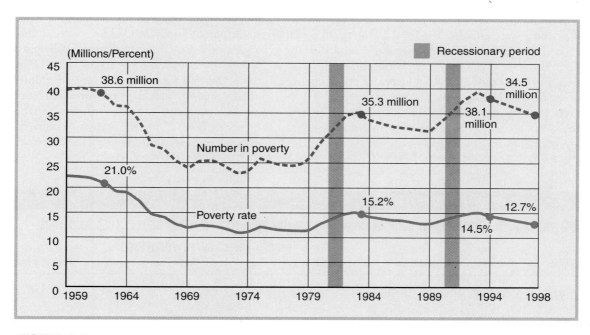

FIGURE 2.3 *Poverty in the United States, 1959 to 1998*
Source: U.S. Bureau of the Census, 1998, 1999b.

The Poverty Line

How is the U.S. poverty line determined? Established in 1965 by the Social Security Administration, the poverty line is based on an assumption that the average family must spend about one-third of its total income on food. Therefore the official poverty line is determined by a minimum family *market basket*—a low-cost food budget that contains a minimum level of nutrition for a family—multiplied by three to allow for nonfood costs such as rent and utilities. Although the poverty line is adjusted for the number of people in the household and is corrected at least annually for changes in the cost of living, essentially the same poverty test has been used since the 1960s.

Today, many social analysts argue that the official poverty line is too low. According to economist Patricia Ruggles (1990, 1992), the poverty line is based on outdated (pre-1960) standards that were established at a time when fewer households were composed of two working parents or of single parents who faced employment-related expenses such as work clothes, transportation, child care, and quick and convenient foods. Ruggles believes poverty thresholds should be increased by at least 50 percent.

 Who Are the Poor?

If poverty were equally distributed among all social groups in the United States, all people regardless of their age, race or ethnicity, sex, household composition, or other attributes would have an equal chance of being among the poor in any given year. However, poverty is not distributed equally: People in some categories are at greater risk for poverty than are people in other categories.

The vast majority of poor people in the United States are women and children. Children under age eighteen—25 percent of the U.S. population—account for more than 40 percent of the poor. About one in five children age eighteen and under lives in poverty (see Table 2.1). The percentage of children under six years of age who live in poverty-level households is even higher: In 1998, about one in four was considered poor. When children under age six live in households headed by women with no adult male present, almost 55 percent are poor. Children of working-poor parents are the fastest growing segment of children living in poverty (Holmes, 1996b). More than half of all poor children live in families in which one or both parents work outside the home (U.S. Bureau of Census, 1998).

About two-thirds of all adults living in poverty are women; households headed by women are the fastest-growing segment of the overall poverty population. Researchers have discovered a number of reasons why single-parent families headed by women are at such a great risk of poverty. Single-parent families typically have fewer employed adults in them and therefore a lower annual income than most two-parent households in the first place, and women generally earn less money than men, even for comparable work. Thus, a single-parent family headed by a woman usually faces a greater risk of poverty than a single-parent family headed by a man. Women also bear the major economic burden for their children. Contributions from absent fathers in the form of child support and alimony payments account for less than 10 percent of family income. About 43 percent of unmarried mothers with incomes above poverty level receive child sup-

TABLE 2.1   CHILDREN (Under 18 Years Old) BELOW THE U.S. POVERTY LEVEL, 1989 AND 1998

| YEAR | PERCENTAGE BELOW POVERTY LEVEL | | | |
	All Races	White	Black	Hispanic Origin
1989	20.1	15.3	44.5	38.1
1998	18.9	16.8	44.7	36.9

Source: U.S. Bureau of the Census, 1998, 1999b.

port from the fathers; however, only 25 percent of unmarried mothers at or below the poverty line receive such support (U.S. House of Representatives, 1994). Sociologist Diana Pearce (1978) refers to the association between gender and poverty as the *feminization of poverty*—**the trend whereby women are disproportionately represented among individuals living in poverty.** On the basis of research on the feminization of poverty, some sociologists suggest that high rates of female poverty are related to women's unique vulnerability to event-driven poverty—poverty resulting from the loss of a job, disability, desertion by a spouse, separation, divorce, or widowhood (Weitzman, 1985; Bane, 1986; Kurz, 1995).

RACE, ETHNICITY, AND POVERTY

African Americans, Latinos/as, and Native Americans are overrepresented among people living in poverty (see Figure 2.4). Across racial-ethnic categories, about three times as many African American

families and Latina/o families lived in poverty in 1999 as non-Latina/o white families (U.S. Bureau of the Census, 1999). Within racial-ethnic categories, fewer than one in ten (non-Latino/a) whites fell below the official poverty level in 1998, in contrast to 12.5 percent of all Asian and Pacific Americans, 26.1 percent of all African Americans, and 25.6 percent of all Latinos/as.

The contrast in poverty rates within racial-ethnic categories becomes especially evident when household composition is considered. In households headed by women with no husband present, about half of all Latina/o families (43.7 percent) and African American families (40.8 percent) had incomes below the official poverty level in 1998, in contrast to 20.7 percent of white (non-Latino/a) families. Recent research suggests that two out of three African American families headed by women were poor before the event that made the woman a single mother (Bane and Ellwood, 1994). According to sociologist Demie Kurz (1995),

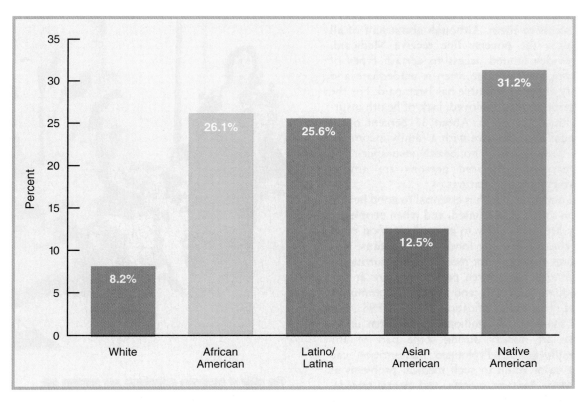

FIGURE 2.4 *People below U.S. Poverty Level, 1998, by Race*

Note: Data on Native Americans are based on 1990 figures.

Source: U.S. Bureau of the Census, 1999b.

the feminization of poverty is intensified by the racialization of poverty—the process by which the effects of low income are made even worse by racial discrimination, which is experienced by all people of color but particularly by women who are single heads of household.

 Consequences of Poverty

Poverty statistics are more than just a snapshot of who is poor and how the poor live: These statistics are predictors. As such, they tend to predict a grim future for individuals who live below the poverty line and for the entire nation (Gleick, 1996). As one social analyst has noted, "Poverty narrows and closes life chances. . . . Being poor not only means economic insecurity, it also wreaks havoc on one's mental and physical health" (Ropers, 1991:25).

HEALTH AND NUTRITION

Although the United States has some of the best high-tech medical facilities in the world, not all people have access to them. Although about half of all people below the poverty line receive Medicaid, which provides limited access to certain types of medical care, the coverage often is inadequate and begins only after a deductible has been paid. For the working poor and unemployed, lack of health insurance is a major problem. About 35 percent of all people under age sixty-five with a family income of less than $16,000 have no health insurance. The highest rates of uninsured persons are among African Americans and Latinas/os.

Good nutrition, which is essential to good health, depends on the food purchased, and when people are poor, they are more likely to go without food or to purchase cheap but filling foods such as beans, rice, and potatoes that may not meet all daily nutritional requirements. Poor children particularly are at risk for inadequate nutrition and hunger (Community Childhood Hunger Identification Project, 1995). It is estimated that about 4 million U.S. children under age twelve are hungry during some part of any twelve-month period. Prolonged malnutrition can contribute to or result in such medical problems as rickets, scurvy, parasitic worms, and mental retardation. Between one-third and one-half of all children living in poverty consume significantly less than the federally recommended guidelines for caloric and nutritional intake (Children's Defense Fund, 1999).

Problems associated with food and shelter are intricately linked. When parents have to decide between paying the rent and putting food on the table, many choose to pay the rent in hopes of keeping a roof over their children's head. Sometimes, however, they cannot afford to do either.

HOUSING

Many regions of the United States have lacked affordable housing for low-income families for some time. In the last decade low-cost housing units in many areas have been replaced by expensive condominiums or single-family residences for affluent residents. This shift to condominiums and single-family residences has made finding housing even more difficult for individuals and families living in poverty. When low-income housing is available, it may be located in racially segregated areas plagued by high crime rates and overcrowded conditions. The housing often has inadequate heating and plumbing facil-

The sight of homeless individuals and families has become all too familiar in both cities and rural areas in the United States. What social factors do you think have caused an increase in homeless families in recent years?

ities, cockroach and rodent infestation, and dangerous structural problems due to faulty construction or lack of adequate maintenance. Although much of the substandard housing exists in central cities, rural areas have more than 50 percent of all inadequate housing units (U.S. House of Representatives, 1994).

In recent years, increasing rates of homelessness reflect one of the most devastating effects of poverty. Today, homeless people include single men, single women, increasing numbers of teenage runaways, older people, and entire families (see studies by Rossi, 1989; Liebow, 1993; Lundy, 1995). Families with children accounted for almost 40 percent of all homeless people in 1994, up from about 27 percent a decade earlier (Children's Defense Fund, 1995). Regardless of age or marital status, homeless people are among the poorest of the poor, and people of color are overrepresented in the homeless population.

EDUCATION

A crucial relationship exists between educational opportunities and life chances. Children from low-income families tend to have inadequate educational opportunities, which keeps them at the bottom of the class system (Bowles and Gintis, 1976). They get fewer years of schooling and are less likely to graduate from high school or college than are children from more affluent families. The schools that poor children attend are more likely to be in areas with lower property values and more limited funding bases for education than are the schools attended by more affluent students, who often live in property-rich suburbs. Schools located in high-poverty rural areas or central cities often are dilapidated, have underpaid and overworked teachers, and must rely on outdated equipment and teaching materials.

Lack of educational opportunity results in lower levels of educational attainment among people from lower-income and poverty-level families and tends to perpetuate poverty by making it significantly more difficult for these individuals to acquire well-paying jobs or a more secure economic future.

SOCIAL WELFARE IN THE UNITED STATES

The initial wave of U.S. welfare programs was established by Roosevelt's New Deal during the Great Depression of the 1930s. These programs marked the beginning of the *welfare state*—**a program under which the government takes responsibility for specific categories of people by offering them certain services and benefits, such as employment, housing, health, education, or guaranteed income.** From their inception, government assistance programs have been viewed as "good" if recipients are thought to be deserving of assistance and "bad" if recipients are considered undeserving (see Box 2.2).

The second wave of welfare programs began with the passage of the Economic Opportunity Act of 1964 and the implementation of the War on Poverty programs, which focused on education and vocational training for low-income children and adults to help them escape poverty. These programs included preschool education (Head Start), compensatory education, and vocational training programs such as Job Corps, Neighborhood Youth Corps, and Manpower Development (Kelso, 1994). With these programs in place, the percentage of people living in poverty dropped from 22 percent in 1960 to 12 percent in

A New Beginning
Welfare to Work

Signing the welfare reform act of 1996, President Bill Clinton stated that he hoped the nation was entering a new era when government-funded welfare payments would no longer be necessary in this country. Do you think we are closer to reaching this goal today than we were when he signed the bill?

SOCIAL PROBLEMS

The End of Welfare as We Know It?

Today we are ending welfare as we know it. But I hope this day will be remembered not for what it ended, but for what it began: a new day that offers hope, honors responsibility, rewards work, and changes the terms of the debate so that no one in America ever feels again the need to criticize people who are poor or on welfare.

—*President Bill Clinton, explaining his hopes for new welfare legislation passed by Congress in 1996 (quoted in Kilborn, 1996:A10)*

On August 22, 1996, President Bill Clinton signed into law the Personal Responsibility and Work Opportunity Reconciliation Act of 1996, which made sweeping changes in the U.S. welfare system. As a result of the act, the Temporary Assistance for Needy Families (TANF) program replaced Aid to Families with Dependent Children (AFDC), the federal program that had provided cash assistance to poor families since 1950. Among other things, TANF guarantees states $16.4 billion in block grants annually and sets limits on the length of time families can receive assistance. With few exceptions, the new law also requires recipients to work after two years of assistance. A recipient's failure to participate in job training programs or to meet work requirements can result in a reduction or termination of benefits for the recipient's family. Because states receive block grants for the program, they are required to enforce a variety of rules concerning the disbursement of funds and the requirements placed on those who receive funds. States are also responsible for trying to reduce the number of "out-of-wedlock births and abortions," and those states that are successful receive bonus monies. States must require unmarried teenage mothers to live with a responsible adult or in an adult-supervised set-

ting. The young mothers must also participate in educational and training programs to enhance their job skills.

What effect have these changes had so far? Although welfare rolls have been cut almost in half and some former recipients of AFDC are now gainfully employed, many remain unemployed, and the number of people below 50 percent of the poverty level has increased sharply. Even as some people have left the welfare rolls, their families have experienced a loss of income. It is estimated that the poorest 20 percent of families once on AFDC have lost $577 a year in income as they have left welfare but have not made up lost benefits with wages (Meckler, 1999). Others have found it impossible to get a job and leave welfare. Debates over why these individuals cannot leave the welfare rolls continue: Liberal politicians usually state that these recipients are held back by child-care difficulties, lack of transportation, weak education, illiteracy, and/or disabilities; conservative politicians usually state that many recipients simply do not want to work or that they are not adequately motivated (Cohen, 1999b).

Why are some of the needy stigmatized more than others? The answer lies in part in the history of the U.S. welfare system. For many years, a distinction has been made between those who are considered deserving of government assistance—widows, orphans, farmers hit by droughts or other natural disasters, the permanently disabled, workers who experience unemployment through no fault of their own, and older workers who retire after many years of employment—and those who are considered undeserving. The undeserving are viewed as able-bodied individuals who are lazy and unwilling to work (Katz, 1989).

The distinction between deserving and undeserving recipients of government largess can be traced back to the Great Depression of the 1930s when the New Deal was implemented and the Social Security Act of 1935 established income transfer programs. Social Security is *age tested*—persons who have paid money into the program are entitled to receive benefits upon reaching retirement age. By contrast, programs such as AFDC and TANF are *means tested*—recipients have to show proof of poverty in order to receive benefits, not proof that they have paid money into the program. Because the majority of TANF recipients are single mothers, this distinction between the two programs has contributed to the stigmatization not only of poverty but also of single motherhood. Thus the 1996 welfare reform act was primarily targeted at single mothers with young children, especially unmarried mothers under age eighteen.

When most people think about appropriate social policy, they do not consider the amount of money spent on "wealthfare" programs, such as defense (Perrucci and Wysong, 1999). In 1999, the U.S. government spent $271 billion on defense and only $16.4 billion on TANF. Indeed, TANF amounted to less than

1 percent of the total $1.7 trillion federal budget in 1999. According to sociologists Robert Perrucci and Earl Wysong (1999:134),

> Of course, some portion of defense spending is legitimate on the grounds of protecting U.S. national security (though how much is open to debate). But large chunks of defense spending exist primarily to juice the profits of military contractor firms and to feed the hundreds of thousands of high-paid scientists, engineers, and civilian employees who work in government, industry, and university research and administration units throughout the "national security state."

Fred Grandy, a former congressman who now heads Goodwill Industries, which finds jobs for those who are difficult to employ, has noted, "Tough love has its place in welfare reform [but] the work of reform is going to get a lot tougher, and love is going to have to get a bit gentler" (Cohen, 1999b:28).

1976 (see Coleman, 1966; Jencks et al., 1972). However, the Reagan and Bush administrations in the 1980s and early 1990s greatly reduced or eliminated funding for Aid to Families with Dependent Children (AFDC), food stamps, subsidized housing, child-nutrition programs, maternal and child health programs, family planning, and job training (see Danziger and Gottschalk, 1995).

In 1996, President Clinton signed into law a welfare reform plan that dramatically changed the U.S. welfare system by requiring recipients to work in exchange for time-limited assistance. This law brought into existence TANF, which replaced AFDC and the Job Opportunities and Basic Skills Training (JOBS) program, ending federal entitlement to assistance (see Box 2.2).

Are welfare programs a problem or a solution for poverty? The answer to this question depends on how poverty itself is explained.

Explanations for Poverty

Poverty can be explained in individualistic, cultural, or structural terms. The framework that is applied influences people's beliefs about how poverty might be reduced. Individual explanations for poverty view poverty as the result of either attitudinal and motivational problems that cause individuals to be poor or the amount of human capital that a person possesses (Rank, 1994). Attitudinal and motivational explanations focus on the United States as the "land of opportunity" and suggest that people who do not succeed have no one to blame but themselves for their lack of motivation, laziness, or other flaws (Feagin, 1975). In contrast, human capital explanations of poverty highlight the individual's lack of *human capital*—the assets that a person brings to the labor market such as education, job training, experience, and specialized knowledge or skills (Becker, 1964).

Reprinted by permission.

Those favoring human capital explanations of poverty have noted, for example, that the introduction of new workplace technologies has resulted in many people having limited human capital to bring to the job market. The 1996 workfare program for welfare recipients appears to be based on individual explanations for poverty and welfare dependency. To many sociologists, however, individual explanations of poverty amount to *blaming the victim*—a practice used by people who view a social problem as emanating from within the individual who exhibits the problem (Ryan, 1976).

Cultural explanations of poverty focus on how cultural background affects people's values and behavior. Among the earliest of these explanations is the culture of poverty thesis by anthropologist Oscar Lewis (1966). According to Lewis, some—but not all—poor people develop a separate and self-perpetuating system of attitudes and behaviors that keeps them trapped in poverty. Among these attitudes and behaviors are an inability to defer gratification or plan for the future; feelings of apathy, hostility, and suspicion toward others; and deficient speech and communication patterns. The culture of poverty thesis has provided political leaders and social analysts with a rationale for labeling the poor as lazy and perpetually dependent on "government handouts."

More recent cultural explanations of poverty have focused on the lack of *cultural capital*—social assets such as the values, beliefs, attitudes, and competencies in language and culture that are learned at home and required for success and social advancement (Bourdieu and Passeron, 1990). From this perspective, low-income people do not have adequate cultural capital to function in a competitive global economy. According to some sociologists, cultural explanations deflect attention from the true sources of poverty and shift blame from the affluent and powerful to the poor and powerless (Sidel, 1996: xvii–xviii).

Unlike individual and cultural explanations of poverty, which operate at the microlevel, structural explanations of poverty focus on the macrolevel, the level of social organization that is beyond an individual's ability to change. One structural explanation of poverty points to changes in the economy that have dramatically altered employment opportunities for people, particularly those who have the least wealth, power, and prestige (see Wilson, 1996). According to the functionalists who espouse this explanation, social inequality serves an important function in society because it motivates people to work hard to acquire scarce resources.

Another structural explanation for poverty is based on a conflict perspective that suggests poverty is a side effect of the capitalist system. Using this explanation, analysts note that workers are increasingly impoverished by the wage squeeze and high rates of unemployment and underemployment. The wage squeeze is the steady downward pressure on the real take-home pay of workers that has occurred over the past two decades. During these same decades, shareholders in major corporations have had substantial increases in dividends and chief executive officers have received extremely lucrative salaries and compensation packages (Gordon, 1996). Corporate downsizing and new technologies that take the place of workers have further enhanced capitalists' profits and contributed to the impoverishment of middle- and low-income workers by creating a reserve army of unemployed people whom the capitalists use for labor and as a means to keep other workers' wages low. In sum, corporations' intense quest for profit results in low wages for workers, a wide disparity in the life chances of affluent people and poor people, and the unemployment and impoverishment of many people. Although some analysts suggest that high rates of poverty will always exist in advanced capitalist societies, others believe that inequality and poverty can be reduced if not eliminated.

◢ Can Class-Based Inequality Be Reduced?

Chapter 1 made the point that how people view a social problem is related to how they believe the problem should be reduced or solved. Poverty and social inequality are no exceptions. Analysts who focus on individualistic explanations of poverty typically suggest individual solutions: Low-income and poverty-level people should change their attitudes, beliefs, and work habits. For example, economist George Gilder (1981) has stated that "the only dependable route from poverty is always work. . . . The poor must not only work, they must work harder than the classes above them."

Similarly, people who use cultural explanations seek cultural solutions, suggesting that poverty can be reduced by enhancing people's cultural capital. They urge the development of more job training and school enrichment programs to enhance people's cultural capital and counteract negative familial and neighborhood influences. Seeking cultural solutions, the federal government developed Head Start programs and the Job Corps to provide children and adolescents from low-income families, especially families of color, with the cultural capital (e.g., white middle-class values) that they need to succeed (see Quadagno and Fobes, 1995).

Although some analysts seeking structural solutions suggest that poverty can be eliminated only if capitalism is abolished and a new means of distributing valued goods and services is established, others state that poverty can be reduced by the creation of "a truly open society—a society where the life chances of those at the bottom are not radically different from those at the top and where wealth is distributed more equitably" (MacLeod, 1995:260). These analysts feel that federal and state governments should play a vital role in reducing poverty and lessening people's dependency on welfare. Recent proposals based on this structural solution include the following:

◢ Establishing a coordinated employment policy that emphasizes the creation of jobs with livable wages and benefits

◢ Building individual assets through government policies that provide incentives and resources for low-income families to acquire and build economic assets

◢ Providing tax benefits such as EITC to assist low-income workers

◢ Giving economic assistance to help families deal with divorce, unwanted teenage pregnancy, and child-care problems

◢ Providing universal medical coverage for low-income families, older people, and individuals with serious health problems without qualifying deductibles that reduce assets and income

◢ Investing in lower-income areas of communities and empowering residents to organize and address problems such as affordable housing and better schools (Rank, 1994)

Although these proposals, if enacted, would not "solve" the problem of poverty, they might temper and reduce the price poor people pay for living in the "land of opportunity" (Rank, 1994). In the meantime, amazingly, many people living in poverty have not given up on the American Dream. Sara, a woman struggling to find opportunities for herself and her children, said,

> I got my vision, I got my dreams. . . . I have goals—I want to be something different from what I have right now. . . . I guess to be somebody in poverty, to see that generation that's coming behind us—it's sad, it's real sad, what do they have to strive for? . . . I just got to believe I only can make the difference. . . . even though obviously the system doesn't really want you to succeed. . . . I can become what statistics has designed me to be, a nothing, or I can make statistics a lie. . . . Today, I am making statistics a lie. (Polakow, 1993:73)

SUMMARY

➡ *Why is social stratification a social problem?*

Social stratification refers to the hierarchical arrangement of large social groups based on their control over basic resources. In highly stratified societies, low-income and poor people have limited access to food, clothing, shelter, education, health care, and other necessities of life.

➡ *What are the major problems of the low-income nations?*

Studies of global inequality distinguish between high-income nations—countries with highly industrialized economies and relatively high levels of national and per capita (per person) income, middle-income nations—countries that are undergoing transformation from agrarian to industrial economies, and low-income nations—countries that are primarily agrarian with little industrialization and low levels of national and personal income. Poverty, food shortages, hunger, and rapidly growing populations are pressing problems in many low-income nations.

➡ *How does the "new international division of labor" perspective explain global inequality?*

According to this perspective, transnational corporations have established global assembly lines of production in which workers in middle- and low-income nations, earning extremely low wages, produce goods for export to high-income nations such as the United States and Japan.

➡ *How is the U.S. class structure divided?*

The U.S. population is divided into a number of classes. The upper, or capitalist, class, the wealthiest and most powerful class is made up of investors, heirs, and executives. The upper-middle class is composed of professionals, business analysts, owners of small businesses, stockbrokers, and business analysts. The middle class includes white-collar office workers, middle-management personnel, people in technical support positions, semiprofessionals, and nonretail salesworkers. Members of the working class hold occupations such as semiskilled machine operators and counter help in fast-food restaurants. The chronically poor include individuals of working age who are outside the labor force and children who live in poor families.

➡ *Who are the poor in the United States?*

The major categories of poor people in the United States are women, children under age eighteen, and people of color, especially African Americans, Latinas/os, and Native Americans.

➡ *What are individual and cultural explanations of poverty?*

Individual explanations of poverty focus on the attitudinal and motivational problems of individuals or the amount of human capital a person possesses. Cultural explanations of poverty focus on how cultural background affects people's values and behavior. These explanations focus on the microlevel, and many sociologists view them as attempts to blame the victim for the problem.

➡ *What are structural explanations of poverty?*

Structural explanations of poverty focus on the macrolevel, the level of social organization that is beyond an individual's ability to change. These explanations consider how changes in the economy have altered employment opportunities or how inequality and exploitation are inherent in the structure of class relations in a capitalist economy.

➤ *What solutions have been suggested for poverty?*
    Most individual and cultural solutions focus on the importance of work. Individual perspectives sug-gest that people should work harder. Cultural perspectives suggest enhancing people's cultural capital to make them better prepared for employment. Structural perspectives are based on the assumption that society can reduce poverty by creating job and training programs and investing in people through provision of child care, health care, and affordable housing.

KEY TERMS

absolute poverty, p. 22
blaming the victim, p. 36
class system, p. 21
cultural capital, p. 36
feminization of poverty, p. 31
high-income nations, p. 22

income, p. 25
life chances, p. 22
low-income nations, p. 22
middle-income nations, p. 22
poverty rate, p. 29
power, p. 25

prestige, p. 25
relative poverty, p. 29
social stratification, p. 23
wealth, p. 25
welfare state, p. 33

QUESTIONS FOR CRITICAL THINKING

1. You have decided to study wealth and poverty in your community. Which of the research method(s) described in Chapter 1 would provide the best data for analysis? What secondary sources might provide useful data? What kinds of information would be easiest to acquire? What kinds of information would be most difficult to acquire?

2. What would happen if all the wealth in the United States were redistributed so that all adults had the same amount? Some analysts suggest that within five years most of the wealth would be back in the possession of the people who hold it today. What arguments can you give to support this idea? What arguments can you give to disprove this idea?

3. How do the lives of assembly line workers in middle- and low-income nations compare with the lives of people who live in poverty in central cities and rural areas of the United States? Should U.S. foreign policy include provisions for reducing the problems of people in middle- and low-income nations? Should it be U.S. government policy to help disadvantaged people in our own country? Why or why not?

4. Pretend that cost is no object and develop a plan for solving the problem of poverty in the United States. What are your priorities and goals? How long will your plan take to implement? Who will be the primary beneficiaries of your plan? Will the plan have any effect on you?

Chapter Three

Racial and Ethnic Inequality

We are unable to get taxis to pick us up in front of office buildings. We are frisked and detained on suburban commuter trains. We are watched in department stores and mistaken for coat-check clerks and restroom attendants while lunching in the best restaurants. We are directed to freight elevators and delivery windows by receptionists who fail to recognize us in our own company offices.

We are black professionals in corporate America in the 1990s.

Although I am at my desk each morning facing the same corporate challenges as my white co-workers, a great deal of my job-related stress comes from sources totally unrelated to my job. . . . The amount of subtle bias I face as a lawyer continues to dismay me. For example, I have worked with clients or co-counsel who have become comfortable with me through phone conversations and correspondence. But upon meeting me, they are suddenly fidgety and wary of my competence.

"Where did you go to law school?" they ask almost immediately.

Unable to focus on anything else until they hear "Harvard," these clients rarely say, "I pay that firm a lot of money. How come they gave me the black lawyer?" But they do practice more subtle, and ultimately more damaging, discrimination. The client, for example, may phrase his immediate dissatisfaction at being assigned to a black as a complaint that is vague yet incriminating ("I don't feel very comfortable working with Larry") or, worse, may complain about my skills ("I don't think Larry is up to the job, so assign me another lawyer").

In both cases, the forthright employer is left thinking there is no bias, and the black employee is left without a client, but with an abiding sense of failure and anger.

—Lawrence Otis Graham, a corporate lawyer and author, describing the experiences of many middle- and upper-middle-class African Americans in corporate America
(Graham, 1995:F13)

As Graham points out, African Americans and other people of color often experience both overt and subtle discrimination in their daily lives, regardless of their educational background and level of income. As described in Chapter 1, *discrimination* is the actions or practices of dominant group members that have a harmful impact on members of subordinate groups (Feagin and Feagin, 1999). Like many other social problems, racial and ethnic discrimination signals a discrepancy between the ideals and realities of U.S. society today. While equality and freedom for all—regardless of race, color, creed, or national origin—are stated ideals of this country, many subordinate group members experience oppression regardless of their class, gender, or age.

RACIAL AND ETHNIC INEQUALITY AS A SOCIAL PROBLEM

As we enter the twenty-first century, race is among the most divisive social problems facing the United States. At the same time, sociologists such as William J. Wilson (1996) suggest that we all—regardless of racial or ethnic background—share certain common interests and concerns that cross racial and class boundaries. Some of the problems are unemployment and job insecurity, declining real wages, escalating medical and housing costs, a scarcity of good-quality child-care programs, a sharp decline in the quality of public education, and the toll of crime and drug trafficking in all neighborhoods. From this perspective, racial and ethnic inequality is a problem for everyone, not just for people of color.

 ### What Are Race and Ethnicity?

Many sociologists view race as a social construct—a classification of people based on social and political values—rather than a biological given (see Omi and Winant, 1994). How does a sociological definition of race differ from a biological one? A biological definition of a race is a population that differs from other populations in the incidence of some genes. In the past, some anthropologists classified diverse categories of peoples into races on the basis of skin color

(pigmentation) and features and build (morphology). However, contemporary anthropologists classify races in terms of genetically determined immunological and biochemical differences. In the process, they have concluded that no "pure" races exist because of multiple generations of interbreeding.

In contrast with the biological definition of race, sociologists define a *racial group* as a category of people who have been singled out, by others or themselves, as inferior or superior, on the basis of subjectively selected physical characteristics such as skin color, hair texture, and eye shape. African American, Native American, and Asian American are examples of categories of people that have been designated racial groups.

Sociologists note that racial groups usually are defined on the basis of real or alleged physical characteristics; ethnic groups are defined on the basis of cultural or nationality characteristics. An *ethnic group* is a category of people who are distinguished, by others or by themselves, as inferior or superior primarily on the basis of cultural or nationality characteristics (Feagin and Feagin, 1999). Briefly stated, members of an ethnic group share five main characteristics: (1) unique cultural traits; (2) a sense of community; (3) a feeling that one's own group is the best; (4) membership from birth; and (5) a tendency, at least initially, to occupy a distinct geographic area (such as Chinatown, Little Italy, or Little Havana). "White ethnics," such as Irish Americans, Italian Americans, and Jewish Americans, are also examples of ethnic groups.

"Official" Racial and Ethnic Classifications

Racial and ethnic classifications have been used for political, economic, and social purposes for many years. During the sixteenth century, northern Europeans used the concept of race to rationalize the enslavement of Africans, who were deemed an "inferior race" (Feagin and Feagin, 1999).

Before the Civil War, race was used to justify the subordination of African Americans—whether they were classified "slaves" in the South or "freemen" in the North. In some southern states, people were classified on the basis of the "one-drop rule"—a person with any trace of African blood was considered "black" and treated as inferior (Davis, 1991). Other states traced "black blood" by fractions, such as one-sixteenth African ancestry, or used an "eyeball test" based on physical features such as hair texture; eye color; and shape of nose, ears, lips, and skull (Funderburg, 1994). Being classified as "Negro," "black," or "colored" had a profound effect on people's life chances and opportunities during slavery and the subsequent era of legally sanctioned separation of the races. Gregory Howard Williams describes how he felt when he learned from his father in the 1950s that he was "colored" rather than white, as he previously had been led to believe:

> [My father said,] "Life is going to be different from now on. In Virginia you were white boys. In Indiana, you're going to be colored boys. I want you to remember that you're the same today that you were yesterday. But people in Indiana will treat you differently. . . ."
>
> No, I answered, still refusing to believe. I'm not colored, I'm white! I look white! I've always been white! I go to "whites only" schools, "whites only" movie theaters, and "whites only" swimming pools! I never had heard anything crazier in my life! How could Dad tell us such a mean lie? I glanced across the aisle [of the bus] to where he sat grim-faced and erect, staring straight ahead. I saw my father as I never had seen him before. . . . My father was a Negro! We were colored! After ten years in Virginia on the white side of the color line, I knew what that meant. (Williams, 1996:33–34)

When Williams and his younger brother went to live with their African American grandmother in Muncie, Indiana, they quickly saw the sharp contrast between the "white" and "black" worlds: The first was one of privilege, opportunity, and comfort, and the second was one of deprivation, repression, and struggle. Since that time, Williams has become a lawyer and a law school dean; however, his memories of the prejudice and discrimination he experienced in Muncie because of the change in his racial classification remain with him (Williams, 1996).

Government racial classifications are based primarily on skin color. One category exists for "whites" (who vary considerably in actual skin color and physical appearance); all the remaining categories are considered "non-white." Until the 2000 census, the Bureau of the Census required respondents to choose from the categories of White, Black, Asian and Pacific American, American Indian, Eskimo or Aleut, or "Other" in designating their racial classification. In an effort to overcome inadequacies in the previous system, the 2000 census allowed people to place themselves in more than one racial category. Although racial classifications may seem unimportant, they affect people's access to employment, housing, social services, federal aid, and many other publicly and privately valued goods and services (Omi and Winant, 1994).

The Meaning of Majority and Minority Groups

When sociologists use the terms *majority group* and *minority group,* they are referring to power differentials among groups, not to the numerical sense in which the words *majority* and *minority* are generally used. **A *majority* (or *dominant*) group is one that is advantaged and has superior resources and rights in a society** (Feagin and Feagin, 1999). Majority groups often are determined on the basis of race or ethnicity, but they can also be determined on the basis of gender, sexual orientation (homosexuality, heterosexuality, or bisexuality), or physical ability. **A *minority* (or *subordinate*) group is one whose members, because of physical or cultural characteristics, are disadvantaged and subjected to unequal treatment by the majority group and regard themselves as objects of collective discrimination** (Wirth, 1945). In the United States, people of color, all women, people with disabilities, and gay men and lesbians tend to be considered minority group members regardless of their proportion in the overall U.S. population.

In the United States, the racial and ethnic majority group typically is associated with the *white-skin privilege,* privilege that accrues to the people who trace their ancestry to Northern Europe and think of themselves as European Americans or WASPs (white Anglo-Saxon Protestants). Women's studies scholar Peggy McIntosh describes white-skin privilege as

> an invisible package of unearned assets that I can count on cashing in each day, but about which I was "meant" to remain oblivious. White privilege is like an invisible weightless knapsack of special provisions, assurances, maps, guides, codebooks, passports, visas, clothes, compass, emergency gear, and blank checks. (McIntosh, 1995:76–77)

Most white Americans are unaware of the benefits that they derive from white-skin privilege (see Frankenberg, 1993; Wellman, 1993; Hacker, 1995; McIntosh, 1995). Nevertheless, the advantage/disadvantage and power/exploitation relationships of majority and minority groups in this country are deeply rooted in patterns of prejudice and discrimination.

RACISM, PREJUDICE, AND DISCRIMINATION

Racism **is a set of attitudes, beliefs, and practices used to justify the superior treatment of one racial or ethnic group and the inferior treatment of another racial or ethnic group.** In the United States, racism is sometimes referred to as white racism. *White racism* refers to socially organized attitudes, ideas, and practices that deny people of color the dignity, opportunities, freedoms, and rewards that are typically available to white Americans (Feagin and Vera, 1995:7). From this perspective, people of color pay a *direct, heavy, and immediately painful price* for racism, while white discriminators pay an *indirect and seldom-recognized price*.

Prejudice **is a negative attitude about people based on such characteristics as race, age, religion, or sexual orientation** (Allport, 1958). If we think of prejudice as a set of negative attitudes toward members of another group simply because they belong to that group, we quickly realize that all people have prejudices, whether or not they acknowledge them. Prejudice is rooted in *ethnocentrism*—the assumption that one's own group and way of life are superior to all others. For example, most schoolchildren are taught that their own school and country are the best. The school song, the pledge to the flag, and the national anthem are forms of *positive ethnocentrism*. However, *negative ethnocentrism* can result if individuals come to believe, because of constant emphasis on the superiority of one's own group or nation, that other groups or nations are inferior and should be treated accordingly (Feagin and Feagin, 1999). Negative ethnocentrism is manifested in stereotypes that adversely affect many people.

Stereotypes **are overgeneralizations about the appearance, behavior, or other characteristics of all members of a group.** For example, second-generation Filipino American Steven De Castro and his friends were the objects of stereotyping throughout their school years:

> "What's up, monkey?" "Hey Ching Chong! Hey eggroll!" "Here comes the gook!" If you are Filipino in America, that is what you grow up hearing in the schoolyard. All you want to do is belong, but white and black classmates never let you forget that you will never belong in their America. (De Castro, 1994:303–304)

Box 3.1, "Racism in Canada," discusses stereotyping and discrimination that occur in most nations that have diverse populations. Discrimination may be carried out by individuals acting on their own or by individuals operating within the context of large-scale organizations or institutions such as schools, corporations, and government agencies. *Individual discrimination* **consists of one-on-one acts by members of the dominant group that harm members of the subordinate group or their property** (Carmichael and Hamilton, 1967). Individual discrimination results from the prejudices and discriminatory actions of bigoted people who target one or more subordinate group members. The taxi driver who refuses to pick up African American passengers is practicing individual discrimination.

In 1996, several black churches in the South were destroyed, apparently in racially motivated acts of arson. Rev. Larry Hill, the pastor of historic Matthews-Murkland Presbyterian Church in Charlotte, North Carolina, is shown here looking at the charred wreckage of that church.

SOCIAL PROBLEMS

Racism in Canada

You feel it every day, but there is no concrete evidence. You see it when you walk into stores, you see that the security is heightened. You see it on the subway. When I get on in the morning to go to work, there aren't too many people. Gradually, the car fills up, but often nobody sits next to me. Sometimes, people are rushing and you may bump into someone and they'll say, "You . . . nigger, why don't you go back where you came from," stuff like that. (quoted in Corelli, 1995:42–43)

Racism is not unique to the Unived States. Sociologists have documented its existence in nations throughout the world. For example, recent studies show that racism directed against African Canadians and recent immigrants is a major social problem in that country. African Canadians make up only 3 percent of the Canadian population, and many trace their ancestry to the 3,500 U.S. slaves who were relocated to Canada after winning their freedom by fighting for the British during the American revolution. For as long as they have been in Canada, African Canadians have been excluded for the most part from churches, schools, and jobs (Blount, 1996). Some social analysts have predicted that racial discrimination will become an even larger issue that African Canadians face in Canada because recent immigration has increased the country's black population and

many newcomers have higher levels of education and better-paying jobs than native-born African Canadians (Blount, 1996).

Racism in Canada is not limited to African Canadians. As immigration by Chinese, Arab, East Indian, and Caribbean peoples has increased so have racial tensions (*Time*, 1999a). According to sociologist Jeffrey Reitz, equal opportunity in employment may be a special problem: "We like to bask in the perception that our race relations are better than those of our southern neighbor. In some respects, that is true" (*Time*, 1999a:1). Still, Reitz believes that Canada is behind the United States in passing legislation that mandates equal opportunity. Moreover, the issue of jobs raises tensions between people living in both immigrant and nonimmigrant communities (*Time*, 1999c). Immigrants are blamed for growing unemployment, high welfare costs, problems in the schools, and increasing crime. Discrimination and racially motivated violence are reinforced by negative stereotypes. Asian Canadians, for example, are viewed as the "new criminal class" that steals, terrorizes, and settles disputes with guns, and Arabs are stereotyped as "sneaky and sly" and "oppressors of women" (Cannon, 1995).

Are the experiences of subordinate racial-ethnic group members in Canada similar to those in the United States? Do you think recent immigration to the United States has affected how people of color are treated in the United States?

In contrast, *institutional discrimination* consists of the day-to-day practices of organizations and institutions that have a harmful impact on members of subordinate groups. For example, many mortgage companies are more likely to make loans to whites than to people of color (see Squires, 1994). Institutional discrimination is carried out by the individuals who implement policies and procedures that result in nega-

tive and differential treatment of subordinate group members. Jewish immigrants in the late 1800s experienced institutional discrimination in accommodations and employment. Signs in hotel windows often read "No Jews Allowed," and many "help wanted" advertisements stated "Christians Only" (Levine, 1992:55). Such practices are referred to as *anti-Semitism—prejudice and discriminatory behavior directed at Jews.*

PERSPECTIVES ON RACIAL AND ETHNIC INEQUALITY

Over the course of the past 100 years, sociologists have developed different perspectives to explain why racial and ethnic inequality occurs and why it persists. Some perspectives are social-psychological; others focus on sociological factors such as migration, assimilation, conflict, and exploitation.

 ## Social-Psychological Perspectives

Are some people more prejudiced than others? Social-psychological perspectives on prejudice emphasize psychological characteristics or personality traits. We will look at the frustration-aggression hypothesis and the authoritarian personality.

Aggression is behavior intended to hurt someone, either physically or verbally, that results from frustration (Weiten and Lloyd, 1994). According to the *frustration-aggression hypothesis,* individuals who are frustrated in their efforts to achieve a highly desired goal tend to develop a pattern of aggression toward others (Dollard et al., 1939). If they have a very high level of frustration and are unable to strike out at the source of their frustration, they may take out their hostility and aggression on a *scapegoat*—a **person or group that is blamed for some problem causing frustration and is therefore subjected to hostility or aggression by others** (Marger, 1994). For example, illegal aliens (people who have entered the United States without permission) have been blamed for a wide variety of societal woes, such as unemployment ("they take our jobs"), economic recession (things were good until they came"), or high taxes ("we pay more taxes to give them health care").

Another major social-psychological perspective suggests that people who have an authoritarian personality are most likely to be highly prejudiced. According to psychologist Theodore W. Adorno and his colleagues (1950), the *authoritarian personality* is characterized by excessive conformity, submissiveness to authority, intolerance, insecurity, a high level of superstition, and rigid, stereotypic thinking. Individuals with this type of personality typically view the world as a threatening place and are highly intolerant of members of subordinate racial, ethnic, or religious groups.

 ## Interactionist Perspectives

Somewhat related to social-psychological explanations of prejudice and discrimination are theories based on the interactionist perspective. One interactionist approach emphasizes how racial socialization contributes to feelings of solidarity with one's own racial-ethnic group and hostility toward all others. *Racial socialization* is a process of social interaction that contains specific messages and practices concerning the nature of one's racial-ethnic status as it relates to (1) personal and group identity, (2) intergroup and interindividual relationships, and (3) one's position in the social stratification system. Although racial socialization may occur through direct statements about race made by parents, peers, teachers, and others, it may also include indirect modeling behaviors, which occur when children imitate the words and actions of parents and other caregivers (Thornton et al., 1990). Racial socialization affects how people view themselves, other people, and the world. Here, for example, racial relations scholar and historian Manning Marable (1995:1) describes how racial socialization makes race a prism through which African Americans and other people of color view their daily lives:

> Black and white. As long as I can remember, the fundamentally defining feature of my life, and the lives of my family, was the stark reality of race. . . . It was the social gravity which set into motion our expectations and emotions, our language and dreams. . . . Race seemed granite-like, fixed and permanent, as the center of the social universe. The reality of racial discrimination constantly fed the pessimism and doubts that we as black people felt about the apparent natural order of the world, the inherent unfairness of it all, as well as limiting our hopes for a better life somewhere in the distant future.

Though all groups practice racial socialization, white racial socialization emphasizes white racial bonding. According to Christine E. Sleeter (1996), white racial bonding occurs when white people act in ways that reaffirm the common stance on race-related issues and draw we–they boundaries, thus perpetuating racism and discrimination. Such people choose to live near other whites, to socialize with other whites, and to vote for other whites, thus maintaining racial solidarity. Although many whites do not support racist beliefs, actions, or policies, they fear breaking bonds with other whites and may simply remain silent in the face of prejudice and discrimination (Sleeter, 1996).

 Functionalist Perspectives

To functionalists, social order and stability are extremely important for the smooth functioning of society. Consequently, racial and ethnic discord, urban unrest, and riots are dysfunctional and must be eliminated or contained. One functionalist perspective focuses on *assimilation*—**the process by which members of subordinate racial and ethnic groups become absorbed into the dominant culture.** Functionalists view assimilation as a stabilizing force that minimizes differences that otherwise might result in hostility and violence (Gordon, 1964). In its most complete form, assimilation becomes *amalgamation,* also referred to as the *melting pot model,* **a process in which the cultural attributes of diverse racial-ethnic groups are blended together to form a new society incorporating the unique contributions of each group.** Amalgamation occurs when members of dominant and subordinate racial-ethnic groups intermarry and procreate "mixed-race" children.

Early assimilation in the United States focused primarily on the Anglo-conformity model, rather than the melting pot model. The *Anglo-conformity model* **refers to a pattern of assimilation in which members of subordinate racial-ethnic groups are expected to conform to the culture of the dominant (white) Anglo-Saxon population.** Assimilation does not always lead to full social acceptance. For example, many successful African Americans and Jewish Americans have been excluded from membership in elite private clubs and parties in the homes of coworkers.

Recently, political conservatives have focused on assimilation and, particularly, adopting English as the country's official language. In her influential book *Out of the Barrio* (1991), social analyst Linda Chavez says Latinas/os in the United States must learn English and adopt the dominant culture if they want economic success and social acceptance. According to Chavez, Latinos/as should forget about entitlement programs such as affirmative

action and focus on assimilating into the U.S. economic mainstream (see Box 3.2).

Another functionalist perspective emphasizes *ethnic pluralism*—**the coexistence of diverse racial-ethnic groups with separate identities and cultures within a society.** In a pluralistic society, political and economic systems link diverse groups, but members of some racial-ethnic groups maintain enough separation from the dominant group to guarantee that their group and ethnic cultural traditions continue (M. M. Gordon, 1964). Ethnic pluralism in the United States typically has been based on *segregation* because subordinate racial-ethnic groups have less power and privilege than do members of the dominant group (Marger, 1994). *Segregation* **is the spatial and social separation of categories of people by race/ethnicity, class, gender, religion, or other social characteristics.** Recent sociological studies have found that when high levels of racial segregation are followed by interracial contact, racial competition may ensue, tending to increase ethnic and racial unrest and the potential for urban riots (Olzak et al., 1996).

 Conflict Perspectives

Conflict theorists explain racial and ethnic inequality in terms of economic stratification and access to power. As discussed in Chapter 1, there are a number of conflict perspectives. However, in this chapter we focus on the critical-conflict approach which explains racial and ethnic inequality in terms of economic stratification and unequal access to power. We will briefly examine class perspectives, split-labor market theory, gendered racism, internal colonialism, and the theory of racial formation.

Class perspectives on racial and ethnic inequality highlight the role of the capitalist class in racial exploitation. For example, according to sociologist Oliver C. Cox (1948), the primary cause of slavery was the capitalist desire for profit, not racial prejudice. African Americans were enslaved because they were the cheapest and best workers that owners of plantations and mines could find to do the heavy labor. One contemporary class perspective suggests that members of the capitalist class benefit from a split-labor market that fosters racial divisions among workers and suppresses wages. According to the *split-labor market theory,* the U.S. economy is divided into two employment sectors: a primary

SOCIAL PROBLEMS

BOX 3.2

Don't Blink: Latinas and Latinos in Television

FACT: Although Latinos/as constitute about 10 percent of the U.S. population, they represent only 1 percent of all speaking characters in prime-time television (Doss, 1996).

FACT: Of the twenty-six programs ABC, CBS, NBC, and Fox announced for fall 1999, none had a minority star (Poniewozik, 1999).

How they are depicted on television is an issue for Latinos/as, because representation of subordinate racial-ethnic groups affects viewers' perceptions of racial inequality (Dawes, 1995).

Given that Latinas/os are the fastest-growing segment of the U.S. population and a ripe market for television advertisers, why don't television executives develop programs featuring Latino/a story lines and characters? Why are Latinas/os and other subordinate group members best represented in workplace settings such as hospitals (*ER*) and police departments (*NYPD Blue*)? Why are situation comedies (sitcoms), which usually take place in family and friendship groupings, either "colorless, color blind, or awkwardly color conscious" (Poniewozik, 1999:2)?

According to actor Jeff Valdez, Hollywood television executives hold socioeconomic and/ or racial-ethnic biases that keep Latinos/as in the background, if not invisible. Gabriel Reyes, a creative affairs director, agrees with Valdez's assessment: "Any time you submit a Latino script, the knee-jerk reaction of the studios and the networks is to Anglicize it, to whitewash it. They don't think the Latino experience sells" (quoted in Mendoza, 1995:B13).

As a result, Latino/a activists have formed the National Hispanic Media Coalition to protest the absence of Latino/a actors in television and film. Through boycotts, demonstrations, and letter-writing campaigns to television networks and major advertisers, the coalition is seeking greater representation of Latinas/os both in front of the camera as actors and behind the scenes as producers, writers, and directors (Mendoza, 1995). Will they be successful? That remains to be seen.

According to José Luis Ruiz, executive director of the nonprofit National Latino Communications Center, which produces Latino-themed programming, the "media is like a big ship. It takes a long time to make a turn. . . . Even when you do change things, networks have a tendency to revert back to their comfort zone" (Doss, 1996:2).

Do the television shows and films that you watch have Latinos/as, African Americans, Asian and Pacific Americans, Native Americans, or other people of color as characters and actors? Does it matter if some subordinate racial and ethnic groups are largely invisible on television? Why or why not?

sector composed of higher-paid workers in more secure jobs and a secondary sector composed of lower-paid workers in jobs that often involve hazardous working conditions and little job security (Bonacich, 1972, 1976). Dominant group members are usually employed in primary sector positions; subordinate group members usually are employed in the secondary sector. Workers in the two job sectors tend to have divergent interests and goals; therefore worker solidarity is unlikely (Bonacich, 1972, 1976). Members of the capitalist class benefit from these divisions because workers are less likely to bind together and demand pay increases or other changes in the workplace. White workers in the primary sector attempt to exclude subordinate group members from higher-paying jobs by barring them from labor unions, supporting discriminatory laws, and opposing immigration.

THE SUPREME COURT SOLVES THE THORNY PROBLEM OF RACISM...

...IT NEVER EXISTED!

AFFIRMATIVE ACTION

BEN SARGENT

Reprinted by permission.

A second critical-conflict perspective links racial inequality and gender oppression. *Gendered racism may be defined as the interactive effect of racism and sexism in exploiting women of color.* According to social psychologist Philomena Essed (1991), not all workers are exploited equally by capitalists. For many years, the majority of jobs in the primary sector of the labor market were held by white men, while most people of color and many white women were employed in secondary sector jobs. Below the secondary sector, in the underground sector of the economy, many women of color worked in sweatshops or the sex trade to survive. Work in this underground sector is unregulated, and people who earn their income in it are vulnerable to exploitation by many people, including unscrupulous employers, greedy pimps, and corrupt police officers (Amott and Matthaei, 1991).

A third critical-conflict perspective examines *internal colonialism—a process that occurs when members of a racial-ethnic group are conquered or colonized and forcibly placed under the economic and political control of the dominant group.* According to sociologist Robert Blauner (1972), people in groups that have been subjected to internal colonialism remain in subordinate positions in society much longer than do people in groups that voluntarily migrated to this country. For example, Native Amer-

icans and Mexican Americans were forced into subordination when they were colonized by European Americans. These indigenous groups lost property, political rights, components of their culture, and often their lives. Meanwhile, the capitalist class acquired cheap labor and land, frequently through government-sanctioned racial exploitation (Blauner, 1972). Vestiges of internal colonialism remain visible today in the number of Native Americans who live in poverty on government reservations, as well as Mexican Americans in *colonias*—poor subdivisions that usually lack essential services such as water, electricity, and sewage disposal—located along the U.S.-Mexico border (see Valdez, 1993).

The last critical-conflict perspective we will look at is the *theory of racial formation,* **which states that the government substantially defines racial and ethnic relations.** From this perspective, racial bias and discrimination tend to be rooted in government actions ranging from passage of race-related legislation to imprisonment of members of groups that are believed to be a threat to society. According to sociologists Michael Omi and Howard Winant (1994), who have said that the U.S. government has shaped the politics of racial inequality in this country through actions and policies that have resulted in the unequal treatment of people of color. Immigration legislation, for example, reveals specific racial biases. The Naturalization Law of 1790 permitted only white immigrants to qualify for naturalization, and the Immigration Act of 1924 favored northern Europeans and excluded Asians and southern and eastern Europeans.

INEQUALITIES AMONG RACIAL AND ETHNIC GROUPS

Although all subordinate racial and ethnic groups have been the objects of prejudice and discrimination and share many problems, each has its own unique identity and concerns. In our examination of Native Americans, African Americans, Latinos/as, and Asian and Pacific Americans, we will note commonalities and differences in the discriminatory practices each group has experienced in contact with members of the dominant group.

 ## Native Americans (American Indians)

Perhaps because they are often somewhat invisible in daily life, Native Americans tend to be viewed more as artifacts of "Indian culture" than real people. As such, they are associated with turquoise jewelry and deerskin clothing, "Indian" Barbie dolls, vehicles such as the Jeep "Cherokee," and the stereotypical images utilized by sports teams with names like "Braves," "Redskins," "Chiefs," and "Seminoles" (Churchill, 1992, 1994; Hilden, 1995; Oxendine, 1995). While such movies as *Dances with Wolves, The Last of the Mohicans, Pocahontas,* and *The Indian in the Cupboard* have increased public awareness of Native Americans to some extent, some also have perpetuated myths and stereotypes.

COLONIZED MIGRATION AND GENOCIDE

When Christopher Columbus arrived in 1492, approximately 15 million indigenous people lived on this continent. They had many distinct cultures, languages, social organizations, technologies, and economies (Thornton, 1987; Sale, 1990; Mohawk, 1992). The arrival of the white Europeans changed the native inhabitants' ways of life forever as *colonization migration*—a process whereby a new immigrant group conquers and dominates an existing group in a given geographical area—occurred (Lauber, 1913; Feagin and Feagin, 1999). During this

period of conquest, white European immigrants engaged in *genocide,* **the deliberate, systematic killing of an entire people or nation.** Hundreds of thousands of Native Americans died during this period. This widespread murder was rationalized by stereotypes depicting Native Americans as subhuman "savages" and "heathens" (Takaki, 1993).

FORCED MIGRATION AND "AMERICANIZATION"

After the Revolutionary War the newly founded federal government negotiated treaties with various Native American nations to acquire additional land for the rapidly growing white population. Even with these treaties in place, federal officials ignored boundary rights and gradually displaced Native Americans from their lands. When the demand for land escalated, Congress passed the Indian Removal Act of 1830, forcing entire nations to move to accommodate white settlers (Green, 1977; Churchill, 1994). During the "Trail of Tears," perhaps the most disastrous of the forced migrations, over half of the Cherokee nation died while being relocated from the southeastern United States to what was called the Indian Territory in Oklahoma during the bitter cold winter of 1832 (Thornton, 1984). After the forced relocation, Native Americans were made wards of the government—a legal status akin to that of a minor or a mental incompetent—and by 1920, about 98 percent of all native lands were controlled by the U.S. government (McDonnell, 1991).

Because Native Americans were regarded as less "civilized" than whites, Native American children were subjected to an extensive Americanization process. Boarding schools and mission schools, cosponsored by the government and churches, were located some distance from the reservations to facilitate assimilation. In these schools, white teachers cut Native American boys' braids, eliminated the children's traditional clothing, handed out new names, and substituted new religious customs for old ones (Oxendine, 1995).

CONTEMPORARY NATIVE AMERICANS

Today, Native Americans number slightly more than 2 million, less than 1 percent of the U.S. population. Most Native Americans live in Oklahoma, California, Arizona, and New Mexico (U.S. Bureau of the Census, 1998). Although the majority of Native Americans live in cities, 38 percent live on reservations or other officially designated areas. They are the most disadvantaged racial or ethnic group in the United States. They have the highest unemployment and school dropout rates in the country. The average family income of Native Americans is $21,750, compared with a national average of more than $35,000 (U.S. Bureau of the Census, 1998). The average life expectancy on reservations is less than forty-five years for men and less than forty-eight years for women (Churchill, 1994). Infant mortality rates and adult death rates from alcoholism, diabetes, tuberculosis, and suicide are much higher than the national averages (Bachman, 1992).

Many Native Americans have organized to resist discrimination and oppression. They actively oppose mining, logging, hunting, and real estate development on native lands without permission or compensation (Serrill, 1992). Groups, such as the American Indian Movement and Women of All Red Nations, have struggled to regain control of native lands, to end centuries of colonization, and to stop cultural exploitation.

 African Americans

The term *African American* does not reflect the diversity of the more than 33 million African Americans who currently make up about 13 percent of the U.S. population. Although some are descendants of families that have been in this country for many generations, others are recent immigrants from the West Indies, South America, Africa, and the Caribbean. Many have Native American, white, or Latino/a ancestors (Feagin and Feagin, 1999; Kivel, 1996).

Although media coverage has improved somewhat over the past decade, stereotypic depictions of African Americans continue to "demonize blackness" (Gray, 1995). Television and films frequently depict African American women as "welfare mothers"; drug addicts; sex objects; prostitutes; and elderly, overweight, aggressive family matriarchs who are made the object of derision by their families and others (see Gray, 1995). African American men are depicted as "menacing black male criminals" who murder, rape, pimp, and sell drugs (Feagin and Feagin, 1999; Kivel, 1996).

SLAVERY AND THE RACIAL DIVISION OF LABOR

From its beginnings in 1619, when the first Africans were brought to North America for forced labor, slavery created a rigid, castelike division of labor between white slave owners and overseers and African slave labor. Southern plantation owners derived large profits from selling raw materials harvested by the slaves. Northern capitalists became rich by converting those raw materials into finished products that could be sold at market (e.g., the cotton fiber used in textile manufacturing). Even white immigrants benefited from slavery because it provided the abundant raw materials needed for their factory jobs.

SEGREGATION AND LYNCHING

After slavery was abolished in 1863, this division of labor was maintained through *de jure segregation,* the passage of laws that systematically enforced the physical and social separation of African Americans from whites in all areas of public life, including schools, churches, hospitals, cemeteries, buses, restaurants, water fountains, and restrooms. (These laws were referred to as Jim Crow laws after a derogatory song about a black man.) African Americans who did not stay "in their place" were subjected to violence by secret organizations such as the Ku Klux Klan and by lynch mobs (Franklin, 1980).

While African Americans in the South experienced de jure segregation, those who migrated to the North experienced *de facto segregation*—racial separation and inequality enforced by custom. African Americans seeking northern factory jobs encountered *job ceilings*—specific limits on the upward job mobility of targeted groups—set up by white workers and their unions (see Baron, 1969; Allen, 1974). Because African American men were barred from many industrial jobs, African American women frequently become their families' primary breadwinners. Most African American women were employed as domestic workers in private households or as personal service workers such as hotel chambermaids (Higginbotham, 1994).

PROTESTS AND CIVIL DISOBEDIENCE

During World War II, new job opportunities opened up for African Americans in northern defense plants, especially after the issuance of a presidential order prohibiting racial discrimination in federal jobs. After the war, increasing numbers of African Americans demanded an end to racial segregation. Between the mid-1950s and 1964, boycotts, nonviolent protests, and *civil disobedience*—nonviolent action seeking to change a policy or law by refusing to comply with it—called attention to racial

Dr. Martin Luther King, Jr., was perhaps the most influential person in obtaining passage of the Civil Rights Acts in the 1960s that have profoundly affected the lives of many African Americans.

inequality. The civil rights movement culminated in passage of the Civil Rights Acts of 1964 and 1965, which signified the end of *de jure* segregation; however, *de facto* segregation was far from over.

CONTEMPORARY AFRICAN AMERICANS

Since the 1960s, African Americans have made significant political gains. Between 1964 and 1994, the number of African American elected officials increased from about 100 to almost 8,000. African Americans won mayoral elections in many major cities that had large African American populations, including Los Angeles, New York, Atlanta, and Washington, D.C. Even with these gains, however, African Americans represent less than 3 percent of all elected officials in this country.

The proportion of African Americans in professional, managerial, sales, clerical, crafts, and factory jobs grew steadily between 1955 and 1972, but this growth slowed dramatically in the late 1970s and 1980s. The continuation of the job ceiling and racial division of labor is evident today in many corporations, including Fortune 500 companies (the 500 highest revenue-producing companies), which have no African American executives (vice presidents or above) (Glass Ceiling Commission, 1995). Approximately one-fourth of the African American work force is employed in the public sector, that is, in federal, state, city, and county governments (Higginbotham, 1994).

The unemployment rate for African Americans (10 percent in 1997) has remained twice as high as that for white Americans (4.2 percent in 1997) for more than three decades. As new technology has been introduced in the workplace and more jobs have moved to suburban areas and to other countries, employment opportunities for African Americans in central cities have declined (see Neckerman and Kirschenman, 1991; Tienda and Stier, 1996; Wilson, 1996).

As is shown in Figure 3.1, a wide disparity exists between the median income of white Americans and that of African Americans. Whereas African American married-couple families with children had median earnings of $47,382 in 1998, the median earnings of white non-Latino married-couple families with children were 20 percent higher ($54,845), but fewer than half (45 percent) of all African American families were married-couple families. Households headed by African American women with children had median earnings of $13,608, or 28 percent of the median for married-couple African American families with children (U. S. Bureau of the Census, 1999a).

Contemporary scholars suggest that the legacies of slavery, segregation, and individual and institutionalized discrimination are evident in both the persistent—though informal—racial discrimination practiced by banks, real estate agencies, mortgage lenders, and other businesses that has resulted in the high percentage of racially segregated schools and residential areas and the daily bias that many African Americans face in the workplace and other public spaces (see Feagin and Sikes, 1994; Feagin and Feagin, 1999). Residential discrimination has proved to be one of the more persistent inequalities experienced by African Americans. Today, African

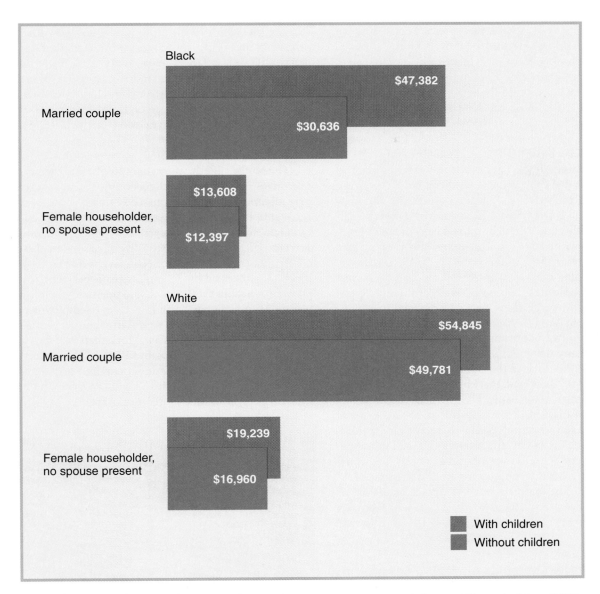

FIGURE 3.1 *Median U.S. Family Income, by Type of Family and Race of Householder, 1998*
Source: U.S. Bureau of the Census, 1999a.

Americans and whites are no more likely to be neighbors than they were forty years ago (O'Hare and Usdansky, 1992). Residential segregation produces a ripple effect on all other areas of social life, including the schools that children attend, the quality of education they receive, the types of jobs people have access to, and the availability and quality of such public facilities as hospitals and transportation systems (Massey and Denton, 1992).

 Latinos/as (Hispanic Americans)

Today, almost two-thirds of the nearly 30 million Latinos/as who make up about 11 percent of the U.S. population are of Mexican origin. After Mexican Americans, the largest groups of Latinos/as are Puerto Ricans and Cuban Americans. The remainder trace their ancestry to Central and South America or to the Dominican Republic.

Latinos/as have been the objects of stereotyping based on skin color and perceived cultural differences, including food preferences and language. In the media, Latinos/as are often depicted as either rich drug lords or illegal aliens (McWilliams, 1968; Morales, 1996). Box 3.2 (see page 48) examines the absence of Latinas/os in the media.

INTERNAL COLONIALISM AND LOSS OF LAND

Beginning in the late 1400s and continuing into the early 1500s, Spanish soldiers took over the island of Puerto Rico, Central America, and that area of the United States now known as the Southwest. Although Mexico gained its independence from Spain in 1810, it lost Texas and most of the Southwest to the United States in 1848. Under the treaty ending the Mexican-American War, Texans of Mexican descent (*Tejanos/as*) were granted U.S. citizenship; however, their rights as citizens were violated when Anglo Americans took possession of their lands, transforming them into a landless and economically dependent laboring class.

When Spain lost the Spanish-American War, it gave Puerto Rico and the Philippine Islands to the United States. Gradually U.S.-owned corporations took over existing Puerto Rican sugarcane plantations, leaving peasant farmers and their families with no means of earning a living other than as seasonal sugarcane laborers. In time, nearly one-third of the Puerto Rican population migrated to the U. S. mainland. The majority of this population settled in the Northeast and found work in garment factories or other light manufacturing.

MIGRATION

In the late 1950s and early 1960s, waves of Latinos/as escaping from Fidel Castro's Communist takeover of Cuba were admitted to the United States. Unlike Puerto Ricans, who have been allowed unrestricted migration between the mainland and the island since Puerto Rico became a U.S. possession in 1917 (Melendez, 1993), these immigrants were admitted as political refugees (Rogg, 1974). Mexicans have been allowed to migrate to the United States whenever there has been a need here for agricultural workers. However, during times of economic depression or recession in this country, Mexican workers have been excluded, detained, or deported (see Moore, 1976; Acuna, 1984).

Many Latinos/as have experienced discrimination as a result of the Immigration Reform and Control Act (IRCA) of 1986. Although IRCA was passed to restrict illegal immigration into the United States, it has adversely affected many Latinos/as. To avoid being penalized for hiring undocumented workers, some employers discriminate against Latinas/os who "look foreign" on the basis of facial features, skin color, or clothing (see Chavez and Martinez, 1996).

CONTEMPORARY LATINOS/AS

Currently, slightly more than 200 Latinos are top executives in Fortune 1000 corporations, most often in companies that actively pursue Latina/o consumers, for example beverage, entertainment, and soap and cosmetic companies; however, Latinos/as hold only 1.4 percent of the senior executive positions in these companies (Zate, 1996). In secondary sector employment, the other end of the employment spectrum, low wages, hazardous workplaces, and unemployment are pressing problems for Latinos/as. The unemployment rate for Latinos/as is about 8 percent, almost twice the rate for white non-Latinos/as. More than one-fourth (25.6 percent) of Latinas/os lived below the poverty level in 1997. Although Latino/a children accounted for almost 12 percent of all U.S. children, they made up 21.3 percent of all children in poverty.

Despite recent gains by some Latinas and Latinos in the workplace, many are still employed in secondary sector jobs, where the wages are low and working conditions are difficult. Many parents work hard to provide better educational opportunities for their children in hopes that they can share the American Dream.

Many Latinas/os continue to experience high levels of segregation in housing and education. According to a recent study by anthropologist Martha Menchaca (1995), landlords, realtors, and bankers in many communities have colluded to keep Mexican Americans in barrios and out of predominantly Anglo neighborhoods. Segregated schools are a major problem for many Latino/a children and their parents. During the mid-1990s, 80 percent or more of all Latina/o students in New York, Illinois, Texas, New Jersey, and California attended schools in which students of color made up between 50 and 100 percent of the school population (DeWitt, 1992).

 ## Asian and Pacific Americans

Asian and Pacific Americans are one of the fastest growing racial-ethnic groups in the United States; their numbers have risen from 1 million in 1960 to 11 million today. In the 1990s, about half of all legal immigrants to this country had Asian or Pacific Island ancestry. Constituting about 3 percent of the U.S. population, most Asian and Pacific Americans reside in California, New York, and Hawaii (U. S. Bureau of the Census, 1998).

Asian and Pacific Americans have been stereotyped as "Orientals." Advertisements often depict Asian and Pacific American women as exotic beauties with silky black hair, heavy eye makeup, and seductive clothing (Shah, 1994). Because many are college-educated and have middle- or upper-income occupations, Asian and Pacific Americans also have been stereotyped as the model minority. However, the model minority stereotype ignores the reality that many Asian and Pacific Americans, especially recent immigrants, are employed in low-paying service jobs or sweatshops.

IMMIGRATION AND OPPRESSION

Among the first Asian and Pacific people to arrive in this country were Chinese immigrants, who came between 1850 and 1880. Some were fleeing political oppression and harsh economic conditions in China; others were recruited to build the transcontinental railroad. Almost immediately, these immigrants were labeled "the yellow peril," a reflection of nineteenth-century prejudice that Asians constituted a threat to Western civilization. In response to demands from white workers who were concerned about cheap labor (employers paid Chinese laborers far less than white workers [Takaki, 1993]), Congress passed the Chinese Exclusion Act of 1882, bringing all Chinese immigration to an abrupt halt. This law wasn't repealed until World War II, when Chinese American workers contributed to the U.S. war effort by working in defense plants (see Chan, 1991).

Facing high levels of overt discrimination, many Chinese Americans opened laundries, stores, and restaurants, doing business primarily with each other (Takaki, 1993). More recently, however, young second- and third-generation Chinese Americans have left these ethnic niches to live and interact with people from diverse racial-ethnic groups (see Chen, 1992).

INTERNMENT

Although Japanese Americans experienced high levels of prejudice and discrimination almost as soon as they arrived in this country, their internment in U.S. concentration camps during World War II remains the central event of the Japanese American experience (Kitano and Daniels, 1995). After Japan bombed Pearl Harbor in 1941, anti-Japanese sentiment soared in the United States. Japanese Americans were forcibly removed to concentration camps on remote military bases surrounded by barbed wire fences and guard towers. During their internment, which lasted for more than two years, most Japanese Americans lost their residences, businesses, and anything else they had owned. Four decades later, the U.S. government issued an apology for its actions and agreed to pay $20,000 to each Japanese American who had been detained in a camp (Kitano and Daniels, 1995). For Japanese Americans and other Asian and Pacific Americans, the struggle for rights has often been played out in the U.S. Supreme Court and other judicial bodies (see Box 3.3).

COLONIZATION

A bloody guerrilla war between Filipino Islanders and U.S. soldiers followed Spain's surrender of the Philippine Islands, as well as Puerto Rico, to the United States in the aftermath of the Spanish-American War. When the battle ended in 1902, the United States established colonial rule over the islands, and Filipinos were "Americanized" by schools that the U.S. government established (Espiritu, 1995).

Most early Filipino migrants were recruited as cheap labor for sugar plantations in Hawaii, agriculture in California, and fish canneries in Seattle and Alaska. Like members of other racial-ethnic groups, Filipino Americans were accused of stealing jobs and

SOCIAL PROBLEMS
AND SOCIAL POLICY

BOX 3.3

Social Justice: Beyond Black and White

Since the Civil Rights Movement of the 1960s, many social analysts have defined issues pertaining to social justice and social policy primarily in terms of "black and white" (Chin, 1999). However, throughout the history of this country, racial and ethnic groups, ranging from Native Americans and Mexican Americans to Jewish Americans and Asian and Pacific Americans, have protested against what they perceive to be racist social policies, and many groups have played key roles in the struggles for civil rights for all.

Think about these experiences of Asian and Pacific Americans:

▲ In the 1880s, Chinese Americans pooled their resources to hire lawyers to fight such unfair immigration laws as the Chinese Exclusion Act of 1882 and other laws that prohibited them from owning land, attending "white-only" public schools, or gaining citizenship (Chin, 1999).

▲ In *People v. Hall* (1854), the California Supreme Court ruled that a white man had been wrongfully convicted of murder because Chinese witnesses had testified against him. The court ruled that the testimony was inadmissible because, according to the justices, the Chinese could be considered "constructive blacks" and thus were covered under a statement in the California state constitution that prohibited "blacks and Indians" from testifying against white Americans (see Foner and Rosenberg, 1993).

▲ Because of fears that Japanese Americans would undermine U.S. efforts against Japan during World War II, Executive Order 9066, issued in 1942, called for the internment of all people of Japanese descent living on the West coast. More than 120,000 Japanese Americans were sent to "relocation camps" (concentration camps) as a result of this order.

Fred Korematsu, a Japanese American living in San Francisco, and several others, sought to avoid internment. Korematsu was arrested, convicted, and sent to an internment camp in Utah. In *Korematsu* v. *United States* (1944), the U.S. Supreme Court upheld his conviction, but the Court never examined the constitutionality of the government policy on internment. In 1983, Korematsu (then in his 80s) was finally exonerated, and his case encouraged other Japanese Americans to seek reparations for their internment (Chin, 1999).

▲ After an increase in anti–Asian and Pacific violence, including several shootings, the National Asian Pacific American Bar Association, along with a number of other organizations and individuals, submitted a 1997 petition to the U.S. Commission on Civil Rights stating that "a climate of racial tension toward Asian and Pacific Americans has become aggravated" and is urging the commission to look into this problem (Chin, 1999:67).

These few examples demonstrate the long struggle for justice and equitable social policies carried on by Asian and Pacific Americans.

Many social analysts believe that our social policies must be designed to improve racial and ethnic relations in this country. For this change to occur, people must become more aware of the vital role that individuals from diverse racial and ethnic groups play in the daily life of this nation. As legal scholar Robert S. Chang (1999:69) has said:

If Asian Americans and other minorities are to feel at home in the United States, it will require an insistent remembering of the past to make America's ideas real. Learning about the historical treatment of people of Asian ancestry is important, not just for Asian Americans but for all Americans, if we are to realize this dream called America.

suppressing wages during the Great Depression, and Congress restricted Filipino immigration to fifty people per year until after World War II.

NEWER WAVES OF ASIAN IMMIGRATION

Today, many of the Asian and Pacific immigrants arriving from India and Pakistan are highly educated professionals. While some immigrants from Korea are also professionals, many have few years of formal schooling. They have developed an ethnic niche in "Koreatowns," which are similar to the communities of earlier generations of Chinese Americans (Kim and Yu, 1996).

Since the 1970s, many Indochinese American refugees have arrived in the United States from Vietnam, Cambodia, Thailand, and Laos. About half of these immigrants live in western states, especially California. Although many early Vietnamese refugees were physicians, pharmacists, and engineers who were able to reenter their professions in the United States, more recent immigrants have had less formal education, fewer job skills, and therefore much higher rates of unemployment. Recent immigrants are more likely to live in poverty and rely on assistance from others (Du Phuoc Long, 1996).

PACIFIC ISLANDERS

More than 1.6 million people live on the Hawaiian Islands. About 13 percent are native or part-native Hawaiians who can trace their ancestry to the original Polynesian inhabitants of the islands. Originally governed as a monarchy and then as a republic, the Hawaiian Islands were annexed by the United States in 1898. In 1959, Congress passed legislation that made Hawaii the fiftieth state. Because of widespread immigration and high rates of intermarriage, contemporary Hawaiians include people of Chinese, Japanese, Filipino, Korean, Puerto Rican, and Portuguese ancestry.

CONTEMPORARY ASIAN AND PACIFIC AMERICANS

Asian and Pacific Americans have high educational levels compared to the overall U.S. population. In 1997, nearly nine out of ten male and eight out of ten female Asian and Pacific Americans age twenty-five and over had at least a high school education. Indeed, Asian and Pacific Americans are almost twice as likely to have a bachelor's degree than are white non-Latinas/os. In 1997, more than 42 percent of

 People from diverse racial and ethnic backgrounds often find an understanding and solidarity within their families that helps them cope with the daily struggles of life in the larger society, particularly with problems of racism and discrimination.

Asian and Pacific Americans held at least a bachelor's degree (U.S. Bureau of the Census, 1998).

The median income of households in this population category exceeded that of non-Latino/a whites: $46,637 to $40,912 in 1998. In fact, the median family income of Japanese Americans is more than 30 percent above the national average. While nearly 14 percent of all Asian and Pacific American families live below the official poverty line, fewer than 4 percent of Japanese American families do.

Summary

As we end our discussion of the experiences of various subordinate racial and ethnic groups in the United States, let's look at the commonalities in their experience: (1) Each has been the object of negative stereotypes and discrimination, (2) each has resisted oppression and continued to strive for a better life for its members and their children, and (3) each has been the object of some government policy that has shaped its place (or lack thereof) in U.S. race and ethnic relations over the past two centuries. Even with these commonalities, however, members of each group have had unique experiences based on the time and circumstances of their arrival in this country and how they were viewed by the dominant members of the racial-ethnic groups.

CAN RACIAL AND ETHNIC INEQUALITIES BE REDUCED?

How do functionalists suggest reducing racial-ethnic inequality? Because they believe a stable society requires smoothly functioning social institutions and people who have common cultural values and atti-

tudes, functionalists suggest restructuring social institutions to reduce discrimination and diffuse racial-ethnic conflict. According to sociologist Arnold Rose (1951), discrimination robs society of the talents and leadership abilities of many individuals, especially people of color. Rose suggests that societies invest time and money fostering racial-ethnic inclusion and eliminating institutionalized discrimination in education, housing, employment, and the criminal justice system. Employing a global perspective, functionalists argue that U.S. racial discrimination should be reduced because it negatively affects diplomatic and economic relations with other nations made up of diverse racial-ethnic groups (Feagin and Vera, 1995).

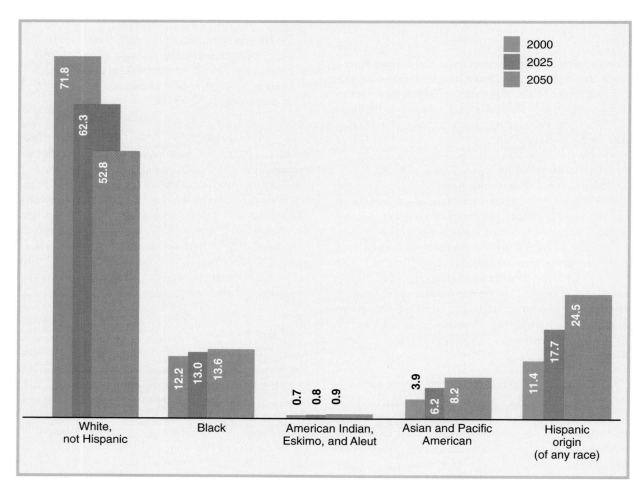

FIGURE 3.2 *Percent of the U.S. Population by Race and Hispanic Origin—2000, 2025, and 2050 (middle-series projections)*

Source: U.S. Bureau of the Census, 1998.

From a conflict perspective, racial and ethnic inequality can be reduced only through struggle and political action. If inequality is based on the exploitation of subordinate groups by the dominant group, conflict theorists believe that political intervention is necessary to bring about economic and social change. They agree that people should mobilize to put pressure on public officials. According to social activist Paul Kivel (1996), racial inequality will not be reduced until there is, in this country, significant national public support and leadership for addressing social problems directly and forcefully.

According to interactionists, prejudice and discrimination are learned, and what is learned can be unlearned. As sociologist Gale E. Thomas (1995:339) notes, "In the areas of race, ethnic, and human relations, we must learn compassion and also to accept and truly embrace, rather than merely tolerate, differences . . . through honest and open dialogue and through the formation of genuine friendships and personal experiential . . . exchanges and interactions with different individuals and groups across cultures." In other words, only individuals and groups at the grass-roots level, not government and political leaders or academic elites, can bring about greater racial equality.

Whether or not the people of the United States work for greater equality for all racial-ethnic groups, one thing is certain: The U.S. population is becoming increasingly diverse at a rapid rate. African Americans, Latinos/as, Asian and Pacific Americans, Native Americans, and people who trace their ancestry to other regions of the world make up more than 25 percent of the U.S. population. In the year 2000, white Americans made up 70 percent or less of the U.S. population (see Figure 3.2); and by the year 2050, most U.S. residents will trace their roots to Africa, Asia, the Hispanic countries, the Pacific Islands, and the Middle East, not white Europe (Henry, 1990). If we fail to recognize the challenges posed by increasing racial-ethnic and cultural diversity and we do not develop a more visionary and inclusive perspective, fires like those that occurred in Los Angeles in the 1960s and the 1990s may spread across the nation, as African American activist James Baldwin (1963) suggested when he spoke of "the fire next time" (Thomas, 1995).

On a more optimistic note, perhaps the future of racial-ethnic relations in the United States is forecast by this newspaper reporter's description of a Chicago kindergarten class:

> They stand with arms outstretched, touching fingertip to fingertip on a yellow circle inscribed on the floor of a kindergarten classroom.
>
> A girl with braids who describes herself as a light-skinned black stands next to a boy who has a white mother and a black father. Just a few feet away is a boy whose mother is black and whose father is white. He is flanked by a classmate born in Sweden of Chinese parents.
>
> He stretches his fingertips to touch the hand of a close friend, a blond girl whose parents are from Idaho. She stands next to two girls with dark ponytails who whisper their secrets in Spanish. They smile at their neighbor, a shy and tiny girl most comfortable speaking Polish.
>
> They are the pupils in Mary Sigman's kindergarten at Ogden Elementary School in Chicago. To much of America, having all these diverse backgrounds in a kindergarten class remains atypical. But that may be changing: These children already are experiencing a multiracial, multiethnic world that increasingly will come to characterize this country by 2008, the year they graduate from high school. (Schreuder, 1996:F1)

SUMMARY

➡ *How do racial and ethnic groups differ?*

According to sociologists, racial groups are defined on the basis of real or alleged physical characteristics, and ethnic groups are defined on the basis of cultural or nationality characteristics.

➡ *What are majority and minority groups?*

When sociologists use the terms *majority group* and *minority group,* they are referring to power differentials. A majority (or dominant) group is one that is advantaged and has superior resources and rights in a society. A minority (or subordinate) group is one whose members, because of physical or cultural characteristics, are disadvantaged and subjected to unequal treatment by the dominant group, and regard themselves as objects of collective discrimination.

➤ *How are prejudice and discrimination related?*

Prejudice is a negative attitude that may or may not lead to discrimination, which is an action or practice of dominant group members that has a harmful impact on subordinate group members.

➤ *How do individual discrimination and institutional discrimination differ?*

Although individual discrimination and institutional discrimination are carried out by individuals, individual discrimination consists of one-on-one acts by members of the dominant group; institutional discrimination refers to actions and practices that are built into the day-to-day operations of large-scale organizations and social institutions.

➤ *How do the interactionist and functionalist perspectives view racial and ethnic relations?*

Interactionists focus on microlevel issues such as how people develop a racial-ethnic identity and how individuals from diverse racial-ethnic groups interact with each other. Functionalists focus on macrolevel issues such as how entire groups of people assimilate into the mainstream of the society.

➤ *What are the major conflict explanations for racial-ethnic inequality?*

Conflict perspectives include class perspectives, split-labor market theory, gendered racism, internal colonialism, and racial formation theory.

➤ *What types of discrimination have been experienced by Native Americans, African Americans, Latinos/as, and Asian and Pacific Americans in the United States?*

Native Americans have experienced internal colonization, genocide, forced migration, and Americanization. African Americans have experienced slavery, *de jure* segregation (Jim Crow laws), and *de facto* segregation—racial separation and inequality enforced by custom. Latinos/as have experienced internal colonialism, exclusionary immigration policies, and segregation in housing and education. Asian and Pacific Americans also have experienced exclusionary immigration policies; Japanese Americans uniquely experienced internment during World War II.

➤ *What commonalities can be seen in the experiences of all subordinate racial-ethnic groups?*

Members of most subordinate racial-ethnic groups have these commonalities in their experiences in the United States: (1) Each has been the object of negative stereotypes and discrimination, (2) each has resisted oppression and continued to strive for a better life for its members and their children, and (3) each has been the object of some government policy that has shaped its place (or lack thereof) in U.S. race and ethnic relations over the past two centuries.

KEY TERMS

amalgamation, p. 47
Anglo-conformity model, p. 47
anti-Semitism, p. 45
assimilation, p. 47
ethnic group, p. 42
ethnic pluralism, p. 47
ethnocentrism, p. 44
gendered racism, p. 49

genocide, p. 50
individual discrimination, p. 44
institutional discrimination, p. 45
internal colonialism, p. 49
majority (dominant) group, p. 43
melting pot model, p. 47
minority (subordinate) group,
   p. 43

prejudice, p. 44
racial group, p. 42
racism, p. 44
scapegoat, p. 46
segregation, p. 47
stereotypes, p. 44
theory of racial formation,
   p. 49

QUESTIONS FOR CRITICAL THINKING

1. Do you consider yourself part of the majority or dominant racial-ethnic group or part of a minority or subordinate racial-ethnic group in the United States? In what specific ways might your life be different if you were in the opposite group?

2. Sociologists suggest that we acquire beliefs about ourselves and others through socialization. What specific messages have you received about your racial-ethnic identity? What specific messages have you received about dealing with people from other racial-ethnic groups?

3. Have all white Americans, regardless of class, gender, or other characteristics, benefited from racial prejudice and discrimination in the United States? Why or why not?

4. Compare recent depictions of Native Americans, African Americans, Latinos/as, and Asian and Pacific Americans in films, television shows, and advertisements. To what extent have we moved beyond the traditional stereotypes discussed in this chapter? To what extent have the stereotypes remained strong?

Chapter Four

Gender Inequality

I have resigned my position as a full tenured professor of a surgical specialty at a prominent U.S. medical school. Hard work over the past 23 years got me to the position I no longer hold and most observers, knowing of my successes, would have said, "You had it all." And I did—except for personal dignity.

Those who administer my work environment at the present time have never been able to accept me as an equal person. Not because I lack professional competence, but because I use a different bathroom. I am minus the appropriate gender identification that permits full membership in the club.

Most medical school classes today across the United States are composed of at least 35 percent women; in many the percentage is higher. . . . [However,] faculty are [still] using slides of *Playboy* centerfolds to "spice up" lectures; sexist comments are frequent and those who are offended are told to be "less sensitive." Unsolicited touching and fondling occur between house staff and students, with the latter having little recourse to object. To complain might affect a performance evaluation. The subsequent ramifications could damage career paths and may extend well into the future. . . .

Will anything be gained by my leaving a truly fine academic position? . . . I hope that the answer is "yes". . . . However, I have no illusions that my leaving will benefit the present classes of medical students who seek institutional change. Instead, I leave in place a validated legacy of sexism, a role model for all men, that women are, indeed, inferior and expected to remain so.

—*Frances K. Conley, M.D., explains why she resigned from the Stanford University medical school faculty, a position to which she later returned after some changes were initiated.* (1998:109–112)

When sociologists conduct research on organizational environments such as medical schools, women students and professors often report experiences like Dr. Conley's. What is sexism, and does it still exist in settings such as medical schools? *Sexism* **is the subordination of one sex, usually female, based on the assumed superiority of the other sex.** According to some social analysts, problems of sexism have been overblown: Sexism was a problem in the past when women were underrepresented in medical schools and other organizations; now, however, women have made significant inroads in education and professions such as medicine and law. Today, for example, they make up almost 45 percent of all first-year medical students whereas, in the late 1970s, they represented slightly more than 20 percent of all medical students (Barzansky, Jonas, and Etzel, 1999). With increases such as these, there are some analysts who suggest that women should learn to take an occasional "joke" on themselves. As one male student said, "If women can't take the heat in medicine, they ought to get out of the kitchen. . . . Taking care of sick and dying people isn't for the thin-skinned" (author's files).

However, most sociologists do not believe that derogatory jokes or sexist comments in organizational settings should be ignored. They argue that such humor creates in-group solidarity among men, particularly in male-dominated occupations, and marginalizes women, thus perpetuating gender inequality (Benokraitis and Feagin, 1995). From this perspective, pervasive sexism (along with racism and class-based inequality) is deeply rooted in many organizational environments and has a negative impact on all organizational participants (see Benokraitis and Feagin, 1995; Myers and Dugan, 1996).

GENDER INEQUALITY AS A SOCIAL PROBLEM

Just as subordinate racial-ethnic group members experience discrimination based on innate characteristics, women experience discrimination based on their sex. Since 51 percent of the people in the United States are female, women constitute the numerical majority. However, they sometimes are referred to as the country's largest minority group because, typically, they do not possess as much wealth, power, or prestige as men.

 Defining Sex and Gender

What is the difference between sex and gender? Although many people use these terms interchangeably, sociologists believe that there are significant differences in their meanings. *Sex* **is the biological differences between females and males.** Our sex is the first label we receive in life. Before birth or at the time of birth we are identified as male or female on the basis of our sex organs and genes. In comparison, *gender* **is culturally and socially constructed differences between females and males based on meanings, beliefs, and practices that a group or society associates with femininity or masculinity.** For many people, being *masculine* means being aggressive, independent, and not showing emotions, and being *feminine* means the opposite—being unaggressive, dependent, and very emotional. Understanding the difference between sex and gender is important, according to sociologists, because what many people think of as *sex differences,* for example, being aggressive or independent, are actually socially constructed *gender differences* based on widely held assumptions about men's and women's attributes (Gailey, 1987). In other words, males are supposed to be aggressive and independent not because they have male sex organs but because that's how people in this society think males should act.

 Biological and Social Bases for Gender Roles

To study gender inequality, sociologists begin with an examination of the biological and social bases for *gender roles,* which are the rights, responsibilities, expectations, and relationships of women and men in a society (Benokraitis and Feagin, 1995). Gender roles have both a biological and social basis. The biological basis for gender roles is rooted in the chromosomal and hormonal differences between men and women. When a child is conceived, the mother contributes an X chromosome, and the father contributes either an X chromosome (which produces a female embryo) or a Y chromosome (which produces a male embryo). As the embryo's male or female sex glands develop, they secrete the appropriate hormones (androgens for males, estrogens for females) that circulate through the bloodstream, producing sexual differentiation in the external genitalia, the internal reproductive tract, and possibly some areas of the brain. At birth, medical personnel and family members distinguish male from female infants by their *primary sex characteristics:* the genitalia used in the reproductive process. At puberty, hormonal differences in females and males produce *secondary sex characteristics,* the physical traits that, along with the reproductive organs, identify a person's sex. Females develop secondary sex characteristics such as menstruation, more prominent breasts, wider hips and narrower shoulders, and a layer of fatty tissue throughout the body. Male secondary sex characteristics include the development of larger genitals, a more muscular build, a deeper voice, more body and facial hair, and greater height. Although both males and females have androgens and estrogens, it is the relative proportion of each hormone that triggers masculine or feminine physical traits.

Is there something in the biological and genetic makeup of boys or girls that makes them physically aggressive or unaggressive? As sociologist Judith Lorber (1994:39) notes, "When little boys run around noisily, we say 'Boys will be boys,' meaning that physical assertiveness has to be in the Y chromosome because it is manifest so early and so commonly in boys." Similarly, when we say, "She throws like a girl" we mean, according to Lorber, that "she throws like a female child, a carrier of XX chromosomes." However, Lorber questions these widely held assumptions: "But are boys universally, the world over, in every social group, a vociferous, active presence? Or just where they are encouraged to use their bodies freely, to cover space, take risks, and play outdoors at all kinds of games and sports?"

According to Lorber, boys and girls who are given tennis rackets at the age of three and encouraged to become champions tend to use their bodies similarly. Even though boys gradually gain more shoulder and arm strength and are able to sustain more concentrated bursts of energy, after puberty girls acquire more stamina, flexibility, and lower-body strength. Coupled with training and physical exercise, these traits enhance, compensate for, or override different physical capabilities (Lorber, 1994). Thus, the girl who throws like a girl is probably a product of her culture and time: She has had more limited experience than many boys at throwing the ball and engaging in competitive games at an early age.

The social basis for gender roles is known as the *gender belief system*—the ideas of masculinity and femininity that are held to be valid in a society (Lorber, 1994). The gender belief system is reflected in what sociologists refer to as the *gendered division of labor*—the process whereby productive tasks are separated on the basis of gender. How do people determine what constitutes "women's work" or "men's work"? Evidence from cross-cultural studies shows that social factors, more than biological factors, influence the gendered division of labor in societies. In poor agricultural societies, for example, women work in the fields and tend to their families' daily needs; men typically produce and market cash crops but spend no time in household work. In developed nations, an increasing proportion of women are in paid employment but still have heavy household and family responsibilities (see Box 4.1). Across cultures, women's domain is the private and domestic, and men's domain is the public, economic, and political. This difference in how labor is divided and how workers are rewarded affects access to scarce resources such as wealth, power, and prestige. Given their domain, men have greater access to wealth, power, and prestige, a situation that leads to gender inequality in other areas.

To explain gender inequality, some sociologists use a *gender role approach,* focusing on how the socialization process contributes to male domination and female subordination. Other sociologists use a *structural approach,* focusing on how large-scale, interacting, and enduring social structures determine the boundaries of individual behavior. Let's look first at how socialization can perpetuate gender stereotyping and inequality.

GENDER INEQUALITY AND SOCIALIZATION

Numerous sociological studies have found that gender-role stereotyping is one of the enduring consequences of childhood gender socialization. Socialization into appropriate "feminine" behavior makes women less likely than men to pursue male-dominated activities, and socialization into appropriate "masculine" behavior makes men more likely than women to pursue leadership roles in education, religion, business, politics, and other spheres of public life (Peterson and Runyan, 1993). We learn our earliest and often most lasting beliefs about gender roles from a variety of *socializing agents*—people, groups, or institutions that teach us what we need

"Shall I Serve Tea at Home, the Office, or Both?": The Dilemma of Women in Japan

My father almost never steps inside the kitchen. If Mom is around, he wouldn't even serve tea. He'd just yell, "Tea!" But of course, if my mother isn't around, he has to do it by himself. Would I marry someone like my dad? No way!

—*Chie Suzuki, a twenty-three-year-old systems engineer in Tokyo (quoted in WuDunn, 1995c:6)*

I pour tea for my boss, there's no question about that. Even when we are far away from them and from the teapot, they come running over to us to tell us that we have to make tea for them. I'm too afraid to say no.

—*Emi Omasa, a thirty-year-old office worker in Tokyo (quoted in WuDunn, 1995a:6)*

As these statements suggest, many women in Japan feel constrained by traditions, such as serving tea, that they believe perpetuate male dominance and female subordination. According to journalist Sheryl WuDunn (1995a: E3), Japanese women have historically been thought of as "accessories to men." Despite some recent changes in women's roles and women's greater presence in the Japanese workplace since World War II, gender stereotyping of women as passive and subservient remains strong. As twenty-three-year-old graduate student Sachiko Nonaka says, "Women in Japan are very changed, but men don't change" (quoted in Deans, 1995:E4).

In the workplace, women are expected to accept routine jobs with much lower pay and less job stability than male workers have. As a result, women's income potential and career opportunities are limited. Over 90 percent of career-track workers are men, who typically are then prepared for jobs as salarymen (white-

collar workers), while women typically are offered jobs as clerks and secretaries (see Brinton, 1988, 1989). Women, on average, earn about 60 percent of what men earn (Landers, 1996). Women college graduates who are hired by major Japanese corporations are responsible for making tea and performing other chores for their male superiors (Deans, 1995). Many women experience sexual harassment, and employers automatically assume that women will leave their jobs when they marry or have their first child. If women keep their jobs after marriage, they often are criticized by both their bosses and their husbands, who believe that married women should be full-time homemakers.

At the beginning of the twenty-first century, more Japanese women are beginning to rebel against making tea and taking orders from men. They are setting up hotlines, organizing pressure groups, and holding nationwide rallies. Some women are choosing to marry later, have fewer children, and challenge sex discrimination in the workplace. However, other women are either remaining at home to serve their husbands and children or pursuing careers in female-dominated fields (for example, flight attendant, or *soochoowadesu*) that reward youth and beauty. As journalist Peter Landers (1996:G5) explains, "In Japan, where female office workers are often expected to make tea and tidy up after their male colleagues, becoming a flight attendant offers women a greater payoff in prestige for the kind of subservience that would probably be expected of them anyway." But the ingrained nature of gender stereotyping is reflected in the alternative explanation given by Kaori Umezawa, a former flight attendant who now trains flight attendants: "The desire to give good service is something that's inherent in women" (quoted in Landers, 1996:G5).

Do you think Japanese women and men will experience greater gender role equality in the future? Why or why not?

to know to participate in society. Among the most significant socializing agents are parents, peers, teachers and schools, sports, and the media.

 ## Gender Socialization by Parents

From birth, parents create and maintain gender distinctions between girls and boys through differential treatment. Because boys are thought to be less fragile than girls, parents are more likely to bounce an infant son, to hold him up in the air, and to play with him more vigorously than they are an infant daughter (MacDonald and Parke, 1986). Parents tend to cuddle infant girls, treat them gently, and provide them with verbal stimulation through cooing, talking, and singing to them (Basow, 1992).

Parents reinforce gender distinctions through their selection of infants' and children's clothing. Most

Across cultures, parents tend to socialize daughters and sons differently, including the assignment of household chores. What gender-specific chores were you assigned as a child? What messages about gender did you receive from your parents? Do you wish to convey the same messages to your children?

parents dress boys in boldly colored "rough and tough" clothing and girls in softly colored "feminine" clothing. They purchase sweatshirts that are decorated with hearts and flowers or female characters such as Minnie Mouse, Tweety Bird, or Pocahontas for girls and sweatshirts that feature male superheroes, athletic motifs, or characters such as Mickey Mouse, Elmer Fudd, or the Lion King for boys.

Parents further reinforce gender stereotyping and gender distinctions through the toys they buy. For example, parents buy blocks and building sets, vehicles, sporting equipment, and action toys such as guns, tanks, and soldiers for boys and dolls, doll clothing, dollhouses, play cosmetics, and homemaking items such as dishes and miniature ovens for girls (Leaper, 1994). However, toys and games do more than provide fun and entertainment; they develop different types of skills and can encourage children to participate in gender-typed activities.

Chores also reinforce gender distinctions. Most research confirms that parents use toys and chores to encourage their sons more than their daughters toward greater independence (Basow, 1992). Thus, boys frequently are assigned such maintenance chores as carrying out the garbage, cleaning up the yard, or helping dad or an older brother. Girls, on the other hand, are given domestic chores such as shopping, cooking, clearing the table, and doing laundry (Weisner et al., 1994). When parents purchase gender-specific toys and give children gender-specific household assignments, they send a powerful message about the gendered division of labor. However, gender socialization varies widely, and the extent of peer group involvement is an important factor.

Peers and Gender Socialization

Peer groups are powerful socializing agents that can reinforce existing gender stereotypes and pressure individuals to engage in gender-appropriate behavior. *Peer groups* are social groups whose members are linked by common interests and, usually, by similar age. Children are more widely accepted by their peer group when they conform to the group's notion of gender-appropriate behavior (Maccoby and Jacklin, 1987; Martin, 1989). Male peer groups place more pressure on boys to do "masculine" things than female peer groups place on girls to do "feminine" things (Fagot, 1984). For example, most girls today wear jeans and many play soccer and softball, but boys who wear dresses or play hopscotch with girls are banished from most male peer groups.

During preadolescence, male peer groups also reinforce gender-appropriate emotions in boys. In a study of a Little League baseball team, for example, sociologist Gary Fine (1987) found that the boys were encouraged by their peers to engage in proper "masculine" behavior—acting tough even when they were hurt or intimidated, controlling their emotions, being competitive and wanting to win, and showing group unity and loyalty. Boys who failed to display these characteristics received instantaneous feedback from their teammates.

Peers are important in both women's and men's development of gender identity and their aspirations for the future (Maccoby and Jacklin, 1987). Among college students, for example, peers play an important part in career choices and the establishment of long-term, intimate relationships (Huston, 1985; Martin, 1989). Even in kindergarten and the early grades, peers influence how we do in school and our perceptions of ourselves and others.

 ### Education and Gender Socialization

Like parents and peers, teachers reinforce gender distinctions by communicating to students that males and male-dominated activities are more important than females and female-dominated activities. Research on education continues to show the existence in schools of *gender bias*—a situation in which favoritism is shown toward one gender. For example, education scholars Myra Sadker and David Sadker (1994) found that teachers subtly convey the message to their students that boys are more important than girls by devoting more time, effort, and attention to boys than to girls. In day-to-day interactions, teachers are more likely to allow boys to interrupt them and give boys more praise, criticism, and suggestions for remediation than girls. Boys are more likely to be called on in class, whether they volunteer or not. When boys make comments, teachers often follow up with additional questions or suggestions; but when girls make comments, teachers often respond with a superficial "OK" and move on to the next student. Teachers praise girls for their appearance or for having a neat paper, but boys are praised for their accomplishments.

Teachers encourage gender-segregated activities when they organize classroom and playground activities by sex ("Boys line up on the left; girls on the right") and when they set up unnecessary competition between the sexes. One teacher divided her class into the "Beastly Boys" and the "Gossipy Girls" for a math game and allowed students to do the "give me five" handslapping ritual when one group outscored the other (Thorne, 1995).

The effects of gender bias become evident when teachers take a "boys will be boys" attitude about derogatory remarks and aggressive behavior against girls. *Sexual harassment*—unwanted sexual advances, requests for sexual favors, or other verbal or physical conduct of a sexual nature—is frequently overlooked by teachers and school administrators. Unfortunately media stories like the one about the first-grade boy who was suspended from school for kissing a female classmate on the cheek trivialize gender bias and sexual harassment, both of which create a hostile environment that makes it more difficult for many girls and young women to learn and accomplish as much as their male counterparts (see Orenstein, 1996; Sadker and Sadker, 1994). Researchers have found that, in some schools, male students regularly refer to girls as "sluts," "bitches," and "hos" without fear of reprimand from teachers and the girls' fear of reprisal keeps them from speaking out against their harassers (Orenstein, 1996). One high school student described her experience in a shop class in this way: "The boys literally pushed me around, right into tables and chairs.

Take a close look at this picture. What do you notice about the two lines? Social scientists have pointed out that gender socialization occurs in many ways, including how teachers organize school activities by sex.

They pulled my hair, made sexual comments, touched me, told sexist jokes. And the thing was that I was better in the shop class than almost any guy. This only caused the boys to get more aggressive and troublesome"(Sadker and Sadker, 1994:127). An American Association of University Women survey found 76 percent of 1,600 middle school and high school girls had experienced unwanted sexual comments, jokes, gestures, or looks at school. Sixty-five percent had been grabbed or pinched. More than one in ten had been forced to perform a sexual act other than kissing. Girls respond to the hostile environment by not speaking in class, letting their grades drop, or saying that they do not want to go to school at all (AAUW Educational Foundation, 1992).

Although it may seem that boys benefit from sexual harassment and teachers' gender bias (or at least are not harmed by it), that is not the case. Boys are limited by stereotypical notions of masculinity and gender-appropriate behavior. According to Sadker and Sadker (1994:220), boys confront "frozen boundaries" of the male role at every turn in their school life. They are taught to "Be cool, don't show emotion, repress feelings, be aggressive, compete, and win"—the same messages that sociologist Gary Fine (1987) found Little Leaguers using to reinforce each other. Such teachings not only limit the range of emotions boys are allowed to feel but also encourage boys to see themselves—and other males—as better than girls and to distance themselves from any activity that is considered "feminine," even though it may be an activity they enjoy.

Male gender norms, which require boys to be active, aggressive, and independent, often conflict with school norms, which require students to be quiet, passive, and conforming. Many boys walk a tightrope between compliance and rebellion. They tend to receive lower grades than girls do and are more likely to drop out of school (Sadker and Sadker, 1994). Although female gender norms conflict less with school norms than male gender norms, sociologist Michelle Fine (1991) has found in a recent study that, for many girls, the price of academic success is being compliant and muting their own voice.

Gender bias also occurs at the college level. Research consistently shows that more educational resources, ranging from athletic programs and dormitories to course offerings and career advising, are targeted primarily at men even though women constitute more than half of all U.S. college students. In the classroom, many professors give more attention

to men than to women (Hall and Sandler, 1982; Hall, 1984). Women tend to be called on less frequently and to receive less encouragement. When they speak out in class, women are more likely to be interrupted, ignored, or devalued than men are (Fox, 1995). Women often experience a drop in self-esteem while in college, yet they tend to have higher grade-point averages and they earn a higher percentage of bachelor's and master's degrees than men do. Even so, women are underrepresented in fields such as engineering, computer and information sciences, and physical sciences and overrepresented in the number of degrees awarded in education, psychology, and nursing and allied health fields (Women's Research and Educational Institute, 1996). Some analysts attribute the underrepresentation of women in math, science, and engineering to the way these courses are taught: "The traditions are based on military applications. The programs started out in military schools and colleges" (Jane Daniels, Women in Engineering, Purdue University, quoted in Urschel, 1996:2D). However, by the doctoral (Ph.D.) level, men outnumber women as recipients of degrees in all fields.

Sports and Gender Socialization

Although girls' participation in athletics has increased dramatically since the 1972 passage of Title IX, which mandates equal opportunities in academic and athletic programs, boys' participation is still almost twice that of girls. When students in a recent study in Michigan were asked about sports participation, most students listed all sports as male domains with the exception of figure skating, gymnastics, and jumping rope, which were identified as female activities (Michigan Department of Education, 1990). Obviously, gender socialization has a profound effect on how girls and boys perceive themselves in relation to sports.

While young boys are socialized to participate in highly competitive, rule-oriented games with many participants, girls are socialized to play in small groups with other girls of their own age and to engage in largely noncompetitive activities such as hopscotch or jump rope (Lever, 1978; Ignico and Mead, 1990). From elementary school through high school, boys are encouraged to play football and other competitive sports while girls are encouraged to become cheerleaders, drill team members, or homecoming queens. For males, competitive sports become a means of developing a masculine identity and a legitimate outlet for feelings of violence and aggression (Lorber, 1994).

Across lines of race or ethnicity and gender, extracurricular activities and sports provide important opportunities for leadership, teamwork, and personal contact with adult role models. However, girls' participation in sports is consistently lower than that of boys despite research indicating that girls, especially those from minority backgrounds, benefit from participation in athletic programs and sporting events. For example, one study found that Latinas who participate in sports are more likely than nonparticipants to improve their academic standing, to graduate from high school, and to attend college (Women's Sports Foundation, 1989).

▲ The Media and Gender Socialization

The media, including newspapers, magazines, television, and movies, are powerful sources of gender stereotyping. While some critics argue that the media simply reflect existing gender roles in society, others point out that the media have a unique ability to shape ideas. From children's cartoons to adult shows, television programs offer more male than female characters. Furthermore, the male characters act in a strikingly different manner than female ones. Male characters in both children's programs and adult programs are typically aggressive, constructive, and direct, while female characters defer to others or manipulate them by acting helpless, seductive, or deceitful (Basow, 1992). Some have argued that even educational programs, such as *Sesame Street,* perpetuate gender stereotypes because most of the characters have male names and masculine voices and participate in "boys' activities."

Daytime soap operas exemplify gender stereotyping. As media scholar Deborah D. Rogers (1995) has noted, even though more contemporary soaps feature career women, the cumulative effect of these programs is to reconcile women to traditional feminine roles and relationships. Whether the scene is laid at home or in the workplace, female characters typically gossip about romances or personal problems or compete for a man. Meanwhile, male characters are shown as superior beings who give orders and advice to others and do almost anything. In a hospital soap, for example, while female nurses gossip about hospital romances and their personal lives

the same male doctor who delivers babies also handles AIDS patients and treats trauma victims (Rogers, 1995).

Recent studies of MTV music videos have found that these videos often show stereotyped gender roles and condone harassment of and discrimination against women. A 1992 study found most female characters were dressed in revealing clothing, made sexual advances toward men, and usually were presented as sex objects. In contrast, male characters routinely pursued fantasy adventures or engaged in aggression and violence (Seidman, 1992).

While changes have occurred in the roles men and women play in movies, most roles still embrace stereotypes. Even though there are many women movie stars, few notable roles exist for women, and even fewer films examine women's lives and issues from their own perspectives. (Exceptions include *Fried Green Tomatoes, A League of Their Own,* and *Thelma and Louise.*) In recent years, boys have tamed a killer whale *(Free Willy),* outwitted burglars *(Home Alone),* helped police solve crimes *(Last Action Hero),* and become hockey champions *(The Mighty Ducks).* Meanwhile, girls and young women in films such as *Clueless* are depicted as "bimbos," shopaholics, and uninterested in school. According to social psychologist Hilary Lips (1993:19), "We are surrounded with the message that masculine males can be powerful, but feminine females cannot, or that women's only effective source of feminine influence is beauty and sex appeal."

Why is awareness of gender socialization important for understanding sex discrimination and gender inequality? Social analysts who use a gender role approach say that because parents, peers, teachers, and the media influence our perceptions of who we are and what our occupational preferences should be, gender role socialization contributes to a gendered division of labor, creates a *wage gap* between women and men workers, and limits the occupational choices of women and men. However, some social analysts say that no direct evidence links gender role socialization to social inequality and that it is therefore important to use social structural analysis to examine gender inequality (see Reskin and Hartmann, 1986). In other words, these analysts believe that the decisions that people make (such as the schools they choose to attend and the occupations they choose to pursue) are linked not only to how they were socialized but they are also linked to how society is structured. We now examine structural features that contribute to gender inequality.

CONTEMPORARY GENDER INEQUALITY

How do tasks in a society come to be defined as "men's work" or "women's work" and to be differentially rewarded? Many sociologists believe that social institutions and structures assign different roles and responsibilities to women and men and, in the process, restrict women's opportunities. According to feminist scholars, gender inequality is maintained and reinforced through individual and institutionalized sexism. The term *individual sexism* refers to individuals' beliefs and actions that are rooted in antifemale prejudice and stereotypic beliefs. The term *institutionalized sexism* refers to the power that men have to engage in sex discrimination at the organizational and institutional levels of society. This pattern of male domination and female subordination is known as *patriarchy*—**a hierarchical system of social organization in which cultural, political, and economic structures are controlled by men.** According to some analysts, the location of women in the workplace and on the economic pyramid is evidence of patriarchy in the United States (Epstein, 1988). In this section, we focus on five structural forms that contribute to contemporary gender inequality: the gendered division of labor, the wage gap, sexual harassment, the glass ceiling and the glass escalator, and the double shift.

▲ The Gendered Division of Paid Work

Whether by choice or economic necessity, women have entered the paid labor force in unprecedented numbers in recent years. In 1940, about 30 percent of working-age women in the United States were employed. Today, women represent more than 45 percent of the work force. Among women age twenty-five to fifty-four, the increase is even more dramatic: 75 percent currently are either employed or looking for a job. In fact, a higher proportion of women of all races, ages, and marital status groups are employed or seeking work than ever before. At the same time the proportion of male employees has gradually declined because of layoffs in the industrial sector and the long-term trend toward early retirement.

While many people who know these statistics are optimistic about the gains U.S. women have made in employment, it should be noted that women's position as a social category in the labor force is lower than men's in terms of status, opportunities, and salaries. Today, most women and men remain concentrated in occupations that are segregated by gender (see Table 4.1). The term *gender-segregated work* refers to the extent to which men and women are concentrated in different occupations and places of work (Reskin and Padavic, 1994). For example, women are predominant in word-processing pools and child-care centers while men are predominant in the construction trades. Other individuals are employed in settings where both men and women are present. In these settings, however, women are employed predominantly in clerical or other support positions while men hold supervisory, managerial, or other professional positions. For example, despite the increasing number of women entering the legal profession, most attorneys are men, and most support-staff workers, such as legal secretaries and paralegals, are women (see Epstein, 1993; Pierce, 1995). Gender-segregated work is most visible in occupations that remain more than 90 percent female (for example, secretary, registered nurse, kindergarten or elementary school teacher, and bookkeeper/auditing clerk) or more than 90 percent male (for example, carpenter, construction worker, mechanic, truck driver, and electrical engineer) (U.S. Bureau of Labor Statistics, 1995). In fact, to eliminate gender-segregated jobs in the United States, more than half of all employed men or women would have to change occupations (Reskin and Hartmann, 1986).

Observers who are optimistic about women's gains point out that government statistics show women employed in a wide variety of organizations and holding nearly every kind of job. It is important to note, however, that the types of work women and men do still vary significantly. The large occupational categories shown in Table 4.1 mask significant underlying differences in employment by gender. While the data show that women and men are most equally represented in the *managerial and professional specialty* category, when we look at specific occupations *within* this category, a different picture emerges. Lumped together are such diverse

▲ TABLE 4.1   EMPLOYMENT PERCENTAGES BY OCCUPATION AND SEX, 1997

Occupation	Men	Women
Total percentage[1]	100.00	100.00
Managerial and professional specialty	28.0	30.8
Executive, administrative, managerial	14.7	13.6
Professional specialty	12.9	17.1
Technical, sales, and administrative support	19.7	41.0
Technical and related support	2.9	3.7
Sales occupations	11.2	13.2
Administrative support, including clerical	5.6	24.2
Service occupations	10.2	17.4
Private household	0.05	1.3
Protective service	2.7	0.7
Service, except private household and protective	7.5	15.4
Precision production, craft, and repair	18.4	2.1
Operators, fabricators, and laborers	19.9	7.6
Farming, forestry, and fishing	4.0	1.1

[1]Percentages may not add to 100 because of rounding.
Source: U.S. Bureau of the Census, 1998.

occupations as prekindergarten, kindergarten, and elementary school teachers (92 percent female); computer systems analysts (70 percent male); and engineers (90 percent male). Therefore 60 percent of all employed women in the United States today are concentrated in *pink-collar occupations*—relatively low-paying, nonmanual, semiskilled positions that are held primarily by women—such as clerical work, counter help in fast-food restaurants, medical assistance, and child-care work.

Women are overrepresented in the contingent work force as well. *Contingent work* is part-time work, temporary work, and subcontracted work that offers advantages to employers but can be detrimental to workers' welfare. Many employers stress that having more contingent workers and fewer permanent, full-time employees keeps corporations competitive in the global marketplace. However, this type of employment actually makes it possible for employers to avoid providing benefits such as health insurance and pen-

sion plans to all employees. While many women are found in contingent work because it often provides greater flexibility for those with family responsibilities, nearly two million women who accepted part-time or temporary work in 1995 did so because they were unable to find permanent jobs (Costello et al., 1996). Although all contingent workers experience problems related to this type of work, women especially are affected by the fact that contingent workers are unlikely to qualify for unemployment compensation if they lose their jobs (see Bassi and Chasanov, 1996), and most do not qualify for pension coverage (see Hounsell, 1996; Patterson, 1996).

Although the degree of gender segregation in the workplace and in professions, such as accounting, law, and medicine, has declined in the last three decades, occupational segregation by race and ethnicity persists. Today, a larger percentage of white women (30 percent) than African American women (21 percent) or Latinas (17 percent) hold managerial

and professional specialty jobs. When African American women become professionals, they often find their employment opportunities more limited than those of white women and men. Sociologist Elizabeth Higginbotham (1994) has found that most African American professional women are concentrated in public sector employment (as public school teachers, welfare workers, librarians, public defenders, or faculty members at public colleges) rather than in private sector employment (e.g., in large corporations, major law firms, and elite private universities).

Both Latinas and African American women are more likely than white women to work in service occupations such as private household workers. Although private household work has become less common among African American women in the last two decades, Latinas remain heavily represented among the 800,000 women who are employed as private household workers. Across racial and ethnic lines, women continue to be concentrated in jobs where they receive lower wages and fewer benefits on average than men.

The Wage Gap

The *wage gap*—the disparity between women's and men's earnings—is the best-documented consequence of gender-segregated work (Reskin and Padavic, 1994). No matter what their race or ethnic group men earn more than women of the same racial or ethnic group. The median earnings for women who worked full time in 1998 were $456 per week compared to $598 for men. This means that a woman who works full time makes about 76 cents for every dollar that a man makes.

The wage gap varies by age: The older the worker, the larger the gap. This may be true in part because younger workers tend to have about the same amount of work experience and to be concentrated in entry-level jobs. Thus, between the ages of twenty and

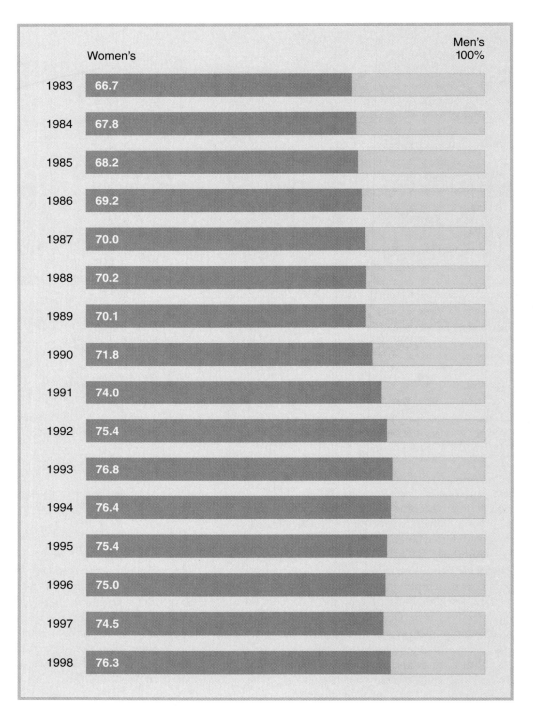

FIGURE 4.1   *The U.S. Wage Gap: Women's Earnings Compared with Men's Earnings, 1983–1998*

Source: U.S. Bureau of Labor Statistics, 1999.

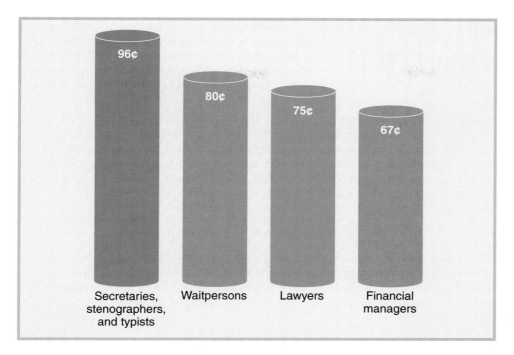

FIGURE 4.2   *U.S. Wage Gap in Selected Occupations*
Source: U.S. Bureau of Labor Statistics, 1999.

twenty-four, women earn an average of 93 cents for every dollar that men earn. However, women between the ages of twenty-five and thirty-four earn only 85 cents for every dollar that men earn. Women between the ages of thirty-five and forty-four earn only 73 cents per dollar; and by ages fifty-five to sixty-four the amount has dropped to only 68 cents for each dollar men earn (U.S. Bureau of Labor Statistics, 1999).

Social analysts suggest that the higher wage gap for older workers probably reflects a number of factors, including the fact that women in those age groups tend to have, on average, less overall work experience and less time with their present employer than have men of the same age (Herz and Wootton, 1996). As Figure 4.1 shows, the wage gap has narrowed somewhat between women and men over the last three decades, but much of the decrease in wage disparity can be attributed to a decline in men's average earnings since 1973 rather than to a significant increase in women's earnings (Roos and Reskin, 1992).

For pay equity to occur between men and women, there has to be a broad-based commitment to *comparable worth*—the belief that wages ought to reflect the worth of a job, not the gender or race of the worker (Kemp, 1994). To determine the comparable worth of different kinds of jobs, researchers break a specific job into components to determine (1) how much education, training, and skills are required; (2) how much responsibility a person in that position has for others' work; and (3) what the working conditions are. Researchers then allocate points for each component to determine whether or not men and women are being paid equitably for their work (Lorber, 1994). For pay equity to exist, men and women in occupations that receive the same number of points must be paid the same. However, pay equity exists for very few jobs. (See Figure 4.2 for a comparison of men's and women's earnings in selected occupations.)

Comparable worth is an important issue for men as well as women. Male workers in female-dominated jobs such as nursing, secretarial work, and elementary teaching pay an economic penalty for their choice of work. If women were compensated fairly, an employer could not undercut men's wages by hiring women at a cheaper rate (Kessler-Harris, 1990).

Sexual Harassment

Millions of men never harass women in the workplace or elsewhere, but so many other men do that it is almost impossible for women to avoid the experience (Langelan, 1993). Sexual harassment is a form of intentional, institutionalized gender discrimination that includes all unwelcome sexual attention affecting an employee's job conditions or creating a hostile work environment. Sexual harassment includes verbal abuse, touching, staring at or making jokes about a woman's body, demands for sexual intercourse, and even rape on the job (Benokraitis and Feagin, 1995). People who are accused of sexual harassment frequently claim that their actions were merely harmless expressions of (supposedly) mutual sexual attraction. However, sexual harassment is not about attraction; it is about *abuse of power*. Sexual harassment constitutes a form of intimidation and aggression: The recipient has no choice in the encounter or has reason to fear repercussions if she or he declines. Some men are able to harass because they hold economic power over women (e.g., bosses, supervisors, and colleagues who have some say over promotions and raises); others are able to harass because they hold gender-based power (e.g., power rooted in cultural patterns of male dominance and backed up by the threat of violence and the ability to rape) (Langelan, 1993). In either case, sexual harassment serves as a means of boundary heightening between men and women in the workplace. For example, male lawyers may exaggerate the differences between women lawyers and themselves by directing unwanted sexual invitations, attention, and behavior at women in their firm. In her recent study of law firms, sociologist Jennifer L. Pierce interviewed many female lawyers who reported incidents similar to the one described by Gabriella, a twenty-six-year-old associate who had slapped a male partner who was harassing her at a firm cocktail party: "Everyone else knew about George, but I was new, I didn't know to avoid him. So, when he tried to grab my breasts, I didn't even think, I just came out swinging. . . . It was so humiliating. Then, afterwards . . . the snide remarks, the knowing glances, the comments, 'How's your left hook?' It was the second public humiliation." (Pierce, 1995:108–109). According to Pierce, the comments made about Gabriella's reaction (slapping George) by the male attorneys show that they considered her behavior (not George's actions) to be inappropriate and worthy of derision.

Sexual harassment is a costly problem for women who may lose employment opportunities and for their employers who lose more than $7 million a year in low productivity, absenteeism, and employee turnover related to harassment (Basow, 1992). Sexual harassment and other forms of blatant and subtle discrimination in the workplace also contribute to the institutional barriers that limit women's opportunities to rise to the top positions in corporations and other occupational settings (see MacCorquodale and Jensen, 1993; Rosenberg et al., 1993).

The Glass Ceiling and the Glass Escalator

More recently, feminist researchers have used the advancement (or lack of advancement) of women into top tier management jobs as a litmus test for how well women are faring in the labor force as a whole. They have found that women hold only a handful of top positions. Although they are inching their way up the corporate ladder, women almost always encounter barriers when they try to enter the lucrative and prestigious top positions of their occupations. This is because of what is known as the *glass ceiling*—the invisible institutional barrier constructed by male management that prevents women from reaching top positions in major corporations and other large-scale organizations. Among the reasons cited for this barrier are male executives who believe that male workers will not work under women supervisors and that women workers are supposed to be in support roles (Benokraitis and Feagin, 1995).

The glass ceiling is particularly evident in the nation's 500 largest companies. In 1996, fewer than 3 percent of the 2,400 people having titles, such as chairman, chief executive, vice chairman, president, chief operations officer, or executive vice president, and the salary that accompanies these titles were women. Women of color occupy fewer than 1 percent of top management positions. According to a recent study by Catalyst (Dobrzynski, 1996a), a nonprofit research group that studies women in upper-level management, fourteen of the top one hundred companies do not have a woman among their top officers (see Table 4.2).

Overall, women are most likely to reach top positions in the service sector (for example, banking and diversified finance, publishing, retailing, food services, and entertainment), a sector in which they have traditionally been employed in great numbers.

TABLE 4.2   TOP 100 CORPORATIONS WITH NO WOMEN AMONG TOP OFFICERS

Fortune 500 Rank	Corporation	Number of Officers
3	Exxon	20
8	Mobil	9
27	Kroger	12
33	Merrill Lynch	17
44	Loews	17
49	Bellsouth	22
59	NationsBank	6
72	Compaq Computer	14
82	Lehman Brothers	18
85	Nynex	27
89	Texas Instruments	12
90	Rockwell International	19
92	Archer Daniels Midland	23
94	IBP	59

Source: Based on Dobrzynski, 1996a.

Women fare the worst in male-dominated businesses such as mining, crude oil, brokerages, and manufacturing. In its research, Catalyst found that women who continue to bump into glass ceilings tend to leave large corporations and start their own businesses (Dobrzynski, 1996a).

Unlike women who enter male-dominated occupations, men who enter female-dominated occupations are apt to find little difficulty in rising to the top of their occupation. In recent research on men working as registered nurses, elementary teachers, librarians, and social workers, sociologist Christine L. Williams (1995) found that they tended to rise in disproportionate numbers to administrative positions at the top of these occupations. Williams (1995:12) calls the upward movement of men in "women's professions" the *glass escalator effect* because, as she notes, "like being on an invisible 'up' escalator, men must struggle to remain in the lower (i.e., 'feminine') levels of their professions." Men also move into more "masculine" specialties within traditionally female-dominated occupations. Male librarians, for example, often move into high-technology computer information specialties and administration. In contrast, women in male-dominated occupations typically find they are bumping their heads on the glass ceiling and working a double shift.

The Double Shift

Although there have been dramatic changes in the participation of women in the labor force, the division of labor by sex has remained essentially unchanged in many families. While more married women now share responsibility for earning part—or all—of the family income, many married men do not participate in routine domestic chores (Reskin and Padavic, 1994). Consequently, many employed women must deal with a double work load. In the words of sociologist Arlie Hochschild (1989), women with dual responsibilities as wage earners and unpaid household workers work "the second shift."

Not only does the relative number of hours spent on housework differ widely between women and men, but the kinds of chores men and women do also vary significantly. Women do most of the *daily* chores such as taking care of children, making beds, and cooking and cleaning up after meals. Men are more likely to do chores that do not have to be done every day. For example, men typically mow the lawn, repair cars or other equipment, and do home improvements (Shelton, 1992). Although some kinds of housework can be put off, young children's needs cannot be ignored or delayed, so daily domestic duties in families with young children consume a great deal of time and energy. A sick child or a school event that cannot be scheduled around work causes additional stress for parents, especially mothers. Furthermore, more and more women are becoming members of "the sandwich generation." In other words, they are caught, sandwiched, between the needs of their young children and those of older relatives for whom they are often the primary caregivers. In an effort to keep up with family obligations while working full-time or part-time, many women spend a large portion of their earnings on day-care and elder-care centers, prepared foods and meals from fast-food restaurants, and laundry and dry cleaning (Bergmann, 1986).

When sociologists conduct research on participation in household work, both men and women state that working couples should share household

As more women have entered the paid work force, they have encountered a double shift at home. According to researchers, employed women still do most of the daily household chores such as taking care of the children. Is this photo a hopeful sign for the future?

responsibilities. However, when it gets down to who actually does what, most studies find that women, even those who hold full-time jobs, do most of the work. According to Arlie Hochschild (1989), many women try to solve their time crunch by forgoing leisure activities and sleep.

PERSPECTIVES ON GENDER INEQUALITY

Unlike functionalist and conflict perspectives, which focus on macrolevel sources of gender inequality, interactionist perspectives typically focus on social constructs such as language. It is language, interactionists say, that structures our thinking and discourse about domination and subordination.

▲ The Interactionist Perspective

For the interactionists, who view society as the sum of all people's interactions, language is extremely significant in defining social realities because it provides people with shared meanings and social realities. Historically, what men have thought, written, and concluded have been the givens of our discourse

(Peterson and Runyan, 1993). Today, however, English and other languages are being criticized for *linguistic sexism,* that is, for words and patterns of communication that ignore, devalue, or make sex objects of one sex or the other, most often women.

Linguistic sexism, some analysts believe, perpetuates traditional gender role stereotypes and reinforces male dominance. These analysts note that the idea that women are secondary to men in importance is embedded in the English language: The masculine form (*he*) is used to refer to human beings generally, and words such as *chairman* and *mankind* are considered to include both men and women (Miller and Swift, 1991). When a woman enters a profession such as medicine or law, she is frequently referred to as a "female doctor" or "woman lawyer"; such terms linguistically protect these male-dominated professions from invasion by females (Lindsey, 1994).

Language can also be used to devalue women by referring to them in terms that reinforce the notion that they are sex objects. Terms such as *fox, bitch, babe,* or *doll* further devalue women by ascribing pet-like, childlike, or toylike attributes to them (Adams and Ware, 1995). According to one analyst, at least 220 terms exist for sexually promiscuous women, but only 22 terms exist for promiscuous men (Stanley, 1972).

Research by scholars in a variety of disciplines has demonstrated not only the importance of language in patterning our thoughts but also how gender—and the hierarchy it constructs—is built into the English language (Peterson and Runyan, 1993). According to sociologists Claire M. Renzetti and Daniel J. Curran (1995:151), "Given that women are denigrated, unequally defined, and often ignored by the English language, it serves not only to reflect their secondary status relative to men in our society, but also to reinforce it."

Linguist Deborah Tannen (1990, 1994) has examined how power differentials between women and men at home and in the workplace are reflected in their communication styles. According to Tannen (1990), men and women speak different *genderlects:* Women speak and hear a language of intimacy and connection, while men speak and hear a language of status and independence. For example, women's conversations tend to focus more on relationships with others and include "rapport talk." Men's conversations are more likely to convey messages about their position in workplace or social hierarchies and include "information talk."

Men's and women's communication styles also differ: Men have a more direct style of communication and are more likely to dominate conversations than women are. Men tend to seek immediate solutions for problems, while women may ponder alternatives before reaching a decision. From this perspective, communication not only reflects women's and men's relative power in society but also perpetuates male domination and female subordination.

According to interactionists, male dominance is also perpetuated through nonverbal communication such as bodily movement, posture, eye contact, use of personal space, and touching. Men typically control more space than women do, whether they are sitting or standing. Men tend to invade women's personal space by standing close to them, touching them, or staring at them. Such actions are not necessarily sexual in connotation; however, when a man nudges and fondles a flight attendant or a coworker in the office, these actions do have sexual overtones that cannot be dismissed. Recent sexual harassment cases show that women do not appreciate such acts and feel threatened by them, especially if the toucher is the employer (Lindsey, 1994:79).

Although the interactionist perspective has been criticized for ignoring the larger, structural factors that perpetuate gender inequality, it is important to note that language and communication patterns are embedded in the structure of society and pass from generation to generation through the socialization process.

 ## The Functionalist Perspective

In focusing on macrolevel issues affecting gender inequality, functionalists frequently examine employment opportunities and the wage gap between men and women.

According to such early functionalists as Talcott Parsons (1955), gender inequality is inevitable because of the biological division of labor: Men generally are physically stronger than women and have certain abilities and interests, whereas women, as the only sex able to bear and nurse children, have their own abilities and interests. Given the biological attributes, Parsons said, men find themselves more suited to *instrumental* (goal-oriented) *tasks* and women to *expressive* (emotionally oriented) *tasks*. In the home, therefore, husbands perform such instrumental tasks as providing economic support and making the most important decisions for the family, while wives perform such

expressive tasks as nurturing children and providing emotional support for all family members. The division of labor by gender ensures that important societal tasks—such as procreation and the socialization of children—are fulfilled and that the family is socially and economically stable.

According to Parsons, this division of labor continues in the workplace, where women again do expressive work and men again do instrumental work. Thus, women cluster in occupations that require expressive work, such as elementary school teaching, nursing, and secretarial work because of their interests and abilities. Women also are concentrated in specific specialties within professions such as law and medicine because of their aptitude for expressive work and their desire to spend more time with their families than men, who are in more lucrative specialties, are able to spend. For example, many women in law specialize in family law, and many women in medicine specialize in pediatrics (infants and children), obstetrics and gynecology (women), or family practice. In corporations, women are thought to be more adept at public relations and human resources; men are viewed as more adept at financial management. In recent years, however, critics have rejected the dichotomy between men's instrumental work and women's expressive work set forth by functionalists (see Scott, 1996). These critics have noted that the functionalist explanation of gender inequality does not take into account sex discrimination and other structural barriers that make some educational and occupational opportunities more available to men than to women. It also fails to examine the underlying power relations between women and men and does not consider the fact that society places unequal value on tasks assigned to men and women (Kemp, 1994).

Other functionalist explanations of gender inequality focus on the human capital that men and women bring to the workplace. According to human capital explanations, what individuals earn is based on choices they have made, including choices about the kinds of training and experience they accumulate. For example, human capital analysts argue that women diminish their human capital when they leave the labor force to engage in childbearing and child-care activities. While women are out of the labor force, their human capital deteriorates from nonuse. When they return to work, they earn lower wages than men do because they have fewer years of work experience and "atrophied human capital," that is, because their education and training may have become obsolete (Kemp, 1994: 70).

Critics of the human capital model note that it is based on the false assumption that all people, regardless of gender, race, or other attributes, are evaluated and paid fairly on the basis of their education, training, and other job-enhancing characteristics. It fails to acknowledge that white women and people of color tend to be paid less even when they are employed in male-dominated occupations and take no time off for family duties (Lorber, 1994).

 Conflict and Feminist Perspectives

Conflict perspectives on gender inequality are based on the assumption that social life is a continuous struggle in which members of powerful groups (males, in this case) seek to maintain control of scarce resources such as social, economic, and political superiority. By dominating individual women and commanding social institutions, men maintain positions of privilege and power. However, conflict theorists note, not all men are equally privileged: Men in the upper classes have greater economic power because they control elite positions in corporations, universities, the mass media, and government (Richardson, 1993).

Conflict theorists using a Marxist approach believe that gender inequality primarily results from capitalism and private ownership of the means of production. Basing their work on this Marxist approach, *socialist feminists* state that under capitalism, men gain control over property and over women. Thus, *capitalism* exploits women in the workplace, and *patriarchy* exploits women at home (Kemp, 1994). According to this perspective, capitalists benefit from the gendered division of labor in the workplace because they can pay women lower wages and derive higher profits. At the same time, individual men benefit from the unpaid work women do at home. The capitalist economic system is maintained because women reproduce the next generation of workers while providing current employees (often including themselves) with food, clean clothes, and other goods and services that are necessary for those who must show up at the workplace each day (Hartmann, 1976).

Unlike socialist feminists, *radical feminists* focus exclusively on *patriarchy* as the primary source of gender inequality. From this perspective, men's oppression of women is deliberate, with ideological justification provided by other institutions such as the media and religion. *Liberal feminists* believe that

According to feminist theorists, women have made major gains in U.S. government and business; however, gender equity is far from a reality in our society. What do you think can be done to reduce the problem?

gender inequality is rooted in *gender-role socialization,* which perpetuates women's lack of equal civil rights and educational opportunities. *Black feminists* believe that women of color face inequalities based on the multiplicative effect of race, class, and gender as simultaneous forces of oppression (Andersen and Collins, 1995).

Conflict and feminist perspectives have been criticized for their emphasis on male dominance without a corresponding analysis of how men may be oppressed by capitalism and/or patriarchy.

CAN GENDER INEQUALITY BE REDUCED?

Although the rights and working conditions of women have improved during the past thirty years, much remains to be done before gender inequality is significantly reduced. As for how, specifically, to go about reducing gender inequality, a point that was made in previous chapters bears repeating: How people view social problems directly affects how they think the problem should be solved. Interactionists, for example, think gender inequality can be reduced only when people redefine social realities such as linguistic sexism. In their view, language should be modified so that it no longer conveys notions of male superiority and female inferiority, which are then transmitted intergenerationally through the socialization process.

Some functionalists believe that traditional gender roles should be redefined for the well-being of individuals and society, but other functionalists suggest that women should become more aware of how their human capital is diminished by decisions they make. From this perspective, to be competitive in the workplace, women must have the same educational background and qualifications for positions that men have. Some functionalists also suggest that overt sex discrimination can be reduced by enforcing existing legislation such as Title VII of the Civil Rights Act of 1964, which forbids discrimination on the basis of sex. However, this approach would not affect covert or institutionalized discrimination, which has a negative and differential impact on white women and people of color.

While some conflict theorists view elimination of sex discrimination as the primary solution for gender inequality, those using a Marxist approach believe that gender equality will occur only when capitalism is abolished. Socialist feminists agree that capitalism should be eliminated and a new economy that eliminates the gendered division of labor and the wage gap between women and men should be developed. Liberal feminists say that we could reduce gender inequality by dramatically changing gender socialization and what children learn from their families,

teachers, and the media about appropriate masculine and feminine attitudes and behavior. Radical feminists suggest that gender inequality can be reduced only when patriarchy is abolished. To achieve this goal, they say that the legal system must continue to provide relief for sex discrimination, especially sexual harassment in schools and the workplace and that alternative institutions must be developed to replace existing gendered social institutions. For example, women's health care centers should replace male-dominated medicine, and child-care and elder-care centers should assume some of women's caregiving burdens. Finally, black feminists believe that equality will occur only when all women—regardless of race, class, gender, age, religion, sexual orientation, and ability or disability—are treated more equitably (Andersen and Collins, 1995).

Clearly, many gender issues remain unresolved. As a result of technological changes and the proliferation of service jobs such as information clerk, nurses' aide, and fast-food restaurant worker, which often are equated with "women's work," gender-segregated jobs may increase rather than decrease. Moreover, if the number and quality of "men's jobs" shrink, many men at all class levels may become more resistant to women entering traditionally male-dominated occupations and professions (Reskin and Padavic, 1994). Many analysts suggest that for a significant reduction in gender inequality to occur, women have to become more involved in the political arena and take action themselves (see Box 4.2 on page 82).

SUMMARY

⇒ *How does sex differ from gender?*
  Sex is the biological aspects of being male or female; gender is the socially constructed differences between females and males. In short, sex is what we (generally) are born with; gender is what we acquire through socialization.

⇒ *What are the primary socializing agents?*
  The key socializing agents are parents, peers, teachers and schools, sports, and the media, all of which may reinforce gender stereotypes and gender-based inequalities as they attempt to teach gender-appropriate behavior.

⇒ *How are sexism and patriarchy related?*
  Individual and institutional sexism are maintained and reinforced by patriarchy, a hierarchical system in which cultural, political, and economic structures are dominated by males.

⇒ *What are some of the primary causes of gender inequality?*
  Gender inequality results from economic, political, and educational discrimination against women as evidenced in gender-segregated work, which in turn results in a disparity—or wage gap—between women's and men's earnings. Even when women are

SOCIAL PROBLEMS
AND SOCIAL POLICY

BOX 4.2

The Women's Movement and Social Policy: "If You Want the Job Done, Do It Yourself"

Throughout history women—individually, collectively, and sometimes with men—have struggled against direct and indirect barriers to their self-development and their full social, political, and economic participation. (Peterson and Runyan, 1993:116)

From the time the Founding Fathers wrote, "All *men* are created equal," some women have realized that they have to take action to bring about greater equality for women. The first wave of the U.S. women's movement began with the Women's Rights Convention in Seneca Falls, New York, in 1848, when early feminists drafted the Declaration of Sentiments, which called for social equality with men, in particular the right to vote and to own property. However, women did not gain the right to vote until 1920, when the suffragist movement succeeded in obtaining the passage of the Nineteenth Amendment.

The civil rights movement of the 1950s and 1960s found women activists advocating voting rights for people of color and an end to racial segregation. This movement culminated in passage of the Civil Rights Act of 1964, which included Title VII, making it illegal to discriminate against women in hiring and promotion.

During the 1970s and 1980s, divisions among women based on race, class, and sexual orientation also became apparent as social legislation was passed that benefited women and children. When the National Women's Political Caucus encouraged women to run for public office, women made some gains in political representation, and more women received political appointments, including one to the U.S. Supreme Court. However, significant setbacks for women's rights occurred when the Equal Rights Amendment was not ratified by the required number of states and pressing issues such as affirmative action, child care, and abortion became highly contested political terrain (Faludi, 1991).

Despite slight political gains in recent decades, the percentage of women holding public office remains low. Although women constitute more than 50 percent of the population, they constitute only 12 percent of Congress with 53 women in the House and 8 women in the Senate (2000). At the state level, women make up about 25 percent of statewide elected officials and 20 percent of state legislators (Women's Research and Education Institute, 1996).

Why are women underrepresented in Congress and other important elected positions? Some social analysts suggest that it is because few women with sufficient experience and credentials choose to run; others believe that the answer lies in the structure of patriarchy, especially the unequal division of labor at home and in the workplace. As a result of this inequality, women have difficulty in finding necessary resources (time, money, and energy) to run for office (Berg, 1994). Female candidates also are targets of sexist assumptions about families. A statement sent out by the Newt Gingrich Congressional Campaign several decades ago is typical of the treatment received by many female candidates, including his opponent, Democrat Virginia Shapard: "The Gingriches have two daughters. . . . When elected, Newt will keep his family together. . . . The Shapards have four children. . . . If elected Virginia will move to Washington, but her children and husband will remain in Georgia" (quoted in Mandel, 1981:90). Do such attitudes persist today? What macrolevel and microlevel changes must occur to increase the proportional representation of women in elective offices? Do you think these changes are possible?

employed in the same job as men, on average they do not receive the same (or comparable) pay.

➡ *What is the second shift and why is it a problem for women?*

The second shift is the unpaid household work performed by employed women. Many women have a second shift because of their dual responsibilities in the workplace and at home. The typical woman in the United States who combines paid work in the labor force and family work as a homemaker does not have enough hours in the average day to fulfill all her responsibilities, and many men have been unwilling or unable to pick up some of the slack at home.

➡ *How do functionalist and conflict analysts explain the gendered division of labor?*

According to functionalist analysts, women's caregiver roles in contemporary industrialized soci-

eties are crucial in ensuring that key societal tasks are fulfilled. While the husband performs the instrumental tasks of economic support and decision making, the wife assumes the expressive tasks of providing affection and emotional support for the family. According to conflict analysts, the gendered division of labor within families and the workplace results from male control and dominance over women and resources.

➡ *What are the major feminist perspectives and how do they explain gender inequality?*

In liberal feminism, gender equality is connected to equality of opportunity. In radical feminism, male dominance is seen as the cause of oppression. According to socialist feminists, women's oppression results from capitalism and patriarchy and women's dual roles as paid and unpaid workers. Black feminism focuses on race and class in analyzing gender inequality.

KEY TERMS

comparable worth, p. 75	gendered division of labor, p. 65	sex, p. 64
contingent work, p. 72	glass ceiling, p. 76	sexism, p. 64
gender, p. 64	patriarchy, p. 71	sexual harassment, p. 68
gender bias, p. 68	pink-collar occupations, p. 72	wage gap, p. 73

QUESTIONS FOR CRITICAL THINKING

1. Examine the various administrative and academic departments at your college. What is the gender breakdown of administrators and faculty in selected departments? Can you identify a gender-related pattern associated with women's and men's majors at your school? What conclusions can you draw about the relationship between gender and education based on your observations?

2. Will the increasing numbers of women in higher education, the workplace, and the military tip the balance of power between men and women and result in greater gender equality in the future? Explain your answer.

3. What kind of study might you develop to examine the effects of children's clothing and toys on the socialization of children? How could you isolate the clothing or toy variable from other variables that influence children's socialization?

4. What steps do you think should be taken to reduce sexism and bring about greater gender inequality in the United States? What resources would you need to implement your plan?

Chapter Five

Inequality Based on Age

A teacher saw my picture [in a newspaper article about ninety-year-olds] in *USA Today* and had her class write to me. I got thirty lovely letters. . . . I've never been to the South, so I flew [to Decatur, Alabama]. . . . I answer any of their questions. Do you still have your own teeth? Do you have a boyfriend? I say, "No, but I'm looking for one who can cook. If you find somebody like that, let me know." They think it's funny.

They want to know how it feels to be ninety. I tell them I feel like myself. Don't you all feel like yourself? Okay, there's a difference. When I was your age, I loved to play basketball and climb mountains and slide down the other side. One thing I didn't want to do was make speeches. It was scary. Now I don't want to climb mountains and play basketball. I love to make speeches. So you see, when you're ninety, you'll do what you feel like doing. In a way, I'm telling them to value old age and respect it.

—Hazel Wolf, age 95, Seattle, Washington, in an interview with author Studs Terkel (1996:140)

As Hazel Wolf's statement indicates, how people of one age view people of another age is relative. Young people may view older people as "over the hill" while older people may consider the young as lacking experience. Throughout one's lifetime, age is a very important ascribed characteristic. Just consider how many times you have been asked, "How old are you?" Most of us answer this question in terms of *chronological age*—age based on date of birth. Although chronological age constitutes our "official" age, most of us view other people in terms of their *functional age*—observable individual attributes such as physical appearance, mobility, strength, coordination, and mental capacity that are used to assign people to age categories (Atchley, 2000). A wide range of physical, psychological, and intellectual factors can influence our functional age (Chudacoff, 1989). Although we may appear to be younger or older than our chronological age, there are some things that we do in life, such as driving a car or voting, that are determined by our chronological age rather than our functional age. Children—regardless of ability—are not allowed to drive and therefore eagerly look forward to the time when they will be "old enough" to drive. For the younger person, then, changes in chronological and functional age are positive. However, as some people age, they begin to lose some of the functional abilities, such as vision or hearing, that are necessary for driving. Thus, the older person may view changes in chronological and functional age negatively. Although age-based restrictions are placed on young drivers, similar restrictions on older drivers are widely viewed as a form of ageism (Stock, 1995).

AGEISM AS A SOCIAL PROBLEM

Ageism—**prejudice and discrimination against people on the basis of age**—is a social problem that particularly stigmatizes and marginalizes older people. Gerontologist Robert Butler (1969) introduced the term *ageism* to describe how myths and misconceptions about older people produce age-based discrimination. According to Butler, just as racism and sexism perpetuate stereotyping and discrimination against people of color and all women, ageism perpetuates stereotyping of older people and age-based discrimination. Most research has therefore focused on the negative and differential impact ageism has on older people.

 ### Age-Based Stereotypes

There are more stereotypes about the physical and mental abilities of older people than there are about the abilities of people in any other age category. This does not mean that children and adolescents are exempt from age-based stereotypes. Comedians often refer to very young children as "crumb crunchers," "curtain climbers," and "little hellions." Animated television characters such as Bart and Lisa Simpson (*The Simpsons*), Beavis and Butt-Head (MTV), and young characters in many situation comedies and movies are simply stereotypic depictions of children and young adolescents.

Older people, however, are stereotyped in numerous ways. Some stereotypes depict them as slow in their thinking and movement; as living in the past and unable to change; and as cranky, sickly, and lacking in social value (Atchley, 2000). Other stereotypes suggest that older people are "greedy geezers," living an affluent lifestyle and ignoring the needs of future generations (Toner, 1995). When age-based stereotypes are accepted by many people, they can affect how people vote and what types of social policies legislators enact. Negative stereotypes of older people reinforce ageism and influence how younger people interact with older people.

Although most of us do not believe that we engage in stereotypical thinking about older people, researcher William C. Levin (1988) found that college students in his study evaluated people differently on the basis of their assumed age. When Levin showed three photographs of the same man, who had been made up to appear twenty-five in the first photo, fifty-two in the second, and seventy-three in the third, to the students and asked them to evaluate these (apparently different) men for employment purposes, many students described the "seventy-three-year-old" as less competent, less intelligent, and less reliable than the "twenty-five-year-old" and the "fifty-two-year-old." Clearly our place in the social structure changes during our life course, and if we live long enough, any of us may become the target of stereotyping and discrimination directed at older people (Hooyman and Kiyak, 1996).

 ### Social Inequality and the Life Course

To study age and social inequality, many sociologists and social gerontologists focus on the *life course*—the age-based categories through which people pass as they grow older. In the United States the life course tends to be divided into infancy and childhood, adolescence and young adulthood, middle age, later maturity, and old age. The field of *gerontology* examines the biological, physical, and social aspects of the aging process. We will focus primarily on *social gerontology*—**the study of the social (non-physical) aspects of aging**—as we examine age classifications in the United States.

CHILDHOOD

Infants (birth to age two) and children (ages three to twelve) are among the most powerless individuals in society. In the past, children were seen as

"My mom and dad are still very sharp."

the property of their parents, who could do with their children as they chose (Tower, 1996). Although we have a more liberal attitude today, children remain vulnerable to problems such as family instability, poverty, maltreatment by relatives and other caregivers, and sexual exploitation. The Children's Defense Fund (1999) reports that *every day* in the United States:

- 2,160 infants are born into poverty
- 80 persons under age 18 die
- 8,219 children are reported abused or neglected
- 1,200,000 latchkey children (children who receive no supervision at home after school because their parents are at work) come home to residences in which there is a gun
- 12 children die from gun wounds

Relatively high rates of single parenthood, a significant increase in the divorce rate in recent decades, and the fact that many parents work several jobs in an attempt to make ends meet have caused many children to face a complex array of problems and social relationships in their families. A large number of children believe that they do not receive enough attention from their parents. Raoul, an eleven-year-old Cuban American, is an example:

I live with my mom. My dad moved to Miami when they broke up and I was about two. So I have a stepdad and a stepbrother. . . . My stepbrother and my mom get along, but not too good. He misses his mom. My stepdad took him because his mom was bad. And then my mom and his dad got married and we became a family. I think he would like to get his mom and dad back together 'cause he gets in trouble a lot. . . .

I've had a nice life so far, for eleven years, but I wish everybody would pay more attention to kids. That's something we really need. Sometimes grown-ups pay attention, but not a lot. They're kind of all wrapped up in their jobs and they don't really pay attention to little children.

I think it wouldn't be so violent [in society] if people paid attention. (quoted in *Children's Express*, 1993:43–45)

ADOLESCENCE

Before the twentieth century, the concept of adolescence did not exist. When children grew big enough to do adult work, they were expected to fulfill adult responsibilities such as making money to support their family (Chudacoff, 1989). Today, the line between childhood and adolescence is blurred. While some researchers define adolescence as the teenage years (ages thirteen to nineteen), others place the lower and upper ages at fifteen and twenty-four, respectively (Corr et al., 1994).

Adolescents tread a narrow path between childhood and adulthood. They are not treated as children, but they are not afforded the full status of adulthood. Early teens are considered too young to drive, to drink alcohol, to stay out late, and to do other things that are considered to be adult behavior by the media, particularly television and movies, and by members of some peer groups. Adolescents face an identity crisis in which they must figure out who they are and what they want to become. They also face difficult decisions pertaining to their sexuality and their relationships with people of the same sex and the opposite sex. Teen pregnancy and parenthood are major concerns for many adolescents.

Many adolescents must deal with conflicting demands for money and school attendance. Most states have compulsory school attendance laws that require young people to attend school from about ages six through sixteen or eighteen. However, some adolescents balk at this requirement; they cannot see what school is doing for them and would prefer to find employment. In fact, many teenagers who live in families that are trapped in poverty may hold jobs to supplement the family income or support themselves. These adolescents may view being required to remain in school as a form of discrimination.

Although child labor laws allegedly control the amount of work and working conditions of young employees, recent studies show that many employed adolescents face hazardous working conditions and work longer than the allowable number of hours per day. There are, for example, few restrictions on farm labor, and teenagers who harvest crops such as strawberries for thirteen hours a day, earning $2.80 per hour or less, may be exposed to harmful pesti-

cides (Lantos, 1992). Teenagers employed in fast-food restaurants have been injured by electric knives that cut off fingers. In one case, a fifteen-year-old boy employed by a bakery died when he was pulled into a dough-mixing machine.

Unemployment rates among adolescents, particularly African American males, are extremely high, and the available jobs are in the service sector, such as fast-food restaurants, which usually pay minimum wage or slightly above. Perceiving a lack of opportunity for themselves in the adult world, many teens, especially males, join gangs. Some social analysts suggest that we should not be surprised that individuals between the ages of fifteen and twenty-four account for almost half of all property crime arrests in the United States. The problems of some young people may be intensified by today's media images of U.S. teenagers (see Box 5.1 on pages 90–91).

YOUNG ADULTHOOD

Typically beginning in the early to mid-twenties and lasting to about age thirty-nine, young adulthood is a period during which people acquire new roles and experience a sense of new freedom. However, many also experience problems finding their niche, particularly when it appears doubtful that they will have as high a standard of living as their parents had. Subsequent chapters examine a variety of issues affecting young adults, including alcohol and drug abuse, divorce, and employment instability. Many of these issues also concern people older than age forty.

MIDDLE AGE

Because life expectancy was lower in the past, the concept of middle age (age forty to sixty or sixty-five) did not exist until fairly recently. *Life expectancy*—the average length of time a group of individuals will live—increased dramatically during the twentieth century. Today, life expectancy at birth is approximately seventy-six years, compared to only forty-seven years in 1900. Moreover, it is predicted that life expectancy will increase to about seventy-eight years by 2010 and about eighty-two years by 2050. Sociologists use an age pyramid to show the distribution of a given population by age and sex groupings at various points in time. As Figure 5.1 (on page 92) shows, the United States is undergoing what some social analysts refer to as the *graying of America*, the aging of the population due to an increase in life expectancy combined with a decrease in the birth rate (Atchley, 2000). As people progress through middle age, they experience *senescence (primary aging),* which results from molecular and cellular changes in the body. Some signs of senescence are visible (e.g., wrinkles and gray hair); others are not (e.g., arthritis or stiffness in connective tissue joints; a gradual dulling of senses such as taste, touch, and vision; and slower reflexes). Vital systems also undergo gradual change; lung capacity diminishes, and the digestive, circulatory, and reproductive systems gradually decline in efficiency (Atchley, 2000). In addition to primary aging, people experience *secondary aging,* which has to do with environmental factors and lifestyle choices. A recent MacArthur Foundation study on aging identified several factors that contribute to "successful aging," including regular physical activity, continued social connections, resiliency—the ability to bounce back readily after suffering a loss—and self-efficacy, a feeling of control over one's life. According to one gerontologist, "Only about 30 percent of the characteristics of aging are genetically based; the rest—70 percent—is not" (Brody, 1996:B9).

Some people fight the aging process by spending billions of dollars on products such as Oil of Olay, Clairol or Grecian Formula, and Buster's Magic Tummy Tightener. Others have cosmetic surgery. In a recent study, one interviewee explained that she had decided to undergo liposuction (a surgical procedure in which fat is removed) because she had started to get a lot of "crepeyness" in her neck and her jowls were "coming down" owing to aging (Dull and West, 1991:57). As her remarks suggest, the United States is a youth-oriented society that tends to equate beauty, stamina, and good health with youth. Because of this, many of the changes associated with growing older are viewed as something to be avoided at all costs.

While women in middle age may believe that they have become less sexually attractive than they were, men tend to begin to realize that their physical strength and social power over others are limited. As if to reinforce their awareness of the passage of time, many women and men also may have to face the fact that their children have grown and left home. However, for some people, middle age is a time of great contentment; their income and prestige are at their peak, the problems of raising their children are behind them, they are content with their spouse of many years, and they may have grandchildren who give them a tie to the future. Even so,

all middle-aged people know that their status will change significantly as they grow older.

LATER MATURITY AND OLD AGE

Later maturity is usually considered to begin in the sixties. The major changes associated with this stage are social. Although many people in their sixties retain sufficient physical strength to be able to carry on an active social life, their peer groups shrink noticeably as friends and relatives die. Many people in later maturity find themselves caring for people of their own age and older people.

Old age is usually considered to begin in the late sixties or in the seventies. Although some people continue to work past age seventy, most have left paid employment by their seventieth birthday. Problems are not just social but also increasingly biological. Some physical changes, such as arteriosclerosis (the loss of elasticity in the walls of the arteries), are potentially life-threatening (Belsky, 1990). As bones become more porous, they become more brittle; a simple fall may result in broken bones that take longer to heal than those of a younger person. Strength, mobility, and height may decline; and the abilities to see, hear, taste, touch, and smell may diminish. Because taste and smell work together to allow us to enjoy food, eating may become less pleasurable and so contribute to poor nutrition in some older adults (Belsky, 1990). Although it is not true of all elderly people, the average person over age sixty-five does not react as rapidly (physically or mentally) as the average person who is younger than sixty-five (Lefrançois, 1999).

The chances of heart attacks, strokes, and cancer increase along with the likelihood of some diseases that primarily affect the elderly. Alzheimer's, a degenerative disease that attacks the brain and severely impairs memory, thinking, and behavior, may be the best-known example. People who have this disease have an impaired ability to function in everyday social roles; in time they cease to be able to recognize people they have always known, and they lose all sense of their own identity. Finally, they may revert to a speechless childishness, at which point others must feed them, dress them, sit them on the toilet, and lead them around by the hand. Alzheimer's strikes one in ten people over age sixty-five and nearly half of those over eighty-five. The disease can last eight to twenty years, ending only with death (Lefrançois, 1999).

SOCIAL PROBLEMS

BOX 5.1

Media Ageism and Reporting on Teenagers

Unplanned pregnancies, HIV infection and AIDS, and other sexually transmitted diseases. Cigarettes, alcohol and drug abuse. Eating disorders. Violence. Suicide. Car crashes.

—*According to FAIR (Fairness and Accuracy in Reporting), a media watchdog group, this lead-in to a* Washington Post *article is typical of how the media portrays teenagers (Males, 1994)*

[A]dolescents—that eager, suspicious, alienated, hyperbolic cohort. . . .

—*A description of contemporary teenagers in a* Time *(1999) cover story, "A Week in the Life of a High School"*

How are teenagers portrayed in the media? Although most research on media ageism focuses on portrayals of older people, activist groups such as FAIR and CYRA (Canadian Youth Rights Association) have also examined media coverage of adolescents.

According to CYRA's (1998) findings, the media perpetuates myths about teenagers in these ways:

▲ The news media seldom report stories about teenagers unless they are involved in a crime or some other "deviant" behavior. The age of the person often is used as a "hook" to catch readers or viewers.

▲ Few news stories describe positive teenager actions, such as volunteer work.

▲ While media reports refer to adults as "women" or "men" and identify them by their last names, teenagers are often referred to by their first names and described as "girls" or "boys."

▲ Entertainment shows and movies typically depict teens as being self-centered, insensitive to the feelings of others, materialistic, sexually promiscuous, involved in alcohol and drug abuse, and prone toward harmful pranks and physical aggression.

Can media stereotyping of teens be changed? According to groups such as FAIR, people must make their criticisms known to members of the media if they want to see

As older people have begun to live longer, gerontologists have come to realize that there are significant differences among the "young-old" (ages sixty-five to seventy-four), the "old-old" (ages seventy-five to eighty-four), and the "oldest-old" (ages eighty-five and older). Although more than half of all people age sixty-five and older are in the young-old category, the oldest-old category has grown more rapidly over the past three decades than has any other age group in the United States (Angier, 1995). As with other age categories, it is difficult to make generalizations about older people, which gerontologists Nancy R. Hooyman and H. Asuman Kiyak (1996:5) have noted:

Older people vary greatly in their health status, their social and work activities, and their family situations. Some are still employed full- or part-time; most are retired. Most are healthy; some are frail, confused, or home-bound. Most still live in a house or apartment; a small percentage are in nursing homes. Some receive large incomes from pensions and investments; many depend primarily on Social Security and have little discretionary income. Most men over age 65 are married, whereas women are more likely to become widowed and live alone as they age. . . . It is . . . impossible to define aging only in

changes. However, Mike Pride (1999), editor of the *Concord Monitor,* a New Hampshire newspaper, notes that it is difficult to gain access to young people. In the aftermath of the Littleton, Colorado, shootings, he tried to arrange interviews for reporters with local young people but found that their parents and school administrators did not want them to talk to journalists. Pride believes that adults are ignorant of the specific cultural influences that affect young people today and most often merely generalize about what all teenagers are doing or thinking.

What would constitute positive journalism about adolescents? Clearly, covering young people's positive endeavors, as well as problematic activities, would be a start. To bring about real change in media portrayals, however, responsible journalists could focus on how problems in the society at large affect young people. For example, journalists could "publicize the enormous racial imbalances inherent in 'youth violence,' the fundamental sexism of the current debate over 'teen' pregnancy, the realities of millions of raped, beaten and neglected children, the skyrocketing rates of youth poverty imposed by ever-richer American elites, and the futility of modern behavior modifica-

tion, laws and treatments aimed at forcing the young to 'adjust' to intolerable conditions" (Males, 1994:5). They also could look for ways to reduce or eliminate these problems.

Whether media coverage of teenagers will change is uncertain, but one thing is apparent: Many young people are "hooked" on media (Haddock, 1999). According to a recent study by the Kaiser Family Foundation, which was based on a representative sampling of 3,155 individuals ages two through eighteen, "children spend so much time watching television, playing video games and the like that media use could qualify as their full-time job" (Haddock, 1999:A32). The typical young person spends more than five hours each day using media, and most of this time is spent watching television. What kinds of images do young people see of themselves when they watch television? Based on media coverage of teenagers, how do adults view today's adolescents? If you would like to know more about how groups monitor media coverage, log on to the FAIR Web site at http://www.fair.org.

(*Note:* Web addresses often change. Those given here were accurate at the time of publication.)

chronological terms, since chronological age only partially reflects the biological, psychological, and sociological processes that define life stages.

As a spokesperson for the AARP (formerly the American Association of Retired Persons) has said, "Age is simply not a measure of competence in any way, shape or form and people need to be judged on their own individual characteristics" (quoted in Berke, 1996:E1). Or, in the words of Virginia McCalmont, age eighty-five, "I feel like I'm about 30 or 40—until I look in a mirror. So I try not to look in the mirror" (quoted in Kolata, 1996b:B10).

 Death and Dying

In previous generations, death was a common occurrence in all stages in the life course, but today most deaths occur among older people. Because of medical advances and the increase in life expectancy, death is now viewed as that stage of the life course that usually occurs in old age. According to social gerontologists, the increased association of *death* with the process of *aging* has caused many people to deny the aging process and engage in ageism as a means of denying the reality of death, particularly their own (Atchley, 2000). Euphemisms, such as "pass away"

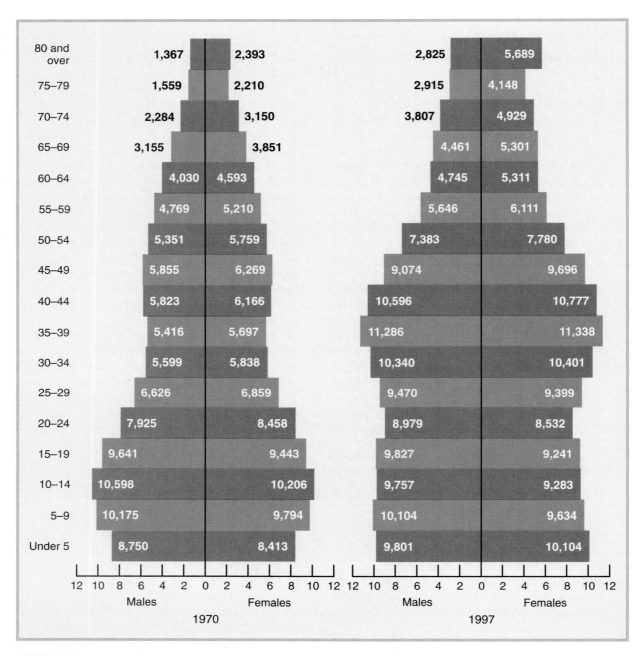

FIGURE 5.1   *U.S. Age Pyramid by Age and Sex, 1970 and 1997*
Source: U.S. Bureau of the Census, 1998.

or "sleep," are often used to refer to death by those who are trying to avoid its reality. Researchers have found, however, that many people do not actually fear death itself as much as they fear the possibility of pain and suffering, loss of control, and the conse- quences of their death for survivors (Marshall and Levy, 1990). Given a chance to choose, most people would choose a painless death over prolonged physi- cal and mental deterioration and the prospect of being a burden on their families. Some researchers

Gerontologists stress that it is hard to generalize about older individuals. The stereotypes don't fit. This couple, for example, in their eighties, apparently enjoy good health—and each other.

have also found that older people have less fear of death than younger people do; others have found that education and religious beliefs are important factors in how people view death and dying (Kalish, 1985). However, little research has focused on attitudes toward death among African Americans, Latinas/os, and other people of color, so it is important to be wary of overgeneralizations about the fear of death (see Kalish and Reynolds, 1981).

There are three widely known frameworks for explaining how people cope with the process of dying: the *stage-based approach*, the *dying trajectory*, and the *task-based approach*. The *stage-based approach* was popularized by Elisabeth Kübler-Ross (1969), who proposed five stages in the dying process: (1) denial ("Not me"), (2) anger ("Why me?"), (3) bargaining and asking for divine intervention to postpone death ("Yes me, but . . ."), (4) depression and sense of loss, and (5) acceptance. According to some social scientists, Kübler-Ross's study is limited because she focused primarily on the attitudes of younger people who had terminal illnesses. These scientists argue that the same stages may not apply

to older people who believe that they have already lived a full life (Marshall, 1980; Kalish, 1985).

In contrast to Kübler-Ross's five stages, the concept of the *dying trajectory* focuses on the perceived course of dying and the expected time of death. From this perspective, not all people move toward death at the same speed and in the same way. A dying trajectory may be sudden (e.g., a heart attack) or slow (e.g., lung cancer) and is usually shaped by the condition causing death. A dying trajectory involves three phases: the acute phase, in which maximum anxiety or fear is expressed; the chronic phase, in which anxiety declines as the person confronts reality; and the terminal phase, in which the dying person withdraws from others (Glaser and Strauss, 1968).

The *task-based approach* suggests that daily activities can still be enjoyed during the dying process and that fulfilling certain tasks makes the process of death easier on everyone involved, not just the dying person. *Physical tasks* are performed to satisfy bodily needs and to minimize physical distress. *Psychological tasks* help to maximize psychological security, autonomy, and richness of experience. *Social tasks* sustain and enhance interpersonal attachments and address the social implications of dying. *Spiritual tasks* are performed to identify, develop, or reaffirm sources of spiritual energy and to foster hope (Corr et al., 1994). Most important in any approach are the rights of the dying person and how care is provided to them.

Technological advances in medicine have helped to focus attention on the physical process of dying and, in recent years, the needs of dying patients and their families. Many people are choosing to sign a *living will*—a document stating their wishes about the medical circumstances under which their life should be allowed to end. Some people reject the idea of being kept alive by elaborate life-support systems and other forms of high-tech medicine, choosing to die at home rather than in a hospital or nursing home. The hospice movement has provided additional options for caring for the terminally ill. **Hospices are organizations that provide a homelike facility or home-based care (or both) for persons who are terminally ill.** Some hospices have facilities where care is provided, but hospice is primarily a philosophy that affirms life, not death, and offers holistic and continuing care to the patient and family through a team of visiting nurses, on-call physicians, and counselors. Home care enables many people to remain in familiar surroundings and maintain dignity and control

SOCIAL PROBLEMS

IN GLOBAL PERSPECTIVE

BOX 5.2

Quantity versus Quality of Life: Suicide and the Graying of the Globe

Ironically, as the number of people age sixty-five and older continues to grow throughout the world, suicide rates among older people seem to be increasing significantly. About 360 million people worldwide are age sixty-five and older, and this population is growing by about *800,000 people a month*. At the same time, in many nations the highest suicide rates are found among older people, particularly men (Kristof, 1996a).

Worldwide, suicide rates tend to (1) increase with age, (2) increase slightly in young adulthood and dramatically in old age, or (3) peak in middle age (ages forty-five to fifty-four or fifty-five to sixty-five). The first pattern is found in nations such as Austria, Italy, Japan, and West Germany, where suicide rates for both women and men increase regularly with age. The second pattern is characteristic of *male* suicides in countries such as Australia, Canada, England, and the United States. The third pattern is characteristic of *female* suicides in the United States, Canada, and France (Lester, 1992).

Although suicide rates among older people are significantly higher than those among other age groups in most countries, older men are up to *twelve times* more likely to commit suicide than older women are. Figure 5.2 shows dramatic differences between suicide rates for men age seventy-five and older per 100,000 people in European countries compared to rates for men of all ages in the same countries. Some analysts suggest that higher rates of suicide among males can be explained by the disparity between images of masculinity, such as independence and productivity, and the realities of growing old, such as dependence on others, loss of occupational and social status, and perhaps chronic illness or disability. Social isolation also may contribute to higher rates of suicide among unmarried older men (Lester, 1992). In the United States, for example, the highest suicide rates are found among older white men who do not have a spouse, children, or other support systems. In recent years, the suicide rate also has increased among African American older people who lack the support systems traditionally provided by families and who lack role models for successfully adapting to the aging process (Alston et al., 1995).

How is quantity of life related to quality of life? Do you think advances in medical technology may have unintended consequences such as high rates of suicide among older people in industrialized nations worldwide? Why or why not?

Additional sources: Albert and Cattell, 1994; Andrews and Fonseca, 1995.

over the dying process (Corr et al., 1994). Sophia Mumford summarizes the feeling of many older people about death:

> I'm afraid of one thing. I want my death to be dignified. My fear is that something will cause me to live past the point where my life has value. I don't want to live on. . . . From now on, if life says it's leaving, I'm not doing anything about it.

If I get a bad pain and it's diagnosed as cancer, then I won't wait, I'll go. I'm ready, because I feel I've had a good life. (Terkel, 1996:429)

Given Mumford's feelings, which mirror the feelings of many others, and a variety of other factors, it is not altogether surprising that older people around the world have a relatively high rate of suicide (see Box 5.2).

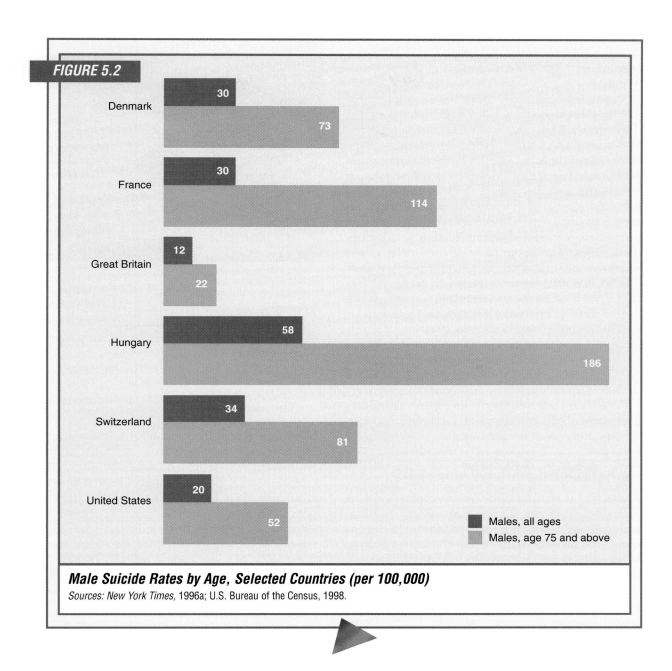

FIGURE 5.2

Denmark — 30 / 73
France — 30 / 114
Great Britain — 12 / 22
Hungary — 58 / 186
Switzerland — 34 / 81
United States — 20 / 52

■ Males, all ages
■ Males, age 75 and above

Male Suicide Rates by Age, Selected Countries (per 100,000)
Sources: New York Times, 1996a; U.S. Bureau of the Census, 1998.

PROBLEMS ASSOCIATED WITH AGING

Age stratification—the inequalities, differences, segregation, or conflict between age groups—occurs throughout the life course (Atchley, 2000). It is a determinant of how education, jobs, and other scarce resources and opportunities are allocated in society. But age stratification also limits roles and opportunities. Many people automatically assume that at age fourteen, a person should be in school; that at age thirty, a person should be married; and that at age sixty-five, a person should retire from full-time employment. Such perceptions about age may create problems for people in all age categories, but the problems typically are most pronounced among older people.

Workplace Discrimination

Despite the Age Discrimination in Employment Act that was passed in 1967 to protect workers age forty-five and above from unfair employment practices based on age, many subtle forms of age discrimination in the workplace remain. Some employers prefer younger workers to older workers, whom they believe have health problems, poor motivation, and low ability. Employers may hire younger workers because they believe that they can pay them less than older workers and make more demands on their time and energy. Older employees may find that their employers have downgraded their job descriptions, failed to promote them or grant them raises, and sometimes are trying to push them out of their jobs so that cheaper workers can be hired. Despite the negative stereotypes, some employers have found it profitable to hire older employees. Days Inns of America, a major hotel chain, in 1986 began a program of hiring older people to work in its national reservation centers. The company found that older people quickly learned to use computers, stayed on the job three times as long, and booked more reservations than their younger counterparts did (Foreman, 1993). Still, at some point, retirement becomes an expected part of the life course.

Retirement and Changing Roles

Retirement is the institutionalized separation of an individual from her or his occupational position, with continuation of income from a retirement pension based on prior years of service (Atchley, 2000). In the past, people in many occupations and professions (including tenured faculty members at universities, police officers, and fire fighters) faced mandatory retirement at age sixty-five regardless of their health or desire to continue working. It was simply assumed that everyone experienced a decline in physical and mental ability at a specific age. Changes in compulsory retirement laws have led many people to view retirement less as a sign of decline than as a newfound period of leisure and opportunity for adaptation and reflection. For some, however, adapting to less income, increased dependency, and the loss of roles and activities can be very difficult (Atchley, 2000).

Typically retirement for African Americans and Latinos/as is different from retirement for white

Retirement is a time for leisure and reflection if it comes by choice and the individual is healthy and financially prepared. But for others, adapting to less income, increased dependency, and the loss of roles can be difficult.

Americans. Racial discrimination in the workplace diminishes the earning power of many minority group members, so older Latinos/as and African Americans who have held lower-paying positions throughout their lifetime often have no employer-sponsored or self-purchased pension plans, only Social Security. When these individuals in the bottom tier of the dual labor market do have pension plans, their pension checks, which are based on income during the working years, are small, leading some to believe that they have no choice but to work into their seventies (Uchitelle, 1995).

Women who are over sixty-five today are less likely to have access to pension and Social Security income in their own name than younger women who are currently employed will. However, many employed women—as well as many men—are losing out on traditional pension coverage because of changes in the economy and the workplace. Many unionized industrial jobs that provided pension coverage have virtually disappeared, and more women than men are employed as part-time workers, who are less likely to have pension coverage than full-time workers. In fact, companies rarely offer pension plans or health insurance to part-time, contingent, and temporary workers.

Health, Illness, and Health Care

At age ninety-three, Malcolm Clarke plays doubles tennis four times a week and sails his boat; he also shops and cooks for himself (Brody, 1996). Although Clarke attributes his longevity and good health to "luck," studies show that many older people are not developing the disabling diseases that were common in the past, and the vast majority function quite well. Improvement in the health status of older people has been attributed, at least in part, to better education (knowing what to do and not do to stay healthy), nutrition, and health insurance through Medicare and sometimes Medicaid (see Box 5.3). Because most people over age sixty-five are covered by Medicare, health care coverage is a greater problem for the young and middle-aged. Lack of health insurance affects substantial portions of all age groups below age sixty-five.

Malnutrition and disease are life-threatening problems for some older people. Although malnutrition is sometimes related to poverty, nutritionists suggest that the condition is pervasive even among older people who are not poor, perhaps in part because diminishing senses make food less appealing. Malnutrition is a problem for 25 percent of people over age sixty-five, and recent studies have found that 16 percent of all older people consume less than 1,000 calories per day (*New York Times*, 1995).

About seven of every ten deaths among older people are due to heart disease, cancer, or stroke. By far, the leading killer of persons over age sixty-five is heart disease. Among white women, cancer has overtaken heart disease as the leading cause of death; breast cancer and lung cancer are responsible for nearly half of all cancer deaths in women. African American women are more likely than white women to die from strokes or diabetes. Men, particularly African Americans, are highly vulnerable to cancer of the prostate, a reproductive gland. Many people over age eighty-five die of multiple organ failure or pneumonia, which has been referred to as the "old folk's friend" (Angier, 1995). Recently, the number of AIDS cases has risen at a faster rate among older people than among other age groups, and AIDS educators are seeking to make older people aware of the risk of becoming infected with HIV, the virus that causes AIDS (*New York Times*, 1994b).

People age sixty-five and older account for about one-third of all dollars spent on health care, and this figure is expected to rise dramatically with the aging of the U.S. population. Many believe the cost problems associated with health care will be further intensified by the *feminization of aging*, the increasing proportion of older women, because these women, on average, have a greater likelihood of being poor and having no spouse to care for them (Weitz, 1996). Chapter 10 discusses health care issues in greater detail.

Victimization

Although older people are in fact less likely than younger people to be victims of violent crime, they fear this type of crime more than people in other age categories do. However, older people are often the targets of other types of crime. Con artists frequently contact them by mail or telephone to perpetrate scams that often promise prizes or involve a "stock-broker" selling a "hot" stock or other commodity (Hays, 1995a). In one scam, an older person would receive a message to call a number beginning with the area code 809 for important information about a family member who had become ill or died or about a prize he or she had won. Callers were charged $25 per minute for the call and often were kept on the line for an extended period of time. Some people received phone bills for more than $100.00 per call, not knowing that the 809 area code covers the British Virgin Islands (the Bahamas) and is a pay-per-call number that is not covered by U.S. regulations regarding 900 numbers (City of Austin, 1996).

Another form of victimization is elder abuse. According to the National Center on Elderly Abuse, the abuse may be physical, emotional, sexual, and/or financial as well as the result of neglect (*Austin American-Statesman*, 1995). The center has estimated that more than 1 million older people were victims of elder abuse in 1996 (Tatara and Kuzmeskus, 1996). Many analysts believe that elder abuse is underreported because people who know of the abuse are unwilling to report it and older people who are the victims are either too ashamed or afraid to notify authorities. As a government official noted, "Seniors are . . . embarrassed to admit that a relative, a loved one, a child is abusing them, either physically or financially, or neglecting or exploiting them"

SOCIAL PROBLEMS

AND SOCIAL POLICY

BOX 5.3

Government-Funded Health Care for Older People: Medicare

Are people entitled to health care regardless of their ability to pay? For years this has been a disputed question in the United States. The issue of health care for older people was partially addressed in 1965 when Congress enacted the Medicare program, a federal program for people age sixty-five and over who are covered by Social Security or railroad retirement insurance or who have been permanently and totally disabled for two years or more. Funded primarily through Social Security taxes paid by current workers, Medicare is an *entitlement program*. Those who receive benefits must have paid something to be covered. Medicare Part A provides coverage for some inpatient hospital expenses (for up to about ninety days) and limited coverage for skilled nursing care at home; Part B, which covers some outpatient expenses, may be purchased for an additional premium that amounts to about $50 per month.

Clearly, Medicare has created greater access to health care services for many older people, but it has serious limitations. Medicare primarily provides for acute, short-term care and is limited to partial payment for ninety days of hospital care and for a restricted amount of skilled nursing care and home health services. It also has a deductible and copayments (fees paid by people each time they see a health care provider), and it pays only 80 percent of *allowable* charges, not the *actual amount* charged by health care providers. Furthermore, Medicare does not include prescription drugs, dental care, hearing aids, eyeglasses, mental health services, long-term care such as nursing homes, or custodial or nonmedical service such as adult day care or homemaker services (Atchley, 2000). Because of these serious gaps in coverage, older people who can afford it often purchase *medigap policies*, supplementary private insurance (Weitz, 1996).

Some low-income older people are eligible for Medicaid, a joint federal-state *means-tested welfare program* that provides health care insurance for poor people of any age who meet specific eligibility requirements. People over age sixty-five constitute about 13 percent of Medicaid recipients but account for more than 40 percent of the program's total expenditures (Hooyman and Kiyak, 1996). However, Medicaid recipients have been stigmatized because Medicaid is a "welfare program." Furthermore, because the administrative paperwork is burdensome and reimbursements are so low—typically less than one-half of what private insurance companies pay for the same services—many physicians refuse to take Medicaid patients.

In sum, Medicare and Medicaid provide broad coverage for older people, but both programs have major flaws: (1) they are extremely expensive, (2) they are highly vulnerable to costly fraud by health care providers and some recipients, and (3) they typically provide higher-quality health care to older people who are white and more affluent than to African Americans, Latinos/as, people with disabilities, and individuals living in rural areas (Pear, 1994). Chapter 10 discusses U.S. health care in greater detail.

What impact do you think the aging of the U.S. population will have on government-funded programs such as Medicare and Medicaid? What solutions can you suggest for providing more adequate health care for older people at less cost?

Additional sources: Harvard Medicare Project, 1986; Women's Research and Education Institute, 1994.

(*Austin American-Statesman,* 1995:A6). Although some analysts initially believed that younger people were likely to exploit older people who were psychologically and economically dependent on them, just the opposite has often proven true: Younger people are more likely to exploit elders on whom they themselves are dependent (Atchley, 2000).

Family Problems and Social Isolation

Older people can easily become socially isolated from their families. Younger members who once asked for advice stop asking, perhaps because they think that their older relatives are out of touch or perhaps because of some miscommunication. Sometimes, younger family members feel unduly burdened by the concerns of their elders, which don't seem truly important to them. For one reason or another, older people come to believe (rightly or wrongly) that they are isolated from the rest of the family.

In 1997, 30 percent of people age sixty-five and above lived alone (U.S. Bureau of the Census, 1998). Many older people live alone voluntarily, but others live by themselves because they are divorced, widowed, or single. Living alone is not the equivalent of social isolation. Many older people have networks of friends with whom they engage in activities. To a large degree, the extent to which they associate with others has to do with social class: People with more money are able to pursue a wider array of activities and take more trips than are those with more limited resources.

Perhaps one of the saddest developments in contemporary society is the growing number of older people who are homeless. While some older homeless people have lived on the streets for many years, others have become homeless because they have been displaced from low-income housing such as single-room occupancy (SRO) hotels. In recent years, many SROs in cities such as New York and San Francisco have been replaced by high-rise office buildings, retail space, and luxury condominiums. Older people who are homeless typically lack nutritious food, appropriate clothing, adequate medical care, and a social support network. They tend to die prematurely of disease, crime victimization, accidents, and weather-related crises such as a winter blizzard, when an individual without shelter can freeze to death on a park bench. Fortunately, the picture is not this bleak for many older people who remain in residences they have occupied for many years.

Housing Patterns and Long-Term Care Facilities

Many people mistakenly assume that most older people live in long-term care facilities such as nursing homes. In fact, however, only about 5 percent of older people live in any kind of institution. More than people of any other age category, older people are likely to reside in the housing in which they have lived for a number of years and own free and clear of debt. White Americans are significantly more likely than African Americans and Latinas/os to own their homes and married couples are more likely to own their homes than are single people. Because of the high cost of utilities, insurance, taxes, and repairs and maintenance, older women, who are more likely to live alone than are older men, are at

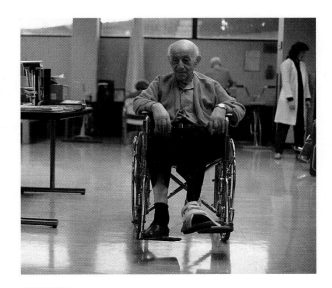

Although only about 5 percent of older people live in nursing homes or other long-term care facilities in the United States, living in an institutional setting remains the only option for some older individuals. What alternative living arrangements can you suggest for older people in the future?

a distinct disadvantage if they attempt to maintain their own homes (Hooyman and Kiyak, 1996).

Some low-income older people live in planned housing projects that are funded by federal and local government agencies or private organizations such as religious groups. Older people with middle and upper incomes are more likely to live in retirement communities (for example, Sun City) or in *congregate housing,* which provides amenities such as housekeeping, dining facilities, and transportation services (Hooyman and Kiyak, 1996). In recent years, religious organizations and for-profit corporations have developed *multilevel* facilities, which provide services ranging from independent living to skilled nursing care all at the same site. Such facilities often are quite expensive. Residents may have to purchase their housing units or pay a substantial initial entry fee and/or sign life care contracts, which provide for nursing home care if it becomes necessary.

Today, only 1.2 percent of people age sixty-five to seventy-four live in nursing homes; however, the percentage increases to almost 24 percent among people age eighty-five and over. Because of their greater life expectancy, higher rates of chronic illness, and higher rates of being unmarried, women are disproportionately represented among the 1.7 million people who reside in nursing homes (U.S. Bureau of the Census, 1998). According to social gerontologists, the primary factors related to living in a nursing home are age (eighty-five and over), being female, having been in the hospital recently, living in retirement housing, having no spouse at home, and having some cognitive or physical impairment that interferes with the activities of daily living (Greene and Ondrich, 1990).

White Americans constitute more than 90 percent of all nursing home residents; 7 percent are African American; 2.5 percent are Latino/a; and fewer than 0.5 percent are Native American or Asian or Pacific American. Ethnic minorities may be underrepresented because their families are less willing to institutionalize them or because more caregivers exist to help meet the needs of older relatives. Racial discrimination and a lack of consideration of residents' ethnic backgrounds also may contribute to the perception among many minority group members that nursing homes are no place for their older family members. Sociologists have found that many nursing home assistants, who often are recent immigrants to the United States, do not speak the same

language as the residents (Diamond, 1992). While some nursing home facilities may be excellent, others have undergone extensive media scrutiny and public criticism for violations of regulations and harmful practices such as elder abuse. As a result, many people select home care, adult day care, or assisted living for older relatives rather than institutional settings, which tend to depersonalize individuals and "reify the image of age as inevitable decline and deterioration" (Friedan, 1993:516).

PERSPECTIVES ON AGING AND SOCIAL INEQUALITY

Although each of the major sociological perspectives focuses on different aspects of aging and social inequality, they all provide insights into how people view the aging process and how ageism contributes to social inequality in society.

 ### The Functionalist Perspective

According to functionalists, dramatic changes in such social institutions as the family and religion have influenced how people look at the process of growing old. Given this, both the stability of society and the normal and healthy adjustment of older people require that they detach themselves from their social roles and prepare for their eventual death (Cumming and Henry, 1961). Referred to as *disengagement theory,* this theory suggests that older people want to be released from societal expectations of productivity and competitiveness. At the same time, disengagement facilitates a gradual and orderly transfer of statuses and roles from one generation to the next instead of an abrupt change, which might result in chaos. Retirement policies, then, are a means of ensuring that younger people with more up-to-date training (for example, computer skills) move into occupational roles while ensuring that older workers are recognized for years of service (Williamson et al., 1992).

Critics of this perspective object to the assumption that disengagement is functional for society and that all older people want to disengage even though they are still productive and gain satisfaction from their work. In fact, according to some social analysts, disengagement as evidenced by early retirement policies has been dysfunctional for society. Social Security and other pension systems have been strained by the proportionately fewer workers who are paying into the plan to support an increasing number of retired workers. Contrary to disengagement theory, these analysts say, older people may disengage not by choice but because of a lack of opportunity for continued activity.

◢ The Interactionist Perspective

Interactionist perspectives on aging and inequality focus on the relationship between life satisfaction and levels of activity. *The interactionist activity theory* is based on the assumption that older people who are active are happier and better adjusted than are less active older persons. According to this the-

Does this photo of participants in the U.S. Senior Sports Classic better represent disengagement theory (a functionalist perspective) or activity theory (an interactionist perspective)?

ory, older people shift gears in late middle age and find meaningful substitutes for previous statuses, roles, and activities (Havighurst et al., 1968). Those who remain active have a higher level of life satisfaction than do those who are inactive or in ill health (Havighurst et al., 1968). In contrast to disengagement theory, activity theory suggests that older people must deny the existence of old age by maintaining middle-age lifestyles for as long as possible. However, an eight-year study found that death rates among older Mexican Americans and whites were not significantly reduced by engaging in such activities as hunting or fishing or by attending movies and sporting events (Lee and Markides, 1990).

Other interactionist perspectives focus on role and exchange theories. Role theory poses the question "What roles are available for older people?" Some theorists note that industrialized, urbanized societies typically do not have roles for older people (Cowgill, 1986). Other theorists note that many older people find active roles within their own ethnic group. Although their experiences may not be valued in the larger society, they are esteemed within their ethnic subculture because they are a rich source of ethnic lore and history. According to sociologist Donald E. Gelfand (1994), older people can exchange their knowledge for deference and respect from younger people.

◢ The Conflict Perspective

Conflict theorists focus on the political economy of aging in analyzing the problems of older people in contemporary capitalistic societies. From this perspective, class constitutes a structural barrier to older people's access to valued resources, and dominant groups attempt to maintain their own interests by perpetuating class inequalities. According to conflict theorists, aging itself is not the social problem. The problem is rooted in societal conditions that older people often face without adequate resources such as income and housing. People who were poor and disadvantaged in their younger years become even more so in old age. Women age seventy-five and over are among the most disadvantaged because, having often outlived their spouses and sometimes their children, they must rely solely on Social Security (Harrington Meyer, 1990).

In the capitalist system, many older people are set apart as a group that depends on special policies and programs. However, to minimize demands for governmental assistance, some services are made punitive and stigmatizing to those who need them (Atchley, 2000). Class-based theories suggest that social and economic policies such as Social Security, Medicare, and Medicaid are a means of social control designed to meet the dominant needs of the economy (Hooyman and Kiyak, 1996). Feminist explanations of age-based inequality suggest that social control policies perpetuate inequality based on gender, class, race, and ethnicity (Harrington Meyer, 1990).

Class-based theorists note that although Social Security and Medicare do benefit some older people, they primarily benefit upper- and middle-income groups and thus perpetuate class inequalities. Conflict analysts draw attention to how class, gender, and race divide older people just as they do everyone else. The conflict perspective adds to our understanding of aging by focusing on how capitalism devalues older people, especially women. Critics assert, however, that this approach ignores the fact that industrialization and capitalism have been positive forces in society, greatly enhancing the longevity and quality of life for many older people.

CAN AGE-BASED INEQUALITY BE REDUCED?

As we have seen, technological innovations and advances in medicine have contributed to the steady increase in life expectancy in the United States. Advances in the diagnosis, prevention, and treatment of diseases associated with old age, such as Alzheimer's, may revolutionize people's feelings about growing older (Atchley, 2000). Technology may bring about greater equality and freedom for older people. Home-based computer services such as banking and shopping make it possible for older people to conduct their daily lives without having to leave home to obtain services. Computerized controls on appliances, lighting, and air conditioning make it possible for people with limited mobility to control their environment. Technology also brings recreation and education into the home. For example, Senior Net is a nationwide computer network that encourages discussion of diverse topics and pro-

vides hands-on classes in computer use. Robotics and computer systems may eventually be used by frail older people who otherwise would have to rely on family or paid caregivers to meet their needs or move to a nursing home. However, class is again a factor: More than 75 percent of home accessibility features currently are paid for by users or their families (Hooyman and Kiyak, 1996).

Economic concerns loom large in the future as baby boomers, those who were born between 1946 and 1964, begin to retire in about 2010, bringing about a dramatic shift in the *dependency ratio*—the **number of workers necessary to support people under age fifteen and over age sixty-three.** Instead of *five* workers supporting one retiree by paying Social Security taxes, *three* workers will be providing support for each retiree. Some social analysts suggest that increased age-based inequality may bring about a "war" between the generations (Toner, 1995). However, advocates of *productive aging* suggest that instead of pitting young and old against each other, we should change our national policies and attitudes. We should encourage older people to continue or create their own roles in society, not to disengage from it. Real value should be placed on unpaid volunteer and caregiving activism, and settings should be provided in which older people can use their talents more productively (Hooyman and Kiyak, 1996).

In order to distribute time for family responsibilities and leisure more evenly throughout the life course, changes must occur in the workplace. Today, younger workers struggle to care for their families, without the support of employers in many cases, and leisure is associated with old age and "being put out to pasture." But people who have had no opportunity to engage in leisure activities earlier in their life are unlikely to suddenly become leisure-oriented. Employment, family responsibilities, and leisure must become less compartmentalized, and changes in technology and employment may make this possible. At present, however, it is difficult for most people to have *free time* and *money* at the same time.

Functionalists suggest that changes must occur in families and other social institutions if we are to resolve problems brought about by high rates of divorce, single-parent households, and cohabitation by unmarried couples, which tend to reduce the individual's commitment to meet the needs of other family members. These analysts argue that individuals must be socialized to care for an increasing number of living generations in their family and must be given economic incentives such as tax breaks for fulfilling their responsibility to children and older relatives. Because adult children may have to provide economic and emotional support for aging parents and grandparents at the same time as they are caring for their own children, more community services are needed, particularly for adult children who are "suitcase caregivers" for frail, elderly relatives living many miles away (Foreman, 1996). Communities should create or expand existing facilities such as day-care centers for children and seniors; provide affordable housing; and build low-cost, community-based health facilities.

Other social analysts suggest that people need to rely more on themselves for their retirement and old age. Younger workers should be encouraged to save money for retirement and not to assume that Social Security, Medicare, and other entitlement programs will be available when they reach old age. As conflict theorists have pointed out, however, many young people do not have jobs or adequate income to meet their current economic needs, much less their future needs. A 1995 Gallup poll found that people with children under age eighteen indicated that they were saving primarily for their children's education and did not have adequate resources to put aside money for retirement (Golay and Rollyson, 1996).

From the conflict perspective, age-based inequality is rooted in power differentials, and short of dramatic changes in the structure of political and economic power in society, the only way for older people to hold onto previous gains is through continued activism. However, this approach does not take into account the fact that some older people have benefited more than others from social programs such as Medicare, Social Security, and the Older Americans Act (the federal law that authorizes and funds direct services such as senior centers, nutrition programs, and referral services). Groups such as the Gray Panthers and the AARP (formerly the American Association of Retired Persons) work for passage of specific legislation that has benefited many older people. Nevertheless, older people as a category are devalued in a society that prizes youth over old age and in a social structure that defines productivity primarily in terms of paid employment.

According to interactionists, however, individuals who maintain strong relationships with others and remain actively involved throughout their lifetime have reason to be optimistic about life when they reach old age. An example is Victor Reuther, age 81, a founder—with his brother Walter—of the United Auto Workers:

> I still have hope. When you lose hope, you bury yourself. I'm not ready for that. I have too much work to do yet. I never did find it comfortable to sit in a rocking chair complaining about my aches and pains. I think society has a lot of aches and pains. We shouldn't become obsessed with them. We've got to be pragmatic and say: There's a challenge. Let's change. Let's turn things over. (Terkel, 1996:96)

SUMMARY

➤ *What is ageism and why is it considered a social problem?*
Ageism is prejudice and discrimination against people on the basis of age. Ageism is a social problem because it perpetuates negative stereotypes and age-based discrimination, particularly against older people.

➤ *What is the life course and why are different stages problematic for some people?*
The life course is generally divided into infancy and childhood, adolescence and young adulthood, middle age, later maturity, and old age. During infancy and childhood, we are dependent on other people and so relatively powerless in society.

Adolescence is a stage in which we are not treated as children but also are not afforded the full status of adulthood. In young adulthood, we acquire new roles and have a feeling of new freedom but also may have problems ranging from alcohol and drug abuse to employment instability that may make life complicated. During middle age, we begin to show such visible signs of aging as wrinkles and gray hair, and roles begin to change in the workplace and family as children leave home. In later maturity, we increasingly find ourselves involved in caring for people of our own age and older people. Problems of older adults vary widely because of the diverse needs of the "young-old" (ages sixty-five to seventy-four), the "old-old" (ages seventy-five to eighty-four), and the "oldest-old" (ages eighty-five and older).

➡ *What types of problems do older people face today?*

Despite laws to the contrary, older workers may experience overt or covert discrimination in the workplace. Retirement brings about changing roles and a loss of status for those older people whose identity has been based primarily on their occupation. For some older people, malnutrition, disease, and lack of health care are life-threatening problems. Older people may become the victims of scams by con artists and elder abuse by family members or nursing home personnel. For most older people, moving into a nursing home represents a loss of autonomy.

➡ *How do people cope with the process of dying?*

Three explanations have been given for how people cope with dying. Kübler-Ross identified five stages that people go through: (1) denial, (2) anger, (3) bargaining, (4) depression, and (5) acceptance. However, the dying trajectory suggests that individuals do not move toward death at the same speed and in the same way. The task-based approach suggests that daily activities can still be enjoyed during the dying process and that fulfilling certain tasks makes the process of death easier on everyone involved (not just the dying person).

➡ *How do functionalist and interactionist explanations of age-based inequality differ?*

According to functionalists, disengagement of older people from their jobs and other social positions may be functional for society because it allows the smooth transfer of roles from one generation to the next. However, interactionists suggest that activity is important for older people because it provides new sources of identity and satisfaction later in life.

➡ *How do conflict theorists explain inequality based on age?*

According to conflict theorists, aging itself is not a social problem. The problem is rooted in societal conditions that older people often face when they have inadequate resources in a capitalist society. In the capitalist system, older people are set apart as a group that depends on special policies and programs.

KEY TERMS

ageism, p. 86
dependency ratio, p. 102

hospices, p. 93

social gerontology, p. 86

QUESTIONS FOR CRITICAL THINKING

1. If you were responsible for reducing ageism, what measures would you suggest to bring about greater equality? What resources would be required to fulfill your plan?

2. Should retirement be compulsory for neurosurgeons (brain surgeons), airline pilots, police officers, and fire fighters? Explain your answer.

3. Does disengagement theory or activity theory more closely reflect how you plan to spend your later years? What other approaches to aging can you suggest?

4. Will future technological advances change how people view growing old? Explain your answer.

Chapter Six

Inequality Based on Sexual Orientation

My son Matthew paid a terrible price to open the eyes of all of us . . . to the unjust and unnecessary fears, discrimination, and intolerance that members of the gay community face every day. . . . I loved my son and . . . was proud of him. He was not my gay son. He was my son who happened to be gay. He was a good-looking, intelligent, caring person. . . . I miss Matt terribly. I think about him all the time—at odd moments when some little thing reminds me of him; when I walk by the refrigerator and see the pictures of him and his brother that we've always kept on the door; at special times of the year, like the first day of classes at [the University of Wyoming] or opening day of sage chicken hunting. I keep wondering almost the same thing that I did when I first saw him in the hospital. What would he have become? How would he have changed his piece of the world to make it better? . . . Matt's beating, hospitalization, and funeral focused worldwide attention on hate. Good is coming out of evil. People have said, "Enough is enough" [and] my son has become a symbol—a symbol against hate . . . a symbol for encouraging respect for individuality; for appreciating that someone is different; for tolerance. I miss my son, but I'm proud to be able to say that he is my son.

—*Dennis Shepard, the*
father of Matthew Shepard,
a college student brutally
murdered because of his
sexual orientation
(matthewsplace.com, 1999)

The Shepard case is an example of a violent hate crime brought about by the prejudice and discrimination that some people experience because of their *sexual orientation*—**a preference for emotional-sexual relationships with individuals of the same sex (homosexuality), the opposite sex (heterosexuality), or both (bisexuality)** (Lips, 1993). The terms *homosexual* and *gay* are most often used in association with males who prefer same-sex relationships; the term *lesbian* is used in association with females who prefer same-sex relationships. Heterosexual individuals, who prefer opposite-sex relationships, are sometimes referred to as *straight* (e.g., "What's it like to be straight?"). It is important to note, however, that heterosexual people are much less likely to be labeled by their sexual orientation than are people who are gay, lesbian, or bisexual.

What criteria do social scientists use to classify individuals as gay, lesbian, or bisexual? In a definitive study of sexuality published in the mid-1990s, researchers at the University of Chicago established three criteria for identifying people as homosexual or bisexual: (1) *sexual attraction* to persons of one's own gender, (2) *sexual involvement* with one or more persons of one's own gender, and (3) *self-identification* as a gay man, lesbian, or bisexual (Michael et al., 1994). According to these criteria, then, engaging in a homosexual act does not necessarily classify a person as homosexual. In fact, many respondents in the Chicago study indicated that although they had at least one homosexual encounter when they were younger, they no longer were involved in homosexual conduct and never identified themselves as lesbians, bisexuals, or gay.

NATURE AND EXTENT OF INEQUALITY BASED ON SEXUAL ORIENTATION

How many homosexuals and bisexuals are there in the United States? Although the Bureau of the Census keeps track of numbers in sex, age, and racial-ethnic categories, it does not specifically count people on the basis of their sexual orientation. Estimates of the homosexual population range from 2 percent to 7 percent of all U.S. men and from 3 percent to 5 percent of all U.S. women. However, lesbian and gay advocates say that these estimates are too low—that more than 10 percent of the population primarily engages in same-sex relationships and an even higher percentage is bisexual (Weinberg et al., 1994).

Although homosexuality has existed in most societies throughout human history, for most of the last two thousand years, there have been groups—sometimes entire societies—that considered homosexuality "a crime against nature," "an abomination," or "a sin" (Doyle, 1995:224). Most societies have norms pertaining to *sexuality*—**attitudes, beliefs, and practices related to sexual attraction and intimate relationships with others.** The norms are based on the assumption that some forms of attraction and sexual relationships are *normal* and *appropriate* while others are *abnormal* and *inappropriate*. In many societies, homosexual conduct has been classified as a form of *deviance*—**a behavior, belief, or condition that violates social norms.** This classification may make people targets of prejudice, discrimination, and even death. Extreme prejudice toward gay men and lesbians is known as *homophobia*—**excessive fear or intolerance of homosexuality.** According to sociologists, homophobia is a *socially determined prejudice,* not a medically recognized *phobia* (Lehne, 1995). Homophobia is intensified by the ideology of *compulsory heterosexism,* a belief system that denies, denigrates, and stigmatizes any gay, lesbian, or bisexual behavior, identity, relationship, or community. Somewhat like institutional racism and sexism, compulsory heterosexism is embedded in a society's social structure and maintained by ideologies that are rooted in religion and law (Herek, 1995).

IDEOLOGICAL BASES OF INEQUALITY BASED ON SEXUAL ORIENTATION

Social analysts such as Bruce Bawer (1994:81), an author and cultural critic, believe that homophobia differs significantly from other forms of bigotry:

In a world of prejudice, there is no other prejudice quite like [homophobia]. Mainstream writers, politicians, and cultural leaders who hate Jews or blacks or Asians but who have long since accepted the unwritten rules that forbid public expression of those prejudices still denounce gays with impunity. For such people, gays are the Other in a way that Jews or blacks or Asians are not. After all, they can look at Jewish or black or Asian family life and see something that, in its chief components—husband, wife, children, workplace, school, house of worship—is essentially a variation of their own lives; yet when they look at gays—or, rather, at the image of gays that has been fostered both by the mainstream culture and by the gay subculture—they see creatures whose lives seem to be different from theirs in every possible way.

According to Bawer, heterosexuals cannot identify with the daily lives of lesbians and gay men, who—unlike them—exist as identifiable categories primarily because there is such strong antigay prejudice in the United States. In fact, the stereotypic beliefs that dominant (heterosexual) group members hold about gay men and lesbians are a major impediment to achieving gay rights and reducing inequalities based on sexual orientation (Nava and Dawidoff, 1994).

Stereotypic beliefs about lesbians and gay men often equate people's sexual *orientation* with sexual *practice*. For example, all gay men and lesbians—regardless of the nature and extent of their sexual activity—are stereotyped as "sex obsessed, sexually compulsive, and sexually predatory" (Nava and Dawidoff, 1994:32). Media depictions tend to reinforce stereotypes of gay men as sexual exploiters or "limp-wristed sissies," while lesbians are "stomping macho soldiers" (Nava and Dawidoff, 1994:32). Recently, television shows such as *Will and Grace* have sought to bring gay lifestyles into prime-time programming. Although some shows have perpetuated negative stereotypes about lesbians and gay men, others have attempted to change public perceptions about issues related to sexual orientation (see Box 6.1).

 ## Religion and Sexual Orientation

Most of the major religions of the world—Judaism, Christianity, Islam, and Hinduism, as well as Confucianism—historically have regarded homosexuality as a sin. Indeed, the only major world religion that does not condemn homosexuality is Buddhism

(Dynes, 1990). Religious fundamentalists in particular denounce homosexual conduct as a sign of great moral decay and societal chaos. In the Judeo-Christian tradition, religious condemnation of homosexuality derives from both the Hebrew Scriptures (e.g., Genesis 19 and Leviticus 18:33) and the New Testament (e.g., Romans 1:26-27 and I Corinthians 6:9) (Kosmin and Lachman, 1993).

Since the early 1990s, same-sex marriages and the ordination of "practicing" lesbians and gay men have been vigorously debated by various religious organizations. For example, the Vatican has directed Roman Catholic bishops in the United States to oppose laws that protect homosexuals, promote public acceptance of homosexual conduct, or give gay relationships equal footing with traditional, heterosexual marriage. However, many Roman Catholics disagree with the directive, stating that it is based on the faulty assumption that lesbians and gay men seek to influence the sexual orientation of children or youths with whom they live or work, that gay people are erotically attracted to every person of their own gender, and that they cannot control their sexual impulses in same-sex environments (cited in Bawer, 1994). Roman Catholics are not the only religious group debating same-sex marriage and the ordination of lesbians and gay men: The Southern Baptist Convention voted to expel two congregations—one for blessing the union of two gay men and the other for licensing a gay divinity student to preach. Although Baptist congregations usually are allowed to be autonomous, religious leaders determined that this autonomy did not extend to "acts to affirm, approve or endorse homosexual behavior" because these acts are deemed to be "contrary to the Bible on human sexuality and the sanctity of the family" (cited in Kosmin and Lachman, 1993:230). Episcopalians have been debating for two decades whether or not "practicing homosexuals" should be ordained. In 1996, an Episcopal bishop was accused of heresy for ordaining a gay deacon (Niebuhr, 1996; Dunlap, 1996).

Still, increasing numbers of lesbians and gay men are carving out their own niches in religious organizations. Some gay men and lesbians have sought to bring about changes in established religious denominations; others have formed religious bodies, such as the Metropolitan Community Church, that focus on the spiritual needs of the gay community. Even so, many gay men and lesbians

SOCIAL PROBLEMS

IN THE MEDIA

BOX 6.1

Depictions of Gay Men and Lesbians in Television Programming: Realistic or Not?

Will: Grace, did you know I was gay when you first met me?
Grace: My dog knew you were gay! (O'Leary, 1998:1)

—Lines from a recent episode of "Will and Grace," an NBC situation comedy (sitcom) about Will Truman (Eric McCormack) and Grace Adler (Debra Messing). Will, a gay man, and Grace, a straight woman, lived together for a period of time after Will ended a long-term relationship with a gay par ner and Grace left her fiancé at the altar.

How are gays and lesbians depicted in television shows? One of the first depictions of a gay male was "Love, Sidney," which aired in 1981, starring Tony Randall. The show was based on a television movie about a single gay man who moved in with a single mother and her young daughter. However, as the story was expanded from a two-hour television movie to a weekly television show, Randall's character was watered down, and no mention was made of his sexuality (O'Leary, 1998). Since that time, most shows featuring two or more men or women living together have depicted the characters as "straight" and often on the look-out for sexual partners of the opposite sex. On those rare occasions when a script has called for a gay or lesbian character, the role usually has been a minor one.

Few programs have had lesbian or gay characters in the lead roles. "Ellen" and "Will and Grace" have been the two exceptions. "Ellen," which aired before "Will and Grace" and starred Ellen Degeneres, was boycotted by the Christian Coalition as well as other conservative religious groups and lost commercial sponsors after Degeneres decided to "come out of the closet" in both her personal life and her television persona (O'Leary, 1998). Shortly thereafter, the network canceled the program.

In contrast, "Will and Grace" has been more widely accepted. Some cultural analysts believe that the program's popularity with viewers is because a gay man–straight woman duo is viewed as "safe." Viewers can see how a successful young woman and man who have been friends for many years might interact if sex were not an issue. According to David Kohan, the executive producer of "Will and Grace,"

When you look out at the television landscape, the men and women you see are either romantically involved, or they want to be romantically involved, or they inevitably will end up romantically involved. What we want to do is to examine a relationship between a man and a woman where sex isn't a factor. (NBC.com/Will&Grace, 1999:1)

Are viewers, critics, and commercial sponsors more tolerant of programs such as "Will and Grace" than they might be of sitcoms based on gay and/or lesbian couples? How might sociologists study the issue of whether or not TV programming perpetuates stereotypes about people based on their sexual orientation?

believe that they should not have to choose between full participation in their church and committed same-sex relationships (Dunlap, 1996).

 ## Law and Sexual Orientation

Throughout U.S. history, moral and religious teachings have been intertwined with laws that criminalize homosexual conduct. It is important to note that the law deals with homosexual *conduct* differently from the way in which it deals with *homosexuality*. To be a homosexual is not a crime, but to engage in homosexual conduct is a crime in some states. Although only a few states today have *sodomy laws* that criminalize oral or anal intercourse between persons of the same sex, about twenty states have laws pertaining to "deviant sexual conduct," "crimes against nature," or "unnatural intercourse." Under these laws, people can be imprisoned for oral or anal intercourse. According to lesbian and gay rights advocates, these laws are unconstitutional or indefensible for two reasons: (1) If the acts are conducted between consenting adults in *private,* any reported violation invades the privacy of

their relationship; and (2) in some states this conduct becomes a crime only if it is between persons of the same sex. However, in 1986, in *Bowers* v. *Hardwick,* the U.S. Supreme Court upheld state laws banning sodomy whether or not the conduct is between persons of the same sex. Thus, in effect, the Court ruled that people do not have a constitutionally protected right to engage in private homosexual conduct. For homosexuals, the Court's ruling virtually eliminates protection for sexual activities and creates the impression that gay or lesbian couples have *no* privacy rights (Aday, 1990). In fact, Justice Harry A. Blackmun's dissenting opinion in this case stated that the Supreme Court had invited the state to "invade the houses, hearts and minds of citizens who choose to live their life differently" (cited in Nagourney, 1996:E4).

Since *Bowers* v. *Hardwick,* the Supreme Court has been asked to rule on civil rights issues pertaining to lesbians and gay men. In 1996, the Court struck down an initiative that Colorado voters had passed, which banned all measures protecting gay men and lesbians against discrimination (Nagourney, 1996). The initiative was a reaction to ordinances

Reprinted by permission.

passed by such Colorado municipalities as Boulder, Denver, and Aspen that barred discrimination against lesbians and gay men (N. A. Lewis, 1995). Many gay rights issues—including those pertaining to same-sex marriages—are won or lost on a case-by-case or state-by-state basis, and some gay rights advocates believe that the fight for equality is far from over (Bawer, 1994).

DISCRIMINATION BASED ON SEXUAL ORIENTATION

As the campaigns for equal rights and an end to antigay discrimination have progressed, more people have come forward to declare that they are gay, lesbian, or bisexual and to indicate their support for gay organizations. Many lesbian or gay couples have sought the statutory right to marry, to obtain custody of their children if they are fit parents, to adopt, and to have their property pass to one another at death—in sum, to do all the things that people in heterosexual marriages are permitted to do. However, because ideas about marriage and the family are at the core of many people's moral or religious objections to homosexuality, gay marriage is still among the most controversial social issues as we begin the twenty-first century.

◢ Lack of Marital Rights

In the United States, many gay or lesbian couples choose to cohabit because they cannot enter into legally recognized marital relationships. In *cohabitation,* partners live together without being legally married. Although some gay men and lesbians take part in social or religious marriage ceremonies (in 1993, more than 3,000 couples participated in a mass wedding at a national gay rights march in Washington, D.C.), their unions are not legally sanctioned.

Over the past decade, some cities and states have given legal recognition to the concept of a *domestic partnership*—a household partnership in which an unmarried couple lives together in a committed, sexually intimate relationship and is granted the same rights and benefits accorded to a heterosexual couple

(Aulette, 1994). Many gay rights advocates consider recognition of domestic partnerships a major step forward because the employment benefits—including health insurance coverage—that are offered to legal spouses (those in heterosexual marriages) are offered to partners of unmarried employees. In this way, domestic partnership agreements benefit all unmarried cohabiting couples, gay and straight. However, certain rights come only with a marriage license and cannot be exercised by unmarried couples. These rights include "the right to joint parenting, through birth or adoption; the right to file joint income tax returns; legal immigration and residency for partners from other countries; benefits such as annuities, pensions, and Social Security for surviving spouses; wrongful death benefits for surviving partners; and immunity from having to testify in court against a spouse" (Findlen, 1995:90).

Although gay rights advocates continue to fight for legal recognition of same-sex marriages, recent rulings by the Hawaii and Vermont supreme courts

Legal analysts suggest that the U.S. Supreme Court eventually will be called on to determine the issue of same-sex marriages. In the meantime, gay rights advocates continue to fight for legal recognition of such marriages, while opponents wage an ongoing battle against legalized marriage for lesbians and gay men.

have raised the question of whether same-sex marriages should receive the same legal status as heterosexual marriages. When the issue first arose in Hawaii, at least thirty other states banned such unions, and in 1996 Congress passed the Defense of Marriage Act, which denies federal recognition of same-sex marriages and allows states to ignore those unions that are legalized elsewhere (DiPietro, 1999: A4).

 ## Parental Rights

There are as many as 5 million lesbian mothers and 3 million gay fathers in the United States. An estimated 6 million to 14 million children have a gay or lesbian parent (Patterson, 1992). Sometimes, when a gay father or lesbian mother has previously had a child with an opposite-sex partner, the other biological parent seeks custody of the child on the grounds that the lesbian or gay parent is "unfit" because of sexual orientation. In several widely publicized cases, lesbian mothers lost custody of their children when their fitness was challenged in court by ex-spouses or the children's grandparents (Gover, 1996a). Gay fathers sometimes face double jeopardy in child custody struggles: Both their sexual orientation and the widespread belief that women make better parents may work against them (Gover, 1996a).

Parental rights are a pressing concern for gay or lesbian partners who are raising children together, particularly when only one partner is legally recognized as the parent or guardian. Many couples rely on legal documents such as special powers of attorney, wills, and guardianship agreements to protect both partners' rights, but these documents do not have the legal force of formal adoption (Bruni, 1996). As more lesbian couples choose donor insemination to become parents, issues arise about the rights of nonbiological gay parents, whose claims often are the least recognized (Gover, 1996c). In recent court custody cases, the nonbiological parent has had no standing because he or she has neither biological nor legal ties to the child. Some lesbian and gay couples draft their own parenting contracts, but for the most part, these agreements are not enforceable in court and can be revoked by the biological parent at any time (Gover, 1996c). As more

states allow unmarried partners—whether gay or straight—to adopt children, more same-sex couples will probably seek joint legal custody of their children. However, the process is extremely time consuming and expensive and involves an invasion of personal privacy (Bruni, 1996).

Many gay men and lesbians experience discrimination when they seek to become foster parents or to adopt a child. Widespread myths about the "homosexual lifestyle" lead to the notion that children living with lesbian or gay parents may witness immoral conduct or be recruited into homosexuality (Singer and Deschamps, 1994). In fact, research shows that children raised by lesbian or gay parents typically are well adjusted, and the parents often serve as role models for equal sharing in the family (Sullivan, 1996).

Gay rights advocates are cautiously optimistic that social norms and laws are gradually changing. They hope that in time sexual orientation alone will not be grounds for denying parental custody or visitation rights to lesbian or gay parents and that courts will rule solely on the basis of which parent can provide a better home for the child (Goldberg, 1996).

 ## Housing Discrimination

In recent years, opponents of gay rights have worked to pass state constitutional amendments that would remove any existing protection afforded to gay men, lesbians, and bisexuals against discrimination in housing, public accommodations, and other areas of life. Carrying signs that say, for example, "God Made Adam and Eve, NOT Adam and Steve," opponents of gay rights maintain that they are not "bashing gays" but rather upholding the family (Dunlap, 1995:10).

Some lesbian and gay people are denied housing because they are gay; others are evicted from apartments where they have lived for some period of time. Even those who successfully rent or purchase property tend to remain targets of discrimination from some heterosexual residents, building managers, and custodial personnel, as Bruce Bawer explains:

> When two gay people decide to move in together, they commit themselves to insult and discrimina-

tion and attack. At one apartment building in which [a male partner] and I lived, the superintendent spit on me one day without provocation; at our next address, members of the building staff, not knowing that I understood Spanish, joked with one another in my presence about the maricones (faggots). Living alone, most gay people can conceal their sexuality; living together, a gay couple advertises theirs every time they step out of the house together. (Bawer, 1994:254)

 ## Discrimination in Medical Care

Like housing, medical care is not exempt from discrimination based on sexual orientation. Studies by the American Medical Association have found that some physicians do not ask about patients' sexual orientation, and many lesbians and gay men do not tell (*JAMA*, 1996). As a result of their failure to ask, when making diagnoses, physicians may overlook diseases that gay men or lesbians are more prone to contract. For example, the risk of developing anal cancer is 25 to 84 times higher for gay men than it is for heterosexual men (*JAMA*, 1996). Gay men also have a greater likelihood than heterosexual men of acquiring gastrointestinal and rectal diseases.

Some physicians and nurses adopt a judgmental stance when dealing with gay and lesbian patients. One study of 100 nurses teaching in nursing programs found that 34 percent believed that lesbians are "disgusting" and 17 percent believed that lesbians molest children (Stevens, 1992). Other physicians and nurses may provide reduced care to gays and lesbians or deny them medical care altogether (*JAMA*, 1996). For example, lesbians may be at risk for terminal breast or ovarian cancer because some doctors do not provide adequate information about the importance of early cancer detection through routine gynecological examinations and mammography screening (Gessen, 1993).

Probably the most controversial topic in health care for gay men, lesbians, and bisexuals is HIV/ AIDS. Although physicians, dentists, nurses, and other health professionals may learn about treating patients who are HIV-positive, many feel inadequate to deal with these patients' psychological and social needs. Today, HIV/AIDS is the eighth leading cause of death in the United States. It is the top cause of death among men between the ages of twenty-five and forty-four and the fourth leading cause of death among women in the same age group (U.S. Bureau of the Census, 1998). Despite the prevalence of HIV/ AIDS among gay men and bisexuals in certain age groups, many medical professionals do not inform their patients about the risks associated with various types of sexual conduct and intravenous drug use or about measures that can be taken to prevent exposure to sexually transmitted diseases and HIV. Although HIV/AIDS has been referred to as "the gay disease," social analysts suggest that it should be viewed as *everyone's* problem.

 ## Occupational Discrimination

Fearing that they may be stigmatized or discriminated against in the workplace, many gay and lesbian people do not reveal their sexual orientation (Woods, 1993). Their fears have some ground in reality. Despite laws in many states prohibiting discrimination in employment on the basis of sexual orientation, openly lesbian and gay people often experience bias in hiring, retention, and promotion in private and public sector employment. More than 100 major companies have stated that they do not discriminate on the basis of sexual orientation. Nevertheless, studies show that about two-thirds of gay employees in private sector employment (e.g., small businesses and large corporations) have witnessed some type of hostility, harassment, or discrimination at their place of employment (Singer and Deschamps, 1994). Many chief executive officers are reluctant to put a lesbian or gay man at the top of the corporate hierarchy, and some employees express concern about working around gay men and lesbians (Woods, 1993). Many who do not reveal their sexual orientation to coworkers are subjected to a general disparagement of gays, as Brian, a gay executive in a large New York corporation, explains:

I was in an office with the boss and another person who is my same level, and we were talking about another professional that we should probably get involved in this transaction. The person who was at the same level as me said,

"Oh, he's really good, but he's a flaming fag-got." What was very shocking to me was that it was an attack on this person in a professional context. You are sort of used to the way straight men sort of banter around, calling each other queer, on a social level. But it's really strange when they talk about it in a professional setting. But this person thought it was okay. I assume that he thought there were three straight men there, so he could still say these things that in mixed company he would never say. (quoted in Mead, 1994:40)

Although the Equal Employment Opportunity Commission, a federal agency, acknowledges that same-sex sexual harassment occurs in the workplace, supervisors frequently do not take it seriously. Because, to prove sexual harassment, victims must show that the harasser targeted a specific category of people such as gay men, charges of harassment reflect the victim's sexual orientation. Victims of same-sex harassment may be blamed for causing the incident. Many fear they will lose their job if they file a grievance, even though gay rights advocates believe sexual orientation should be irrelevant in determining whether harassment has occurred (Gover, 1996b).

Same-sex sexual harassment and blatant discrimination in hiring and promotion are also problems in public sector positions at the federal and state government level, as well as in local law enforcement agencies. Consider, for example, the blatant discrimination of the executive order signed in 1953 by President Dwight D. Eisenhower mandating that "sexual perverts" be fired from federal jobs. For many years, most law enforcement agencies and police departments did not employ lesbian or gay people. Until 1993, the Dallas police department refused to hire gay men or lesbians because of Texas sodomy laws criminalizing same-sex conduct. Today, gay and lesbian people are employed in law enforcement agencies throughout the country because of antibias policies that preclude the agencies from asking job applicants about their sexual orientation. Despite such provisions, sociologist Stephen Leinen (a former lieutenant in the New York City police department) found in his study of "gay cops" that many remain "totally closeted" for fear of how other police officers and gay people will treat them. The total secrecy

among lesbians and gay men in many large police departments is illustrated by one gay police officer's surprise on learning that his partner, with whom he had worked for some time, also was gay: "I was deeply shocked when he told me. We had worked together for over three years and neither of us knew about the other. He said, 'How the hell could we have worked together for so long and neither one of us knew it?'" (Leinen, 1993:3)

In recent years, some gay advocates have encouraged people to "come out" (identify their sexual orientation) at work and to make the biases against people based on their sexual orientation known to the media and the general public so that demands for change will be met. As long as people remain "in the closet," the advocates argue, workplace discrimination will not be eliminated (Nava and Dawidoff, 1994). However, extensive media coverage about openly lesbian and gay soldiers in the U.S. armed forces has not led to lifting the ban against gays and lesbians in the military.

 Discrimination in the Military

According to the U.S. military—the nation's largest employer—lesbians and gay men are unfit to serve their country, especially if they make their sexual orientation known to others. Although many closeted gay men and lesbians have served in various branches of the military over the years, the official government policy has been one of exclusion, based on the assumption that homosexuals are a security risk because they might be blackmailed by someone who finds out about their sexual orientation. Accordingly, tens of thousands of gay and lesbian military service personnel have sought to appear as conventional as possible and behave exactly like heterosexual people. This course of action often has devastating personal consequences for closeted soldiers and sailors (see Shilts, 1993).

When the Clinton administration attempted to lift the ban on gays in the military, the outcry by many military and religious leaders forced the administration to promulgate a compromise policy known as "don't ask, don't tell." Under this policy, commanders may no longer ask about a serviceperson's sexual orientation, and gay men and lesbians can serve in the military as long as they do not reveal their sexual orientation. While some social analysts believe the policy provides gay men and lesbians with the same opportunity to serve their country as heterosexuals, others believe that this compromise is a form of institutionalized discrimination: "while heterosexuals would continue to enjoy their right to lead private lives and to discuss those lives freely, gays would be allowed to remain in the armed forces only so long as they did not mention that they were gay or lesbian or have relationships on or off base" (Bawer, 1994:61).

A recent study by the Servicemembers Legal Defense Network appears to support the belief that the "don't ask, don't tell" policy has led to differential treatment of some gay men and lesbians in the military. Some commanders continue to ask about sexual orientation. The number of army, navy, marines, and air force personnel discharged for homosexuality doubled between 1993 and 1998, the latest year for which figures are available. Internal navy documents have shown, for example, that the navy has sought evidence of homosexual conduct if sailors have acknowledged being gay or were reported to have told friends or others that they were gay. In some cases, heterosexual women have indicated that they were falsely accused of being lesbians after they filed sexual assault or sexual harassment charges against male military personnel (Shenon, 1996c). In other cases, gay men have been victims of hate crimes. In 1999, for example, former U.S. Army private, Calvin Glover was convicted and sentenced to life in prison for the brutal murder of Private First Class Barry Winchell, a gay soldier who had confronted Glover about the latter's "outrageous, macho bragging" during a beer drinking session with other soldiers outside their barracks at Ft. Campbell, Kentucky. This case raises new questions about whether "don't ask, don't tell" is an unfulfilled promise rather than an actual functioning policy in the U.S. military (Thompson, 1999).

 Victimization and Hate Crimes

Before the early 1990s, few acts of violence against gays and lesbians were ever reported in the media. Indeed, hate crimes against gay men and lesbians were not acknowledged as such, even though civil rights groups had been tracking increasing violence motivated by group prejudice for over a decade.

Hate crimes appear to be most prevalent where homophobic attitudes and behaviors are tolerated or at least overlooked. However, some behaviors are too reprehensible to be overlooked. As discussed at the beginning of this chapter, one of the most brutal hate crimes perpetrated against a gay man occurred when Matthew Shepard, a college student, was brutally murdered because of his sexual orientation. In 1999, Shepard's killer, a 22-year-old man, was given two life sentences for beating the gay University of Wyoming student to death. Shepard had been lured from a bar by two men posing as homosexuals. The men drove him to the outskirts of Laramie, Wyoming, tied him to a fence, savagely pistol-whipped him, and left him to die in a snowstorm. Had it not been for an appeal for mercy in remarks to the jury by Matthew's father, Dennis Shepard, the killer might have received the death penalty. But Dennis Shepard ended his remarks with one final comment to the killer: "You robbed me of something very precious, and I will never forgive you for that" (matthewsplace.com, 1999).

The Shepard incident was not an isolated hate crime. In other incidents around the country, pipe-wielding youths yelling "kill the faggot" beat a gay man unconscious in Laguna Beach, California; a gay man was so seriously injured in an act of "gay bashing" in Boston that doctors initially believed he might not survive; and another gay man was killed by an antigay cruiser who had "picked up" his victim on the Internet (Meers, 1996). Lesbians have been assaulted, raped, and sometimes killed when they have been seen in public with their partners (Dunlap, 1995).

Before enactment of the Hate Crimes Statistics Act of 1990, hate crimes were classified as such only on the basis of race, ethnicity, or religion. However, during debate over the passage of the act, gay rights advocates argued that not including sexual orientation in the law created a double standard in the United States: Crimes against gay men and lesbians would be classified as "less significant, less pervasive, and less reprehensible" than crimes motivated by racial, religious, or ethnic prejudice. In contrast, some senators argued that the law gave undue protection and respectability to gay men and lesbians (Fernandez, 1991). Information gathered since passage of the act shows that more than 50 percent of all reported

SOCIAL PROBLEMS
AND SOCIAL POLICY

BOX 6.2

School's Out: Closing the Books on Homophobia

History, as taught, is devoid of gays or lesbians. Without knowing that history, it's no surprise that many consider their present-day presence strange or unnatural.

—*Kevin Jennings, founder of the Gay Lesbian Straight Education Network (cited in Seavor, 1996:E11)*

Recently, some U.S. schools have modified their curricula to incorporate information on lesbians, gays, and bisexuals. However, journalist Dan Woog (1995), author of a book on the impact of gay and lesbian issues in schools, suggests that much remains to be done. According to Woog, within the administration of each school, there should be at least one advocate to address gay issues—a person who is available to gay, lesbian, and bisexual students; who makes sure that the school complies with its responsibility to all students; and who helps with referrals to outside support groups, counseling agencies, hot lines, and organizations for family members. Woog also suggests that schools define harassment on the basis of sexual orientation and make clear that inappropriate use of language, jokes, graffiti, and vandalism based on sexual orientation is unfair, offensive, and harmful to everyone in the school community.

In the twenty-first century, we are still concerned about how gay men and lesbians are treated in school. The Gay, Lesbian and Straight Education Network (GLSEN) "school climate" survey, which was conducted in 1999 among nearly 500 gay, lesbian, bisexual and transgender students across thirty-two states, found that 91 percent of the participants had heard words like "faggot," "dyke," or "queer" used regularly at school. Sixty-nine percent stated that they had experienced direct verbal harassment; 24 percent reported incidences of physical harassment. Are other students the primary perpetrators of prejudice and discrimination? Not necessarily. The GLSEN survey found that more than one-third of the participants had heard negative remarks about sexual orientation from faculty or staff. Judy Shepard, the mother of Matthew Shepard, a college student who was brutally murdered because of his sexual orientation, decries this type of negative behavior among teachers, administrators, and students:

I sort of get the feeling that teachers and administrators feel that they grew up with that teasing in school, and they made it through—they treat it almost as a rite of passage. "We survived it, you survive it. This is how you grow." Oh, ignorant people! Kids have scars—from being teased because they have big ears. What kind of scars do they have from being teased because they're black, or gay? (Cullen, 1999:3)

What suggestions do you have for reducing the problems described in the GLSEN study? According to Judy Shepard, education is where change must begin first: "Kids go to school to learn how to behave in society. . . . And if we don't start doing that in the schools soon, it's harder to do as an adult" (Cullen, 1999:2). Arguing that discrimination and violence against gays must be taken seriously in any and all settings, including schools, GLSEN and other organizations conduct teacher training workshops in an effort to make teachers and administrators more aware of this pressing problem.

antigay harassment and violence is perpetrated by young males age twenty-one or under (Comstock, 1991). In some situations, police officers and judges do not take hate crimes against lesbians and gay men seriously. According to a former Dallas judge, "I put prostitutes and queers at the same level . . . and I'd be hard-put to give somebody life for killing a prostitute" (quoted in Singer and Deschamps, 1994:68). One way (see Box 6.2 on page 117) to decrease homophobia and hate crimes, say some social analysts, is to change school curricula.

PERSPECTIVES ON SEXUAL ORIENTATION AND SOCIAL INEQUALITY

Sexual orientation and social inequality can be understood from various perspectives. Biologists take one approach, and psychologists take another. Sociological explanations focus primarily on how sexual orientation and homophobia are associated with social learning and/or social structural factors in society. We'll look at each perspective separately.

▲ Biological and Psychological Perspectives

If biologists could determine that sexual orientation was genetic in origin and that gay men and lesbians do not choose to be homosexuals, would homophobia decrease? There is no simple answer to this question, but some gay advocates applaud recent studies that suggest sexual orientation may be determined by a person's genetic inheritance. According to this view, homosexuality—like heterosexuality—is an ascribed characteristic, present from birth, that cannot be changed through counseling or therapy; therefore, gay men and lesbians cannot be blamed for their sexual orientation.

Over the past two decades, research has produced some evidence that sexual orientation may be partially linked to genetic inheritance. For example, some researchers believe they have isolated a specific marker on the sex chromosome that may increase the likelihood of homosexuality among members of the same family (LeVay and Hamer, 1994). Other researchers are searching for a "gay gene." So far, they have found some support for the presence of such a gene in their studies of identical twins (twins who have the same genetic material), and fraternal twins (twins who share some, but not all, genetic material), which have shown that identical twins are much more likely to both be gay (if one is gay) than fraternal twins (see Bailey and Pillard, 1991; Bailey and Benishay, 1993). Still other researchers have identified an area (but not the specific gene) on the X chromosome that may carry the predisposition for homosexuality (see Angier, 1993; Travis, 1995). Although these studies are promising, critics suggest that biological explanations alone cannot account for sexual orientation (Doyle, 1995).

Unlike biologists, who typically focus on genetic determinants of sexual orientation, psychologists associate homosexuality with mental processes and childhood experiences. Early psychological approaches considered homosexuality a form of *maladjustment*. Sigmund Freud, founder of the psychoanalytic approach, believed that humans are constitutionally bisexual—meaning that masculine and feminine currents coexist in everyone—but children as they progress toward adulthood move toward heterosexuality. According to Freud, not everyone makes it down the difficult path to heterosexuality because it is fraught with dangers and problems. According to Freud, for example, sons whose mothers were domineering and overprotective found it difficult to achieve heterosexuality. Following in Freud's footsteps, later psychologists equated heterosexuality with good mental health and homosexuality with mental illness (see Bieber et al., 1962).

In 1942, the American Psychiatric Association formally classified homosexuality as a form of mental illness and suggested that treatments ranging from castration to electroshock therapy might remedy the problem (Marcus, 1992). However, the association's classification did not go undisputed. By administering standard personality tests to two groups of men—one heterosexual and the other homosexual—and asking a panel of psychiatrists and psychologists to tell her the sexual orientation of each subject on the basis of those tests, psychologist Evelyn Hooker (1957; 1958) showed that not all homosexuals are maladjusted or mentally ill. The judges were unable to differentiate between the heterosexuals and homosexuals. In 1973, the American Psychiatric Association removed homosexuality from its list of mental disorders.

Many psychologists believe that biological and psychosocial factors interact in the formation of sexual orientation. Psychologist Daryl J. Bem, for example, thinks that genetic factors and gender roles in childhood interact to produce sexual orientation. According to Bem, "In most societies, including our own, most boys and girls are raised so that they tend to feel more similar to children of their own sex and different from children of the opposite sex" (cited in Shea, 1996:A11). These feelings of similarity and difference are often formed on the playground, where boys are more aggressive than girls. Over time, children's belief that people of the opposite gender are different—and somewhat mysterious—translates into heterosexual desire. However, some children see themselves as more similar to children of the opposite gender. For example, boys who do not like rough-and-tumble play or sports but like to play with dolls or other "girls' toys" may grow up feeling different from other boys. Similarly, girls who prefer "boys' sports" frequently feel awkward around other girls. According to Bem, the best predictor of sexual orientation is the degree to which children are gender-conforming or nonconforming; children who fit in sometimes but not others are likely to become bisexual.

Advocates of Bem's theory point out that it is supported by earlier studies showing that 66 percent of gay men (compared to 10 percent of heterosexual men) did not enjoy activities typical of their own gender. Critics point out that Bem's theory does not take into account the fact that what is defined as gender-appropriate behavior differs widely across cultures and over time. For example, thirty years ago, girls who wanted to play soccer might have been viewed as tomboys with few female friends; whereas today, many girls—and boys—play soccer, and their sports participation does not single them out as different from others of their gender. Bem's theory also does not explain the stages in the process of taking on a homosexual identity or how labeling by others may influence people's perceptions of themselves as homosexual, heterosexual, or bisexual.

◢ Interactionist Perspectives

In contrast to biological and psychological perspectives, interactionist perspectives view heterosexual and homosexual conduct as learned behavior and focus on the process by which individuals come to identify themselves as gay, lesbian, bisexual, or straight. According to interactionists, most people acquire the status of *heterosexual* without being consciously aware of it because heterosexuality is the established norm and they do not have to struggle over their identity. But the same is not true of people who identify themselves as *homosexual* or *bisexual.* In fact, some sociologists suggest that sexual orientation is a master status for many gay men, lesbians, and bisexuals (Schur, 1965). **A *master status* is the most significant status a person possesses because it largely determines how individuals view themselves and how they are treated by others.** Master status based on sexual orientation is particularly significant when it is linked to other subordinate racial-ethnic group statuses. For example, working-class gay Latinos are more hesitant than white, middle-class gay men to come out to their families because of cultural norms pertaining to *machismo* (masculinity) and the fear that relatives will withdraw the support that is essential for surviving at the subordinate end of race and class hierarchies (see Almaguer, 1995).

Interactionists have identified several stages in the process of accepting a lesbian, gay, or bisexual identity (Weinberg et al., 1994). First, people experience identity confusion—a situation in which they feel different from other people and struggle with admitting that they are attracted to individuals of the same sex. For example, someone who identified

Individuals seem to accept their identities as lesbian, gay, or bisexual in stages. Initially there is identity confusion. But seeking out others who are open about their sexual orientation and experimenting sexually can eventually lead to acceptance.

himself as a fourteen-year-old boy posted the following note on an Internet newsgroup:

> I feel like my life is over. Am I gay? God, I hope not. I walk around going, "God, I hope not." I walk around going, "Do I like him?" "Do I like her?" "How would it feel to do it with him/her?" WHY DOES THIS HAVE TO HAPPEN TO ME!! The funny thing is, I absolutely detest everything about sex with men, and relationships with men. But somehow, I feel attracted to them anyway!! (Gabriel, 1995b:1)

In the past, many gay and lesbian people had nowhere to turn in their quest for answers and support from others; today, many use the Internet and other forms of global communication to connect with others who share their concerns (Gabriel, 1995b).

The second stage in establishing a lesbian or gay identity is seeking out others who are openly lesbian or gay and perhaps engaging in sexual experimentation or making other forays into the homosexual subculture. In the third stage, people attempt to integrate their self-concept and acceptance of a label such as "homosexual," "gay," or "lesbian" by pursuing a way of life that conforms to their definition of what those labels mean (Cass, 1984; Coleman, 1981/2; Ponse, 1978). Like most "stage" theories, however, not all people go through these stages. Even those who do may not go through each stage in the same way, and some may move back and forth between stages (Weinberg et al., 1994).

Studies on how people come to accept their sexual identity as gay, bisexual, or lesbian show the significance of labeling and how it can create barriers to full participation in U.S. society. However, these studies typically are based on a relatively narrow selection of people, which makes it difficult to generalize the findings to larger populations. That is, respondents who openly identify themselves as gay or bisexual may not be characteristic of the larger homosexual or bisexual population (Weinberg et al., 1994).

▲ Functionalist and Conflict Perspectives

Unlike the interactionist approach, which focuses primarily on how individuals come to identify themselves as homosexual, bisexual, or heterosexual, functionalist perspectives focus on the relationship between social structure and sexual orientation. To functionalists, social norms and laws are established to preserve social institutions and maintain stability in society. From this perspective, then, many societies punish homosexual conduct because it violates the social norms established by those societies and thus undermines the stability of the societies. Sociologist David P. Aday, Jr., provides an overview of this perspective:

> Marriage and family are structural arrangements that contribute to the continuity of our contemporary society. . . . [Homosexuality undermines] arrangements that currently operate to replace societal members in an orderly way—that is, the arrangement has survival value. . . . If homosexual conduct were allowed to exist unchallenged and unpunished, then it might in time undermine norms and laws that underpin monogamous marital sex, at least some of which results in the production of offspring to repopulate the society. . . . The punishment of homosexual conduct, from ridicule and discrimination to imprisonment, reinforces expectations about heterosexual and marital sex and defines the boundaries of society. (Aday, 1990:25)

Does this photo tend to support or reject some functionalist analysts' assumption that gay or lesbian families destroy "family values" in this country? Why or why not?

The functionalist perspective explains why some people do not believe homosexual conduct or marriages between lesbian or gay couples should be protected legally. It also explains why some religious and political leaders call for a renewal of "family values" in this country.

Critics suggest that the functionalist approach supports the status quo and ignores a need for new definitions of marriage and family. If marriage is understood to be the decision of two people to live together in a partnership—be a family—then the intention or the capacity to have children should not be a condition. These critics say that nothing but custom mandates that marital partners must be of different genders (Nava and Dawidoff, 1994).

Whereas the functionalist approach focuses on how existing social arrangements create a balance in society, the conflict approach focuses on *tensions* in society and *differences* in interests and power among opposing groups. From this perspective, people who hold the greatest power are able to have their own attitudes, beliefs, and values—about sexual orientation, in this case—represented and enforced while others are not (Aday, 1990). Therefore norms pertaining to *compulsory heterosexuality* reflect the beliefs of dominant group members who hold high-level positions in the federal and state government, the military, and other social institutions. However, critics assert that the conflict approach fails to recognize that some people who have wealth and power are gay or lesbian yet take no action to reduce discrimination based on sexual orientation.

According to Karl Marx, conflicts over values are an essential element of social life, and less-powerful people often challenge the laws imposed on them by those in positions of power. For example, adverse decisions by state courts and the U.S. Supreme Court often result in increased political activism by gay and lesbian rights groups. In recent years, more openly lesbian and gay people can be found in public office as elected or appointed officials, in the medical and legal professions, as educators and business leaders, and in all walks of life. However, regardless of their location in the power structure, most gay men, lesbians, and bisexuals remain acutely aware that many social barriers have not been lifted and there has not been a major shift in people's attitudes toward homosexuality and bisexuality.

With rapid Internet communications, lesbians and gay men around the world keep informed about political decisions that may adversely affect them. Many coalitions have been formed to organize gay pride marches and protests around the world. For example, the International Lesbian and Gay Association reports that more than three hundred lesbian and gay groups exist in more than fifty nations (Hendriks et al., 1993).

CAN INEQUALITIES BASED ON SEXUAL ORIENTATION BE REDUCED?

As we have emphasized in previous chapters, how people view a social problem is related to how they believe the problem should be reduced or solved. Inequality based on sexual orientation is no exception. From an interactionist perspective, homosexual conduct is learned behavior, and people go through stages in establishing a lesbian or gay identity. Society should therefore be more tolerant of people as they come to accept their sexual identity. Legal and social barriers that prevent homosexuals from fully participating in society should be removed, thus making the complex psychological and social process of coming out to friends, family, and coworkers easier for those who choose to do so.

According to the functionalist perspective, social norms and laws exist to protect the family and maintain stability in society. Given this, sexual orientation becomes a social issue: gay activists' demands for equal rights, including the reversal of sodomy laws and legal recognition of same-sex marriage, become major threats to the stability of society. In the face of these perceived threats, groups, such as the Alliance for Traditional Marriage, advocate passage of a constitutional amendment making marriage the legal union between a man and a woman. If gay advocates succeed in getting legally sanctioned marriage redefined, these groups say there will be no stopping others who wish to strike down what remains of "foundational truths once thought to be self-evident" (Thomas, 1996:A15). Some advocates of this position believe that lesbians and gay men can change their sexual orientation:

Homosexuals can and do change. My files bulge with stories of those who once engaged in sex with people of the same gender, but no longer do. They testify to the possibility of change for those who want to.

The struggle to maintain what remains of the social fabric will ultimately determine whether we will continue to follow ancient Rome on the road to destruction, or come to our senses, turn around and re-enter a harbor of safety ordained by God for our own protection. (Thomas, 1996:A15)

Whether gay, lesbian, and bisexual individuals can or should change their sexual orientation is the subject of widespread disagreement. However, most functionalists agree that homosexuality may be dysfunctional for society if it does not contribute to society's need for new members or if it undermines social norms and laws that preserve the family unit and maintain stability in society.

Conflict theorists believe that prejudice and discrimination against lesbians, gay men, and bisexuals are embedded in the social structure of society and are reinforced by those who hold the greatest power and thus are able to perpetuate their own attitudes, beliefs, and values about what constitutes "normal" sexual conduct. From this perspective, homophobia is similar to racism, sexism, and ageism, and the overt and covert discrimination that gay men and lesbians experience is similar to the discrimination experienced by people of color, white women, and older people. According to the conflict approach, the best way to reduce inequality based on sexual orientation is to repeal laws prohibiting sexual acts between consenting adults and to pass laws that ban all forms of discrimination against gay men, lesbians, and bisexuals. However, to gain equal rights, activism is necessary: People must continue to demand social change.

In the twenty-first century, gay advocacy is perhaps the most effective means of reducing homophobia and bringing about greater equality for gay men and lesbians. In fact, it took a small riot to make the general public aware of inequality based on sexual orientation and the need for social change. In 1969, police raided the Stonewall Inn, a bar patronized by gay men in New York City's Greenwich Village, for alleged liquor law violations. The angry response by militant gay activists caused police to stop raiding the Stonewall Inn and other gay bars and clubs on Christopher Street and ushered the Gay Liberation movement into existence (Weinberg and Williams, 1975). However, by the late 1970s and the 1980s,

the opponents of gay rights had rallied, and groups such as "Save Our Children" defeated gay rights bills in a number of states. With the emergence of HIV/AIDS as a major problem in the 1980s, many gay advocates shifted the focus of their lobbying from civil rights to the need for medical research (Shilts, 1988). Today, more than 2,500 organizations seek equal rights and protections for gay men, lesbians, and bisexuals; these groups represent a wide cross-section of the U.S. population. For example, the Association of Lesbian and Gay Asians focuses on the unique needs and concerns of gay and lesbian Asian and Pacific Americans (Leong, 1996), and groups such as the Bisexual Resource Group,

Source: Advertising in the *New York Times* by the Empire State Pride Agenda, New York State's lesbian and gay political organization, as part of a "Lesbian and Gay Values Are American Values" public affairs campaign to get out the vote.

BiWomen of Color, BiAdult Children of Alcoholics, and BiStar Trekkies focus on the needs of bisexual people (Gabriel, 1995a; Leland, 1995).

Despite some changes in the attitudes and laws pertaining to homosexuality, discrimination remains strong. According to a recent study, gay, lesbian, and bisexual sociologists who advocate gay rights are more likely than their heterosexual colleagues to encounter difficulty in obtaining academic positions, to experience bias in the tenure and promotion process, and to be excluded from social and professional networks (Taylor and Raeburn, 1995). However, not all of the study's findings were negative: for some sociologists, being involved in gay rights issues brings professional visibility, recognition, and opportunities for advancement (Taylor and Raeburn, 1995).

Gay rights advocates argue that gay men, lesbians, and bisexuals should not be the only ones responsible for reducing or eliminating inequality based on sexual orientation:

It all comes down to this: Are people equal in this society by virtue of their citizenship, or not? If the answer is no, then we will be saying that equality does not exist in America anymore but has been replaced by tiers of citizenship, and that what tier you occupy depends on whether people like you or not. And if we accept this, then we will have repudiated the constitutional principles of liberty and equality upon which America was founded and which have been its historic challenge to the world. . . . We believe that you will join in this cause because it is your cause, too, the cause of individual liberty and human equality. (Nava and Dawidoff, 1994:167)

Some analysts suggest that people in the future will ask, "What was all the fuss over gay men and lesbians (or sexual orientation) about?" What do you think?

SUMMARY

➤ *What criteria do sociologists use to study sexual orientation?*

Sociologists define sexual orientation as a preference for emotional-sexual relationships with persons of the same sex (homosexuality), the opposite sex (heterosexuality), or both (bisexuality). Recent studies have used three criteria for classifying people as homosexual or bisexual: (1) sexual attraction to persons of one's own gender, (2) sexual involvement with one or more persons of one's own gender, and (3) self-identification as a gay man, lesbian, or bisexual.

➤ *How do religion and law influence people's beliefs about homosexuality?*

Most major religions regard homosexuality as a sin. Contemporary religious fundamentalists denounce homosexual conduct as a sign of great moral decay and societal chaos. Throughout U.S. history, moral and religious teachings have been intertwined with laws that criminalize homosexual conduct. Some states have sodomy laws or other

laws pertaining to "deviant sexual conduct," "crimes against nature," or "unnatural intercourse" whereby people can be imprisoned for oral or anal intercourse.

➤ *How does cohabitation differ from domestic partnership?*

In cohabitation, same-sex or opposite-sex partners live together without being legally married. Many gay or lesbian couples cohabit in this country because they cannot enter into legally recognized marital relationships. However, some cities and states have given legal recognition to domestic partnerships—household partnerships in which unmarried couples live together in a committed, sexually intimate relationship and are granted the same rights and benefits as those accorded to heterosexual couples. Domestic partnership agreements benefit some couples by providing health insurance coverage and other benefits that were not previously afforded them.

➡ *What types of discrimination do gay and lesbian people experience?*

Although lesbians and gay men experience discrimination in most aspects of daily life, some of the principal areas are (1) child custody and adoption, (2) housing, (3) medical care, (4) occupations, and (5) the military. In each of these areas, gains have been made over the past three decades. However, discrimination against lesbians and gay men remains among the most blatant of all forms of prejudice and discrimination experienced by members of subordinate groups.

➡ *How have changes in the definition of hate crimes affected gay men and lesbians?*

Before the early 1990s, hate crimes against gay men and lesbians were not acknowledged. The enactment of the Hate Crime Statistics Act of 1990 enabled hate crimes to be classified on the basis of sexual orientation, race, ethnicity, religion, or other characteristics that are devalued or "hated." Hate crimes against gays and lesbians appear to be most prevalent where homophobic attitudes are tolerated or overlooked.

➡ *How do biologists and psychologists explain sexual orientation?*

Biologists suggest that sexual orientation may be determined by a person's genetic inheritance. Researchers have identified an area (but not the specific gene) on the X chromosome that may carry the predisposition for homosexuality. Until fairly recently, psychologists associated homosexuality with maladjustment or mental illness. Today, however, social psychologists believe that genetic and social factors combine to produce sexual orientation. According to Bem's theory, the best predictor of sexual orientation is the degree to which children are gender-conforming or nonconforming; children who fit in sometimes but not others are likely to become bisexual.

➡ *How do interactionists explain problems associated with sexual orientation?*

According to interactionists, most people acquire the status of heterosexual without being consciously aware of it. For lesbians, gay men, and bisexuals, however, sexual orientation may be a master status because it largely determines how individuals view themselves and how they are treated by others. Interactionists identify several stages in the process of accepting the identity of lesbian, gay, or bisexual: (1) experiencing identity confusion, (2) seeking out others who are openly lesbian or gay and sometimes engaging in sexual experimentation, and (3) attempting to integrate self-concept and acceptance of a label such as "homosexual," "gay," or "lesbian."

➡ *How do functionalists explain problems associated with sexual orientation?*

Functionalists focus on how social norms and laws are established to preserve social institutions, such as the family, and to maintain stability in society. They also analyze reasons why societies find it necessary to punish sexual conduct that violates social norms prohibiting nonmarital sex and same-sex sexual relations. According to functionalists, homosexual conduct is punished because it undermines social institutions and jeopardizes the society.

➡ *How do conflict theorists explain problems associated with sexual orientation?*

Conflict theorists believe that the group in power imposes its own attitudes, beliefs, and values about sexual orientation on everyone else. Thus norms enforcing compulsory heterosexuality reflect the beliefs of dominant group members in the federal and state governments, the military, and other social institutions. According to conflict theorists, social change can occur only if people demand that laws be changed to bring about greater equality for gay men and lesbians.

➡ *How have gay rights advocates sought to reduce inequality based on sexual orientation?*

Beginning with the Gay Liberation movement in the 1960s, advocates have argued that lesbians and gay men are citizens and entitled to the same rights and protections that other citizens enjoy, including the right to equal employment and housing, legally sanctioned marriage, and protection from harassment and hate crimes. Some analysts suggest that future social change depends on the continued vigilance of gay and lesbian advocacy organizations.

KEY TERMS

deviance, p. 108
domestic partnership, p. 112

homophobia, p. 108
master status, p. 119

sexuality, p. 108
sexual orientation, p. 108

QUESTIONS FOR CRITICAL THINKING

1. How is homophobia similar to racism, sexism, and ageism? How is it different?

2. As a sociologist, how would you study the problem of discrimination against lesbians and gay men? What are the strengths and weaknesses of using survey research, interviews, and observations to study discrimination based on sexual orientation?

3. Some people think that state laws should be changed to give legal recognition to same-sex marriage. How would you find out what students at your college or university believe about this issue? If student organizations for gay men and lesbians exist on your campus, how might you find out about members' beliefs on this topic? Do you think their responses would differ from those of a cross-section of the student population? Why or why not?

4. In Chapters 2 through 6, we have examined inequality and discrimination as it relates to class, race-ethnicity, gender, age, and sexual orientation. If you could do one thing to reduce these problems, what would it be? What resources would be needed to implement your plan?

Chapter Seven

Prostitution, Pornography, and the Sex Industry

I was a minister's daughter. As far as I was concerned, prostitution was the last thing in the entire world I would think of. . . . Then I met my man. That's how I got into it. . . . They meet you. They're nice to you. They take you out. It's like you think you're meeting a normal guy and falling in love . . . . Some of them, they tell you right up front that you have to work for them. My man told me after two weeks. He said he cared for me, he liked me, and he felt deeply, but this is what he does and the only way I could be with him is by coming out here and working. He drove me around here. He said, "See those girls? They have furs, diamonds, houses. They have everything." I fell for it. My first day, I made $100. One hundred dollars! I couldn't believe it! After a while, you're not thinking about the sex. There's no intimacy. You don't [care] about your date. If he dropped dead, fine. Just leave your wallet behind.

—*Nadia, a nineteen-year-old prostitute in New York City*
(Kasindorf, 1988:56)

To some, like Nadia, sex work is a career choice— with willing buyers and sellers, a purely economic exchange—that is no more or less degrading than any other profession (McWilliams, 1996). Certainly in this country, it is a thriving multi-billion-dollar industry that includes prostitution, the adult film and video trade, printed pornography, escort services, massage parlors, and strip and table dancing clubs. However, prostitution and other types of sex work have always been controversial; not all social scientists even agree on whether or not the sex industry is a social problem. To better understand the controversy over prostitution, pornography, and other sex work, let's look at what constitutes deviant behavior.

DEVIANCE, THE SEX INDUSTRY, AND SOCIAL PROBLEMS

Chapter 6 defined *deviance* as a behavior, belief, or condition that violates social norms. To learn about deviance, sociologists ask such questions as the following: Why are some types of behavior considered deviant while others are not? Who determines what is deviant? Whose interests are served by stigmatizing some people as deviants but not others?

Sociologists generally take one of three approaches in studying deviance. The first approach assumes that deviance is *objectively given:* A deviant is any person who does not conform to established social norms—specifically, folkways, mores, and laws. *Folkways* are informal norms or everyday customs that may be violated without serious consequences. Contemporary U.S. folkways include eating certain foods with silverware and shaking hands when introduced to someone. In comparison, *mores* are strongly held norms with moral and ethical connotations. College football players who scalp (sell at inflated prices) the free game tickets they receive from their school for their family members and friends behave unethically and violate social mores. *Laws* are formal, standardized norms enacted by legislatures and enforced by formal sanctions such as fines and imprisonment. Laws may be either civil or criminal. *Civil law* deals with disputes between people or groups, such as an argument between a landlord and a tenant over the provisions of an apartment lease. *Criminal law* deals with public safety and well-being and defines the behaviors that constitute a *crime*—**a behavior that violates criminal law and is punishable by a fine, a jail term, or other negative sanctions.** Crimes range from relatively minor offenses, such as traffic violations, to major offenses, such as murder.

If deviance is considered to be objectively given, then prostitution and pornography are viewed as violations of deeply held convictions (folkways or mores) about good taste or morality or as significant departures from existing criminal laws (Smith and Pollack, 1994). To limit the amount of deviance and criminal behavior in society, in this view, societies employ social control mechanisms. *Social control* **refers to the systematic practices developed by social groups to encourage conformity and discourage** deviance. Social control may be either internal or external. Internal social control occurs through socialization: People learn to adhere to the norms of social groups and the larger society. Internal social control mechanisms are strengthened by external mechanisms such as the criminal justice system, which enforces laws whether or not individuals choose to adhere to them.

The second approach to studying deviance considers it to be *socially constructed:* A behavior, belief, or condition is deviant because it is labeled as such (Goode, 1996; Rubington and Weinberg, 1996). Sociologist Howard S. Becker (1963:8) summed up this approach when he wrote, "Social groups create deviance by making rules whose infraction constitutes deviance, and by applying those rules to particular people and labeling them as *outsiders*." According to Becker and other interactionists, deviance is not a quality of any act the person commits; rather, a deviant is one to whom the label of deviant has been successfully applied. Thus, street prostitutes who openly solicit customers ("johns") are more likely to be labeled deviant than are women and men who work for high-priced escort services, even though their actions are essentially the same.

The third approach assumes that deviance is rooted in *the social structure of society*, particularly in power relations. In fact, according to this approach, deviance is defined—initially and disproportionately—by the most powerful members of the dominant class, racial, and gender groups (Feagin and Feagin, 1997). Rule makers and rule enforcers protect the power and privilege of dominant group members, often at the expense of subordinate group members. Thus, prostitutes are more likely than their customers or pimps to be apprehended and punished for their alleged sexual deviance.

What is sexual deviance? Although all societies have social norms regulating sexual conduct, not all societies regulate it in the same way. In the United States alone, definitions of what is sexually deviant have varied from time to time, from place to place, and from group to group. Traditionally, at least four types of sexual conduct between heterosexual partners have been regarded as deviant: (1) premarital sex or fornication—sexual relations between two people who are not married to each other; (2) extramarital sex or adultery—sexual relations between a married person and a partner other than her or his spouse; (3) promiscuous sex—casual sexual relations with many partners; and (4) underage sex or statutory rape—sexual relations with children below the age of consent as defined by state law, usually about age fourteen, fifteen, or sixteen. Prostitution crosses several lines of *proscribed* (prohibited) sexual conduct and is viewed as deviance because it involves promiscuous behavior between two (or more) people, who may be married to other people, and sometimes involves underage sex. Despite changes in prescribed rules of sexual conduct during the twentieth century, the United States is one of the few highly industrialized nations that still defines prostitution as a crime (Jolin, 1994).

PROSTITUTION IN GLOBAL PERSPECTIVE

Narrowly defined, *prostitution* **is the sale of sexual services (of oneself or another) for money or goods and without emotional attachment.** More broadly defined, systems of prostitution refer to any industry in which women's and/or children's—and sometimes men's—bodies are bought, sold, or traded for sexual use and abuse (Giobbe, 1994). According to this definition, systems of prostitution include pornography, live sex shows, peep shows, international sexual slavery, and prostitution as narrowly defined. The vast majority of prostitutes around the globe are women and children. A certain amount of male prostitution does exist, although most boys and men in the sex industry engage in sexual encounters with other males (see McNamara, 1994; Browne and Minichiello, 1995; Snell, 1995).

 ### The World's Oldest Profession?

Prostitution has been referred to as the "world's oldest profession" because references to it can be found throughout recorded history. Still, over the past 4,000 years, prostitution has been neither totally accepted nor completely condemned. For example, while prostitution was widely accepted in ancient Greece, where upper-class prostitutes were admired and frequently became the companions of powerful Greek citizens, the prostitutes themselves were refused the status of wife—the ultimate affirmation of legitimacy for women in Greek society—and were negatively compared with so-called virtuous women in a "bad woman–good woman" dichotomy (see Bullough and Bullough, 1987; Roberts, 1992; Jolin, 1994).

In other eras, attitudes and beliefs about prostitution have ranged from generally tolerant to strongly averse. Such early Christian leaders as St. Augustine and St. Thomas Aquinas argued that prostitution was evil but encouraged tolerance toward it. According to Aquinas, prostitution served a basic need that, if unmet, would result in greater harm than prostitution itself. Later Christian leaders such as Martin Luther in sixteenth-century Europe believed that prostitution should be abolished on moral grounds (Otis, 1985; Jolin, 1994).

In the nineteenth-century feminist movement, women for the first time voiced their opinions about prostitution. Some believed that prostitution led to promiscuity and moral degeneracy in men and should therefore be eradicated. Others believed that prostitution should be legitimized as a valid expression of female sexuality outside of marriage. Recently, some advocates have suggested that prostitution should be viewed as a legitimate career choice for women (prostitute as sex worker), but others have argued that prostitution is rooted in global gender inequality (prostitute as victim of oppression).

 ### The Global Sex Industry

The past three decades have seen the industrialization, normalization, and globalization of prostitution. Although *industrialization* typically refers to the mass production of manufactured goods and services for exchange in the market, sociologist Kathleen Barry (1995:122) suggests that this term should also apply to commercialized sex manufactured within the human self. Prostitution becomes *normalized* when sex work is treated as merely a form of entertainment and there are no legal impediments to promoting it as a commodity. The *globalization* of prostitution refers to the process by which the sex industry has become increasingly global in scope (e.g., international conglomerates of hotel chains, airlines, bars, sex clubs, massage parlors, brothels, and credit card companies that have an economic interest in the global sex industry), which

SOCIAL PROBLEMS

IN GLOBAL PERSPECTIVE   BOX 7.1

Economic Development or Childhood Sexual Slavery?

Tens of thousands of children in Asia . . . are slaves working in the plantations of the 1990s: the brothels of Cambodia, India, China, Thailand, the Philippines, Taiwan, and other countries. . . . Americans and other Westerners helped build the child prostitution trade in Asia, and many of the brothel districts date . . . from the Vietnam War, or surround former American military bases. Now they sustain it with an appetite for what at home would be child molestation and rape. A result is a partnership between local people, who run the brothels, and Westerners like the one who posted an item on the Internet informing sex tourists that in Cambodia "a six-year-old is available for US$3." (Kristof, 1996b:1,6)

Although it is impossible to know exactly how many child prostitutes there are in the world, recent estimates suggest that as many as 1 million girls and boys aged seventeen and younger engage in prostitution in Asia alone. Initially, social analysts believed that the end of

the Vietnam War and economic development would end child prostitution in Asian cities such as Shanghai, Hong Kong, and Hanoi, where brothels have existed for many years. But this has not happened. Instead, sex tourism has emerged as a form of economic development, and the AIDS scare has dramatically increased child prostitution in some nations. Brothel owners purchase girls as young as twelve and force them to become house prostitutes. Girls who try to escape are caught, severely beaten, and sometimes starved. While imprisoned in the brothel, they are forced to have sex with many customers each night (Kristof, 1996b).

In Thailand, a large sex industry services Thai men and foreigners. Most of the prostitutes are younger than fifteen years old. In impoverished areas young girls can no longer earn a living in agriculture, and their opportunities in the labor market are limited to extremely low-wage production and service jobs—often assembly-line work for transnational corporations. In contrast, sex work offers a rate of pay that—though still very low—can be 25 times higher than the wages for seamstresses or domestics. Sex-based tourism in Thailand is estimated at $4 billion

---

has occured as people's political, economic, and cultural lives have become linked globally (Barry, 1995; Davidson, 1996). For evidence of this globalization, one has only to look at recent investigations by journalists and sociologists of the use of child prostitutes in the sex tourism industry (see Box 7.1).

The demand for prostitution is greatest when large numbers of men are congregated for extended periods of time in the military or on business far from home. A connection between wartime rape and increased prostitution has been documented for the Vietnam War and more recently for the wars in El Salvador and Bosnia. Large populations of refugees

and victims of rape and sexual violence tend to be exploited by networks of pimps and organized crime gangs such as the yakuza in Japan (Women's International Network, 1995).

Although recent research has indicated that the global sex industry, especially prostitution, contributes to the transmission of HIV, the virus that causes AIDS (Gil et al., 1996; Purvis, 1996), many agencies and governments have not come to grips with the problem. For example, the Japanese Foundation for AIDS Prevention, an organization affiliated with the Japanese government, launched a poster campaign featuring a grinning, middle-aged man

Do the two in this photo look like mother and daughter? Actually, both are employed in a Cambodian brothel. What global social and economic factors contribute to the growing number of young girls working in the sex industry?

a year. In fact, because many foreign visitors consider sex the country's chief attraction, on the macroeconomic level sex is now part of the economy of international domination.

Some families sell their daughters into prostitution out of economic necessity. Indenturing a daughter to sex industry recruiters makes it possible for an entire rural family to survive. However, others simply do not want another mouth to feed or want to acquire material possessions. One woman in Manila periodically sells the sexual services of her two daughters, ages ten and twelve, to a Japanese man for cash so that she can purchase amenities such as a karaoke music system, which costs several hundred dollars, for her shack, where the stench of garbage and an open sewer waft into the room (Kristof, 1996b:6).

Analysts have recently suggested that the prostitution industry has become more thoroughly capitalistic and globalized than ever before. From this point of view, advocates of social change suggest that sex workers should be thought of as working people entitled to human rights and workers' rights (see Kempadoo and Doezema, 1998). How is the global sex industry linked to the international division of labor and other forms of globalization?

wearing a business suit and displaying his passport, with a caption reading, "Have a nice trip! But be careful of AIDS." The Japanese government is obviously aware that many businessmen participate in sex tourism abroad (Sachs, 1994), but the poster gives a mixed message rather than a strong warning.

The global sex industry reflects the economic disparity between the poorest regions of the world—where women and children may be bought, sold, or traded like any other commodity—and the richest regions, such as Europe and North America, where many of the global sex industry's consumers reside (see Bauerlein, 1995; Davidson, 1996).

PROSTITUTION IN THE UNITED STATES

Trafficking in women and children is as great a problem in the United States as it is in low-income nations. In recent years, organized prostitution networks have been identified in urban, suburban, and rural areas of the country. Newspaper accounts over the past decade have described thousands of incidences in which immigrant women have been forced to have sex with many men to pay off their passage to the United States. Women and children from Asia and Mexico have been among the most frequently exploited by smugglers. Today, the U.S. mail-order bride industry is a multimillion dollar business that markets women from low-income nations as "brides" to men in the United States and other Western nations (*Factbook on Global Sexual Exploitation,* 1999).

 The Nature of Prostitution

Clearly not all prostitutes are alike: Life experiences, family backgrounds, years of formal education, locales of operation, types of customers, and methods of doing business vary widely. Even with these differences, however, sociologists have identified five levels or tiers of prostitution, ranging from escort prostitutes to street prostitutes and women exchanging sex for drugs in crack houses.

Top-tier prostitutes typically are referred to as *escorts* or *call girls* and *call boys*. They are considered the upper echelon in prostitution because they tend to earn higher fees and have more selectivity in their working conditions and customers than do other prostitutes (see Macy, 1996). Escort prostitutes typically have more of formal education than other types of prostitutes do. Most of them do not think of themselves as prostitutes. Many dress nicely—and often conservatively—so that they do not call undue attention to themselves at luxury hotels, clubs, and apartment buildings. Sydney Biddle Barrows (1986:69), the former owner of a well-known New York escort service, explains:

> While good looks were generally important [for escort prostitutes], I was more concerned with the *right* look. Men have always responded to the way I dress, and I decided that the elegant, classic look that worked for me would also work for the girls. . . . Quite a few of the new girls had no money and nothing appropriate to wear, so I would either lend them something of mine or take them to Saks and charge whatever they needed on my credit card. They would pay me back from their future earnings.

Escort prostitutes work "on call," going out to see customers who are referred to them by their escort service, pimp, or other procurers such as hotel concierges and taxi drivers who receive a percentage of the prostitute's fees. Although their work is not as visible as that of other prostitutes, they face some of the same hazards, including abusive customers and sexually transmitted diseases.

The second tier of prostitutes is comprised of hustlers, strippers, and table dancers who engage in prostitution on the side. People in this tier work out of night clubs, bars, and strip joints primarily. The hustlers are sometimes referred to as *bar girls* or *bar boys* because they are supposed to pressure (hustle) customers to buy drinks. Most hustlers are not paid by the bar but earn their livelihood by negotiating sexual favors with potential customers, who often are lonely and want someone to talk to as well as to have sex with (Devereaux, 1987).

The third tier is made up of *house girls* who work in brothels (houses of prostitution) run by a madam or a pimp who collects up to half of the fees earned by the women. Customers choose "dates" from women lined up in a parlor or receiving room. House prostitutes are not allowed to engage in "dirty hustling" (winking, running one's tongue over one's lips, or shaking a leg) or to turn down a customer (Devereaux, 1987). Since prostitution is illegal in most states, houses of prostitution typically operate as body-painting studios, massage parlors, or other businesses. The only legal brothels in the United States are located in eleven counties in Nevada where prostitution has been decriminalized. However, the state of Nevada requires house prostitutes to register, be fingerprinted, pay a state business fee, and provide up-to-date medical certification that they are free of sexually transmitted diseases.

Near the bottom tier of prostitution are *streetwalkers,* who publicly solicit customers and charge by the "trick." Most street prostitutes work a specific location and defend it from other prostitutes, as Nadia (whom we met earlier) explains:

> I only work this corner, 'cause this is the first-class street. . . . Even here, you know there's always the chance you're going with someone who might want to kill you. My [pimp] drives around to make sure I'm okay, but not every day. So you're always alert. You watch your date's every move. You're sexy, you're smiling, you're teasing, everything, but you're watching their every move. You're always listening to their conversation so you can know what they're leading up to. Then you're okay. (quoted in Kasindorf, 1988:56)

Nadia and other streetwalkers derive status and some degree of protection from their pimps. However, researchers have also documented the exploitative and sometimes violent nature of the pimp–prostitute relationship.

The very bottom tier of prostitution is occupied by women who are addicted to crack cocaine and engage in crack-for-sex exchanges (Fullilove et al., 1992). Researchers have found that many crack-addicted women perform unprotected oral sex on men in crack houses in exchange for hits of crack. According to one study,

> Some men will enter a crack house, purchase enough rocks for two people for several hours, and then make it clear to every woman in the house what he has in mind. . . . [There] seems to be an expectation [in the crack house] that if a man wants to have sex with a woman, she will not oppose the offer. The expectations are implicit. Everyone involved—the house owner, the male user/customer, and the female user/prostitute are all aware of what is expected. (Inciardi et al., 1993b:74–75)

Although less research has been done on prostitution tiers in male prostitution, the tiers appear to be similar to those of female prostitution except that most customers are of the same gender as the prostitute. For example, in her report on escort services, journalist Marianna Macy (1996:249) found that some male escorts exist but that "Men normally go see men." Some male prostitutes work as hustlers in bars and night clubs, where they typically wear blue jeans, leather jackets, and boots, seeking to project a strong heterosexual image. Sexual orientation is frequently an issue with male prostitutes, some of whom do not define themselves as gay and limit the types of sexual acts they are willing to perform. Others view sex strictly as an economic exchange by defining work-related sex as "not real sex" (Browne and Minichiello, 1995).

 The Extent of Prostitution

Estimates of the number of working prostitutes in the United States range from 100,000 to more than 500,000, but accurate estimates are impossible for several reasons (Reynolds, 1986). First, there is the question of how prostitution is defined. Second,

because of its illegal nature, much prostitution is not reported. Third, arrest records—which are about the only source of official information on prostitution—do not reflect the extent of prostitution. Because they visibly solicit customers, streetwalkers are more likely to be apprehended, tried, and convicted of prostitution than are prostitutes working for exclusive escort services. Finally, many people drift into and out of prostitution, considering it temporary work between full-time jobs or as part-time work while attending school (Potterat et al., 1990).

 Prostitution and Age, Class, and Race

Although some prostitutes are as young as thirteen or fourteen, the vast majority are between the ages of seventeen and twenty-four. The peak earning age appears to be about twenty-two (Clinard and Meier, 1989; DePasquale, 1999). In contrast, the typical male customer is middle-aged, white, and married, although some teenage and college-age males also hire prostitutes (National Victims Resource Center, 1991). Often, the age difference between teenage prostitutes and older customers is striking, as a woman forced into prostitution at age thirteen by a pimp explains:

> The men who bought me—the tricks—knew I was an adolescent. Most of them were in their 50s and 60s. They had daughters and granddaughters my age. They knew a child's face when they looked into it. . . . It was even clearer that I was sexually inexperienced. So they showed me pornography to teach me and ignored my tears as they positioned my body like the women in the pictures, and used me. (Giobbe, 1993:38)

Although a small percentage of teenagers enter prostitution through coercion, most are runaways who have left home because of sexual abuse or other family problems. Some teen prostitutes are "throwaways"—thrown out of their homes by parents or other family members (Snell, 1995; Vissing, 1996). Regardless of their prior history, many teens become prostitutes because prostitution is the best—or only—job they can get.

Social class is directly linked to prostitution: Lower-income and poverty-level women and men are far more likely to become prostitutes than are more affluent people (Miller, 1986). Some people with little formal education and few job skills view prostitution as an economic necessity. As one woman stated, "I make good money [as a prostitute]. That's why I do it; if I worked at McDonald's for minimum wage, then I'd feel degraded" (quoted in McWilliams, 1996: 340). However, women working for exclusive escort services are more likely to have attended college and come from the middle or upper-middle class. For example, Heidi Fleiss—the so-called Hollywood madam—is the daughter of a prominent California physician.

Race is also an important factor in prostitution. Sociologist Patricia Hill Collins (1991) suggests that

African American women are affected by the widespread image of black women as sexually promiscuous and therefore potential prostitutes. Collins traces the roots of this stereotype to the era of slavery when black women—and black men and children—were at the mercy of white male slave owners and their sexual desires. According to Collins (1991:175), prostitution exists within a "complex web of political and economic relationships whereby sexuality is conceptualized along intersecting axes of race and gender." Today, prostitution remains linked to the ongoing economic, political, and social exploitation of people of color, especially women. At the same time, since 1971, there has been a significant reversal in the racial composition of people arrested for

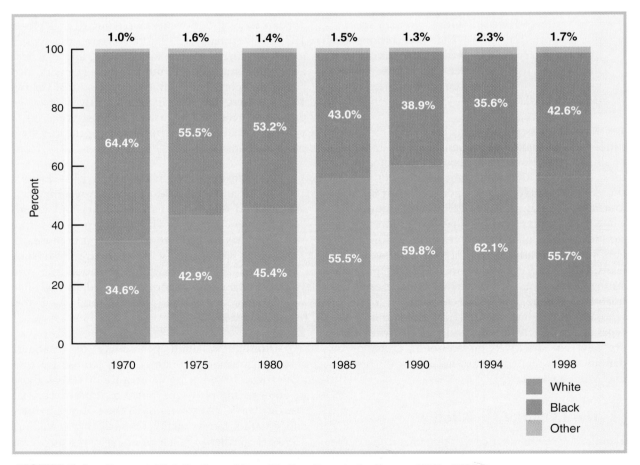

FIGURE 7.1   *Percent Distribution of Prostitution Arrests by Race, 1970–1998*
Sources: Federal Bureau of Investigation, 1999; U.S. Bureau of the Census, 1998.

prostitution and commercialized vice, which includes keeping a brothel, procuring (pimping), and transporting women for immoral purposes (see Figure 7.1).

SOCIOLOGICAL PERSPECTIVES ON PROSTITUTION

Sociologists use a variety of perspectives to examine prostitution as a social problem. Functionalists focus on how deviance—including prostitution—serves important functions in society. Interactionists investigate microlevel concerns, such as how and why people become prostitutes and how the stigmatization affects their self-esteem. Conflict perspectives seek to explain how the powerful enact their moral beliefs into law and how prostitution is related to capitalism and/or patriarchy.

 ### The Functionalist Perspective

Functionalists believe that the presence of a certain amount of deviance in society contributes to its overall stability. According to early sociologist Emile Durkheim, deviance clarifies social norms and helps societies to maintain social control over people's behavior. By punishing those who engage in deviant behavior such as prostitution, the society reaffirms its commitment to its sexual norms and creates loyalty to the society as people bind together to oppose the behavior.

According to sociologist Kingsley Davis (1937), in societies that have restrictive norms governing sexual conduct, including the United States, prostitution will always exist because it serves important functions. First, it provides quick, impersonal sexual gratification that does not require emotional attachment or a continuing relationship with another person (Freund et al., 1991). Second, prostitution provides a sexual outlet for men who do not have ongoing sexual relationships because they are not married or have heavy work schedules. Third, prostitution provides people with the opportunity to engage in sexual practices—multiple sex partners, fellatio (oral stimulation of the male genitalia), cunnilingus (oral stimulation of the female genitalia), anal intercourse, or sado-

masochism (S&M), including the use of such devices as handcuffs, whips, and chains—that regular sex partners or spouses might view as immoral or distasteful. Fourth, prostitution protects the family as a social institution by making a distinction between "bad girls" or "bad boys"—with whom one engages in promiscuous sexual behavior—and "good girls" and "good boys"—with whom one establishes a family. Finally, prostitution benefits the economy by providing jobs for people who have limited formal education and job skills.

 ### The Interactionist Perspective

Why do people become prostitutes? Do some prostitutes like their work? Interactionists investigate questions such as these by using a social psychological framework, for example, by examining people's lived experiences. Here is an excerpt from an interview with a prostitute named Dolores:

> I set my own schedule. I set my own limits and made my own rules, and I didn't have to answer to anyone. I learned a lot about myself: what I would and would not do for money, and what I was willing to do for the right amount of money. . . . I didn't have to see anyone I didn't want to see. If a man was too boring or too rough or too crude or took too much time, I didn't have to see him again. I loved it. (French, 1988:180)

Dolores's remarks suggest that some people become prostitutes because it provides them with greater autonomy and more career options than they otherwise would have. These reasons fit with sociologist Howard Becker's (1963) suggestion that entering a deviant career is similar in many ways to entering any other occupation. The primary difference is the labeling that goes with a deviant career. Public labeling of people as deviant and their acceptance or rejection of that label are crucial factors in determining whether or not a person stays in a deviant career. Some people are more willing than others to accept the label "deviant" or may believe they have no other option.

Why do men seek out prostitutes? Research by interactionists suggests that some young men seek out prostitutes to fulfill what they believe is a rite of passage from boyhood to manhood. Consider, for example, John's comments after several trips to a house of prostitution:

> We went back to school, Mike and I, after going to that first whorehouse. We were probably the only two guys in the class that had done it. We were celebrities. We had crowds around us when we'd tell them all the details, how great it was, what studs we were. . . . My reaction to all this was it wasn't really very exciting. After all the talk you hear about it, all the writing, all the pictures, all the taboos about sex, I thought, "For this? This is what it was about?" . . . It wasn't something bad; it just wasn't nearly as exciting as I thought it would be. But we thought, "This is a good chance to learn," so we went back several times. . . . I can remember up to eleven. . . . I always thought I'd keep count all my life; that was part of what being a man was all about. (quoted in Raphael, 1988:74–75)

Social analysts suggest that the need of men of all ages to validate their sexual prowess or reaffirm their masculinity is an important factor in their seeking out prostitutes (Raphael, 1988). Interactionist perspectives such as these highlight how people define social realities—such as the importance of sexual prowess or masculinity—in light of competing and often contradictory values they have learned through socialization.

 The Conflict Perspective

Conflict perspectives on prostitution highlight the relationship between power in society and sex work: The laws that make prostitution illegal are created by powerful dominant group members who seek to maintain cultural dominance by criminalizing sexual conduct that they consider immoral or in bad taste (Barry, 1995).

Conflict analysts using a liberal feminist framework believe that prostitution should be *decriminalized*—meaning that laws making prostitution a crime should be repealed. These analysts argue that prostitution is a *victimless crime*—a **crime that many people believe has no real victim because it involves willing participants in an economic exchange.** Therefore sex workers should not be harassed by police and the courts. According to Margo St. James, a former prostitute and founder of

an activist group called COYOTE (Call Off Your Old Tired Ethics), "The profession itself is not abusive; it's the illegality; it's the humiliation and degradation that is dealt to them at the hands of the police" (quoted in McWilliams, 1996:340). In other words, prostitution is sex work in the sex industry and should be treated as a labor issue.

Conflict perspectives using Marxist feminist and radical feminist frameworks suggest that women become prostitutes because of structural factors such as economic inequality and patriarchy (Jolin, 1994). Capitalism and patriarchy foster economic inequality between women and men and force women to view their bodies as simply commodities: "when a man has bought a woman's body for his use as if it were like any other commodity . . . the sex act itself provides acknowledgment of patriarchal right. When women's bodies are on sale as commodities in the capitalist market . . . men gain public acknowledgment as women's sexual masters" (Pateman, 1994:132).

According to Marxist feminists, the only way to eliminate prostitution is to reduce disparities in income levels between women and men and eliminate poverty. However, radical feminists believe that prostitution will not be eliminated until patriarchy is ended.

Conflict theorists who focus on the interrelationship of race, class, and gender in examining social problems suggest that criminalizing prostitution uniquely affects poor women, especially poor women of color, who are overrepresented among street prostitutes. According to these theorists, white male supremacy—which traditionally preserves the best-paying jobs for men—makes women of color particularly vulnerable to recruitment or coercion into prostitution. As one woman explains: "As a Black coming up in Indiana in the steel mill industry up there, they hired men. All the men got jobs in the mills there; very few women. . . . but there were lots of jobs for you in strip joints, dancing, or even down at some of the restaurants and bars outside of the steel mills for when the guys came in" (quoted in Giobbe, 1994:122).

Analysts using this framework also note that discrimination in law enforcement uniquely affects women of color. For example, law enforcement officials target street prostitutes and other sex workers, particularly when political elites decide to crack down on "deviant" behavior such as prostitution and pornography (Barry, 1995).

PORNOGRAPHY

Nina Hartley, founder of the Pink Ladies club, a group of women in the pornography industry, wrote of herself (1994, 176–177):

> "A feminist porno star?" Right, tell me another one, I can hear some feminists saying . . . why porno? Simple—I'm an exhibitionist with a cause: to make sexually graphic (hard core) erotica, and today's porno is the only game in town. . . . As I examine my life, I uncover the myriad influences that led me to conclude that it was perfectly natural for me to choose a career in adult films. . . . I stripped once a week while getting my bachelor's degree in nursing, magna cum laude. . . . I went into full time [adult] movie work immediately following graduation.

Pornography **is the graphic depiction of sexual behavior through pictures and/or words—including by electronic or other data retrieval systems—in a manner that is intended to be sexually arousing.** Although Hartley claims to be a feminist porn star, many social analysts, as Hartley herself notes, believe that this is a contradiction in terms. Most of these analysts believe pornography is a pressing social problem. But what kind of social problem is it? Religious groups typically construe pornography as a social problem because they say it is obscene. On the other hand, social analysts, particularly feminists, usually frame the problem in terms of patriarchy—male oppression of women (Leong, 1991). Thus, the specific nature of pornography as a social problem is not clear cut, as sociologist Wai-Teng Leong (1991:91) explains:

> Some religious groups preach that pornography propagates perverse sexualities and its proliferation portends the poverty of morality. Some women promulgate the view that pornography preserves and promotes patriarchal power. Some other women claim that pornography in popular music leads to all kinds of teenage pathology. On the other hand, producers of pornography argue that their products have the positive potential of catharsis, channeling off sexual desires into masturbatory fantasies. And many people who purchase pornography consume it in the privacy of

their homes and cannot comprehend why a private matter should become a public problem.

Adding to the confusion over the nature of pornography as a social problem is the difficulty social scientists have in determining what constitutes pornography. Over time public attitudes change regarding what should be tolerated and what should be banned because of *obscenity*—**the legal term for pornographic materials that are offensive by generally accepted standards of decency.**

Who decides what is obscene? According to what criteria? In *Miller* v. *California* (1973), the U.S. Supreme Court held that material can be considered legally obscene only if it meets three criteria: (1) The material as a whole appeals to prurient interests (lustful ideas or desires), (2) the material depicts sexual conduct in a patently offensive way as defined by state or federal law, and (3) the work as a whole lacks serious literary, artistic, political, or scientific value (Russell, 1993). But according to some analysts, including Leong (1991), the Court's decision has contributed to the social construction of pornography as a social problem.

◢ The Social Construction of Pornography as a Social Problem

The social construction of pornography as a social problem involves both a cognitive framework and a moral framework. The cognitive framework refers to the reality or factualness of the situation that constitutes the "problem." In regard to pornographic materials, one cognitive framework might be based on the assumption that pornography *actually affects* people's actions or attitudes; an opposing cognitive framework might be based on the assumption that pornography is a fantasy mechanism that allows people to express the forbidden without actually engaging in forbidden behavior (Kipnis, 1996). The moral framework refers to arguments as to whether something is immoral or unjust. In the case of pornography, moral condemnation arises from the belief that graphic representations of sexuality are degrading, violent, and sinful. From this perspective, pornography is less about sex than about violating taboos in society. The moral framework often distinguishes between pornography and *erotica*—**materials that depict consensual sexual activities that are sought by and pleasurable to all parties involved.** According to sociologist Diana E. H. Russell (1993), materials can be considered erotic—rather than obscene—only if they show respect for all human beings and are free of sexism, racism, and homophobia. Contemporary erotica might include romance novels that describe two consenting adults participating in sexual intercourse (see Snitow, 1994). On the other hand, materials depicting violent assault or the sexual exploitation of children would be considered pornographic or obscene. However, the distinction appears to be highly subjective, as feminist scholar Ellen Willis (1981:222) notes: "Attempts to sort out good erotica from bad porn inevitably come down to 'What turns me on is erotic: what turns you on is pornographic.'"

 ## The Nature and Extent of Pornography

As part of the multibillion-dollar sex industry, pornography is profitable to many people, including investors, film makers, and owners of stores that distribute such materials. *Hard-core* pornography is material that explicitly depicts sexual acts and/or genitals. In contrast, *soft-core* pornography is suggestive but does not depict actual intercourse or genitals.

Technological innovations such as digital media have greatly increased the variety of pornographic materials available as well as methods of distribution. Although some people visit live peep shows and "X-rated" adult bookstores and video arcades, sexually explicit materials are available at home or in the office through mail-order services, movies on "X-rated" cable television channels, dial-a-porn, digitized scans and striptease QuickTime movies, and private computer bulletin boards and Usenet newsgroups specializing in adult chat areas and graphics exchanges on the Internet.

Hard-core pornographic films gross over $400 million a year in the United States alone. It is not uncommon for a small production company that shoots, manufactures, and distributes such videos to gross more than $1 million a year (*New York Times*, 1993). However, "Ron," who works in the pornography industry, suggests that these profits do not extend to most actors in the films:

> You'd have to go a long way to find an industry with worse labor practices. They work people very hard; they pay them very little, really, for what they do. . . . As a porn performer, you're

putting up with a couple of days of hard, even abusive, behavior that compromises your ability to do anything else in your life ever again, because the piece of evidence of your past misbehavior continues to exist. . . . But after you've done porn films, you can't do anything else. You can't even do commercials. . . . Another thing. There's an endless appetite for new faces and new bodies, which means they work [actors] to death for about six months or a year, put out twenty to thirty videos with them. And then they can't get work any more. New ones have come along. The audience is sick of looking at the old ones and wants to see new ones. (quoted in Stoller 1991:209–210)

According to some social analysts, pornography is a prime example of the principle of supply and demand. As long as demand remains high, pornographers will continue to market their goods and services and find new ways to use technology. According to Walter Kendrick, a scholar whose research focuses on pornography:

> Pornographers have been the most inventive and resourceful users of whatever medium comes along because they and their audience have always wanted innovations. Pornographers are excluded from the mainstream channels, so they look around for something new, and the audience has a desire to try any innovation that gives them greater realism or immediacy. (quoted in Tierney, 1994:H18)

Each new development in technology changes the meaning of pornography and brings new demands for regulation or censorship. Today, interactive media presentations and pornography on the Internet are widely believed to be a far more powerful influence on people, especially children, than the printed word is (see Box 7.2).

Research on Pornography

During the past three decades, two presidential commissions have examined pornography and reached contradictory conclusions. The 1970 U.S. Commission on Pornography and Obscenity found no conclusive links between pornography and sex crimes or antisocial behavior. However, the 1986 Attorney

Are there any businesses like this in your community? Why do many people believe that establishments such as this not only harm individuals and their families but also the larger community?

General's Commission on Pornography (known as the Meese Commission) concluded that pornography is dangerous, causes sex crimes, increases aggression in males, inspires sexism against women, and encourages *pedophilia* (adults engaging in sexual intercourse with children). Although some members strongly disagreed, the Meese Commission concluded that sexually explicit materials should be further restricted and obscenity laws should be more stringently enforced.

Sociologists do not agree on the extent to which pornography that depicts excessive sex, violence, and the domination of one person by another affects behavior. More than 80 percent of X-rated films in one study included scenes showing women dominated and exploited by men. The vast majority of these films portrayed physical aggression against women, and about half explicitly depicted rape (Cowan et al., 1988; Cowan and O'Brien, 1990). Explicit violence is also part of many videos in the adult section of video stores (see Duncan, 1991). Nevertheless, studies have not established that watching such films and videos contributes to aggressive or violent behavior in viewers, and most people therefore do not support efforts to censor adults' access to pornographic material.

Pornography and Age, Gender, Class, and Race

Because viewing pornography is a secretive activity, data on the consumers of various forms are limited. Some studies have found that the typical customer of an adult bookstore is a white, relatively well-educated, married middle-class man between the ages of twenty-five and sixty-six. Other studies have found that younger and more educated adults express more accepting attitudes toward pornography than do older, less educated adults (Lottes, 1993).

Overall, men watch more sexually explicit material and hold more favorable attitudes toward it than women do. Some analysts attribute this difference to gender role socialization. In a society in which men are socialized to be sexual initiators and often fear rejection, pornography is satisfying because it typically shows a willing female partner. In contrast, women have been socialized to respond negatively to material showing nude bodies and male pleasure that may occur at the expense of a woman's sense of safety and dignity (see Reiss, 1986). However, in recent years, more women have become consumers of *Playgirl* magazine, erotic novels and videos such as those by Candida Royalle, a former porn star, that are made specifically for women (see Lottes, 1993; Macy, 1996).

In general, women are more vocal than men in opposing pornography. According to sociologist Michael Kimmel (1990), men are relatively silent for several reasons: embarrassment or guilt for having enjoyed pornography, anger at women's interference in male privilege, lack of interest in what they perceive to be a nonissue, fear that speaking out will lead to questions about their masculinity, reluctance to talk openly about their sexual feelings, and confusion about "what it means to be a 'real man' in contemporary society" (Kimmel, 1987:121).

According to film scholar Laura Kipnis (1996), much of the sentiment against pornography is rooted in class-based elitism: Opposition to pornography is a form of snobbery related to maintaining class distinctions in society. From this perspective, rejecting pornography amounts to rejecting all that is vulgar, trashy, and lower class. Although Kipnis does not suggest that all consumers of pornography are lower class, she believes that members of the upper classes typically view pornography consumers as lower-class people who may imitate the images

SOCIAL PROBLEMS

AND INFORMATION TECHNOLOGY

BOX 7.2

Cracking Down on Internet Child Pornography

Anonymity on the Internet makes it difficult to detect child pornography and to apprehend those who distribute or consume such materials. (Simon, 1999)

Since its inception in 1989, the Internet has become the source of vast amounts of beneficial information. However, this new form of information technology has also facilitated the dissemination of child pornography. According to one legal analyst, the Internet has changed the manner in which pornography can be created, distributed, and accessed:

Prior to the invention of the Internet, consumers and distributors of child pornography had to know each other or have connections to exchange materials. Underground networks facilitated the trade of photographs or videos through the mail or in person. Currently, however, subscribers . . . can simply download graphic images through their modems to be able to view and print images.

The anonymity available on the Internet hinders the detection of child pornography. A user can create any identity and transmit a message from California, through New Zealand, and then to Arkansas, making it impossible to determine the origin. Furthermore, "anonymous remailers" enable a user to re-route outgoing messages by removing the source address, assigning an anonymous identification code number with the remailer's address, and forwarding it to the final destination. (Simon, 1999:7)

Just as the distribution of child pornography has been facilitated by the Internet, sexually explicit visual depictions of children (and adults) have become much easier to create and mass produce. Scanners, video cameras, and graphics software packages are an integral part of the production of child pornography today (Simon, 1999).

What social policy issues are raised by the increasing availability of pornographic materials? One major consideration is the use of children under the age of 18 in porno-

---

they see. Similarly, women who appear in pornography or consume it are seen as brainwashed or unenlightened people who lack "class."

In another class analysis of pornography, philosopher Alan Soble (1986) linked men's use of pornography with their feelings of boredom and powerlessness, which are the result of capitalist work relations, the nature of labor, and the centralization of economics and politics. For these men, pornography becomes a diversion—a means of escaping from the dull, predictable world of work. Soble suggests that consumers of pornography use the material to construct fantasies and gain a sense of control; it gives men the opportunity—otherwise rarely available—to organize the world and conduct its events according to their own wishes and tastes.

In Soble's eyes, pornography consumption is not an expression of men's power as much as it is an expression of their lack of power (Soble, 1986).

In other research, sociologists Alice Mayall and Diana E. H. Russell (1993) have detailed how different racial-ethnic groups are portrayed in pornography. Examining materials in a heterosexual pornography store, the researchers found that skin color is a highly salient issue: White women were featured in 92 percent of the pornography, perhaps because they fulfill traditional stereotypes equating female beauty with white skin and Caucasian features (Mayall and Russell, 1993).

People of color were more likely to be found in materials featuring rape, bondage and sadomasochism, anal sex, sex with children, and sex between

graphic depictions. Another is the question of whether or not child pornography contributes to pedophilia (defined as an abnormal condition in which an adult has a sexual desire for children). Further complicating this issue is the fact that some child pornographers claim that the actors they use are over the age of 18 and simply appear to be younger or that the children shown are not actual children but rather computer-generated images—"virtual" actors.

The Child Pornography Prevention Act (CPPA) of 1996 sought to address some of the larger issues surrounding the controversial topic of child pornography on the Internet. Although previous legislation had criminalized child pornography, CPPA was passed by Congress specifically to address growing concerns about child pornography, particularly depictions of what *appear to be* minors (persons below age 18) engaging in sexually explicit conduct. According to CPPA, child pornography includes sexual depictions that allow observers to believe they are actually seeing minors engaged in sexual conduct. Thus, under CPPA, possession of any type of child pornography, whether or not the material involves actual children and whether or not the children are actually engaged in sexual conduct, is a criminal offense if it has been transported or produced using materials that have been transported in interstate commerce. (Because the Internet involves the use of telephone lines or other means of transmitting information from place to place and state to state, data received via the Internet is considered to be part of interstate commerce that can be regulated by the federal government.)

What social policy issues are raised by CPPA? Some critics argue that freedom of expression involving youthful-looking adults is limited by this statute; therefore, the statute is unconstitutional. Other critics raise the issue of privacy, asserting that people should be able to read and view whatever they want. Suppose, they say, someone else used your computer, downloaded child pornography, you were accused of possessing that pornography. On the other hand, supporters of laws such as CPPA argue that these concerns are outweighed by the necessity of protecting children from being victimized by child pornographers. What do you think?

women. Among women of color, African American women were most frequently featured, followed by Asian or Asian American women, and Latinas. African American men who consume pornography have a choice of buying magazines portraying only whites, white men with African American women, or African American men with white women. The researchers were unable to determine whether these options were based on the preferences of consumers or those of the makers of pornography (Mayall and Russell, 1993). Sociologist Patricia Hill Collins (1991) suggests that racism in pornography can be traced to the oppression of black women in slavery: African American women were depicted as animals and used as sex objects for the pleasure of white men. Others have noted that at the same time that the white man was exploiting the black woman, he was obsessive about protecting the white woman from the black man (Gardner, 1994).

THE FUTURE OF PORNOGRAPHY AND THE SEX INDUSTRY

Public opinion polls show that people in the United States are ambivalent about pornography and other aspects of the sex industry. While they acknowledge that the sex industry may produce goods and services that serve as a "safety valve" for some, many believe that these goods and services can be a "trigger" for others. There does seem to be consensus

Sexually explicit sites on the Internet are available to many students through their university computer accounts. Should colleges and universities be able to restrict students' access to computer pornography? Why or why not?

regarding children and pornography: Children should be shielded from some materials. At this point, however, the consensus breaks down. Who should do the shielding and what materials should be banned?

The controversy over sexually explicit materials is particularly strong in schools, and some school boards have banned books and audiovisual materials they consider obscene. For example, *Our Bodies, Ourselves,* a women's health manual, has been banned in some schools because of its written material and pictures. Many adults would also like to see children shielded from sexually explicit movies, television shows, and rock music videos—to say nothing of the sophisticated adult entertainment on child-oriented gaming platforms such as the CD-equipped Sega Genesis (Stefanac, 1993).

Children also have access to sexually explicit materials on the Internet. Although Congress passed the Communications Decency Act in 1996, which made it a crime for a person to knowingly circulate "patently offensive" sexual material to on-line sites

that are accessible to users under age eighteen, the law was held to be unconstitutional. The censorship wars—both on line and in real life—continue to pose serious social policy questions.

All of the issues pertaining to pornography and censorship that we've discussed bring us to a point we've made in previous chapters: How people view social problems affects how they believe such problems should be solved. People seem to view pornography in one of four ways: liberal, religious conservative, antipornography feminist, and anticensorship feminist (Segal, 1990; Berger et al., 1991). Each point of view espouses a different solution to the problem of pornography.

According to the *liberal* point of view, pornography may offend some people but brings harmless pleasure to others. It may even serve as a safety valve for those who have no other sexual outlet. Moreover, no scientific evidence links pornography to actual sexual violence or degradation of women. Therefore the social problem is not really pornography but censorship—people attempting to impose their morals on others and thereby violating First Amendment rights (Cottle et al., 1989).

In contrast, from a *religious conservative* point of view, pornography is a threat to the moral values of society, especially family values. Pornography encourages people to have sexual intercourse outside marriage and to engage in deviant sexual behavior. Therefore sexually explicit and violent materials should be censored to protect families and societal values.

Feminist analysts are generally critical of pornography because it is sexist in its portrayal of women, emphasizes male dominance and female submission, and encourages the valuing of women according to their ability to please men. However, not all feminists agree on what—if anything—should be done about pornography. *Antipornography feminists* believe that pornography is a primary source of male oppression of, and violence against, women. Viewing pornography as a form of sexual discrimination that diminishes women's opportunities in all areas of life, including employment, education, and freedom of movement, they believe it should be restricted or eliminated (see MacKinnon, 1987; Dworkin, 1988). In this view, pornography becomes a a civil rights issue, and antipornography feminists argue that communities should pass antipornography ordinances that would enable people who have been victimized by pornography to sue pornographers for damages (see Russell, 1993).

In contrast, *anticensorship feminists* do not believe that any single factor such as pornography causes women's subordination. Focusing on pornography as the primary source of sexual oppression, they say, "downplays the sexism and misogyny at work within all of our most respectable social institutions and practices, whether judicial, legal, familial, occupational, religious, scientific, or cultural" (Segal, 1990:32). Therefore pornography should not be censored because open discussions about sexuality and sexual practices promote women's sexual freedom and their right to express themselves (Willis, 1983; Kaminer, 1990).

The controversy over censorship may be rapidly becoming obsolete in a world linked by the Internet and other rapid sources of communication. In such a world, whose community standards should be applied in determining whether on-line materials are obscene? Should we use the standards of Berkeley, California, or those of Tokyo, Japan? Should we use the standards of the community where the image is posted, or the community where it is viewed, or both? Censorship is a very complicated proposition in the global marketplace. To restrict local access to a picture, story, or idea on the Internet, access must be blocked to computer users all over the world. What are Internet service providers such as CompuServe

and America Online to do? For instance, German authorities asked one U.S.-based corporation in 1996 not to let German subscribers access 200 discussion groups and picture databases that allegedly violated German pornography laws. To meet this request, CompuServe had to block worldwide access to those sites. Although the ban was only temporary, it sent shock waves throughout the community of Internet users, who became concerned that material deemed pornographic or obscene by people anywhere in the world could become unavailable everywhere. Among the materials Germany sought to ban were sexuality support groups for the handicapped and a bulletin board for gay men and lesbians that provided a network for gay youths (*Time*, 1996b).

In this chapter, we have focused on prostitution and materials that are defined as pornographic, obscene, and erotic. However, it is important to note that mainstream media—including magazines, movies, videos, television programming, and specifically music videos shown on MTV and other channels—also may contribute to negative images of women and the exploitation of children. Furthermore, the mainstream media can desensitize people to sexual assault, rape, violence, and murder through repeated exposure to depictions of women as victims and sex objects and men as aggressors, rapists, and killers.

SUMMARY

➡ *How do sociologists view deviance?*

Some sociologists view deviance as objectively given: Social problems such as prostitution and pornography are violations of folkways, mores, or laws. Others view deviance as socially constructed: A behavior, belief, or condition is deviant because it is labeled as such. Still others believe that deviance is rooted in the social structure of society: People in positions of power maintain their cultural dominance by defining as deviant the behaviors they consider immoral, distasteful, or threatening to them.

➡ *What kinds of behavior have traditionally been defined as sexual deviance in the United States?*

Four types of sexual conduct among heterosexual partners have traditionally been regarded as deviant: premarital sex (fornication), extramarital sex (adultery), promiscuous sex (casual sexual relations with many partners), and underage sex (statutory rape).

➡ *What is prostitution and how has it changed in recent years?*

Prostitution is the sale of sexual services (one's own or another's) for money or goods and without emotional attachment. According to some social analysts, prostitution has recently become industrialized, normalized, and globalized. The industrialization of prostitution refers to commercialized sex as a product manufactured within the human self. Normalization is the process whereby sex work comes to be treated as a form of entertainment with no legal impediments to promoting it as a commodity. The globalization of prostitution refers to the process by which the sex industry has increasingly become global in scope.

➡ *What levels, or tiers, of prostitution have sociologists identified?*

Sociologists have identified several categories: Escort prostitutes (call girls or call boys) earn higher fees and can be more selective in their working conditions and customers than other prostitutes. Hustlers (bar girls or bar boys) work out of night clubs, bars, and strip joints, where they solicit their customers. House prostitutes (house girls) work in brothels, and a substantial portion of their earnings goes to the house madam or pimp. Street prostitutes (streetwalkers) publicly solicit customers and charge by the "trick." At the very bottom of the tiers are those who exchange crack cocaine for sex.

➡ *How do functionalists view prostitution?*

Functionalists point out that prostitution—like other forms of deviance—is functional for society. Prostitution continues because it provides people with (1) quick, impersonal sexual gratification without emotional attachment; (2) a sexual outlet for those who have no ongoing sexual relationships; (3) the opportunity to engage in nontraditional sexual practices; (4) protection for the family as a social institution; and (5) jobs for low-skilled people.

➡ *How do interactionists view prostitution?*

Interactionists believe that prostitution—like other forms of deviance—is socially constructed. Entering a deviant career such as prostitution is like entering any other occupation, but public labeling—and the individual's acceptance or rejection of that label—determines whether a person stays in a deviant career.

➡ *How do conflict theorists view prostitution?*

There are several conflict perspectives on prostitution. Liberal feminists consider prostitution a victimless crime—involving a willing buyer and a willing seller—that should be decriminalized. Marxist feminists see prostitution as linked to the capitalist economy. Radical feminists trace the roots of prostitution to patriarchy in society. Conflict theorists who focus on the intersection of race, class, and gender believe that the criminalization of prostitution is a form of discrimination against poor women, particularly poor women of color.

➡ *Does pornography differ from obscenity and erotica?*

Sometimes it is difficult to distinguish among these categories, but pornography usually refers to the graphic depiction of sexual behavior through pictures and/or words—including delivery by electronic or other data retrieval systems—in a manner that is intended to be sexually arousing. Obscenity is the legal term for pornographic materials that are offensive by generally accepted standards of decency. Erotica refers to material depicting consensual sexual activities that are sought by and pleasurable to all parties involved.

➡ *Has pornography changed in recent years?*

Yes, technological innovations have greatly increased the variety of pornographic materials available as well as their methods of distribution. According to some analysts, as long as the desire for such materials is high, the multibillion-dollar pornography industry will continue to produce and market goods and services, adapting to new technologies as they become available.

➡ *Does research indicate that pornography contributes to sexual violence?*

No conclusive answer has been found to this question. Some studies have found that hard-core pornography is associated with aggression in males and sexual violence in society, but other studies have found no conclusive evidence that pornography contributes to sexual violence. However, most feminist scholars suggest that pornography exploits all women and sometimes men and children.

➡ *How do people react to the censorship of pornography?*

Reactions to the censorship of pornography are varied. People with a liberal view of pornography believe that it is a safety valve for society and censorship—not pornography—is the social problem. Religious conservatives consider pornography a threat to moral values and encourage censorship of some materials. Antipornography feminists view pornography as a primary source of male oppression and violence against women and argue for its restriction or elimination. Anticensorship feminists believe that some pornography is bad but censorship is worse because it suppresses free speech.

KEY TERMS

crime, p. 128
erotica, p. 137
obscenity, p. 137

pornography, p. 137
prostitution, p. 129

social control, p. 128
victimless crime, p. 136

QUESTIONS FOR CRITICAL THINKING

1. Suppose you are going to participate in a class debate on decriminalizing prostitution. What arguments would you present in favor of decriminalization? What arguments would you present against decriminalization?

2. Are prostitution and pornography the result of sexism, racism, homophobia, and class-based inequality? Why or why not?

3. On the basis of the text discussion of pornography, obscenity, and erotica, find examples from the mainstream media (including films, music videos, talk shows, and fashion ads in magazines) that might fit each category.

4. Peter McWilliams suggests that the problem with censorship can be summed up in two words: Who decides? Who do you think should decide what materials—if any—should be censored as pornographic or obscene? Besides deciding what's acceptable and what isn't, who should decide on the punishment for violating these standards?

Chapter Eight

Alcohol and Other Drugs

I knew I had hit a person. . . . You don't have to be legally intoxicated to be dangerous. I used to think drunk drivers were guys who were alcoholics and staggered into their car. I know now that they are kids and adults like myself. . . . When I got into my car [after leaving the bar] . . . it never occurred to me at any time that I was intoxicated. I didn't stumble. I wasn't sick. I started the car easily. Nothing indicated to me that I was not in control. . . . That's the danger of so-called social drinking. How can you judge that you are intoxicated when your judgment is already impaired? Just a little alcohol can do it.

—*Cesilee Hyde, age 23, describes the night in 1995 that her car struck and killed a police officer directing traffic at an accident site* (quoted in Banta, 1996:A1)

When most people think of alcohol abuse as a social problem, they picture someone with slurred speech, a flushed face, and slow responses. As Hyde's situation shows, however, not all alcohol-related problems involve alcoholics. Even occasional overconsumption of alcoholic beverages can have dire consequences, especially when combined with driving an automobile. In 1995, for example, there were 17,274 alcohol-related deaths on U.S. streets and highways (Wald, 1996a). In this chapter, we'll examine this and other issues pertaining to alcohol and other types of drug abuse.

DRUG USE AND ABUSE

What is a drug? There are many answers to this question, so the definition is not always consistent or clear. For our purposes, a **drug is any substance—other than food or water—that, when taken into the body, alters its functioning in some way.** Drugs are used for either therapeutic or recreational purposes. *Therapeutic* use occurs when a person takes a drug for a specific purpose such as reducing a fever or controlling an epileptic seizure. Sometimes, individuals who take prescription drugs for therapeutic purposes cross the line to drug abuse. *Recreational* drug use occurs when a person takes a drug for no other purpose than achieving some pleasurable feeling or psychological state. Alcohol and tobacco (nicotine) are *licit* (legal) drugs that are used for recreational purposes; heroin and cocaine are *illicit* (illegal) recreational drugs (Levinthal, 1996). Licit drugs, which include such substances as vitamins, aspirin, alcohol, tobacco, and prescription drugs, are legal to manufacture, sell, possess, and use. Illicit drugs such as marijuana, cocaine, heroin, and LSD (lysergic acid diethylamide) are socially defined as deviant, and using them is criminal behavior and hence a social problem. We live in a society that is saturated with both licit and illicit drugs, some of which are difficult to obtain, others of which are as available as the local drugstore (Akers, 1992).

 Defining Drug Abuse

What is drug abuse? *Drug abuse* is the excessive or inappropriate use of a drug that results in some form of physical, mental, or social impairment. A more difficult question to answer is "What constitutes drug abuse?" When looked at from this perspective, drug abuse has both objective and subjective components. The *objective component* is physical, psychological, or social evidence that harm has been done to individuals, families, communities, or the entire society by the use of a drug. The *subjective component* refers to people's perceptions about the consequences of using a drug and the social action they believe should be taken to remedy the problem.

Sometimes when people talk about drug abuse, the subjective component—the perception of consequences—overrides the objective component. Consider, for example, the subjective and objective components underlying our society's view of the use of marijuana. The subjective component of marijuana use is the general belief that marijuana is harmful and therefore should not be legal, even though there is little evidence that marijuana use is detrimental to health. The subjective component of alcohol use is the general belief that it is harmless and acceptable, even though there is considerable evidence that it impairs more people and produces greater costs to

Signe Wilkinson, CARTOONISTS & WRITERS SYNDICATE/cartoonweb.com

individuals and society than marijuana use. Thus, the use of alcohol is legal.

 Drug Addiction

The term *drug addiction (or drug dependency)* **refers to a psychological and/or physiological need for a drug to maintain a sense of well-being and avoid withdrawal symptoms.** Drug dependency has two essential characteristics: tolerance and withdrawal. *Tolerance* **occurs when larger doses of a drug are required over time to produce the same physical or psychological effect that was originally achieved by a smaller dose.** Tolerance is a matter of degree: Some drugs produce immediate and profound levels of tolerance, whereas others produce only mild tolerance. For example, when a person first drinks a five-ounce cup of coffee, containing about 100 milligrams of caffeine, the stimulant effect is usually quite pronounced. After that person drinks the same amount of coffee over a period of several days or weeks, the effect is greatly diminished, and a second or third cup of coffee (for a total of 200 to 300 milligrams of caffeine) becomes necessary to duplicate the earlier feeling (Levinthal, 1996). *Withdrawal* **refers to a variety of physical and/or psychological symptoms that habitual drug users experience when they discontinue drug use.** For example, people who suddenly terminate their alcohol intake after long-term, heavy drinking experience various physical symptoms ranging from insomnia to DTs (*delirium tremens,* or mental confusion often accompanied by sweating and tremor) and psychological symptoms such as a reduced sense of self-worth.

ALCOHOL USE AND ABUSE

The use of alcohol—ranging from communion wine in religious ceremonies to beer, wine, and liquor at business and social gatherings—is considered an accepted part of the dominant culture in the United States. *Alcohol* and *alcoholic beverages* are terms that refer to the three major forms in which ethyl alcohol (ethanol) is consumed: *wine,* which is made from fermentation of fruits and contains between 12 and 14 percent ethyl alcohol; *beer,* which is brewed from grains and hops and usually contains 3 to 6 percent; and *liquor,* which includes whiskey, gin, vodka, and other distilled spirits and usually con-

tains 40 percent (80 proof) to 50 percent (100 proof) alcohol. In the United States, adults consume an average of 2.7 gallons of wine, 32 gallons of beer, and 1.8 gallons of liquor a year. In fact, adults consume more beer on average than milk (24.3 gallons) or coffee (23.1 gallons) (U.S. Bureau of the Census, 1998). But statistics on average alcohol consumption do not indicate how much *each* person drinks during a given year. Some people do not drink at all, and others drink heavily. Among those who drink, 10 percent account for roughly half the total alcohol consumption in this country (Levinthal, 1996).

Many people do not think of alcohol as a drug because it can be purchased legally—and without a prescription—by adults. It is, however, a psychoactive drug that is classified as a *depressant* because it lowers the activity level of the central nervous system. The impairment of judgment and thinking associated with being drunk is the result of alcohol's depressing brain functions. Alcohol also affects mood and behavior. One to two drinks often bring a release from tensions and inhibitions. Three to four drinks affect self-control—including reaction time and coordination of hands, arms, and legs—and judgment, muddling the person's reasoning ability. Five to six drinks affect sensory perception, and the person may show signs of intoxication such as staggering, belligerence, or depression. At seven to eight drinks, the drinker is obviously intoxicated and may go into a stupor. Nine or more drinks affect vital centers, and the drinker may become comatose or even die. Of course, factors such as body weight, physical build, and recent food and fluid consumption must be taken into account in estimating the rate of alcohol absorption in the body.

Although negative short-term effects of drinking are usually overcome, chronic heavy drinking or alcoholism can cause permanent damage to the brain or other parts of the body (Fishbein and Pease, 1996). Social scientists divide long-term drinking patterns into four general categories. *Social drinkers* consume alcoholic beverages primarily on social occasions; they drink occasionally or even relatively frequently. *Heavy drinkers* are more frequent drinkers who typically consume greater quantities of alcohol when they drink and are more likely to become intoxicated. *Acute alcoholics* have trouble controlling their use of alcohol and plan their schedule around drinking. *Chronic alcoholics* have lost control over their drinking and tend to engage in compulsive behavior such as hiding liquor bottles and sneaking drinks when they are not being observed.

Alcohol Consumption and Class, Gender, Age, and Race

Although people in all social classes consume alcohol, income and class differences are associated with alcohol use. For example, studies show that people who earn more than $50,000 a year tend to drink expensive special or imported beers and more wine than liquor, whereas those who earn less than $20,000 tend to consume less expensive domestic beers and drink more beer than wine or liquor (Levinthal, 1996). The relationship between social class and rates of alcohol abuse is not as clear. Some studies show that people in the middle and upper classes are *less* likely to be heavy drinkers or have high rates of alcoholism; however, other studies show that alcohol consumption and abuse tend to be *higher* in the middle and upper classes than in the lower class (Akers, 1992). In any case, more affluent people typically have greater resources and more privacy than lower-income individuals have and can often protect themselves from the label "drunk" or "alcoholic." A member of the upper-middle or upper class who drinks to excess at the country club is less visible to the public and less likely to be negatively sanctioned by law enforcement officials—unless the person drives while under the influence—than a lower-income or poverty-level person who sits on a public sidewalk drinking beer or wine.

Gender, age, and race are also associated with drinking behavior. More men than women drink, and men are more likely than women to be labeled as problem drinkers or alcoholics. Women who drink alcoholic beverages tend to be lighter drinkers than men, who are more likely to consume alcohol daily and experience negative personal and social consequences from drinking. However, drinking patterns in the teen years are similar for males and females.

In a recent national survey, about half of all respondents between the ages of twelve and seventeen reported that they had tried alcohol at least once, and slightly more than 15 percent reported that they were current users. Among respondents in the eighteen to twenty-five age category, the vast majority (86.8 percent) reported that they had tried alcohol at least once, and over 60 percent indicated

that they were current users (U.S. Bureau of the Census, 1998). Among first-year college students, about half the respondents in a national survey reported that they consumed alcohol frequently or occasionally (see Figure 8.1). Young adults—particularly men—between the ages of twenty-one and thirty are at greater risk of alcohol abuse if they remain single or become divorced than they are if they marry or remain married and become parents (Chilcoat and Breslau, 1996).

Most research on race and alcohol consumption has focused on male drinking patterns; studies show that young African American males as a category are less likely than their white counterparts to abuse alcohol, but later in life this pattern is reversed. After age thirty, African American men have higher rates of heavy drinking and alcoholism than white males have. Some analysts attribute this difference to structural inequalities that uniquely affect men of color, such as high rates of unemployment in central cities, racial discrimination in employment practices, and inadequate housing conditions (Herd, 1988). Low-income Native American men living on government-controlled reservations are especially vulnerable to chronic alcohol abuse and alcoholism. Our knowledge of alcohol consumption among Latinas and African American women is limited, but studies show that such factors as physical health, marital status, religious orientation, and previous life experiences apparently play a role in consumption (Taylor and Jackson, 1990). For example, Latinas and African American women who have higher levels of income and education typically consume alcohol more frequently than do their counterparts with lower incomes and education levels (Parker et al., 1995).

Alcohol-Related Social Problems

Alcohol consumption in the United States has been declining across lines of class, gender, race, and age over the past two decades. Nevertheless, chronic alcohol abuse and alcoholism are linked to many social problems. Here we will examine health problems, workplace and driving accidents, and family problems.

HEALTH PROBLEMS

Although not all heavy drinkers and chronic alcohol abusers exhibit the major health problems that are typically associated with alcoholism, their

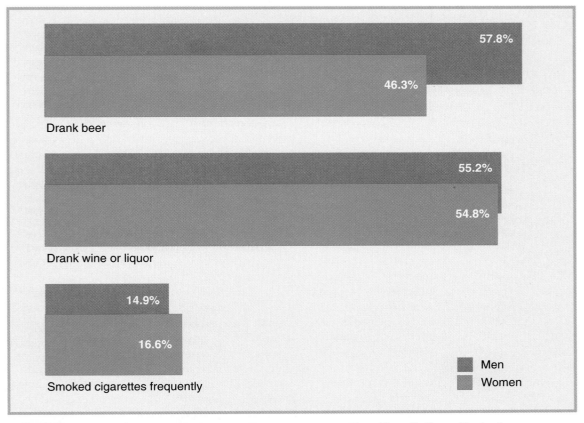

FIGURE 8.1 *Alcohol Consumption and Smoking among First-Year College Students.*
*Based on survey responses of 275,811 freshmen entering two-year and four-year institutions
in the fall of 1998.*
Source: *Chronicle of Higher Education,* 1999.

risk of them is greatly increased. For alcoholics, the long-term health effects include *nutritional deficiencies* as a result of poor eating habits. Chronic heavy drinking contributes to high caloric consumption but low nutritional intake. Alcoholism is also associated with fluctuations in blood sugar levels that can cause adult-onset diabetes. Structural loss of brain tissue may produce *alcoholic dementia,* which is characterized by difficulties in problem solving, remembering information, and organizing facts about one's identity and surroundings (Levinthal, 1996).

Chronic alcohol abuse is also linked to *cardiovascular problems* such as inflammation and enlargement of the heart muscle, poor blood circulation, reduced heart contractions, fatty accumulations in the heart and arteries, high blood pressure, and cerebrovascular

disorders such as stroke (Levinthal, 1996). However, studies show that moderate alcohol consumption—such as a glass of wine a day—may improve body circulation, lower cholesterol levels, and reduce the risk of certain forms of heart disease.

Over time, chronic alcohol abuse also contributes to irreversible changes in the liver that are associated with *alcoholic cirrhosis*—a progressive development of scar tissue in the liver that chokes off blood vessels and destroys liver cells by interfering with their use of oxygen. Alcoholic cirrhosis is the ninth most frequent cause of death in the United States, and most deaths from it occur between ages forty and sixty-five (U.S. Bureau of the Census, 1998). Given all the possible health problems, perhaps it is not surprising that alcoholics typically have a shorter life expectancy—often

SOCIAL PROBLEMS

BOX 8.1

A Fading Drumbeat against Drunken Driving?

It's harder and harder for us to get major media coverage. . . . If anyone would have told me 15 years ago that this many people, 17,000 people, would still be dying on the road, I would not have believed it.

—*Katherine Prescott, former National President, Mothers Against Drunk Driving (quoted in Wald, 1996a)*

Like many other members of Mothers Against Drunk Driving (MADD), including Candace Lightner, who founded the organization in the early 1980s when her daughter was killed, Katherine Prescott has a personal reason for confronting the problem of drunk driving: Her son was killed by a drunk driver in an automobile crash. Over the past two decades, MADD has campaigned for stricter laws against drunk driving and mounted media campaigns against driving and drinking.

Through public information messages in newspapers and on television, MADD continues to put human faces on the problem of drunk driving and to encourage people to mobilize for action. Two periods of unusually high media attention are credited with reducing the number of people killed in drunk-driving accidents: Between 1983 and 1984, the MADD campaign focused on making the public more aware of the problem; between 1989 and 1992, it focused on the importance of having a designated driver when people have been drinking. MADD also originated the "Friends Don't Let Friends Drive Drunk" ad campaign.

But in 1995—the same year that the mass media ran fewer public service ads on drinking—the number of people killed in drunk-driving accidents rose by 4 percent, the first increase in 10 years. In 1999, MADD issued its report card on the war on drunk driving and gave the United States a C+ for its efforts to control alcohol-related traffic deaths (MADD, 1999). According to MADD, drunk driving—as well as underage drinking—is the number one youth drug problem.

In 1998, about 16,000 people were killed, and 900,000 others were injured in alcohol-related traffic crashes, an average of one death every thirty-three minutes or one injury every twenty seconds.

Over $1 billion is spent each year on alcoholic beverage advertising in the United States; about $626 million is spent annually on television advertising by the beer industry alone. If liquor manufacturers decide to ease a decades-old voluntary restraint on television liquor ads in the future, these revenues may increase dramatically (Jung, 1994).

Some politicians want a reassessment of beer and wine advertising in sports programming, which has a huge percentage of viewers younger than the legal drinking age (Seelye, 1997b). In one study, researchers found that beer commercials appear more frequently than commercials for any other beverage during televised sports events (Madden and Grube, 1994).

Despite the fact that the annual number of alcohol-related auto accidents in this country remains high, images and fantasies associated with drinking make it seem far more exciting, romantic, and adventurous to drink than to abstain. Do you think that alcoholic beverage manufacturers have a responsibility to inform the public about the potential consequences of their products? Why or why not?

by as much as ten to twelve years—than nondrinkers or occasional drinkers who consume moderate amounts of alcohol.

Abuse of alcohol and other drugs by a pregnant woman can damage the fetus. The greatest risk of *fetal alcohol syndrome (FAS)*—**a condition characterized by mental retardation and craniofacial malformations that may affect the child of an alcoholic mother**—occurs during the first three months of pregnancy. Binge drinking during the third week of gestation has been linked particularly with this syndrome because that is when crucial craniofacial formation and brain growth take place in the fetus.

ALCOHOL IN THE WORKPLACE

A recent study by the National Institute on Alcohol Abuse and Alcoholism found that lost productivity and time spent in treatment programs as a result of alcoholism cost about $100 billion annually in the United States (Pedersen-Pietersen, 1997). Other job-related problems associated with drinking include absenteeism, tardiness, and workplace accidents. Excessive alcohol consumption impairs the sensorimotor skills necessary to operate machinery, heavy equipment, and motor vehicles. Numerous studies have shown a relationship between alcohol—and other drugs—and many workplace injuries or fatalities (Macdonald, 1995). On the basis of Bureau of Labor Statistics reports of more than 1,300 fatal occupational accidents, researchers have concluded that alcohol, cocaine, and marijuana are the three leading substances involved in workplace injuries and deaths (Marine and Jack, 1994).

DRIVING AND DRINKING

Drivers who have been drinking often do not realize how much alcohol they have consumed or what effects it has on their driving ability. As a result, many people drive dangerously even when they are not legally drunk, which in most states requires a minimum blood alcohol level of 0.08 or 0.10 and is referred to as driving while intoxicated (DWI) or driving under the influence (DUI). Alcohol-related driving accidents occur, for example, when drivers lose control of their vehicles or fail to see a red traffic light or a car or pedestrian in the street, or a sharp curve in the road (Gross, 1983). Alcohol has been implicated in about 41 percent of all fatal motor vehi-cle accidents in the United States; among people sixteen to twenty-four years of age, alcohol is involved in 30.8 percent of all motor vehicle fatalities (U.S. Bureau of the Census, 1998). As high as these figures are, the exact size of the problem is unknown because only 68 percent of the drivers killed in automobile crashes are tested for alcohol, and only 24 percent of the drivers who survive accidents in which someone else dies are tested (Wald, 1996b). Moreover, despite the efforts to educate people about the hazards of drinking and driving made by some alcoholic beverage manufacturers and groups such as Mothers Against Drunk Driving, public interest in the issue appears to be declining (see Box 8.1).

FAMILY PROBLEMS

Chronic alcohol abuse or alcoholism makes it difficult for a person to maintain social relationships and have a stable family life. For every person who has a problem with alcohol, an average of at least four other people are directly affected on a daily basis (Levinthal, 1996). Domestic abuse and violence in families are frequently associated with heavy drinking and alcohol abuse by one or more family members. Growing up in a family that is affected by alcohol can have a profound impact on children. The extent to which alcohol abuse affects other family members depends on the degree of alcoholism and the type of alcoholic. Some alcoholic parents are violent and abusive; others are quiet and sullen or withdrawn. To outsiders, the family of an alcoholic may appear to be normal, but family members may feel as though they have an "elephant in the living room," as journalist Joyce Maynard (1994:80–81) explains:

> I grew up in an alcoholic household. But as difficult as it was dealing with my father's drinking, the greater pain for me was the secret keeping. Adult children of alcoholics refer to the phenomenon as "the elephant in the living room": You have a huge, inescapable fact about your life that affects everything in your home, but nobody mentions it, although everybody's behavior is altered to accommodate or deal with it. . . . Our family squeezed past the elephant in the living room, felt his breath on our faces, and rearranged furniture to make room for him. I

hid liquor bottles if a friend was coming over. To prevent my father from driving, I even stashed away the keys to his car. But I never uttered a word, and neither did the rest of my family, about what was behind those actions. . . . It wasn't until I became an adult myself that I recognized the unhealthiness of our family's conspiracy of silence.

As Maynard suggests, family members of alcoholics frequently become *enablers*—people who adjust their behavior to accommodate an alcoholic. Enabling often takes the form of lying to cover up the alcoholic's drinking, absenteeism from work, and/or discourteous treatment of others. Enabling leads many families to develop a pattern of *codependency*—a reciprocal relationship between the alcoholic and one or more nonalcoholics who unwittingly aid and abet the alcoholic's excessive drinking and resulting behavior (Jung, 1994). When codependency occurs, the spouse or another family member takes on many of the alcoholic's responsibilities and keeps the alcoholic person from experiencing the full impact of his or her actions. Children who grow up in alcoholic families tend to have higher than normal rates of hyperactivity, antisocial

The relationship between alcohol abuse and family problems is extremely complex. Does this young mother view alcohol use as the **cause** of her problems or a **solution** to them? What might be the long-term effects of her drinking on her child?

behavior, low academic achievement, and cognitive impairment (Fishbein and Pease, 1996). However, although the statistical risks of becoming an alcoholic increase if one's parent has been an alcoholic, most children of alcoholics (as many as 59 percent) do not become alcoholics themselves (Sher, 1991).

TOBACCO (NICOTINE) USE AS A SOCIAL PROBLEM

The nicotine in tobacco is a toxic, dependency-producing psychoactive drug that is more addictive than heroin. It is categorized as a *stimulant* because it stimulates central nervous system receptors, activating the release of adrenaline, which raises blood pressure, speeds up the heartbeat, and gives the user a sense of alertness. Some people claim that nicotine reduces their appetite, helps them to lose weight, and produces a sense of calmness and relaxation (Akers, 1992). Perhaps these physical and psychological effects of nicotine dependency help to explain why about one in every four U.S. adults over the age of seventeen smokes, and about 70 percent of all smokers have more than fifteen cigarettes a day.

Although the overall proportion of smokers in the general population has declined somewhat since the 1964 Surgeon General's warning that smoking is linked to cancer and other serious diseases, tobacco is still responsible for about one in every five deaths in this country (Akers, 1992). People who smoke cigarettes, cigars, or pipes have a greater likelihood of developing lung cancer and cancer of the larynx, mouth, and esophagus than nonsmokers because nicotine is ingested into the bloodstream through the lungs and soft tissues of the mouth (Akers, 1992). In fact, smokers are ten times more likely than nonsmokers to contract lung cancer. Nearly 90 percent of the more than 140,000 lung cancer deaths annually are attributed to cigarette smoking (Fishbein and Pease, 1996; Levinthal, 1996). Furthermore, many cases of bronchitis, emphysema, ulcers, and heart and circulatory disorders can be traced to nicotine consumption. When tobacco burns, it forms carbon monoxide, which disrupts the transport of oxygen from the lungs to the rest of the body and hence contributes to cardiovascular disease (Levinthal, 1996).

Smoking typically shortens life expectancy. It is estimated that about a half a pack (ten cigarettes) a day on average reduces a person's life expectancy by four years, and smoking more than two packs a day (forty cigarettes) reduces life expectancy by eight years. When a person uses both tobacco and alcohol, the cancer-causing effects of tobacco are exacerbated (Fishbein and Pease, 1996).

Even people who never light up a cigarette are harmed by *environmental tobacco smoke—the smoke in the air as a result of other people's tobacco smoking* (Levinthal, 1996). When someone smokes a cigarette, about 75 percent of the nicotine ends up in the air. Researchers have found that nonsmokers who carpool or work with heavy smokers are more affected by environmental smoke than nonsmokers who are only occasionally exposed to it. Therefore, smoking has been banned in many public and private facilities throughout the country.

Not surprisingly, cigarette smoking adversely affects infants and children. Infants born to women who smoke typically have lower than average birth weights and sometimes slower rates of physical and mental growth. When a pregnant woman smokes, blood vessels constrict, which reduces the amount of oxygen reaching the fetus. Carbon monoxide transmitted from the mother's blood to the fetus interferes with the distribution of oxygen that does reach the fetus (DiFranza and Lew, 1995). Children who grow up in households where one or both parents smoke are more apt to suffer from frequent ear infections, upper respiratory infections such as bronchitis and sinusitis, allergies, asthma, and other health problems than children whose parents do not smoke.

Today, at least 3 million teenagers smoke, and many report that they started in the sixth or seventh grade (Johnston et al., 1994). The National Institute on Drug Abuse reports that almost 20 percent of eighth-graders say they smoke—an increase of nearly one-third since the early 1990s (Hostetler, 1995). About 19 percent of high school seniors report that they smoke on a daily basis, and about 11 percent indicate that they smoke as much as half a pack of cigarettes a day. Like smokers of all ages, high school–age smokers differ from nonsmokers on the basis of educational level and socioeconomic status. High school seniors who are not planning to attend college are three times more likely to smoke half a pack a day than college-bound seniors. Those who drop out of high school are four times more likely to smoke cigarettes daily than are those who remain in high school through graduation. College students have

lower rates of smoking than do individuals of the same age who are not attending college (Levinthal, 1996).

In recent years, young people have been targeted for smokeless tobacco products such as chewing tobacco and moist snuff, which is placed between the cheek and the gum. White teenage boys and young adult males, particularly in the South and West, are the primary consumers of these products. However, since oral smokeless tobacco is absorbed through the membranes of the mouth into the bloodstream, it increases the risk of cancer of the tongue, cheeks, gums, and esophagus. Most habitual snuff users have *leukoplakia*—a white, thick precancerous patch that is visible on tissues in the mouth—and *erythroplakia*—a red precancerous spot inside the mouth and nasal cavity (Akers, 1992).

Why do so many people use nicotine if it is so dangerous? Several reasons have been suggested. First, nicotine creates a high level of dependency, so once a person has begun to use tobacco regularly, the withdrawal symptoms may be strong enough to make the person light up another cigarette. Some researchers have found that the majority of people who smoke recognize that smoking is bad for them and would like to quit but cannot (Fishbein and Pease, 1996:213). Second, sophisticated marketing campaigns associate smoking with desirable cultural attributes such as achieving maturity, gaining wealth and happiness, or being thin and sexy. Although cigarette manufacturers are no longer allowed to advertise their products on radio or television, there are other venues open to them. More than $4 billion dollars is spent annually on magazine and newspaper advertising, billboards, sponsorship of sports events, and other forms of cigarette promotions (Hostetler, 1995). Some cigarette ad campaigns appear to specifically target young people, and they appear to work. Researchers have found that 86 percent of all children who smoke prefer heavily advertised brands such as Marlboro, Camel, or Newport.

Efforts by the U.S. government in the late 1990s to regulate the tobacco industry appear to have failed, at least for now. Attempts to pass legislation under which tobacco products would have become more regulated and less readily available to the public were defeated in Congress. Some advocates of tobacco regulation believe that it will be extremely difficult to get legislation passed as long as tobacco companies remain a major source of campaign contributions.

PRESCRIPTION DRUGS, OVER-THE-COUNTER DRUGS, AND CAFFEINE

When most people think of drug abuse, they picture unscrupulous drug dealers in dark alleys selling illegal drugs. But legal drugs also may be abused. Legal drugs fall into two categories: *prescription drugs,* which are dispensed only by a registered pharmacist on the authority of a licensed physician or dentist, and *over the counter (OTC) drugs,* which are available off the shelf and are restricted only by the customer's ability to pay.

 Prescription Drugs

Pain medication is probably the prescription drug that is most frequently abused. Though millions of people benefit from *narcotics*—natural or synthetic opiates such as morphine (brand names Duramorph and Roxanol), propoxyphene (Darvon), and codeine—that relieve pain, suppress coughing, control chronic diarrhea, and reduce heroin withdrawal symptoms, there are risks of short-term abuse and long-term psychological and physical dependence. Over time, users develop tolerance for the drug they are taking and must continue to increase dosages to obtain the same effect that was derived from the lower dose. Drug dependency that results from physician-supervised treatment for a recognized medical disorder is called *iatrogenic addiction.* Iatrogenic addiction is most likely to occur with long-term use and/or high dosages of a prescription drug; it most often affects people from the middle or upper class who have no previous history of drug abuse or addiction (Fishbein and Pease, 1996).

Two widely prescribed drugs that have been the subject of controversy regarding their use and abuse are methylphenidate (Ritalin) and fluoxetine (Prozac). Ritalin is a stimulant that is prescribed for children who are diagnosed with *attention-deficit hyperactivity disorder* (ADHD). According to the American Psychiatric Association, ADHD is characterized by "emotionality, behavioral hyperactivity, short attention span, distractibility, impulsiveness, and perceptual and learning disabilities" (Fishbein and Pease, 1996). Although some children are probably correctly diagnosed with this disorder, one survey has concluded that

Ritalin is overprescribed. In the United States, 3 to 5 percent of all schoolchildren take Ritalin. Boys are three times more likely than girls to be diagnosed with ADHD, and it is estimated that 10 percent to 12 percent of boys between the ages of six and fourteen take or have taken the drug (Crossette, 1996a). Advocates believe that children with normal to above average intelligence who are performing poorly in school can benefit from Ritalin, which has proven to be safe for more than 40 years. But critics argue that many parents, doctors, and teachers see Ritalin as a quick fix for dealing with troublesome children and note that the drug typically is prescribed to be taken *only* during the school year (Crossette, 1996a).

One of the most abused prescription drugs for adults is Prozac, an antidepressant. Introduced in 1987 as a breakthrough medication for clinical depression, Prozac has become a "cure-all for the blues," a far milder form of depression. Advocates believe that the more than 4.5 million prescriptions for Prozac that are filled annually enhance the quality of life for many people, freeing them from depression and suicidal thoughts. But the long-term side effects of the drug are unknown, and there is some evidence that Prozac is associated with intense, violent suicidal thoughts in some patients. Both Prozac and Ritalin are approved by the U.S. Food and Drug Administration (FDA) and are considered safe and effective if taken as directed (Angier, 1990; Kramer, 1993).

 Over-the-Counter Drugs

A fine line exists between prescription and over-the-counter (OTC) drugs. Today, both types of drugs are advertised directly to the consumer in the electronic and print media with suggestions to "ask your doctor or pharmacist about [our product] on your next visit." Some drugs are available both by prescription and over the counter, depending on their strength and dosage. For example, medication for stomach ulcers (e.g, Zantac and Tagamet) are sold over the counter in lower doses and by prescription in higher doses. Some drugs that are now sold over the counter were previously available only by prescription.

Widely used OTC drugs include analgesics, sleep aids, and cough and cold remedies. Abuse of aspirin and other analgesics can cause gastric bleeding, problems with blood clotting, complications in surgery patients and pregnant women in labor and delivery, and Reye's syndrome (a potentially life-threatening condition that can arise when children with flu, chicken pox, or other viral infections are given aspirin). Overdoses of analgesics such as acetaminophen (e.g., Tylenol and Anacin-3), aspirin, and ibuprofen (e.g., Motrin, Advil, and Midol) have been linked to cases of attempted suicide, especially by white females between the ages of six and seventeen years. Few of these suicide attempts have resulted in death except when the analgesics were combined with alcohol or other drugs (Levinthal, 1996). Like analgesics, sleep aids are dangerous when combined with alcohol or some cough and cold remedies because they are depressants that slow down the central nervous system. Even cough and cold medications alone have side effects, such as drowsiness, that can be hazardous if users attempt to drive a car or operate heavy machinery. To counteract drowsiness, some drug companies add caffeine to their product.

 Caffeine

Although it is a relatively safe drug, caffeine is a dependency-producing psychoactive stimulant (Gilbert, 1986). Caffeine is an ingredient in coffee, tea, chocolate, soft drinks, and stimulants such as NoDoz and Vivarin. Most people ingest caffeine because they like the feeling of mental alertness and reduced fatigue that it produces. The extent to which caffeine actually improves human performance, however, is widely debated. Caffeine may improve concentration when a person is performing boring or repetitive tasks, but it has little effect on the performance of complex tasks such as critical thinking and decision making (Curatolo and Robertson, 1983; Dews, 1984). The short-term effects of caffeine include dilated peripheral blood vessels, constricted blood vessels in the head, and a slightly elevated heart rate (Levinthal, 1996). Long-term effects of heavy caffeine use (more than three cups of coffee or five cups of tea per day) include increased risk of heart attack and osteoporosis—the loss of bone density and increased brittleness associated with fractures and broken bones (Kiel et al., 1990). Overall, the social problems associated with the abuse of caffeine and prescription and OTC drugs are relatively minor when compared with the social problems associated with illegal drugs.

ILLEGAL DRUG USE AND ABUSE

Are some drugs inherently bad and hence classified as illegal? What constitutes an illegal drug is a matter of social and legal definitions and thus is subject to change over time. During the nineteenth and early twentieth centuries, people in the United States had fairly easy access to drugs that are currently illegal for general use. In the early 1800s, neither doctors nor pharmacists had to be state licensed. *Patent medicines,* which sometimes contained such ingredients as opium, morphine, heroin, cocaine, and alcohol, could be purchased in stores, through mail-order advertisements, and from medicine wagons run by people who called themselves doctors and provided free entertainment to attract crowds (Young, 1961). Over time, because of the rapidly growing number of narcotics addicts, prescriptions became required for some drugs. Some forms of drug use were criminalized because of their association with specific minority groups. For example, opium could legally be consumed in cough syrup, but smoking the same amount of opium was declared illegal in 1908 because opium smoking was a favorite pastime of the Chinese workers building railroads in the western United States (James and Johnson, 1996). Other forms of opium use were regulated when Congress passed the Harrison Narcotics Act in 1914.

The Harrison Act required anyone who produced or distributed drugs to register with the federal government, keep a record of all transactions, and pay a tax on habit-forming drugs such as heroin, opium, and morphine; it also required that certain drugs be purchased only from physicians (James and Johnson, 1996). However, the Harrison Act and drug-related legislation that has followed it have not been able to eliminate illegal drug use in this country (Bertram et al., 1996). Today, the most widely used illegal drugs are marijuana, stimulants such as cocaine and amphetamines, depressants such as barbiturates, narcotics such as heroin, and hallucinogens such as LSD.

 Marijuana

Marijuana is the most extensively used illicit drug in the United States: About one in three people over the

SOCIAL PROBLEMS

The Battle over Marijuana: Medicalization or Legalization?

Perhaps the most persuasive argument for medicinal marijuana I've encountered came two years ago, when the California Assembly was debating a medical-marijuana bill. One GOP assemblyman said he had had a great deal of trouble with the issue. But when a relative was dying a few years before, the family had used marijuana to help her nausea. That story helped the bill pass. Wouldn't it be awful if people changed their minds only after someone close to them had died?

—Marcus Conant (1997:26), a doctor at the University of California, San Francisco, who has treated more than 5,000 HIV-positive patients in his private practice

[Until adequate testing is done on marijuana] . . . it is inconceivable to allow anyone of any age to have uncontrolled use of marijuana for any alleged illness—without a doctor's exam-

ination or even a prescription. But that is precisely what the California law lets people do. Can you think of any other untested, home-made, mind-altering medicine that you self-dose, and that uses a burning carcinogen as a delivery vehicle? I think it's clear that a lot of people arguing for the California proposition and others like it are pushing the legalization of drugs, plain and simple.

—Barry R. McCaffrey (1997:27), a retired army general who is director of the Office of National Drug Control Policy, Washington, D.C.

As these statements suggest, the controversy over marijuana is far from resolved. Advocates of *legalization* suggest that marijuana use should no longer be subject to legal control. Some states have adopted some form of decriminalization for the possession of small amounts—usually less than one ounce or so—of marijuana. Other states have passed medical-marijuana laws that permit use of the drug

---

age of twelve has tried marijuana at least once. It is ingested by smoking a hand-rolled cigarette known as a *reefer* or a *joint* or through a pipe or other smoking implement. Potent marijuana—marijuana with high levels of the plant's primary psychoactive chemical, delta-9 tetrahydrocannabinol (THC)—has existed for many years, but potency has increased in recent years because of indoor gardens in the United States. Indoor crops have levels of THC up to four times as high as plants grown outdoors and in other nations (Navarro, 1996).

Although most marijuana users are between the ages of eighteen and twenty-five, use by teens between the ages of twelve and seventeen has more than doubled over the past decade (Substance Abuse and Mental Health Services Administration, 1996). Many teenage users report that marijuana is as easy to acquire as alcohol or cigarettes. According to one

teenager, "It is so popular, so well known, it is around everywhere. Nobody is afraid of the consequences of selling it or buying it. . . . It is really easy to get" (quoted in Friend, 1996:2A). Many young people buy the drug from friends who grow their own plants.

Marijuana is both a central nervous system depressant and a stimulant. In low to moderate doses, the drug produces mild sedation; in high doses, it produces a sense of well-being, euphoria, and sometimes hallucinations. Marijuana slightly increases blood pressure and heart rate and greatly lowers blood glucose levels, causing extreme hunger. The human body manufactures a chemical that closely resembles THC, and specific receptors in the brain are designed to receive it. Marijuana use disrupts these receptors, impairing motor activity, concentration, and short-term memory (Cowley, 1997).

under specific medical circumstances. Advocates of these laws believe doctors should be allowed to prescribe marijuana or that the federal government should lift the ban on the medical use of this drug altogether. Advocates of medical legalization believe marijuana's benefits in treating certain medical conditions far outweigh its possible adverse consequences. For example, marijuana can help to control glaucoma, an eye disease that eventually produces blindness. It also can forestall AIDS-related complications, ease the nausea brought on by cancer chemotherapy, and counter some of the symptoms of epilepsy and multiple sclerosis (Kalb, 1999; *Time,* 1999a). Advocates envision a physician-controlled, prescription-based system or a legalized regulatory system something like that in place now for alcohol and tobacco. If marijuana were treated as a legal substance, it could be subject to restrictions on advertising, content, purchase age, and other regulations for production, distribution, and sale (Akers, 1992).

In sharp contrast, federal drug enforcement officials and other opponents of medical-marijuana laws or legalization argue that the medical benefits of marijuana are modest at best and the drug is useless or dangerous at worst. Opponents believe that medical-marijuana laws or legalization would increase the general level of use and open the door for legalization of drugs such as cocaine, heroin, amphetamines, and hallucinogens, which are far more dangerous. Although problems associated with the criminalization of drugs, such as drug smuggling and global drug trafficking, might be lessened by legalization, the costs to society would be too great. According to sociologist Ronald L. Akers (1992:160), marijuana use "has the potential to grow to the same level as tobacco and alcohol use with basically the same magnitude of threat to health and life. . . . The benefits of legalization . . . are no more certain than are the harmful consequences of legalization."

Do you think marijuana for medical use should be treated differently than for recreational use? What pros and cons would you give in a debate over the legalization of marijuana?

As a result, complex motor tasks such as driving a car or operating heavy machinery are dangerous for a person who is under the influence of marijuana. Some studies show that heavy marijuana use can impair concentration and recall in high school and college students (Wren, 1996b). Users become apathetic and lose their motivation to perform competently or achieve long-range goals such as completing their education. Overall, the short-term effects of marijuana are typically milder than the short-term effects of drugs such as cocaine (Fishbein and Pease, 1996).

High doses of marijuana smoked during pregnancy can disrupt the development of a fetus and result in lower than average birth weight, congenital abnormalities, premature delivery, and neurological disturbances (Fishbein and Pease, 1996). Furthermore, some studies have found an increased risk of cancer and other lung problems associated with inhaling because marijuana smokers are believed to inhale more deeply than tobacco users.

Over the past decade, medical uses of marijuana have been widely debated. In 1985, the Food and Drug Administration approved a synthetic version of THC, called Marinol, for prescription use to ease the nausea and vomiting that are common side effects of chemotherapy in cancer patients. Marinol is now also used to help AIDS patients regain their appetites (Cowley, 1997). Although recent reports by the Institute of Medicine have confirmed the medical merits of marijuana, the study did not give blanket approval of marijuana as a medicine (Kalb, 1999), and thus the debate over what to do about this widely used—but still controlled—substance continues (see Box 8.2).

Stimulants

Cocaine and amphetamines are among the major stimulants that are abused in the United States. Cocaine is an extremely potent and dependency-producing drug derived from the small leaves of the coca plant, which grows in several Latin American countries. In the nineteenth century, cocaine was introduced in the United States as a local anesthetic in medical practice and a mood-enhancer in patent medicines (Akers, 1992). It was an ingredient in Coca-Cola from the 1880s to the early 1900s (Miller, 1994). Today, cocaine is the third most widely used psychoactive drug after alcohol and marijuana. Users typically sniff, or "snort," the drug into their nostrils, inject it intravenously, or smoke it in the form of crack, a potent form of cocaine that is specially processed for smoking.

About 23 million people over the age of twelve in this country report that they have used cocaine at least once, and about 1 million acknowledge having used it during the past month (Substance Abuse and Mental Health Services Administration, 1996). According to recent research, more males than females use cocaine, and the majority of users are in their twenties (Fishbein and Pease, 1996). In the mid-1980s, extensive media coverage of the hazards of cocaine use resulted in decreased usage by middle-class white high school and college students; however, an upswing in use occurred among young minority group members living in central cities (Fishbein and Pease, 1996). For some central city residents living in poverty, with no hope of gainful employment, cocaine is a major source of revenue and an entry point for other drug-related crime. Here's how one fourteen-year-old male in Miami, Florida, described his involvement in the drug business (quoted in Inciardi et al., 1993a:86–87):

> I was sort of a scout, a lookout, for Mr. George. That was the name of the man who delivered the stuff [cocaine] to the places that sold it. . . . I was 11, an' Mr. George had a kid like me probably on every block. . . . I'd be in my front yard, see, watchin' for the cops. Mr. George would drive by my house . . . a few times. I'd watch and see if he was being followed. If everything looked OK, I'd go over to his car an' he'd give me the stuff, and tell me where to take it, or who to give it to. Sometimes he'd just give me a key an' say some-

thin' like "blue Pontiac 75/25." That would mean that near the corner of 75th Street and 25th Avenue there'd be a blue Pontiac. The stuff, and instructions, or maybe something else, would be in the trunk. Mr. George was real careful. When I'd drop it off I'd collect the money too. . . . For each job I'd get $10.

This young man's experience is not unique; studies indicate that selling drugs such as cocaine, crack, and heroin is the fastest-growing means of economic survival for men in locations ranging from Miami to Harlem (New York City) and Los Angeles (Bourgeois, 1995).

The effects of cocaine on the human body depend on how pure the dose is and what effect the user expects. Most cocaine users experience a powerful high or "rush" in which blood pressure rises and heart rate and respiration increase dramatically. Reactions vary in length and intensity, depending on whether the drug is injected, smoked, or snorted. When the drug wears off, users become increasingly agitated and depressed. Some users become extremely depressed and suicidal; others develop such a powerful craving that they easily become addicted to the drug (Gawin and Ellinwood, 1988). Occasionally, cocaine use results in sudden death by triggering an irregular heart rhythm.

People who use cocaine over extended periods of time have higher rates of infection, heart disturbance, internal bleeding, hypertension, cardiac arrest, stroke, hemorrhaging, and other neurological and cardiovascular disorders than nonusers. Although these problems may develop gradually as cocaine use continues, some users experience the problems after a single dose. Intravenous cocaine users who share contaminated needles and syringes are also at risk for AIDS. The risk of contracting AIDS is especially high in crack houses, where women addicts often engage in prostitution (see Chapter 7) to acquire drugs.

Cocaine use is extremely hazardous during pregnancy. Children born to crack-addicted mothers usually suffer painful withdrawal symptoms at birth and later show deficits in cognitive skills, judgment, and behavior controls. "Crack babies" must often be cared for at public expense in hospitals and other facilities because their mothers cannot meet their basic needs or provide nurturance. But social scientist Philippe Bourgeois suggests that blame for the problem cannot be placed on the women alone.

 Extensive media coverage of the arrest, conviction, and incarceration of film star Robert Downey, Jr. for felony drug possession called attention to the fact that drug abuse cuts across lines of race, class, and gender. Do you believe that media reports about Downey's prison sentence will make young people more aware of the problems associated with illicit drug use? Or does such coverage sometimes glamorize such behavior?

Many mothers of crack babies desperately seek meaning in their lives and refuse to sacrifice themselves to the impossible task of raising healthy children in the inner city. Instead, Bourgeois blames the problem on patriarchal definitions of "family" and the dysfunctional public sector that relegates the responsibility for nurturing and supporting children almost exclusively to women. For change to occur,

fathers and the larger society must share the women's burden (Bourgeois, 1995).

Like cocaine, amphetamines ("uppers") stimulate the central nervous system. Amphetamines in the form of diet pills and pep formulas are legal substances when they are prescribed by a physician, but many people, believing that they cannot lose weight or have enough energy without the pills, become physically and/or psychologically dependent on them. Speed freaks—heavy users who inject massive doses of amphetamines several times a day—often do "runs," staying awake for extended periods of time, eating very little, and engaging in bizarre behavior such as counting cornflakes in a cereal box or pasting postage stamps on the wall before "crashing" and sleeping for several days (Goode, 1989). Recent concern about amphetamine abuse has focused on a smokable form called ICE that contains a high percentage of the pure drug and produces effects that last from four to twenty-four hours (Lauderback and Waldorf, 1993). Chronic amphetamine abuse can result in *amphetamine psychosis,* which is characterized by paranoia, hallucinations, and violent tendencies that may persist for weeks after use of the drug has been discontinued. Overdosing on amphetamines can produce coma, brain damage, and even death.

Depressants

Many people who abuse stimulants also abuse depressants—drugs, including alcohol, that depress the central nervous system and may have some painkilling properties. The most commonly used depressants are barbiturates (e.g., Nembutal and Seconal) and antianxiety drugs or tranquilizers (e.g., Librium, Valium, and Miltown). Relatively low oral doses of depressants produce a relaxing and mildly disinhibiting effect; higher doses result in sedation. Users may develop both physical addiction to and psychological dependence on these depressants. Users sometimes use depressants for *potentiation*—the interaction that takes place when two drugs are mixed together to produce a far greater effect than the effect of either drug administered separately. Heroin users, for example, will sometimes combine heroin and barbiturates in hopes of prolonging their high and extending their heroin supply (Fishbein and Pease, 1996).

Recently, Rohypnol and GHB (gamma-hydroxybutyrate), also known as "Grievous Bodily Harm" or "Liquid X," have been topics of discussion on college campuses. Rohypnol is used as an anesthetic and sleep aid in other countries, but it is not approved for use in the United States. Before it was banned by the FDA in 1990, GHB was sold in health food stores and used by body builders to increase muscle growth. Currently, GHB is manufactured illegally, and some people acquire the recipe on the Internet. Rohypnol and GHB are popular among young people because they are inexpensive ("lunch money") drugs, and they produce a "floaty" state, a mild euphoria, increased sociability, and lowered inhibitions. For some people, Rohypnol works like a powerful sleeping pill. Jenny Altick was a college student when she tried the drug: "I'd just pass out. . . . it seemed like a very safe thing to take. It wasn't like acid or something that was totally chemical and bad. If you're thinking about trying coke [cocaine], you've heard how bad it is. There's that little thing in your head. But this one, no one had heard about it. It was one of those new things everyone was doing" (quoted in Bonnin, 1997: E1). For other users, however, the consequences are more dire. Rohypnol is known as the "date rape drug" because a number of women have reported that they were raped after an acquaintance secretly slipped the drug into their drink. The combination of alcohol and Rohypnol or GHB has also been linked to automobile accidents and deaths from overdoses, which occur because it is difficult to judge how much intoxication will result when depressants are mixed with alcohol (Bonnin, 1997).

 Narcotics

Narcotics or opiates are available in several forms: natural substances (e.g, opium, morphine, and codeine), opiate derivatives, which are created by making slight changes in the chemical composition of morphine (e.g., heroin and Percodan), and synthetic drugs, which produce opiatelike effects but are not chemically related to morphine (e.g., Darvon and Demerol). Because heroin is the most widely abused narcotic, we will focus primarily on its effects.

Who uses heroin? Young people are among the heaviest heroin users; however, only 1 percent of people between eighteen and twenty-nine years of age acknowledge that they have ever used the drug. Some people who try the drug have adverse side effects such as nausea and vomiting and never use it again; others become addicted. Current estimates of the number of U.S. heroin abusers range from 300,000 to 700,000. Most studies conclude that the typical heroin abuser is a young male, often a minority group member, under age thirty, who lives in a low-income area of a large urban center such as New York City (Fishbein and Pease, 1996).

What effect does heroin have on the body? Most heroin users inject the drug intravenously—a practice known as *mainlining* or *shooting*—which produces a tingling sensation and feeling of euphoria that is typically followed by a state of drowsiness or lethargy. Heroin users quickly develop a tolerance for the drug and must increase the dosage continually to achieve the same effect. Heroin and other opiates are highly addictive; users experience intense cravings for the drug and have physical symptoms such as diarrhea and dehydration if the drug is withdrawn.

What are the long-term effects of heroin? Although some users experience no long-term physical problems, there are serious risks involved in use. In high doses, heroin produces extreme respiratory depression, coma, and even death. Because the potency of street heroin is unknown, overdosing is always a possibility. Street heroin also tends to be diluted with other ingredients that produce adverse reactions in some users. Shooting up with contaminated needles can lead to hepatitis or AIDS. Heroin use also has been linked more directly to crime than have some other types of drug use. Because hardcore users have difficulty holding a job and yet need a continual supply of the drug, they often turn to robbery, burglary, shoplifting, pimping, prostitution, or working for the underground drug industry (Johnson et al., 1985).

 Hallucinogens

Hallucinogens or psychedelics are drugs that produce illusions and hallucinations. Mescaline (peyote), lysergic acid diethylamide (LSD), phencyclidine (PCP), and MDMA (Ecstasy) produce mild to profound psychological effects, depending on the dosage. Mescaline or peyote—the earliest hallucinogen used in North America—was consumed during ancient Native American religious celebrations.

In the 1960s, LSD became a well-known hallucinogen because of Dr. Timothy Leary's widely publicized advice, "turn on, tune in, drop out." LSD is one of the most powerful of the psychoactive drugs; a tiny dose (10 micrograms) of the odorless, tasteless, and colorless drug can produce dramatic, highly unpredictable psychological effects for up to 12 hours. These effects are often referred to as a *psychedelic trip,* and users report experiences ranging from the beautiful (a good trip) to the frightening and extremely depressing (a bad trip). Consequently, some LSD users take the drug only with the companionship of others who are familiar with the drug's effects. However, some studies have found that there is a possibility of *flashbacks* in which the user reexperiences the effects of the drug as much as a year after it was taken. Most long-term psychiatric problems associated with the drug involve people who are unaware that they have been given LSD, who show unstable personality characteristics before taking the drug, or who experience it under hostile or threatening circumstances (Levinthal, 1996).

Among the most recent hallucinogens are PCP ("angel dust") and MDMA ("Ecstasy"). PCP can be taken orally, intravenously, or by inhalation, but it is most often smoked. Initially, PCP was used as an anesthetic in surgical procedures, but it was removed from production when patients who received it showed signs of agitation, intense anxiety, hallucinations, and disorientation. Production then went underground, and PCP became a relatively inexpensive street drug that some dealers pass off as a more expensive drug such as LSD to unknowing customers.

In the mid-1980s, MDMA ("Ecstasy") hit the street market. Manufactured in clandestine labs by inexperienced chemists, Ecstasy, or "E," is a "designer drug" that is derived from amphetamines and has hallucinogenic effects. Users claim that it produces a state of relaxation, insight, euphoria, and heightened awareness without the side effects of LSD. Ecstasy has a high abuse potential and no recognized medical use (Milkman and Sunderwirth, 1987).

EXPLANATIONS OF DRUG ABUSE

Why do people abuse drugs? Various explanations have been given. Some focus on biological factors; others emphasize environmental influences. Social scientists believe that drug abuse is associated with continuous and cumulative influences from the time of conception throughout the life course (Fishbein and Pease, 1996). Thus to answer the question of why people abuse drugs, we must examine the intertwining biological, psychological, and sociological factors that affect people's behavior.

Biological Explanations

Some biological explanations of alcohol and other drug addiction focus on genetic factors. Some studies of alcoholism have found that children who have an alcoholic birth parent have a higher than normal risk of becoming alcoholics themselves, even if they are adopted at birth and reared by nonalcoholic parents. These studies suggest that the child of an alcoholic parent inherits a biological predisposition (or vulnerability) to problem drinking or alcoholism. For example, the child may inherit increased sensitivity to alcohol as indicated by impaired enzyme production, brain function, and physiological responsivity during alcohol intake. The child also may inherit cognitive or learning impairments (e.g., hyperactivity, attention deficit disorder, or language delay) or psychological features (e.g., impulsivity, sensation seeking, anxiety, or aggressiveness) that increase the risk of alcohol abuse by exaggerating the rewarding biological and psychological properties of alcohol (Fishbein and Pease, 1996).

Other biological studies focus on the relationship between the brain and drug addiction. These studies have found convincing evidence that drugs such as alcohol, heroin, and cocaine act directly on the brain mechanisms responsible for reward and punishment. As the drugs stimulate the areas of the brain that create the sensation of pleasure and suppress the perception of pain, the user receives reinforcement to engage in further drug-taking behavior. According to these findings, then, drugs that provide an immediate rush or intense euphoria (e.g., cocaine and heroin) are more likely to be abused than drugs that do not. Similarly, drugs that produce pleasant but rapidly dissipating effects (e.g., alcohol) tend to encourage users to take additional doses to maintain the pleasurable effects. Biological explanations provide some insights on drug abuse, but biological factors alone do not fully explain alcoholism and other drug dependency.

Psychological Explanations

Psychological explanations of drug abuse focus on either personality disorders or the effects of social learning and reinforcement on drug-taking behavior. Some studies have found that personality disorders—antisocial personality, psychopathy, impulsivity, affective disorder, and anxiety, among others—are more common among drug abusers than among nonabusers (Shedler and Block, 1990). Hyperactivity, learning disabilities, and behavioral disorders in childhood are also associated with a greater risk of substance abuse in adolescence or young adulthood. When people have low self-esteem or lack motivation, their desire to get away from problems is intensified, and drugs often provide the most available option for escape.

Social psychologists explain drug behavior in terms of social learning. According to *social learning theory,* drug and alcohol use and abuse are behaviors that are acquired and sustained through a learning process. Learning takes place through instrumental conditioning (positive reinforcement or punishment) and modeling (imitation) of other people's behavior. Every person learns attitudes, orientations, and general information about drug use from family members, friends, and significant others, so he or she comes to associate positive consequences (positive reinforcement) and negative consequences (punishment) with drug use. Therefore, whether the person abstains from, takes, or abuses drugs depends on the past, present, and anticipated rewards and punishments he or she associates with abstinence, use, or abuse. In a nutshell, the more an individual defines drug behavior as good, or at least excusable, the more that person is likely to use drugs (Akers, 1992).

 Sociological Explanations

The social psychological perspective on drug abuse and the interactionist perspective overlap. In contrast, functionalists focus on how drug use and abuse fulfills a function in society, and conflict theorists emphasize the role of powerful elites in determining what constitutes legal or illegal drug use.

THE INTERACTIONIST PERSPECTIVE

Like social psychologists, sociologists who use an interactionist framework believe that drug behavior is learned behavior that is strongly influenced by families, peers, and other people. In other words, individuals are more likely to use or abuse drugs if they have frequent, intense, and long-lasting interactions with people who use or abuse drugs. For example, some children learn to abuse alcohol or other drugs by watching their parents drink excessively or use illegal drugs. Other young people learn about drug use from their peer group. In his classic study of marijuana

users, sociologist Howard S. Becker (1963) concluded that drug users not only learn how to "do" drugs from other users but also what pleasurable reactions they should expect to have from drug use.

People also are more prone to accept attitudes and behaviors favorable to drug use if they spend time with members of a *drug subculture*—**a group of people whose attitudes, beliefs, and behaviors pertaining to drug use differ significantly from those of most people in the larger society.** Over time, people in heavy drinking or drug subcultures tend to become closer to others within their subculture and more distant from people outside the subculture. Given this, participants in hard-core drug subcultures quit taking drugs or drinking excessively only when something brings about a dramatic change in their attitudes, beliefs, and values regarding drugs. Although it is widely believed that most addicts could change their behavior if they chose to do so, according to *labeling theory,* it is particularly difficult for individuals to discontinue alcohol and other drug abuse once they have been labeled "alcoholics" or "drug addicts." Because of the prevailing ideology that alcoholism and drug addiction are personal problems rather than social problems, individuals tend to be held solely responsible for their behavior.

THE FUNCTIONALIST PERSPECTIVE

Why does the level of drug abuse remain high in the United States? Functionalists point out that social institutions such as the family, education, and religion, which previously kept deviant behavior in check, have become fragmented and somewhat disorganized. Because they have, it is now necessary to use formal mechanisms of social control to prohibit people from taking illegal drugs or driving under the influence of alcohol or other drugs. External controls in the form of law enforcement are also required to discourage people from growing, manufacturing, or importing illegal substances.

Functionalists believe that activities in society continue because they serve important societal functions. Prescription and over-the-counter drugs, for example, are functional for patients because they ease pain, cure illness, and sometimes enhance or extend life. They are functional for doctors because they provide a means for treating illness and help to justify the doctor's fee. They are functional for pharmacists because they provide a source of employment; without pills to dispense, there would be no

This man may be playing double jeopardy with his life. The purity of street drugs often is in doubt, and shooting up with contaminated needles is a significant source of new AIDS cases in the United States.

need for pharmacists. But dysfunctions also occur with prescription drugs: Patients may experience adverse side effects or develop a psychological dependence on the drug; doctors, pharmacists, and drug companies may be sued because they manufactured, prescribed, or sold a drug that is alleged to cause bodily harm to users.

Illicit drugs also have functions and dysfunctions. On the one hand, illicit drug use creates and perpetuates jobs at all levels of the criminal justice system, the federal government, and social service agencies that deal with problems of alcoholism and drug addiction. What, for example, would employees at the Drug Enforcement Administration (DEA)—the principal federal narcotics control agency—do if the United States did not have an array of illicit drugs that are defined as the "drug problem"? On the other hand, the dysfunctions of illicit drug use extend throughout society. At the individual level, addictive drugs such as heroin, cocaine, and barbiturates create severe physical and mental health problems as well as economic crises for addicts, their families, and acquaintances. At the societal level, drug abuse contributes to lost productivity, human potential and life, and money. Billions of dollars in taxpayers' money that

might be used for education or preventive health care are spent making and enforcing drug laws and dealing with drug-related crime and the spread of AIDS by addicts who shoot up with contaminated needles. Addiction to illegal drugs, the abuse of legal drugs, and the abuse of alcohol and tobacco exacerbates the loss of human potential and undermines the stability of society.

THE CONFLICT PERSPECTIVE

According to conflict theorists, people in positions of economic and political power make the sale, use, and possession of drugs abused by the poor and the powerless illegal. We mentioned earlier that opium smoking was outlawed because it was associated with the Chinese. Similarly, marijuana smoking, which was associated primarily with Mexican workers who were brought to the United States during the 1920s to work in some fields and factories, was restricted by the Marijuana Tax Act of 1937. Although the name of this legislation suggests that its purpose was to raise tax revenues, the intent was to criminalize marijuana and provide a mechanism for driving Mexican workers back across the border so that they would not be a threat to U.S.-born workers who couldn't find jobs during the Great Depression. As middle- and upper-middle-class, college-educated people took up marijuana smoking in the 1950s and 1960s, many states reduced the penalties for its use. In sum, restricting the drugs that members of a subordinate racial-ethnic group use is one method of suppressing the group and limiting its ability to threaten dominant group members or gain upward mobility in society (Fishbein and Pease, 1996). Whether a drug is legal or illegal is determined by those who control the nation's political and legal apparatus.

Conflict theorists also point out that powerful corporate interests perpetuate the use and abuse of legal drugs. Corporations that manufacture, market, and sell alcohol, tobacco, and pharmaceuticals reap huge profits from products that exact a heavy toll on the personal health and well-being of abusers, their families and communities, and the larger society. Recent congressional hearings on the tobacco industry's alleged manipulation of nicotine levels to make cigarette smoking more addictive have helped to highlight this point. However, by contributing millions of dollars each year to election campaigns, these corporations position themselves to manipulate political decisions that could affect them. Members of

Congress who control most tobacco-related regulations typically receive large campaign contributions from political action committees funded by the tobacco industry and often represent districts where tobacco companies are among the largest employers. Using their wealth and political clout, elites in tobacco companies have spent years vigorously fighting measures, including those that would classify and regulate tobacco as a drug, affecting the industry's more than $50 billion annual revenue (Kluger, 1996).

THE FUTURE OF ALCOHOL AND DRUG ABUSE

How to prevent abuse of alcohol and other drugs and how to treat drug-related problems after they arise are controversial issues in contemporary society. What kinds of drug abuse prevention programs are available? Will future treatment programs for alcoholics and drug addicts differ from the ones that are available today?

 Prevention Programs

Drug and alcohol prevention programs can be divided into three major categories: primary, secondary, and tertiary prevention. *Primary prevention* **refers to programs that seek to prevent drug problems before they begin.** Most primary prevention programs focus on people who have had little or no previous experience with drugs. In contrast, *secondary prevention* programs seek to limit the extent of drug abuse, prevent the spread of drug abuse to substances beyond those already experienced, and teach strategies for the responsible use of licit drugs such as alcohol (Levinthal, 1996). For example, a program directed at college students who already consume alcohol might focus on how to drink responsibly by emphasizing the dangers of drinking and driving. Finally, *tertiary prevention* programs seek to limit relapses by individuals recovering from alcoholism or drug addiction. The purpose of tertiary prevention is to ensure that people who have entered treatment for some form of drug abuse become free of drugs and remain that way.

In the United States, a variety of primary and secondary prevention strategies have been employed, including (1) reduction in the availability of drugs,

(2) punishment of drug addicts, (3) scare tactics and negative education, (4) objective-information approaches, (5) promotional campaigns, and (6) self-esteem enhancement and affective education (Levinthal, 1996). We'll look at each in more detail.

In an attempt to reduce the supply and availability of drugs, U.S. law enforcement agencies have expended vast resources to control the domestic production, sale, and consumption of illicit drugs, but their efforts have removed only a small fraction of drugs (Wren, 1996a). The U.S. government has also tried to reduce the influx of drugs from other countries. However, estimates of global retail sales of illicit drugs range from $180 billion to more than $300 billion annually, making the underground drug economy one of the most expansive commercial activities in the world. In North America and Europe alone, the combined sales of heroin, cocaine, and marijuana add up to about $122 billion annually (Stares, 1996). Despite drug laws and an array of sanctions against drug trafficking, drug use and abuse have not been significantly deterred in the United States or elsewhere. Map 8.1 shows the volume of drugs that continue to arrive in the United States from other nations.

Efforts to punish offenders of U.S. drug laws have clogged the criminal justice system and overcrowded prisons without noticeably reducing the sale and consumption of illegal drugs in this country. In fact, scare tactics and negative education programs have not fared much better; they turn students off and do not achieve their desired goal. In fact, scare tactics appear to pique some students' curiosity about drugs rather than deter their use. Objective information programs often begin in kindergarten and progress through grade 12. Using texts, curriculum guides, videos, and other materials, teachers impart factual information about drugs to students, but as with scare tactics, students sometimes become more—instead of less—interested in drug experimentation. "Just Say No" and other magic bullet promotional campaigns for preventing drug abuse have also had limited success in deterring drug use. An eighteen-year-old student who smoked his first marijuana joint at age thirteen explains why he thinks these programs are ineffective: "When someone tells you not to do it, that makes you want to do it even more" (Kolata, 1996a:A12). Self-esteem enhancement and affective education programs focus on the underlying emotional and attitudinal factors that are involved in drug abuse while building character through teaching

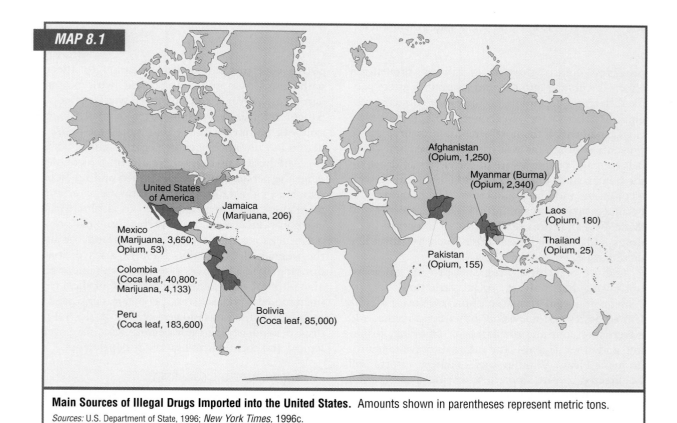

MAP 8.1

United States of America

Jamaica
(Marijuana, 206)

Mexico
(Marijuana, 3,650;
Opium, 53)

Colombia
(Coca leaf, 40,800;
Marijuana, 4,133)

Peru
(Coca leaf, 183,600)

Bolivia
(Coca leaf, 85,000)

Afghanistan
(Opium, 1,250)

Myanmar (Burma)
(Opium, 2,340)

Laos
(Opium, 180)

Thailand
(Opium, 25)

Pakistan
(Opium, 155)

Main Sources of Illegal Drugs Imported into the United States. Amounts shown in parentheses represent metric tons.

Sources: U.S. Department of State, 1996; *New York Times*, 1996c.

positive social values and attitudes. These programs are most effective when they are incorporated into more comprehensive prevention programs.

If the purpose of prevention programs is to reduce actual drug-taking behavior, what types of programs have the greatest likelihood of success? Many social analysts suggest that family and school-based primary and secondary prevention programs are the most effective. Previously, some prevention programs focused on high school students, but today elementary schools are among the first lines of attack because drug-taking behavior now starts at younger ages. Nearly 75 percent of U.S. public schools have a program known as DARE (Drug Abuse Resistance Education), which is taught by specially trained police officers who teach children how to resist drugs. Critics suggest that police officers, whom many young people view as authority figures, are not the best people to teach adolescents that drug use is not cool. Critics also note that one-shot programs that are forced on students may not prevent drug abuse. Children who have been through the DARE program are no less likely to smoke, drink, or use other drugs than children who have not been through the program (Kolata, 1996a).

Prevention programs for the future that look hopeful emphasize *life skills training*. The Life Skills Training Program developed by Gilbert Botvin at Cornell Medical School consists of a fifteen-session curriculum directed toward seventh-grade students. Booster sessions are offered in the eighth and ninth grades. The program provides information on the short-term consequences of alcohol or other drug use and teaches participants critical thinking skills, independent decision making, ways to reduce anxiety and resist peer pressure to take drugs, and ways of gaining a sense of personal control and self-esteem (Botvin and Tortu, 1988). Unlike programs that primarily tell students to stay off drugs, life skills training attempts to give students the tools they need to stay drug free. Although the short-term effects of life skills programs are impressive, according to social scientist Charles F. Levinthal, they erode over time (1996). Still, Levinthal believes that we can learn important lessons from prevention strategies that have failed in the past, lessons that we can use to create better approaches in the future.

Future prevention programs will be family, school, and community based. They will offer alternative activities and outlets to drug use. These programs—like other drug abuse prevention efforts—will take into account issues that affect people differently depending on their race/ethnicity, religion, or other factors. Reaching across lines of race, class, and gender, the next generation of drug abuse prevention programs will use cable television channels to make people aware of the effects of drugs on the human body and how to get help in dealing with alcoholism and drug addiction. The Internet will become a vital source of information. Current World Wide Web sites provide an array of information on drugs and offer unique features such as an on-line dictionary of street drug slang.

Future prevention programs provide cause for optimism, but only if social structural factors change. If illegal drugs continue to flow into the United States and television, other mass media, and advertising continue to glamorize smoking, drinking, and other drug use, the future of preventive programs is bleak. Without social change, efforts will be directed toward apprehension and incarceration of drug offenders and treatment programs for drug addicts and alcoholics, not at primary or secondary prevention strategies.

 Treatment Programs

Tertiary prevention programs are programs that aim to ensure that people who have sought help for some form of drug abuse remain drug free. It follows from the biological and social learning explanations for substance abuse and alcohol addiction that treatment must deal with the body's physiological and psychological responses. Therefore, *alcohol and drug treatment* involves the use of activities designed to eliminate physical and psychological addiction and to prevent relapse—returning to abuse and/or addiction (Fishbein and Pease, 1996). Most treatment programs are based on a medical model or therapeutic community.

THE MEDICAL TREATMENT MODEL

The *medical treatment model* considers drug abuse and alcoholism to be medical problems that must be resolved by medical treatment by medical officials. Treatment may take the form of *aversion therapy* or *behavioral conditioning*. For example, drugs such as Cyclazocine and Nalozone are given to heroin and opiate addicts to prevent the euphoric feeling that they associate with taking the drugs. Supposedly, when the pleasure is gone, the person will no longer abuse the drug. Some heroin addicts

also receive methadone detoxification to alleviate withdrawal symptoms associated with stopping heroin use. Over a one- to three-week period, the patient receives decreasing doses of methadone, a synthetic opium derivative that blocks the desire for heroin but does not have its negative side effects.

Antabuse is used in the treatment of alcoholism. After the person has been detoxified and no alcohol remains in the bloodstream, Antabuse is administered along with small quantities of alcohol for several consecutive days. Because this combination produces negative effects such as nausea and vomiting, the individual eventually develops an aversion to drinking, which becomes associated with uncomfortable physical symptoms. Although the medical treatment model works for some people, it is criticized for focusing on the physiological effects of alcohol and drug dependency and not dealing with the psychological and sociological aspects of dependency.

THE THERAPEUTIC COMMUNITY

When substance abusers are perceived to have an underlying psychological problem, treatment generally involves counseling, rehabilitation, and/or the therapeutic community. Counseling often employs rehabilitated alcoholics or addicts who encourage participants to take more responsibility for their lives so that they can function better in the community. Some counseling and rehabilitation programs take place on an outpatient basis or as day treatment; others involve residential treatment. *Outpatient programs* allow drug abusers to remain at home and continue working while attending regular group and individual meetings. *Day treatment* takes place in a hospital setting where the abuser participates in daylong treatment groups and individual counseling sessions and returns home in the evening. The *therapeutic community approach* is based on the idea that drug abuse is best treated by intensive individual and group counseling in either a residential or a nonresidential setting. Residential treatment takes place in a special house or dormitory where alcoholics or drug addicts remain for periods of time ranging from several months to several years. One of the most widely known residential treatment centers is the Betty Ford Clinic in California, but many others exist throughout the country. Residents in these programs receive therapy and try to establish new behavior patterns outside of their drinking or drug abuse environments (Bertram et al., 1996).

Perhaps the best known nonresidential therapeutic communities are Alcoholics Anonymous (AA), founded in 1935, and its offshoot, Narcotics Anonymous (NA). Both AA and NA provide members with support in their efforts to overcome drug dependence and addiction. AA was established in 1935 by two alcoholics who were seeking a way of returning to sober life (Fishbein and Pease, 1996). Today, the organization has more than 30,000 chapters with more than 600,000 members. Members use only their first names to ensure anonymity, and recovering alcoholics serve as sponsors and counselors for others. AA and NA are based on a twelve-step program that requires members to acknowledge that they are alcoholics or drug addicts who must have the help of God and other people to remain sober or drug free. Group support is central to success in these programs, as journalist Caroline Knapp (1996:253–254) explains:

> A few months after my one-year anniversary [of sobriety] I went to the meeting . . . on the ground floor of a church outside of Boston. . . . One person tells his or her story for the first half hour, and then the meeting opens up, first to those in their first month of sobriety, then to those with three months or less, then six months or less, and so on. . . . At the end of the meeting there was a presentation for a young guy named John, who was celebrating one year without a drink. . . . He was so happy that evening, so grateful to get that one-year medallion, and so moved by the amount of support he'd gotten over the year, that his eyes welled up and his voice kept cracking. "I can't thank you all enough," he said, and his face was the picture of hope. . . . Then I had an image of every person in that room . . . getting into our beds clean and sober, another day without a drink behind us. It was a simple image but it filled me with a range of complicated feelings: appreciation for the simple presence of all those people; admiration for their courage and strength; a tinge of melancholy for the amount of pain it must have taken each and every one of them to put down the drink; affection for their humanity. I didn't realize until hours later that there was a name for that feeling. It's called love.

Sociologists believe AA is successful because it gives former alcoholics the opportunity to be de-labeled as stigmatized deviants and relabeled as former and repentant deviants. It should be kept in mind, however, that social class and personality factors affect people's ability to enter into the repentant role, which requires a public admission of guilt and repentance, and to interact successfully with others in the program (Trice and Roman, 1970).

All the approaches for reducing alcohol and drug abuse that we have discussed can help certain individuals, but none address what to do about social structural factors that contribute to the drug problem. Because drug- and alcohol-related problems and their solutions are part of deeper social issues and struggles, they cannot be dealt with in isolation, as social scientist Philippe Bourgeois (1995: 319, 327) explains:

> Drugs are not the root of the problems . . . they are the expression of deeper, structural dilemmas. Self-destructive addiction is merely the medium for desperate people to internalize their frustrations, resistance, and powerlessness. In other words, we can safely ignore the drug hysterias that periodically sweep through the United States. Instead we should focus our ethical concerns and political energies on the contradictions posed by the persistence of inner-city poverty in the midst of extraordinary opulence. In the same vein, we need to recognize and dismantle the class- and ethnic-based apartheids that riddle the U.S. landscape. . . . The problem of substance abuse in the United States is worse in the 1990s than in the recent past because of a polarization of the structural roots that generate self-destructive behavior and criminal activity. The economic base of the traditional working class has eroded throughout the country. Greater proportions of the population are socially marginalized. The restructuring of the world economy by multinational corporations, finance capital, and digital electronic technology, as well as the exhaustion of social democratic models for public sector intervention [e.g., welfare programs] on behavior of the poor, has escalated inequalities around class, ethnicity, and gender. . . . There is no technocratic solution. Any long-term paths out of the quagmire will have to address the structural and political economic roots, as well as the ideological and cultural roots of social marginalization. The first step out of the impasse, however, requires a fundamental ethical and political reevaluation of basic socioeconomic models and human values.

If the United States sets out to reduce inequalities in all areas of social life, perhaps the drug problem will be alleviated as well. What do you think it would take to make this happen?

SUMMARY

➤ *What are the major patterns of drinking?*

Social scientists divide long-term drinking patterns into four categories: (1) *social drinkers* consume alcoholic beverages primarily on social occasions and may drink either occasionally or relatively frequently; (2) *heavy drinkers* are more frequent drinkers who typically consume greater quantities of alcohol when they drink and are more likely to become intoxicated; (3) *acute alcoholics* have trouble controlling their use of alcohol and plan their schedule around drinking; and (4) *chronic alcoholics* have lost control over their drinking and tend to engage in compulsive behavior such as hiding liquor bottles.

➤ *What are the major hazards associated with tobacco use?*

Nicotine is a toxic, dependency-producing drug that is responsible for about one in every five deaths in the United States. People who smoke have a greater likelihood of developing cardiovascular disease, lung cancer, and/or cancer of the larynx, mouth, and esophagus. Even those who do not smoke may be subjected to the hazard of environmental tobacco smoke—the smoke in the air as a result of other people's tobacco smoking. Infants born to women who smoke typically have lower than average birth weights and sometimes have slower rates of physical and mental growth.

➤ *What problems are associated with use of prescription and over-the-counter drugs?*

Some prescription drugs have the potential for short-term abuse and long-term psychological and physical dependence. This form of dependency is known as *iatrogenic addiction*—drug dependency that results from physician-supervised treatment for a recognized medical disorder. Over-the-counter drugs, which are widely advertised and readily available, may be dangerous when combined with alcohol or other drugs.

➤ *What categories of people are most likely to use marijuana?*

Most marijuana users are between the ages of eighteen and twenty-five; however, use by twelve- to seventeen-year-olds more than doubled in the 1990s. More men than women smoke marijuana; however, teenage girls are slightly more likely than boys to have used marijuana at least once.

➤ *In the United States, what are the major stimulant drugs?*

Cocaine and amphetamines are the major stimulant drugs abused in the United States. Cocaine is an extremely potent and dependency-producing stimulant drug. Amphetamines can be obtained legally in the form of diet pills and pep formulas when they are prescribed by a physician.

➤ *What are depressants and what health-related risk do they pose?*

As the name indicates, depressants depress the central nervous system; they also may have some pain-killing properties. The most common depressants are barbiturates and antianxiety drugs or tranquilizers. Users may develop both physical addiction and psychological dependency on these drugs. There is also the risk of *potentiation*—the drug interaction that takes place when two drugs are mixed together and the combination produces a far greater effect than that of either drug administered separately.

➤ *What other drugs are widely abused in the United States?*

Narcotics or opiates, including natural substances (e.g, opium, morphine, and codeine), opiate derivatives (e.g., heroin and Percodan), and synthetic drugs with opiatelike effects (e.g., Darvon and Demerol) are frequently abused. Hallucinogens or psychedelics such as mescaline (peyote), lysergic acid diethylamide (LSD), phencyclidine (PCP), and MDMA (Ecstasy) are also widely abused.

➤ *How do biological and psychological perspectives view alcohol and drug addiction?*

Biological explanations of alcohol and drug addiction focus on inherited biological factors and on the effects of drugs on the human brain. Psychological explanations of drug abuse focus on personality disorders and the effects of social learning and reinforcement on people's drug-taking behavior.

➤ *How do sociological perspectives view alcohol and drug addiction?*

Interactionists believe that drug use and abuse are learned behaviors that are strongly influenced by families, peers, and others who serve as role models. People are more prone to accept attitudes and behaviors that are favorable to drug use if they spend time with members of a drug subculture. Functionalists believe that drug-related problems have increased as social institutions such as the family, education, and religion have become fragmented and somewhat disorganized. However, use of alcohol and other drugs serves important functions even though some aspects of their use are dysfunctional for society. According to conflict theorists, people in positions of economic and political power are responsible for making the sale, use, and possession of some drugs illegal. Conflict theorists also point out that powerful corporate interests perpetuate the use and abuse of alcohol, tobacco, and other legal drugs.

➤ *What is the purpose of prevention and treatment programs?*

Primary prevention programs seek to prevent drug problems before they begin. Secondary prevention programs seek to limit the extent of drug abuse, prevent the spread of drug abuse to other substances beyond the drugs already experienced, and teach strategies for the responsible use of licit drugs such as alcohol. Tertiary prevention programs seek to limit relapses by individuals recovering from alcoholism or drug addiction. They may be based either on a medical model or the therapeutic community. The best-known therapeutic community is Alcoholics Anonymous (AA).

➤ *What other factors must be taken into account in efforts to reduce the drug problem?*

Alcoholism and drug abuse are intertwined with other social problems such as dramatic changes in the economic and technological bases of the society, the growing gap between the rich and poor, and inequalities based on race/ethnicity and gender.

KEY TERMS

codependency, p. 154
drug, p. 147
drug addiction, p. 149
drug dependency, p. 149
drug subculture, p. 164

environmental tobacco smoke, p. 155
fetal alcohol syndrome (FAS), p. 153

primary prevention, p. 166
tolerance, p. 149
withdrawal, p. 149

QUESTIONS FOR CRITICAL THINKING

1. Does public tolerance of alcohol and tobacco lead to increased use of these drugs? Why do many people view the use of alcohol and tobacco differently from the use of illicit drugs?

2. If stimulants, depressants, and hallucinogens have such potentially hazardous side effects, why do so many people use these drugs? If drug enforcement policies were more stringently enforced, would there be less drug abuse in this country?

3. As a sociologist, how would you propose to deal with the drug problem in the United States? If you were called upon to revamp existing drug laws and policies, what, if any, changes would you make in them?

4. How have changes in technology affected the problem of alcohol and drug abuse over the past century? How have changes in the global economy affected drug-related problems in this country and others?

Chapter Nine

Crime and
Criminal Justice

A bunch of us were sitting on the curb on our block, shooting the breeze, when the ice cream man drove up the street. . . . The ice cream man rang his bell and stopped a half block from us as excited young children ran outdoors, flailing their arms. . . .

There was no special plan. We just got up, drifted on over, and studied the scene. The ice cream man was so busy serving children that he didn't notice us surrounding him. While the fellas stood in back, watching the man go in and out of the freezer, I walked to the front of the truck and peeked inside the cab. . . . I noticed he'd left the engine running. I quietly opened the door and slid inside, then stomped the accelerator and pulled away. As I drove down the street, I glanced into the big rearview mirror and saw the shocked ice cream man standing in the middle of the street, holding Popsicles in each hand.

▲—*Journalist Nathan McCall remembers the day that he and other members of his gang stole an ice cream truck*
(McCall, 1994: 87–88)

As McCall tells the story, what he did seems nothing more than a youthful escapade, but his theft of the ice cream truck is an example of opportunistic crime. Some sociologists believe that for crime to occur, people must have access to *illegitimate opportunity structures*—circumstances that allow people to acquire through illegitimate activities what they cannot achieve legitimately (Cloward and Ohlin, 1960). In this chapter, we examine types of crimes and explanations of crime, as well as the criminal justice system.

CRIME AS A SOCIAL PROBLEM

Many people in the United States fear crime and are somewhat obsessed with it even though they have no direct daily exposure to criminal behavior. Their information about crime comes from the media (Chermak, 1995) and sometimes from watching real-crime dramas such as *America's Most Wanted* and fictionalized crime stories such as *N.Y.P.D. Blue* on television. Media coverage of crime is extensive and may in fact contribute to our widespread perception that crime has increased dramatically in this country. The truth, however, is rather different. With the exception of the rate of serious and violent crime, which has continued to fall during the last five years, crime rates have remained relatively stable over the past two decades (Butterfield, 1997). That is not to say that crime isn't a problem. Crime statistics tell only part of the story. Crime *is* a significant social problem because it endangers people's lives, property, and sense of well-being. About 35 million people annually are victims of crimes in the United States, and 100 billion tax dollars are spent annually on law enforcement and the administration of justice (Donziger, 1996). Even individuals who are not directly victimized by crime are harmed because they have to pay increased taxes to fight it (Barlow, 1996).

 Problems with Official Statistics

Over the past two decades, sophisticated computer-based information systems have not only improved rates of detection, apprehension, and conviction of offenders but also provided immediate access to millions of bits of information about crime, suspects, and offenders (Barlow, 1996). The leading source of information on crimes reported in the United States is the *Uniform Crime Report* (UCR). It is published annually by the Federal Bureau of Investigation and is based on data provided by federal, state, and local law enforcement agencies. The UCR tracks two categories of reported crimes: index crimes and nonindex crimes. There are eight *index crimes:* murder, rape, robbery, assault, burglary (breaking into private property to commit a serious crime), motor vehicle theft, arson, and larceny (theft of property worth $50 or more). All other crimes (including arrests for prostitution and drug- and alcohol-related offenses) are considered *nonindex crimes.* The UCR also includes a "Crime Clock" (see Figure 9.1), showing how often (on average) the index crimes are committed in this country. In 1998, for example, a murder occurred in the United States an average of once every 31 minutes, a robbery every minute, and a forcible rape occurred every six minutes (FBI, 1999). During the same year, there were about 14.5 million arrests for

all criminal offenses (excluding traffic violations). Because these statistics are highly publicized, it is easy to see why people are concerned for their personal safety, their property, and their very lives.

How accurate are these crime statistics? Any answer to this question must take into account the fact that legal definitions of some offenses vary from jurisdiction to jurisdiction and that the statistics reflect only crimes that are reported to law enforcement agencies or that police officers see occur. According to the UCR, overall rates of crime (number of crimes per 100,000 people), which increased sharply between 1987 and 1991, have decreased annually since then. This downward trend probably reflects several factors, including a shift in population. The percentage of the U.S. population under age twenty-six—the age group most likely to commit crimes—began to decline in 1992. The FBI is in the process of replacing the UCR with a more comprehensive system called the National Incident-Based Reporting System (NIBRS). This system will keep more detailed information about offenders and allow sophisticated statistical analysis, but it too will be limited to data on reported crimes.

Because the number of crimes *reported* is not necessarily the number of crimes *committed,* the Bureau of Justice Statistics conducts an annual National Crime Victimization Survey (NCVS) of 100,000 randomly selected households to identify crime victims, whether the crime was reported or not (see Chapter 1). These surveys indicate that the number of crimes committed is substantially higher than the number reported. However, the NCVS has limitations too: (1) Responses are based on recall, and some people don't remember specifically when a crime occurred; (2) for various reasons, respondents may not be truthful; and (3) the surveys focus on theft and assault and do not measure workplace crimes such as embezzlement or bribery (Vito and Holmes, 1994).

 Defining Crime and Delinquency

Crime is behavior that violates the criminal law and is punishable by fine, jail term, or other negative sanctions. In the United States, criminal laws can be enacted at the local, state, and federal levels. As a result, some laws apply uniformly throughout the states while others vary from state to state or apply only in the local jurisdiction where they were passed. Whether the law that is broken is federal, state, or

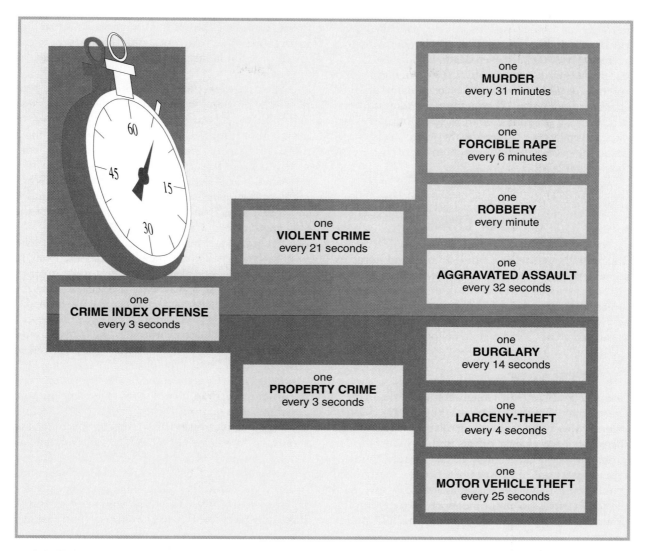

FIGURE 9.1 *Crime Clock, 1998*
The crime clock should be viewed with care. Being the most aggregate representation of UCR data, it is designed to convey the annual reported crime experience by showing the relative frequency of occurrence of the Index Offenses. This mode of display should not be taken to imply a regularity in the commission of the offense; rather, it represents the annual ratio of crime to fixed time intervals.
Source: FBI, 1999.

local, there are two components to every crime: the act itself and *criminal intent*, expressed in the concept of *mens rea*, meaning "guilty mind." An individual's intent in committing a crime may range from willful conduct (hiring someone to kill one's spouse) to an unintentional act of negligence that is defined as a crime (leaving a small child unattended in a locked automobile in extremely hot weather, resulting in the child's death).

Criminal law is divided into two major categories: misdemeanors and felonies. *Misdemeanors* **are relatively minor crimes that are punishable by a fine or less than a year in jail.** Examples include public drunkenness, shoplifting, and traffic violations. *Felonies* **are** more serious crimes, such as murder, rape, or aggravated assault, that are punishable by more than a year's imprisonment or even death. Children and adolescents below a certain age (usually eighteen) who commit illegal or antisocial acts usually are not charged with criminal conduct but are adjudicated as *delinquent* by a juvenile court judge. However, when older juveniles are charged with violent crimes, it is becoming increasingly common to *certify* or *waive* them to adult court.

TYPES OF CRIMES

To make the study of crime—a large and complex subject—manageable, sociologists and criminologists categorize types of crime. In this section, we will look at six categories of crime: violent crime, property crime, occupational crime, corporate crime, organized crime, and juvenile delinquency.

Violent Crime

In the United States, a violent crime occurs an average of once every 21 seconds (FBI, 1999). *Violent crime* consists of actions involving force or the threat of force against others and includes murder, rape, robbery, and aggravated assault. Violent crimes are committed against people; nonviolent crimes are usually committed against property. People tend to fear violent crime more than other kinds of crime because victims are often physically injured or even killed and because violent crime receives the most sustained attention from law enforcement officials and the media (see Parker, 1995; Warr, 1995).

MURDER

The *UCR* defines *murder* as the unlawful, intentional killing of one person by another. (Killing in self-defense or during wartime is not murder.) By this definition, murder involves not only an unlawful act but also *malice aforethought*—the *intention* of doing a wrongful act. A person who buys a gun, makes a plan to kill someone, and carries out the plan has probably committed murder. In contrast, *manslaughter* is the unlawful, *unintentional* killing of one person by another. An intoxicated person who shoots a gun into the air probably holds no malice toward the bystander who is killed by a stray

bullet. Sometimes a person's intentions are clear, but many times they are not, and the lines between intentional, unintentional, and accidental homicides are blurred.

Mass murder **is the killing of four or more people at one time and in one place by the same person.** Unfortunately, there is no shortage of examples of mass murder in the United States. Among the most notorious "Texas killers" are George Hennard, who shot and killed twenty-two people at a Luby's Cafeteria in Killeen, Texas, in 1991, and Charles Whitman, who shot fifteen people fatally and wounded fourteen others from a tower on the campus of the University of Texas at Austin in 1965.

According to criminologists, mass murderers tend to kill in the areas where they live. They are likely to be male, problem drinkers, and collectors of firearms and other weapons, which they often hide (Dietz, 1986). Some recent mass murderers have been disgruntled employees or former employees who seek out supervisors and coworkers in the workplace; a number of these violent eruptions have occurred in post offices (Holmes and Holmes, 1993).

Serial murder **is the killing of three or more people over more than a month by the same person.** Serial murders account for fewer than 5,000 victims annually but receive extensive media coverage. Ted Bundy, John Wayne Gacy, and Jeffrey Dahmer are among the most well-known serial killers. Bundy, who was convicted of three murders and suspected in more than thirty-six other killings, was executed in Florida in 1989. Gacy was convicted of thirty-three murders of young men in Illinois, and Dahmer was convicted of fifteen counts of first-degree intentional homicide in Wisconsin after the murders of many young males.

It's difficult to characterize serial killers, outside of the fact that the best-known ones are white males. Some travel extensively to locate their victims; others kill near where they live. One study identified four basic types of serial killers: (1) *visionaries*, who kill because they hear a voice or have a vision that commands them to commit the murderous acts; (2) *missionaries*, who take it on themselves to rid the community or the world of what they believe is an undesirable type of person; (3) *hedonists*, who obtain personal or sexual gratification from violence; and (4) *power/control seekers*, who achieve gratification from the complete possession of the victim (Holmes, 1988).

Nature and Extent of the Problem. Statistics on murder are among the most accurate official crime statistics available. Murders rarely go unreported, and suspects are usually apprehended and charged (FBI, 1999). Although annual rates vary slightly, murder follows certain patterns in terms of gender, age, race, and region of the country. Men make up the vast majority of murder victims and offenders. Of the 22,000 to 23,000 murders that are reported annually in this country, about 80 percent of the victims and 90 percent of the offenders are male. Males kill other males in about 86 percent of cases. Females kill 14 percent of the male victims, often because the females think they are in a life-threatening situation.

Age patterns are clearly evident in murder rates. Almost 90 percent of all murder victims are eighteen or older; nearly half of these are between ages twenty and thirty-five. Murder arrest rates per 100,000 for youths age ten through seventeen decreased significantly for the fifth year in a row in 1998. According to one analyst, the decrease is due to "some of the glamour of being a thug, walking around with a gun . . . [being gone] . . . because people 13, 14, and 15 years old have seen so many of their friends or relatives being killed or going to prison" (Butterfield, 1996:A9).

Most murders are intraracial. More than half of all murder victims in the United States are African American, and more than 90 percent of them are killed by other African Americans. Similarly, about 80 percent of white murder victims are killed by other white people (FBI, 1999). Murder takes a greater toll on young African American males than on any other group in society. Race and class factors are often intertwined: Poor people are much more likely to kill than are members of the middle and upper classes, and a higher proportion of people of color live below the U.S. poverty level because of racial discrimination and generations of inequality in education and employment.

Large metropolitan areas of the nation have a murder rate of about 10 victims per 100,000 residents; rural counties and cities outside metropolitan areas have a rate of about 5 per 100,000 (FBI, 1999). However, the incidence of murder is unevenly distributed within cities. Many suburbs have extremely low rates of murder compared to those of central cities. In the United States overall, murder is most likely to occur in the Southern states. Not only is the South the most populous region, it also views the possession and use of guns and other weapons more positively than other regions.

In the past, most murder victims knew their killers, but this pattern seems to be gradually changing. Today, slightly less than half of all murder victims know their assailants. About 12 percent are related to their assailants, and 35 percent are acquainted with them well enough to at least engage in an argument. Of the remaining victims, 13 percent are murdered by strangers, and in about 40 percent of cases, the relationship between victim and offender is unknown. This pattern does differ somewhat when we look at gender differences in victimization. Among female murder victims, almost 25 percent are slain by a husband or boyfriend, whereas only 3 percent of male victims are killed by a wife or girlfriend (FBI, 1999).

Across the nation, guns are used in approximately 70 percent of all murders annually—a fact that leads to ongoing political debate over gun control, especially of handguns. The death rate from guns among African American males aged 15 to 19 is about 153 per 100,000 as contrasted with about 28 per 100,000 among their white peers. Cutting or stabbing instruments are used in slightly more than 10 percent of murders, and hands, fists, and feet are used as weapons about 5 percent of the time (FBI, 1999).

Social Responses to Murder. Even though most murders are not random, many people have a deep and persistent fear of strangers. According to one analyst:

> We have responded [in various ways to the threat of murder]. Some of us by minimizing our time in public space for fear of encountering the random menace; many by purchasing a range of weapons, locks, bolts, alarms, and insurance; parents, by acting as virtual bodyguards for our children; governments, by dispensing crime prevention advice which promotes individual responsibility for keeping crime at bay. But has this reduced our fear? Or contributed to our greater security? Clearly not. (Stanko, 1990:viii)

Individual responses are intensified by media coverage of violent personal crimes, especially murder. The special newsworthiness of murder is discussed in Box 9.1.

At state and federal levels, the government has responded to the public's fear of murder by increasing

What Makes Murder So Newsworthy?

"If it ain't a homicide, then I'm not interested."

—*A newspaper reporter as he leafed through the morning police blotter reports (Chermak, 1995:55)*

"Do you have any bodies for me?"

—*A reporter making her daily calls to police divisions, hospitals, and the coroner's office (Chermak, 1995:55)*

Crime is the fourth largest category of news reported in the media. In fact, if we exclude sports and business, which take up so much space that they get their own newspaper sections, and television programs, the only topic that gets more news space and time than crime is general interest (the arts, entertainment, people, etc.). Politics, foreign affairs, environmental issues, scientific discoveries, medical and health issues, natural disasters, plane crashes, power outages, chemical explosions, school strikes, accidents, ceremonies, parades—all get less coverage than crime. Moreover, almost 25 percent of the crime reported in the news is murder (Chermak, 1995:53). What makes murder so newsworthy?

First, of course, there is the issue of seriousness. Reporters look for breaking stories on murder because the law says that murder is the most serious crime and society adds moral and humane reasons. At the same time, however, not every homicide is reported. As one television newsperson put it, "You can't cover every homicide—it's just not of interest. You need more unusualness" (Chermak, 1995:58). In other words, murder is newsworthy, but some murders are more newsworthy than others.

Certain characteristics of the victim make a murder more newsworthy. Age is very important. Children and the elderly are considered special groups within society and therefore get special media attention. Children

are innocents, and the elderly are believed to deserve a peaceful life; when such people are murdered, the public thinks that the system has let them down.

The victim's occupation is also important. When a criminal justice professional—especially a police officer—is murdered, or someone in the helping professions (e.g., a nurse, doctor, teacher, or social worker), the case gets a great deal of attention.

Murder victims from the suburbs are more newsworthy than residents of the inner city because educated, middle-class people are less often victimized, they may hold an important position, and more of the media audience can relate to them. Moreover, reporters get better human interest stories from the survivors: "[People] are so fatalistic in the inner city; it is almost like they expected it to happen" (Chermak, 1995:68). Sometimes reporters are afraid to go to inner-city neighborhoods to interview friends and relatives of the victim. Murder in the suburbs, especially a wealthy suburb, also gets more attention because educated and affluent residents have contacts in the media and—just as important—because they give reporters more to report by posting flyers, offering rewards, and so forth.

It is not, of course, only the victim who can increase the newsworthiness of a murder. So can the defendant. Age is a factor if the defendant is very young. If the defendant is a politician or in the criminal justice system, the story immediately becomes important because these people have betrayed a public trust. Occupation is also important. A defendant who is a doctor, teacher, or priest—a guardian of life—is very newsworthy. In certain cases, it is the relationship between the victim and the defendant that makes a murder newsworthy, as when a parent murders a child.

Are you surprised by the way the media decide which murders are newsworthy and which are not? Do the media have a responsibility to present more balanced coverage?

expenditures on fear reduction programs and crime prevention programs that supposedly will help people to make their homes and neighborhoods safe. Lawmakers and enforcers continue to seek longer prison sentences—often without possibility of parole—for anyone convicted of murder (especially mass or serial murder).

RAPE

Many people think of rape as a sexually motivated crime, but it is actually an act of violence in which sex is used as a weapon against a powerless victim (Vito and Holmes, 1994). Although both men and women can be victimized by rape, the legal definition of *forcible rape* is the act of forcing sexual intercourse on an adult of legal age against her will. Sexual assaults or attempts to commit rape by force or threat of force are included in FBI statistics on this crime. Unlike murder or other violent crimes, the age of the victim is a central issue in charging a person with rape. *Statutory rape* refers to sexual intercourse with a person who is under the legal age of consent as established by state law (some states now use the term *illegal intercourse* instead of *statutory rape*). In most states, the legal age of consent is between ages sixteen and eighteen. A few states have attempted to include male victims of sexual assault in definitions of rape. However criminologists estimate that (excluding men who are raped in prison) only about 1 percent of reported rape victims are men.

Acquaintance rape is forcible sexual activity that meets the legal definition of rape and involves people who first meet in a social setting (Sanday, 1996). This definition is preferred by some scholars because it encompasses dates and casual acquaintances but excludes spouses (marital rape) and relatives (incest). The phrase was coined to distinguish forced, nonconsensual sex between people who know one another from forced, nonconsensual sex between strangers— but both are rape.

Acquaintance rape is often associated with alcohol or other drug consumption, especially among college students. We probably know much less about the actual number of acquaintance rapes than we do about the number of stranger rapes because victims are less likely to report sexual attacks by people they know. A study by the National Victim Center (1992) found that most rapes involve people who are at least acquaintances, and these rapes have the lowest probability of being reported to the police. It is estimated that fewer than 20 percent of the victims of acquaintance rape report the crime to the police, and 69 percent of the victims believe that they will be blamed by others for having caused the rape (Martin, 1992).

On college campuses acquaintance rape sometimes takes the form of gang or party rape. Unlike individual acquaintance rape, gang rape is used as a reinforcing mechanism for membership in the group of men (Warshaw, 1994). In fact, men who rape in groups might never commit individual rape. As they participate in gang rape, they experience a special bonding with each other and use rape to prove their sexual ability to other group members and thereby enhance their status among members.

Nature and Extent of the Problem. Statistics on rape are misleading at best because rape is often not reported. According to national victimization studies, however, since the 1950s, on average, one in five women in the United States has been the victim of forced sex at some time during her life (Sanday, 1996). Some women are victimized more than once. Although some women may not report that they have been raped because they believe that nothing will be done about it, arrests have been made in more than half the forcible rapes reported to law enforcement officials in recent years (FBI, 1999).

Like murder, rape follows certain patterns in terms of gender, age, race, and region of the country. Because of the definition that law enforcement officials use, rape is gender specific; that is, the victims of forcible rape are always female, and men make up the vast majority of offenders. Occasionally, women are charged as accomplices to male companions. Of the approximately 102,000 rapes reported annually, almost 90 percent of the victims were raped and the remaining 10 percent were the victims of attempted rape or sexual assaults (FBI, 1999).

Rape is committed by men of every class, race, ethnicity, and cultural background and across a wide range of age and educational levels (Fairstein, 1995). While there is no single profile of a rapist, most rapists tend to be under age twenty-five; their typical victims are also under twenty-five, white, divorced or separated, poor, and unemployed or in school (Vito and Holmes, 1994). In most reported rapes, the victim is under eighteen years of age. Although females of all ages are raped, the rate of victimization drops off sharply after age thirty-four.

Offenders and victims are usually of the same race and class. Although numerically more white women are raped than African American women and more white men commit rape than African American men, the probabilities of being a rape victim or an offender are significantly higher for African Americans than for whites (FBI, 1999). Moreover, in an intersection of class and race, young poor women of color who live in central cities are much more likely to be rape victims than other women generally are.

The rate of reported rape varies geographically; the most populous Southern states account for almost 40 percent of the total each year, followed by states in the Midwest, the West, and the Northeast. Across all regions, the rate of rape is approximately 80 victims per 100,000 females in large metropolitan areas, 77 per 100,000 in cities outside metropolitan areas, and 51 per 100,000 females in rural areas. Although most regions have experienced recent declines in reported rape (ranging from 2 percent in the South to 7 percent in the Northeast), the primary decrease has been in the metropolitan areas of these regions. This decrease, however, has been paralleled by an 88 percent increase in the rate of reported rapes in cities outside metropolitan areas and a 46 percent increase in rural areas over the past 10 years (FBI, 1999).

Social Responses to Rape. As the discrepancies between official statistics and victimization studies indicate, societal attitudes toward rape primarily affect the victims of rape. Many rapes are never reported. The extremely traumatic nature of the crime may prevent some victims from coming forward. They may believe that if they don't think about it or talk about it, the experience will "go away." Often, the fear generated by the attack is carried over into a fear that the attacker may try to get even or attack again if the crime is reported. This is a particularly significant issue for women who are still in proximity to their attacker. Suppose the attacker is in the same college class or works at the same place as the victim. How can the woman file a report without disrupting her whole life? Many women also fear how they will be treated by the police and, in the event of a criminal trial, by prosecutors and defense attorneys. Many victims also fear publicity for themselves and their families (Sanday, 1996).

GANG VIOLENCE AND HATE CRIMES

Gang violence includes murder, rape, robbery, and aggravated assault. Typically gangs are com-

posed primarily of young males of the same race or ethnicity. Some gangs are basically peer groups that hang out together, but others are well organized and violent. In recent years, gang activity and gang-related violence have increased significantly not only in large metropolitan areas but also in smaller cities and suburbs. Incidents involving gang violence are among the most frequently mentioned memories of some students in Chicago's public high schools:

> One day in the halls the gangs came up to me and asked what I was doing. They said if I were in a gang they would kill me right there. . . . Another time a car came up to me and [they] started shooting.
>
> The gangs killed one of my best friends. In high school, I always feel afraid because the gangs hang around the school and try to recruit the current students. (quoted in Hutchison and Kyle, 1993)

Some analysts have suggested that gang violence may be exacerbated by socialization of males for male dominance and by patriarchal social structures. Sociologist Martín Sánchez Jankowski (1991) suggests that violence attributed to gangs is often committed by gang members acting as *individuals* rather than as agents of the organization. According to Jankowski, most gang members do not like violence and fear that they may be injured or killed in violent encounters. As a result, gang members engage in collective violence only to accomplish specific objectives such as asserting authority or punishing violations by their own members who are incompetent or who break the gang's code. Violence against other gangs occurs primarily when a gang feels threatened or needs to maintain or expand its operations in a certain area. In general, according to Jankowski, collective violence is used to achieve the goals of gang membership (proving masculinity and toughness, providing excitement, and maintaining reputation) mainly when gang members are provoked by others or when they are fearful.

Sociologists Jack Levin and Jack McDevitt (1993) suggest that gangs look for opportunities to violently attack "outgroup" members because they are seeking a thrill and view their victims as vulnerable. When violent attacks are made because of a person's race, religion, skin color, disability, sexual orientation, national origin, or ancestry, they are considered to be *hate crimes* (see Chapter 1) (Levin and McDevitt, 1993).

Of course, not all hate crimes are committed by gang members. In Chapter 1, we discussed the cases of Matthew Shepard and James Byrd, Jr. The case of Joseph Paul Franklin is equally shocking. Franklin believes that it is his mission to rid the United States of African Americans and Jews. He has been convicted of bombing a Jewish synagogue and killing several interracial couples, and he has expressed no remorse for his actions:

> In his confession to the police, after he detailed every step of the synagogue attack, Franklin was asked if there was anything he'd like to say. He stared thoughtfully over the top of his glasses. There was a long silence. "I can't think of anything," he answered. Then he was asked if he felt any remorse. There was another silence. "I can't say that I do," he said. He paused again, then added, "The only thing I'm sorry about is that it's not legal."
>
> "What's not legal?"
>
> Franklin answered as if he'd just been asked the time of day: "Killing Jews." (Gladwell, 1997: 132)

When people with beliefs and attitudes like this join violent gangs or paramilitary groups, they can perpetrate devastating acts of violence, terrorism, and even war.

Social Responses to Gang Violence and Hate Crimes.
For many years now, the threat of gang violence—particularly such seemingly random events as drive-by shootings—has contributed to a climate of fear in low-income and poverty-level areas of central cities. People living in smaller cities and suburban areas often believed that gang violence was not their problem. As gangs have spread and become increasingly violent, however, it has become apparent that no one is immune. Thus, the demand for harsher penalties for youthful offenders, who often are under the jurisdiction of juvenile courts not the adult criminal justice system, has grown.

In some urban areas, law enforcement officials have been slow to deal with hate crimes perpetrated by gang members against recent immigrants to the United States and against persons of color. Intervention by law enforcement officials and the criminal justice system has had only limited success in dealing with the structural problems—lack of educational opportunities and jobs, inadequate housing,

and racial and ethnic discrimination—that accompany much gang behavior. The best solution seems to come from former gang members and former felons who band together to help break the cycle of crime and hopelessness that they believe produces gang violence. For example, the Alliance of Concerned Men of Washington, D.C., a collection of middle-aged former felons, substance abusers, and inmates, mediated a truce between two factions of a gang that had been terrorizing a southeast Washington neighborhood. Members of the alliance not only reduced gang violence in the city but also helped gang members to find jobs, giving them hope that they would be able to reach their eighteenth birthdays (Janofsky, 1997).

◢ Property Crime

Property crime **is the taking of money or property from another without force, the threat of force, or the destruction of property.** Burglary, larceny-theft, motor vehicle theft, and arson are examples of property crimes. According to victimization surveys, the most frequent property crime is *burglary*—the unlawful or forcible entry or attempted entry of a residence or business with the intent to commit a serious crime. Burglaries usually involve theft: The burglar illegally enters by, for example, breaking a window or slashing a screen (forcible entry) or

Property crimes such as this one occur far more frequently than violent crime, yet the media give far greater coverage to violence than to acts like auto burglary. Should the media's motto be "If it bleeds, it leads"? Why or why not?

through an open window or unlocked door (unlawful entry). Although burglary is normally a crime against property, it is more serious than most nonviolent crimes because it carries the possibility of violent confrontation and the psychological sense of intrusion that is associated with violent crime. To fully grasp the possibility of violent confrontation, consider the following explanations by two burglars of the pressures—both internal and external—that motivate them to commit burglary:

> Usually what I'll do is a burglary, maybe two or three if I have to, and then this will help me get over the rough spot. . . . Once I get it straightened out, I just go with the flow . . . the only time I would go and commit a burglary is if I needed the money at that point in time. That would be strictly to pay the light bill, gas bill, rent. (Dan Whiting, quoted in Wright and Decker, 1994:37)

> You ever had an urge before? Maybe a cigarette urge or a food urge, where you eat that and you got to have more and more? That's how that crack is. You smoke it and it hits you [in the back of the throat] and you got to have more. I'll smoke that sixteenth up and get through, it's like I never had none. I got to have more. Therefore, I gots to go do another burglary and gets some more money. (Richard Jackson, quoted in Wright and Decker, 1994:39)

According to victimization surveys, African Americans and Latinos/as have a higher than average risk of being burglarized than whites. Risk of victimization is also much higher for families with incomes under $7,500 living in rental property or in central city areas. In contrast, people who live in well-maintained residences with security systems on well-lit streets or cul-de-sacs are less likely to be victimized (Vito and Holmes, 1994). The *UCR* does not accurately represent the number of burglaries committed because people tend to report them only when very valuable goods are taken.

The most frequently reported index crime is *larceny-theft*—unlawfully taking or attempting to take property (with the exception of motor vehicles) from another person. Larceny-theft includes purse snatching and pickpocketing. Although most people arrested for larceny-theft are white, African Americans are overrepresented in arrests for this type of

crime given the proportion of the total population that is African American. The average age of arrest for larceny-theft is twenty-five, and many offenders are under the influence of alcohol or other drugs at the time of their arrest (Gentry, 1995).

Statistics on auto theft are more accurate than those for many other crimes because insurance companies require claimants to report the theft to police. Analysts have identified four basic motives for auto theft: (1) joyriding—the vehicle is stolen for the fun of riding around in it and perhaps showing off to friends; (2) transportation—the vehicle is stolen for personal use; (3) as an aid in the commission of another crime; and (4) profit—the vehicle is sold or taken to a "chop shop," where it is dismantled for parts, which are then sold separately (Barlow, 1996). Middle-class youths tend to steal cars for fun and joyriding; urban lower-class minority youths are responsible for most auto thefts for economic profit.

Shoplifting accounts for billions of dollars in losses to retail business each year. For some stores, the annual loss can be as high as 2 to 5 percent of the total value of inventory (Vito and Holmes, 1994). Early criminologists thought that shoplifters fell into three categories: the *snitch*—someone with no criminal record who systematically pilfers goods for personal use or to sell; the *booster* or *heel*—the professional criminal who steals goods to sell to fences or pawnshops; and the *kleptomaniac*—someone who steals for reasons other than monetary gain (e.g., for sexual arousal) (Holmes, 1983). Most experts think that shoplifting is committed primarily by amateurs across lines of race, class, gender, and age (Barlow, 1996).

The last type of nonviolent property crime that we will examine is *credit card fraud*—using a credit card or account number to obtain property, services, or money under false pretenses. Despite the security measures taken by banks and other credit card issuers, credit card fraud is perpetrated in many ways. A lost or stolen wallet or purse can provide a potential offender with all the identification necessary to open up charge accounts in the victim's name and run up large bills before the individual becomes aware of what has happened. Sometimes credit cards are obtained by pickpockets, purse snatchers, robbers, burglars, and sometimes by prostitutes who go through their customers' pockets. There are companies using the Internet to sell personal information—such as a person's Social Security number and mother's maiden name—that can be used to apply for and activate some credit cards (Hansell, 1996). Credit card information can also be stolen by people with legitimate access to personal data (e.g., airline or hotel reservationists or department or grocery store personnel) or by computer hackers.

 ## Occupational (White-Collar) Crime

Occupational (white-collar) crime **refers to illegal activities committed by people in the course of their employment or normal business activity.** When sociologist Edwin H. Sutherland (1949) first introduced the term *white-collar crime,* he was referring to such acts as employee theft, fraud (obtaining money or property under false pretenses), embezzlement (theft from an employer), and soliciting bribes or kickbacks. With the advent of personal computers, some white-collar crimes have become easier to commit, and some criminals have developed new types of crime based on computer technology. One type of white-collar crime that has been in the news lately is insider trading of securities: An offender buys or sells stocks on the basis of information that isn't publicly known and that he or she obtained only as a corporate insider. For individual investors, losses may be in the thousands of dollars, but for institutional investors such as pension funds, losses may be in the millions (Friedrichs, 1996) and a devastating effect on retired people who depend on pensions.

 ## Corporate Crime

Some white-collar offenders engage in *corporate crime*—**illegal acts committed by corporate employees on behalf of the corporation and with its support.** Examples include antitrust violations (seeking an illegal advantage over competitors); deceptive advertising; infringements on patents, copyrights, and trademarks; unlawful labor practices involving the exploitation or surveillance of employees; price fixing; and financial fraud. These crimes arise from deliberate decisions by corporate personnel to profit at the expense of competitors, consumers, employees, and the general public. According to a study by the Computer Security Institute and the FBI, the biggest threat to a U.S. company's trade secrets, research and development plans, pricing lists, and customer information is a competing company that engages in electronic snooping. "People do things in the computer

environment that they would never do outside," one criminal lawyer who works with high-tech companies has noted. "An attorney in a courtroom would never look in the briefcase of another who stepped out of the room. And yet I have a case in which one attorney looked at the computer files of another. There is something [alluring] about the anonymity" (quoted in Young, 1996:71).

Corporate crime has both direct and indirect economic effects. Direct economic losses from corporate crime are immense in comparison to the money lost in street property crime. For example, losses from twenty years of street crime are estimated at less than half of the losses from savings and loan (S&L) failures, which occurred in the 1980s (Friedrichs, 1996). Some of these failures involved bank fraud and other crimes. Failed S&Ls cost U.S. taxpayers hundreds of billions of dollars (Pizzo et al., 1991).

The indirect costs of corporate crime include higher taxes, increased cost of goods and services, and higher insurance rates. Although personal injury and loss of life are usually associated with homicides and conventional street crimes, deaths resulting from such corporate crimes as deliberately polluting the air and water, manufacturing defective products, or selling unsafe foods and drugs far exceed the number of homicides each year. Of course, any consideration of the indirect costs of corporate crime must include its effects on the moral climate of society (Friedrichs, 1996; Simon, 1996).

 ## Organized Crime

Organized crime **is a business operation that supplies illegal goods and services for profit.** These illegal enterprises include drug trafficking, prostitution, gambling, loan-sharking, money laundering, and large-scale theft such as truck hijackings (Simon, 1996). No single entity controls the entire range of corrupt and illegal enterprises in the United States (Chambliss, 1988). Instead, there are many groups—syndicated crime networks—that can thrive because there is great demand for illegal goods and services. Sometimes these groups form alliances with businesspeople, law enforcement officials, and politicians. Some law enforcement and government officials are corrupted through bribery, campaign contributions, and favors that are intended to buy them off. Known linkages between legitimate businesses and organized crime exist in banking, hotels

SOCIAL PROBLEMS

IN GLOBAL PERSPECTIVE

BOX 9.2

Organized Crime: The Global Empire

Five nights a week, at least $100 million in crisp new $100 bills is flown from JFK [International Airport] nonstop to Moscow, where it is used to finance the Russian mob's vast and growing international crime syndicate. State and federal officials believe it is part of a multimillion-dollar money-laundering operation. When the money arrives in Moscow, it is transported by armored trucks to Russian banks, which have purchased the $100 bills on behalf of clients, who typically pay for the cash with wire transfers from London bank accounts. (Friedman, 1996:24)

This is one of many recent reports of international organized crime, in this instance allegedly involving the Russian mob and U.S. banks. The mob supposedly uses a steady supply of freshly minted U.S. currency to finance its vast and growing international crime syndicate and to invest in legitimate businesses across Europe and in the United States.

The "dirty" money allegedly comes from Russian *Mafiya* alliances with other crime syndicates such as the Sicilian Mafia, the Brighton Beach gang (a criminal gang of Russian immigrants living in Brooklyn, New York), and Colombian drug lords. The Russian banking system is considered one of the world's leading money-laundering centers (Friedman, 1996).

Despite a 1992 law requiring U.S. banks to verify that they are not knowingly doing

business with criminals or their agents, money laundering continues to flourish in the United States. Combating money laundering is difficult because there are about 700,000 wire transfers a day, totaling $2 trillion. About $300 million of that—less than one-sixtieth of 1 percent—is believed to be laundered funds. Because existing technology can identify only the most obvious money trading irregularities, a great deal of money laundering goes undetected (Friedman, 1996). Major U.S. cities such as New York, Los Angeles, Dallas, and Miami have become primary points of international entry or exit for money-laundering operations, as well as drug-trafficking operations.

Globally, seven or eight crime syndicates often operate in collusion. In addition to the Russian syndicate and the Sicilian Mafia, other organized crime groups allegedly include the Colombian cocaine cartels, which have operations in Spain, and ethnic Chinese from East and Southeast Asia, who have overseas bases in Rotterdam and London. At a lower level, the transport and marketing of drugs and other contraband is managed by syndicates of Nigerians, Moroccans, Pakistanis, Lebanese, Albanians, and others (Viviano, 1995).

What can the United States do about global organized crime? Can any one nation or organization—such as the United Nations—reduce international money laundering and drug trafficking? What do you think?

and motels, real estate, garbage collection, vending machines, construction, delivery and long-distance hauling, garment manufacture, insurance, stocks and bonds, vacation resorts, and funeral parlors (National Council on Crime and Delinquency, 1969). Syndicated crime networks operate at all levels of society and even globally (see Box 9.2).

 Juvenile Delinquency

Juvenile delinquency involves a violation of law or the commission of a status offense by a young person under a specific age. Many behaviors that are identified as juvenile delinquency are not criminal acts per se but *status offenses*—acts that are illegal

This picture reflects the changing face of gangs in the United States. Today's gang members come from a wide diversity of racial and ethnic groups, and many gangs have both male and female members. What factors do you think are most significant in determining whether or not a person joins a gang?

because of the age of the offender—such as cutting school, buying and consuming alcoholic beverages, or running away from home. In most states, the age range for juvenile delinquency is from seven to seventeen. Older offenders are considered adults and are tried in a criminal court.

The statistics for juvenile delinquency are astounding. People under age eighteen account for almost one-fifth of all arrests in the United States. About 29 percent of people arrested in 1998, for the eight index crimes, were under the age of eighteen. In that year, people under age eighteen were responsible for 17 percent of the violent crime arrests and 33 percent of the property crime arrests. More than 27 percent of the people arrested for robbery and 32 percent of the people arrested for larceny-theft were under age eighteen (FBI, 1999). Note that these are arrest figures and do not necessarily reflect the true nature and extent of crime and status violations among juvenile offenders.

Juveniles who are apprehended are processed by the juvenile justice system, which is based on the assumption that young people can do better if they are placed in the right setting and receive guidance. Thus, unlike adult offenders, whose cases are heard in criminal courts, most juveniles' cases are heard in juvenile courts or by specially designated juvenile judges. Unfortunately, most juvenile correction facilities or "training schools" hold large numbers of young people in overcrowded conditions and provide only limited counseling and educational opportunities for rehabilitation (Donziger, 1996).

WHO COMMITS CRIMES?

The most significant factor in any study of delinquency and crime arrest rates is gender. Men are more likely than women to commit major property crimes (for example, robbery and larceny-theft), whereas women are more likely than men to be involved in minor property crimes (for example, larceny and fraud) and in prostitution offenses (Steffensmeier and Allan, 1995). Men have higher arrest rates than women for violent crimes such as homicide, aggravated assault, robbery, and burglary; women are most often arrested for such nonviolent crimes as shoplifting, passing bad checks, credit card fraud, and employee pilferage. Although a considerable number of arrests and convictions for larceny and theft occur among women, men still account for the vast majority of these arrests and convictions. Criminologists estimate that 15 to 20 percent of all homicides in this country are committed by women. Most of these are linked to domestic violence and self-defense (Harlow, 1991; Belknap, 1996).

Although there are significant gender differences in the types of crimes committed, there are also commonalities. First, for both sexes, the most common offenses are driving under the influence of alcohol or drugs (DUI), larceny, and minor or criminal mischief. These three categories account for about 47 percent of all male arrests and about 49 percent of all female arrests. Second, liquor law violations (such as underage drinking), simple assault, and disorderly conduct are middle-range offenses for both men and women. Third, the rate of arrests for murder, arson, and embezzlement are relatively low for both men and women (Steffensmeier and Allan, 1995).

Age is also an important factor in any study of delinquency and crime arrest rates. The proportion of the population involved in serious crimes, such as homicide, rape, and robbery, tends to peak during the teenage years or early adulthood and then decline with age. Several reasons have been advanced for age-crime patterns including differential access to legitimate or illegitimate opportunity structures at various ages; differences in social factors such as peer influences; physiological factors such as the effects of aging on strength, speed, and aggression; and building up deviant networks that make it possible for people such as bookies or fences to commit less visible crimes (Steffensmeier and Allan, 1995).

Although individuals from all social classes commit crimes, some kinds of crimes are more associated with lower or upper socioeconomic status. People from lower socioeconomic backgrounds are more likely to be arrested for violent and property crimes; people from the upper classes generally commit white-collar or corporate crimes. Moreover, the majority of crimes committed by doctors, lawyers, accountants, and other professionals are ignored because of the prestige associated with these professions. Friends and neighbors assume that these people are law-abiding citizens, and law enforcement officials are not likely to scrutinize their behavior (Coleman, 1995).

When we examine the intersection of race and class in arrest data, we see that low-income African Americans are overrepresented. In 1998, whites accounted for 65 percent of all property crime arrests and 58 percent of all violent crime arrests; African Americans accounted for 32 percent of property crime arrests and 40 percent of violent crime arrests (FBI, 1999). However, African Americans comprise a little over 12 percent of the U.S. population. Compared with the arrest rates for African Americans, arrest rates for whites are higher for nonviolent property crimes such as fraud and larceny-theft but lower for violent crimes such as

robbery and murder. It should be recognized, however, that the eight index crimes are crimes that are more likely to be committed by low-income people, among whom African Americans and other people of color are overrepresented.

Having considered who commits crimes, let's look at who the victims are. Most people fear the violent stranger, but the vast majority of murders are committed by family members, friends, neighbors, or coworkers. In slightly less than half the cases, the murderers are members of the victim's family or acquaintances. As we have already noted, most murder is intraracial. That is, whites most often murder whites (85 percent of the time), and African Americans most often murder African Americans (95 percent of the time) (see Table 9.1).

According to the NCVS, men are the most frequent victims of crimes of violence and theft, although women are more fearful of crime, particularly crime directed toward them, such as forcible rape (Warr, 1995). The elderly also tend to be more fearful of crime but are the least likely to be victimized. Young men of color between the ages of twelve and twenty-four have the highest rates of criminal victimization (Karmen, 1995).

The NCVS data on robbery victims indicates that males are robbed at more than twice the rate of females. African Americans are more than three times as likely to be robbed as whites. Young people have a much greater likelihood of being robbed than middle-aged and older people do. People from lower-income families are more likely to be robbed than those from higher-income families (Karmen, 1995). Risk of being a crime victim varies by region of the country, too. Risk of violent crime or property

TABLE 9.1   RACE OF KILLERS AND VICTIMS, 1998

Victims	Killers		
	WHITE	BLACK	OTHER/UNKNOWN
WHITE	83%	15%	3%
BLACK	6%	92%	2%

Source: FBI, 1999.

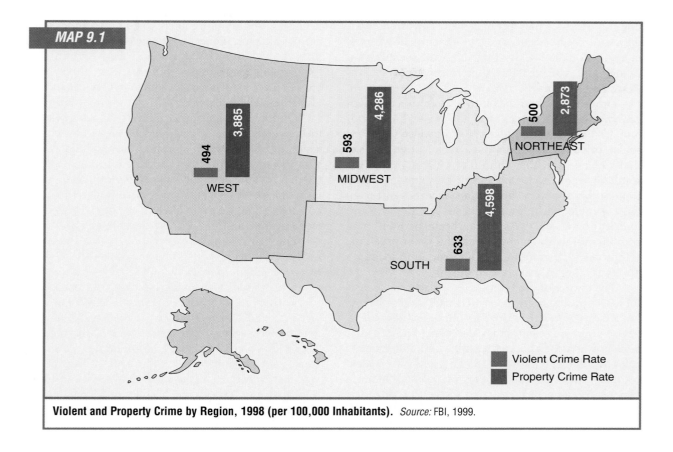

MAP 9.1

494
3,885
WEST

593
4,286
MIDWEST

500
2,873
NORTHEAST

633
4,598
SOUTH

■ Violent Crime Rate
■ Property Crime Rate

Violent and Property Crime by Region, 1998 (per 100,000 Inhabitants). *Source:* FBI, 1999.

crime is greatest in the Western states and the South (see Map 9.1).

BIOLOGICAL AND PSYCHOLOGICAL EXPLANATIONS OF CRIME

As with other social problems, crime and delinquency have been explained in biological, psychological, and sociological terms. Most biological and psychological explanations assume that criminal behavior is an inherent or acquired individual trait with genetic, biological, or psychological roots. Sociological perspectives, in contrast, focus on external factors.

 Biological Explanations

One of the earliest biological explanations of criminality came from the *positivist school,* which created physical typologies that were used to classify and study criminals (Barlow, 1996). The biological approach of Cesare Lombroso, a nineteenth-century Italian physicist, is probably the best known. Lombroso suggested that some people were born criminals or *atavists*—biological throwbacks to an earlier stage of evolution—and could be recognized by their low foreheads and smaller than normal human cranial capacities. A later theory, also based on physical traits, that received some attention for a time was proposed by physician William Sheldon (1949). According to Sheldon's *somatotype theory, mesomorphs*—people who are muscular, gregarious, aggressive, and assertive—are more prone to delinquency and criminal behavior than are *endomorphs*—people who are fat, soft, round, and extroverted—or *ectomorphs*—people who are thin, wiry, sensitive, and introverted.

Contemporary biological approaches based on genetics have attempted to link higher rates of aggression in men to levels of testosterone or chromosomal abnormality (an extra Y chromosome).

But this research has produced no consistent findings, and social scientists argue that the differences in aggression may be due to gender role socialization of men and women rather than to biological factors (Katz and Chambliss, 1995).

Other contemporary biological approaches suggest that violence is a natural and inevitable part of human behavior that can be controlled only by social organization. Some scientists, however, say that violence is neither natural nor inevitable but the result of traumatic brain injury or some combination of brain injury and other factors. Although most people with brain injuries are not violent, injuries to certain parts of the brain or injuries in combination with an abusive childhood or psychotic symptoms (e.g., paranoia) can affect an individual's ability to conform to societal norms.

The cortex of the brain—particularly the frontal lobes—is most closely associated with violent behavior. It is the cortex that modifies impulses, allowing us to use good judgment, make decisions, and organize behavior; it also facilitates learning and adherence to rules of conduct (Gladwell, 1997). Using various neurological and psychiatric examinations, medical experts try to determine whether violent offenders have frontal-lobe impairment, were abused as children, or have any psychological disorders. These factors, especially in combination, make people prone to violent behavior because they have fewer inhibitions.

 ## Psychological Explanations

Like biological explanations of delinquency and crime, psychological explanations focus on individual characteristics. Some researchers have used personality inventories in hopes of identifying abnormal personality traits in individuals who have committed crimes or engaged in delinquent behavior. Other researchers have investigated the effects of social learning and positive reinforcement (e.g., rewards such as money or special attention) and negative reinforcement (e.g., the withdrawal of reward or lack of attention) on delinquent and criminal behavior.

The most enduring psychological explanations of delinquency and crime seem to be the ones that bridge the biological explanations by linking intelligence and crime. Since the introduction of IQ (intelligence quotient) tests in the early 1900s, some analysts have suggested that people with lower intelligence scores are more likely to commit crimes than are people with higher intelligence scores. However, both the validity of IQ tests and the assertion that low intelligence causes delinquency or crime have come under great scrutiny and much criticism (see Hirschi and Hindelang, 1977).

Of course, some social analysts do acknowledge the possibility of a relationship between low intelligence and delinquency or crime. These analysts note that low intelligence may indirectly promote delinquency because it affects school performance. Similarly, less intelligent offenders may commit more obvious crimes and be more likely to be apprehended by law enforcement officials (Vito and Holmes, 1994).

One psychological explanation of violent crime focuses on *aggression*—behavior intended to hurt someone, either physically or verbally—that results from frustration (Weiten and Lloyd, 1994). According to the *frustration-aggression hypothesis,* people who are frustrated in their efforts to achieve a highly desired goal become aggressive toward others (Dollard et al., 1939). The object of the aggression becomes a *scapegoat,* a substitute for the actual source of frustration, who can be blamed, especially if that person or group is incapable of resisting the hostility or aggression (see Chapter 3).

Explaining violence in biological and/or psychological terms suggests responses based on some type of psychiatric or other medical intervention. After all, if violent behavior is associated with specific neurological problems, it can be diagnosed like any other neurological illness and treated with drugs, including, possibly, anticonvulsants, antidepressants, and antihypertensive medications that act on the cortex to moderate violent behavior.

SOCIOLOGICAL EXPLANATIONS OF CRIME

Unlike biological and psychological explanations that focus on individual behavior, sociological explanations focus on those aspects of society that may contribute to delinquent or criminal behavior.

The Functionalist Perspective

Although there are numerous functionalist perspectives on crime and delinquency, we will focus on two

TABLE 9.2   MERTON'S STRAIN THEORY

Mode of Adaptation	Method of Adaptation	Agrees with Cultural Goal	Follows Institutional Means
Conformity	Accepts culturally approved goals; pursues them through culturally approved means	Yes	Yes
Innovation	Accepts culturally approved goals; adopts disapproved means of achieving them	Yes	No
Ritualism	Abandons society's goals but continues to conform to approved means	No	Yes
Retreatism	Abandons both approved goals and the approved means to achieve them	No	No
Rebellion	Challenges both the approved goals and the approved means to achieve them	No—seeks to replace	No—seeks to replace

Source: Adapted from Merton (1968).

perspectives: strain theory and control theory as illustrated in social bond theory.

Functionalist explanations for why people commit crimes can be traced to Emile Durkheim, who believed that the macrolevel structure of a society produces social pressures that result in high rates of deviance and crime. Durkheim introduced the concept of *anomie* to describe a social condition that engenders feelings of futility in people because of weak, absent, or conflicting social norms. According to Durkheim (1964/1895), deviance and crime are most likely to occur when anomie is present in a society. On the basis of Durkheim's theory, sociologist Robert Merton (1938, 1968) developed strain theory to explain why some people conform to group norms while others do not. **Strain theory states that people feel strain when they are exposed to cultural goals that they cannot reach because they do not have access to a culturally approved means of achieving those goals.** When some people are denied legitimate access to cultural goals such as success, money, or other material possessions, they seek to acquire these things through deviant—and sometimes criminal—means.

Merton identified five ways in which people respond to cultural goals: conformity, innovation, ritualism, retreatism, and rebellion (see Table 9.2). *Conformity* occurs when people accept the culturally approved goals and pursue them through the approved means. People who choose conformity work hard and save their money to achieve success. Someone who is blocked from achieving a high level of education or a lucrative career typically conforms by taking a lower-paying job and attending school part-time, joining the military, or trying alternative (but legal) avenues, such as playing the lottery. People who choose *innovation* accept society's goals but use illegitimate means to achieve them. Innovations for acquiring material possessions include shoplifting, theft, burglary, cheating on income taxes, embezzling money, and other kinds of occupational crime. *Ritualism* occurs when people give up on societal goals but still adhere to socially approved means for achieving them. People who cannot obtain expensive material possessions or wealth seek to maintain the respect of others by being "hard workers" or "good citizens" to an extreme degree. *Retreatism* occurs when people abandon both the approved goals and the approved means of achieving them. Retreatists include hardcore drug addicts and some middle- or upper-income people who reject conventional trappings of success and the means to acquire them, choosing to "drop out" instead. *Rebellion* occurs when people reject both the approved goals and the approved means for achieving them and advocate an alternative set of goals and means. Rebels may use violence (such as vandalism or rioting) or nonviolent tactics (such as civil disobedience) to change society and its cultural beliefs. Or they may withdraw from mainstream society, like the Amish, to live their own life.

Another functionalist perspective—control theory—seeks to answer the question: Why do people *not* engage in deviant behavior? According to control theory, people are constantly pulled and pushed toward deviant behavior. Environmental factors (pulls), such as adverse living conditions, poverty, and lack of educational opportunity, draw people toward criminal behavior while, at the same time, internal pressures (pushes) such as feelings of hostility or aggressiveness make people not want to act according to dominant values and norms (Reckless, 1967). If this is true, why doesn't everyone who is poor or has a limited education commit crimes? According to control theorists, people who do not turn to crime or delinquent behavior have *outer containments*—supportive family and friends, reasonable social expectations, and supervision by others—or *inner containments*—self-control, a sense of responsibility, and resistance to diversions.

The best-known control theory is **social bond theory—the proposition that criminal behavior is most likely to occur when a person's ties to society are weakened or broken.** According to Travis Hirschi (1969), who proposed this theory, social bonding consists of (1) *attachment* to other people, (2) *commitment* to conformity, (3) *involvement* in conventional activities, and (4) *belief* in the legitimacy of conventional values and norms. When a person's social bonds are weak and when peers promote antisocial values and violent behavior, the probability of delinquency and crime increases (Massey and Krohn, 1986).

When analyzing violent crime, some functionalists believe that a sense of anomie is the root cause. Others believe that violence increases when social institutions such as the family, schools, and religious organizations weaken and the primary mechanisms of social control in people's everyday lives become external—law enforcement and the criminal justice system.

Several other functionalist perspectives on violence were discussed in Chapter 1. The *subculture of violence hypothesis* notes that violence is part of the normative expectations governing everyday behavior among young males in the lower classes (Wolfgang and Ferracuti, 1967). These violent subcultures are most likely to develop when young people, particularly males, have few legitimate opportunities available in their segment of society and when subcultural values accept and encourage violent behavior.

According to the *lifestyle-routine activity approach,* the patterns and timing of people's daily movements and activities as they go about obtaining the necessities of life—such as food, shelter, companionship, and entertainment—are the keys to understanding violent personal crimes and other types of crime in our society (Cohen and Felson, 1979). In other words, changes in social institutions, such as more families in which both parents (or the sole parent) work outside the home or shopping hours being extended into the night, put some people at greater risk of being victims of violent crime than others (Parker, 1995).

Functionalist explanations contribute to our understanding of crime by emphasizing that individuals who engage in such behavior are not biologically or psychologically impaired but are responding to social and economic conditions in society. However, functionalists are not without their critics. Strain theory may point out that people from low-income and poverty-level backgrounds are prevented from achieving success goals through legitimate channels, but it is still criticized for focusing almost exclusively on crimes committed by the lower classes and ignoring crimes committed by people in the middle and upper classes. Critics of social bond theory say that it is limited in its ability to explain more serious forms of delinquency and crime (Krohn, 1995).

 ## The Conflict Perspective

Conflict theorists explain criminal behavior in terms of power differentials and/or economic inequality in society. One approach focuses on how authority and power relations can contribute to some people—but not others—becoming criminals. According to Austin Turk (1966, 1971), crime is not a *behavior* but a *status* that is acquired when people with the authority to create and enforce legal rules apply those rules to others.

A second conflict approach focuses on the relationship between economic inequality and crime. Having roots in the work of Karl Marx, the *radical-critical conflict approach* argues that social institutions (such as law, politics, and education) create a superstructure that legitimizes the class structure and maintains capitalists' superior position. In fact, say these theorists, the crimes people commit are based on their class position. Thus, crimes committed by low-income people typically involve taking things by force or physical stealth, while white-collar crime usually involves nonphysical means such as paper transactions or computer fraud. Some critical theorists believe that affluent people commit crimes because they are greedy and continually want more than they have, whereas poor people commit street crimes such as robbery and theft to survive (Bonger, 1969/1916).

Finally, some conflict explanations are based on feminist scholarship and focus on why women commit crimes or engage in delinquent behavior. Scholars who use a *liberal feminist* framework believe that women's delinquency or crime is a rational response to gender discrimination in society. They attribute crimes such as prostitution and shoplifting to women's lack of educational and job opportunities and stereotypical expectations about roles women should have in society (Daly and Chesney-Lind, 1988). Scholars who espouse *radical feminism* believe that patriarchy contributes to crimes such as prostitution, because, according to society's sexual double standard, it is acceptable for a man to pay for sex but unacceptable for a woman to accept money for such services. A third school of feminist thought, *socialist feminism*, believes that women are exploited by capitalism and patriarchy. Because most females have relatively low-wage jobs and few economic resources, crimes such as prostitution and shoplifting become a means of earning money and acquiring consumer products. Feminist scholars of color, however, point out that none of the feminist theories include race/ethnicity in their analyses. As a result, some recent studies have focused on the relationship between crime and the simultaneous effects of race, class, and gender (Arnold, 1990).

In sum, the conflict approach is useful for pointing out how inequalities of power, class, race, and gender can contribute to criminal or delinquent behavior. Nevertheless, critics say that conflict theorists have not shown that powerful political and economic elites manipulate law making and enforcement for their own benefit. Rather, say these critics, people of all classes share a consensus that acts such as murder, rape, and armed robbery are bad (Klockars, 1979).

The Interactionist Perspective

Interactionists emphasize that criminal behavior is learned through everyday interaction with others. We will examine two major interactionist theories: differential association theory and labeling theory. *Differential association theory* states that individuals have a greater tendency to deviate from societal norms when they frequently associate with people who tend toward deviance rather than conformity. According to sociologist Edwin Sutherland (1939), who formulated this theory, people learn not only the techniques of deviant behavior from people with whom they associate but also the motives, drives, rationalizations, and attitudes. Former gang member Nathan McCall (1994:93–94) describes such a learning process in his own life:

> Sometimes I picked up hustling ideas at the 7-Eleven, which was like a criminal union hall: Crapshooters, shoplifters, stickup men, burglars, everybody stopped off at the store from time to time. While hanging up there one day, I ran into Holt. . . . He had a pocketful of cash, even though he had quit school and was unemployed. I asked him, "Yo, man, what you been into?" "Me and my partner kick in cribs and make a killin'. You oughta come go with us sometimes. . . . " I hooked school one day, went with them, and pulled my first B&E [breaking and entering]. . . . After I learned the ropes, Shell Shock [another gang member] and I branched out, doing B&Es on our own. We learned to get in and out of houses in no time flat.

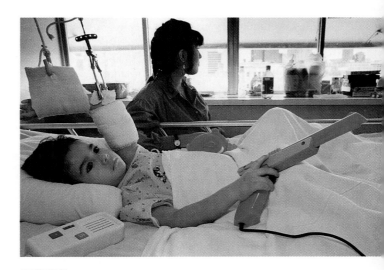

Gang violence not only harms gang members but also innocent bystanders such as this three-year-old boy who was the victim of a drive-by shooting. Do you find it ironic that he is playing with a toy gun at the hospital?

As McCall's description indicates, criminal activity often occurs within the context of frequent, intense, and long-lasting interactions with people who violate the law. When more factors favor violating the law than not, the person is likely to become a criminal. Although differential association theory contributes to our knowledge of how deviant behavior reflects the individual's learned techniques, values, attitudes, motives, and rationalizations, critics note that many individuals who are regularly exposed to people who break the law still conform most of the time. Many critics think that the theory does not adequately take into account possible connections between social inequality and criminal behavior.

Labeling theory, which was mentioned briefly in Chapter 1, takes quite a different approach from differential association theory. According to *labeling theory,* **delinquents and criminals are people who have been successfully labeled as such by others.** No behavior is inherently delinquent or criminal; it is defined as such by a social audience (Erikson, 1962). According to sociologist Howard Becker (1963), labeling is often done by *moral entrepreneurs*—people who use their own views of right and wrong to establish rules and label others "deviant." Furthermore, the process of labeling is directly related to the power and status of the people who do the labeling and those who are being labeled. In support of this theory, one study of juvenile offenders has found that youths from lower-income families were more likely to be arrested and indicted than were middle-class juveniles who did the same things (Sampson, 1986). Sociologists have also noted that the criminal justice system generally considers such factors as the offender's family life, educational achievement (or lack thereof), and social class in determining how to deal with juvenile offenders. According to one study, the individuals who are most likely to be apprehended, labeled delinquent, and prosecuted are people of color who are young, male, unemployed, and undereducated and who live in urban high-crime areas (Vito and Holmes, 1994).

Sociologist Edwin Lemert (1951) expanded labeling theory by distinguishing between primary and secondary deviance. *Primary deviance* **is the initial act of rule breaking** in which the individual does not internalize the delinquent or criminal self-concept. *Secondary deviance* **occurs when a person who has been labeled a deviant accepts that new identity and continues the deviant behavior.** The concept of secondary deviance is important to labeling theory because it suggests that when people accept a negative label or

stigma that has been applied to them, the label may actually contribute to the behavior it was meant to control. In other words, secondary deviance occurs if a person is labeled a juvenile delinquent, accepts that label, and then continues to engage in delinquent behavior. Labeling theory is useful for making us aware of how social control and personal identity are intertwined. Critics, however, do not think that labeling theory explains what causes the original acts that constitute primary deviance, nor do they think that it adequately explains why some people accept deviant labels and others do not (Cavender, 1995).

THE CRIMINAL JUSTICE SYSTEM

The term *criminal justice system* is misleading because it implies that law enforcement agencies and courts constitute one large, integrated system when actually they are a collection of somewhat interrelated, semi-autonomous bureaucracies (Sheley, 1995). The *criminal justice system* **is the network of organizations, including the police, courts, jails, and prisons, involved in law enforcement and the administration of justice** (Donziger, 1996). Originally, the criminal justice system was created to help solve the problem of social disorder and crime. Today, however, some social analysts wonder whether the criminal justice system is part of the *problem*. Most cite two reasons for concern: (1) The criminal justice system fails in its mission to prevent, control, or rehabilitate offenders; and (2) unequal justice occurs because officials discriminate against people on the basis of race, class, gender, age, sexual orientation, or other devalued characteristics. We'll examine both issues in greater depth. First, though, let's look at each component of the justice system, starting with the police.

 ## The Police

The police are the most visible link in the criminal justice system because they determine how to apply the law to control crime and maintain order. The police arrest and jail about 11 million people each year. Four factors seem to influence the occurrence of an arrest: (1) the nature of the alleged offense or problem; (2) the quality of available evidence; (3) the age, race, and sex of the alleged offender; and (4) the level of deference shown to police officers (Mastrofski, 1995). Given these factors, law enforcement officials have fairly wide *discretion*—use of personal judgment regarding whether and how to proceed in a given situation—in deciding who will be stopped and searched and which homes and businesses will be entered and for what purposes (Donziger, 1996). Because they must often make these decisions in a dangerous environment, sociologist Jerome Skolnick (1975) argues, police officers develop a sense of suspicion, social isolation, and solidarity. A New York City police officer describes this feeling:

> Guys . . . will eat you alive, even with the uniform on. They can sense fear, smell it like a dog smells it. Some of the mopes will come right out and tell you you're nothing, and you don't want that, oh no. If you're going to do this job, wear this uniform, you definitely don't want that. If it gets around that you're soft, that without your nightstick and gun you can't fight, that's bad. If you allow someone to smoke a joint in front of you or curse you out, word will spread throughout the neighborhood like a disease. You're a beat cop, out here every day, alone, so you set standards right away. (Norman, 1993:64)

Most officers feel that they must demand respect on the streets, but they also know that they must answer to their superiors, who expect them to handle situations "by the book."

The problem of discretion is most acute in the decision to use deadly force. Generally, deadly force is allowed only when a suspect is engaged in a felony, is fleeing the scene of a felony, or is resisting arrest and has endangered someone's life (Barlow, 1996). But police officers' lives are often on the line in confrontations with suspects, and sometimes the officers have less firepower than the individuals they are attempting to apprehend. In a Los Angeles bank robbery, for example, the robbers were wielding AK-47 automatic rifles and using 100-round ammunition drums and 30-round clips from which they were firing steel-jacketed bullets capable of penetrating the police officers' body armor (Story, 1997).

People of color often have a negative image of police because they believe that they receive differential treatment from the police (Anderson, 1990; Cose, 1993; Mann, 1993). Some analysts feel that studies of police shootings lend credence to this belief. Rates of police shootings vary widely from one jurisdiction to another, but the percentage of shooting incidents involving African American suspects is disproportion-

ately high. African Americans are from five to thirteen times more likely than whites to be killed by police officers (Mann, 1993). Historically, criminal justice personnel at all levels have been white and male. The composition may be slowly changing, but white Americans still made up more than 80 percent of all police officers in 1995 (U.S. Bureau of the Census, 1996b).

In the past, women were largely excluded from law enforcement because of stereotypical beliefs that they were not physically and psychologically strong enough for the work. By 1995, however, women accounted for slightly more than 10 percent of all police officers (U.S. Bureau of the Census, 1996b). Still, research shows that although more females have entered police work, they sometimes receive lower evaluations from male administrators even when objective measures show that they are equally effective on patrol (Reid, 1987).

How can police departments become more effective in reducing crime as a social problem? According to some analysts, police departments with entrenched problems must first reform their own agencies and win the respect of the communities they serve. One way to do this is to be sure that police departments reflect the racial and ethnic composition of the communities they serve. It is difficult for an all-white police force to build trust in a primarily African American neighborhood (Donziger, 1996). Greater representation of women in police departments may reduce complaints that domestic violence, child abuse, and other family-related problems are sometimes minimized or ignored by police officers.

Some police departments have begun *community policing* as a way of reducing crime. Community policing involves integrating officers into the communities they serve—getting them out of their patrol cars and into a proactive role, recognizing problems and working with neighborhood citizens to find solutions. In cities where community policing has been implemented, crime rates appear to have dropped; however, it should be noted that there has also been a general trend toward fewer crimes, especially violent crimes, in some cities where community policing is not employed (Donziger, 1996).

 The Courts

Criminal courts are responsible for determining the guilt or innocence of people who have been accused of committing a crime. In theory, justice is determined in an adversarial process: A prosecutor (an attorney who represents the state) argues that the accused is guilty and a defense attorney argues that the accused is innocent. In reality, judges have a great deal of discretion. Working with prosecutors, they decide who will be released, who will be held for further hearings, and—in many instances—what sentences will be imposed on people who are convicted.

Because courts have the capacity to try only a small fraction of criminal cases, prosecuting attorneys also have considerable discretion in deciding when to prosecute and when to negotiate a plea bargain with a defense attorney. About 90 percent of criminal cases are never tried in court; they are resolved by *plea bargaining*—a process whereby the prosecution negotiates a reduced sentence in exchange for a guilty plea. In other words, defendants (especially those who are poor and cannot afford to pay an attorney) plead guilty to a lesser crime in return for not being tried for the more serious crime for which they were arrested. As cases are sifted and sorted through the legal

machinery, steady attrition occurs. At each stage, various officials determine what alternatives will be available for the cases that remain in the system (Hills, 1971). Now that many jurisdictions specify mandatory minimum sentences, offenders typically spend a longer time in prison. In fact, mandatory sentencing guidelines have removed sentencing power from judges and transferred it to prosecutors, who determine what charges will be brought against the defendant. Unless the defendant is found not guilty, the judge must sentence him or her according to the statutory prescription for the offense regardless of any facts that might have led a different prosecutor to charge differently or of any mitigating circumstances in the case.

 Punishment and the Prisons

Punishment is any action designed to deprive a person of things of value (including liberty) because of an

"My client pleads great wealth."

offense the person is thought to have committed (Barlow, 1996). Punishment is seen as serving four functions:

1. *Retribution* imposes a penalty on the offender. Retribution is based on the premise that the punishment should fit the crime: The greater the degree of social harm, the more the offender should be punished. An individual who murders, for example, should be punished more severely than one who steals an automobile.
2. *Social protection* results from restricting offenders so that they cannot continue to commit crimes.
3. *Rehabilitation* seeks to return offenders to the community as law-abiding citizens. However, the few rehabilitation programs that exist in prisons are seriously understaffed and underfunded. Often, the job skills (such as agricultural work) that are taught in prison do not transfer to the outside world, and offenders are not given help in finding work that fits the skills they might have once they are released.
4. *Deterrence* seeks to reduce criminal activity by instilling a fear of punishment. Criminologists debate, though, whether imprisonment has a deterrent effect, given that 30 to 50 percent of those who are released from prison commit further crimes.

According to the text, punishment serves four functions: retribution, social protection, rehabilitation, and deterrence. Which of these functions is shown in this photo?

Today, about 1.5 million people are behind bars in the United States. One million of these are in state and federal prisons; another half million are in local jails (U.S. Bureau of the Census, 1998). This is the highest rate of incarceration in relation to population in any high-income country. Moreover, another 11 million people are annually booked in jails at the city or county level, where they spend at least one night of incarceration. Most of these individuals are charged with disorderly conduct or misdemeanor offenses such as public drunkenness, traffic violations, shoplifting, or drug possession.

Disparate treatment of the poor and people of color is evident in the prison system. Although incarceration rates have risen overall in recent years, the rate for minorities (with the exception of Asian Americans, who are the least likely to be incarcerated) is disproportionately higher than for whites. For example, African Americans are incarcerated at a six times greater rate than whites: 1,947 per 100,000 African Americans as compared to 306 per 100,000 white Americans. Nearly half of all prison admissions are African Americans, even though the majority of violent crime nationwide is committed by whites (FBI, 1999).

Jail and prison conditions often do little to rehabilitate offenders. In fact, three out of four inmates are housed in such overcrowded facilities that two people often live in a space only slightly larger than a walk-in closet. Some inmates suffer physical abuse by prison officials or other inmates. A videotape was recently shown on national television of an African American inmate restrained in a chair with a metal face mask over his head while a guard danced around, teasing him with a soft drink. The inmate was suffering from a drug overdose and begging for help; he eventually died.

Because of plea bargains, credit for "good time" served, and overcrowded prison conditions, most convicted criminals do not serve their full sentences. They are released on either probation (close supervision of their everyday lives in lieu of serving time) or parole (early release from prison). About 3.8 million people are currently on probation or parole (U. S. Bureau of the Census, 1998). If offenders violate the conditions of their probation or parole, they may be returned to prison to serve their full sentence. Some courts use *shaming penalties*—named for punishments used by the seventeenth-century Puritans—with probationers or as alternatives to incarceration. Shaming penalties typically take the form of a message to the community, just as the public stocks did in the seventeenth-century. For example, as a condition of his probation, one Illinois man had to put this sign at the end of his driveway: "Warning. A Violent Felon Lives Here. Travel at Your Own Risk" (Hoffman, 1997:A1). Drunk drivers may get special license plates; men who have been convicted of soliciting prostitutes may be identified in the media or on billboards; and shoplifters have been required to walk in front of the stores from which they stole, carrying signs admitting their guilt. Because these sentences are usually the result of a guilty plea, they cannot be appealed except under very special circumstances (Hoffman, 1997).

Aside from their deterrent effect, shaming penalties are a way of avoiding the high cost of incarceration, another taxpayer burden. The average cost of building a new cell in a state prison is $54,000, and the cost per prisoner averages $22,000 per year, excluding food and medical services. Increasing numbers of older prisoners add to the costs because they often have chronic health conditions that require long-term medical care. The $22,000 average per prisoner actually comes closer to $69,000 a year for elderly state prison inmates (Camp and Camp, 1994).

The Death Penalty

About 4,000 people have been executed in the United States since 1930, when the federal government began collecting data on executions (Smith, 1995). The death penalty—or *capital punishment*—is a highly controversial issue. Removal—not just expulsion—from the group is considered the ultimate form of punishment. In the United States, capital punishment is considered an appropriate and justifiable response to very serious crimes.

In 1972, the U.S. Supreme Court ruled (in *Furman* v. *Georgia*) that *arbitrary* application of the death penalty violates the Eighth Amendment to the Constitution but that the death penalty itself is not unconstitutional. In other words, determining who receives the death penalty and who receives a prison term for similar offenses should not be done on a lotterylike basis (Bowers, 1984). To be constitu-

tional, the death penalty must be imposed for reasons other than the race/ethnicity, gender, and social class of the offender.

Opponents of capital punishment argue that the death penalty is discriminatory because people of color, especially African Americans and poor people, are at greater risk of receiving a death sentence than their white, more affluent counterparts (Smith, 1995). In fact, the former slave states are more likely to execute criminals than are other states, and African Americans are eight to ten times more likely to be sentenced to death for crimes such as homicidal rape than are whites (non-Latinos/as) who commit the same offense (Marquart et al., 1994).

People who have lost relatives and friends because of a crime often see the death penalty as justifiable compensation—"an eye for an eye." Others fear that innocent individuals may be executed for crimes they did not commit. However controversial the death penalty is, it is likely to remain in place well into the twenty-first century because many political leaders and U.S. Supreme Court justices have expressed support for it. In fact, today, more people await execution than ever before. California, Florida, and Texas each have over 300 death row prisoners.

Is the solution to our "crime problem" to build more prisons and execute more people? Only about 20 percent of all crimes result in arrest, only half of these lead to a conviction, and fewer than 5 percent of convictions result in a jail term. The "lock 'em up and throw away the key" approach has little chance of succeeding. As for individuals who commit occupational and corporate crime, the percentage that enters the criminal justice system is so minimal that prison is relatively useless as a deterrent to others. Furthermore, the high rate of recidivism strongly suggests that the rehabilitative efforts of our existing correctional facilities are sadly lacking. One thing is clear: The existing criminal justice system cannot solve the crime problem. Some people believe that the way to reduce street crime, at least, is to short-circuit criminal behavior (see Box 9.3).

Is equal justice under the law possible? As long as racism, sexism, classism, and ageism exist in our society, equal justice under the law may not be possible for all people; however, that does not keep it from being a goal that citizens and the criminal justice system can strive to reach.

SOCIAL PROBLEMS

AND SOCIAL POLICY

BOX 9.3

Crime Prevention or the Prison-Industrial Complex?

I know something serious has happened when I wake up well before dawn to discover two guards wearing armored vests and riot helmets taking a head count. . . . It's apparent that the prison is on "full lockdown status." At the minimum, we will be locked in our cells twenty-four hours a day for the next several days. . . . The experienced prisoner knows to be prepared for a few weeks of complete isolation. (Hopkins, 1997:66)

With these words, author Evans D. Hopkins describes the day at the Nottoway Correctional Center in Virginia when two correctional officers and two nurses were taken hostage by three prisoners after a botched escape attempt. On that day, officials declared a lockdown that ultimately lasted four and a half months.

Although some politicians and social analysts believe that building more prisons and giving long sentences to offenders is the way to reduce the crime problem in the United States, others think that we should spend our money and energy on crime prevention instead. According to *prevention ideology,* the best way to reduce delinquency and crime is early intervention and prevention (Bynum and Thompson, 1996). Prevention typically takes three avenues: (1) early childhood and youth socialization that contributes to law-abiding behavior; (2) attacking the roots of delinquency and crime—poverty, unemployment, racism, sexism, drug abuse, and other problems discussed in this book; and (3) specific programs or services that intervene before individuals who have already engaged in delinquent or criminal behavior become immersed in deviant subcultures.

Current U.S. social policy is not based on prevention but consists of programs that include hiring more police officers, strengthening and enforcing gun control laws, and implementing the "three strikes" law, which requires a mandatory life sentence without parole for an individual who is convicted of a third felony. In fact, recent studies show that the government and private security companies spend nearly the same amount on crime control each year as the Pentagon spends on national defense (Donziger, 1996). The "war on crime" approach has contributed to the growth of a *prison-industrial complex*—a network of private companies, the government, and politicians—that greatly influences crime policy. In the past, most money spent on crime control went to public prisons; today, many state and local governments contract with private companies to build and operate correctional facilities, generating an annual revenue to these companies of more than $250 million. Other private enterprises also benefit from the prison-industrial complex, including investment houses that underwrite jail and prison construction and companies that provide food service, transportation, and health care for the facilities. Still other companies benefit from the sale of protective vests for guards, security systems, closed-circuit television systems, and other surveillance apparatus. Some analysts suggest that the prison-industrial complex, with its interlocking financial and political interests, has good reason to support the "war on crime" instead of developing social policies that prevent delinquency and crime before it happens (Donziger, 1996).

Does living in a prison environment with full lockdown status, as Hopkins describes, turn inmates into law-abiding citizens when they are released? What strategies can you suggest for rehabilitating prisoners? For preventing crime before it occurs?

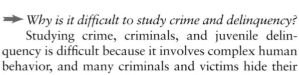

➤ *Why is it difficult to study crime and delinquency?*

Studying crime, criminals, and juvenile delinquency is difficult because it involves complex human behavior, and many criminals and victims hide their involvement. There also are problems inherent in using official sources of data such as the *Uniform Crime Report* because they reflect crimes that are reported rather than crimes that are committed, and they do not provide detailed information about offenders.

➤ *How does violent crime differ from property crime?*

Violent crime consists of actions involving force or the threat of force against others and includes murder, rape, robbery, and aggravated assault. Property crime consists of taking money or property from another without force, the threat of force, or the destruction of property.

➤ *Why is rape as a violent crime not well understood, and how is this lack of understanding reflected in our social response to rape?*

First, many people think that rape is a sexually motivated crime, but it is actually an act of violence in which sex is used as a weapon against a powerless victim. Moreover, statistics on rape are misleading at best because rape is often not reported. Many reasons keep victims from coming forward. Some victims may be so traumatized that they just want to forget about it. Others fear the attacker will try to get even. Many also fear how they will be treated by the police and, in the event of a trial, by prosecutors and district attorneys.

➤ *What is occupational crime?*

Occupational (white-collar) crime refers to illegal activities committed by people in the course of their employment or normal business activity. Occupational crime includes computer and other high-tech crimes, as well as more traditional crimes such as employee theft, fraud (obtaining money or property under false pretenses), embezzlement (theft from an employer), soliciting bribes or kickbacks, and insider trading of securities.

➤ *How does occupational crime differ from corporate crime?*

Occupational crimes are illegal activities committed by people in the course of their employment or normal business activity. Corporate crimes are illegal acts committed by corporate employees on behalf of the corporation and with its support.

➤ *What is organized crime and why does it flourish in the United States?*

Organized crime is a business operation that supplies illegal goods and services for profit. These illegal enterprises include drug trafficking, prostitution, gambling, loan-sharking, money laundering, and large-scale theft. Organized crime thrives because there is great demand for illegal goods and services.

➤ *How does juvenile delinquency differ from adult crime?*

Juvenile delinquency refers to a violation of law or the commission of a status offense by people who are younger than a specific age. Many behaviors that are identified as juvenile delinquency are not criminal acts per se but status offenses—acts that are illegal because of the age of the offender—such as cutting school or purchasing and consuming alcoholic beverages. Juvenile hearings take place in juvenile courts or before juvenile judges, whereas adult offenders are tried in criminal courts.

➤ *Who is most likely to be arrested for a crime in the United States?*

Men are more likely to be arrested than women. Teenagers and young adults are most likely to be arrested for serious crimes such as homicide, rape, and robbery. Although individuals from all social classes commit crimes, people from lower socioeconomic backgrounds are more likely to be arrested for violent and property crimes, whereas people from the upper classes generally commit white-collar or elite crimes. Low-income African Americans are overrepresented in arrest data.

➤ *How do functionalists explain crime?*

Functionalists use several theories to explain crime. According to strain theory, people are socialized to desire cultural goals, but many people do not have institutionalized means to achieve the goals and therefore engage in criminal activity. Control perspectives, such as social bond theory, suggest that delinquency and crime are most likely to occur when a person's ties to society are weakened or broken.

➤ *How do conflict theorists explain crime?*

Conflict theorists explain criminal behavior in terms of power differentials and/or economic inequality in society. One approach focuses on the relationship between authority and power and crime; another focuses on the relationship between economic inequality and crime. Feminist approaches offer several explanations of why women commit crimes: gender discrimination, patriarchy, and a combination of capitalism and patriarchy.

➤ *How do interactionists explain crime?*

Interactionists emphasize that criminal behavior is learned through everyday interaction with others. According to differential association theory, individuals have a greater tendency to deviate from societal norms when they frequently associate with people who are more likely to deviate than conform. Labeling theory says that delinquents and criminals are those people who have been successfully labeled by others as such.

➤ *What are the components of the criminal justice system?*

The criminal justice system is a network of organizations involved in law enforcement, including the police, the courts, and the prisons. The police are the most visible link in the criminal justice system because they are responsible for initially arresting and jailing people. Criminal courts are responsible for determining the guilt or innocence of people who have been accused of committing a crime. Imprisonment, probation, and parole are mechanisms of punishment based on retribution, social protection, rehabilitation, and deterrence.

➤ *Why is the death penalty controversial?*

The death penalty—or capital punishment—is a highly controversial issue because removal from the group is considered the ultimate punishment. Some people believe that it is an appropriate and justifiable response to very serious crimes; others view this practice as discriminatory because people of color—especially African Americans—and poor people are at greater risk of receiving a death sentence than are their white, more affluent counterparts.

KEY TERMS

acquaintance (date) rape, p. 179
corporate crime, p. 183
criminal justice system, p. 192
differential association theory,
  p. 191
felony, p. 176
forcible rape, p. 179
illegitimate opportunity
  structures, p. 173

juvenile delinquency, p. 184
labeling theory, p. 192
mass murder, p. 176
misdemeanor, p. 175
murder, p. 176
occupational (white-collar)
  crime, p. 183
organized crime, p. 183
plea bargaining, p. 194

primary deviance, p. 192
property crime, p. 181
punishment, pp. 194–195
secondary deviance, p. 192
serial murder, p. 176
social bond theory, p. 190
statutory rape, p. 179
strain theory, p. 189
violent crime, p. 176

QUESTIONS FOR CRITICAL THINKING

1. Why doesn't the United States use all of its technological know-how to place known criminals and potential offenders under constant surveillance so that the crime rate can be really reduced?
2. If most of the crimes that are committed are property crimes, why do so many people fear that they will be the victims of violent crime?

3. Does the functionalist, conflict, or interactionist perspective best explain why people commit corporate crimes? Organized crimes? Explain your answer.
4. If money were no object, how would you reorganize the criminal justice system so that it would deal more equitably with all people in this country?

Chapter Ten

Health Care
Problems of Physical and Mental Illness

THE SUSAN G. KOMEN BREAST CANCER FOUNDATION
RACE FOR THE **CURE**®
Presented by JCPenney

I am a very different person now: more open, much more honest, and more self-knowing. . . . I turned it [cancer] into a possibility of opening up to myself, of discovering, and for exploring new areas. I've realized that I want to list the ways in which cancer can do that. You can get courage to take larger risks than you ever have before. I mean, you're already sick, so what can happen to you? You can have much more courage in saying things and in living than you ever had before. . . . And you can do the things you've always wanted to do. Cancer, by giving you the sense of your own mortality, can entice you into doing those things you've been postponing. . . . You have this sense of urgency. And you can turn this urgency—you can harness this energy that propels you—so that you go ahead and do these things and discover new parts of yourself. . . . Cancer has put me in touch with that. And then also, it has taught me to enjoy the tenderness and the preciousness of every moment. Moments are very important because there may not be any after that—or you may throw up. Cancer exquisitely places you in the moment. I have become very human to myself in a way that I would never have imagined. I've become a bigger person, a fuller person. This to me is one of the greatest lessons: just being human. Having cancer doesn't mean that you lose yourself at all. For me it meant that I discovered myself.

—Sociologist Barbara Rosenblum explaining how cancer reshaped her thoughts about life sometime before her death at age forty-four of breast cancer
(Butler and Rosenblum, 1991:160–161)

Diseases like Barbara Rosenblum's breast cancer tend to be viewed as *personal problems,* but cancer and other diseases are also *social problems.* For one thing, they affect large numbers of people; for another, they are problems that cannot be reduced or eliminated in the population as a whole without a significant social response such as additional funding for research and programs for prevention and early detection. Consider for a moment the impact that breast cancer has on a woman and then add to your thoughts these facts: one out of every nine women in the United States will be diagnosed with breast cancer in her lifetime; each year, nearly 200,000 new cases are reported, and about 50,000 women die from the disease; even with early detection and treatment, breast cancer takes an average of nineteen years off a woman's life (Neuman, 1992). Breast cancer is only one of many diseases that affect individuals, families, and the health care industries in the United States and other countries. This chapter examines health care problems, including both physical and mental illness, and current problems in providing health services in this country.

HEALTH CARE AS A SOCIAL PROBLEM

According to the World Health Organization (1946: 3), *health* is a state of complete physical, mental, and social well-being. In other words, health is not only a biological issue, it is also a social issue. Many people think there is a positive relationship between the amount of money a society spends on health care and the overall physical, mental, and social well-being of its people. After all, physical and mental health are intertwined: Physical illness can cause emotional problems; mental illness can produce physical symptoms. Based on this belief, spending a great deal of money on health care should result in physical, mental, and social well-being. If this is true, however, people in the United States should be among the healthiest and most fit in the world. We spend almost $950 billion—the equivalent of $3,510 per person—on health care each year. The health service industry accounts for almost 14 percent of the gross domestic product, a proportion that has increased substantially since the 1960s (U.S. Bureau of the Census, 1998). Table 10.1 shows the increase in health service expenditures between 1980 and 1996.

However, although we, as individuals, pay more for health services than people in other high-income nations, our expenditures do not translate into improved life expectancy for everyone. *Life expectancy* **is an estimate of the average lifetime of people born in a specific year.** During this century, overall life expectancy has increased in the United States. Right now, individuals born in 2000 can expect to live 76.4 years, compared to only 47.3 years for people born in 1900. But today's life expectancy statistics vary by sex and race. Overall, females born in 2000 can expect to live about 79.7 years, compared to 73.0 years for males. African American males born in 2000, however, have a life expectancy of only 64.6 years, compared to 74.7 years for African American females (U.S. Bureau of the Census, 1998).

In high-income nations, life expectancy has increased as a nation's infant mortality rate has decreased. The *infant mortality rate* **is the number of deaths of infants under 1 year of age per 1,000 live births in a given year.** The infant mortality rate is an important indication of a society's level of preventive (prenatal) medical care, maternal nutrition, childbirth procedures, and care for infants. For all our expenditures in health care, however, infant mortality in the United States is considerably higher than it is in a number of other high-income nations (see Table 10.2). Perhaps the single most important cause of infant mortality is lack of prenatal care. Drinking, smoking, taking drugs, and maternal malnutrition all contribute (Stewart, 1995). Divergent infant mortality rates for African Americans and whites indicate another problem: unequal access to health care. Even with today's high-tech medicine, the infant mortality rate for African American infants is twice as high as the rate for white infants. In 1996, for example, the U.S. mortality rate for African American infants was 14.2 per 1,000 live births compared to 6 per 1,000 live births for white infants (U.S. Bureau of the Census, 1998).

▲ Acute and Chronic Diseases and Disability

Life expectancy in the United States and other developed nations has increased largely because vaccinations and improved nutrition, sanitation, and personal hygiene have virtually eliminated many acute diseases, including measles, polio, cholera, tetanus, typhoid, and malaria. *Acute diseases* **are illnesses that strike suddenly and cause dramatic incapacita-**

TABLE 10.1   NATIONAL HEALTH EXPENDITURES, BY TYPE: 1980 TO 1996

Type of Expenditure*	1980	1985	1990	1995	1996
Totals	247.3	428.7	699.5	991.4	1,035.1
Annual percentage change[1]	14.9	9.9	12.2	4.8	4.4
Private expenditures	142.5	254.5	415.1	536.2	552.0
Health services and supplies	138.0	248.0	404.9	525.3	540.9
Out-of-pocket payments	60.3	100.7	144.4	166.7	171.2
Insurance premiums[2]	69.8	132.8	238.6	326.9	337.3
Other	8.0	14.5	21.9	31.7	32.4
Medical research	0.3	0.5	1.0	1.3	1.4
Medical facilities construction	4.2	6.0	9.3	9.6	9.7
Public expenditures	104.8	174.2	284.4	455.2	483.1
Federal percentage	68.7	70.7	68.9	72.2	72.6
Health services and supplies	97.6	164.3	270.1	435.4	462.7
Medicare[3]	37.5	72.1	112.1	187.9	203.1
Public assistance medical payments[4]	28.0	44.4	80.4	145.6	153.1
Temporary disability insurance[5]	0.1	0.1	0.1	0.1	0.1
Workers' compensation (medical)[5]	5.1	8.0	16.1	18.2	17.3
Defense Dept. hospital, medical	4.4	7.5	11.6	13.4	13.4
Maternal, child health programs	0.9	1.3	1.9	2.4	2.4
Public health activities	6.7	11.6	19.6	31.5	35.5
Veterans' hospital, medical care	5.9	8.7	11.4	15.6	16.7
Medical vocational rehabilitation	0.3	0.4	0.6	0.7	0.7
State and local hospitals[6]	5.6	7.0	11.3	12.3	12.5
Other[7]	3.1	3.3	5.0	7.7	7.9
Medical research	5.2	7.3	11.3	15.3	15.6
Medical facilities construction	2.0	2.6	3.0	4.5	4.8

1. Change from immediate prior year.
2. Covers insurance benefits and amount retained by insurance companies for expenses, additions to reserves, and profits (net cost of insurance).
3. Represents expenditures for benefits and administrative cost from federal hospital and medical insurance trust funds under old-age, survivors, disability, and health insurance programs.
4. Payments made directly to suppliers of medical care (primarily Medicaid).
5. Includes medical benefits paid under public law by private insurance carriers and self-insurers.
6. Expenditures not offset by other revenues.
7. Covers expenditures for Alcohol, Drug Abuse, and Mental Health Administration; Indian Health Service; school health; and other programs.

*In billions of dollars, except percentages; includes Puerto Rico and outlying areas.

Source: U.S. Bureau of the Census, 1998.

tion and sometimes death (Weitz, 1996). Acute diseases that are still common in the United States are chicken pox and influenza. Recently, too, multidrug-resistant strains of tuberculosis, Lyme disease, and HIV (the virus that causes AIDS) have become pressing health problems.

With the overall decline in death from acute illnesses in high-income nations, however, has come a

TABLE 10.2   INFANT MORTALITY RATES IN SELECTED COUNTRIES

Country or Area	Infant Mortality Rate 1996	2000 proj.	Country or Area	Infant Mortality Rate 1996	2000 proj.
United States	6.7	6.2	India	71.1	63.5
Afghanistan	149.7	137.5	Indonesia	63.1	55.4
Angola	138.9	125.9	Iran	52.7	45.1
Argentina	28.3	26.1	Iraq	60.0	50.1
Australia	5.5	5.0	Israel	8.5	7.5
Bangladesh	102.3	93.0	Italy	6.9	6.4
Belgium	6.4	6.1	Japan	4.4	4.3
Brazil	55.3	47.7	Kenya	55.3	54.9
Bulgaria	15.7	14.8	Korea, North	25.9	22.2
Canada	6.1	5.5	Korea, South	8.2	7.4
Chad	120.4	113.6	Malawi	139.9	135.8
Chile	13.6	11.9	Mexico	25.0	20.7
China	39.6	32.6	Netherlands	4.9	4.7
Cuba	9.0	8.6	Pakistan	96.8	90.3
Czech Republic	8.4	8.0	Peru	52.2	44.4
Denmark	4.8	4.7	Philippines	35.9	33.2
Egypt	72.8	65.7	Poland	12.4	11.8
El Salvador	31.9	27.2	Portugal	7.6	7.1
Ethiopia	122.8	117.7	Russia	24.7	21.6
Finland	4.9	4.8	Rwanda	118.8	118.8
France	6.2	5.7	Somalia	121.1	111.6
Germany	6.0	5.7	Spain	6.3	5.7
Greece	7.4	6.6	Sweden	4.5	4.4
Guatemala	50.7	44.6	Switzerland	5.4	5.2
Haiti	103.8	98.4	Taiwan	7.0	6.3
Hong Kong	5.1	4.5	Thailand	33.4	28.3
Hungary	12.3	11.7	United Kingdom	6.4	6.0

Rate = number of deaths of children under 1 year of age per 1,000 live births in a calendar year.

Source: U.S. Bureau of the Census, 1998.

corresponding increase in *chronic diseases,* **illnesses that are long term or lifelong and that develop gradually or are present from birth** (Weitz, 1996). Chronic diseases are caused by various biological, social, and environmental factors. In Chapter 8 we discussed two of the most common sources of chronic disease and premature death: tobacco use, which increases mortality among both smokers and people who breathe the tobacco smoke of others, and alcohol abuse. According to some social analysts, we can attribute many chronic diseases in our society to the *manufacturers of illness*, groups that promote illness-causing

behavior and social conditions, such as smoking (McKinlay, 1994). The effect of chronic diseases on life expectancy varies because some chronic diseases are progressive (e.g., emphysema worsens over time), whereas others are constant (e.g., paralysis after a stroke); also, some are fatal (lung cancer), but others are not (arthritis and sinusitis).

Some chronic diseases produce disabilities that significantly increase health care costs for individuals and for society. Disability can be defined in several ways. Medical professionals tend to define it in terms of organically based impairments—that is, the problem is entirely within the body (Albrecht, 1992). However, disability rights advocates believe that disability is a physical or health condition that stigmatizes or causes discrimination. Perhaps the best way to define disability is, as medical sociologist Rose Weitz (1996:428) has said, in terms of both physical and social factors: *Disability* **is a restricted or total lack of ability to perform certain activities as a result of physical limitations or the interplay of these limitations, social responses, and the social environment.** An estimated 48 million people in the United States have one or more physical or mental disabilities, and the number continues to increase for several reasons. First, with advances in medical technology, many people who in the past would have died from an accident or illness now survive with an impairment. Second, as people live longer, they are more likely to experience chronic diseases (such as arthritis) that may have disabling consequences (Albrecht, 1992). Third, people born with serious disabilities are more likely to survive infancy because of medical technology. (However, fewer than 15 percent of people with a disability today were born with it; accidents, disease, violence, and war account for most disabilities in this country.) For many people with chronic illness and disability, life takes on a different meaning. Knowing that they probably will not live out the full life expectancy for people in their age category, they come to treasure each moment. Today, some of the most tragic instances of life cut short are because of AIDS.

 The AIDS Crisis

AIDS—acquired immune deficiency syndrome—has reached crisis proportions in the United States and other nations. An estimated 200,000 people in this country have AIDS, and about 2 million are estimated to be infected with the human immunodeficiency virus (HIV); 40,000 new infections occur each year (Kolata, 1995). In the 25–44 age group, AIDS is the leading cause of death among men and the fourth leading cause among women. It is the eighth leading cause of death for the overall U.S. population (see Table 10.3). The U.S. Centers for Disease Control in Atlanta estimates that more than 400,000 people in the United States have died from AIDS-related complications over the past two decades (U.S. Bureau of the Census, 1998). We should note, however, that people do not technically die of AIDS; they die because HIV gradually destroys their immune systems by attacking the

TABLE 10.3   TEN LEADING CAUSES OF DEATH IN THE UNITED STATES

Cause	Number of Deaths (in thousands)
Heart disease	733.8
Cancer	544.3
Cerebrovascular disease (stroke)	160.4
Chronic lung disease	106.1
Accidents	93.9
Pneumonia	82.0
Diabetes	61.6
Homicide and legal intervention	39.7
HIV infection	39.2
Suicide	30.9

Source: U.S. Bureau of the Census, 1998.

white blood cells, making them vulnerable to diseases such as pneumonia, tuberculosis, yeast infection, Kaposi's sarcoma, and other forms of cancer.

How is AIDS transmitted? AIDS is transmitted primarily through bodily fluids, such as semen (through oral, anal, or vaginal sex with someone who is infected with HIV) or blood (usually by sharing drug needles and syringes with an infected person). It can also be transmitted by blood transfusions (although testing donated blood for the presence of HIV has made this rare in high-income nations) and by infected mothers before or during birth or while breast-feeding. AIDS is *not* transmitted by routine contact such as a handshake or hugging a person who has the disease.

Who is most likely to become infected with the HIV virus? Initially, AIDS was referred to as a "gay disease" because in this country it was most frequently diagnosed in gay men between the ages of twenty and forty. According to the World Health Organization, however, about 75 percent of the people who are infected with AIDS worldwide became infected through heterosexual intercourse. Today in the United States, most new AIDS cases are linked to heterosexual relations and to sex with prostitutes (Kolata, 1995). Some women acquire the disease through sex with an infected male partner who may have contracted the disease from a prostitute, a

AIDS in Thailand and India: Two Different Patterns

A ribbon of acrid, pale yellow smoke rose from the crematory as a Buddhist monk approached, clutching one end of his saffron robe in a bony, withered hand. . . . "I know that my body will end up here," said the AIDS-stricken monk. . . . "Of course I accept that." In a corner, set beneath a gilded statue of the Buddha, there was a pile of dozens of fist-sized white cotton bags, each containing the ashes from an earlier cremation. The 38-year old monk gently picked up some of the bags. "All of these people died of AIDS, and the ashes stay here because the families are afraid to claim them," he said. "They are afraid that they will get sick if they hold the ashes."

—*Phra Kamthorn Kitisalo, a Buddhist monk abandoned by his monastery, waiting with others to die at the temple crematory (Shenon, 1996a)*

Phra Kamthorn was infected with the AIDS virus during "his playboy days," before he entered the monastery: "I would see prostitutes every day." His story is not unusual in Thailand, one of the first countries in Asia hit by the AIDS epidemic as a result of its widespread sex industry. But Thailand confronted the problem in 1991 by distributing condoms, shutting down brothels that didn't use them, and requiring radio stations to broadcast AIDS prevention information hourly. These actions have been effective. In 1990 there were 215,000 new cases of HIV; by the early 2000s the number of new cases should be down to about 90,000 (Shenon, 1996a).

The story is different in India, where AIDS appeared in 1991, ten years after it was recognized as a new disease (Altman, 1996b). The number of people with AIDS is exploding in India, and the World Health Organization projects that the country will soon be the world center of the disease, with one-fourth of all infected people (Burns, 1996). One immediate source of the problem is India's truck drivers, who often have long layovers with nothing to do, and the many prostitutes available along the roadsides, flying gaily colored scarves. Drivers who pick up the disease carry it to other prostitutes in previously uninfected regions as well as home to their wives and future children. The red-light districts of Bombay, Calcutta, and New Delhi are another source of the growing epidemic. An estimated 52 percent of the brothel "cage girls" (enslaved child prostitutes who are kept in cages during the day so they don't escape) in Bombay are infected with HIV (Burns, 1996).

Fighting AIDS in India means fighting more than the disease. It means fighting the caste system because prostitutes and AIDS victims are discriminated against. It means fighting social taboos against talking about sex. It means fighting poverty because prostitutes who use condoms lose clients and starve. And it means fighting the denial of political leaders; only $35 million of a five-year $100 million dollar AIDS prevention program has been spent in four years (Burns, 1996).

Though India may be the worst future case, with 14 million cases, Africa is the hardest-hit continent, and now AIDS is sweeping Russia and the Ukraine (Altman, 1996c). Each day, there are an estimated 8,500 new HIV infections in the world, and 1,000 are children; 42 percent of the adults infected are women (Altman, 1996c). "No country is free of HIV infection, nor is any province of India or China," Dr. Peter Piot, a United Nations official, said at the eleventh international AIDS meeting in 1996 (Altman, 1996a). "Developed countries should act out of 'enlightened self-interest' to ensure adequate treatment of AIDS in the third world."

Should the United States and other high-income countries act to stop the global spread of AIDS? What should they do? What does Dr. Piot mean by "enlightened self-interest"? Could the United States, where the spread of AIDS has been stabilized, learn from Thailand, which has *reversed* the spread of AIDS in its country? What do you think?

homosexual encounter, or an infected needle during intravenous drug use. In fact, a woman is 12 times as likely as a man to be infected with HIV during heterosexual intercourse, and she is more likely to die quickly from the disease. Although not all people who carry HIV develop AIDS, they can transmit the disease to others. In some cases, ten years or more may elapse between the time of infection with HIV and the development of full-blown AIDS.

Is there a cure for AIDS? No, thus far there is no cure for AIDS. Though drugs, such as AZT in combination with protease inhibitors (which attack the virus during its reproductive process within the human body), have led to dramatic improvements in the health of many people with AIDS, once HIV develops into AIDS, it is fatal. The only way to reduce the rate of AIDS, then, is to prevent its initial occurrence. Many believe the U.S. health care industry was slow to respond to the emergence of AIDS as a life-threatening illness because of the stigma attached by its initial association with gay men and drug users. Like many other people, sociologist Philip Kayal (1993:xi, xii) realized that he had ambivalent feelings about the disease when a relative died from an AIDS-related illness:

> When my cousin Paul died in his prime, nearly everyone knew his pneumonia was AIDS related. . . . There were so many people at Paul's wake, from so many disparate walks of life and so many distinct parts of his own life, that it was impossible to find a common way to symbolize our shared loss. . . . Were we, his mourners, ashamed of Paul? Did we blame him? Were we angry at him for dying? Did he disappoint us? Did we think deep down that something about his life and death should be hidden from the neighbors, from ourselves? Would Paul want us to bury him secretly? He lived his life openly and with pride. Why don't we accept why he, like all the others, really had to die? We need to accept that homophobia, like AIDS, also kills. I suppose that if Paul had died an ordinary death in ordinary times, it would not be as important to raise these questions. But he didn't, and his death remains as much a personal loss as a political issue.

Gradually public attitudes are changing and people are coming to understand that AIDS is not an isolated problem that does not affect them. Public service advertising campaigns encouraging people to abstain from sex or to practice "safer sex" by using condoms have raised awareness, and many cities have started needle exchange programs for intravenous drug users in an effort to reduce the number of new AIDS cases. But efforts to control the spread of HIV have raised many moral and ethical questions. Should people be required to submit to testing for HIV? Should people who test positive for the virus be required to provide the names of sexual partners or people with whom they have shared hypodermic needles? Should schools distribute condoms to students? No doubt, politicians, educators, and religious leaders throughout the country will continue to debate these issues for decades to come.

Not all social scientists agree on how AIDS will ultimately affect life expectancy, mortality rates, or the health care industry in the United States. Treatment for AIDS-related illnesses, perhaps even more than for other chronic diseases, is complex and costly and typically requires lengthy stays in a hospital or hospice. The incidence of AIDS, the number of AIDS patients, and the cost of caring for AIDS patients are highest and most concentrated in central cities where clinics, hospitals, and other medical facilities are overcrowded, underfunded, and understaffed. Some analysts estimate that more people in the United States will die from AIDS-related illnesses in the future than have died in all the wars fought by this nation (Petersen, 1994). Unfortunately, too, the AIDS problem in the United States is only a small part of the global picture of devastation caused by this disease (see Box 10.1).

MENTAL ILLNESS AS A SOCIAL PROBLEM

Mental illness is a social problem because of the number of people it affects, the difficulty of defining and identifying mental disorders, and the ways in which mental illness is treated. Although most social scientists use the terms *mental illness* and *mental disorder* interchangeably, many medical professionals distinguish between a *mental disorder*—a condition that makes it difficult or impossible for a person to cope with everyday life—and *mental illness*—a condition that requires extensive treatment with medication, psychotherapy, and sometimes hospitalization.

1. Disorders first evident in infancy, childhood, or adolescence	These disorders include mental retardation, attention-deficit hyperactivity, anorexia nervosa, bulimia nervosa, and stuttering.
2. Organic mental disorders	Psychological or behavioral disorders associated with dysfunctions of the brain caused by aging, disease, or brain damage.
3. Substance-related disorders	Disorders resulting from abuse of alcohol and/or other drugs such as barbiturates, cocaine, or amphetamines.
4. Schizophrenia and other psychotic disorders	Disorders with symptoms such as delusions or hallucinations.
5. Mood disorders	Emotional disorders such as major depression and bipolar (manic-depressive) disorder.
6. Anxiety disorders	Disorders characterized by anxiety that is manifest in phobias, panic attacks, or obsessive-compulsive disorder.
7. Somatoform disorders	Psychological problems that present themselves as symptoms of physical disease such as hypochondria.
8. Dissociative disorders	Problems involving a splitting or dissociation of normal consciousness such as amnesia and multiple personality.
9. Eating or sleeping disorders	Includes such problems as anorexia and bulimia or insomnia and other problems associated with sleep.
10. Impulse control disorders	Symptoms include the inability to control undesirable impulses such as kleptomania, pyromania, and pathological gambling.
11. Personality disorders	Maladaptive personality traits that are generally resistant to treatment such as paranoid and antisocial personality types.

FIGURE 10.1 *Mental Disorders Identified by the American Psychiatric Association*
Source: Adapted from American Psychiatric Association, 1994.

The most widely accepted classification of mental disorders is the American Psychiatric Association's (1994) *Diagnostic and Statistical Manual of Mental Disorders IV* (*DSM-IV*) (see Figure 10.1). The *DSM* is now in its fourth edition, and with each revision, its list of disorders has changed and grown. Listings change partly because of new scientific findings, which permit more precise descriptions that are more useful

than broad terms covering a wide range of behaviors, and partly because of changes in how we view mental disorders culturally (at one time, for example, homosexuality was considered a mental disorder).

Despite the changes, some social analysts still question the extent to which mental health professionals can accurately detect and treat mental disorders. Given this, how many people are affected by

MENTAL ILLNESS AS A SOCIAL PROBLEM   **209**

mental illness? Some answers to this question come from the National Comorbidity Survey, a national study conducted by Ronald C. Kessler and his colleagues (1994:346). The term *comorbidity* refers to the combination of physical and mental conditions—such as physical illness and depression—that compound each other and undermine an individual's overall well-being (Angel and Angel, 1993). The researchers found that 50 percent of respondents between the ages of fifteen and fifty-four years were diagnosed with a mental disorder at some time in their lives (Kessler, 1994). Severe mental illness—such as schizophrenia, bipolar affective disorder (manic-depression), and major depression—typically affected fewer than 15 percent of all U.S. adults at some time in their lives (Bourdon et al., 1992; Kessler, 1994). The National Comorbidity Survey showed that mental disorders in the United States were more prevalent than most analysts had thought. It also indicated that the proportion of people who obtain treatment is low. Even among people with a lifetime history of three or more diagnosed mental disorders, fewer than 50 percent seek treatment (Kessler, 1994).

 Treatment of Mental Illness

Even though statistics indicate that people with mental disorders usually do not seek professional treatment, the leading cause of hospitalization for men between the ages of fifteen and forty-four and the second leading cause (after childbirth) for women in that age group is mental disorders, particularly disorders related to substance abuse (Kessler, 1994; U.S. Bureau of the Census, 1998).

People who do seek professional help are treated with medication and psychotherapy to help them understand the underlying reasons for their problem. Sometimes they are treated in psychiatric wards of local hospitals or in private psychiatric hospitals (Mechanic and Roche-fort, 1990). Because medication is used so routinely today, we tend to forget that institutionalization used to be the most common treatment for severe mental illness. In fact, it was the development of psychoactive drugs that made possible the deinstitutionalization movement of the 1960s.

Deinstitutionalization **is the practice of discharging patients from mental hospitals into the community.** Although deinstitutionalization was originally devised as a solution for the problem of warehousing mentally ill patients in large, prisonlike mental hospi-

Although there are many causes of homelessness ranging from lack of affordable housing to drug dependency, some analysts believe that the deinstitutionalization of patients from mental hospitals has significantly increased the number of people living on the streets of our nation. What other alternatives can you suggest for dealing with mental illness?

tals in the first half of the twentieth century, many social scientists now view deinstitutionalization as a problem. To understand how this solution evolved into a problem, one must understand the state of mental health care in the United States in the 1950s and 1960s. Involuntary (i.e., without a patient's consent) commitment allowed many patients to be warehoused in state mental hospitals for extended periods of time with only minimal and sometimes abusive custodial care. According to sociologist Erving Goffman (1961), mental hospitals are a classic example of a *total institution*—**a place where people are isolated from the rest of society for a period of time and come under the complete control of the officials who run**

the institution. Patients are stripped of their individual identities—or depersonalized—by being required to wear institutional clothing and to follow a strict regimen of activities, meals, and sleeping hours and sometimes by being referred to impersonally as "a CMI" (a person who is chronically mentally ill) (see Grobe, 1995). The deinstitutionalization movement sought to release patients from the hospitals so that they could live at home and go about their daily activities. Professionals believed that the patients' mental disorders could be controlled with medication and treatment through community-based mental health services. Other advocates hoped that it would remove the stigma attached to hospitalization for mental illness. This stigma is described by Susanna Kaysen (1993:123–124), who, at age eighteen, was committed to a private mental hospital for two years:

> The hospital had an address, 115 Mill Street. . . .
>
> In Massachusetts, 115 Mill Street is a famous address. Applying for a job, leasing an apartment, getting a driver's license: all problematic. . . .
>
> "You're living at One fifteen Mill Street?" asked [one prospective employer]. . . . "And how long have you been living there?"
>
> "Oh, a while." I gestured at the past with one hand.
>
> "And I guess you haven't been working for a while?" He leaned back, enjoying himself.
>
> "No," I said. "I've been thinking things over."
>
> I didn't get the job.
>
> As I left the shop my glance met his, and he gave me a look of such terrible intimacy that I cringed. I know what you are, said his look. . . . In the world's terms . . . all of us [at the hospital] were tainted.

Although deinstitutionalization had worthwhile goals—protection of civil rights, more humane and less costly treatment—in too many cases, it simply moved people out of mental hospitals into the streets and jails. Many social analysts believe that the movement was actually triggered by changes in public health insurance. With the introduction of Medicare and Medicaid in 1965, states were more than willing to move patients from state-funded mental hospitals to nursing homes that would be paid for largely by federal government funding (Weitz, 1996). Today,

critics of deinstitutionalization argue that it exacerbated long-term problems associated with treating mental illness. Often, the mental problems were never treated. As John A. Chiles, professor of psychiatry at the University of Texas Health Science Center in San Antonio, writes (quoted in Lawrence, 1996:20):

> Some people [with schizophrenia] never find their way into the system. If they do, it's often into the legal system through petty crime. One local patient attempted a bank robbery while pointing a paintbrush at the teller. "Give me some money," he demanded. "How about $6.25?" asked the skeptical teller. "OK," he agreed. He was apprehended outside the bank and charged with armed robbery. There are more schizophrenics in the Bexar County Jail than there are in the San Antonio State Hospital. And this is similar to many cities across the country.

If schizophrenia and other serious mental illnesses do not lead to jail, they often result in homelessness. One study concluded that as many as 30 percent of homeless people were previously patients in mental hospitals and about 80 percent have some diagnosable mental disorder (Searight and Searight, 1988). However, it is difficult to determine which came first—the mental disorder or homelessness. If you or I were homeless, for instance, what are the chances that we might develop mental health problems if we tried to survive on the streets or in-and-out of shelters and city jails? In any case, social scientists and homeless advocates agree that most homeless shelters and other community services cannot adequately meet the needs of people known as "the homeless mentally ill" (see Torrey, 1988).

Although involuntary commitment to mental hospitals has always been controversial, it remains the primary method by which police officers, judges, social workers, and other officials deal with people—particularly the homeless—whom they have reason to believe are mentally ill and imminently dangerous to themselves and others (Monahan, 1992). However, it should be recognized that involuntary commitment is a social control mechanism, used to keep people with a history of mental illness off the streets so that they cannot engage in violent crime. It does little—if anything—to treat the medical and social conditions that contribute to mental disorders (Catalano and McConnell, 1996). Given this, state mental hospitals tend to function as revolving doors to poverty-level board and care homes, nursing homes, or homelessness; patients who can pay private psychiatric facilities through private insurance coverage or Medicare are not part of this cycle (Brown, 1985).

Race, Class, Gender, and Mental Disorders

Studies of race, class, and gender-based differences in mental disorders show that some of these factors are more important than others. While there are no significant differences in diagnosable mental illness between African Americans and white Americans (the two groups that are most often compared), studies of racism show interesting implications for mental health. For example, in a study of the effects of racism on the everyday lives of middle-class African Americans, social scientists Joe R. Feagin and Melvin P. Sikes (1994) found that repeated personal encounters with racial hostility deeply affect the psychological well-being of most African Americans, regardless of their level of education or social class. In a subsequent study, Feagin and Hernán Vera (1995) found that white Americans also pay a high "psychic cost" for the prevalence of racism because it contradicts deeply held beliefs about the American dream and equality under the law. In earlier work on the effects of discrimination on mental well-being, social psychologist Thomas Pettigrew (1981) suggested that about 15 percent of whites have such high levels of racial prejudice that they tend to exhibit symptoms of serious mental illness. According to Pettigrew, racism in all its forms constitutes a "mentally unhealthy" situation in which people do not achieve their full potential.

Only a few studies have focused on mental disorders among racial-ethnic groups such as Mexican immigrants and Mexican Americans, and they have yielded contradictory results. One study found that strong extended (intergenerational) families—which are emphasized in Mexican culture—provide social support and sources of self-esteem, even if the individuals have low levels of education and income (Mirowsky and Ross, 1980). Another study found the opposite: that maintaining a strong connection to Mexican culture, rather than adopting an Anglo (white/non-Latino/a) culture, is not the primary consideration in whether or not Mexican Americans develop mental disorders (Burnham et al., 1987).

A more recent study from a national survey of people of Mexican origin found that "dark and

Indian-looking Chicano men" in the United States are more likely to develop depression than are "lighter, European-looking Chicanos and their dark-skinned female counterparts" (Codina and Montalvo, 1994). This study also found that women and men who lose their fluency in Spanish while living in the United States experience more depression than those who remain fluent in the language and keep closer ties to their culture (Codina and Montalvo, 1994), findings that support the Mirowsky and Ross study.

Most researchers agree that social class is related to mental illness. For example, one study that examined the relationship between mental disorders, race, and class (as measured by *socioeconomic status*—a combined measure of income, occupation, and education) found that as social class increases for both white Americans and African Americans the rate of mental disorders decreases (Williams et al., 1992). However, although researchers agree that there is a relationship between class and mental disorders, they do not agree on whether lower social class status causes mental illness or mental illness causes lower social class (Weitz, 1996). Analysts using the *social stress framework* to examine schizophrenia—the disorder that is most consistently linked to class—believe that stresses associated with lower-class life lead to greater mental disorders. In contrast, analysts using the *social drift framework* argue that mental disorders cause people to drift downward in class position. To support their argument, they note that individuals who are diagnosed with schizophrenia typically hold lower-class jobs than would be expected on the basis of their family backgrounds (Eaton, 1980; Weitz, 1996).

Gender also appears to be a factor in mental illness. Researchers have consistently found that the rate of diagnosable depression is about twice as high for women as for men, that this gender difference typically emerges in puberty (Cleary, 1987), and that the incident rate rises as women and men enter adulthood and live out their unequal statuses (Mirowsky, 1996). Although women have higher rates of minor depression and other disorders that cause psychological distress, men have higher rates of personality disorders (for example, compulsive gambling or drinking) as well as higher rates of maladaptive personality traits such as antisocial behavior (Link and Dohrenwend, 1989; Weitz, 1996). Some analysts suggest that the difference in types of mental disorders is linked to gender role socialization, which instills aggressiveness in men and learned helplessness in women. According to the *learned helplessness theory*, people become depressed when they think they have no control over their lives (Seligman, 1975). Because this theory emphasizes that people think they have no control, it assumes a *subjective perception* and therefore implies that women contribute to their own helplessness. But feminist analysts argue that the powerlessness in many women's lives is an *objective condition* (Jack, 1993). Support for the feminist view comes from numerous studies indicating that women in high-income, high-status jobs usually have higher levels of psychological well-being and fewer symptoms of mental disorders regardless of their marital status (Horowitz, 1982; Angel and Angel, 1993).

Although numerous studies have been done on women with mild depression, women with serious mental illnesses have been nearly ignored (Mowbray et al., 1992). Furthermore, mental disorders in women have often been misdiagnosed, and on many occasions, physical illnesses have been confused with psychiatric problems (see Busfield, 1996; Lerman, 1996; Klonoff, 1997). It is generally agreed that additional studies of women's diversity across lines of race, class, age, religion, and other factors are necessary before we can accurately assess the relationship between gender and mental illness and how women are treated in the mental health care industry (Gatz, 1995).

THE CRISIS IN U.S. HEALTH CARE

The United States and the Union of South Africa are the only high-income nations without some form of universal health coverage for all citizens. After considering the state of health care in this country, many professional and political advisors have suggested that we look to countries such as Canada and Great Britain for models of government-subsidized medical services (see Box 10.2).

▲ Health Care Organization, Rising Costs, and Unequal Access

Medical care in the United States is provided on a *fee-for-service* basis: Patients are billed individually for each service they receive, including treatment by doctors, laboratory work, hospital visits, prescriptions, and other health-related services. Fee-for-service is an expensive way of delivering health care because there are few restrictions on the fees charged by doctors, hospitals, and other medical providers.

PRIVATE HEALTH INSURANCE

Costly to begin with, fee-for-service health care became even more so with the development of the health insurance industry. During the Great Depression of the 1930s, the American Hospital Association, fearing that many hospitals would go bankrupt because patients could not pay their hospital bills, founded Blue Cross—a nonprofit company—to sell health insurance to people so that they could pay their hospital bills. Shortly thereafter, the American Medical Association established Blue Shield to provide coverage for physicians' bills. Under Blue Cross/Blue Shield and other private insurance programs, patients do not pay doctors and hospitals directly. Instead they pay premiums into a fund that in turn pays doctors and hospitals for each treatment a patient receives as long as the services are covered and the patient has met the annual deductible.

According to medical sociologist Paul Starr (1982), the main reason for medical inflation in this country is third-party fee-for-service because it gives doctors and hospitals an incentive to increase medical services. That is, the more services they provide, the more fees they charge and the more money they make. At the same time, patients have no incentive to limit their visits to doctors or hospitals because they have already paid their premiums and feel entitled to medical care (Starr, 1982).

Health care costs began to spiral with the expansion of medical insurance programs in the 1960s. At that time, third-party providers (public and private insurers) began picking up large portions of doctor and hospital bills for insured patients. Recently, in an effort to reduce the demand for health care services and medical costs, many insurance companies have established an option known as *preferred provider organizations* (PPOs), with such names as HealthSelect (a Blue Cross/Blue Shield entity). In a PPO, doctors work out of their own offices on a fee-for-service basis but contract with an insurance company to provide care for insured patients. The doctors agree to charge set fees for particular services; these fees may be higher or lower than those for other patients who are not covered by the PPO. This model of health care delivery shares certain commonalities

SOCIAL PROBLEMS

AND SOCIAL POLICY

BOX 10.2

Health Care: The Canadian Model

The United States spends more on health care than any other high-income country, yet many people go without health care because it is too expensive. Furthermore, access to health care is often limited by race, class, or gender. Do people have a *right* to health care? No, say some; it is unfortunate that some people suffer illness or disability, but it is not up to society to make the world a fair place (Engelhardt, 1996). On the contrary, say others; health care is a right, not a privilege or a choice, because the choice is ultimately between life and death and every individual has inherent worth (Rawls, 1971). So far, the nays have it in the United States, but among developed nations, only the United States and the Union of South Africa stand together; all others—Canada, Great Britain, France, and Germany, to name only a few—provide universal health coverage for their citizens. Should our system be reformed? How well, for example, does Canada's plan work?

A Canadian citizen never sees a medical bill or insurance form or pays for a prescription. Canada's national health insurance system pays all medical costs directly. Hospitals get a yearly budget, and doctors bill the provincial governments (equivalent to our state governments), which administer the health care system, on a fee-for-service basis. Fees are negotiated annually between doctors and the provincial government. Individuals choose any primary-care doctor they wish, but they need a referral to a specialist.

But are Canadians actually healthier? What about those stories in the newspaper about people in Canada dying because they have to "wait in line" for surgery? First, those stories are not true. Across the board, Canadi-

ans have better access to health care than U.S. citizens do. Canadians pay more visits to the doctor, are hospitalized more often and for longer times, and have higher immunization rates; 85 percent of one-year-olds in Canada are fully immunized compared to 45 percent in the United States (Himmelstein and Woolhandler, 1994). And, yes, Canadians are healthier; they have longer life expectancies and a lower infant mortality rate than do U.S. citizens.

Is there any fly in this ointment? Well, one. The cost of health care is skyrocketing, and Canada—like the United States—must find ways to control costs. So far, that has mostly meant cutting services. For instance, the Ontario Health Insurance Plan no longer pays for a pre-employment physical or electrolysis (hair removal) and is reviewing other procedures, including vasectomies, circumcision of newborns, and psychoanalysis (Farnsworth, 1993). But service cuts have not stopped the cost of medical care from outstripping government funds, and the next step is to ask individuals and employers to pay a share of essential services.

Part of the reason for skyrocketing costs is, of course, new medical technology. The Canadian government also thinks that an oversupply of doctors is contributing to the problem. There are no restrictions on doctor visits or types of treatment, and doctors charge on a fee-for-service basis. Therefore the more doctors there are, the more available care becomes, and the more the bills add up. Also, as in the United States, hospital stays are very expensive (Farnsworth, 1993).

What should the United States do? Is health care a right? Should we reform our health care system to provide universal coverage? Would the Canadian system be a good model? Would some modified version of the Canadian model be better? What do you think?

WILL WORK FOR
HUNDREDS OF THOUSANDS
OF DOLLARS

Rini

with the health maintenance organization and managed care models.

Like other private insurance plans, HMOs emerged during the Great Depression as a means of providing workers with health coverage at a reasonable rate by keeping costs down. A *health maintenance organization* (HMO) **provides, for a fixed monthly fee, total heath care with an emphasis on prevention to avoid costly treatment later.** The doctors do not work on a fee-for-service basis, and patients are encouraged to get regular checkups and to practice good health habits (exercise and eat right). As long as patients use only the doctors and hospitals that are affiliated with their HMO, they pay no fees, or only small copayments, beyond their

insurance premium (Anders, 1996). Believing that the HMO model could be a source of high profits because of its emphasis on prevention, many for-profit corporations moved into the HMO business in the 1980s (Anders, 1996). However, research has shown that preventive care is good for the individual's health but does not necessarily save money. Early detection of HIV infection, diabetes, or high cholesterol, for example, often means a lifetime of costly treatments and drugs. Indeed, some health experts have suggested that for-profit HMOs are unlikely to provide top-notch early detection and prevention programs because of the costs—especially future costs—involved (Rosenthal, 1997). Some critics have even charged that some HMOs require their physicians to withhold vital information from their patients if it is going to cost the HMO money to provide the needed procedure or hospitalization (Gray, 1996). Recently, some HMOs have responded to such criticism (and threats of lawsuits) by allowing doctors and patients greater participation in the HMO's process of determining treatment.

Another approach to controlling health care costs is known as *managed care*—**a term that is used to refer to any system of cost containment that closely monitors and controls health care providers' decisions about medical procedures, diagnostic tests, and other services that should be provided to patients** (Weitz, 1996). In most managed care programs, patients choose a primary-care physician from a list of participating doctors. When patients need medical services, they first contact the primary-care physician; then, if a specialist is needed for treatment, the primary-care physician refers the patient to a specialist who participates in the program. Doctors must get approval before they perform certain procedures or admit a patient to the hospital. If they do not, the insurance company has the prerogative of not covering part of the cost. While managed care does contain some medical care costs, many physicians are opposed to it and HMOs. As one doctor explains (Williams, 1997:A19):

> I was a physician for more than 20 years. Now I am a provider. "Provider" is the term used by health maintenance organizations to refer to physicians and other health-care professionals. They attempt to suppress the very word "physician," and for good reason: It has connotations of expertise, authority and respect, which are incompatible with the managed-care agenda. . . . I have a busy and previously successful internal medicine practice. An hour of my time is now worth approximately 60 percent of its value several years ago. I work more than 60 hours a week. My current personal income, after office expenses, works out to less than $35 per hour. I know many internists who are doing no better. I find myself very discouraged and sometimes rather angry. . . . It is the apparent intent of those who drive managed care that medicine be reduced to a commodity, and a cheap commodity at that, to be bought, sold and manipulated solely for the financial benefit of their industry. I believe this portends very serious problems ahead, not only

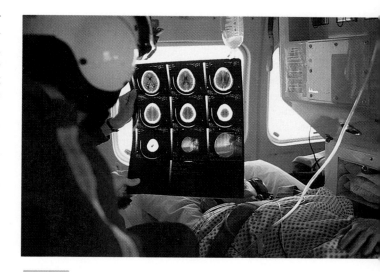

Contemporary high-tech medicine takes place in a wide variety of locales. Because of advanced technologies, this patient is receiving medical attention while being transported to a hospital in a helicopter. Does your city have "life flight" services such as this? Is it important to have such services, or do they merely run up the cost of medical care?

for the profession but for the future of patient care and the well-being of the population at large.

Not only are physicians' revenues reduced under managed care, but so are revenues to hospitals, which means that hospitals can no longer afford to treat uninsured patients who come through their doors seeking treatment for everything from flu to heart disease. In the past, hospitals passed much of the cost of treating uninsured patients to paying patients, but managed care has cut out any margin for doing this (Preston, 1996). Finally, despite cost containment measures, health care continues to be a significant expenditure in the United States, partly because of the for-profit structure of much medical care and partly because of the fragmented health care provided by government-funded insurance programs.

PUBLIC HEALTH INSURANCE

Today, of the total U.S. health care bill, patients pay slightly less than 25 percent; insurance companies pay about 33 percent, and the government pays more than 40 percent (Pear, 1996). Although private health insurance companies were well established by the 1950s, and almost all working people and their immediate families had hospitalization insurance, those who did not work—the elderly and the poor—were often uninsured. Federal legislation extending health care coverage to the elderly and the poor was not passed until the 1960s. From its inception, federally funded health care assistance was a two-tiered system: a medical entitlement program for older people (Medicare) and a medical welfare system for the poor (Medicaid). Medicare is a program that covers most people age 65 and over who are eligible for Social Security or who buy into the program by paying a monthly premium. The largest single insurance program in the country, Medicare is made up of two separate programs: Part A, a hospital insurance program, and Part B, a supplementary medical insurance program. Although Medicare provides coverage for many older people who otherwise would have no health insurance, there are large gaps in its coverage, and elderly near-poor individuals often find it difficult to pay the required deductibles (an initial specified amount that the patient pays before the insurance begins payments) and copayments (shared costs). Also, Medicare provides only limited coverage for costly and sometimes long-term expenses such as post-hospital nursing services, home health care, nursing homes, and hospice services (Toner and Pear, 1995).

Unlike Medicare coverage, which is based primarily on age, Medicaid provides medical, hospital, and long-term care for people who are poor *and* either aged, blind, disabled, or pregnant. Also, whereas Medicare is funded by people's payments into the Social Security system, Medicaid is funded by federal and state governments. As a result, many people view Medicaid as a welfare program and Medicare as an entitlement program—people are assumed to have earned medical coverage through years of hard work and paying into the system. Perceptions aside, both Medicare and Medicaid, like other forms of health insurance, dramatically expand the resources for supplying and financing medical services, especially for people with chronic disabling illnesses that extend over months or years. Analysts therefore suggest that these programs are extremely costly to the public because they provide no incentive for keeping costs down or managing resources. For example, many hospitals use Medicare funds to build new buildings, buy the latest high-tech equipment, and pay nonmedical

personnel in marketing and fund-raising positions. Some physicians abuse the system by operating "Medicaid mills" that charge excessive fees for unnecessary tests and treatments.

During the past fifteen years the growing number of Medicaid recipients with AIDS has increased Medicaid costs. These costs have been driven still higher by AIDS patients, who, on losing their jobs, also lose their company-provided private insurance coverage and therefore seek Medicaid. It seems likely that Medicare costs will also increase in the future as more people over age fifty are being diagnosed with AIDS. In 1996, for example, AIDS was diagnosed in 56,000 people over age fifty (Gross, 1997).

◢ The Uninsured and the Underinsured

Despite public and private insurance programs, about one-third of all U.S. citizens are without health insurance or had difficulty getting or paying for medical care at some time in the last year. An estimated 44.3 million people in the United States had no health insurance in 1998—an increase of about 1 million people since 1997 (U.S. Bureau of the Census, 1999a). About one-fourth of the people not covered by health insurance are children. Excluding the elderly and members of the military and their families—who are covered by the federal government—the majority of the uninsured are full-time workers (about 41 percent) (Toner, 1993). About 70 percent of the uninsured said that they had been employed some of the time they were without health insurance. Jobs in agriculture, personal services, construction, business and repair services, retail, self-employment, and recreation and entertainment have higher-than-average percentages of uninsured employees (Toner, 1993; Pear, 1996). One study has found that some corporations are cutting medical benefits for rank-and-file employees or moving them into managed care programs that strictly limit benefits while company executives continue to have health plans that provide full coverage for office visits and hospitalization for monthly premiums of less than $10 and no annual deductible or out-of-pocket expenses (Myerson, 1996). The bitter reality of being uninsured was best expressed by Tommy Markham, who at age forty-eight was disabled by a stroke: "You could be damn near dying, and the first thing they ask is 'Do you have insurance?'" (Abraham, 1993:3).

◢ Race, Class, Gender, and Health Care

Just as deinstitutionalization was initially seen as the solution to mental health care and is now viewed by many as the problem, health insurance plans were initially considered a solution but have now become a problem, especially when they perpetuate unequal access to health care because of race, class, or gender. According to a large federal study, even when people are covered by Medicare or Medicaid, the care they receive and their overall life expectations are influenced by their race and income. Among other things, people of color across class lines and low-income whites typically receive less preventive care and less optimal management of chronic diseases than others (Leary, 1996). Under Medicaid the poorest people sometimes receive the fewest services because of limitations placed on eligibility and the way in which payment of fees to doctors is structured. For example, many doctors are unwilling to work in a central city area for a Medicaid reimbursement of $13 a visit (Rosenthal, 1993). Even with private health insurance, people living in central cities where there are high levels of poverty and crime or in remote rural areas have difficulty getting medical treatment because most doctors prefer to locate their practices in "safe" areas, particularly ones with a patient base that will produce a high income.

Like race and class, gender is an important factor in health care. Numerous researchers have found pervasive gender inequality in health care in the United States (Nechas and Foley, 1994; Rosser, 1994). The long-term exclusion of women from medicine continues to have a detrimental impact on their health in this country and elsewhere. Women are underrepresented in the medical profession, representatively less research is done on health care issues specifically pertaining to them, and women have differential access to medical treatment.

Although more women have become physicians in recent years, about 80 percent of medical doctors in the United States today are men. The underrepresentation of women in medicine can be traced back to 1910 and the publication of the Flexner Report, a study on the state of medical education in the United States commissioned by the American Medical Association and the Carnegie Foundation. According to educator Abraham Flexner (1910), the only way to make the practice of medicine more sci-entific was to make medical education more rigorous, and the way to accomplish this was to close a number of medical schools. Flexner's plan was implemented, but not in an even-handed way: Only one of the three women's medical schools and two schools for African Americans survived. As a result, white women and people of color were largely excluded from medical education for the first half of the twentieth century. Until the civil rights movement and the women's movements of the 1960s and early 1970s, virtually all physicians were white, male, and upper- or upper-middle class. Today, however, women make up more than 42 percent of medical students. Given this, the gender ratio in the profession will change rather dramatically early in the twenty-first century (Association of American Medical Colleges, 1999).

While the more equitable gender enrollments in medical schools are welcome and long overdue, there is still a male-centered focus on human health and health care delivery in both medical school and medical practice. Funding for research on women's health issues and diseases is lacking, and women have been excluded from most experimental drugs trials, which are conducted to determine the positive and negative effects that a specific drug has on a given category of patients (Laurence and Weinhouse, 1994). Many clinical studies virtually ignore women. For example, although women are in the group with the most rapidly increasing incidence of AIDS, very little AIDS research relating to women is being conducted (Nechas and Foley, 1994). Similarly, in a widely reported study on the effects of aspirin on heart disease, all of the patients were men, even though heart disease is the leading cause of death for both women and men (Steering Committee of the Physicians' Health Group Study, 1989).

The failure to include women in research contributes to their differential treatment for certain kinds of medical problems. For example, women with the same symptoms of kidney failure as men are much less likely to receive an organ transplant (Steingart et al., 1991). Similarly, far fewer women than men with an abnormal heart scan are referred for a procedure known as cardiac catheterization to remedy the problem. Without adequate studies, diseases in women may go unrecognized, be misdiagnosed, or be attributed to a nonphysical factor. According to medical sociologists, both male and female doctors need more training in health issues pertaining to women so that they can treat the majority of the U.S. population (Rosser, 1994).

SOCIOLOGICAL EXPLANATIONS FOR HEALTH CARE PROBLEMS

What are the primary causes of health care problems in the United States? How can health care be improved? The answers that social scientists give to these questions depend on their theoretical framework. Analysts approaching these questions from a functionalist perspective focus on how illness affects the smooth operation of society and on the functions medicine serves as a social institution. Some sociologists using a conflict perspective focus on how a capitalist economy affects health and health care delivery; others look at inequalities of race, class, and gender. Finally, sociologists who use an interactionist framework look at the social and cultural factors affecting communication between doctors and patients.

 The Functionalist Perspective

The functionalist perspective views illness as a threat to a smoothly functioning society because it is necessary for all people to fulfill their appropriate social roles. According to this view, when people become ill, they cannot fulfill their everyday responsibilities to family, employer, or the larger society and instead adopt the *sick role*—patterns of behavior expected from individuals who are ill. Sociologist Talcott Parsons (1951) identified four role expectations of the sick role: (1) sick people are not responsible for their incapacity; (2) they are exempted from their usual role and task obligations; (3) they must want to leave the sick role and get well; and (4) they are obligated to seek and comply with the advice of a medical professional. In other words, illness is a form of deviance that must be controlled. According to Parsons, physicians are the logical agents of social control. By certifying that a person is physically or mentally ill and by specifying how the ill person should behave, doctors use their professional authority to monitor people with illnesses, thereby granting them only a temporary reprieve from their usual social roles and responsibilities. Today, however, the dramatic increase in

chronic illness and the disorganization in the delivery system for medical services mean that many people have less access to doctors and doctors have less control over those aspects of patients' lives that can increase their chances of becoming ill. Patients thus end up incurring large medical bills and being unproductive in society.

Functionalists believe that the problems in U.S. health care are due to macrolevel changes, such as the development of high-tech medicine, overspecialization of doctors, erosion of health insurance coverage, and increased demand for health care by consumers. Since World War II, functionalists say, the rapid growth of medical knowledge has produced a glut of information, new technologies, and greatly improved surgical techniques. To remain competitive in the face of this new technology and the demand for it, hospitals operating in the same city have often purchased the same extremely expensive equipment. The costs of the equipment are passed on to consumers in the form of higher medical bills and insurance premiums. In the same way that hospitals believe they must have all the latest technology, most medical students have come to believe that they have to specialize—rather than enter general or family practice—to build a large patient base and thereby increase their income and prestige. Thus, both doctors and hospitals have begun to view health care as a commodity and to provide a far wider array of services (treatment for substance abuse, day care for the mentally ill, and elective procedures such as cosmetic surgery) to sell to consumers (potential patients). At the same time, most individuals have come to view health care as a right to which they are entitled. As both the supply of and demand for medical treatment have grown, lobbying organizations such as the American Medical Association and the American Hospital Association and business, labor, and consumer (especially the elderly) groups have entered into battle with Congress over the extent to which federal and state government should regulate health care.

Although functionalists agree that the disorganization in U.S. health care is clearly dysfunctional for both individuals and society, they do not agree on what should be done. Some believe that the whole health care system should be reorganized; others think that managed care is the best answer. Most attempts at reorganization have ended up on the rocks. In 1993, for example, the Clinton administration proposed a vast restructuring of the health care system that was to be phased in over several years. Under the plan, financial incentives would have been used to encourage consumers to join low-cost HMOs and push doctors, hospitals, and insurance companies to join together in networks. The plan would have made consumers conscious of the costs of their care and fostered competition among health plans in an effort to reduce costs and provide better services. However, as employers would have paid the bulk of the cost (because they would have paid the premiums for their workers), many small business owners and others who feared the financial impact of the plan adamantly opposed it.

Without proper planning, the United States cannot have a fully functioning health care system. Instead, we have many individual components—ranging from doctors in private practice to for-profit HMOs, pharmaceutical companies, and insurance companies—each with its own agenda for health care delivery. Also, say the functionalists, health care must shift its focus from acute diseases to problems associated with chronic illness and disability.

 ## The Conflict Perspective

The conflict approach is based on the assumption that problems in health care delivery are rooted in the capitalist economy, which views medicine as a commodity produced and sold by the medical-industrial complex. The *medical-industrial complex* **encompasses both local physicians and hospitals as well as global health-related industries such as the pharmaceutical and medical supply companies that deliver health care** (Relman, 1992). Although wealthy patients and patients with good insurance may receive high-quality care in the medical-industrial complex structure, low-income and poverty-level people often do without. In this view, physicians hold a legal monopoly over medicine and benefit from the existing structure because they can charge inflated fees. Similarly, hospitals, clinics, and other medical facilities control how health care is delivered and what various services will cost patients. From this perspective, managed care and other cost-containment strategies are ways of reducing the control of physicians and other players in the medical-industrial complex and thereby reducing inequalities in the system. But managed care, conflict theorists are quick to point out, is no more than a bandage on the hemorrhaging cost of health care because it does not deal with the larger systemic problem of how health care is delivered.

Radical conflict theorists say that only when race-, class-, and gender-based inequalities in society are reduced will inequalities in health care be reduced. As long as societal conditions—environmental pollution, lack of affordable housing, high levels of stress associated with working conditions or unemployment, inadequate nutrition, and lack of early diagnosis for diseases such as breast cancer and heart disease—affect people according to their race, class, and gender, health care will be unequal. Most conflict theorists believe that short of a dramatic change in the economic system, the primary way to deal with health care is to treat it as a common good that should be provided and regulated by the government just as highways, schools, courts, and national defense are (Shweder, 1997).

Some conflict theorists also suggest that the doctor–patient relationship should be demystified. These theorists argue that if patients were given the information and resources they need for prevention, self-treatment, and home care, the need and demand for expensive medical care would be greatly reduced (Stewart, 1995). In the past, most patients relied on doctors for heath-related information. Today, many people receive medical information from the media and the Internet. Thousands of web sites are devoted to health and medical information, ranging from potentially life-saving research in top medical journals to alternative therapies such as herbal preparations and colonic irrigation (Fisher, 1996; Kolata, 1996c). Many computer bulletin boards, chat groups, and Usenet newsgroups have emerged to support people with diseases such as AIDS and multiple sclerosis (Kantrowitz, 1993). Capitalism also thrives on the Internet. Corporations have on-line ventures that offer not only research on any health care topic but also information on physicians, nurses, hospitals, HMOs, and preferred provider organizations. In most cases, fees come from the providers, not from users viewing the pages (Fisher, 1996). Because of the proliferation of medical information on the Internet, the Food and Drug Administration is working to regulate promotion of drugs and medical devices to protect patients who may not be able to distinguish between science and quackery (Neergaard, 1996). Whether or not this proliferation of information helps to demystify doctor–patient relationships remains to be seen.

▲ The Interactionist Perspective

Interactionists believe that many problems pertaining to health and illness in our society are linked to social and cultural factors that influence how people define physical illness and mental illness. According to interactionists, we socially construct "health" and "illness" and how both should be treated. As a result, both medical and nonmedical "experts" play a role in determining what constitutes physical and mental illnesses and how these illnesses should be treated by society. For example, in 1997 under the Americans with Disabilities Act, the Equal Employment Opportunity Commission established guidelines requiring that employers take "reasonable steps" to accommodate employees with mental illnesses—the same requirement that previously applied only to people with physical disabilities (Stolberg, 1997a). What exactly does "reasonable steps" mean? According to one analyst, "That could mean anything from a flexible schedule for an anxious person, to a desk near a window for a person who grows depressed with too little light, to a quiet work space for a schizophrenic" (Stolberg, 1997a:E1).

Interactionists also examine how doctors and patients interact in health care settings. For example, medical schools provide future doctors with knowledge and skills that laypeople do not have. Given this competence gap, some physicians do not think it is necessary—or possible—to communicate certain kinds of medical information to patients. Some may hesitate to communicate the diagnosis of a fatal illness or, more often, may simply not explain why they are prescribing certain medications or what side effects or drug interactions may occur.

One way to solve this communication problem, according to interactionists, is to increase the number of family practice doctors as these doctors usually focus on patient care and communication, not just the scientific and technological aspects of health care. Another way is to emphasize prevention and work with patients on behaviors to practice and avoid if they want to stay healthy. A third way to change health care is to limit the bureaucracies in mental hospitals where individuals are labeled by their diagnosis and not viewed as people with specific emotional and physical needs to be met. Finally, interactionists say, more public health campaigns are needed to make people aware of issues in health care and health care reform. The 1993 Clinton health reform proposal, they note, was debated by politicians and interest groups with very little input from everyday people whose lives would be affected by the new health care policy—or the lack of one. Consider, for example, the Patten family. Leo Patten has emphysema from smoking and breathing foul air in the factories where he worked as a machinist. Elma Patten has had heart bypass surgery, a mastectomy, a hysterectomy, and two wrist operations for a repetitive motion injury related to her work (Kilborn, 1993). After decades of middle-class security, the Pattens have dwindling savings and fear that another medical setback will drive them out of their $65,000 home and onto the welfare rolls. According to Elma Patten, "A person keeps their nose to the grindstone, works hard, pays their bills on time. Then when your health goes bad they kick you into a corner" (Kilborn, 1993:4A14). The Pattens wonder whether they will be able to pay their doctor, whom they like because she communicates with them. However, the Pattens' future—like that of many people with chronic illnesses—is caught up in political and economic issues about health care delivery that will apparently remain with us for decades.

Since Clinton withdrew his health care reform package, federal health officials have focused on reforming the Medicare/Medicaid system and on health coverage for children, particularly for families where parents are temporarily out of work. One plan would increase the cigarette tax to subsidize medical premiums for all children in families earning less than 185 percent of the poverty level. Another would offer refundable tax credits to low-income families. However, interactionists point out that these are not long-term solutions. Problems with access to health care will inevitably worsen as costs soar, increasing demands are placed on health care systems, and cuts are made in Medicaid and Medicare reimbursement rates for doctors and hospitals. Further cost-cutting by private insurers will squeeze out whatever is left of the financial slack that once paid for much charity health care, placing even more pressure on state and local governments that are already hard-pressed to come up with money for health coverage as they try to deal with the side effects of cuts in welfare programs.

According to interactionists, three factors will inevitably perpetuate inequalities of U.S. health care: (1) high health care costs due to advanced medical services and the use of expensive medications and technology; (2) abuse of existing systems by some health care professionals, particularly those who overcharge patients, provide unnecessary services, or charge for expensive services that were never rendered; and (3) the aging population that will continue to increase sharply and place greater strain on Medicare, Medicaid, and other health resources (Bagby, 1997). As one woman explained to her granddaughter, "Your generation is giving my generation a free ride and the sooner we stop it the better. There is no way on earth to eliminate the [federal] debt without touching entitlements" such as Medicare (Bagby, 1997:21).

SUMMARY

➡ *Why is health care a social problem?*

Health care is a social problem because, according to the World Health Organization, health is a state of complete physical, mental, and social well-being. In other words, health is a social issue. Although people in the United States pay more for health services than people in other high-income nations, our expenditures do not translate into improved life expectancy for everyone.

➡ *What kinds of health problems cause most of today's high health care costs?*

Since acute illnesses (e.g., measles, polio) are largely under control with vaccinations and improved public health practices, most health problems today are chronic diseases (e.g., arthritis, diabetes, heart disease) or disabilities (e.g., back injuries, hearing or vision problems, mental retardation), which require long-term treatment. Medical advances mean that many people born with serious disabilities survive, as do many who would have died from acute illnesses or accidents in earlier times. As more people survive and live longer, more are likely to experience chronic illnesses and disabilities.

➡ *Why is AIDS considered a health crisis in the United States and other nations?*

First, the number of cases is rising annually. Second, about 75 percent of people infected worldwide are infected through heterosexual intercourse—it is not a disease restricted to any single group. Third, there is no cure; once HIV develops into AIDS, it is fatal. Fourth, treatment is complex and costly and typically requires lengthy stays in a hospital or hospice. Finally, numerous ethical issues (e.g., issues relating to testing) have yet to be resolved.

➡ *Why is mental illness a social problem?*

Mental illness is a social problem because of the number of people it affects, the difficulty in defining and identifying mental disorders, and the ways in which it is treated. Deinstitutionalization—discharging mental patients from hospitals into the community—was considered a solution to the problem of warehousing patients, but it has created new problems.

➡ *Historically, what kinds of health care have been available in the United States?*

Originally, there was fee-for-service care in which patients paid directly for treatment they received from doctors and hospitals. The Great Depression brought about third-party fee-for-service care—patients pay premiums to private or public health insurance companies that in turn pay the doctors and hospitals. Both of these health care structures are expensive because there are few restrictions on fees charged by health care providers.

➡ *What new types of health care are available in the United States?*

Some insurance companies now offer preferred provider organizations (PPOs) in which doctors contract to treat insured patients for set fees; these fees may be higher or lower than the fees for other patients who are not enrolled in the PPO. For a set monthly fee a health maintenance organization

(HMO) provides total care with an emphasis on prevention; patients must use the doctors and hospitals affiliated with the HMO. Managed care refers to any system of cost containment that closely monitors and controls health care providers' decisions about what medical tests, procedures, and other services should be provided to patients; a patient's primary-care physician must get approval to send the patient to a specialist or order hospitalization and costly tests or procedures. Since many for-profit companies have entered health care, there is some concern that quality of care is sacrificed to cost containment.

What is the difference between Medicare and Medicaid?

Medicare is public health insurance for people age sixty-five and over that is funded by Social Security payments. Medicaid is public health insurance for people who are poor and either aged, blind, disabled, or pregnant; it is funded by federal and state governments. Both programs are considered costly to the public because there are no incentives to keep costs down.

How do race, class, and gender affect health care?

Research shows that people of color across class lines and low-income whites typically receive less preventive care and less optimal management of chronic diseases than others do. Women have been underrepresented in the medical profession (though that is changing); medical training, practice, and research are male-centered; and women receive differential treatment for certain kinds of medical problems.

What are the sociological explanations for health care problems?

Functionalists consider the sick role a form of deviance that medicine as an institution controlled until recently. Today, however, the supply of and demand for health care means that patients incur large medical bills and are unproductive to society. Some functionalists believe that the whole health system must be reorganized; others think that managed care is the best answer. Some conflict theorists believe that our health problems are rooted in capitalism and the medical-industrial complex; others believe that only when race-, class-, and gender-based inequalities are reduced will inequalities in health care be reduced. Interactionists believe that communication problems between doctors and patients create many of our health problems and that people must, among other things, become more involved in health care issues and health care reform.

KEY TERMS

acute diseases, pp. 202–203
chronic diseases, p. 204
deinstitutionalization, p. 209
disability, p. 205

health maintenance organization (HMO), p. 214
infant mortality rate, p. 202
life expectancy, p. 202

managed care, p. 215
medical-industrial complex, p. 219
total institution, pp. 209–210

QUESTIONS FOR CRITICAL THINKING

1. Because the United States takes pride in its technological and social standing in the world, people are usually surprised to learn that our infant mortality rate is higher than the rates in most other high-income countries. Why is it and what do you think individuals can do at the community level to save these young lives?

2. In what ways are race, class, and gender intertwined with mental disorders? Consider causes and treatments.

3. Reread the doctor's statement on page 215. Do you agree that managed care is detrimental to patient care, or do you side with conflict theorists who believe that doctors uphold the fee-for-service system because it allows them to inflate the cost of treatment? Is there a middle ground?

4. Do you think the U.S. health care system needs reforming? If so, what would you propose?

Chapter Eleven

The Changing Family

I was working from six-thirty in the morning to seven at night without breaks. I wasn't eating. I was irritable. I couldn't deal with anybody. I was fighting with my wife all the time. We were breaking apart. I wasn't communicating anymore. The job took control of me. I was possessed. I didn't feel patient with my daughter anymore. It was taking a big toll on me, and I didn't like it at all. I decided it wasn't worth it and the only way to stop it was to leave.

—Ernie, a physical therapist, explaining that he resigned from a managerial position in a large corporation when he discovered that his job was damaging his family relationships
(Gerson, 1993:145)

—A 35-year-old white secretary, who was married for sixteen years and had one child
(Kurz, 1995:90)

Since the divorce what's been hard is worrying about paying the bills—having enough money for food for my son. I don't even get to think about buying him new sneakers.

I wish my parents had had some time to spend with me when I was growing up. They were basically absentee parents. I'm not going to do that to my kids. I'm going to be there for them!

—A student in introductory sociology discussing the importance of early childhood socialization
(Author's files, 1997)

—Renee, an African American woman who was considering marriage to her current companion
(Jarrett, 1997:353)

I could do bad by myself. . . . If we got married and he's working, then he lose his job. I'm going to stand by him and everything. I don't want to marry nobody that don't have nothing going for themselves . . . . I don't see no future . . . . I could do bad by myself.

Many people today experience the family-related problems described by these individuals: the family-work dilemma, economic hardship after divorce, lack of time for family life, and feelings of hopelessness brought about by unemployment and poverty. Although most sociologists believe that the family as a social institution is here to stay in one form or another, they also acknowledge that family-related problems are a challenge not only to individuals but to our entire society.

THE NATURE OF FAMILIES

What is a family? According to sociologist Robin Wolf (1996), that question generates heated debate: Some say that any definition of the family must emphasize tradition and stability; others argue that any useful definition must take into account diversity and social change. Traditionally, *family* has been defined as a group of people who are related to one another by blood, marriage, or adoption and who live together, form an economic unit, and bear and raise children (Benokraitis, 1993). According to this definition, families are created through childbearing, and it is the parent–child relationship that links generations (Beutler, Burr, Bahr, and Herrin, 1989). Today, however, the traditional definition of family is often modified to incorporate diverse living arrangements and relationships such as single-parent households, cohabiting unmarried couples, domestic partnerships of lesbian or gay couples, and several generations of family members (grandparent, parent, and child) living under the same roof. To encompass these arrangements, we will use the following definition as we look at family-related social problems: *families* **are relationships in which people live together with commitment, form an economic unit and care for any young, and consider the group critical to their identity** (Benokraitis, 1993; Lamanna and Riedmann, 1994).

Changing Family Structure and Patterns

The basis of the traditional family structure is *kinship,* **a social network of people based on common ancestry, marriage, or adoption.** Kinship is very important in preindustrial societies because it serves as an efficient means of producing and distributing food and goods (clothing, materials for building shelter) and transferring property and power from one generation to the next. In many preindustrial societies the primary kinship unit is the *extended family*—**a family unit composed of relatives in addition to parents and children, all of whom live in the same household.** Extended families typically include grandparents, uncles, aunts, or other relatives in addition to parents and children. When the growing and harvesting of crops is the basis of economic production, extended families mean that large numbers of people participate in food production, which can be essential to survival. Living together also enables family members to share other resources, such as shelter and transportation. Though extended families are not common in the United States, they are in some countries in Latin America, Africa, Asia, and parts of Eastern and Southern Europe (Busch, 1990).

With industrialization, other social institutions begin to fulfill kinship system functions. The production and distribution of goods and services, for example, largely shifts to the economic sector. The form of kinship that is most typical in industrialized nations is the *nuclear family*—**a family unit composed of one or two parents and their dependent children that lives apart from other relatives.** The nuclear family in an industrialized society functions primarily to regulate sexual activity, socialize children, and provide family members with affection and companionship. Although many people view the two-parent nuclear family as the ideal family, only one out of four U.S. families is composed of a married couple and one or more children under age eighteen (U.S. Bureau of the Census, 1998). This is a 15 percent decrease since 1970, when two out of five families were two-parent households. Sociologists attribute the decrease to a greater number of births among unmarried women, a trend toward postponing or forgoing marriage and childbearing, and high rates of separation and divorce.

Are U.S. Families in Decline?

Will the family as a social institution disappear in the future? Social analysts answer this question differently, depending on whether they adopt a traditional definition of the family or a modified def-

"So how's the family? Still disintegrating?"

inition. Sociologist David Popenoe (1988, 1996) uses a traditional definition and believes that three trends mark the coming end of the traditional nuclear family:

▲ The divorce rate has increased sharply (it currently exceeds 50 percent), and parents increasingly decide to forgo marriage, so a sizable number of children are being raised in single-parent households apart from other relatives.

▲ Large numbers of married women have left the role of full-time mother and housewife to go into the labor market, and not all the functions of the former role are being fulfilled.

▲ The focus of many families has shifted away from childbearing to the needs of the adult members. Increasingly, even when parents have young children to raise, they break up if their psychological and self-development needs are unmet in the marriage relationship. (Popenoe, 1995:16)

Some sociologists have suggested that if marriage and the family weaken enough and no satisfactory substitute for marriage emerges, industrial societies like the United States will not survive (Davis and Grossbard-Shechtman, 1985).

Some analysts point out that research has shown that the structure of the family is undergoing profound changes around the world, in both rich and poor nations (see Box 11.1). These analysts say the family isn't declining, it's simply changing. From

SOCIAL PROBLEMS

The Changing Family around the World

Ms. Polyakovskaya lives with her 6-month-old baby, relying on friends and baby sitters to watch Aleksandr when she is at work. The father, an unmarried journalist, has never seen his child. Her 6-year-old son, Simeon, is being raised by his grandmother and great-grandmother in Kiev. Ms. Polyakovskaya says she hopes to bring him to Moscow, but cannot even afford train fare to visit him.

She loves her job covering music and ballet, but it is ill paid. In her bare one-room apartment, she sleeps on a tiny, fold-out couch next to the baby's crib. An ironing board serves as a desk. But like many women raising children alone, she said she does not want to marry again.

"My life is difficult," she said, "but God, if I had to come home from work and clean, cook and iron for a husband who keeps telling me I am doing it wrong, it would be even worse."

—*Yelena Polyakovskaya, age 32, a television reporter in Russia (Stanley, 1995)*

Yelena Polyakovskaya is one of a growing number of women in Russia raising her family without a husband. Approximately 15 to 20 percent of Russian families are single-parent households. This is a lower figure than in the United States (with about 27 percent single-parent households), but in Russia, single mothers span all social strata; in the United States, single-parent households are largely in the poorest urban areas (Stanley, 1995). In Japan, single-parenthood because of abandonment or divorce is rare, but a practice called *tanshin hunin* has the same effect. When middle-managers are transferred, they go without their families so that their children don't have to change schools. When possible, the fathers commute home on weekends, but the mothers are essentially single parents (O'Connell, 1994).

this social change perspective, families are becoming more complex and diverse—they are not in a state of irreversible decline (Skolnick, 1991; Cherlin, 1992). In fact, according to sociologist Andrew Cherlin (1992), the family will last as a social institution precisely because it can adapt to social change and modify its form. However, Cherlin goes on to say that the best way to minimize the costs of change in the family unit is to modify the other social institutions of daily life—such as the economy and workplace.

Changing Views on Marriage and Families

The term *marriage* refers to a legally recognized and/or socially approved arrangement between two individuals that carries certain rights and obligations and usually involves sexual activity. In the United States the only legal form of marriage is *monogamy*—**a marriage between one woman and one man.** The marriage rate (number of marriages per 1,000 population) in the United States is about 9 percent annually.

Marriage was once a cultural imperative. There was "something wrong" with a person who didn't marry. But since the 1970s, people's attitudes toward marriage and the family have changed as other aspects of society have changed. Cultural guidelines on marriage and childbearing have grown weaker as our society has experienced a broader cultural shift toward autonomy and personal growth. In the 1970s, according to Cherlin (1992:127), "Family life became a matter of personal choice in which individuals made decisions based on a calculus of self-interest and self-fulfillment. Marriage was still desirable, but

Increasing single-parenthood is just one worldwide trend. According to Judith Bruce, author of a report published by the Population Council, a nonprofit group in New York, "trends like unwed motherhood, rising divorce rates, smaller households and the feminization of poverty are not unique to America, but are occurring worldwide" (Lewin, 1995). Among the report's findings are the following:

▲ Divorce rates are rising. In many developed countries, the divorce rates doubled between 1970 and 1990; in less developed countries, about one-fourth of first marriages end by the time women are in their forties.
▲ Unwed motherhood is increasing virtually everywhere.
▲ Children in single-parent households are more likely to be poor than are children in two-parent households, especially when the parent is the mother (often termed the *feminization of poverty*).
▲ Though the reason varies from country to country, more women are entering the work force and taking increasing economic respon-

sibility for children. In Bangladesh, for example, where older husbands take young wives, when a husband dies, the wife must find work to support their children. In Asia, if a father who migrates for better work opportunities stops sending money, the mother must support the family herself. In sub-Saharan Africa a woman's husband may go on to another polygamous marriage and support those children instead (Lewin, 1995).

The fact that families around the world are changing in similar ways shows that there is nothing inevitable about the form of the family or the roles of women and men even within a single society (O'Connell, 1994). The fact of so much change in the most basic unit of society also poses important questions for the twenty-first century. Is the basic problem really inequality between women and men? Would shared responsibilities in the home and equal opportunities in the workplace create better families? Can some general principles for social policies be developed, given vastly different societal conditions? What do you think?

no one any longer had to be married to be a proper member of society." Marriage also became much less of an economic necessity for women in the 1970s because of new job opportunities and rising incomes. Although women's wages remained low in comparison to men's during this time, their wages rose in absolute terms (Cherlin, 1992).

Still, marriage is a persistent preference for most people today, especially those who plan to have children. In a national survey conducted by sociologist Arland Thornton (1989), more than 75 percent of high school seniors reported that marriage and family life were extremely important to them. Most also indicated that if they married, it was very likely that they would stay married to the same person for life. Carrying out such intentions may not be easy. According to another national study, more than half the married people interviewed indicated that if they

had it to do over again, they would marry the same person, but 20 percent said that they would definitely not marry their current partner again, and another 25 percent said that they weren't sure (Patterson and Kim, 1991).

The divorce rate (number of divorces per 1,000 population) in the United States during the twentieth century has varied from a low of 0.7 in 1900 to an all-time high of 5.3 in 1981; by 1996 it had stabilized at 4.3 (U.S. Bureau of the Census, 1998). Though many believe marriage should last "until death do us part," others feel marriage is a commitment "for as long as love allows." Through a pattern of marriage, divorce, and remarriage, many people reaffirm their belief in the institution of marriage but not to the individual they initially married. This pattern of successive marriages, in which a person has several spouses over a lifetime but is legally married to only one partner at a time, is referred to as *serial monogamy*. Some social analysts consider serial monogamy a natural adaptation to other social changes in society; others think it is detrimental to individuals and to society and serves as further evidence of the decline of the family (see Popenoe, 1996). Who is right? As with other social problems we have examined, the causes, effects, and possible solutions for family-related problems depend on the theoretical framework the analyst uses.

SOCIOLOGICAL PERSPECTIVES ON FAMILY-RELATED PROBLEMS

What purposes do families serve in contemporary societies? Do families create problems for society or solve them? The latter, say functionalists, who believe that the family fulfills important functions for individuals at the microlevel and for the entire society at the macrolevel. Conflict and feminist theorists, on the other hand, consider families a primary source of inequality—and sometimes abuse and violence—in society. Taking a microlevel approach, interactionists analyze family-related social problems in terms of socialization and social interactions among family members.

Functionalist Perspectives

Functionalists emphasize the importance of the family in maintaining the stability of society and the well-being of individuals. According to Emile Durkheim, marriage is a microcosmic replica of the larger society; both marriage and society involve a mental and moral fusion of physically distinct individuals (Lehmann, 1994). Durkheim also believed that a division of labor contributed to greater efficiency in marriage and families (and all areas of life). In his study of family life in the United States, Talcott Parsons (1955) also viewed a division of labor as important. He saw the husband in an ideal nuclear family as fulfilling an *instrumental role*—meeting the family's economic needs, making important decisions, and providing leadership—and the wife as fulfilling an *expressive role*—running the household, caring for children, and meeting family members' emotional needs.

Using Durkheim's and Parsons's work as a basis for their model of the family, contemporary func-

tionalists believe that a division of labor makes it possible for families to fulfill a number of functions that no other social institution in high-income nations can perform as efficiently and effectively:

1. *Regulate sexual behavior and reproduction.* Families are expected to regulate the sexual activity of their members and thus control reproduction so that it occurs within specific boundaries. Sexual regulation of family members by the family is supposed to protect the *principle of legitimacy*—the belief that all children should have a socially and legally recognized father (Malinowski, 1964).
2. *Socialize and educate children.* Parents and other relatives are responsible for teaching children the values and norms of their culture.
3. *Provide economic and psychological support.* Families are responsible for providing for their members' physical (food, shelter) and emotional needs.
4. *Provide social status.* Families confer social status on their members, including *ascribed statuses* such as race, ethnicity, nationality, class, and religious affiliation, although some of these statuses may change later in life.

Considering their view of the family, functionalists believe that problems in the family are a social crisis. The functional family provides both social order and economic stability by providing for the survival and development of children; the physical and emotional health of adults; and the care of the sick, injured, elderly, and disabled. The family is also the front line for reinforcing society's norms and values. Functionalists consider the family to be part of the solution to many problems faced by people in contemporary societies. In this view, dysfunctions in families are problems that threaten the well-being of individuals, groups, and nations.

Functionalists believe that changes in other social institutions, such as the economy, religion, education, law, medicine, and the government, contribute to family-related problems. For example, some functionalists think that changing the law to recognize no-fault divorce contributes to higher rates of divorce and dramatically increases single-parent households, which do not provide children with the nurturance and guidance they get in a two-parent home (Popenoe, 1996).

Conflict and Feminist Perspectives

Most conflict and feminist analysts believe that functionalist views on family problems are idealized and inadequate. Rather than operating harmoniously and for the benefit of all members, families are sources of social inequality and conflict over values, goals, and access to resources and power.

Conflict theorists who focus on class relations in capitalist economies compare family members to workers in a factory. Women are dominated by men in the home just as workers are dominated by managers and capitalists in factories (Engels, 1972). As wives and mothers, women contribute to capitalism by producing the next generation of workers and providing the existing labor force with food, clean clothes, and emotional support. Not only does women's work in the family benefit the capitalist class, it reinforces women's subordination because the work is unpaid and often devalued. In support of this view, conflict theorists note that women who work solely in their own homes for many years usually do not have health insurance or a retirement plan apart from sharing in their husbands' employment benefits.

Many feminist theorists, however, think that male dominance and female subordination began long before capitalism and the private ownership of property arose as an economic system (Mann, 1994). They see women's subordination as rooted in patriarchy, particularly in men's control over women's labor power. At the same time that women's labor in the home is directed by men, it is undervalued, which allows men to benefit from their status as the family breadwinner (Firestone, 1970; Goode, 1982). In a more recent study, sociologist Jane Riblett Wilkie (1993) found that most men are reluctant to relinquish their status as family breadwinner. Although only 15 percent of the families in the United States are supported solely by a male breadwinner, many men continue to construct their ideal of masculinity based on this role. It is acceptable for wives to enter the paid work force if their role is simply to earn money; they should not, however, challenge the ideal roles of male breadwinner and female homemaker.

In sum, both conflict and feminist theorists think that family problems derive from inequality—not just within the family, but in the political, social, and economic arenas of the larger society as well (Aulette, 1994). In fact, pervasive societal inequality leads to one of the most tragic family problems: wife batter-

ing. According to these theorists, wife battering and other forms of domestic violence may even be conscious strategies that men use to control women and perpetuate gender inequality (Kurz, 1989). Almost 30 percent of all female murder victims are killed by current or former husbands or boyfriends. In a study of women killed in New York City from 1990 through 1994, researchers found that one-third of the women killed by their husbands were married but not living with their spouses at the time of their deaths, a finding that suggests that these women were trying to leave the relationships at the time (Belluck, 1997). In contrast, only 3 percent of all male murder victims are killed by current or former wives or girlfriends. According to conflict and feminist theorists, then, family-related problems, including domestic violence and wife battering, can be solved only if all social institutions work to eliminate the subordination of women in society.

 Interactionist Perspectives

Some interactionists view the family communication process as integral to understanding the diverse roles that family members play; therefore these analysts examine how husbands, wives, and children act out their roles and react to the parts played by others. Although societies differ widely on the rules and norms that shape family and kin relationships, people are socialized to accept their society's form of the family as the acceptable norm. According to sociologists Peter Berger and Hansfried Kellner (1964), marital partners develop a shared reality through their interactions with each other. Although newlyweds bring separate identities to a marriage, over time they construct a shared reality as a couple. In the process, the partners redefine their past identities to be consistent with their new realities. Interactionists say that the process of developing a shared reality is continuous and occurs not only in the family but in any group in which the couple participates together. In cases of separation and divorce, the process is reversed: Couples may start with a shared reality but once again become individuals with separate realities in the process of uncoupling their relationship.

How do interactionists explain problems in a family? Some look at the subjective meanings and interpretations people give to their everyday lives. According to sociologist Jessie Bernard (1982), women and men experience marriage differently.

While the husband may see *his marriage* very positively, the wife may feel less positive about *her marriage*. The reverse may also be true. Evidence for the different realities of marriage comes from research that shows that husbands and wives often give very different accounts of the same event (Safilios-Rothschild, 1969).

Still other interactionists view family problems in terms of partners' unrealistic expectations about love and marriage, which can lead to marital dissatisfaction and sometimes divorce. These analysts note that our culture emphasizes *romantic love*—a deep and vital emotion based on significant need satisfaction, caring for and acceptance of another person, and the development of an intimate relationship (Lamanna and Riedmann, 1994). Indeed, most couples in the United States get married because they are in love, but being a "nation of lovers" doesn't mean that men and women have the same ideas about what constitutes romantic love. According to sociologist Francesca Cancian (1990), women tend to express their feelings verbally, whereas men tend to express their love through nonverbal actions such as fixing dinner or doing household repairs. Women may not always interpret these actions as signs of love. One man complained (Rubin, 1976:146), "What does she want? Proof? She's got it, hasn't she? Would I be knocking myself out to get things for her—like to keep up this house—if I didn't love her? Why does a man do things like that if not because he loves his wife and kids? I swear, I can't figure what she wants." His wife replied, "It's not enough that he supports us and takes care of us. I appreciate that, but I want him to share things with me. I need for him to tell me his feelings."

Whatever their different viewpoints on marriage and family, most social theorists agree on one fact: Three decades ago, the nuclear family was the most common family form, and today it is only one of many patterns.

DIVERSITY IN INTIMATE RELATIONSHIPS AND FAMILIES

Greater diversity in intimate relationships and families in the United States has come about because of dramatic increases in (1) singlehood, (2) postponing

marriage, (3) living together without marriage (cohabitation and domestic partnerships), (4) dual-earner marriages, and (5) one-parent families.

 ## Singlehood

Although some will eventually marry, there are 42 million adults in the United States who have never been married. The proportion of the U.S. population that has never been married has continued to grow since the 1960s. Some people choose singlehood over marriage because it means greater freedom from commitments to another person. Others choose it because of more career opportunities (especially for women), the availability of sexual partners without marriage, the belief that the single lifestyle is full of excitement, and because of the desire for self-sufficiency and freedom to change and experiment (Stein, 1976, 1981). Though some analysts think that individuals who prefer to remain single hold more individualistic values and are less family-oriented than are people who choose to marry, sociologist Peter Stein (1981) has found otherwise: Many singles still feel a strong need for intimacy, sharing, and continuity and, as a result, develop relationships with other singles, valuing friends and personal growth more highly than marriage and children (Cargan and Melko, 1982; Alwin, Converse, and Martin, 1985).

Some people are single not by choice but by necessity. Because of structural changes in the economy, many young working-class people cannot afford to marry and set up their own households. Indeed, some college graduates have found that they cannot earn enough money to set up households separate from those of their parents.

The proportion of never-married singles varies significantly by racial and ethnic group. Among males age eighteen and over, about 42 percent of African Americans have never been married, compared to about 36 percent of Latinos and 20 percent of whites. Among women age eighteen and over, about 37 percent of African Americans have never married, compared to almost 25 percent of Latinas and 17 percent of whites (U.S. Bureau of the Census, 1998). Lower marriage rates among African American women seem to be associated with these factors:

1. Young African American men have higher rates of mortality than young African American women.

2. More African American women are college-educated and tend to make more money than African American men.

3. Some African American men have less to offer in a marriage because they have experienced high levels of discrimination and limited educational opportunities.

4. Rates of homosexuality are higher among African American men than women.

5. More African American men than women marry members of other racial-ethnic groups (Staples, 1994).

There is a scarcity of research on singlehood among Latinos/as, Native Americans, and Asian and Pacific Americans. Apparently the diverse experiences among Latinas/os, who may be Mexican Americans, Cuban Americans, or Puerto Ricans (among others), and Asian and Pacific Americans, who may trace their roots to many parts of Asia and the Pacific Islands, is one of the primary reasons for the lack of research.

 Postponing Marriage

Young people today are less eager to get married than they were two decades ago; many are remaining single into their late twenties. The median age at which men first get married is 26.7 years, and the median age for women is 24.5 years. (*Median* is a statistical midpoint; therefore half of all men who marry do so before age 26.7 and half marry after.) Although the age at which people marry for the first time has been rising steadily since the 1950s, it has accelerated since the 1970s. Between 1970 and today, the proportion of women aged 25 to 29 who have never married has tripled.

Why are more people postponing first marriages? Although some reasons are the same as those for staying single, sociologist Robin Wolf (1996) suggests four key factors: (1) economic uncertainty due to the changing job structure in the United States; (2) women's increasing participation in the labor force; (3) the sexual revolution of the 1970s that made sexual relationships outside marriage more socially acceptable; (4) the rising divorce rate—young people watching their parents divorce may be less anxious to jump into marriage themselves. Other analysts suggest that a significant increase in cohabitation and domestic partnerships also contributes to

the percentage of people who are counted as single or postponing marriage.

Cohabitation and Domestic Partnerships

The popularity of cohabitation has increased in the past two decades. *Cohabitation* **is two unmarried adults living together in a sexual relationship without being legally married.** It is not known how many people actually cohabit because the U.S. Bureau of the Census refers to couples who live together simply as "unmarried couple households" and does not ask about emotional or sexual involvement. According to Census Bureau data, however, the heterosexual couples who are most likely to cohabit are under age forty-five and have been married before or are older individuals who do not want to lose financial benefits (such as retirement benefits) that are contingent on not remarrying. Among younger people, employed couples are more likely to cohabit than college students are.

For some couples, cohabitation is a form of trial marriage and constitutes an intermediate stage between dating and marriage. According to anthropologist Margaret Mead (1966), dating patterns in the United States do not adequately prepare people for marriage and parenting responsibilities. Mead proposed a two-stage marriage process, each with its own ceremony and responsibilities. In the first stage, the individual marriage, two people would make a serious commitment to each other but agree not to have children during this stage. In the second stage, the parental marriage, the couple would decide to have children and to share responsibility for their upbringing. Unlike cohabitation, Mead's two stages of marriage would both be legally binding.

For other couples, cohabitation is not necessarily a first step toward marriage. In one study, researchers found that slightly more than 50 percent of cohabitation relationships eventually culminated in marriage, whereas 37 percent broke up and 10 percent were still ongoing at the time of the study (London, 1991).

Does cohabitation contribute to marital success? The evidence is mixed. Some studies show that cohabitation has little or no effect on marital adjustment, emotional closeness, satisfaction, and intimacy (Watson and DeMeo, 1987). Other studies indicate that couples who cohabit first are more likely to divorce than those who do not (Bennett, Blanc, and Bloom, 1988). Apparently, partners in this study who had cohabited were less satisfied with their marriage and less committed to the institution of marriage than were those who had not lived together before marrying. The researchers theorized that cohabitation may contribute to people's individualistic attitudes and values while making them more aware that alternatives to marriage exist (Axinn and Thornton, 1992; Thomson and Colella, 1992).

Many gay and lesbian couples consider themselves married and living in a lifelong commitment. Because the law does not allow them to marry legally, they establish *domestic partnerships* (see Chapter 6). To make their commitment public, some couples exchange rings and vows under the auspices of churches such as the Metropolitan Community Church (the national gay church) and even some mainstream churches. One reason people prefer legal marriage to domestic partnerships is that employee health insurance coverage and other benefits are offered to legal spouses, although today some employers offer similar benefits to domestic partners.

In the age of dual-earner marriages, it has become increasingly important for fathers to assume child care and household duties. How does this photo show the competing demands faced by many employed parents?

 Dual-Earner Marriages

More than 50 percent of all marriages in the United States are *dual-earner marriages*—**marriages in which both spouses are in the labor force.** Over half of all employed women hold full-time, year-round jobs, and in a change from the past, there are more married women with young children in the paid labor force today than there were in the past. In 1997, 61.3 percent of all women with a child under age three were in the paid work force, and 73.7 percent of African American women with a child under age three were in the paid work force (U.S. Bureau of the Census, 1998).

Many married women who are employed outside the household face hours of domestic work and child care when they go home. Sociologist Arlie Hochschild (1989) refers to a women's dual workdays as the *second shift*—**the domestic work that many employed women perform at home after completing their work day on the job.** According to Hochschild, the unpaid housework that women do on the *second shift* (see Chapter 4) amounts to an extra month of work each year. In households with small children or many children, the amount of housework increases (Hartmann, 1981). Across race and class, numerous studies confirm that domestic work remains primarily women's work (Gerstel and Gross, 1995).

In recent years, more husbands share some of the household and child-care responsibilities, especially when the wife's earnings are essential to family finances (Perry-Jenkins and Crouter, 1990). But even when husbands assume some of the household responsibilities, they typically spend much less time in these activities than do their wives (see Coverman, 1989). Women and men perform different household tasks, and the deadlines for their work vary widely. Recurring tasks that have specific times for completion (such as bathing a child or cooking a meal) tend to be the women's responsibility, whereas men are more likely to do the periodic tasks that have no highly structured schedule (such as mowing the lawn or changing the oil in the car) (Hochschild, 1989).

Couples with more egalitarian ideas about women's and men's roles tend to share more equally in food preparation, housework, and child care (Wright, Shire, Hwang, Dolan, and Baxter, 1992). An *egalitarian family* is one in which the partners share power and authority equally. As women have gained new educational and employment opportunities, a trend toward more egalitarian relationships has become evident in the United States. Some degree of economic independence makes it possible for women to delay marriage or to terminate a problematic marriage (O'Connell, 1994). For some men, the shift to a more egalitarian household occurs gradually, as the following quotation indicates:

> It was me taking the initiative, and also Connie pushing, saying, "Gee, there's so much that has to be done." At first I said, "But I'm supposed to be the breadwinner," not realizing she's also the breadwinner. I was being a little blind to what was going on, but I got tired of waiting for my wife to come home to start cooking, so one day I surprised the hell out [of] her and myself and the kids, and I had supper waiting on the table for her. (Gerson, 1993:170)

Problems associated with providing economic support for the family and rearing children are even more pressing in many one-parent households.

Comparing Two-Parent and One-Parent Households

When the mother and father in a two-parent household truly share parenting, children have the benefit of two primary caregivers. Some researchers have found that when fathers take an active part in raising the children, the effect is beneficial for all family members. Fathers find increased contact with their children provides more opportunities for personal and emotional gratification (Coltrane, 1989).

However, living in a two-parent family does not guarantee children a happy childhood. Children whose parents argue constantly, are alcoholics, or abuse them have a worse family experience than do children in a single-parent family where there is a supportive environment. Women who are employed full-time and are single parents probably have the greatest burden of all. These women must fulfill their paid employment duties and meet the needs of

their children and the household, often with little help from ex-husbands or relatives.

How prevalent are one-parent households? The past two decades have seen a significant increase in one-parent households due to divorce, death of a parent, and births outside of marriage. Many more children under the age of eighteen are living with just one parent today than were a generation ago. In 1970, about 12 percent of all children lived with one parent; by 1995, 27 percent did (Seelye, 1997). About 42 percent of all white children and 86 percent of all African American children spend part of their childhood in a household headed by a single mother who is divorced, separated, never-married, or widowed (Garfinkel and McLanahan, 1986).

Who heads most one-parent households? Today, 88 percent of all one-parent families are headed by single mothers. Men are heads of about 17 percent of white one-parent families, 12 percent of Latino/a one-parent families, and 5 percent of African American one-parent families. Interestingly, a study of one-parent households headed by fathers found that most of the men had very positive relationships with their children (Risman, 1987).

What effect does a one-parent household have on children? According to one study based on six nationally representative data sets of more than 25,000 children from various racial and social class backgrounds, children growing up with only one biological parent are at risk of serious problems, including poor academic achievement, dropping out of school, drug and alcohol abuse, teen pregnancy, early marriage, and divorce (McLanahan and Sandefur, 1994). Obviously, living in a one-parent family does not necessarily cause these problems. Factors such as poverty, discrimination, unsafe neighborhoods, and high crime rates must also be considered. In fact, other researchers have found some benefits to growing up in a one-parent family (Lauer and Lauer, 1991). For example, children in one-parent families are often less pressured to conform to rigid gender roles. Rather than having chores assigned by gender, as is common in two-parent families, single-parent children typically take on a wider variety of tasks and activities. Many single-parent children also show high levels of maturity and self-sufficiency earlier because they have to help out at a younger age than do children in other families (Lauer and Lauer, 1991).

What about the fathers of children in one-parent households headed by women? Although some fathers remain involved in their children's lives, others become "Disneyland daddies"—occasionally taking their children out for recreational activities or buying them presents on birthdays and holidays. Personal choice, workplace demands on time and energy, location of the ex-wife's residence, and limitations placed on visitation by custody arrangements are all factors that affect how often absentee fathers visit their children. As more parents are receiving joint custody of their children, it appears that joint custody can minimize the disruption of divorce in a child's life if the ex-spouses cooperate with each other and live in relatively close geographical proximity. Ex-spouses who constantly argue or live far away from each other can create serious problems for "commuter" children, as author David Sheff (1995:64) describes:

My son began commuting between his two homes at age 4. . . . The commuter flights between San Francisco and Los Angeles were the only times a parent wasn't lording over him, so he was able to order Coca-Cola, verboten at home. . . . But such benefits were insignificant when contrasted with his preflight nightmares about plane crashes. . . . Like so many divorcing couples, we divided the china and art and our young son. . . . First he was ferried back and forth between our homes across town, and then, when his mother moved to Los Angeles, across the state. For the eight years since, he has been one of the thousands of American children with two homes, two beds, two sets of clothes and toys, and two toothbrushes.

The transition from a two-parent family to a one-parent family is only one of many child-related family issues that many people today must deal with, as we discuss in the next section.

CHILD-RELATED FAMILY ISSUES

One of the major issues facing many individuals and families today is reproductive freedom, a term that implies both the desire of individuals *to have* and the desire *not to have* a child. As sociologists Leslie King and Madonna Harrington Meyer (1997:8) explain:

The average woman is fertile, and therefore must attempt to control her reproductivity, for one-half of her life. For most women, it is the preoccupation with preventing births that consumes their health care dollars and energies; for a small minority, it is the preoccupation with achieving a birth that dominates. The ability to control fertility is, to a great extent, linked to access to various forms of reproductive health services, including contraceptives and infertility treatments. Yet, in the United States, insurance coverage of contraceptive and infertility treatments is fragmented.

Reproductive Freedom, Contraception, and Abortion

Reproductive freedom has been a controversial issue throughout much of U.S. history. In the nineteenth century, the government instituted formal, legal policies to ensure that some people would not produce children. By incarcerating "wayward girls" and limiting their right to marry and by passing laws that permitted the sterilization of the poor, the criminal, or the "feebleminded," political leaders attempted to prevent people who were thought to be "unfit" from reproducing (Luker, 1996). Today, say some researchers, the government discourages births among the poor by mandating the coverage of contraceptives for women on Medicaid (King and Harrington Meyer, 1997).

Contraceptive devices such as condoms and diaphragms were widely available and relatively technologically sophisticated in the first half of the nineteenth century. By the 1850s, however, the government had begun to establish policies limiting their availability in order to prevent a drop in the birth rate among white Americans (Luker, 1996). Abortion became illegal in most states by 1900. Physicians—among others—had begun to crusade against it in the 1800s because most procedures were done by people (such as barbers) who had no medical training. Some physicians apparently believed that if these abortionists could be stopped, physicians would become the

For a number of decades, one of the most intense public confrontations in the United States has been between abortion rights advocates and members of the anti-abortion movement. These demonstrators are a familiar sight outside the Supreme Court building in Washington, D.C., where the justices frequently make decisions on abortion-related issues.

arbiters of whether or not women should have abortions. The ban on abortion and the limited availability of contraceptives did not prevent wealthy women from practicing birth control or procuring an abortion (Luker, 1996).

It was not until the introduction of the birth control pill in 1960 that women gained almost complete control of their fertility. The "Pill" quickly became the most popular contraceptive among married women in the United States. During this time and into the early 1970s, public opinion about women's reproductive freedom began to change somewhat. In 1971, the U.S. Supreme Court upheld women's right to privacy in reproductive matters in *Griswold* v. *Connecticut*. The Court ruled that laws prohibiting the use of contraception by married couples violated the constitutional right to privacy. In subsequent cases, the Court included unmarried adults and minors in this protection.

Many U.S. women spend about 90 percent of their fertile years trying to avoid pregnancy (Gold and Richards, 1994). An estimated 60 percent of all women between the ages of fifteen and forty-four are using contraceptives at any specific time. Unplanned pregnancies, then, are usually the result of not using contraceptives or using contraceptives that do not work or are not used as intended. Of the 6.4 million pregnancies in the United States each year, about 3.6 million (56 percent) are unintended, and about 2.8 million (44 percent) are intended (Gold and Richards, 1994). The most effective forms of birth control, however, are the most expensive: Oral contraceptives cost about $300 a year, and five-year contraceptive implants average $500. In 1993, people in this country spent $1.5 billion for contraceptives (King and Harrington Meyer, 1997).

Over the past three decades, the roles that government, religious organizations, physicians, and the legal establishment should play in reproductive decisions continue to be highly controversial in this country. Perhaps the most significant legal action involving reproductive rights was the Supreme Court decision in *Roe* v. *Wade* (1973) that women have a constitutionally protected right to choose abortion and the state cannot unduly interfere with or prohibit that right. The court distinguished between trimesters of pregnancy in its ruling. During the first three months, decisions about the pregnancy are strictly private—made by women in consultation with their physicians; in the second trimester, the state may impose some restrictions but only to safeguard women's health; in the third trimester, the state may prohibit abortion—because of the fetus's viability (ability to survive outside a woman's womb)—except when necessary to preserve the woman's life or health.

Although the Court has not overturned *Roe* v. *Wade*, subsequent decisions have eroded some of women's reproductive rights and made abortions more difficult to obtain, particularly for poor women and unmarried pregnant teenagers. For example, in

1993 the Supreme Court ruled that requiring a minor to get written permission from both parents for an abortion did not constitute an "undue burden" for a fourteen- or fifteen-year-old girl. And as of this writing, members of Congress have failed to reach a consensus on whether or not to ban partial birth (late term) abortions. Indeed, there is a lack of consensus over how many partial birth abortions are actually performed and under what circumstances.

Opposition to abortion has resulted in violence against physicians and the personnel of clinics where abortions are performed, which has caused a number of facilities to close. In response, in 1993, Congress passed the Freedom of Access to Clinic Entrances Act, making it a federal offense to attack an abortion clinic or obstruct clients from going to one. In 1994, the Supreme Court ruled that organizers of violent protests against abortion clinics may be prosecuted under federal racketeering laws. Nevertheless, antiabortion activists continue to try to make it difficult for women to have abortions. Some social analysts fear that women will once again seek abortions in "back rooms," as they did in the era of illegal abortions, if abortion is restricted (see Miller, 1993; Messer and May, 1994). The Food and Drug Administration's recent approval of the drug RU-486,

which is used for abortions in France, may reduce the number of direct confrontations between vocal—and sometimes violent—factions on all sides of the abortion debate (Rosser, 1994).

At the microlevel, abortion is a solution for some pregnant women and their families but a problem for others, particularly when they face religious or family opposition. At the macrolevel, abortion is both a problem and a solution when activists try to influence the making and enforcement of laws pertaining to women's reproductive rights and the control of new reproductive technologies.

◤ Infertility and New Reproductive Technologies

Infertility is defined as an inability to conceive after a year of unprotected sexual relations. Today, infertility affects nearly 5 million U.S. couples, or one in twelve couples in which the wife is between the ages of fifteen and forty-four. In 40 percent of the cases, the woman is infertile, and in another 40 percent it is the man; 20 percent of the time, the cause is impossible to determine (Gabriel, 1996).

Sexually transmitted diseases are a leading cause of infertility: Each year, 100,000 to 150,000 women

◤ **TABLE 11.1   FORMS OF ASSISTED REPRODUCTIVE TECHNOLOGY**

Name	Description
In vitro fertilization (IVF)	Eggs that were produced as a result of administering fertility drugs are removed from the woman's body and fertilized by sperm in a laboratory dish. The embryos that result from this process are transferred to the woman's uterus.
Micromanipulation	Viewing the process through a microscope, a specialist manipulates egg and sperm in a laboratory dish to improve the chances of a pregnancy.
Cryopreserved embryo transfer (CPE)	Embryos that were frozen after a previous assisted reproductive technology procedure are thawed and then transferred to the uterus.
Egg donation	Eggs are removed from a donor's uterus, fertilized in a laboratory dish, and transferred to an infertile woman's uterus.
Surrogacy	An embryo is implanted in the uterus of a woman who is paid to carry the fetus until birth. The egg may come from either the legal or the surrogate mother, and the sperm may come either from the legal father or a donor.

Source: Gabriel, 1996.

become infertile as a result of a sexually transmitted disease that develops into pelvic inflammatory disease (Gold and Richards, 1994). There are also some women—both married and unmarried—who would like to have a child but cannot because of disabilities. Still other women in lesbian relationships would like to be parents. Some analysts point out that a growing number of prospective parents delay childbearing into their thirties and forties when it may be more difficult for them to conceive.

About 50 percent of infertile couples who seek treatment can be helped by conventional, low-tech treatments such as fertility drugs, artificial insemination, and surgery to unblock fallopian tubes. The other 50 percent require advanced technology, sometimes called assisted reproductive technology (ART). Many middle- and upper-income couples, for example, receive in vitro fertilization (IVF), which costs between $8,000 and $11,000 per attempt (see Table 11.1). Despite the popularity of such treatments and the growth of fertility clinics (from 30 slightly over a decade ago to more than 300 today), only one in five couples who receive ART actually become parents (Gabriel, 1996). For couples like Michael and Stephanie Plaut, who have spent three years and thousands of dollars trying to have a baby through IVF and other procedures, every unsuccessful attempt is traumatic. Journalist Felicia Lee (1996:A1) has documented the trauma the couple undergoes: "Michael Plaut answered the telephone . . . [and the] call confirmed his worst fear: the pregnancy test was negative. The Plauts sobbed, held each other and then had a glass of Scotch. 'It's like we're in a period of mourning,' Mrs. Plaut said. 'You just get to the point where you want this to be over.'" Couples like the Plauts who have their hopes raised by the new reproductive technologies only to find that they do not work for them often form support groups. Many couples finally decide to remain childless, but some adopt one or more children.

◢ Adoption

Adoption is a legal process through which the rights and duties of parenting are transferred from a child's biological and/or legal parents to new legal parents. The adopted child has all the rights of a biological child. In most adoptions, a new birth certificate is issued, and the child has no further contact with the biological parents, although some states have right-

Many parents who adopt one or more children also add to the racial and ethnic diversity of their household. What can children and adolescents learn from growing up with others whose background is not identical to their own?

to-know laws under which adoptive parents must grant the biological parents visitation rights.

Matching children who are available for adoption with prospective adoptive parents can be difficult. The children often have specific needs, and prospective parents often specify the kind of children they want to adopt. Because many prospective parents do not want to adopt children who are nonwhite (most prospective parents are white), older, or have disabilities or diseases, children available for adoption move from foster home to foster home (Zelizer, 1985).

Prospective parents frequently want infants, but fewer infants are available for adoption than in the past because better means of contraception exist,

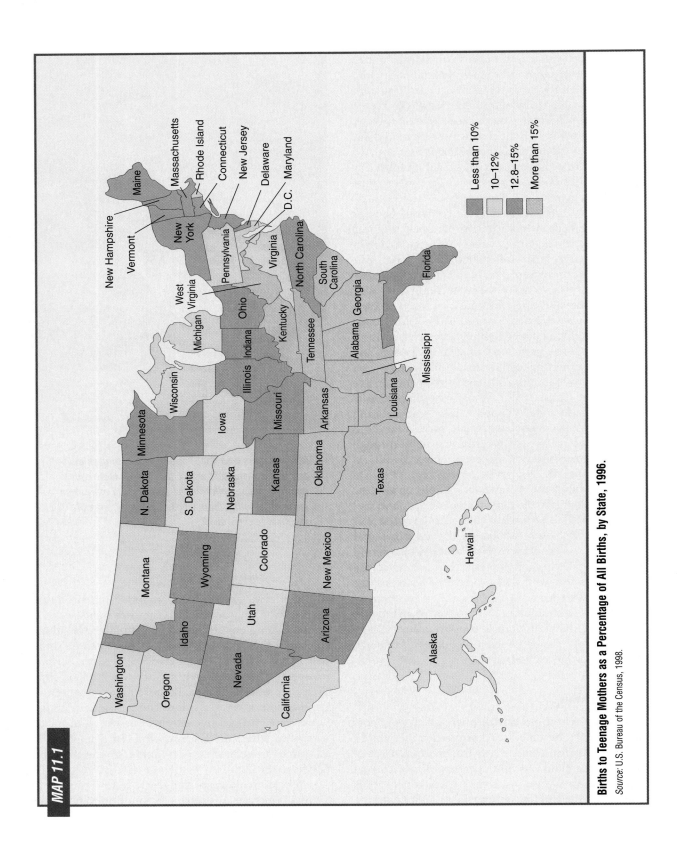

MAP 11.1

Births to Teenage Mothers as a Percentage of All Births, by State, 1996.

Source: U.S. Bureau of the Census, 1998.

Legend:
- Less than 10%
- 10–12%
- 12.8–15%
- More than 15%

abortion is more readily available, and more unmarried teenage parents are deciding to keep their babies. Some teenagers, however, believe that adoption is the best way to solve the problem of early childbearing. Christina, one of many teenagers facing the realities of an early pregnancy and lack of resources to meet the child's needs, explained her decision this way:

> I know I can't keep my baby. I can't give it all the things a baby needs and I sure can't dump it on my parents because they can't afford to take care of their own family. I've decided to give it up for adoption. I think it's better for the baby to give it up to parents who can't have a baby themselves. I think that I'm really doing a favor to my baby, although I'm always going to wonder what it looks like and what it's doing. (Luker, 1996:163)

▲ Teen Pregnancies and Unmarried Motherhood

The birth rate among teenagers is higher in the United States than in any other high-income nation. Although the pregnancy rate among *all* female teenagers has actually decreased over the past three decades, the number of births among *unmarried* teenaged females has jumped from about 22 to 45 per 1,000 in the last three decades (U.S. Bureau of the Census, 1998). About 500,000 children are born each year to girls aged thirteen to nineteen, three-fourths of whom are unmarried (Holmes, 1996a).

Although a popular myth claims that most births to unmarried teenagers occur in the central cities of large urban areas, the greatest number of teens giving birth occurs in the South and in less urbanized areas (see Map 11.1). Similarly, although it is widely believed that teens from minority racial and ethnic groups are the most likely to be unwed mothers, the majority of births occur among white teenagers. At the same time, given their relative numbers in the population, African American males and females are five times more likely than white teenagers to become unwed parents. One of the key factors behind this statistic is the poverty and lack of employment opportunity for African American males, as we discussed in Chapter 3.

According to social analysts, the outcome of teen pregnancies is problematic because teenage mothers are typically unskilled at parenting, are likely to drop out of school, and have no social support other than relatives (Chase-Lansdale et al., 1992). Family support is extremely important to unmarried pregnant teens because emotional and financial support from the fathers of their children is often lacking (Nath et al., 1991). Without this support, teen mothers rely on their own mothers and grandmothers to help with childrearing. As a result, many unmarried teenage mothers do not make the same transition from the family of orientation to the family of procreation that most people make when they become parents. The *family of orientation* **is the family into which a person is born and in which early socialization takes place.** When teenage mothers and their children live with their grandmothers or other relatives, they do not establish the separate family unit known as a *family of procreation*—**the family that a person forms by having or adopting children,** which married couples with young children create.

The picture for the children of teenage mothers without parental support is especially bleak because few of these mothers have adequate parenting skills or knowledge of child development. Children of unwed teenage mothers tend to have severely limited educational and employment opportunities and a high likelihood of living in poverty (Benokraitis, 1993). In addition, about 43 percent of the teenagers who first give birth between the ages of fifteen and nineteen have a second child within three years (Benokraitis, 1993). The future of these children is in even greater jeopardy today because of the 1996 welfare reform law that reduces assistance to single mothers with young children, especially unmarried mothers under age eighteen (see Chapter 2).

Teenagers are not the only ones having children without getting married these days. Since 1990 the birth rate for unmarried women between the ages of twenty and twenty-four has increased to 70.3 births per 1,000, followed by that for women ages fifteen to nineteen (44.3 per 1,000). According to demographer Charles Westoff, these rates reflect "the declining significance of marriage as a social obligation or a social necessity for reproduction. Increasing proportions of white women who have not been married are deciding that having a child is more important than any kind of disapproval they might face" (quoted in Connell, 1995). With less of a social stigma attached to unmarried pregnancy, fewer women seem to be seeking abortion and are deciding instead to raise the child themselves whether the pregnancy was planned or not.

DIVORCE AND REMARRIAGE

Divorce is the legal process of dissolving a marriage that allows former spouses to remarry if they so choose. Have you heard such statements as "One out of every two marriages ends in divorce"? Statistics might initially appear to bear out this statement, but consider the following: Most sociologists use a statistic called the *refined divorce rate* to calculate the incidence of divorce. The number of divorces each year is divided by the total number of marriages in that year. According to the refined divorce rate, approximately 2.4 million marriages take place in the United States each year, and about 1.2 million divorces are granted. However, it is misleading to compare the number of marriages with the number of divorces from year to year because couples who divorce in any given year are very unlikely to have come from the group that married that year. Also, some people go through several marriages and divorces, which skews the divorce rate because the likelihood of divorce goes up with each subsequent marriage.

Why do divorces occur? A number of factors contribute to a couple's statistical likelihood of becoming divorced, including the following:

▲ Getting married during the teenage years (Martin and Bumpass, 1989)
▲ Getting married after only a short acquaintanceship (Goode, 1976)
▲ Having relatives and friends disapprove of the marriage (Goode, 1976)
▲ Having limited economic resources and earning low wages (Spanier and Glick, 1981)
▲ Both partners having a high school education or less (Houseknecht et al., 1984)
▲ Having parents who were divorced or who had unhappy marriages (Goode, 1976)
▲ Having children present at the beginning of the marriage (Rankin and Maneker, 1985; Morgan et al., 1988; Martin and Bumpass, 1989)

Because these factors are interrelated with such other factors as class, race, and age, determining the likelihood of divorce is very complicated. For example, age is intertwined with economic resources and people from low-income families typically marry earlier than do people from more affluent families, but if divorce occurs, which factor—age or economic resources—is more closely associated with it?

The relationship between race and divorce is also complex. Although African Americans are more likely than whites to get divorced, factors such as income level and the extent of racial discrimination in society must be taken into account. Latinos/as share some of the problems faced by African Americans, but their divorce rate is only slightly higher than the divorce rate among whites of European ancestry. Religion may affect the divorce rate of some Latinos/as who are Roman Catholic, although the divorce rate among Catholics is now approximately equal to the rate for Protestants (Lamanna and Riedmann, 1994).

Divorce laws in many states once required the partner seeking the divorce to prove misconduct on the part of the other spouse. Under today's *no-fault divorce laws*, however, proof of blameworthiness is no longer necessary, and most divorces are granted on the grounds of *irreconcilable differences*, which means that a breakdown has occurred in the marital relationship and neither partner is to be specifically blamed.

With or without blame, divorce usually has a dramatic economic and emotional impact on family members. An estimated 60 percent of divorcing couples have one or more children. By age sixteen, about one out of every three white children and two out of every three African American children experience divorce in their families (Kurz, 1995). Indeed, some children experience more than one divorce during their childhood because one or both of their parents may remarry and subsequently divorce again.

Divorce not only changes relationships for the couple and children involved but also for other relatives. Some grandparents feel that they are the big losers. Grandparents who wish to see their grandchildren have to keep in touch with the parent who has custody, but if the grandparents are in-laws, they are less likely to be welcomed and may be seen as taking the "other side" simply because they are the parents of the ex-spouse. Recently, some grandparents have sued for custody of minor grandchildren. For the most part, these suits have not been successful except when there has been some question about the emotional stability of the biological parents or the suitability of a foster care arrangement.

Most people who divorce remarry (Ihinger-Tallman and Pasley, 1987). In fact, in more than 40 percent of all marriages, either the bride, the groom, or both have previously been married. Among individuals who divorce before age thirty-five, about half remarry within three years of their first divorce (Bumpass, Sweet, and Martin, 1990). Most divorced people marry others who have been divorced (London and Wilson, 1988), though remarriage rates vary by gender and age. At all ages, a greater proportion of men than women remarry, often relatively soon after the divorce. Among women, the older a woman is at the time of divorce, the lower her likelihood of remarrying (Wallerstein and Blakeslee, 1989). Women who have not graduated from high school and have young children tend to remarry relatively quickly. Women with a college degree and without children are less likely to remarry (Glick and Lin, 1986).

Divorce and remarriage often creates complex family relationships. **Blended families consist of a husband and wife, children from previous marriages, and children (if any) from the new marriage.** At least initially, stress in blended families may be fairly high because of rivalry among the children and hostilities directed toward stepparents or babies born into the family. In some cases, when parents divorce and marry other partners, the children become part of a *binuclear family,* living with one biological parent and a stepparent part of the time and with the other biological parent and another stepparent the rest of the time.

As sociologist Andrew Cherlin (1992) points out, the norms governing divorce and remarriage are ambiguous, so people must make decisions about family life (such as who should be invited to a birthday celebration or a wedding) on the basis of their own feelings about the people involved. But in spite of the problems, many blended families succeed.

DOMESTIC VIOLENCE

The term *domestic violence* obscures the fact that most victims of domestic violence are women and children. Women are more likely to be assaulted, injured, or raped by their male partners than by any other type of assailant. Children are extremely vulnerable to abuse and violence because of their age

and economic and social dependence on their parents or other adult caregivers.

 ## Child Abuse

According to the 1974 Federal Child Abuse Prevention and Treatment Act, child abuse and neglect is the physical or mental injury, sexual abuse, or negligent treatment of a child under the age of eighteen by a person who is responsible for the child's welfare. While most of us, when we hear the words *child abuse,* think in terms of physical injury or sexual abuse, the most frequent form of child maltreatment is *child neglect*—not meeting a child's basic needs for emotional warmth and security, adequate shelter, food, health care, education, clothing, and protection. We will focus primarily on physical injury and sexual abuse because these actions are classified as violent personal crimes.

In the past, children in the United States were considered the property of their parents and could be punished or ignored as the parents wished. With passage of the Social Security Act in the 1930s, however, children became legally protected even from their own parents. Still, many physical injuries to children are intentionally inflicted by parents and other caregivers. Parental violence can, in fact, lead to the *battered child syndrome,* a psychological disorder in which a child experiences low self-esteem and sometimes clinical depression associated with former or current abuse perpetrated by a biological or custodial parent (Kempe et al., 1962).

The physical abuse of children in the United States is a serious social problem that remains largely hidden unless an incident results in the death or serious injury of a child. Some researchers have found that children are most likely to be assaulted in their own homes if their parents were abused, neglected, or deprived as children and if their parents are socially isolated as adults. Parents who lack a support network and suddenly face a crisis tend to make their children the targets of their frustration and sometimes their aggression (Kempe and Kempe, 1978). Other researchers have found that abusive parents characteristically feel unloved and unworthy and totally unprepared to cope with their circumstances (Tower, 1996).

The signs of physical abuse include bruises, particularly on the back of the legs, upper arms and chest, neck, head, or genitals. Fractures in infants under twelve months of age are a strong indication of abuse, as are head injuries and burns, especially cigarette burns. Most physicians and emergency room personnel are specially trained to identify signs of child abuse so that parents or guardians can be reported to the appropriate authorities. In fact, reporting of suspected child abuse has improved significantly in recent years because of increased training, awareness, and legislation, including the Federal Child Abuse Prevention and Treatment Act of 1974, which established that reports of suspected abuse would be investigated promptly and fully. In the past, even when physicians suspected abuse, they often chose to treat the child but not to report the incident, believing that abuse would be too difficult to prove (Tower, 1996).

One of the most disturbing forms of physical abuse of children is sexual abuse. Unfortunately, there is a lack of consensus on how to define sexual abuse. In one study, child sexual abuse was defined in terms of three actions: intrusion, molestation with genital contact or other forms of fondling, and inadequate supervision of a child's sexual activity (see Tower, 1996). Another study included all behaviors ranging from "sexual overtures" to sexual intercourse occurring between a child age thirteen or under and someone five or more years older or between adolescents aged thirteen to sixteen and someone ten or more years older (Finkelhor, 1984).

Although it is difficult to estimate the incidence and prevalence of sexual abuse, it appears that between 10 and 15 percent of girls and boys experience some form of sexual contact as children (Finkelhor, 1984). At all ages, females are more likely than males to be victims of sexual abuse as well as *incest*, or sexual relations between individuals so closely related that they are forbidden to marry by law. Males are more likely to experience assault in public places, by strangers or nonrelatives; girls are more likely to experience long-term victimization by relatives or family acquaintances in their own home. Both male and female victims are more likely to be abused by male offenders, and offenders are known to their victims in the vast majority of cases (Knudsen, 1992).

▲ Spouse Abuse

From the days of early Rome to current times, spouse abuse has been acknowledged to exist, but until recently, it was largely ignored or tolerated. Today, it is estimated that as many as 5 million spouses, primarily wives, are abused each year. Women are much more likely than men to be victims of domestic violence of all types. The U.S. Attorney General's office estimates that at least 94 percent of all cases of spouse abuse involve a man beating a woman. In fact, physical abuse by husbands or boyfriends is the single most common source of injury among women (Murphy-Milano, 1996). Injuries sustained by victims of spouse abuse are as serious as, or more serious than, the injuries incurred in 90 percent of all rapes, robberies, and other aggravated assaults. Spouse abuse ranges in intensity from slapping, kicking, and hitting with a closed fist to inflicting critical injuries or death (Straus et al., 1980). Spouse abuse occurs across lines of race, class, region, religion, and other factors. Charlotte Fedders, for example, was abused by her husband, John Fedders, a powerful young lawyer in the Reagan administration:

> I was in the bathroom sitting on a closed toilet, bathing two of the boys in the tub. John came home, went upstairs, and saw my note [that she had written a check for $80 to a marriage counselor]. He came into the bathroom and started beating me with his fists and pulling on my hair. I turned away to protect myself, and he beat me on my back. I managed to get out and run into Luke's [an older son] room, because I didn't think that he'd hit me in front of Luke. But he ran after me. I can remember crouching in the corner. He beat my neck and shoulder and back. Then he chased me into our bedroom. He yelled at one point, "I don't give a . . . if I kill you." It was one of the worst beatings John ever gave me. And I hadn't done anything but written a check. (Fedders and Elliott, 1987:158–159)

Although Fedders had the financial means to divorce her husband and to go on to become an advocate for battered women, many abused women come from low-income backgrounds and have few options. Unfortunately, many of these women end up victims of homicide. Women are more than three times as likely to be killed by their spouses than men are with the exception of African American husbands, who are at greater risk of being killed by their spouses than are African American wives or white spouses of either gender. Moreover, the risk of being killed by one's spouse is greater for individuals in interracial marriages than it is for those who marry within their race (Mercy and Saltzman, 1989). When women kill their spouses, it is often because they have been physically and sexually abused over a long period of time and see themselves as hopelessly trapped in a dangerous relationship.

Related to the issue of spouse abuse is marital rape. In *marital rape,* a husband forces sexual intercourse on his resisting wife. The federal criminal code and most state laws now identify marital rape as a crime. Analysts have identified three types of marital rape: (1) battering rape, in which sexual violence is part of a larger pattern of abuse; (2) nonbattering rape, in which the husband and wife do not agree over when, where, and whether or not to have sex; and (3) obsessive rape, which involves male sexual obsessions, sometimes related to use of pornography or force to become aroused (Finkelhor and Yllo, 1985). Many victims of spouse abuse and/or marital rape fear that if they try to leave the abusive husband, they will endanger themselves and their children. Studies have shown that women who have been severely sexually assaulted by their husbands and do not have adequate support services for victims of domestic violence where they live are the most likely to kill their spouses (Browne and Williams, 1987).

▲ Social Responses to Domestic Violence

The civil and criminal trials of O.J. Simpson, the former professional football star, actor, and media celebrity who was accused of brutally slaying his ex-wife, Nicole Brown Simpson, and her friend, Ronald L. Goldman, put domestic violence in the forefront of public consciousness (Gross, 1994). Photographs of the battered and bruised face of Nicole Brown Simpson were splashed across supermarket tabloids, daily newspapers, and television screens around the world. Even so, many people who are aware of domestic abuse don't do anything about it, feeling that they do not want to become involved in a "private matter."

Historically, in the United States, an *ideology of nonintervention*—a strong reluctance on the part of outsiders to interfere in family matters—has led people and police officers to ignore or tolerate domestic violence (Lauer, 1995). Unfortunately, the pattern of violence that ultimately results in a homicide is eerily similar in many cases of domestic abuse, and in most of those cases, death might have been prevented by earlier intervention. Positive changes are now being made in how law enforcement officials handle domestic violence calls—changes that are long overdue.

FAMILY-RELATED PROBLEMS IN THE TWENTY-FIRST CENTURY

As we have seen, families and intimate relationships have changed dramatically during the twentieth century. Because of these changes, some people believe

Why is high-quality, affordable day care a pressing problem in our society? How can we more effectively meet the needs of both children and their parents?

SOCIAL PROBLEMS
AND SOCIAL POLICY

BOX 11.2

Day Care: Jump-Starting the Stalled Revolution

▲ About 50 percent of all women with children under one year of age now work outside the home. (*New York Times,* 1997b)

▲ Sixty percent of women with children under six and 76 percent of women with school-age children are in the work force. (Hays, 1995b)

▲ Women make up 45 percent of the U.S. labor force. (Scarr, 1995)

In the 1960s, the women's movement sent women into the workplace, and in the 1970s, economic forces and changes in the family sent even more women into the workplace. But, says sociologist Arlie Hochschild, we are in a "stalled revolution" (Smolowe, 1996). The need for good-quality child care far outdistances its availability, and most experts put that problem at the feet of government and business: "The workplace really hasn't changed much, and public policies haven't kept up with the social changes," says Paula Rayman, director of the Public Policy Institute at Radcliffe College.

The United States and Great Britain are the only two industrialized countries that do not provide tax-supported child care, and in recent elections in Britain, both parties have pledged reform (Scarr, 1995). The United States also does not have national standards for child care; individual states set the ratio of children to caregiver, decide what job training (if any) is required, and regulate facilities.

As for business, several studies show that men with working wives are paid less and pro-moted less than men with nonworking wives, apparently because they are not sufficiently visible at work (Morris, 1997). According to Karen Nussbaum, Director of the Women's Bureau of the Labor Department, "We expect women and men to be at work, but we've made no provision for their children" (Hays, 1995b).

The problem is big, and it's going to get worse with increases in shift work and state and federal welfare reforms. According to the U.S. Department of Labor, one in five full-time workers works nonstandard hours in our increasingly twenty-four-hour, global economy (Hays, 1995b). At one time, only manufacturing and some service occupations required shift work, but today, banks and law offices routinely hire shift clerical help. Still, many day-care centers are open only 7 A.M. to 6 P.M., Monday through Friday. Parents—especially single parents—who work rotating schedules or on weekends are constantly scrambling among friends, relatives, home day care with extended hours, and standard day-care centers.

The demand for odd-hour care will grow only as more welfare parents enter the work force. According to Marianne Duddy, a child-care consultant in Boston, "If there's a job opening, it's going to be in that second shift in many communities, and that's going to force parents into the dilemma of 'What do I do with my children?'" (Hays, 1995b).

What are we going to do about the work–family dilemma? What role should the government play in providing good-quality child care? What role should businesses play? What do you think?

that the family as we know it is doomed; others think that returning to traditional family values can save this important social institution and create a more stable society. Another point of view, however, comes from sociologist Lillian Rubin (1994), who suggests that clinging to a traditional image of families is hypocritical in light of our society's failure to support the family, whether through family allowances or decent public-sponsored child care facilities (see Box 11.2). Some laws even hurt children whose families do not fit the traditional model. Welfare cuts, for example, affect children as well as the adults who are trying to provide for them.

Although many people demonstrate their faith in the future of the family as a social institution by choosing to have children, a macrolevel societal commitment is needed, as sociologist Demie Kurz (1995:232) states:

As a society we should make a commitment to helping all families—traditional nuclear families, two-parent, two-earner families, and single-parent families—and to providing adequately for their members, particularly their children. To help families we must reduce female and male poverty, making special efforts to end institutionalized discrimination against minorities. We must also promote equality between men and women in the family. This includes creating new conceptions of what it means to be a father and what it means to be a partner in a marriage and share family life and household work. It also means taking decisive steps to end violence toward women and children. While the costs of creating humane and just social policies are high, the cost of failing to promote the welfare of family members is far higher.

SUMMARY

➡ *What is a family?*

A family is a relationship in which people live together with commitment, form an economic unit, care for any young, and consider the group critical to their identity. This definition modifies the traditional definition to account for today's greater diversity in living arrangements and relationships in families.

➡ *Are U.S. families in decline?*

Not at all, say analysts who take a social change perspective. Families are becoming more complex and diverse, adapting to other changes in society. For one thing, marriage is no longer a cultural imperative; for another, many people reaffirm their belief in the institution through serial monogamy, a succession of marriages over a lifetime.

➡ *What are the sociological perspectives on family-related problems?*

Functionalists believe that the family provides social order and economic stability; the family is the solution to many societal problems, and dysfunctional families threaten the well-being of individuals and the whole of society. Conflict and feminist theorists see the family as a problem in society, not a solution; they believe that the family is a major source of inequality in society. Interactionists view the family first in terms of socialization. Some speak of the shared reality of marriage; some view family problems in terms of the subjective meanings that people give to their everyday lives; and some cite partners' unrealistic expectations about love and marriage.

➡ *What characterizes singlehood in the United States today?*

The proportion of the U.S. population that has never married has continued to grow since the 1960s. Some people remain single by choice, others by necessity; many working-class young people cannot afford to marry and set up a household.

➡ *Why do young people postpone marriage today?*

Four factors are important: The changing job structure in the United States leads to economic uncertainty; more women are in the labor force;

sexual relationships outside of marriage are more socially acceptable than before; and young people observing the rising divorce rate may be cautious about jumping into marriage.

➡ *Does cohabitation usually lead to a successful marriage? What is a domestic partnership?*

According to one recent study, only about 50 percent of cohabiting couples marry, and evidence on whether those marriages succeed is mixed. Some studies show little or no effect; others show that partners who cohabit are more likely to divorce than partners who do not. A domestic partnership is a household partnership in which an unmarried couple lives together in a committed, sexually intimate relationship and is granted the same rights and benefits as married heterosexual couples.

➡ *What does research show about dual-earner marriages?*

More than 50 percent of all marriages in the United States are dual-earner marriages, that is, marriages in which both spouses are in the labor force. Many women in these marriages do the domestic work at home after completing their workday jobs though there seems to be a trend toward more egalitarian families.

➡ *Is a two-parent family always preferable to a one-parent family?*

If the parents argue constantly, are alcoholics, or abuse the children, a supportive single-parent family would be preferable. However, growing up in a single-parent household poses serious risks to a

child that are complicated by other factors, such as poverty, discrimination, unsafe neighborhoods, and high crime rates.

➡ *Why is reproductive freedom such a controversial issue?*

Reproductive freedom implies the desire to have or not to have a child, and the roles that religious organizations, physicians, and the legal establishment should play in controlling a woman's fertility continue to be debated. Contraception, abortion, and the new reproductive technologies all raise personal and—when activists on either side get involved—societal issues.

➡ *Are teen pregnancies increasing or declining?*

Teen pregnancies have decreased over the past thirty years, but the teenage birth rate is higher in the United States than in any other high-income nation. Most unwed mothers are white teenagers, though, given their relative numbers in the population, African American teens are five times more likely than white teens to become unwed parents.

➡ *Who gets divorced, and do most people remarry?*

Many factors affect who gets divorced (e.g., marrying during the teen years or having limited economic resources), and these factors are interrelated with class, race, and age, so it is very difficult to determine any kind of statistical likelihood of divorce. Most people do remarry, and divorce and remarriage leads to complex family relationships, such as blended families.

KEY TERMS

blended family, p. 243
cohabitation, p. 233
dual-earner marriages, p. 234
extended family, p. 226

family, p. 226
family of orientation, p. 241
family of procreation, p. 241
kinship, p. 226

monogamy, p. 228
nuclear family, p. 226
second shift, p. 234

QUESTIONS FOR CRITICAL THINKING

1. Sociologist Andrew Cherlin says that the family is a highly adaptable social institution, but we can minimize the costs of change in the family unit by modifying other social institutions of daily life, such as the economy and workplace. What specific suggestions can you give for modifications in these and other areas?

2. What do you think of Margaret Mead's proposal of a two-stage marriage? What problems might it forestall? Would it create any new ones?

3. What suggestions can you offer to help offset the potentially detrimental effects of single-parent households, especially when the parent is a woman who is employed full-time?

Chapter Twelve

Problems in Education

One fateful day, in the second grade, my teacher decided to teach her class more efficiently by dividing it into six groups of five students each. Each group was assigned a geometric symbol to differentiate it from the others. There were the Circles. There were the Squares. There were the Triangles and Rectangles.

I remember being a Hexagon.

I remember something else, an odd coincidence. The Hexagons were the smartest kids in the class. These distinctions are not lost on a child of seven. . . . Even in the second grade, my classmates and I knew who was smarter than whom. And on the day on which we were assigned our respective shapes, we knew that our teacher knew, too. . . . We knew also that, along with our geometric shapes, our books were different and that each group had different amounts of work to do. . . . Not surprisingly, the Hexagons had the most difficult books of all, those with the biggest words and the fewest pictures, and we were expected to read the most pages. . . . What I had been exposed to, and in truth had benefited from, in that dusty elementary school was the educational practice of ability-grouping, or tracking. . . . it was tracking, along with the support of my family and my own effort and talent, that had ultimately carried me from a small farming town to [Harvard University]. . . . In essence, my ascension to the heights of academic privilege was orchestrated almost twenty years earlier by the well-intentioned grade school teachers and an assortment of odd geometric shapes. . . . Still, the more I learned about the insidious nature and harmful consequences of tracking, consequences even for its benefactors, the less I felt like thanking anyone.

—*Ruben Navarette, Jr., describes how he feels about ability-grouping in his school*
(Navarette, 1997:275–276)

As Navarette explains, educational practices such as *tracking*—**assigning students to specific courses and educational programs on the basis of their test scores, previous grades, or both**—can have a positive effect on some students' educational achievements and aspirations but a negative effect on those of other students. Tracking benefited Navarette, but in racially integrated schools, it often harms Latinos/as, African Americans, and Native Americans. The harm isn't intentional. The United States and other industrialized nations highly value *education*—**the social institution responsible for transmitting knowledge, skills, and cultural values in a formally organized structure.** But a wide gap exists between the ideals of U.S. education and the realities of daily life in many schools. As a result, business and political leaders, parents, teachers, and everyday people tend to complain about the state of education in this country, even as many parents report feeling relatively positive about the schools their children attend. In this chapter, we examine problems in education, such as tracking, and analyze how issues in education are often intertwined with other social problems. We'll begin with an overview of sociological perspectives on problems in education.

SOCIOLOGICAL PERSPECTIVES ON EDUCATION

The way a sociologist studies education depends on the theoretical perspective he or she takes. Functionalists, for example, believe that schools should promote good citizenship and upward mobility and that problems in education are related to social disorganization, rapid social change, and the organizational structure of schools. Conflict theorists believe that schools perpetuate inequality and that problems in education are the result of bias based on race, class, and gender. Meanwhile, interactionists focus on microlevel problems in schools, such as how communication and teachers' expectations affect students' levels of achievement and dropout rates.

▲ Functionalist Perspectives

Functionalists believe that education is one of the most important social institutions because it contributes to the smooth functioning of society and provides individuals with opportunities for personal fulfillment and upward social mobility. According to functionalists, when problems occur, they can usually be traced to the failure of educational institutions—schools, colleges, universities—to fulfill one of their manifest functions. *Manifest functions* are **open, stated, and intended goals or consequences of activities within an organization or institution.** While the most obvious manifest function of education is the teaching of academic subjects (reading, writing, mathematics, science, and history), education has at least five major manifest functions in society:

1. *Socialization.* From kindergarten through college, schools teach students the student role, specific academic subjects, and political socialization. In kindergarten, children learn the appropriate attitudes and behavior for the student role (Ballantine, 1997). In primary and secondary schools, students are taught specific subject matter that is appropriate to their age, skill level, and previous educational experience. At the college level, students expand their knowledge and seek out new areas of study. Throughout, students learn the democratic process.

2. *Transmission of culture.* Schools transmit cultural norms and values to each new generation and play a major role in *assimilation*, the process whereby recent immigrants learn dominant cultural values, attitudes, and behavior so that they can be productive members of society.

3. *Social control.* Although controversy exists over whose values should be taught, schools are responsible for teaching values such as discipline, respect, obedience, punctuality, and perseverance. Schools teach conformity by encouraging young people to be good students, conscientious future workers, and law-abiding citizens.

4. *Social placement.* Schools are responsible for identifying the most qualified people to fill available positions in society. Students are often channeled into programs on the basis of their individual ability and academic achievement. Graduates receive the appropriate credentials for entering the paid labor force.

5. *Change and innovation.* Schools are a source of change and innovation. To meet the needs of student populations at particular times, new programs—such as AIDS education, computer education, and multicultural studies—are created.

College and university faculty members are expected to conduct research and publish new knowledge that benefits the overall society. A major goal of change and innovation in education is to reduce social problems.

In addition to these manifest functions, education fulfills a number of *latent functions*—hidden, **unstated, and sometimes unintended consequences of activities in an organization or institution.** Consider, for example, these latent functions of education: Compulsory school attendance keeps children and teenagers off the streets (and, by implication, out of trouble) and out of the full-time job market for a number of years (controlling the flow of workers). High schools and colleges serve as matchmaking institutions where people often meet future marriage partners. By bringing people of similar ages, racial and ethnic groups, and social class backgrounds together, schools establish social networks.

Functionalists acknowledge many dysfunctions in education, but one seems overriding today: Our public schools are not adequately preparing students for jobs and global competition. In comparative rankings of students across countries on standardized reading, mathematics, and science tests, U.S. students are lagging. For example, in the 1996 International Mathematics and Science Study, a comprehensive study of science and math achievement by students in forty-one countries, U.S. students ranked slightly below average in math and slightly above average in science (Bagby, 1997). Countries that outperformed the United States in math included Singapore, where all students are tracked individually and expected to perform, and Japan, where teachers are generally better trained and prepared than their U.S. counterparts (see Box 12.1). Almost every top-ranked country has national educational standards set by the national government, unlike the largely decentralized educational system in the United States (Bagby, 1997).

◢ Conflict Perspectives

Sociologists using a conflict framework for analyzing problems in education believe that schools—which are supposed to reduce social inequalities in society—actually perpetuate inequalities based on class, race, and gender (Apple, 1982). In fact, conflict theorists such as Pierre Bourdieu argue that education *reproduces* existing class relationships (see Bourdieu

and Passeron, 1990). According to Bourdieu, students have differing amounts of *cultural capital* that they learn at home and bring with them to the classroom (see Chapter 2). Children from middle- and upper-income homes have considerable cultural capital because their parents have taught them about books, art, music, and other forms of culture. According to Bourdieu, children from low-income and poverty-level families have not had the same opportunities to acquire cultural capital. Some social analysts believe it is students' cultural capital—rather than their "natural" intelligence or aptitude—that is measured on the standardized tests used for tracking. Thus, test results unfairly limit some students' academic choices and career opportunities (Oakes, 1985).

Other sociologists using the conflict framework focus on problems associated with the hidden curriculum, a term coined by sociologist John C. Holt (1964) in his study of why children fail. The *hidden curriculum* **refers to how certain cultural values and attitudes, such as conformity and obedience to authority, are transmitted through implied demands in the everyday rules and routines of schools** (Snyder, 1971). These conflict theorists suggest that elites use a hidden curriculum that teaches students to be obedient and patriotic—values that uphold the status quo in society and turn students into compliant workers—to manipulate the masses and maintain their power in society (Bowles and Gintis, 1976).

Although students from all social classes experience the hidden curriculum to some degree, working-class and poverty-level students are the most adversely affected (Ballantine, 1997). When middle-class teachers teach students from lower-class backgrounds, for example, the classrooms are very structured and the teachers have low expectations about the students' academic achievement (Alexander et al., 1987). In one study of five elementary schools with students from different class backgrounds, researchers found significant differences in how knowledge was transmitted despite similar curricula (Anyon, 1980). Schools for working-class students emphasize procedures and rote memorization without much decision making, choice, or explanation of why something is done a particular way. In contrast, schools for middle-class students stress the processes that are involved in getting the right answer. Elite schools develop students' analytical powers and critical thinking skills, teaching them how to apply abstract principles to problem solving. These

SOCIAL PROBLEMS

Education in Japan: The Underside of Excellence

Everyone is still afraid of saying the truth: . . . that there are some things all students should know regardless of what state they live in.

—*Bruce Alberts, president of the National Academy of Sciences (Applebome, 1996d)*

Until recently, the education system was very uniform, producing children like manufactured goods.

—*Michiro Iida, a teacher at Shingakai Educational Institute, a nationwide chain of cram schools in Japan (WuDunn, 1996)*

In the United States, education is a local enterprise. States and local school districts decide on standards, set curricula, and assess—or do not assess—students' achievement. This system would seem to be just fine except that in international math and science tests, the United States ranks low in comparison to other modern, industrialized countries. Worse, some students graduate from high school barely able to read a menu or fill out a job application. Critics say that we need higher standards, which must be national standards backed up by a common nationwide curriculum that culminates in standardized achievement tests (Applebome, 1996b).

Countries that rank highest in international pupil achievement tests have national standards. Take Japan, which has nearly universal literacy and high school students who can solve complicated math problems. In Japan, at age three, sometimes earlier, children prepare for preschool entrance exams by entering the first of a series of cram schools—called *juku*. Some juku are national chains; others are held in small neighborhood apartments. The best are known only by word of mouth and charge more than $9,000 a year (WuDunn, 1996) but the discipline and thinking skills they teach set students on the path to a first-rate future. In Japan, the job you get depends on the university you attended, which depends on the high school you went to, which in turn depends on your elementary school, which, finally, depends on where you went to preschool. Thus, the sooner a child begins cramming, the better. The following excerpt describes a scene from Keiokai Educational Institute, where three- and four-year-olds sit at little desks in a ninety-minute class designed to improve performance on IQ tests (WuDunn, 1996).

---

schools also emphasize creative activities so that students can express their own ideas and apply them to different areas of study. Compare the following comments from students in high-track and low-track classes who were asked what they learned in a particular class (Oakes, 1985:86–89):

"I want to be a lawyer and debate has taught me to dig for answers and get involved. I can express myself." (High Track English).

"To understand concepts and ideas and experiment with them. Also to work independently." (High Track Science).

"To behave in class." (Low Track English).

"To be a better listener in class." (Low Track English).

"I have learned that I should do my questions for the book when he asks me to." (Low Track Science).

As these comments show, the hidden curriculum teaches working-class and poverty-level students that they are expected to arrive on time, follow bureaucratic rules, take orders from others, and experience high levels of boredom without complaining (Ballantine, 1997). The limitations on what and how these

The children followed the teacher's instructions: first, string as many colored beads as possible within two minutes; second, string only six beads or ten beads; third, string colored beads without letting two beads of the same color touch.

Then the teacher pinned pictures of fruits on the blackboard, arranging them in a line. Which fruit is in the middle? Which is second from the left? Second from the right? Then the fruits were rearranged vertically and the exercise was repeated. To a U.S. student, a cram school for 3-year-olds may sound cruel, but many students enjoy the classes. That is not to say the system is perfect: Some Japanese parents and educators feel students become "trained seals"—mechanical thinkers—and there is a movement today to nurture more individuality and independent thinking.

Another problem comes from the competition for elite schools: "Preparation for entrance exams makes students turn everyone into rivals, so they come to find pleasure in another's failure," says one Japanese headmaster. "What is most important for human society [compassion] is not nurtured in Japan" (WuDunn, 1996).

Then there are the children who cannot function in the Japanese system: "school refusers"—children as young as eight or nine who will not go to school. They cannot handle the academic pressure, rigid dress and hairstyle codes, and corporal punishment during the day followed by cram school at night. Truancy is a growing problem, especially among junior high school students (Pollack, 1996b). Traditionally, truants have been considered psychologically ill and sent to strict private schools that teach discipline or to mental hospitals. With 210 beds, Tokyo Metropolitan Umegaoka Hospital is the world's largest psychiatric hospital devoted solely to treating truant students. Today, though, the Ministry of Education acknowledges that the school system itself may play a role in the problem, and one mother has even started an alternative school for truants (Pollack, 1996b).

Japan's educational system is admired throughout the world, but do Japan's children pay too high a price? On the other hand, how can the United States compete in the global economy of the twenty-first century without improving its children's academic performance? If state and local school districts don't seem able to accomplish the goal, should we adopt national standards? Is there, perhaps, a middle road—something between our current laissez-faire system and national tests—that would lead to academic excellence? What do you think?

students are taught mean that many of them do not get any higher education and therefore never receive the credentials to enter high-paying professions (Bowles and Gintis, 1976). Our society emphasizes *credentialism*—a process of social selection that gives class advantage and social status to people who possess academic qualifications (Collins, 1979). Credentialism is closely related to *meritocracy*—a social system in which status is assumed to be acquired through individual ability and effort (Young, 1994). People who acquire the appropriate credentials for a job are assumed to have gained the position through what they know, not who they are or who they know.

According to conflict theorists, however, the hidden curriculum determines in advance that credentials will stay in the hands of the elites, so the United States is not a meritocracy even if it calls itself one.

 Interactionist Perspectives

Whereas functionalists examine the relationship between the functions of education and problems in schools and conflict theorists focus on how education perpetuates inequality, interactionists study classroom dynamics and how practices such as labeling affect students' self-concept and aspirations.

Interactionists believe that education is an integral part of the socialization process. Through the formal structure of schools and interpersonal relationships with peers and teachers, students develop a concept of self that lasts long beyond their schooling. Overall, social interactions in school can be either positive or negative. When students learn, develop, and function effectively, their experience is positive. For many students, however, the school environment and peer group interactions leave them discouraged and unhappy. When students who might do better with some assistance from teachers and peers are instead labeled "losers," they may come to view themselves as losers and thus set the stage for self-fulfilling prophecies. As noted in Chapter 1, a *self-fulfilling prophecy occurs when a false definition of a situation evokes a new behavior that makes the original false conception come true.*

Standardized tests can also lead to labeling, self-fulfilling prophecies, and low self-esteem. In fact, say interactionists, standardized tests such as IQ (intelligence quotient) tests particularly disadvantage racial, ethnic, and language minorities in the United States (see Haney, 1993). IQ testing first became an issue in the United States in the early 1900s when immigrants from countries such as Italy, Poland, and Russia typically scored lower than immigrants from Northern Europe. As a result, teachers did not expect them to do as well as children from families with Northern European backgrounds and therefore did not encourage them or help them overcome educational obstacles (Feagin and Feagin, 1997). In time, these ethnic groups became stigmatized as less intelligent.

Today, the debate over intelligence continues, but the focus has shifted to African Americans. In their highly controversial book *The Bell Curve: Intelligence and Class Structure in American Life,* Richard J. Herrnstein and Charles Murray (1994) argue that intelligence is genetically inherited and people cannot be "smarter" than they are born to be, regardless of their environment or education. According to Herrnstein and Murray, certain racial-ethnic groups differ in average IQ and are likely to differ in "intelligence genes" as well. To bolster their arguments, Herrnstein and Murray point out that on average, people living in Asia score higher on IQ tests than white Americans and that African Americans score 15 points lower on average than white Americans.

Many scholars have refuted Herrnstein and Murray's conclusions, but the idea of inherited mental infe-riority tends to take on a life of its own when there are people who want to believe that such differences exist (Duster, 1995; Hauser, 1995; Taylor, 1995). Thus, on the basis of IQ testing and psychological evaluations, many minority students, particularly boys, are designated *learning disabled* and placed in special education programs. Nearly 75 percent of all special education students are boys, and about 25 percent are African American (Bagby, 1997). Studies in California and Texas show that many African American and Mexican American children are placed in special education classes on the basis of IQ scores and other tests when their real problems are cultural influences and lack of English language skills and understanding (Brooks and South, 1996). Some analysts believe that 80 percent of students in special education classes are initially placed there because they do not know how to read (Bagby, 1997).

According to interactionists, labels such as *learning disabled* stigmatize students, *marginalize* them— put them at the lower or outer limits of a group—in their interactions with parents, teachers, and other students, and lead to self-fulfilling prophecies (Carrier, 1986; Coles, 1987). As a result, about 70 percent of special education students either drop out of school or are expelled (Bagby, 1997).

Labeling students *gifted and talented* may also result in self-fulfilling prophecies. Students who are identified as having above average intellectual ability, academic aptitude, creative or productive thinking, or leadership skills may achieve at a higher level because of the label. However, this is not always the case. Girls who are identified as gifted may deny their intelligence because of cultural norms about the proper roles of women and men (see Eder, 1985; Eder and Parker, 1987). Afraid that their academic achievement will make them unpopular, high-achieving girls, and sometimes boys, can become victims of *anti-intellectualism*—hostility toward people who are assumed to have great mental ability or toward subject matter that is thought to require significant intellectual ability or knowledge. White students are overrepresented in gifted-and-talented programs, whereas students of color are underrepresented. For example, in Austin, Texas, African American students are five times less likely to be placed in gifted and talented programs than are whites (Brooks and South, 1996). As one social scientist put it, if students are not given equal opportunities for gifted education, it is "a mythology that schools represent the great equalizing force in society . . . [and] . . . every child has an equal chance at success and achievement" (Sapon-Shevin, 1993:43–44).

PROBLEMS IN U.S. EDUCATION

Although we have already identified a variety of problems in education, other issues must be addressed in planning for the future of this country. These issues include the problem of illiteracy; the impact of high rates of immigration on educational systems; race, class, and gender inequalities in educational opportunities; and growing concerns about violence in schools.

▲ What Can Be Done about Illiteracy?

In a book by Jonathan Kozol (1986:7), a mother described her reading problem: "Donny wanted me to read to him. I told Donny: 'I can't read.' He said, 'Mommy, you sit down. I'll read it to you.' I tried it one day, reading from the pictures. Donny looked at me. He said, 'Mommy, that's not right.' He's only five. He knew I couldn't read. . . . Oh, it matters. You *believe* it matters." Kozol uses this example to show how illiterate people make up a growing but largely invisible minority in our country. Today, one in four U.S. adults is *functionally illiterate*—**unable to read and/or write at the skill level necessary for carrying out everyday tasks.** Illiteracy is much higher for minority group members than for U.S.-born whites; 16 percent of white adults are illiterate, compared to 44 percent of adult African Americans and 56 percent of adult Latinos/as.

When functional literacy is measured not just in terms of reading words from a page but also in regard to such practical matters such as understanding a bus schedule, filling out a bank deposit slip, or computing the cost of having some work done, many more people qualify as illiterate. A 1993 U.S. Department of Education study concluded that nearly half (95 million people) of the adult population in this country was functionally illiterate when it came to tasks such as those just described (Kaplan, 1993). Astoundingly, many people who are functionally illiterate have graduated from high school. In the 1993 study, 50 percent of those who scored in the lowest 20 percent were

Volunteers and trained professionals are an important link in reducing adult illiteracy. How can we make it easier for people to learn to read without experiencing embarrassment?

high school graduates. Among urban high school graduates, 15 to 20 percent cannot read at the sixth-grade level (Kaplan, 1993).

Can illiteracy be reduced in the United States? In an effort to improve education and eliminate illiteracy in this country, Congress passed the Goals 2000: Educate America Act in 1994. One of the eight goals set forth was that every adult in this country be literate by the year 2000. Unfortunately, we have made little headway in reaching this goal or the others (Bagby, 1997). Acknowledging that illiteracy is a social problem is an important first step in finding a solution, but so far, the primary solution proposed has been to raise standards. For example, in 1997, the standards for high school dropouts seeking a high school equivalency certificate—known as General Equivalency Diploma (GED)—were raised because current GED holders were not uniformly performing at the average literacy level. At the time, one director at the American Council on Education, the Washington organization that oversees GED testing, said: "With all the movement on higher standards and people in the workplace who were saying they were getting people who could not perform adequately, we could not make the claim that they could" (Arenson, 1997b: A18). Between 450,000 and 500,000 people take the

GED exam annually, and individuals are allowed to take the test up to three times each year until they pass it (Arenson, 1997b). For all its merits, however, sociologists examining high dropout rates among Latino/a students have found that some schools use the GED as a way to rid themselves of high-risk minority students who might graduate from high school if they were given the services and encouragement they need (Romo and Falbo, 1996).

Some social analysts believe that illiteracy will not be as big a problem in the future because new technologies will make reading and writing as we know it obsolete. These analysts note that the information age increasingly depends on communication by computers, not on basic reading and math computation skills. Still other educators and community leaders believe that illiteracy can be overcome through televised instruction in basic skills and courses on the Internet. However, not all social analysts believe that technology is the answer. As Jonathan Kozol (1986) points out, knowing how to read the printed word remains the access route to every other form of intellectual information. People need basic literacy skills before they can benefit from computers and other information technologies. Business and industry are now playing a role in solving the problem; it is estimated that employers spend over $50 billion annually to educate functionally illiterate workers in the effort to increase their skill levels and productivity (Kaplan, 1993).

Some critics say that the illiteracy problem is largely an immigration problem. Recent immigrants to this country continue to speak their own languages rather than learn English. However, Kozol (1986) argues that high rates of illiteracy should not be blamed on U.S. immigration policies. According to Kozol, illiteracy is a home-grown problem that would exist even without immigration.

▲ Immigration and Increasing Diversity in Schools

Debates over the role of schools in educating immigrants for life in the United States are not new. In fact, high rates of immigration—along with the rapid growth of industrial capitalism and the factory system during the Industrial Revolution—brought about the free public school movement in the second half of the nineteenth century. Many immigrants arriving in U.S. cities during this time spoke no English and could neither read nor write. Because of the belief that democracy requires an educated citizenry, schools were charged with the responsibility of "Americanizing" immigrants and their children. Workers needed basic reading, writing, and arithmetic skills to get jobs in factories and offices. Initially, an eighth-grade education was considered sufficient for many jobs, but soon a high school diploma became a prerequisite for most jobs above the level of the manual laborer. Schooling during this era was designed primarily to give people the means to become self-supporting. Educational systems were supposed to turn out workers with the knowledge and skills needed to enter the labor market and produce profits for managers and owners.

In the second half of the twentieth century, this country is again experiencing high rates of immigration from many nations around the world, and many of the newcomers are school-age children (Portes and MacLeod, 1996). Although some of the recent groups of immigrants, including many Koreans and Asian Indians, are well educated, most have limited formal education and few job skills. Today, about 14 percent of U.S. residents age five and older—or some 32 million people—speak a language other than English at home (see Table 12.1). Since we use language to communicate with others, develop a sense of personal identity, and acquire knowledge and skills necessary for survival, schools must cope with language differences among students.

Although most recent immigrants rely on public schools to educate their children, some supplement school efforts with additional educational opportunities. For example, some Asian and Pacific American parents have established weekend cram schools, which are similar to the *juku* in Japan, *buxiban* in China, and *hagwon* in Korea. Students spend a full day on subjects such as math and English and get specialized help in building study skills and learning test-taking strategies. Their parents are willing to sacrifice so that they will not experience language and cultural barriers that limit opportunities (Dunn, 1995).

How best to educate children of recent immigrants with lower levels of education and income is a pressing problem in states that have high levels of immigration, such as California, Texas, Illinois, and New York. Some school districts establish transitional programs for newcomers, six months to four years of classes taught in English and in the student's native language (Belluck, 1995). Some schools offer

TABLE 12.1   PRINCIPAL LANGUAGES SPOKEN AT HOME (UNITED STATES)

Language Used at Home	Persons Five Years Old and Over Who Speak It
English only	198,601,000
Spanish	17,339,000
French	1,702,000
German	1,547,000
Italian	1,309,000
Chinese	1,249,000
Tagalog	843,000
Polish	723,000
Korean	626,000
Vietnamese	507,000
Portuguese	430,000
Japanese	428,000
Greek	388,000
Arabic	355,000
Hindi (Urdu)	331,000
Russian	242,000
Yiddish	213,000
Thai (Laotian)	206,000
Persian	202,000
French Creole	188,000
Armenian	150,000
Navaho	149,000
Hungarian	148,000
Hebrew	144,000
Dutch	143,000
Mon-Khmer (Cambodian)	127,000
Gujarathi	102,000

Source: U.S. Bureau of the Census, 1998.

bilingual education in as many as ten languages in major subjects such as math, science, and social studies. Preliminary studies of newcomer programs show that many children not only learn English and about U.S. culture but also get help in overcoming traumatic experiences and educational deficits suffered in their country of origin.

Although some school officials believe that newcomer programs are the most efficient way to bring together students who speak the same language and teachers who can communicate with them, others consider them a form of segregation because recent immigrants are isolated from the mainstream (Belluck, 1995). Segregation is also still a problem for many students born in the United States.

Educational Opportunities and Race, Class, and Gender

Most research on access to educational opportunities for minority students has focused on how racially segregated schools affect student performance and self-esteem. Indeed, some forty years after the 1954 Supreme Court ruling in *Brown* v. *The Board of Education of Topeka, Kansas*—which stated that "separate but equal" schools are unconstitutional because they are inherently unequal—racial segregation appears to be increasing in education rather than decreasing (Brooks and South, 1996). Progress in bringing about racial *desegregation* (the abolition of legally sanctioned racial-ethnic segregation) and *integration*, which, for schools, involves taking specific action to change the racial or class composition of the student body, has been extremely slow for African Americans because segregated schools mirror race- and class-based residential segregation. Today, students of color comprise the vast majority of the student body in some urban school districts, whereas middle- and upper-class white students make up the majority of the student body in private urban schools or suburban public schools. For example, African Americans and Latinas/os make up 93 percent of the 24,000 public school students in Hartford, Connecticut, and 66 percent of these students come from families with incomes below poverty level (Gleick, 1995). According to sociologists, schools in which racial and ethnic minorities are in the majority typically have high teacher-student ratios (more students per teacher), inexperienced teachers who are sometimes less qualified, lower expectations of students, and high dropout rates (Feagin and Feagin, 1997).

What are the future educational prospects for African Americans, Latinas/os, and other students of color? On the one hand, although racial segregation is still prevalent in some areas of the country, the education gap appears to be narrowing between whites and African Americans; young African Americans are earning high school diplomas at about the same rate as their white counterparts (Holmes, 1996c). On the other hand, the President's Advisory Commission on Educational Excellence for Hispanic Americans recently concluded that segregation of

Latina/o students in poorly funded schools contributes to Latino/a students' low educational attainments (Shannon, 1996). Latino/a students are more likely than white (Anglo) students to attend schools in which racial and ethnic minorities make up the majority of the student body, and there are few Latino/a teachers to serve as role models and mentors. Although Latina/o youth accounted for more than 12 percent of the public school population in 1994, fewer than 4 percent of public school teachers were Latinos/as. In fact, the faculty of most public schools usually does not reflect the racial-ethnic or gender composition of the student body. Both Latinas/os and African Americans are underrepresented among teachers, administrators, and school board members in most systems. About 85 percent of public school teachers are white (roughly the same proportion as twenty years ago), and nearly 75 percent are women.

Moreover, fewer Latina/o children than white (Anglo) children have had an opportunity to attend preschool programs such as Head Start. The average Latino/a child's school-readiness skills—such as identifying colors and shapes—are less well developed than the average white (Anglo) child. As children move through high school and college, the dropout rate for Latinas/os between sixteen and twenty-four years of age grows dramatically: In 1993 it was 28 percent (Shannon, 1996). The percentage of Latinos/as who have not finished high school has been higher than the percentage of whites (Anglos) and African Americans over the past two decades (see Figure 12.1).

One explanation for the high dropout rate comes from a comprehensive study of Latino/a high school graduates in Texas. Researchers found that high dropout rates were more closely linked to practices in schools and attitudes within the community than to individual or family problems (Romo and Falbo, 1996). Across lines of race and ethnicity, students from poor families are three to four times

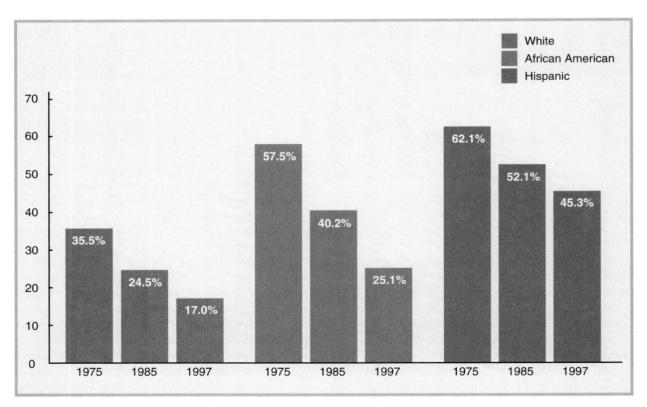

FIGURE 12.1   *Percentage of Persons Not Completing High School by Race and Hispanic Origin, 1975, 1985, and 1997*

Source: U.S. Bureau of the Census, 1998.

To overcome gender bias in schools, some parents are now enrolling their children in same-sex schools such as this New York City public school that enrolls only girls.

more likely to become school dropouts than are students from affluent families.

Even racially integrated schools often recreate segregation in the classroom when tracking or ability grouping is used (Mickelson and Smith, 1995). Lower-level courses and special education classes are disproportionately filled with children of color, while gifted-and-talented programs and honors courses are more likely to be filled with white and Asian and Pacific American students (McLarin, 1994). Moreover, even though roughly as many African Americans as whites are earning high school diplomas today, African American and white students do not achieve at the same level—and achievement differences increase with every year of schooling. The achievement gap between African American and white first-graders is less than the gap between white and African American twelfth-graders. According to some researchers, schools typically reinforce—rather than reduce—the effects of race and class inequalities in society (Mickelson and Smith, 1995).

How does gender bias in schools negatively affect female students? Contemporary gender bias has its roots in historical assumptions about the divergent roles of women and men in society, including the belief that males should be educated for the public sphere (i.e., work and civic involvement) and females

for the private sphere (i.e., home and childrearing). An extensive national survey on gender and self-esteem by the American Association of University Women (1992) found that young women and young men are treated differently in our educational system. First, teachers pay less attention to girls than to boys. In observing thirty physical science and chemistry classes, researchers found that teachers encouraged boys to talk in class and to volunteer for demonstrations and experiments more often than girls; girls were more likely to be observers and to be self-conscious and quiet (Jones and Wheatley, 1990). Many teachers also encourage boys to be problem solvers by asking them more complicated questions than they ask girls. In addition, reading materials may use language in biased ways (e.g., using masculine pronouns throughout), or they may stereotype women or ignore them. Finally, since boys tend to be more boisterous than girls, classroom activities are geared to holding boys' interest. Thus, through teacher reactions and classroom reading materials, female students come to learn that they are less important than male students. Over time, differential treatment undermines females' self-esteem and discourages them from taking courses—such as mathematics and science—that are dominated by male teachers and students (Raffalli, 1994).

Some analysts believe that schools are "gender-sorting machines" that steer girls and young women into outdated female roles and contribute to permanently low self-esteem (Schrof, 1993). At best, low self-esteem is associated with reduced expectations for the future and less self-confidence; at worst, it is associated with depression and sometimes even attempted suicide (American Association of University Women, 1992; Orenstein, 1994).

School Violence

According to the National School Safety Center, about fifty students are killed on school grounds during the school day each academic year, and about 3 million felony or misdemeanor-level crimes are committed annually at school (Applebome, 1995a). As discussed in Chapter 1, violence is a growing problem in schools throughout the country. Today, some school buildings look like fortresses or prisons with high fences, bright spotlights at night, and armed security guards. Many schools have installed metal detectors at entrances, and some search students for weapons, drugs, and other contraband as they enter. Consider this journalist's description of how one

Prison, airport, or school? Security guards and metal detectors have become an increasingly visible scene in many social institutions, including schools throughout the United States. Do such measures deter school violence? Why or why not?

school district is attempting to reduce violence (Applebome, 1995a:A1):

> The sprawling new brick building next to the Dallas County Probation Department has 37 surveillance cameras, six metal detectors, five full-time police officers and a security-conscious configuration based on the principles of crime prevention through environmental design. It is not the Big House. It is a schoolhouse: Dallas's $41 million state-of-the-art Townview Magnet Center.

Most educational analysts acknowledge that technology alone will not rid schools of violence and crime. Organizations such as the American Federation of Teachers have called for enhancing safety in schools by requiring higher student standards of conduct and achievement and giving teachers and administrators the authority to remove disruptive students. Some school districts now require students to wear uniforms in an effort to reduce violence, crime, and even truancy. The Clinton administration advocates such a policy on the basis that young people are less likely to be killed for a pair of sneakers

or for jewelry or designer clothes if all students are required to dress alike (Mathis, 1996). We do not know yet whether the positive effects of school uniforms outweigh the negative consequences—such as the embarrassment of poor families who cannot purchase the uniforms (Muto, 1995; Mathis, 1996).

Teachers, too, are the victims of violence on school premises. One study found that about 5,000 teachers are attacked or assaulted at schools each month; about 1,000 of the victims require medical attention (Applebome, 1995a). According to a spokesperson for one teacher's organization, "In the long run, we will not solve the problems of the schools by turning them into fortresses. But for the short term, we're going to have to cope with problems that are not immediately going away" (Applebome, 1995a:B8). Providing safety at school for students and teachers alike is only one crisis facing school districts that are burdened with shrinking budgets, decaying buildings, and heightened demands for services.

PROBLEMS IN SCHOOL FINANCING

Because financing affects all other aspects of schooling, perhaps it is the biggest problem in education today. Although many people believe that the federal government makes significant contributions to public education, most funds come from state legislative appropriations and local property taxes. State and local governments contribute about 47 percent each toward total education expenses, and the federal government pays the remaining 6 percent, largely for special programs for students who are disadvantaged (e.g., Head Start) or have disabilities (Bagby, 1997). In recent years, however, major industries in central cities have either gone out of business or relocated, resulting in the erosion of property tax revenues. This problem has been made worse by the move of middle- and upper-income families to suburban areas that have their own property tax. Without the funds from property taxes, schools in the central cities cannot purchase the latest textbooks and computer technology that today's students need (see Kozol, 1991; Ballantine, 1997). However, in what many see as a controversial move, some corporations are now providing supplies and media technology to some schools (see Box 12.2 on pages 264–265).

At the same time that educational funds are growing more scarce, a record number of students are entering the nation's schools—51.7 million in 1996. According to the Department of Education, enrollment increases will continue through 2006, when 3 million more students than today will enter the public school system annually. Unfortunately, many schools are already overcrowded and in need of major repairs. A report on New York City's public schools, for example, noted that one school in the borough of Queens was so overcrowded that science classes were held in a boys' shower room off the gymnasium (Applebome, 1996a). This same report found that many buildings had crumbling brickwork, rotting window frames, and rusted steel beams that were about as resistant to stress as a chocolate chip cookie (Applebome, 1995b). According to the U.S. General Accounting Office, at least $112 billion is needed immediately for building repairs and upgrades in the nation's 80,000 schools (Bagby, 1997).

Is there a way to resolve problems of unequal funding among the states, among school districts within states, and among schools within school districts? In recent years, the federal courts have held some states accountable for the unequal funding that has resulted in "rich" and "poor" school districts. However, most proposals to improve educational funding have been limited in scope and seem to benefit some groups at the expense of others. One plan—a voucher system—would give students and their families a specified sum of government money to purchase education at the school of their choice. Advocates of the voucher system say that the U.S. Department of Education should be eliminated and federal funds should be given to the states in the form of block grants that would then be dispersed as vouchers, approximately $1,000 per student regardless of family income. These advocates argue that schools would have to provide better-quality instruction at lower costs because they would be competing for students. However, critics say that the voucher system would offer only a limited number of students better opportunities and would not resolve the larger problem of underfunded schools. They note that a fully operational voucher system might mark the end of public education in this country. As the debate over solutions goes on, some parents have formed organizations, such as Parents for Public Schools, to support public education and build alliances among parents from different races and economic backgrounds.

Some of these organizations focus on raising bond issues; others organize public rallies to call attention to problems in education (Applebome, 1997).

Some analysts believe that the problem of underfunding could be solved by significantly reducing expenditures for administration and other non-instructional activities and using that money in the classroom. For example, spending on administration and other noninstructional functions grew by 107 percent between 1960 and 1984, but teachers' salaries dropped over 56 percent during the same period (Bagby, 1997). Problems in education are not limited to the elementary and secondary levels; higher education has its problems, too.

PROBLEMS IN HIGHER EDUCATION

Higher education serves several important functions in society: the transmission of specialized knowledge and skills, production of new information and technologies, and preparation of the next generation of professionals and scholars. Over the past decade, however, many public colleges and universities have come under increasing financial pressure as appropriations by state legislatures and federal funding have been cut. In response, some schools have intensified their fund-raising efforts, pursuing corporations, nonprofit foundations, and alumni. To remain solvent, many of these schools have also had to increase tuition and student fees.

▲ The Soaring Cost of a College Education

A recent study by the College Board found that the increases in average yearly tuition for four-year colleges in 1996–1997 were higher than the rate of inflation (Bagby, 1997). Although public community colleges and state colleges and universities typically have lower tuition rates than private colleges because they are funded primarily by tax dollars, some have grown too expensive for low-income students, particularly with the decline in scholarship funds and grants during the 1990s. Many students today must take out student loans and go into debt to attend college. Although some students find part-time jobs, their earnings make only a small dent in the cost of tuition and books. Students from more affluent families with

SOCIAL PROBLEMS

BOX 12.2

Channel One: Commercialism in the Classroom

The TV set is mounted atop the front chalkboard. Seated at desks facing the center of the classroom, most of the eighth graders peer sideways and upwards in the semidarkness. . . . [The Channel One logo appears.]. . . . Next, a few moments of rock music and music-video–style graphics. . . . Dissolve to Lisa Ling and Rawley Valverde, two casually dressed young anchors, in the game room–like Channel One news set. Mr. Valverde, talking forcefully and seriously—the Channel One anchor style—reports briefly on President Clinton's trip to an Asian Pacific economic summit in Manila. Cut to: commercials for M&M candies and Nintendo video games. . . . Then back to Ms. Ling, who introduces a mini-documentary [on] China.

—*Channel One at Pliny Haskell Junior High, Cerritos, California (Meisler, 1995)*

Channel One is a television network that broadcasts ten minutes of news and two min-

utes of commercials daily to 8 million students in 12,000 public, private, and parochial schools—approximately 40 percent of the twelve-to-eighteen-year-olds in the country (Jayson, 1997). It was founded by Whittle Communications in 1989 and sold in 1994 to K-III Communications Corporation, which still owns it, for $300 million. The arrangement is simple: Schools agree to broadcast the twelve-minute segment daily; in return they get a satellite dish and closed-circuit television system with a nineteen-inch television for every classroom in grades six through twelve (paid for by the advertisers).

Since its beginning, Channel One has been controversial. Proponents say that two minutes of advertising is a small price to pay for bringing news and public affairs programming to students who often don't read newspapers or watch TV newscasts. Then, of course, there's the $25,000 worth of free equipment that most schools can't otherwise afford. Paulette Fuller, principal at Haskell Junior High, which no longer has sports teams or after-school activities because of budget cuts, says firmly, "We like Channel One. The bene-

---

two parents present are more likely to attend private colleges, where annual costs range from an average of $12,823 annually to more than $30,000.

Some social analysts maintain that a college education is still a bargain at about $90 a day for private schools and $35 for public schools, because students receive instruction, a room, and three meals a day, as well as athletic facilities, counseling, job placement help, and other services. But social scientists applying a conflict framework to the problem of soaring college costs say that the high cost of a college education reproduces the existing class system: Some students lack access to higher education because they do not have adequate financial resources, and those who attend college are stratified according to their ability to pay. Among people of color from lower-income families, Latina/o enrollment as a percentage

of total college attendance increased from about 3.5 percent to 6.0 percent between 1976 and 1990. However, for African American men, college enrollment decreased from 9 percent in 1976 to 8.4 percent in 1990; for African American women, enrollment decreased from 11.5 percent to 10.6 percent. Also discouraging is the fact that college enrollment rates among Native Americans stagnated at about 0.8 percent from 1976 to 1990. The disproportionately low number of people of color enrolled in colleges is reflected in later educational achievement. The underrepresentation of people of color among those receiving doctorate degrees is striking.

What can be done about the cost of higher education? Some colleges have tried to reduce tuition, but most say they cannot do so and provide the same level of instruction and services. Since most federal

fits greatly outweigh the disadvantages" (Meisler, 1995).

What are the disadvantages? Are those two minutes of advertising really so awful? Yes, says social analyst Ellen Wartella. Business leaders may say they're becoming partners in education, but in actuality, they're becoming "partners in the increasing commercialization of American youth" (Wartella, 1995:451). Wartella isn't alone in her views. Edward Miller, former editor of the *Harvard Education Newsletter*, says that advertising to a captive audience of sixth-through twelfth-graders is an ethical issue: "By and large, educators are aware of these ethical issues, but . . . they are incredibly squeezed when it comes to resources and materials, and they'll take help where they can get it" (Stead, 1997).

Commercials are only part of the problem with Channel One. The media watchdog group Fairness & Accuracy in Reporting (FAIR) hired sociologist William Hoynes, an expert in analyzing news programs, to evaluate Channel One. Here are some of Hoynes's findings (Jayson, 1997):

▲ News is presented as drama, not reportage. The style is quick-cutting, like MTV, and, says Hoynes, "The news is filtered through youthful and very hip and attractive anchors. It becomes kind of a news drama that focuses on their lives and feelings."

▲ Racial and ethnic diversity is largely limited to the anchors. The news sources are not diverse. For example, Hoynes found that 69 percent of the sources were government officials or politicians, and they were primarily white males. Over half the African American sources were athletes or prisoners.

▲ Only one minute of every four is about breaking news. Political coverage is shallow, and economic coverage amounts to promoting consumption.

When Channel One was for sale in 1994, many parents, teachers, and social analysts hoped that the federal government would buy it and provide commercial-free news coverage. Unfortunately, that didn't happen, and the controversy continues. Is it immoral to sell tennis shoes and soda in the classroom? Or is two minutes of advertising a good trade-off for an educational tool that many schools couldn't otherwise provide? What about the other content problems—dramatization instead of reportage, bias in the news sources, and poor or slanted coverage? What do you think?

aid to students is in the form of loans, not outright grants, recent proposals have included a two-year, $1,500 annual tax credit for families with students in college and a cash grant for families with insufficient taxable income (Bagby, 1997).

▲ The Continuing Debate over Affirmative Action

Affirmative action programs in higher education—programs that take race, ethnicity, and gender into consideration for admissions, financial aid, scholarships, fellowships, and faculty hiring—were the subject of debate among academics and nonacademics alike even before the 1978 U.S. Supreme Court decision in *Bakke* v. *The University of California at Davis*.

In that case, Allan Bakke, a white male, sued the University of California at Davis, claiming that its policy of allocating 16 of 100 places in the first-year class to members of underrepresented minority groups was discriminatory. Bakke claimed he had been denied admission to the university's medical school even though his grade point average and Medical College Admissions Test score were higher than those of some minority applicants who were admitted under the university's affirmative action program. Although the Court ruled that Bakke should be admitted, it left the door open for schools to increase diversity in their student population.

The affirmative action controversy intensified in the 1990s with the 1995 decision of the regents of the University of California to discontinue any special consideration of "race, religion, sex, color, ethnicity,

Reprinted by permission.

or national origin" as a criterion for admission; the passage of Proposition 209 in California, a sweeping prohibition of affirmative action; and the 1996 U.S. Fifth Circuit Court of Appeals ruling in *Hopwood* v. *State of Texas*, which declared that school affirmative action programs unconstitutionally discriminated against whites. This case was named for Cheryl Hopwood, one of four white students rejected by the University of Texas law school who claimed that they were more qualified than some minority students who were admitted. Having declared the school's affirmative action policies discriminatory, the Court went on to rule that colleges and universities in Texas, Louisiana, and Mississippi (the states in the jurisdiction of the Fifth Circuit) could not use race as a factor in deciding which applicants to admit, even if the intention was to (1) achieve a diverse student body, (2) combat the perceived effects of a hostile environment, (3) alleviate a school's poor reputation in the minority community, or (4) eliminate any present effects of past discrimination by actors other than the school (*Texas Lawyer*, 1997). The U.S. Supreme Court refused to overrule the Fifth Circuit's decision (Brooks, 1997).

Whether affirmative action policies will continue to apply to college and university admissions is uncertain. What does seem clear, however, is that minority enrollments have dropped in many schools that have reduced or eliminated affirmative action programs. For example, after the *Hopwood* ruling, the University of Texas's admissions procedures changed, and minority applicants and enrollment dropped sharply. African Americans showed a 21 percent decrease, and Latinos/as showed a 17 percent decrease (Brooks, 1997). Concerned about the drop in minority enrollments, presidents and chancellors of major research universities who belong to the Association of American Universities issued a statement strongly supporting diversity in university admissions (*New York Times*, 1997a:A17). The statement reads, in part:

We believe that our students benefit significantly from education that takes place within a diverse setting. In the course of their university education, our students encounter and learn from others who have backgrounds and characteristics very different from their own. . . . [A] very substantial portion of our curriculum is enhanced by the discourse made possible by the heterogeneous backgrounds of our students. . . . a significant part of education in our institutions takes place outside the classroom, in extracurricular activities where students learn how to work together, as well as to compete; how to exercise leadership, as well as build consensus. If our institutional capacity to bring together a genuinely diverse group of students is removed—or severely reduced—then the quality and texture of the education we provide will be significantly diminished.

According to spokespeople for the Association of American Universities, applicants for college admission cannot be evaluated solely on such statistical definitions of merit as academic grades and standardized test scores. They must also be assessed on the basis of unquantifiable human qualities and capacities, including their potential to become leaders in a diverse society (Arenson, 1997a).

Some say that we must explicitly address problems of racial inequality in university admissions (Takagi, 1992). The areas to be examined include (1) minimum qualifications, (2) racial differences in academic achievement, and (3) race relations in campus academic, social, and political life. Although some admissions officers believe that minimum qualifications can be easily determined, others—including those at such elite private schools as Brown, Harvard, Princeton, Stanford, and Yale—argue that minimum standards are not clear-cut and depend on other factors such as academic promise, motivation, and ability to grasp concepts and ideas. Even when schools decide to eliminate affirmative action in admissions, they rarely dismantle "special talents" categories such as athletics, which is a crucial money-maker for many universities. Student athletes get special academic advising and help, whereas academic services for nonathlete members of racial minorities are very limited on many campuses (Takagi, 1992).

Some sociologists believe racial differences in academic achievement should not be completely ignored. For example, to make her point, sociologist Dana Takagi (1992:203) points out differences in Asian Americans' achievement compared to that of other students:

How should admissions officers evaluate an Asian American with a below-average SAT verbal score, an above-average SAT math score, outstanding grades, and strong extracurriculars against others? Because grade point average is a better predictor of Asian American undergraduate grades than test scores, should the admissions officer weigh the high school grade point averages of Asian Americans more heavily than those of whites? The important issue underlying racial differences in academic achievement is whether selection decisions are based on a universal set of criteria or are keyed to the indicators of success for different racial groups.

Takagi believes that a social policy dealing with differences in the performance of students of different racial categories is preferable to simply ignoring the problem or denying its existence.

Finally, students of different races often self-segrate in academic, social, and political life, a tendency that some people view as symbolic of resentment among various groups. However, Takagi (1992:204) believes that such self-segregation is more accurately viewed as "the loss of language and hope necessary to talk and act on racial differences." If problems of racial inequality were dealt with more specifically, affirmative action might eventually cease to be a problem in higher education.

EDUCATIONAL PROBLEMS IN THE TWENTY-FIRST CENTURY

Many problems remain unsolved in U.S. education. Rising rates of illiteracy are so worrisome that some members of Congress are proposing plans to expand spending on literacy programs. Still, some analysts believe that the best models for fighting illiteracy can be found in local programs, such as Literacy Austin, that use volunteers to teach basic reading skills to adults (*Austin American-Statesman*, 1997b). Perhaps the best way to give the greatest number of people the opportunity to learn how to read and thus more opportunities in society is to address illiteracy at both the national and local levels.

What about the issue of U.S. students not achieving at the levels of students in other high-income nations? Goals 2000: Educate America Act included these eight education goals to be met by the year 2000:

▲ All children in the United States will start school ready to learn.

▲ The high school graduation rate will be 90 percent or higher.

▲ Students will leave grades four, eight, and twelve showing competency in challenging subject matter.
▲ American students will be the best in the world in mathematics and science.
▲ Every American adult will be literate.
▲ Schools will be free of drugs, guns, and violence.
▲ Schools will promote partnerships with parents.
▲ Teachers will have the means for professional development.

These goals have not been met within the time allotted; and in the case of two, we've lost ground: Drug activity and classroom disruptions have increased, and reading achievement among twelfth graders has declined. Some state governors, corporate leaders, and educators believe that the goals are too broad to be implemented nationally and should be implemented at the state and local levels. These individuals feel states and local school districts should jointly develop rigorous, concrete standards in basic subject areas, such as English, mathematics, and science. Local districts would then be responsible for implementing plans that would bring students up to the standards (Applebome, 1996d). However, critics of Goals 2000, whether implemented nationally or locally, point out that being first in the world in mathematics or science does little for African American children in underfunded, drug- and crime-plagued central city schools or Native American children in substandard classrooms on U.S. government-run reservations.

Some parents are avoiding the problems of school safety and quality by home schooling their children. By the mid-1990s, home schooling was legal in every state, and the number of children being taught at home exceeded 500,000 (Gibbs, 1994). Some children seem to like home schooling or not know the difference because they have never attended school with other children. Others, such as Lydia Kiefer, age six, have mixed feelings about it: "Sometimes I like playing school. I'll get up in the morning, get my backpack, put some books in it, come downstairs, and sit down at my little brown table and pretend I have a teacher and other kids next to me. But I'm not so sure it would be so much fun in real life" (Gibbs, 1994).

A dozen states have charter schools. A charter school is an autonomous public school. The school has full authority and is freed from the bureaucracy

of a larger school district. Some charter schools have a special emphasis, such as science or special education; others offer the same curricula as other public schools but in an "improved," more creative version. However, many people believe charter schools create more problems than they solve because they take money away from already financially strapped, conventional public schools (Wallis, 1994).

In some cases, for-profit companies have been hired to operate public schools on a contract basis. The Edison Project took over management of schools in Boston; Mount Clemens, Michigan; Sherman, Texas; and Wichita, Kansas. Initially, the project was hailed as a rousing success because academic performance improved and students received such extras as home computers. Now, however, there is some question about for-profit corporations delivering the same quality of instruction over time. Some argue that demands from investors for increased profits are likely to result in cost-cutting measures and lack of public accountability (Applebome, 1996c).

Innovative approaches to improving the quality of public schools are being tried by individuals and groups across the country. For example, two professors at San Francisco State University became co-principals of an elementary school that educated needy urban children; the professors recruited minority students who were education majors at their university to serve as interns at the elementary school. Not only did the college students gain experience, the children's test scores went up and discipline problems went down as they were exposed to minority role models and given an improved curriculum and instruction (Nicklin, 1996).

What should education be like in the future? According to one analyst, the education we need for the future is different from that which was needed in the past (Fenstermacher, 1994):

For this education [in the future] is not bent on assimilation, to . . . melting . . . different cultures and languages into some common American pot, or to merely readying today's children for tomorrow's workforce. In contrast, the education that must engage us today and in the future is how to form common space and common speech and common commitment while respecting and preserving our differences in heritage, race, language, culture, gender, sexual orientation, spiritual values, and political ideologies. It is a new challenge for America.

During the twenty-first century, we must not underestimate the importance of education as a social institution. It is a powerful and influential force that imparts the values, beliefs, and knowledge necessary for the social reproduction of individual personalities and entire cultures (Bourdieu and Passeron, 1990). But in what direction should this tremendous social force move? Some educators, parents, and political leaders believe that we should continue to focus on a core curriculum and instilling discipline in students. We must also provide safety and order in our public schools (Loury, 1997).

Others argue that education must prepare students for today's high-tech living. They believe learning how to use the computer and how to access information on the Internet and the World Wide Web are perhaps the most important skills schools can teach contemporary students (MacFarquhar, 1996). But will computers, the Internet, and the World Wide Web improve education? Here is what author Clifford Stoll (1996:E15) says:

> What's most important in a classroom? A good teacher interacting with motivated students. Anything that separates them—filmstrips, instructional videos, multimedia displays, E-mail, TV sets, interactive computers—is of questionable education value. . . . Yes, kids love these high-tech devices and play happily with them for hours. But just because children do something willingly doesn't mean that it engages their minds. Indeed, most software for children turns lessons into games. The popular arithmetic program Math Blaster simulates an arcade shoot-'em-down, complete with enemy flying saucers. Such instant gratification keeps the kids clicking icons while discouraging any sense of studiousness or sustained mental effort. . . . For decades, we've welcomed each new technology . . . as a way to improve teaching. Each has promised better students and easier learning. None has succeeded. Except that it is even more expensive, I suspect that classroom computing isn't much different.

Stoll—and others, no doubt—would endorse the following statement by Ennis Cosby, the late son of actor Bill Cosby, writing on why he was becoming a teacher (Cosby, 1997:E13):

> First, I have a natural love for children, and children get along with me very well. It is one of those nonobservable variables that exists between me and children. I am far from being perfect, but I get along very well with most children.
>
> Second, I believe in chances, so I do not give up on people or children. I know that if I have a class full of kids, I would want all of them to be successful students. I believe in finding solutions to any and every problem. I don't believe in quitting because of my academic experiences [with dyslexia]. With all of the chances I was given, I am going to give all of my students as many chances as they need to find themselves as students.
>
> Third, I believe teachers need to bond with students. When I reflect on my favorite teachers in my life, they were teachers who were my friends, too. I see teachers wearing many titles besides TEACHER. I see psychologist, mother, father, friend and adviser. I believe students react to my behavior. The more I give of myself, the more they will give back to me. Fourth, I believe in a saying one of my favorite teachers told me: "Whatever you teach a child, it will not be digested completely by that student until they leave your classroom." I feel that learning is a slow process, and patience is a very crucial quality to have as a teacher.
>
> Lastly, my best quality is that I am very personal with all students. I work with kids and try to make them feel that I understand them. I am very stern on good morals and manners. I am not old-fashioned. I just believe in respect, honesty and truthfulness. I feel that children will be better students if they become better people. . . . I believe in fairness within the [school] system. I just want all students to have an equal opportunity. I have a lifetime to devote to making the school system more balanced any way I can.

Unfortunately, we will never know what kind of teacher Ennis Cosby would have become; he was murdered as he changed a tire late one night on the side of a Los Angeles freeway. But perhaps other future teachers will pursue similar goals, helping individual students to succeed and thereby remedying problems in U.S. schools.

SUMMARY

➤ *What is education?*

Education is the social institution responsible for transmitting knowledge, skills, and cultural values in a formally organized structure.

➤ *What is the functionalist perspective on education?*

Functionalists believe that education contributes to the smooth functioning of society when it fulfills its manifest functions, the open, stated, and intended goals or consequences of its activities. Education has at least five major manifest functions: socialization, transmission of culture, social control, social placement, and change and innovation. Schools also fulfill a number of latent functions—hidden, unstated, and sometimes unintended consequences of its activities.

➤ *What is the conflict perspective on education?*

Conflict theorists believe that schools, which are supposed to reduce inequality in society, actually perpetuate inequalities based on class, race, and gender. The sociologist Pierre Bourdieu, for example, says that children from low-income and poverty-level families come to school with less cultural capital (values, beliefs, attitudes, and competencies in language and culture) than middle- and upper-income children. Conflict theorists also think that elites manipulate the masses and maintain their power in society through a hidden curriculum that teaches students to be obedient and patriotic and thus perpetuates the status quo in society.

➤ *What is the interactionist perspective on education?*

Interactionists study classroom dynamics and how practices such as labeling affect students' self-concept and aspirations. If students are labeled "learning disabled" for example, the label may become a self-fulfilling prophecy, that is, an unsubstantiated or erroneous belief that results in behavior that makes the false belief come true. A student who is erroneously labeled "learning disabled" may stop trying and teachers may lower their expectations, with the result that the student doesn't succeed in the long run.

➤ *What is illiteracy and what can be done about it?*

Functional illiteracy is being unable to read and/or write at the skill level necessary for carrying out everyday tasks. Today, one in four adults in the United States is illiterate; the problem is greatest among minorities. On the national level, the United States took action toward solving the illiteracy problem by passing the Goals 2000: Educate America Act in 1994, though progress in achieving the goals has been slow. At the local level, business and industry are taking a leading role, spending over $50 billion annually to educate functionally illiterate workers. Volunteer organizations that teach adults basic reading skills have been very successful.

➤ *Why are high rates of immigration a problem for U.S. schools?*

Though some immigrants are well educated, most have limited formal education and few job skills. Also, many immigrants are children, so schools must cope with language differences among students. Some school districts offer transitional newcomer programs with bilingual instruction, but critics say that these programs are a form of segregation.

➤ *How do race, class, and gender affect educational opportunities?*

The Supreme Court outlawed segregation in 1954, but segregated schools still exist because segregated schools mirror race- and class-based residential segregation. Schools in which racial and ethnic minorities are in the majority typically have high teacher-student ratios, less qualified teachers, lower expectations of students, and high dropout rates. Despite such disadvantages, young African Americans are earning high school diplomas at the same rate as white Americans. Latino/a students face many educational obstacles, including few school-readiness programs (like Head Start), few Latino/a teachers as role models, and high dropout rates. An extensive survey on gender shows that teachers treat boys and girls differently in the classroom, so females' self-esteem and life expectations suffer.

➡️ *How has violence affected our schools?*

Many schools now look like fortresses and use metal detectors and security guards to screen entering students. To lessen the possibility of students being killed for shoes, jewelry, or designer clothes, some school districts now require students to wear uniforms.

➡️ *What is the crisis in school financing?*

Most educational funds come from state legislative appropriations and local property taxes, but the eroding tax base in central cities leaves schools underfunded. At the same time, record numbers of students are entering the public school system, and many schools are overcrowded and need major repairs. One proposed solution is the voucher system, whereby families are given vouchers to "buy" education at the school of their choice. Critics say that this plan would offer only a limited number of students better opportunities and wouldn't solve the funding problem.

➡️ *What are the major problems in higher education?*

The soaring cost of a college education is a major problem because, say conflict theorists, it reproduces the existing class system: Those who attend college are stratified according to their ability to pay. There is also the question of affirmative action. Should race, ethnicity, and gender be taken into consideration for admissions, financial aid, scholarships, and faculty hiring? While the debate continues, one thing is certain: Minority enrollments have dropped in many schools that have reduced or eliminated affirmative action programs either voluntarily or as the result of a court order.

➡️ *What are the urgent educational problems of the twenty-first century?*

To compete in the global economy, we must come to terms with illiteracy in our adult population and we must provide *all* children with safe, high-quality education. Some experts say that the best way to achieve both goals is to reframe the Goals 2000 program so that it can be implemented at the local level. Some parents deal with issues of school safety and quality by home schooling their children or starting charter schools, which are autonomous public schools. Other innovative approaches are being tried by individuals and groups across the country.

KEY TERMS

education, p. 252
functionally illiterate, p. 257

hidden curriculum, p. 253
latent functions, p. 253

manifest functions, p. 252
tracking, p. 252

QUESTIONS FOR CRITICAL THINKING

1. Are you for or against school uniforms? What psychological effects of uniforms might improve student behavior and academic performance? What are the drawbacks to school uniforms?

2. Even though the Goals 2000 objectives were not met by the year 2000, should we continue to try to achieve these goals? Which goals appear to be more attainable? Which appear to be the least attainable?

3. What creative solutions can you propose for the school financial crisis? That is, if the federal government doesn't increase its contribution and voters resist increased taxes, where can state legislatures find more money for education?

Chapter Thirteen

Problems in Politics and the Global Economy

I think this Seattle movement has legs. The issues that brought these people to Seattle are enduring issues. They are not the subject of a single egregious policy, like Vietnam. It's not just about the W.T.O.—it's about the dominance of huge corporate power over globalization. The greenie-Sweeney [environmentalists and labor activists] alliance has a future.

—*New York University sociologist Todd Gitlin gives his view on the confrontation among global trade organization leaders, environmentalist activists, labor leaders, and others at the 1999 World Trade Organization (WTO) meeting in Seattle, Washington.*
(Greenhouse, 1999:A26)

—*University of Texas at Austin journalism professor Robert Jensen gives his view on the real meaning behind the Seattle demonstrations, which brought together labor, environmental, and human rights groups, each with its own specific concerns.*
(Jensen, 1999)

Corporations shouldn't run the world, people should. . . . When rising corporate profits coincide with stagnating real wages for the majority of Americans and continued sweatshop conditions in the developing world, that's an increasingly hard line to sell. Slowly, people are coming to understand a few obvious truths about the corporate entities that control much of our lives: Corporations are authoritarian institutions that are incompatible with democracy.

Perhaps nothing better signifies our growing awareness and the intertwining of politics and the economy in today's global economy than the abrupt end of the World Trade Organization (WTO) meeting in Seattle, Washington, in 1999. At that time, a series of global trade talks deteriorated into angry confrontations between diverse protesters who demanded that large corporations and the U.S. government become more accountable for their actions. Although the delegates to the meeting went home frustrated and empty handed, the WTO meeting served to highlight some problems that lie at the heart of the global economy and thus affect and are affected by U.S. politics. Among these problems, which will continue well into the twenty-first century, are sweatshop conditions, child labor, and the environmental problems brought about by increased industrialization (*New York Times*, 1999a).

Although there have been protests throughout the history of the United States, especially during the 1960s, the radical activism seen in Seattle had not been visible for many years. Some analysts believe that a new mood has arisen as more people feel a "loss of control in a world of rapid change and turbocharged global capitalism" (Elliott, 1999:37). Today, however, the Internet offers protesters and social activists a much wider audience than ever before and makes it possible to mobilize a worldwide campaign against political decisions or economic maneuvers that are viewed as harmful (Elliott, 1999).

TYPES OF ECONOMIES

Before examining how individuals and nations are affected by problems in politics and the global economy, let's briefly look at the economic organization of societies in the past. Depending on its major type of economic production, a society can be classified as having a preindustrial, industrial, or postindustrial economy.

 ### Preindustrial Economies

Hunting and gathering societies, horticultural societies, and agrarian societies are all preindustrial economies. Most workers engage in *primary sector production*—**the extraction of raw materials and natural resources from the environment.** In this type of production, materials and resources are used without much processing. Today, extracting gold and silver from mines in Indonesia is an example of primary sector production. In early hunting and gathering societies families produced the goods they consumed, and the division of labor typically was based on age and gender. Inequality was minimal. However, in horticultural societies, in which production shifts somewhat away from the family unit, the division of labor is more complex. Because more than enough food is produced to feed everyone, some people can engage in work-related activities other than food production. In agrarian societies, people can assume even more specialized tasks—becoming warriors and priests, for example—in addition to working in food production.

At each stage in preindustrial economies, inequality grows more distinct as some people are more able than others to put the surplus to their own use.

 ### Industrial Economies

Social inequality grows still more pronounced in industrial economies where most workers are engaged in *secondary sector production*—**the processing of raw materials (from the primary sector) into finished products.** Work in industrial economies is much more specialized, repetitious, and bureaucratically organized than in preindustrial economies. Consider, for example, Ben Hamper's first day on the rivet line at the General Motors' truck and bus division in Flint, Michigan (Hamper, 1991:88–89):

> The Rivet Line was the starting point for all that went on during the three-day snake trail needed to assemble a truck. The complex birth procedure began right here. It started with a couple of long black rails. As the rails were hoisted onto crawling pedestals, the workers began riveting them together and affixing them with various attachments. There weren't any screws or bolts to be seen. Just rivets. Thousands upon thousands of dull gray rivets. They resembled mushrooms. . . . For the next couple of hours I stood back and studied the routine. You were given three days to learn your assignment. I didn't plan on jumpin' in until absolutely necessary. I looked around at those who would soon be my neighbors. I'd seen happier faces on burn victims.

Hamper describes the work in the General Motors factory as specialized, repetitious, and highly bureaucratic. There were rules to follow, and workers were assigned to be sure that everyone obeyed them.

Although many workers are involved in the production process in industrial economies, most jobs are done by machines and other "things" rather than through workers interacting.

Over the last two decades, there are some sectors of the industrial economy that have undergone *deindustrialization*—**the process by which capital is diverted from investment in basic industries (in the form of economic resources, plants, and equipment) to business practices such as mergers and acquisitions and foreign investment** (Bluestone and Harrison, 1982). According to some social analysts, deindustrialization has brought about "shuttered factories, displaced workers, and a newly emerging group of ghost towns" (Bluestone and Harrison, 1982:6). Although it might seem natural that deindustrialization would transform the United States into a postindustrial economy, this has not yet been the case.

Postindustrial Economies

Postindustrial economies are characterized by *tertiary sector production—providing services rather than goods as the primary source of livelihood.* Tertiary sector production includes work in such areas as fast-food service, transportation, communication, education, real estate, advertising, sports, and entertainment. Although some tertiary sector jobs are personally fulfilling and economically rewarding, many of them are not. Here's what one college student had to say about working her way through college in fast-food service (Loeb, 1994:289):

> I came here . . . as a freshman. I didn't know about the previous tuition hikes. I didn't care. I thought it wouldn't affect me. Then I started hearing rumors and I freaked. I'm the youngest

of seven children trying to get a degree. Right now I work at Roy Rogers flipping chicken and baking biscuits for $4.25 an hour—[then] minimum wage. Is my career being a biscuit babe for the rest of my life?

In postindustrial economies, people in highly paid, primary tier jobs may work at home or network with business contacts virtually anywhere in the world, using computers and modems to connect to employers' or clients' offices.

Almost three decades ago, sociologist Daniel Bell (1973) predicted that the United States would eventually become a postindustrial economy characterized by service and information processing. That may be, but Hodson and Sullivan (1995:206) do not think we are there now and we may never be:

> The current economy, with a large share of the labor force in services, has not gone *beyond* being an industrial society. Rather, it is based on a highly productive industrial base in which it is possible to produce more goods with fewer workers. Because the need for manufactured goods can be expanded to a greater extent than the need for agricultural products, the economy will probably never reach a state in which only a tiny fraction of workers is producing manufactured goods.

According to sociologists, the United States is best characterized as an *advanced industrial society* that has a small sector of primary production, a larger manufacturing sector, and a growing service sector (Hodson and Sullivan, 1995).

An advanced industrial society is characterized by greater dependence on an international division of labor. For example, when U.S. manufacturers are faced with stiff international competition, they use foreign assembly plants such as the ones in Indonesia, China, and Vietnam where labor costs are low. Some manufacturers have set up *maquiladora* plants—factories in Mexico where components manufactured in the United States are assembled into finished goods and shipped back to the United States for sale. Of course, when U.S. manufacturing workers are displaced by workers in other nations, their earnings are diminished. At the same time, technological innovations have led to considerable deskilling (and consequently lower pay) in work that is available. The

In postindustrial economies, work may become more flexible and more demanding at the same time. Working at home has both its pleasures and its frustrations for this woman. What do you think the office of the future will look like?

result is a decrease in the absolute number of well-paid workers in the United States (Wilson, 1992).

Another characteristic of an advanced industrial society is a shift toward flexible production. *Flexible production* involves small batch production rather than mass production, product innovation rather than product standardization, and responsiveness to rapid changes in market opportunities rather than dependence on mass markets (Wilson, 1992). Flexible production is sometimes referred to as "post-Fordism" and differs from mass production, or Fordism, in three important ways: (1) Technology is based on programmable automated machines that allow a variety of products or models to be produced without downtime or retooling; (2) factories are organized so that workers are rotated through a variety of tasks, usually as a team; and (3) firms subcontract activities that they cannot easily or cheaply perform to other firms that can. In *subcontracting,* a larger company hires other (usually smaller) firms to provide specialized components, products, or services. Many U.S. companies—ranging from manufacturers of athletic shoes to high-tech industries—find that it is more cost efficient (and therefore profitable) to subcontract certain work to small contractors than to do it in-house.

THREE MAJOR MODERN ECONOMIC SYSTEMS

There are three major modern economic systems: capitalism, socialism, and mixed economies. The U.S. economy is a form of capitalism, which, as we explained in Chapter 1, is characterized by private ownership of the means of production. **Socialism is characterized by public ownership of the means of production, the pursuit of collective goals, and centralized decision making.** Unlike capitalist economies, in which the primary motivation for economic activity is personal profit, the primary motivation in a socialist economy is the collective good of all citizens. For Karl Marx, socialism was only an intermediate stage to an ideal communist society in which the means of production and all goods would be owned by everyone. Under communism, Marx said, people would contribute according to their abilities and receive according to their needs. Moreover, government would no longer be necessary, since it existed only to serve the interests of the capitalist class.

No economy is purely capitalist or purely socialist; most are mixtures of both. A *mixed economy* **combines elements of both capitalism (a market economy) and socialism (a command economy).** Sweden, Great Britain, and France have an economic and political system known as *democratic socialism,* in which private ownership of some of the means of production is combined with governmental distribution of some essential goods and services and free elections. Although most industry in mixed economies is privately owned, there is considerable government involvement in setting rules, policies, and objectives. The government is also heavily involved in providing services such as medical care, child care, and transportation. Debates about problems in the U.S. economy often involve comparisons of capitalism with other types of economic systems.

There are four distinctive features of "ideal" capitalism: private ownership of the means of production, pursuit of personal profit, competition, and lack of government intervention. First, capitalism is based on the right of individuals to own various kinds of property, including those that produce income (e.g, factories and businesses). Second, capitalism is based on the belief that people should be able to maximize their individual gain through personal profit, which is supposed to benefit everyone, not just capitalists. Third, capitalism is based on competition, which is supposed to prevent excessive profits. For example, when companies are competing for customers, they must offer innovative goods and services at competitive prices. The need to do this, it is argued, prevents excessive profits. Finally, capitalism is based on a lack of government intervention in the marketplace. According to this *laissez-faire* (meaning "leave alone") policy, also called *free enterprise,* competition in a free marketplace—not the government—should be the force that regulates prices and establishes workers' wages.

PROBLEMS IN THE GLOBAL ECONOMY

Twenty-five years ago, about one-third of the world's workers lived in countries with centrally planned economies—economies in which the government decides what goods will be produced and in what quantities—and another third lived in countries only weakly linked to international commerce because of protective barriers to trade and investment. Today, however, it is possible that fewer than 10 percent of the world's workers live in countries that are largely disconnected from world markets (World Bank, 1995). While the breakdown in trade barriers and the turn to economies based on the demands of the marketplace have brought new goods, capital, and ideals to many, they have also brought new fears:

> Rapid change is never easy. In rich and poor countries alike there are fears of rising insecurity, as technological change, expanding international interactions, and the decline of traditional community structures seem to threaten jobs, wages, and support for the elderly. Nor have economic growth and rising integration solved the problem of world poverty and deprivation. Indeed, the numbers of the poor could rise still further as the world labor force grows . . . to a projected 3.7 billion in thirty years' time. The bulk of the more than a billion individuals living on a dollar or less a day depends . . . on pitifully low returns to hard work. In many countries workers lack representation and work in unhealthy, dangerous, or demeaning conditions. Meanwhile 120 million or so are unemployed worldwide, and millions more have given up hope of finding work. (World Bank, 1995:4).

The rapid changes in economies have also raised concerns about the accountability of transnational corporations.

◤ Transnational Corporations and the Lack of Accountability

Today, the most important corporate structure is the *transnational corporation*—**a large-scale business organization that is headquartered in one country but operating in many countries.** Some transnational corporations constitute a type of international monopoly capitalism that transcends the boundaries and legal controls of any one nation. The largest transnationals are headquartered in the United States, Japan, Korea, other industrializing Asian nations, and Germany. Currently, transnational corporations account for more than 25 percent of total world production. Not all large U.S. corporations that do business abroad are transnational; for exam-

ple, General Motors doesn't qualify because only about one-third of its assets and one-third of its sales are outside the United States, and most of these are in other high-income nations such as Australia, Canada, and various European countries. Examples of true transnational corporations are Asea Brown Boveri, a Swiss-Swedish engineering group, and Philips, a Dutch electronics firm. Both have 85 percent of their sales outside the country in which they are headquartered (Waters, 1995). Transnationals dominate in petrochemicals, motor vehicles, consumer electronics, tires, pharmaceuticals, tobacco, soft drinks, fast food, financial consulting, and luxury hotels (Waters, 1995).

The shareholders in transnational corporations live throughout the world. Although corporate executives may own a great number of shares, most shareholders have little control over where plants are located, how much employees are paid, or how the environment is protected.

Because transnational corporations are big and powerful, they play a significant role in the economies and governments of many countries. At the same time, by their very nature, they lack accountability to any government or any regulatory agency. Because transnationals do not depend on any one country for labor, capital, or technology, they can locate their operations in countries where political and business leaders accept their practices and few other employment opportunities exist. For example, when Nike workers went on strike in Indonesia, Nike subcontracted to Korean entrepreneurs operating assembly plants in Vietnam, where employees work for barebones wages and, according to media coverage, plant managers physically abuse some of the women. Although many workers in low-income nations earn less than a living wage from transnational corporations, the products they make are often sold for hundreds of times the cost of raw materials and labor. Designer clothing and athletic shoes are two examples of this kind of exploitation. Young women working in Nike factories in Indonesia and Vietnam, for example, go barefoot and cannot afford to buy the shoes they assemble (Goodman, 1996).

Still another concern is that transnational corporations foster global consumerism through advertising and strategic placement of their business operations around the world. McDonald's golden arches and Coca-Cola signs can be seen from Times Square in New York to Red Square in Moscow (see

SOCIAL PROBLEMS

IN GLOBAL PERSPECTIVE

BOX 13.1

Global Consumerism: Something for Everyone?

Chen Jingwen has a symbol of China's rising affluence tucked away near the dinner table in his two-bedroom apartment just outside Beijing.

It is an Ab-Rotor, a stomach exerciser he bought in September through a new television home shopping program for about $24, more than one-fifth of his monthly salary.

Mr. Chen, 33, a Communist Party member who works as a youth league organizer, reported just one glitch on his path to a trimmer stomach: He did not have a telephone to order the contraption. So instead of buying the product on impulse from home, he had to wait a day and make the call from his office.

"My next plan is I want to buy a jogging machine or a stationary bicycle, if the price is fair," said Mr. Chen, dressed in a new yellow warm-up suit and running shoes as he headed home after work to do some stomach crunches.

—*From a report on China's new home shopping networks, which sell primarily Western goods (Hilsenrath, 1996)*

The Chinese consumer market is largely undeveloped—but it won't be for long. With the demise of heavy industry in the United States, our major export is our consumer culture and its products (Ritzer, 1995:170). At the same time, economic success in any country—or even a hint of it—prompts consumption, which is fed by U.S. advertising. In Russia, for example, where Christmas has returned after seventy years, a twelve-foot Christmas tree in front of Moscow's biggest toy store "glimmers with unsubliminal advertising. It is trimmed with huge fake boxes of Nesquik, the Nestle chocolate powder" (Stanley, 1996). At Christmastime, billboards all over the city show

Box 13.1). Both companies are conquering other nations as aggressively as they have the United States. Coca-Cola has 33,000 employees on its payroll, 70 percent of whom work outside the United States (Hardy, 1996).

PROBLEMS IN THE U.S. ECONOMY

Although an economic boom occurred late in the twentieth century, corporate wealth became increasingly concentrated. *Economic concentration* refers to the extent to which a few individuals or corporations control the vast majority of all economic resources in a country. Concentration of wealth is a social problem when it works to society's detriment, particularly when people are unable to use the democratic process to control the actions of the corporations.

Concentration of Wealth

The concentration of wealth in the United States can be traced through several stages. In the earliest stage (1850–1890), most investment capital was individually owned. Before the Civil War, about 200 families controlled all major trade and financial organizations. By the 1890s, even fewer—including such notables as Andrew Carnegie, Cornelius Vanderbilt, and John D. Rockefeller—controlled most of the investment capital in this country (Feagin and Feagin, 1997).

In early monopoly capitalism (1890–1940), ownership and control of capital shifted from individuals to corporations. As monopoly capitalism grew, a few

Santa drinking Coca-Cola, and parents can buy their children nonalcoholic champagne in bottles decorated with Disney's Pocahontas and the Lion King.

Sometimes, though, U.S. business has to really work for its market share. In the 1960s, when Mattel, Inc., the world's largest toy company, introduced the Barbie doll to Japan, the world's second largest toy market, it was a crashing failure (Pollack, 1996a). Barbie was simply too threatening to Japanese girls and their mothers. So instead of a toothy smile, Mattel gave Barbie a closed mouth because, in Japan, many women still cover their mouths when they laugh. And instead of presenting her as a fashionable professional woman, Barbie was given a stroller for pushing baby sister Kelly, a more nurturing look that fit with Japan's family-oriented values. These changes helped to make Barbie a success, but not nearly as much as another factor: the simple passage of time and, with it, massive U.S. marketing of *everything*—from Levi's to Holiday Inn to Visa to Friskies cat food. Over time, as Japanese tastes became Americanized in general, Barbie became more

popular (Pollack, 1996a). Today, in fact, Barbie has a cult following—young women can buy Barbie clothing, and the most popular weight-loss diet is "the Barbie diet."

Some critics see global consumerism in strictly negative terms, leading to global homogenization—the loss of cultural practices and distinctive features of a society (Ritzer, 1995:173). But others say that along with homogenizing comes differentiating: If something can be sold in one locale, it can be sold in any locale (Waters, 1995:142). In other words, we're all enriched by global consumerism. Britishers may eat Big Macs instead of fish and chips, but Americans now eat fish and chips—and we drink Perrier mineral water, buy Chanel perfume, and drive Volvos, Toyotas, Volkswagens, and Hyundais. We import from other cultures just as other countries import American culture.

Where do you stand on the global consumerism debate? Can global consumerism be stopped? If it can't be stopped, can it be controlled? Should it be controlled? What do you think?

corporations gained control over major U.S. industries, including the oil, sugar, and grain industries. A *monopoly* exists when a single firm controls an industry and accounts for all sales in a specific market. In early monopoly capitalism, some stockholders derived massive profits from such companies as American Tobacco Company, Westinghouse Electric Corporation, F. W. Woolworth, and Sears, which held near-monopolies on specific goods and services (Hodson and Sullivan, 1995).

In advanced monopoly capitalism (between 1940 and the present), ownership and control of major industrial and business sectors became increasingly concentrated. After World War II, there was a dramatic increase in *oligopoly*—a situation in which a small number of companies or suppliers control an

entire industry or service. Today, a few large corporations use their economic resources—through campaign contributions, PACs, and lobbying—to influence the outcome of government decisions that affect their operations. Smaller corporations have only limited power and resources to bring about political change or keep the largest corporations from dominating the economy.

Today, mergers often occur *across* industries. In this way, corporations gain near-monopoly control over all aspects of the production and distribution of a product because they acquire both the companies that supply the raw materials and the companies that are the outlets for the product. For example, an oil company may hold leases on the land where the oil is pumped out of the ground, own the refineries that convert the oil into gasoline, and own the individual gasoline stations that sell the product to the public. Corporations that have control both within and across industries and are formed by a series of mergers and acquisitions across industries are referred to as *conglomerates*—combinations of businesses in different commercial areas, all of which are owned by one holding company. Media ownership is a case in point (see Chapter 14).

Further complicating corporate structures are *interlocking corporate directorates*—members of the board of directors of one corporation who also sit on the board of one or more other corporations. Although the Clayton Antitrust Act of 1914 made it illegal for a person to sit on the boards of directors of two corporations that are in direct competition with each other at the same time, a person may serve simultaneously on the board of a financial institution (a bank, for example) and the board of a commercial corporation (a computer-manufacturing company or a furniture store chain, for example) that borrows money from the bank. Directors of competing corporations also may serve together on the board of a third corporation that is not in direct competition with the other two. The problem with such interlocking directorates is that they diminish competition by producing interdependence. People serving on multiple boards are in a position to forge cooperative arrangements that benefit their corporations but not necessarily the general public. When several corporations are controlled by the same financial interests, they are more likely to cooperate with one another than to compete (Mintz and Schwartz, 1985). Compensation for board members of top corporations ranges from $15,000 to $50,000 annually, plus stock, stock options, and pensions in the $100,000 to $400,000 range, making the total compensation package as high as $400,000 to $500,000 per board position (Dobrzynski, 1996b).

▲ The National Debt and Consumer Debt

As recently as 1997, the federal government was spending more money each year than it was making. In 1997, for example, the government spent $75 billion dollars more than it took in. A prolonged period of economic expansion in the late 1990s and slower growth in some spending areas has allowed the government to produce a surplus, estimated at $120 bil-

This photo shows an important irony in our consumer society. Just as credit cards and automated gasoline pumps make it easier for consumers to purchase gasoline, these same factors also have significant downside risks. One risk is a substantial increase in consumer debt. What are other risks affecting U.S. workers and the overall economy?

lion in 1999 and $161 billion in 2000 (Congressional Budget Office, 1999); but even with these surpluses, the national government remains deeply in debt. The *national debt* consists of the total amount of money the federal government has borrowed over the years from U.S. citizens and foreign lenders to finance overspending. In late 1999, the national debt was in excess of $5 trillion. How much is that in everyday language? According to political analysts, "If you laid the debt out in dollars from end to end, it would reach out into space four times the distance between the earth and the sun" (Bagby, 1997:47). What would it take to pay off the debt? Consider this: "If Congress paid down the deficit at a dollar every second, it would take 130,000 years, or roughly the amount of time that has passed since the Ice Age, to pay down the present debt" (Bagby, 1997:47).

Like the federal government, many individuals and families in this country are deeply in debt. Consumer debt rose significantly during the 1980s and 1990s; even more worrisome to analysts is the fact that the ratio of consumer debt to income increased. According to a definitive study of bankruptcy, "the most distinguishing characteristic of bankrupt debtors is their high debts in relation to their incomes" (Sullivan et al., 1989:331). Although an increase in consumer debt may benefit the U.S. and global economies, it is detrimental to individuals who cannot pay their bills and must declare bankruptcy (Sullivan et al., 1989).

Two factors contribute to high rates of consumer debt. The first is the instability of economic life in modern society; unemployment and underemployment are commonplace. The second factor is the availability of credit and the extent to which credit card companies and other lenders extend credit beyond people's ability to repay. One study of credit card debt found that about 15 percent of this country's wage earners owe more than half a year's income on credit card debt alone (Sullivan et al., 1989). Some people run up credit card charges that are greatly out of proportion to their income; others cannot pay off the charges they initially believed they could afford when their income is interrupted or drops. For example, "Sally Bowman" (a pseudonym) ran up $20,000 in charges, a sum that was more than half her total yearly income:

> It all started when I graduated from college and took a low-paying job. . . . I didn't want to live like a student so I used credit cards to buy myself furniture and eat dinners out. I wasn't extravagant, I just didn't want to deprive myself. . . . When I got a new card with a $5,000 credit limit, it felt like someone just handed me $5,000. . . . The reality has been that I got in the hole financially. (Tyson, 1993:E1; cited in Ritzer, 1995:67)

Having a high level of consumer debt is a personal problem for people like "Sally Bowman," but it is also a public issue, particularly when credit card issuers negligently give fifth, sixth, or seventh credit cards to people who are already so far in debt that they cannot pay the interest, much less the principal, on their other cards (Sullivan et al., 1989). One businessman had accumulated a total debt of $183,000 on forty-one cards when he received an unsolicited application for still another card, which he accepted and quickly "maxed out" at $5,000 (Ritzer, 1995). According to sociologist George Ritzer, both consumers and credit card companies must become more responsible if consumer debt is to be reduced. Ritzer (1995:71) is particularly critical of banks and credit card companies that entice students in high school or college to become accustomed to buying on credit, saying that it lures many people into a "lifetime of imprudence and indebtedness." He believes that the government should restrain credit card companies by limiting the profits they can make and by restricting mail and telephone campaigns offering incentives to accept new credit cards (Ritzer, 1995). But many people are adamantly opposed to any kind of government intervention in the marketplace, whether it relates to credit cards or anything else. Of course, what some refer to as "government intervention" is viewed by others as corporate welfare.

▲ Corporate Welfare

Corporate welfare occurs when the government helps industries and private corporations in their economic pursuits. Corporate welfare is not new in the United States. Between 1850 and 1900, corporations received government assistance in the form of public subsidies and protection from competition. To encourage westward expansion, the federal government gave large tracts of land to privately owned railroads. Antitrust laws that were originally intended to break up monopolies were used against labor unions that supported workers' interests (Parenti, 1988). Tariffs, patents, and trademarks all serve to protect corporations from competition.

Today, government intervention includes billions of dollars in subsidies to farmers, tax credits for corporations, and large subsidies or loan guarantees to auto makers, aircraft companies, railroads, and others. In 1996, government subsidies included $1.1 million to Campbell Soup for product promotion, $2.6 million to E & J Gallo Winery for product promotion, and $3 million to a cargo ship owner for making his vessel available to the United States during wartime even though the Pentagon no longer wants to use it (Tumulty, 1996). U.S. taxpayers have spent $1 million promoting Uncle Ben's rice in Poland, Turkey, and Saudi Arabia and $2 billion to help keep electric power a bargain in resort communities like Aspen, Colorado, and Hilton Head, South Carolina (Tumulty, 1996). Overall then, most corporations have gained much more than they have lost as a result of government involvement in the economy.

Why do we have corporate welfare programs today? Some can be traced back to the Great Depression in the 1930s, when programs were initiated to bail out companies and stabilize the U.S. economy. Today, for example, billions of dollars in federal subsidies are given to the shipbuilding industry to protect it from foreign competition and to appease maritime unions that want to salvage high-paying jobs for workers. However, even existing ships have difficulty making a profit, so it hardly makes sense to build new ones. Some analysts say that the subsidies continue because of lobbying efforts and political contributions by labor unions and the shipbuilding industry (Tumulty, 1996). As a result, many members of Congress find it is easier to cut back on domestic spending, including Medicare and Medicaid, than to cut corporate handouts (Tumulty, 1996).

PROBLEMS IN U.S. POLITICS

Social scientists distinguish between politics and government: *Politics* **is the social institution through which power is acquired and exercised by some people and groups.** The essential component of politics is *power*—the ability of people to achieve their goals despite opposition from others (see Chapter 2). People who hold positions of power achieve their goals because they have control over other people; those who lack power carry out the wishes of others. Powerful people get others to acquiesce to their demands by using persuasion, authority, or force.

In contemporary societies, the primary political system is *government*—**a formal organization that has legal and political authority to regulate relationships among people in a society and between the society and others outside its borders.** The government (sometimes called *the state*) includes all levels of bureaucratized political activity such as executive, central, and local administrations; the legislature; the courts; and the armed forces and police (Perdue, 1993).

The United States is a *democracy,* **a political system in which the people hold the ruling power either directly or through elected representatives.** In a *direct participatory democracy,* citizens meet regularly to debate and decide issues of the day. Ancient Athens was a direct democracy, as was colonial New England with its town meetings. Even today, many New England towns use the town meeting. However, even in its beginnings, the United States was not a direct democracy. The framers of the Constitution believed that decisions should be made by representatives of the people. To ensure that no single group could control the government, they established a *separation of powers* among the legislative, executive, and judicial branches of government and a *system of checks and balances,* giving each branch some degree of involvement in the activities of the others.

In countries that have some form of *representative democracy,* such as the United States, citizens elect representatives who are responsible for conveying the concerns and interests of those they represent. If these representatives are not responsive to the wishes of the people, voters can unseat them through elections. This is not to say that representative democracy is equally accessible to all people in a nation. The framers of the U.S. Constitution, for example, gave the right to vote only to white males who owned property. Eventually, nonlandowners were given the vote, then African American men, and finally, in 1920, women. Today, democratic participation is at least theoretically available to all U.S. citizens age eighteen and over.

Unfortunately, today voter apathy and influence-buying through campaign contributions threaten to undermine the principles on which our government is based. We'll look at voter apathy first.

Voter Apathy and the Gender Gap

Since 1986, fewer than 40 percent of the eligible voters nationally have participated in elections for the United States Senate and House of Representatives (36.4 percent in 1998). Overall, voter turnout was lower in the 1996 presidential election than it was in the 1992 presidential election, even though the Motor Voter Law of 1995 had made it possible for 15 million people to register to vote when they applied for a driver's license (Bagby, 1997).

What causes voter apathy? According to studies by the Pew Research Center for the People and the Press, many people did not vote in the election because of the strong economy (so they saw no reason to change their representation, though, of course, this is spurious reasoning), excessive polling by media and other groups (people saw no point to voting if the outcomes were predictable), negative advertising by candidates and parties, and because the issues didn't seem as important as those in previous elections. Economic issues are usually the issues that garner the most voters. A nationwide telephone poll by media analysts before the 1992 election found that the U.S. economy and jobs were the top-priority issue of 52 percent of respondents; in a similar poll conducted before the 1996 election, the economy and jobs were the top-priority issue for 11 percent of respondents (*New York Times*, 1997c).

Along with voter apathy, the emergence and persistence of the *gender gap*—**the difference between a candidate's number of votes from women and men**—is a dominant feature of U.S. politics today. Political analysts first noticed a gender gap in the early 1980s, but the gap grew wider and more apparent in the 1996 election. In 1980, the gender gap was about eight points (men were 8 percent more likely than women to support Ronald Reagan for president). In 1996, the gap increased to eleven points (women were eleven percent more likely than men to vote for Bill Clinton). For voters under age thirty, the gap was even wider: Women were 17 percent more likely than men to vote for Clinton. In the forty-five to fifty-nine age category, the gap narrowed; women were only 8 percent more likely than men to vote for Clinton (Bagby, 1997).

Why is there a gender gap? Most analysts agree that the gap is rooted in how women and men view economic and social issues, such as welfare reform, abortion, child care, and education, and what they believe the nation's priorities should be.

Voter apathy and an increase in the gender gap received attention after the 1996 election, but nothing like the scrutiny given to allegations of political influence-buying by large campaign contributors.

▲ Politics and Money in Political Campaigns

Presidential and congressional candidates and their supporters raised and spent more than $2 billion during the 1996 elections—almost double what was spent in the 1992 national elections (Rosenbaum, 1996). Where does all the money go? The cost of running for political office has skyrocketed. Advertising

and media time, staff, direct-mail operations, telephone banks, computers, consultants, travel expenses, office rentals, and many other campaign expenses have increased dramatically over the past two decades. Unless a candidate has private resources, contributions can determine the success or failure of his or her bid for election or reelection.

Certain kinds of campaign contributions are specifically prohibited by law: Corporate contributions to presidential and congressional candidates have been illegal since 1907, and contributions from labor unions were outlawed in 1943. In 1974 (in the Watergate scandal era), Congress passed a law limiting an individual's total contribution to federal candidates to $25,000 a year and no more than $1,000 per candidate. However, these individual limits can be sidestepped by *bundling*, which occurs when a donor collects contributions from family members, business associates, and others and then "bundles" them together and sends them to a candidate. For example, Steve Wynn, a major contributor to Bob Dole's 1996 presidential campaign, bundled money from family members and ninety-nine employees to give Dole a contribution of $78,300 (Gup, 1996).

Federal law also limits individual contributions to a political action committee to a maximum of $5,000. *Political action committees (PACs)* **are special-interest groups that fund campaigns to help elect (or defeat) candidates based on their positions on specific issues.** PACs were originally organized by unions to get around the laws that prohibited union gifts. Today, there are thousands of PACs representing businesses, labor unions, and various single-issue groups (such as gays and lesbians and environmental groups).

Finally, federal law limits contributions made to political parties for campaigning to $25,000, but there is no limit on contributions made for purpose of party-building, such as distributing "vote Democratic" or "vote Republican" bumper stickers or organizing get-out-the-vote drives (Rosenbaum, 1996). However, both the Democratic and Republican parties use these contributions to pay for administrative expenses and overhead, thus freeing up other party money to support candidates. This *soft money loophole*—contributing to a political party instead of to a specific candidate—was a particular issue in the 1997 election. In fact, most of the money donated to campaigns in the 1996 election came through the soft money loophole (Bagby, 1997). Table 13.1 shows how much money the twenty-five largest contributors donated to political parties and federal candidates in

TABLE 13.1   THE 25 LARGEST POLITICAL CONTRIBUTORS

CONTRIBUTIONS TO CANDIDATES, 1997–1998

Contributor	Amount Contributed
Realtors Political Action Committee	$2,474,133
Association of Trial Lawyers of America Political Action Committee	2,428,300
American Federation of State, County & Municipal Employees—People, Qualified	2,374,950
American Medical Association Political Action Committee	2,336,281
Democratic Republican Independent Voter Education Committee	2,183,250
Dealers Election Action Committee of the National Automobile Dealers Association (NADA)	2,107,800
UAW-V-Cap (UAW Voluntary Community Action Program)	1,915,460
International Brotherhood of Electrical Workers Committee on Political Education	1,884,470
National Education Association Political Action Committee	1,853,390
Build Political Action Committee of the National Association of Home Builders	1,807,240
Committee on Letter Carriers Political Education (Letter Carriers Political Action Fund)	1,760,496
Machinists Non-Partisan Political League	1,637,300
NRA Political Victory Fund	1,633,211
United Parcel Service of America Inc. Political Action Committee (UPSPAC)	1,527,149
United Food & Commercial Workers, Active Ballot Club	1,505,951
American Federation of Teachers Committee on Political Education	1,415,400
Laborers' Political League—Laborers' International Union of NA	1,413,850
Carpenters Legislative Improvement Committee, United Brotherhood of Carpenters & Joiners of America	1,372,423
National Association of Life Underwriters Political Action Committee	1,336,000
National Beer Wholesalers' Association Political Action Committee	1,301,719
Service Employees International Union Political Action Committee	1,295,099
United Transportation Union Transportation Political Education League	1,290,875
CWA-COPE Political Contributions Committee	1,219,613
National Federation of Independent Business/Save America's Free Enterprise Trust	1,209,836
American Bankers Association BANKPAC	1,205,350

Source: Federal Election Commission, 1999.

1997–1998. No doubt a large proportion of this money was given through the soft money loophole.

The Federal Election Commission—the enforcement agency that monitors campaign contributions—is considered "one of the most toothless agencies in Washington" (Cohn, 1997). Violations, when discovered, are typically not punished until some time after an election is over. As a result, a very small percentage of the U.S. population is contributing extraordinarily large amounts to get their candidates elected:

The Federal Election Commission's records indicate that in the first 21 months of the Presidential race, both parties took in nearly $470 million in "soft dollars." Republicans raised $274 million in soft money, significantly more than the Democrats, who raised only $195 million. These 21-month totals amount to more than double what was raised in the entire two years of the 1992 Presidential race. . . . To put things in perspective, 99.97% of Americans do not make political contributions over $200. In other words, .03% of the population has the strongest political influence. (Bagby, 1997:76)

During the 1990s, allegations arose that the Republican and Democratic national parties had accepted unethical and/or illegal campaign contributions. After the 1994 congressional elections, it was alleged that a Hong Kong businessman had helped the Republican party raise money to take over Congress. However, the most widely reported allegations of influence-buying by foreign governments, lobbyists, or other special interests involved the Democratic National Committee and the 1996 presidential elections. According to media accounts, in the days and weeks prior to the election, President Bill Clinton and more than twenty-four members of Congress received donations from individuals associated with the Lippo Group, a powerful Indonesian banking group formerly headed by James Riady, a longtime friend and supporter of Clinton. The reports stated that the Lippo Group was hoping to buy influence with a number of government agencies and regulators that could help the group invest millions of dollars in a California bank (*Austin American-Statesman*, 1997a). Through the fund-raising activities of John Huang, a Commerce Department official who formerly worked for the Lippo Group, other foreign contributors also allegedly gave money to the Democratic National Committee, though the committee returned these donations after information about them became public (*Austin American-Statesman,* 1997a). An FBI investigation found that top Chinese officials may have approved financial contributions to U.S. politicians in an effort to influence votes on decisions affecting Chinese interests in this country and elsewhere (Woodward, 1997). But, as one analyst noted, the subsequent Senate inquiry into campaign funding abuses merely proved "the dictum that politics stops at the water's edge" (Clines, 1997:A9). Because the Senate committee's authority is nonexistent outside the United States, senators could not search foreign bank accounts or interview crucial witnesses who were not in the United States or who claimed a constitutional right against self-incrimination (Clines, 1997:A9).

Are influence-buying and unethical campaign contributions recent phenomena? According to journalist Kevin Phillips (1995), influence-buying, particularly by representatives of foreign interests, has been going on for some time in this country. Most political candidates and elected officials do not refuse such contributions or suggest campaign finance reform:

> Were most senators and presidential candidates to refuse contributions from foreign lobbyists or interests, and then further refuse to let lobbyists for foreign interests raise money for them or serve on their campaign committees, the Washington lobbying community would receive a powerful message. This, however, was not an idea anyone ever wanted to discuss. Striking at an accepted culture is not how things are done. . . . A significant overhaul of campaign finance, unlikely through federal legislation, could also come, if it can come at all, from a broader uncorking of populist politics. . . . But attempts to change campaign finance and regulation of lobbyists too often resemble shooting paper clips at a tank because the system is so resistant. Massive infusions of direct democracy and blistering public discussion are the most plausible flamethrowers of change. (Phillips, 1995:247–248)

While the general public realizes that special-interest groups and lobbyists often have undue influence on political decisions and the outcome of elections, most people believe that they are powerless to do anything about it. When respondents in a recent Gallup Poll survey were asked, "Would you say the government is pretty much run by a few big interests looking out for themselves or that it is run for the benefit of all the people?" 76 percent said they believed "big interests" ran the country, only 18 percent believed the government operates for the "benefit of all," and 6 percent had no opinion (Golay and Rollyson, 1996). However, campaign finance reform appears unlikely at the federal level at this time (see Box 13.2).

◢ Government by Special-Interest Groups

What happens when special-interest groups have a major influence on how the government is run? Some special-interest groups exert their influence on single issues such as the environment, gun control, abortion, or legislation that affects a particular occupation (e.g., the American Medical Association) or business (e.g., the National Restaurant Association). During the 1996 elections two of the best-funded and most politically active special-interest groups were the Christian Coalition, which placed political pressure on Republican candidates to stay "right" on issues such as abortion, and the AFL-CIO, which sought to influence candidates to take a prolabor stance on relevant issues (Bagby, 1997).

SOCIAL PROBLEMS

AND SOCIAL POLICY

BOX 13.2

Campaign Reform

[T]he money flowing into the coffers of political candidates and political parties is staggering. It comes from corporations, wealthy individuals, political action committees and other interest groups—all with agendas that often are at odds with what is good for average Americans.

—Donald L. Barlett and James B. Steele of the Philadelphia Inquirer (1996)

It's a real movement that's beginning. People are just tired of money buying influence.

—Ben Senturia of the Missouri Alliance for Campaign Reform (Weiss, 1996)

In the wake of recent elections, several campaign finance reform bills have been put before the U.S. House and Senate. The bipartisan McCain-Feingold bill, for example, seeks to close the soft money loophole.

However, some reformers believe we should strengthen the Federal Election Commission (FEC), the agency that is responsible for enforcing campaign laws. The six commissioners, who must approve all investigations and prosecutions, are "in perpetual deadlock" because each party appoints three commissioners (Cohn, 1997). Nonpartisan watchdogs would make more sense. So would electronic reporting of contributions. Currently, campaign contributions need be reported only monthly for presidential campaigns and quarterly for congressional campaigns; instantaneous electronic reporting would be much easier to monitor.

Other critics say that the only hope for campaign finance reform comes from the state level, where some progress is already evident. Among the states that have passed campaign finance measures are California, Florida, Minnesota, Missouri, Montana, Oregon, and Rhode Island (Weiss, 1996). But even when campaign finance reform passes at the state level, it can be a matter of two steps forward, one back: The laws passed by several of these states have been challenged in court—with mixed results.

Campaign finance reform is a difficult issue. Must we make sweeping national reforms to have any impact? For example, should PAC contributions to candidates be banned? Or should we cut out corporate welfare subsidies and use that money to publicly finance campaigns? The $60 billion a year in subsidies would more than cover the $2.7 billion spent in 1996 federal campaigns (Cohn, 1997). Or is it unrealistic to think that campaign reform can be legislated by the same representatives and senators who must campaign for reelection? Must we begin with average citizens at the state level? What do you think?

Other special-interest groups represent specific industries and make contributions to candidates who will protect their interests and profits. For example, representatives of the tobacco industry make significant contributions to members of Congress who are from states where tobacco is grown, such as Virginia, North Carolina, Kentucky, Missouri, and Mississippi (Fisher, 1995). Officials from tobacco companies and their lobbyists also testify before congressional committees and attend administrative hearings conducted by various federal agencies, including the Food and Drug Administration (about the effects of nicotine on health) and the Federal Trade Commission (about advertising by tobacco companies) (Kluger, 1996). The political power wielded by tobacco company lawyers, lobbyists, and other representatives was evident in 1997 when a federal judge in North Carolina ruled that the Food and Drug Administration could regulate nicotine as a drug but a spokesperson for the FDA said that the agency was not going to regulate the ingredients in cigarettes because so many people were already addicted to the product. In other words, as one journalist put it, "So officials are charting a delicate course. . . . the agency is keeping a watchful distance, focusing instead on how to negotiate the political minefield of tobacco regulation" (Stolberg, 1997b:A1). Although it appears possible that some nationwide agreement may be reached regarding tobacco, some analysts have suggested that issues pertaining to the FDA and the tobacco industry will be tied up in the courts for years to come (Stolberg, 1997b).

Another strong lobby is the sugar industry, which makes major contributions to members of Congress in hopes of maintaining price supports, special loans, and protective restrictions on imports that help to prop up the price of sugar. The price of raw sugar in this country is about 21 cents a pound, roughly double the world price (*New York Times*, 1997d). Higher raw sugar prices translate into higher retail prices for U.S. consumers. Although the price support program may have kept some marginal sugar producers in business, its primary beneficiaries are corporations such as Flo-Sun, which is controlled by José and Alfonso Fanjul (Boller, 1997). The Fanjuls are major contributors to political candidates and to both the Democratic and Republican parties, though it is difficult to determine the amount they give because they bundle contributions from family members and company executives, give through PACs, and make large soft money contributions through companies they own or control (*New York Times*, 1997c). Estimates place their overall 1996 contributions at $902,580 (Boller, 1997), but according to the General Accounting Office, the sugar subsidy adds about 65 million dollars in annual profits to the Fanjuls' bottom line (*New York Times*, 1997d).

Of course, not everyone is represented by a PAC or a special-interest group. As one Senator pointed out, "There aren't any Poor PACs or Food Stamp PACs or Nutrition PACs or Medicare PACs" (quoted in Greenberg and Page, 1993:240). Conversely, "big business" interest groups wield disproportionate power in U.S. politics, undermining the democratic process (Lindblom, 1977; Domhoff, 1978).

 ## Government by Bureaucracy

Special-interest groups wield tremendous political power, but so does the federal bureaucracy. The federal bureaucracy, or *permanent government,* **refers to the top-tier civil service bureaucrats who have a strong power base and play a major role in developing and implementing government policies and procedures.** The federal government played a relatively limited role in everyday life in the nineteenth century, but its role grew during the Great Depression in the 1930s. When faced with high rates of unemployment and persistent poverty, people demanded that the government do something. Public welfare was instituted, security markets were regulated, and programs for labor-management relations were set in place. With better technology and demands that the government "do something" about the problems facing society, government has continued to grow. In fact, since 1960, the federal government has grown faster than any other segment of the U.S. economy. Today, more than 3 million people are employed by the federal bureaucracy, in which much of the actual functioning of the government takes place.

Sociologists point out that bureaucratic power in any sphere tends to take on a life of its own over time, and this is evident in the U.S. government. Despite efforts by presidents, White House staffs, and various presidential cabinets, neither Republican nor Democratic administrations have been able to establish control over the federal bureaucracy (Dye, 2000). In fact, many federal bureaucrats have seen a number of presidents come and go. The vast majority of top-echelon positions have been held by white men for many years. Rising to the top of the bureaucracy may take as long as twenty years, and few white women and people of color have reached these positions (Weiner, 1994).

The government bureaucracy is able to perpetuate itself and expand because many of its employees possess highly specialized knowledge and skills and cannot easily be replaced. As the issues facing the United States have grown in number and complexity, offices and agencies have been established to create rules, policies, and procedures for dealing with such things as nuclear power, environmental protection, and drug safety. These government bureaucracies announce about twenty rules or regulations for every one law passed by Congress (Dye, 2000). Today, public policy is increasingly made by agencies rather than elected officials. The agencies receive little direction from Congress or the president, and while their actions are subject to challenge in the courts, most are highly autonomous.

The federal budget is the central ingredient in the bureaucracy. Preparing the annual federal budget is a major undertaking for the president and the Office of Management and Budget, one of the most important agencies in Washington. Getting the budget approved by Congress is an even more monumental task. However, as Dye (2000) points out, even with the highly publicized wrangling over the budget by the president and Congress, the final congressional appropriations usually are within 2 to 3 percent of the budget originally proposed by the president.

As powerful as the federal bureaucracy has become, it is not immune to special interest groups. Special-interest groups can help an agency to get more operating money. Although the president has budgetary authority over the bureaucracy, any agency that believes that it did not get its fair share can raise a public outcry by contacting friendly interest groups and congressional subcommittees. This outcry can force the president to restore funding to the agency or prod Congress into appropriating money that was not requested by the president, who may go along with the appropriation to avoid a confrontation. Special-interest groups also influence the bureaucracy through the military-industrial complex.

 The Military-Industrial Complex

The term *military-industrial complex* **refers to the interdependence of the military establishment and private military contractors.** The complex is actually a three-way arrangement involving one or more private interest groups (usually corporations that manufacture weapons or other military-related goods), members of Congress who serve on congressional committees or subcommittees that appropriate money for military programs, and a bureaucratic agency (such as the Defense Department). Often, a revolving door of money, influence, and jobs is involved: Military contractors who receive contracts from the Defense Department also serve on advisory committees that recommend what weapons should be ordered. Many people move from job to job, serving in the military, then in the Defense Department, then in military industries (Feagin and Feagin, 1997).

In the 1970s, sociologist C. Wright Mills (1976) stated that the relationship between the military and

The U.S. Air Force F-117 stealth fighter has played a key role in the destruction of targets in nations such as Iraq. What are the benefits of having advanced military technologies such as this? What are the costs?

private industry was problematic and could result in a "permanent war economy" or "military economy" in this country. But economist John Kenneth Galbraith (1985) argued that government expenditures for weapons and jet fighters stimulates the private sector of the economy, creating jobs, and encouraging spending. In other words, military spending by Congress is not an economic burden but a source of economic development. It also enriches those corporations that build jet fighters and other warplanes, such as McDonnell Douglas, Lockheed Martin, and Boeing. According to one executive who has spent much of his career building jet fighters for the U.S. military, getting a $1 trillion Pentagon contract for a new generation of jet fighters is of utmost important to his company: "It's the Super Bowl. It's winner takes all. It's the huge plum. It's the airplane program of the century. If you don't win this program, you're a has-been in tactical aircraft" (quoted in Shenon, 1996b:A1).

The 1997 federal budget allocated $244 billion for military programs, including $44 billion for weapons procurement and $800 million for two attack submarines and other major military systems. This budget also included funding for ongoing military operations in Bosnia and southern Iraq (Bagby, 1997). In budget negotiations, President Clinton and the Republican-controlled Congress agreed to $85 billion in military cuts over the five-year period from 1997 through 2002 (Stevenson, 1997). Even so, many members of Congress actively support military spending, particularly if it benefits their local constituencies economically in the form of defense contracts or support for military bases or space centers. When members of Congress secure government funding for projects that will bring jobs and tax money to their home districts, it is called *pork barreling* (Greenberg and Page, 1993).

Despite the large sums in the federal budget for defense spending, the overall amount that we spend on defense is lower than it was in the 1980s. For example, in 1997 the United States spent only 3.6 percent of its gross domestic product—the total value of the nation's annual output of goods and services—on the military, compared to 6.3 percent in 1986 (Bagby, 1997). When the Cold War ended in the 1980s, the United States downsized its defense industries and found new markets for arms made by U.S. manufacturers. We are now the major supplier of weapons to the developing nations of the world; in fact, the United States and Western Europe combined provide over 75 percent of all arms transfers to developing nations.

From one point of view, the United States will always have an active military-industrial complex because of our emphasis on *militarism*—a societal focus on military ideals and an aggressive preparedness for war. The belief in militarism is maintained and reinforced by values such as patriotism, courage, reverence, loyalty, obedience, and faith in authority, as sociologist Cynthia H. Enloe (1987: 542–543) explains:

Military expenditures, militaristic values, and military authority now influence the flow of foreign trade and determine which countries will or will not receive agricultural assistance. They shape the design and marketing of children's toys and games and of adult fashions and entertainment. Military definitions of progress and security dominate the economic fate of entire geographic regions. The military's ways of doing business open or shut access to information and technology for entire social groups. Finally, military mythologies of valor and safety influence the sense of self-esteem and well-being of millions of people.

SOCIOLOGICAL PERSPECTIVES ON THE POLITICAL ECONOMY

Politics and the economy are so intertwined in the United States that many social scientists speak of the two as a single entity, the *political economy.* At issue for most social scientists is whether political and economic power are concentrated in the hands of the few or distributed among the many in this country. Functionalists adopt a pluralistic model of power, while conflict theorists adopt an elitist model.

 The Functionalist Perspective

Pluralism is rooted in the functionalist perspective, which assumes that people generally agree on the most important societal concerns—freedom and security—and that government fulfills important functions in these two regards that no other institution can fulfill. According to the early functionalists, government serves to socialize people to be good citizens, to regulate the economy so that it operates effectively, and to provide necessary services for citizens (Durkheim, 1933/1893). Contemporary functionalists identify four similar functions: A government maintains law and order, plans society and coordinates other institutions, meets social needs, and handles international relations, including warfare.

But what happens when people do not agree on specific issues or concerns? Functionalists say that divergent viewpoints lead to political pluralism; that is, when competing interests or viewpoints arise, government arbitrates. Thus, according to the *pluralist model,* **power is widely dispersed throughout many competing interest groups in our political system** (Dahl, 1961). In the pluralist model, (1) political leaders make decisions on behalf of the people through a process of bargaining, accommodation, and compromise; (2) leadership groups (such as business, labor, law, and consumer organizations) serve as watchdogs to protect ordinary people from the abuses of any one group; (3) ordinary people influence public policy through voting and participating in special-interest groups; (4) power is widely dispersed in society (the same groups aren't equally influential in all arenas); and (5) public policy reflects a balance among competing interest groups, not the majority group's view (Dye, 2000).

How might a social analyst who uses a functionalist framework address problems in politics and the economy? Such an analyst might begin by saying that since dysfunctions are inevitable in any social institution, it is important to sort out and remedy the specific elements of the system that are creating the problems. It should not be necessary to restructure or replace the entire system. Consider, for example, government regulations: Some regulations are good, and some are bad. The trick, functionalists say, is to keep the good ones and get rid of the bad (Barlett and Steele, 1996). Too often, the U.S. government moves between two extremes: overregulation of business and society or seeking to end most, if not all, regulation. As social analysts Donald L. Barlett and James B. Steele (1996:214) suggest, "We must preserve the rules that assure the quality of American life: the food you eat, the medicines you take, the air you breathe and the water you drink. They have evolved over a century." Barlett and Steele go on to say, however, that demanding that U.S.-owned companies comply with regulations that are not required of their competitors in foreign countries creates an uneven playing field. Hence a tariff should be imposed on imported products equal to the amount of money that U.S. businesses must spend to comply with government regulations (Barlett and Steele, 1996). This perspective is based on the belief that a certain amount of government intervention in the economy is appropriate but that too much—or the wrong kind—is detrimental.

The Conflict Perspective

Most conflict theorists believe democracy is an ideal, not a reality, in our society today because the government primarily benefits the wealthy and the politically powerful, especially business elites. In fact, according to conflict theorists, economic and political elites use the powers of the government to impose their will on the masses. According to the **elite model, power in political systems is concentrated in the hands of a small group, whereas the masses are relatively powerless.** In the elite model, (1) elites possess the greatest wealth, education, status, and other resources and make the most important decisions in society; (2) elites generally agree on the basic values and goals for the society; (3) power is highly concentrated at the top of a pyramid-shaped social hierarchy, and those at the top set

public policy for everyone; (4) public policy reflects the values and preferences of the elite, not of ordinary people; and (5) elites use the media to shape the political attitudes of ordinary people (Dye, 2000).

According to sociologist C. Wright Mills (1959a), the United States is ruled by a **power elite, which at the top is composed of business leaders, the executive branch of the federal government, and the military (especially the "top brass" at the Pentagon).** The corporate rich—the highest-paid CEOs of major corporations—are the most powerful because they have the unique ability to parlay their vast economic resources into political power. The next most powerful level is occupied by Congress, special-interest groups, and local opinion leaders. The lowest (and widest) level of the pyramid is occupied by ordinary people, the unorganized masses who are relatively powerless and vulnerable to economic and political exploitation.

Individuals in the power elite have similar class backgrounds and interests and interact on a regular basis. Through a revolving door of influence, they tend to shift back and forth between and among the business, government, and military sectors. It is not unusual for people who have served in the president's cabinet to become directors of major corporations that do business with the government, for powerful businesspeople to serve in the cabinet, or for former military leaders to become important businesspeople. Through such political and economic alliances, people in the power elite can influence many important decisions, including how federal tax money will be spent and to whom lucrative subsidies and government contracts are awarded.

In his analysis of the political economy, sociologist G. William Domhoff (1978) speaks of a *ruling class,* which is made up of the corporate rich, a relatively fixed group of privileged people who wield power over political processes and serve capitalist interests. The corporate rich influence the political process in three ways: (1) by financing campaigns of candidates who favor their causes; (2) by using PACs and loophole contributions to obtain favors, tax breaks, and favorable regulatory rulings; and (3) by gaining appointment to governmental advisory committees, presidential commissions, and other governmental positions. For example, some members of the ruling class influence international politics through their involvement in banking, business services, and law firms that have a strong interest in overseas sales, investments, or raw materials extraction (Domhoff, 1990).

Some analysts who take a conflict perspective say that the only way to overcome problems in politics and the economy is to change the entire system. Our present system exploits poor whites, people of color, women of all colors, people with disabilities, and others who consider themselves disenfranchised from the political and economic mainstream of society.

Other conflict theorists think that we can solve many problems by curbing the abuses of capitalism and the market economy and thereby reducing the power of political and economic elites. Political scientist Benjamin R. Barber believes that we cannot rely on the capitalist (market) economy to look after common interests:

It is the job of civil society and democratic government and not of the market to look after common interests and make sure that those who profit from the common planet pay its common proprietors their fair share. When governments abdicate in favor of markets, they are declaring *nolo contendere* [no contest] in an arena in which they are supposed to be primary challengers, bartering away the rights of their people along the way. . . .

Markets simply are not designed to do the things democratic polities do. They enjoin private rather than public modes of discourse, allowing us as consumers to speak via our currencies of consumption to producers of material goods, but ignoring us as citizens speaking to one another about such things as the social consequences of our private market choices. . . . They advance individualistic rather than social goals. . . . Having created the conditions that make markets possible, democracy must also do all the things that markets undo or cannot do. It must educate citizens so that they can use their markets wisely and contain market abuses well. (Barber, 1996:242)

PROBLEMS IN POLITICS AND THE ECONOMY IN THE TWENTY-FIRST CENTURY

What will U.S. politics and the economy be like as we progress through the twenty-first century? There is no single vision, of course, but many social analysts think that *digital democracy*—the use of information technologies such as the Internet and the World Wide Web—will dramatically change not only economic relationships but also the way in which politics and government are conducted. For example, digital democracy can inform people about political candidates and issues. Volunteers use e-mail and Web sites to encourage people to go to the polls and vote for their candidate. They also send messages to voters who indicate an interest in a specific topic.

Most analysts agree that the 1996 election was just the beginning of digital grass-roots activism in U.S. politics. The World Wide Web, cable access channels, and other new information technologies have radically democratized access to political information. However, critics point out that there are some major problems with trying to maintain a pluralist democracy through digital democracy:

The ultimate threats to American democracy in the digital age aren't the rise of splinter groups, or new tycoons, or government-imposed limits on speech. The dangers are more subtle and insidious. One is the lack of a common starting point for discussion. . . . If anyone can see the world from any angle—if everything is relative and the dominant reality virtual—where's the place called America?. . . . The other danger is that leadership as we knew it . . . will disappear as politicians become all too connected to the voters. . . . What if our presidents become nothing more than the sum of our whims and misinformation? The netizens of the future will have to take their jobs seriously. Are we ready for this much democracy? Let's hope so. (Fineman, 1997:52)

Is it possible that the U.S. economy and democratic politics will become obsolete in the face of the global economy and digitized democracy? Despite digital democracy and the transnational nature of politics and the economy, scholars such as Paul Kennedy (1993:134) argue that individual nations will remain the primary locus of identity for most people. Regardless of who their employers are and what they do for a living, individuals pay taxes to a specific government, are subject to its laws, serve in its armed forces, and can travel only by having its passport. Therefore, as new challenges arise, most people in democracies will turn to their own governments and demand solutions.

SUMMARY

➤ *How are societies classified by their predominant type of work?*

Societies are classified as preindustrial, industrial, or postindustrial. Preindustrial societies engage in primary sector production—the extraction of raw materials and natural resources from the environment. Industrial societies engage in secondary sector production—the processing of raw materials (from the primary sector). Two major problems in industrial societies are job deskilling (doing a job with fewer skills) and deindustrialization (diverting capital from investment in basic industries to mergers and acquisitions and foreign investment). Postindustrial societies engage in tertiary sector production—providing services rather than goods.

➤ *What kind of economic system does the United States have?*

The United States has a capitalist economy. Ideally, capitalism is characterized by private ownership of the means of production, pursuit of personal profit, competition, and lack of government intervention.

➤ *What are transnational corporations, and why do they pose social problems?*

Transnational corporations are large-scale business organizations headquartered in one country but operating in many countries. Transnationals lack accountability to any government or regulatory agency. They are not dependent on any one country for labor, capital, or technology. They can play important roles in the economies and governments of countries that need them as employers and accept their practices.

➤ *Why is the national debt a serious problem? How is consumer debt a public issue?*

When we increase the national debt, we are borrowing from future generations, which will leave them with higher taxes, fewer benefits, and a lower rate of economic growth. Consumer debt becomes a public issue when people cannot repay their credit card loans.

➤ *What is corporate welfare?*

Corporate welfare occurs when the government helps industries and private corporations in their economic pursuits. Many subsidies that were originally put in place to help stabilize the economy continue unnecessarily because of labor union and PAC lobbying and campaign contributions.

➤ *Why is voter apathy a problem? What is the gender gap?*

Voter apathy undermines the basis on which representative democracy is built; if large numbers of people don't vote, the interests of only a few are represented. The gender gap is the difference between a candidate's number of votes from women and men. More than ever today, women and men seem to view economic and social issues differently.

➤ *Why have campaign contributions become an issue in recent elections?*

Campaign contributions are regulated, but individuals, unions, and corporations circumvent the law through the soft money loophole—contributing to a political party instead of to a specific candidate—and through political action committees. Political action committees (PACs) are special-interest groups that fund campaigns to help elect (or defeat) candidates on the basis of their positions on specific issues. Because running for office is expensive, contributions can make the difference between a candidate's success or defeat. However, there is always the risk that special-interest groups use campaign contributions as a means of buying political influence, as has been alleged with the tobacco and sugar industries.

➤ *What is the military-industrial complex?*

The military-industrial complex refers to the interdependence of the military establishment and private military contractors. The military-industrial complex can be a revolving door of money, influence, and jobs.

➤ *What are the sociological perspectives on the political economy?*

The functionalists use a pluralist model, believing that power is widely dispersed through many competing interest groups in our political system. Functionalists therefore believe that problems can be solved by identifying dysfunctional elements and correcting them. Conflict theorists use an elite model, believing that power in political systems is concentrated in the hands of a small group, whereas the masses are relatively powerless. Sociologist C. Wright Mills used the term *power elite* for this small group of top business leaders, the executive branch of the federal government, and the "top brass" of the military.

KEY TERMS

deindustrialization, p. 274
democracy, p. 282
elite model, p. 290
gender gap, p. 283
government, p. 282
military-industrial complex, p. 288
mixed economy, p. 276
monopoly, p. 279

oligopoly, p. 279
permanent government, p. 287
pluralist model, p. 289
politics, p. 282
political action committees (PACs), p. 283
power elite, p. 290
primary sector production, p. 274

secondary sector production, p. 274
socialism, p. 276
tertiary sector production, p. 275
transnational corporation, p. 277

QUESTIONS FOR CRITICAL THINKING

1. Imagine that you are given unlimited funds and resources to reverse the trend in voter apathy. What would you do at the local level? What would you do at the state and national levels?

2. How would you respond to the Gallup Poll survey question: "Would you say the government is pretty much run by a few big interests looking out for themselves or that it is run for the benefit of all the people?" Explain your answer.

3. Do you favor or oppose sociologist George Ritzer's proposal that the government restrain credit card companies? Do you agree with his means—limiting profit and restricting incentives for accepting new credit cards? Would you propose other means?

Chapter Fourteen

Problems in the Media

On the highway these days, you can't help noticing the familiar flicker of the television set shining in the windows—of other vehicles. Not just luxury limousines; some buses now have rows of little TV sets suspended over the seats. . . . [T]his trend of TV in buses disturbs [me]. It means there's almost *no place* left in this country where you can go without being entertained. Americans today demand entertainment. We expect it. We're surprised when there's not entertainment everywhere. We punish those who dare to be dull.

When I was a boy . . . we didn't have television sets on buses, or in many homes. Now they're even putting TV sets in public bathrooms. (Why should anybody miss a minute of *General Hospital*?)

—Dan Rather, anchor and managing editor of CBS Evening News, describing how omnipresent he believes television sets have become in the United States (1999:183–184)

Suddenly, I'm worried. Like so many other Americans, I'm using the Internet a lot now and am enjoying its complexity and enormity—even its chaos. But I'm aware that with every click I'm being watched, perhaps as I've never been watched before. When I consider my cyber future, how should I conceptualize my privacy?

—Colin Harrison, deputy editor of Harper's Magazine, discussing his concerns about privacy in the age of information technology (*Harper's Magazine*, 2000:58)

The media play a vital role in the daily lives of many people. Whether we realize their existence or try to ignore their influence, various forms of the media are with us constantly. What constitutes the media? Media is the plural of *medium,* which refers to any device that transmits a message. Thus, as we noted in Chapter 4, the media include newspapers, magazines, television, and movies among other things. When sociologists refer to the media (or mass media), however, they are usually speaking of the *media industries*—**major businesses that own or own interests in radio and television production and broadcasting; motion pictures, movie theaters, and music companies; newspaper, periodical (magazine) and book publishing; and Internet services and content providers; and that influence people and cultures worldwide.** To understand how pervasive media industries are in our daily lives, consider one day in the life of Scott Schatzkamer, a college student who reported that on October 6, 1999, he awakened to the sound of an AM/FM adult-contemporary radio station and, during the day and evening, watched ESPN's *SportsCenter* (owned by Disney), read part of Time Warner's *Sports Illustrated,* listened to a radio station owned by Disney, played Electronic Arts' *Madden NFL 2000* on his fraternity's Sony PlayStation, checked his e-mail several times on AOL, logged on to ESPN.com for sports scores, read assignments in *General Chemistry* (published by Houghton Mifflin) and *Psychology in Perspective* (published by Pearson), and watched a baseball game on News Corporation's Fox Network (Heilbrunn, 2000). Recent estimates show that the average person in the United States spends more than one-half of his or her waking hours in some media-related activity. Indeed, today, many people spend more time in media-related activities (see Table 14.1) than they do in any other single endeavor, including sleeping, working, eating, or talking with friends and family (Biagi, 1998).

Is this time well spent? Most analysts and media scholars agree that the media industries that emerged in the twentieth century are one of the most significant social institutions at work in the United States and many other nations. They facilitate human communication and provide news and entertainment. By doing so, however, they have a powerful influence on all other social institutions, including education, health care delivery, religion, families, and politics. Some aspects of this influence are positive, but other

TABLE 14.1 HOW MUCH TIME DO PEOPLE SPEND WITH MASS MEDIA?

It is estimated that the average U.S. adult age 18 and older (except as noted) spent the following number of hours with various forms of media in 1998:

TYPE OF MEDIA	NUMBER OF HOURS
Television (including pay cable)	1,552
Radio	1,085
Recorded music*	303
Daily newspapers	157
Books	96
Magazines	80
Home video	54
Home video games*	31
Consumer-online Internet access	30
Movies in theaters*	11
Educational software	2

*Includes people age twelve and older
Source: U.S. Bureau of the Census, 1998.

aspects may be negative. Some critics who are concerned about possible negative influences note that we are experiencing a media glut and increasing commercialization of all aspects of life (Biagi, 1998). For example, commercialization of the Internet and the rise of the World Wide Web in the 1990s has magnified the amount of media messages and products that confront people who use computers and online services (McChesney, 1999). Other critics question the effects of contemporary media ownership on U.S. democracy (McChesney, 1999). They point out that radio, television, newspapers, and the Internet are the main sources of news and entertainment for most people; therefore, it is important to know who owns the media and to assess the quality of the information that is disseminated (Biagi, 1998; McChesney, 1999).

THE POLITICAL ECONOMY OF MEDIA INDUSTRIES

How did the contemporary media industries come to be known as "Big Media"? The answer seems to lie in one word—technology. Technology, in the form of motion pictures, radio, and television, increased competition and broadened markets in the twentieth century. Prior to that, newspapers and books had been the primary means of disseminating information and entertainment to large numbers of people simultaneously. The companies involved in these forms of media were usually small and focused on a single output: Newspapers were produced by companies whose only business was newspapers, and books were published by companies whose only business was books (Biagi, 1998). However, at least two factors limited the market for the information and entertainment provided by the newspaper and publishing industries: the length of time it took to get the product to consumers and the consumer's literacy. Radio, on the other hand, offered consumers immediate access to information and entertainment from coast to coast. Introduced in 1920, radio promptly became a competitor to the newspaper and publishing industries. Simply by turning a knob, consumers could listen to the latest news (sometimes even as it happened), hear the latest song, laugh with their favorite comedian, or thrill to the adventures of their favorite detective. Both consumers and corporate executives alike felt that radio's dominance in the media industries could not be shaken. Still, in the 1950s, a new technology emerged to threaten the newspaper and radio industries—television. Television had all the advantages of radio and one more, moving images. Now consumers could not only listen to the world around them, they could watch it.

 ## Media Ownership and Control

Just as technology played a significant role in the development of the media industries, it has played a significant role in the changes that have occurred within these industries.

Consider, for a moment, the effects that fiber optic cable, broadcast satellites, and computers have had on these industries. The introduction of cable television, for example, brought about a significant shift in media ownership. The development of more sophisticated space satellites in the 1970s made it possible for cable television systems to become interconnected throughout the United States and contributed to the success of cable networks such as Home Box Office (HBO) and Cable News Network (CNN), for which viewers pay a monthly fee. Having a variety of cable channels to watch increased the number of cable TV subscribers, resulting in more broadcast stations being built and the creation of

additional cable channels. At the same time, the dramatic increase in cable television viewers drastically reduced the audience share previously held by the "Big Three" television networks—NBC, CBS, and ABC (Budd, Craig, and Steinman, 1999)—and led to rapid changes in the ownership and control of these networks. Within a few months in the mid-1980s, the three major networks, which had seemed indomitable, all changed ownership through purchases, takeovers, and mergers.

Although these changes seemed to have occurred overnight, some analysts point out that since the 1960s, media ownership has become increasingly more concentrated, and the trend has been for a few megacorporations to own most media businesses and for companies to own more than one form of the media business (Biagi, 1998). Still, as a result of the changes in the "Big Three," a few megacorporations gained a great deal of control over all aspects of the television industry, from program production to distribution to the audience. In their never ending search for profit, these corporations also consolidated their holdings in other sectors of the media, ranging from film and music production to books and magazine publishing. They also acquired interests in technologies such as computers and direct broadcasting from satellite (Budd, Craig, and Steinman, 1999). At the beginning of 2000, America Online (AOL) and Time Warner agreed to enter into the largest media merger to date. Why would the largest worldwide media company, Time Warner, agree to join AOL? The answer lies in access to the Internet, which is central to the contemporary music, publishing, and television industries (Hansell, 2000). Through the merger, AOL's 22 million subscribers (as of January 2000) would be linked to Time Warner's cable television systems, which have about 13 million customers. Analysts describe these types of mergers in the media industries as *convergence,* meaning that a melding of the communications, computer, and electronics industries has occurred. Convergence in the media industry has led to media concentration (Rosenwein, 2000). **Media concentration refers to the tendency of the media industries to cluster together in groups with the goal of enhancing profitability** (Biagi, 1998). Figure 14.1 shows some of the top media industries.

As this definition suggests, profit is the driving force in media concentration. According to media scholar Shirley Biagi (1998:263), "Media companies are owned by people who want to make money." Since profits in this sector are high compared with

NEWS CORP.	AOL TIME WARNER	UNIVERSAL/SEAGRAM	WALT DISNEY
Avon Books British Sky 　Broadcasting Fox Broadcasting 　Company Fox News Channel Fox Television Fox Television 　Stations FX Networks HarperCollins Los Angeles Dodgers *New York Post* William Morrow 　Publishing	America Online Atlanta Braves Atlanta Hawks Book of the Month 　Club Cartoon Network CNN CNNfn CNN/*Sports Illustrated* *Fortune* *In Style* Little, Brown and 　Company New Line Cinema *Parenting* *People* *Southern Living* *Sports Illustrated* TBS Superstation *Time* Turner Network 　Television Warner Bros. Studio 　Stores Warner Music Group World Championship 　Wrestling	A&M Records Interscope Records Island Def Jam Music 　Group Motown Records Spencer Gifts Universal Pictures Universal Studios 　Hollywood Wet 'n Wild	ABC Radio Network ABC Television 　Network ABC radio and 　television stations Anaheim Angels *Discover* magazine Disney Channel Disneyland Resort Go Network Hyperion Books *Los Angeles* 　magazine Mighty Ducks of 　Anaheim Miramax Films The Disney Store Walt Disney Studios

FIGURE 14.1 *Big Media Conglomerates*

profits in the manufacturing sector, businesspeople view investments in the media industries positively. Thus far, corporate megamergers have led to the following changes in the media industries (based on Biagi, 1998):

1. *Concentration of ownership within one industry.* For example, ten newspaper chains own 20 percent of all the daily newspapers in the United States. Among the top ten are the Gannett Company, Knight-Ridder, Newhouse, Times Mirror, Dow Jones, the New York Times Company, and Thomson. These chains control more than 280 daily newspapers. Each firm is ranked among the 1000 largest firms in the world and does over $1 billion in business per year (Biagi, 1998; McChesney, 1999).

2. *Cross-media ownership.* Cross-media ownership occurs when media companies own more than one type of media property. Today, a single giant media corporation may own newspapers, magazines, radio, and television stations. Even among smaller media corporations, cross-media ownership is common. For example, the A. H. Belo Corporation of Dallas, Texas, owns seventeen television stations and eight newspapers around the country (dmnweb, 1999). In some cases, the newspapers and TV stations are the prevalent information source in one geographic region. When people in Central Texas, for example, wanted to find out about the 1999 tragedy at Texas A&M University in Bryan/College Station, Texas, in which eleven students and one former student were killed while building a massive bonfire site, they turned to the *Bryan-College Station Eagle,* the *Dallas Morning News,* and *WFAA TV* in Dallas, all of which are owned by the Belo Corporation.

3. *Conglomerate ownership.* Conglomerates occur when a single corporation owns companies that

operate in different business sectors. General Electric, one of the leading electronics and manufacturing firms in the United States, owns NBC Television Network, NBC Studios, thirteen local NBC television stations, and (with Microsoft) MSNBC. Universal/Seagram is a conglomerate created by the acquisition of MCA/Universal by Seagram, the Canadian liquor company (*Brill's Content,* 2000). Seagram Company owns theme parks, concert halls, motion picture production companies, movie theaters, and retail stores such as Spencer Gifts (Budd, Craig, and Steinman, 1999).

4. *Vertical integration.* Vertical integration occurs when the corporations that make the media content also control the distribution channels. Walt Disney Company, for example, owns film and television production companies (Touchstone Pictures and ABC Entertainment Television Group), which supply programming for its television network (ABC), which helps to promote cable channels that are owned in part by Disney (ESPN, Lifetime TV, E! Entertainment TV, and the History Channel). These in turn have ties with Hyperion, the Disney book publishing unit (Rosenwein, 2000; *Brill's Content,* 2000).

Supporters of convergence believe that much can be gained by these corporate strategies and speak of synergy. The term *synergy* is often used to describe the process used in capitalizing on a product to make all the profit possible. Media analysts believe that synergy is created, for example, when a corporation acquires ownership of both a production studio and a television network. Theoretically, the products made by one branch of the company may be distributed and sold by the other branch of the company in a more efficient and profitable manner than if separate companies were involved. Rupert Murdoch's News Corporation is a good example of synergy. News Corporation produces the television program "X-Files," airs it over its Fox network as well as its worldwide television channels, and then shows reruns on twenty-two Fox television stations and the FX cable network. "X-Files" books and other related merchandise are created and sold through subsidiaries of News Corporation. A movie version of the "X-Files" was made by Twentieth Century Fox, which is also owned by News Corporation.

Most people in the media industries do not see consolidation as a problem. For example, the editor of

Time, Inc., a unit of Time Warner, believes that "the real story of the last 20 years is the proliferation of media" (Rosenwein, 2000:94). However, some media executives have acknowledged that the close link between their sectors may lead to conflicts of interest or accusations of collusion. Michael Eisner, chairman of Disney, has stated that he believes ABC News (which is owned by Disney) should not cover Disney: "I think it's inappropriate for Disney to be covered by Disney. . . . By and large, the way you avoid conflict of interest is to, as best you can, not cover yourself" (Rosenwein, 2000:94). However, according to *Brill's Content,* Eisner's comments were made only days before ABC News killed a story about Disney's unintentionally hiring convicted pedophiles to work at its theme parks (Rosenwein, 2000).

◣ Problems Associated with Convergence

As Table 14.2 indicates, concentration and conglomeration are profitable for investors and media executives. In 1999, 62 members of the *Forbes* list of the 400 wealthiest people in the United States had gained their wealth from media and entertainment, and 71 had gained their wealth from technology and software (*Forbes,* 1999). However, many analysts believe that convergence has reduced the amount of *message pluralism,* the "broad and diverse representation of opinion and culture," available to the public (Biagi, 1998:265). As one media scholar has noted, as a result of convergence

> . . . media fare is even more closely linked to the needs and concerns of a handful of enormous and powerful corporations, with annual revenues approaching the [Gross Domestic Product] of a small nation. These firms are run by wealthy managers and billionaires with clear stakes in the outcome of the most fundamental political issues, and their interests are often distinct from those of the vast majority of humanity. By any known theory of democracy, such a concentration of economic, cultural, and political power into so few hands—and mostly unaccountable hands at that—is absurd and unacceptable. On the other hand, media fare is subjected to an ever-greater commercialization as the dominant firms use their market power to squeeze the greatest possible profit from their products. (McChesney, 1999:29–30)

TABLE 14.2	SELECTED MEDIA MOGULS AND THEIR WEALTH	
PERSON	**KEY MEDIA BUSINESS INTERESTS**	**ESTIMATED WEALTH**
Sumner Redstone	Viacom (MTV, Nickelodeon, Paramount)	$9.4 billion
Robert E. (Ted) Turner	Television; founder of Cable News Network (CNN)	6.9 billion
Rupert Murdoch	News Corporation (FOX, cable channels, Web sites)	6.8 billion
David Geffen	Recording industry and movies (Dreamworks)	2.7 billion
Michael Bloomberg	Cable television, radio (covering financial industry)	2.5 billion
George Lucas	Film producer (*Star Wars*)	2.5 billion
Steven Spielberg	Film producer/director (*Saving Private Ryan; Schindler's List*)	2.0 billion
Barry Diller	Television (USA Networks; Ticketmaster, BET.com)	950 million
Roy Disney	Nephew of Walt Disney (*The Lion King*)	900 million
Oprah Winfrey	Television talk show host; with Disney Corporation produces television movies, books, videos, and feature films	725 million

Source: Forbes, 1999:238–248.

Do you see the Starbucks coffee on the table? That distinctive cup did not get into the Austin Powers 2 film accidentally. Corporations such as Starbucks pay millions of dollars for "product placements" in the media so that consumers will be constantly reminded to buy their brand. How is branding such as this changing films and the Internet?

As this statement suggests, other industries have used convergence in the media industries to increase their own market shares. Advertising agencies have found that convergence has allowed them to perfect the process of branding. Consider the following example:

Coca-Cola not only spent $30 million running Diet Coke ads with characters from *Friends* during episodes of that and other shows, but it organized a contest around matching actors' names with Diet coke caps. . . . [The company gave] away *Friends* sunglasses and T-shirts, and sponsored a special one-hour episode after the 1996 Super Bowl that had been filmed before an audience that included 100 contest winners and a special commercial for *Friends*/Diet Coke. . . . A Coke executive told reporters, "It's no longer a promotion—it's a lifestyle." (Budd, Craig, and Steinman, 1999:164)

Commercialization and branding have already found their way to the Internet, which, even as it is hailed as a new source of news and entertainment that is relatively free from corporate constraints (see Box 14.1 on pages 302 and 303), has experienced criticism similar to the criticism leveled at more established forms of media.

Among the problems that analysts believe have been brought about by convergence are (1) the decline of journalism as a public service profession, (2) constant pressure for all journalistic endeavors to be immediately profitable, (3) a significant decrease in the quantity and quality of international news available to U.S. audiences, (4) the quashing of public debate about the power of the media industries and how they deal with important social issues, and (5) a dramatic increase in the influence of powerful Washington lobbyists who represent the interests of the media conglomerates (McChesney, 1999; Phillips, 1999). Because the reach of the media industries is worldwide, these concerns are not limited to the United States.

GLOBAL MEDIA ISSUES

To understand the effect transnational media corporations may have on other nations of the world, consider this: Six major media conglomerates—Time Warner, Sony, Viacom, Disney, Bertelsmann, and News Corporation—control most of the publishing, recording, television, film, and mega–theme park business in the high-income nations of the world. Of these, Time Warner and Disney have the largest media and entertainment operations. Time Warner has 200 subsidiaries worldwide. The corporation owns controlling interest not only in CNN (Cable News Network) in the United States but also CNN International, which broadcasts in several languages to more than 200 nations (McChesney, 1999).

Perhaps it should not be surprising that advertising by transnational corporations has fueled the rise of commercial television, and consequently the profitability of media conglomerates, around the world. For example, more than half of the advertising on the ABN-CNBC Asia network (which is co-owned by Dow Jones and General Electric) is for transnational corporations, most of which are U.S.-based businesses (McChesney, 1999). As international agreements over trade, such as NAFTA (the North American Free Trade Agreement) and GATT (the General Agreement on Tariffs and Trade) have come into effect, companies in fields such as oil production, aerospace engineering, and agribusiness have used transnational media corporations to improve their communication base and extend their international operations

(Schiller, 1996). All in all, then, the global economy has proved profitable for media conglomerates. It has been estimated that between 50 and 60 percent of all the revenues generated by U.S. film and television production companies is made in nations other than the United States (McChesney, 1999).

Among analysts, however, there is growing concern about the amount of control a few media giants have over the world's information. Some have predicted that major media conglomerates will soon control about 90 percent of all global information (Kilbourne, 1999). These same few giant media companies are rapidly gaining ownership and control of both the hardware and software that will make it possible for them to fully control messages and images appearing in any format (Schiller, 1996; Kilbourne, 1999). This fact may be particularly alarming to those who are already critical of how the media giants depict other nations (see Box 14.2 on pages 304 and 305).

While global media industries obviously provide news and entertainment to people who otherwise might not know what is going on in the world, according to media critic Robert McChesney (1999), they also contribute to the development of "neo-liberal" democracies in those nations in which people have the formal right to vote but the wealthy actually hold political and economic power:

> The global commercial media system is *radical,* in the sense that it will respect no tradition or custom, on balance, if it stands in the way of significantly increased profits. But it ultimately is politically *conservative,* because the media giants are significant beneficiaries of the current global social structure, and any upheaval in property or social relations, particularly to the extent it reduced the power of business and lessened inequality, would possibly—no, probably—jeopardize their positions. (McChesney, 1999:100).

Many critics also worry that the U.S.-based giants undermine traditional cultural values and beliefs, replacing them with U.S. values, particularly those supporting materialism and consumerism. According to media critic Jean Kilbourne (1999:55), "Although the conglomerates are transnational, the culture they sell is American. . . . Today we export a popular culture that promotes escapism,

SOCIAL PROBLEMS

Virtual Media versus the Mainstream Press

It's 8:30, do you know where your brains are?

—*This question starts off each half-hour show on Paper Tiger TV, a public access television organization in New York City, San Francisco, and several other large media markets (Jenik, 1999).*

You're no longer just restricted to what gets fed to you on the evening news. Individuals are able to access content on their own.

—*Eileen Quigley, director of Real Impact, a company that specializes in streaming technology, which allows a computer to receive digital information and show it on-screen at the same time, and thus allows people to observe events as they happen, without editing or commercial interruptions (quoted in Paton, 1999)*

As the corporate media industries have become increasingly concentrated, some people have grown outraged at what they consider

to be centralized control over information resources. They believe that "Big Media's" control over news and entertainment results in a variety of problems, including unverified information, media bias hidden under the cloak of objectivity, and a narrowing of the voices, ideas, and opinions that are available to the general public. Accordingly, alternative media organizations such as Paper Tiger TV, Deep Dish Television, RealNetworks, and Free Speech TV seek to provide viewpoints different from those found in the mainstream media.

During the 1999 World Trade Organization meeting in Seattle, alternative television and Internet sources provided divergent perspectives on the protests led by environmentalists, labor activists, and others. Unlike such mainstream media sources as NBC, CBS, ABC, FOX, and CNN, these virtual media groups did not claim to be neutral or objective. They were and still are activist journalists who want to balance the corporate media's coverage of events with wider and—for them—more accurate perspectives on social problems. These alternative media groups state that they want to serve as role models for how democratic reporting can occur (Paton, 1999).

---

consumerism, violence, and greed." Kilbourne (1999:56) provides this example:

In 1980 the Gwich'in tribe of Alaska got television, and therefore massive advertising for the first time. Satellite dishes, video games, and VCRs were not far behind. Before this, the Gwich'in lived much the way their ancestors had for a thousand generations. Within ten years, the young members of the tribe were so drawn by television they no longer had time to learn ancient hunting methods, their parents' language, or their oral history. Legends told around campfires could not compete with *Beverly Hills 90210*. Beaded moccasins gave way to Nike

sneakers, sled dogs to gas-powered skimobiles, and "tundra tea" to Folger's instant coffee.

As Kilbourne and other media scholars point out, for the first time in history, people are hearing most stories of life not from their parents, schools, churches, or friends, but from transnational media conglomerates that have something to sell. If it is true that the media are a crucial influence in shaping and creating global cultural perceptions, then all of us must give careful consideration to the images and information offered to us. Of particular significance is how the news is framed. *Framing* **refers to how content and its accompanying visual images are linked together to create certain audience perceptions and give specific**

Social scientists who examine activist groups and and social movements are interested in how these groups disseminate their ideas and information. Alternative presses and nonmainstream media sources such as Access TV and Web sites provide options for individuals and organizations that wish to challenge existing social and/or economic arrangements. For example, the Institute for Global Communications (http://www.igc.org) provides accessible computer networking tools for movements such as EcoNet, PeaceNet, LaborNet, WomensNet, and ConflictNet (Budd, Craig, and Steinman, 1999).

Are you interested in learning more about alternative media sources? If so, you may wish to visit the web sites of one or more of the national alternative media organizations or read Project Censored's annual list of the most important under-reported stories. Published annually, *Censored: The News that Didn't Make the News* is authored by Peter Phillips and Project Censored and is published by Seven Stories Press in New York. More than 150 people participate in the selection process that designates the top twenty-five censored stories of each year. Among the participants are Sonoma State University students who, under the auspices of the sociology depart-

ment, read thousands of news stories; academic evaluators from various departments at the university; community experts; and national judges who rank the top twenty-five stories. In 1999, topics of these stories ranged from "secret government-sponsored trade deals, terminator seeds, radioactive spoons, and death squads to militarized police and government/media propaganda" (Phillips, 1999:11). For more information, contact:

Project Censored
Sociology Department
Sonoma State University
1801 East Cotati Avenue
Rohnert Park, CA 94928
e-mail address: censored@sonoma.edu

Some media analysts believe that the Internet and the World Wide Web will open up many new opportunities for decentralized and democratized communication on a global scale (Budd, Craig, and Steinman, 1999). Do you believe that a need exists for such alternative media sources? Why or why not?

(Note: Web addresses often change. Those given here were accurate at the time of publication.)

impressions to viewers and readers. When framing occurs in a news story, some analysts use the term "spin," because the process involves presenting information from a particular angle, or point of view.

POTENTIAL MEDIA EFFECTS

Today, as we have said, the global media industries are the primary source of news and entertainment for many people. Although these industries may have greater influence over some people than others, media analysts suggest that all of us are more profoundly—and often negatively—influenced by media

messages than we realize. In at least two areas—the portrayal of aggression and violence and the presentation of race, class, and gender stereotypes—the influence may be negative.

 Aggression, Violence, and the Media

The recent outbreak of violence in schools, discussed in Chapter 1, has renewed concerns about how the media depict aggressive and/or violent behavior. A number of media analysts assert that the need of media industries to capture public interest and thus increase the size of their markets has contributed to the use of violence or incidences of violence as a means of selling newspapers, television

SOCIAL PROBLEMS

BOX 14.2

The Depiction of Africa by the Global Media: Omissions and Commissions

There has been a precipitous drop in the quantity and quality of international news coverage in recent years. . . . Without adequate information we lack the ability to form responsible personal and societal responses to events that affect many and may one day affect us.

—*Joelle Tanguy, executive director of the U.S. office of Doctors Without Borders (quoted in Phillips, 1999:233)*

How the "Africa Story" is told in U.S. news is a serious concern to organizations such as the Africa-America Institute, an organization that seeks to promote cooperation between Africa and the United States and to encourage trade, investment, and economic development (aaionline, 1999). According to spokespersons for the Africa-America Institute, Western media sources often provide

inadequate or misleading information about Africa to other nations. The institute has identified several problems with how the mainstream U.S. media report on Africa:

1. *Cultural bias frequently is shown.* Journalists use metaphors such as "heart of darkness" in describing complex African stories. The use of such language and imagery suggests that the people of Africa are strange and exotic and that they live in a dangerous place (McLean, 1999).
2. *Geopolitical considerations are placed above accuracy in reporting.* U.S. national interests influence how reporters cover Africa and sometimes lead to distortions about realities in Africa. An example was the portrayal of Africa nations as pawns of the superpowers during the Cold War years (McLean, 1999).
3. *There has been less, rather than more, coverage of Africa in recent years.* Some attribute this change to the overall decrease in foreign affairs news provided to the U.S. people; others believe that people in this country have

programs, movies, heavy metal and rap music, and other media-related commodities. According to an extensive study conducted in the mid-1990s by the Center for Communications and Social Policy at the University of California at Santa Barbara, violent television shows made up 60 percent of all television programming during the three years of the study. Moreover, that percent continued to increase over the course of the study (Stern, 1998). A comprehensive economic analysis of television programming led one researcher to conclude that violent fare emerges as a logical extension of commercial broadcasting. While television executives claim their programs reflect audience desires, they do so in a commercially exploitable manner (Hamilton, 1998). In other words, when audiences say they want to see justice triumph, television executives make sure justice does triumph in their programs but only after

several violent fights or shootings that hold viewers in their seats even during commercials.

What effect does the depiction of violence have on audiences? There is no definitive answer to this question. Most scholars do not believe that the media *cause* aggressive behavior in people. Although there have been some studies that have shown a relationship between at least short-term aggressive behavior and media depictions of violence, other studies have suggested that the media may actually prevent acts of violence by providing people with an outlet for pent-up feelings and emotions. According to the *cathartic effect hypothesis,* television shows, videos, motion pictures, and other forms of media offer people a vicarious outlet for feelings of aggression and thus may reduce the amount of violence engaged in by the media consumer. Believing that research does not support this hypothesis, other ana-

become more interested in themselves and less interested in the issues and concerns of other people around the world (McLean, 1999).

4. *Human crises in Africa (with the exception of HIV/AIDS) are largely ignored by the U.S. media.* According to Doctors Without Borders, the world's largest independent international medical relief agency, humanitarian stories about Africa are seldom carried by U.S.-based media outlets. Among the underreported stories of 1998 were the "devastating famine in southern Sudan, the growing number of multidrug-resistant diseases, and a cholera epidemic that swept East Africa" (Phillips, 1999:233). Gaining media coverage regarding the HIV/AIDS epidemic in Africa was difficult until this disease began to increase in Asia. Today, there is more coverage of HIV/AIDS in Africa, partly because the weakening of the work force by this disease is a key problem in sub-Saharan Africa (Jeter, 2000).

What might be done to promote more accurate and balanced media coverage of Africa? According to the Africa-America Institute, the

news media typically are guided by U.S. policymakers' priorities; therefore, policymakers must become more aware of why greater involvement with Africa is in the best interests of the U.S. government. Likewise, the Institute encourages U.S. policymakers and journalists to invite recent African immigrants to the United States to participate in shaping and informing U.S. policy toward Africa (McLean, 1999).

New information technologies are beginning to have a significant role in altering trends in how news is covered. Alternative media sources, including the Internet and the World Wide Web, may become vehicles for projecting Africans' images of themselves to people around the globe (McLean, 1999). Currently, Africa News Service (http://www.africanews.org) disseminates stories from African news organizations. A comparative studies perspective on South Africa, Asia, and the Middle East is available at: http://www.duke.edu/web/dupress.

(*Note:* Web addresses often change. Those given here were accurate at the time of publication.)

lysts have suggested that continual depictions of violence tend to desensitize viewers and create values that contribute to aggressive behavior and feelings of fear and frustration (Gerbner, 1995). These analysts point out that depictions of violence do not require the use of language; thus, global audiences are drawn to violence because it needs no translation. Over time, however, desensitization makes it necessary for films and television programming to become even more violent in order to attract the potential audience's attention. This theory may help to explain the recent popularity of animal documentaries showing "kill sequences" and blood fights among animals (McElvogue, 1997). At a minimum, constant exposure to violence-laden media content may contribute to an individual's feelings of fear and a need for greater security and protection in everyday life.

According to media scholar Jean Kilbourne, one of the many ways in which the media perpetuate violence against women is through advertising. Kilbourne (1999) analyzed tens of thousands of advertisements to determine what effect they might have on viewers. According to Kilbourne, "The poses and postures of advertising are often borrowed from pornography, as are many of the themes, such as bondage, sadomasochism, and the sexual exploitation of children" (Kilbourne, 1999:271). She points out that advertisements showing women as dead or in the process of being killed are particularly popular themes among perfume advertisers. Advertising in other nations can be even more explicit. An Italian version of *Vogue* showed a man aiming a gun at a nude woman who was wrapped in plastic and had a leather briefcase covering her face (Kilbourne, 1999).

Media advertising also tends to treat women as sexual objects. In order to sell products, advertisements frequently show women in compromised positions or as the victims of rape or other violence and thus contribute to the ongoing subordination of women. Such depictions may also suggest that forcing sex on a woman is an acceptable norm, as Kilbourne (1999:273) points out:

> Men are also encouraged [by advertisements] to never take no for an answer. Ad after ad implies that girls and women don't really mean "no" when they say it, that women are only teasing when they resist men's advances. "NO" says an ad showing a man leaning over a woman against a wall. Is she screaming or laughing? Oh, it's an ad for deodorant and the second word, in very small print, is "sweat." Sometimes it's "all in good fun," as in the ad for Possession shirts and shorts featuring a man ripping the clothes off a woman who seems to be having a good time. And sometimes it is more sinister. A perfume ad running in several teen magazines features a very young woman, with eyes blackened by makeup or perhaps something else, and the copy, "Apply generously to your neck so he can smell the scent as you shake your head 'no.'" In other words, he'll understand that we don't really mean it and he can respond to the scent like any other animal.

As studies continue on the relationship between violence in the media and in everyday life, we will no doubt learn more about the causes and consequences of extensive media violence in society.

 Perpetuation of Race and Gender Stereotypes in the Media

Although a growing number of media consumers are not members of the dominant racial or ethnic groups or of the privileged classes, some media may reinforce existing racial, ethnic, and gender stereotypes and even create new ones. As defined previously, a *stereotype* is an overgeneralization about the appearance, behavior, or other characteristics of all members of a group.

RACIAL AND ETHNIC STEREOTYPING
Numerous media scholars have documented the long history of stereotyping of African Americans in film, television programming, and other media forms. More recently, studies have examined the effects of stereotyping on perceptions about Latinos/Latinas and Asian and Pacific Americans.

No matter which racial or ethnic group is depicted, stereotyping often involves one or more of the following:

1. Perpetuating images that appear to be positive in nature and thus flattering to members of a specific racial or ethnic group. For example, some stereotypes attribute superior traits, such as being "naturally" better at activities such as music and sports or mathematics and science, to members of one racial or ethnic category. In the case of Asian Americans, the term "the model minority" is used to praise the achievements of Vietnamese Americans, Japanese Americans, Chinese Americans, and others. However, this stereotype also is used to question why some people have been able to achieve the "American Dream" while others have not.
2. Exaggerating the physical appearance of subordinate group members or suggesting that all people in a specific category "look alike."
3. Creating racial or ethnic characters who have undesirable attributes, ranging from laziness and unwillingness to work to lack of intelligence or so-called lower class attitudes and behavior.
4. Using statements and visual images that link subordinate racial or ethnic group members to illegal actions, such as gang or organized crime activity, prostitution, drug dealing, or other deviant or criminal conduct.

These four examples of stereotyping can be found in a number of television programs, including "The PJs," an animated comedy created by actor Eddie Murphy and shown on the Fox Network. According to the Fox Network, "The PJs" is a "cutting-edge satire" that looks at African Americans living in a big city housing project (Fox Network, 1999); but is it? Many of the characters, including building superintendent Thurgood Stubbs and his wife, Muriel, are overweight and/or have exaggerated facial features such as large flat noses, thick lips, bulging eyes, and "nappy" hair. Other characters are alcoholics, drug addicts, "voodoo ladies," constantly complaining older women, and rather

Do the media seek to reduce racial stereotypes or do they sometimes perpetuate them? Some media critics believe that programs such as Fox Network's "The PJs" seek to end stereotypical treatment of African Americans and other minorities. However, others believe that depictions of characters like Thurgood Stubbs and his wife, Muriel, perpetuate negative images of subordinate racial and ethnic group members.

While some media critics and viewers believe that "The PJs" seeks to end stereotypical treatment of African Americans and other minorities, other critics believe that the show simply perpetuates negative images of subordinate racial and ethnic group members.

Of course, sometimes stereotypes are unintentional, but other times they are intentional. When media creators and producers become aware of the negative effects that stereotypical depictions may have on subordinate group members, particularly children, will they continue to perpetuate these images? Perhaps as the media industries and those who use them to advertise their goods begin to view nonwhite racial and ethnic groups around the globe as viable consumers of their products, greater concern will be shown over stereotypical images. After all, the estimated buying power of middle-income and affluent African Americans alone is about $450 billion, a figure that is more than the gross domestic product of Switzerland (Kilbourne, 1999).

Despite this fact, John Hoberman (1997) argues that damaging media images of African American men have increased rather than decreased in recent years. According to Hoberman, the commodification and aggressive marketing of sports figures, gangster rap artists, and others has created a stereotype of the African American athlete, criminal, and gangster rap artist as a "single black male persona." Some research appears to support this argument. In a study of more than 2,500 issues of *Time* and *Newsweek* magazines, researchers found that African American men were featured on the covers of these magazines ninety-eight times, and over 50 percent of those featured were athletes, alleged criminals, or rioters (Farrey, 1999).

GENDER STEREOTYPING

According to scholars who have conducted studies of gender stereotypes in the contemporary media, such stereotyping may result, at least in part, from the underrepresentation of women as producers, directors, and executives in the largest media industries. Regardless of the cause, some studies of female roles in television programs and films have shown the following:

1. *The intertwining of gender and age bias.* Gender-specific age bias is apparent in the casting of many female characters. Older men and significantly

"slow"-thinking children. Although Thurgood Stubbs is shown as successfully caring for maintenance problems at the housing project, he has a "lazy streak" that aggravates his wife. Stubbs often hangs out in the boiler room, watching the game show "Wheel of Fortune" and hiding from the tenants and sometimes his wife. Thurgood's chess-playing friend, Sanchez, is a Latino who constantly pines for his late wife, Esperanza, and Thurgood's Korean brother-in-law routinely makes assertions about his own "blackness."

younger women are often cast in leading roles in films, causing some women actors to ask "where are the roles for older women in Hollywood?"

2. *The perpetuation of traditional roles for women and the maintenance of cultural stereotypes of femininity.* Female characters who do not live up to the gendered expectations associated with femininity are overtly or subtly punished for their conduct.

3. *Impulsive conduct by women holding professional positions.* When television shows portray professional women, they often are shown as engaging in compulsive behavior. A recent example is "Ally McBeal," the television show about a law firm in which the lead character, Ally McBeal (played by Calista Flockhart) has a variety of impulsive sexual encounters, including one with a male stranger in a car wash and another with a female in her law firm.

4. *Women in positions of power as abusing their positions.* Prior to the 1990s, most female characters were depicted in lower-status occupations or in roles that were clearly subordinate to those of men. Although recently, more female characters on prime-time television shows have been lawyers or judges, these characters are often shown as "seducers, harassers, and wimps in black robes" (Goodman, 1999:AR 47). In programs such as "The Practice" and "Ally McBeal," writer/producer David E. Kelley has capitalized on harassment in the workplace by having women do the harassing (Goodman, 1999). When female characters are not seducing men, they are often depicted as "bitches" or "bimbos." On "Judge Judy," Judy Sheindlin, a former family court judge in New York, berates and demeans people appearing in her court (Goodman, 1999). On "Family Law," a woman judge frequently yells, "Shut up. Just shut up," along with a few four-letter words, at attorneys practicing before her.

5. *Women overwhelmed by their work.* In "Judging Amy," the young family court judge makes important decisions regarding child custody, foster care, and other family-related situations but appears overwhelmed by her caseload, her

Even when women are shown in professional careers in a television series, their characters are sometimes depicted as "bimbos" who wear extremely short skirts and engage in impulsive behavior that would not be typical of a "real life" professional. An example is Ally McBeal (right), a lawyer on the hit show by the same name, who often engages in bizarre behavior in the law firm or in the middle of a courtroom trial.

aggressive mother, and even her child's kindergarten teacher (Goodman, 1999).

Although the depiction of women characters in television programs, films, and other forms of media has improved significantly in recent decades, much remains to be done if women are to be shown in the wide diversity of occupations and endeavors in which real-life women participate on a daily basis.

SOCIOLOGICAL PERSPECTIVES ON MEDIA-RELATED PROBLEMS

Just as they do in regard to other social issues, functionalist, conflict, and interactionist approaches to media-related problems start with differing assumptions about these problems.

 ### The Interactionist Perspective

Perhaps the earliest interactionist theory concerning the media's effect on individuals and groups was the *hypodermic needle theory,* which suggested that audiences were made up of passive individuals who were equally susceptible to the messages of the media. However, a World War II study of military personnel who were shown movies designed to portray the enemy as evil and to increase morale among soldiers concluded that most of the subjects showed little change in their morale level. Based on these findings, researchers suggested an alternative explanation: the theory of limited effects. The *theory of limited effects states that the media have a minimal effect on the attitudes and perceptions of individuals.* According to this theory, people may not always be selective about what they watch or read, but they gather different messages from the media, and many people carefully evaluate the information they gain. This theory notes that when people are interested and informed about an issue, they are less likely to be influenced by what members of the media report. Those who are poorly informed or have no personal information about a particular topic or issue are likely to be affected by what other people, including reporters and journalists, say about the social concern.

A similar theory, known as *use and gratification theory,* suggests that people are active audience participants who make conscious decisions about what they will watch, listen to, read, and surf on the Internet. However, this theory assumes that people using different media have specific wishes or desires and will choose media sources that gratify their desires. In other words, people use the media to entertain and inform themselves but are aware of the limitations the media have in their coverage of topics and the forms of entertainment.

Another interactionist theory, mentioned in previous chapters, is *social learning theory,* **which is based on the assumption that people are likely to act out the behavior they see in role models and media sources.** To support this theory, social psychologist Albert Bandura (1977) conducted a series of experiments on aggression in children. For the experiment, children were divided into four groups. One group watched a film of a man attacking and beating a large, inflatable doll and being rewarded for his behavior. The second group saw a similar film, except in this version the man was punished for attacking the doll. The third group was shown a version in which the man was neither rewarded nor punished for his behavior. The final group was not shown any film. Prior to the experiment, researchers believed that the children who saw the man rewarded for hitting the doll would be the most likely to show aggressive behavior toward the doll. However, this did not prove to be true. Regardless of which version of the film they saw, children who were prone to aggression before the film tended to act aggressively toward the doll but other children did not. As a result, the researchers concluded that many factors other than the media influenced aggressive behavior in children, including their relationship with their parents, how much formal education their parents possessed, and the personality of the children.

More recent theories have sought to explain the effects of media on individuals by emphasizing the part that viewers, listeners, and readers play in shaping the media. According to the *audience relations approach,* people use their own cultural understandings to interpret what they hear and see in the media. Factors involved in the audience relations approach include how much previous knowledge individuals have about a topic and the availability of other sources of information. This viewpoint is somewhat in keeping with functionalist approaches, which highlight the important contemporary functions of the media.

The Functionalist Perspective

Functionalist approaches to examining the media often focus on the functional—and sometimes dysfunctional—effects the media have on society. Functionalists point out that the media serve several important functions in contemporary societies. First, the media provide news and information, including warnings about potential disasters such as an approaching hurricane. Second, the media facilitate public discourse regarding social issues and policies such as welfare reform. Third, the media pass on cultural traditions and historical perspectives, particularly to recent immigrants and children. (Lasswell, 1969). Fourth, the media are a source of entertainment, providing people with leisure-time activities (Biagi, 1998). Finally, the media confer status on individuals and organizations by frequently reporting on their actions or showing their faces and mentioning their names. According to sociologist Joshua Gamson (1994:186), becoming a media celebrity is a means of gaining power, privilege and mobility: "Audiences recognize this when they seek brushes with it and when they fantasize about the freedom of fame and its riches and about the distinction of popularity and attention."

As Gamson notes, some people become celebrities because the media confers that status on them. In other words, as the popular saying goes, "Some people are famous for being famous." For example, Monica S. Lewinsky, a former White House intern, became a media celebrity in the late 1990s because of her sexual involvement with then-president Bill Clinton. Constant media attention not only brought Lewinsky temporary notoriety but also several Internet fan clubs, a book contract, an international media tour, and a stint as a spokesperson for the Jenny Craig diet plan.

According to the functionalist approach, the media are dysfunctional when they contribute to a reduction in social stability or weaken other social institutions such as the family, education, politics, and religion. For example, television has brought about significant changes in family interaction patterns, as one media scholar explains:

> The most pervasive effect of television—aside from its content—may be its very existence, its readily available, commanding, and often addictive presence in our homes, its ability to reduce hundreds of millions of citizens to passive spectators for major portions of their waking hours. Television minimizes interactions between persons within families and communities. One writer I know only half-jokingly claims, "I watch television as a way of getting to know my husband and children." Another associate, who spent years in Western agrarian regions, relates how a farmer once told her: "Folks used to get together a lot. Now with television, we see less of each other." (Parenti, 1998:188)

Over time, the media not only change how people interact with each other but also may have a profound influence on individuals' perceptions of one another and their impressions of the world. When dysfunctions occur, the problems should be addressed for the benefit of individuals, families, and the larger society. Some functionalist approaches suggest that individuals and families are responsible for social change in regard to the media. Analysts who favor this approach suggest that rather than changing the nature of television programming, parents should monitor their children's television watching and schools should offer media education for parents and children to make them aware of the classic persuasion and propaganda techniques often used in programming and advertising (Minow and LaMay, 1999).

The Conflict Perspective

Conflict theorists typically link the media industries with the capitalist economy. From this approach, members of the capitalist class own and control the media, which, along with other dominant social institutions, instruct people in the values, beliefs, and attitudes that they should have (Curran, Gurevitch, and Woollacott, 1982). According to this perspective, the *process of legitimization* takes place as media consumers are continually provided with information that supports the validity of existing class relations. As a result, members of the working class are lulled into a sense of complacency in which they focus more on entertainment and consumption than on questioning existing economic and social relations. This perspective is sometimes referred to as *hegemony theory*—**the view that the media are instruments of social control and are used by members of the ruling classes to create "false consciousness" in the working classes.** Although there are various conflict approaches, most view ownership and economic control of the media as a key factor in determining what kinds of messages are disseminated around the globe. Media analysts such as Michael Parenti (1998:149) believe that media bias is inevitable as transnational media industries become concentrated in the hands of a few mega-corporations:

> Media bias usually does not occur in random fashion; rather, it moves in the same overall direction again and again, favoring management over labor, corporations over corporate critics, affluent whites over inner-city poor, officialdom over protestors, the two-party monopoly over leftist third parties, privatization and free-market "reforms" over public-sector development, U.S. domination of the Third World over revolutionary or populist social change, investor globalization over nation-state democracy, national security policy over critics of that policy, and conservative commentators and columnists . . . over progressive or populist ones.

According to Parenti, the built-in biases of the media reflect the dominant ideology that supports the privileged position of members of the capitalist class. Parenti (1998) lists a number of ways in which media manipulation occurs: (1) sponsors control broadcasting decisions, (2) information may be suppressed by omitting certain details of a story or the entire story, particularly if the story may have a negative effect on a person or organization to whom members of the media feel beholden, (3) a story may be attacked or the reporting may not present a balanced view of the diverse viewpoints involved, (4) negative labels that subsume a large number of people, for example, "Islamic terrorists," "inner-city gangs," may be used, and (5) stories may be framed to convey positive or negative connotations through the use of visual effects, placement, and other means. Like other conflict theorists, Parenti (1998:157) believes that the media tell people what to think before they have had

a chance to think about an issue for themselves: "When we understand that news selectivity is likely to favor those who have power, position, and wealth, we move from a liberal complaint about the press's sloppy performance to a radical analysis of how the media serve the ruling circles all too well with much skill and craft."

In an era marked by increased concentration of all forms of media, including the Internet and the World Wide Web, conflict perspectives on media ownership and control raise important questions. Although people engaged in political dissent and social activism, such as the U.S. environmental movement, have been able to marshal the media on their behalf, the media often implicitly support the status quo because of their own corporate interests and the need to maintain and enhance advertising revenues.

Regardless of which theoretical perspective on the media industries most closely resembles our own thinking, each of us should take a closer look at the ideas, images, and advertisements that bombard us daily. While most of us may believe that we are not affected by the constant stream of advertisements that we encounter, we should realize, as media scholar Jean Kilbourne (1999:27) states, "The fact is that much of advertising's power comes from this belief that advertising does not affect us. The most effective kind of propaganda is that which is not recognized as propaganda." Although individuals alone cannot solve the problems associated with the media industries, they can become more aware of the pervasive impact of television, films, newspapers, the Internet, and other forms of mass communication.

THE MEDIA IN THE TWENTY-FIRST CENTURY

Problems associated with the media will continue well into this century, and many of the issues will probably become even more complex. For example, it has been suggested that the Internet and e-commerce will affect all aspects of life, particularly in high-income nations such as the United States. Some analysts have suggested that U.S. cities will lose more of their tax base to untaxed Internet commerce, bringing about a need

Around the globe, U.S. media conglomerates influence local cultures through continual marketing of films, television programming, and other media. This movie-goer in Beijing, China, is purchasing tickets for the movie Titanic. *According to media sources, the film was a gigantic box office success in Beijing and other cities worldwide.*

to restructure relations between cities, states, and the federal government (Friedman, 2000a). Indeed, the ability of a single government to control the activities of transnational media industries may be weakened as globalization continues to occur. Thus, according to journalist Thomas L. Friedman (2000a:A31), a world of global communications means that many issues that were once considered the domain of individual nations and governments will have to be rethought:

> Issues such as freedom of speech and libel are going to have to be rethought as the Internet makes everyone a potential publisher in cyberspace—but with no censor or editor in charge. Privacy protection is going to have to be rethought in a world where for $39 Web sites will search out anyone's assets and home address for you. And our safety nets are going to have to be rethought in a world in which access to the Internet is going to be viewed as a human right, essential for basic survival—especially as governments move more services to the Web.

In the years to come, new communication technology will undoubtedly continue to change our lives. While new forms of media offer many potential benefits, they also raise serious concerns about social life as many of us know it.

SUMMARY

→ *What are the media industries? How much time do individuals spend in media-related activities?*

According to social scientists, the media industries are media businesses that influence people and cultures worldwide and own interests in radio and television production and broadcasting; motion pictures, movie theaters, and music companies; newspaper, periodical (magazine) and book publishing; and Internet services and content providers. Today, many people spend more time in media-related activities than they do in any other single endeavor, including sleeping, working, eating, or talking with friends and family; therefore, some analysts believe

the media have a major influence on how people think, feel, and act.

→ *What part does technology play in how various media industries change over time?*

For many years, newspapers were the primary source of news. However, new technologies brought about radio as the media phenomenon of the 1920s and television as the phenomenon of the 1950s. With the introduction of communications technologies such as computers, fiber optic cable, and broadcast satellites, the media industries continue to change rapidly.

➡️ *How has media ownership changed?*

Although there once were a variety of independent companies that produced books, records, television programs, and films, there are now large corporate conglomerates that own more than one form of the media business.

➡️ *What is convergence? How does it relate to media concentration?*

Convergence refers to a melding of the communications, computer, and electronics industries that gives a few huge corporations control over an increasing proportion of all media sources. Convergence contributes to greater concentration in the media. Media concentration refers to the tendency of the media industries to cluster together in groups.

➡️ *What forms may media concentration take?*

Media concentration may take place in several forms: (1) within one industry (such as newspaper chains), (2) cross-media ownership in which media companies own more than one type of media property (such as newspaper chains and television stations), (3) conglomerate ownership in which corporations own media properties but also own other businesses, (4) vertical integration in which the corporations that make the media content also control the distribution channels (such as film and television production companies, television networks, and movie theaters).

➡️ *Why do some people favor media convergence whereas others do not?*

Supporters believe that much can be gained from the synergy created by media convergence because it makes it possible to take a media brand and capitalize on it. This process is clearly profitable for investors and media executives; however, media critics believe convergence limits the news and entertainment that the public receives by reducing message pluralism. Other problems include (1) the decline of journalism as a public service profession, (2) constant pressure for all journalistic endeavors to be immediately profitable, (3) a significant decrease in the quantity and quality of international news available to U.S. audiences, (4) the quashing of public debate about the power of the

media industries and how they deal with important social issues, and (5) a dramatic increase in the influence of powerful Washington lobbyists representing the interests of the media giants.

➡️ *What potential problems are associated with global media concentration?*

A few large media conglomerates are rapidly gaining control over most of the publishing, recording, television, film, and mega–theme park business worldwide. One major problem is the extent to which a few media giants have almost complete control over the world's information. Some people in other nations have been critical of how the media conglomerates depict nations around the globe and the influence, often negative, that they have on the politics and culture of other nations.

➡️ *What is framing and how does it affect media coverage?*

Framing refers to how news content and its accompanying visual images are linked together to create certain audience perceptions and give specific impressions to viewers and readers. This process of "spinning" information provides audiences with a particular angle, which usually is favorable to the media and the interests they favor while minimizing or eliminating coverage of other issues and concerns.

➡️ *Why are some media critics concerned about depictions of violence in the media?*

Although most scholars do not believe that the media *cause* aggressive behavior in people, a number of media analysts assert that the media's need to capture public interest has contributed to the gratuitous use of violence as a means of selling newspapers, television programming, movie tickets, heavy metal and rap music, and other media-related commodities. According to a recent study, violent television shows made up 60 percent of all television programming. Some studies have shown a relationship between short-term aggressive behavior and media depictions of violence; however, others have suggested that the media may prevent acts of violence by providing people with an outlet for pent-up feelings and emotions.

➡ *What forms of media communication typically show violence against women?*

According to media scholar Jean Kilbourne, advertising, which often uses semi-pornographic images and themes such as bondage, sadomasochism, and the sexual exploitation of children to sell products, is one of the ways in which the media perpetuate violence against women. The media also contribute to the view of women as sexual objects that do not need to be taken seriously.

➡ *What is a stereotype and how may the media perpetuate stereotypes about racial and ethnic groups?*

A stereotype is an overgeneralization about the appearance, behavior, or other characteristics of all members of a group. The media may perpetuate stereotypes by casting some groups as having superior traits such as being "naturally" better at music and sports or mathematics and science and then using the "model minority" image to question why some people succeed while others do not. Other media stereotyping includes exaggerating people's physical appearance, suggesting that all people in a specific category "look alike," creating racial or ethnic characters who have undesirable attributes, and using statements and visual images that continually link subordinate racial or ethnic group members to illegal actions.

➡ *Why is gender stereotyping pervasive in the media? What major forms does this problem take?*

Underrepresentation of women as producers, directors, and executives in the largest media industries may be a factor in the more limited range of roles available to women in television programs and films. First, gender-specific age bias is apparent in the casting of many female characters. Second, television shows and films often perpetuate traditional roles for women and maintain cultural stereotypes of femininity.

➡ *How do interactionists explain the influence of the media on individuals?*

According to the theory of limited effects, the media have a minimal effect on individuals' attitudes and perceptions. The use and gratification theory suggests that people are active audience participants who make conscious decisions about what they will watch, listen to, read, and surf on the Internet. However, social learning theory is based on the assumption that people are likely to act out the behavior they see in role models and media sources. The audience relations approach states that people interpret what they hear and see in the media by using their own cultural understandings as a mental filtering device.

➡ *How do functionalist and conflict perspectives on the media differ?*

According to some functionalist analysts, the media fulfill several important functions in contemporary societies, including providing news and information, facilitating public discourse on social issues and policies, passing on cultural traditions and historical perspectives, and entertaining people. In contrast, conflict theorists assert that members of the capitalist class (either intentionally or unintentionally) use the media to provide information that supports the validity of existing class relations. Hegemony theory states that the media are an instrument of social control that is used by members of the ruling classes to create false consciousness in the working classes.

KEY TERMS

framing, pp. 302–303
hegemony theory, p. 311

media concentration, p. 297
media industries, p. 296

social learning theory, p. 309
theory of limited effects, p. 309

QUESTIONS FOR CRITICAL THINKING

1. Why is media concentration a potentially greater social problem than concentration in other industries?

2. If you were an owner or large shareholder in a major media company, how might you view synergy? What negative effects might synergy have on those who are in your reading, listening, viewing, and/or Internet audiences?

3. Is continued consolidation in the media a serious threat to democracy? Should we be concerned about the ability of some companies to "buy" political influence? Why or why not?

Chapter Fifteen

Population and the Environmental Crisis

You see, there are only nine cabins in the steamer launch which comes from Dhaka to Patuakhali. In the nine cabins only 18 people can travel. The ticket is expensive, so only the rich people travel in the cabins. The rest of the common passengers travel in the deck. The latrine facility [restroom] is provided only for the cabin passengers. But sometimes the passengers from the deck want to use the latrines. The cabin passengers allow them to use the latrine because they are afraid that if the poor deck passengers get angry then they might go down and make a hole in the launch. Then the launch will sink; they will die no doubt but the rich cabin passengers will not survive either. So, my dear sisters, do not give birth to more children as they cause a problem for the cabin passengers.

▲ —*Writer Farida Ahkter*
recalls the story she heard
one family planning officer
tell a group of poor and
illiterate women in a
remote village in
Bangladesh
(*The Ecologist*, 1993:143)

Global population control policies are the subject of international controversy. Although some people believe that government policies are essential for curbing overpopulation, others argue that government policies are a means by which dominant group members decide "*who* will be born, *how* many will be born, and of *what* race, class, sex and 'quality' they will be" (*The Ecologist,* 1993:143). In this chapter, we will examine the problem of global overpopulation, including its impact on the environment.

GLOBAL OVERPOPULATION

During the past fifty years, the world's population has more than doubled, growing from 2.5 billion in 1950 to over 6 billion today. At this rate, the world population will double again in the next fifty years. Even today, more than 1 billion of the world's people do not have enough food and lack basic health care (Hauchler and Kennedy, 1994). Will the earth's resources be able to support such a population? This is an urgent question and one for which we need answers.

Population Growth

Growth rates vary among nations; high-income nations (for example, the United States) have a lower population growth rate than low-income nations, especially those in Africa, Asia, and Latin America. A *population* is all the people living in a specified geographic area. In some nations, the population growth rate is negative; that is, fewer people are added to the population through birth and immigration than are lost through death and emigration. Current estimates suggest that countries such as Italy, Romania, Russia, and Spain will shrink in population over the next fifty years (Sanger, 2000).

Demography is the study of the size, composition, and distribution of populations. Global population changes are important because they have a powerful influence on social, economic, and political structures both within societies and between societies. For example, the population growth imbalance between high-income and middle- and low-income nations is a potential source of global conflict, particularly if world hunger and environmental destruction increase. Three primary factors affect the rate of population growth in any nation or area: fertility (births), mortality (deaths), and migration (movement between geographic areas). We'll look at each in turn.

FERTILITY

Fertility refers to the number of children born to an individual or a population. The most basic measure of fertility is the *crude birth rate*—the number of live births per 1,000 people in a population in a given year. In 1998, there were 3.9 million live births in the United States, yielding a crude birth rate of 14.4 per 1,000. This rate was down slightly from 16.6 per 1,000 in 1990 (U.S. Bureau of the Census, 1998). The crude birth rate is used to gauge fertility because it is based on the entire population and does not take into account the variables that affect fertility, such as age, marital status, and race/ethnicity.

The level of fertility in a society is associated with social, as well as biological, factors. For example, countries that have high rates of infant and child mortality often have high birth rates. By having many children, parents in these nations are more likely to see a few of them survive to adulthood. In nations without social security systems to provide old-age insurance, parents may view children as an "insurance plan" for their old age. In patriarchal societies, having many children—especially sons—is

proof of manliness. Finally, in cultures in which religion dictates that children are God-given and family planning is forbidden because it "interferes with God's will," many more children are usually born (Hauchler and Kennedy, 1994).

Although men obviously are important in the reproductive process, the measure of fertility focuses on women because pregnancy and childbirth are more easily quantified than biological fatherhood. One factor in determining how many children will be born in a given year is the number of women of childbearing age (usually between the ages of fifteen and forty-five) who live in the society. Other biological factors that affect fertility include the general health and nutrition level of women of childbearing age. However, on the basis of biological capability alone, most women could produce twenty or more children during their childbearing years. In industrialized nations, therefore, many people limit their biological capabilities by practicing abstinence, refraining from sexual intercourse before a certain age, using contraceptives, being sterilized, or having one or more abortions over the course of their reproductive years. Fertility rates also are affected by the number of partners available for sex and/or marriage, the number of women of childbearing age in the work force, and government policies regarding families. China, for example, has a one-child policy, so abortion or sterilization can be required by the government when there is an unauthorized pregnancy (Mosher, 1994).

MORTALITY

Birth rates are one factor in population growth; another is a decline in **mortality—the number of deaths that occur in a specific population.** The simplest measure of mortality is the *crude death rate*—the number of deaths per 1,000 people in a population in a given year. In 1998, there were 2.4 million deaths in the U.S. population, which yields a crude death rate of 8.8 deaths per 1,000 (U.S. Bureau of the Census, 1998). In many nations, mortality rates have declined dramatically as diseases, such as malaria, polio, cholera, tetanus, typhoid, and measles, have been virtually eliminated by vaccinations and improved sanitation and personal hygiene (Weeks, 1998).

In addition to measuring the crude death rate, demographers often measure the *infant mortality rate*—the number of deaths of infants under one year of age per 1,000 live births in a given year. In general, infant mortality has declined worldwide over the past two decades because many major childhood and communicable diseases are now under control. Still, infant mortality rates vary widely between nations. In high-income nations, the average was 6 deaths per 1,000 live births in 1997 (Japan had a low of 4 deaths per 1,000 live births), in sharp contrast to about 72 deaths per 1,000 live births in southern Asia and about 105 deaths per 1,000 live births in sub-Saharan Africa (United Nations Development Programme, 1999).

In any nation, the infant mortality rate is an important reflection of a society's level of preventive (prenatal) medical care, maternal nutrition, childbirth procedures, and neonatal care for infants. In the United States, differential levels of access to these services are reflected in the gap between infant mortality rates for African Americans and whites. In 1998, for example, mortality for African American infants was 15 deaths per 1,000 live births, compared to 6 per 1,000 live births for white infants (U.S. Bureau of the Census, 1998).

Demographers also study *life expectancy,* the estimated average lifetime of people born in a specific year. For example, in 1998, the life expectancy at birth for a person born in the United States was 76.1 years, compared to 80.0 years in Japan and less than 50.0 years in the African nations of Burundi, Chad, Rwanda, and Uganda (U.S. Bureau of the Census, 1998). In fact, the estimated life expectancy for people in Uganda and Zambia has dropped significantly over the past two decades. In Uganda, life expectancy has dropped from 48 to 43 years for women and from 45 to 41 years for men (United Nations, 1995). Life expectancy varies not only by nation but also by sex. Females born in the United States in 2000 have a life expectancy of about 80 years, whereas males born in that year have a life expectancy of about 73 years. Life expectancy also varies by race. African American men, for example, have a life expectancy at birth of about 65 years, compared to 74 years for white males (U.S. Bureau of the Census, 1998).

MIGRATION

Migration **is the movement of people from one geographic area to another for the purpose of changing residency.** Migration takes two forms: *immigration*—the movement of people *into* a geographic area to take up residency—and *emigration*—the movement of people *out of* a geographic area to take up residency elsewhere. Today, more than 23 million people live outside their countries of origin (Kane, 1995).

In the early 1990s, about 1 million people were entering the United States each year, but this number has since decreased to about 900,000 annually because of more restrictive U.S. immigration policies and stricter enforcement. However, it should be noted that official immigration statistics do not reflect the actual number of immigrants who arrive in this country. The U.S. Immigration and Naturalization Service records only legal immigration based on entry visas and change-of-immigration-status forms. Some people who enter the country as temporary visitors, coming for pleasure or business, as students, or as temporary workers or trainees do not leave when their stated purpose has been achieved and their permits expire.

Approximately 130,000 refugees are also admitted to this country annually as permanent residents. According to the 1951 United Nations Convention on Refugees, the term *refugee* applies solely to those who leave their countries because of persecution for reasons of race, religion, nationality, membership in a particular social group, or political opinion (Kane, 1995). People who leave home to escape famine, for example, do not officially qualify as refugees.

The largest proportion of immigrants entering the United States each year arrive illegally. Many come from Mexico, El Salvador, Guatemala, Poland, Haiti, the Bahamas, and Nicaragua (U. S. Bureau of the Census, 1998). Government officials estimate that between 3.5 million and 4 million people annually enter this country illegally (U.S. Bureau of the Census, 1998). Of course, it is not known how many of them return to their countries of origin or how many people enter, leave, and reenter, as is often done by undocumented workers who come and go between the United States and Mexico or Canada (Weeks, 1998).

Many immigrants come to the United States because it offers them greater job opportunities and freedom from the political, religious, sexual, or racial/ethnic oppression of their home countries. For example, researchers have found that many women migrate to this country from the Dominican Republic to improve their economic position and to escape a repressive patriarchal environment. When both husband and wife migrate from the Dominican Republic, the wife is more likely to remain in this country than the husband because she finds that working gives her more economic security and power at home. Many husbands save their money and return to the Dominican Republic (Grasmuck and Pessar, 1991).

To determine the effects of immigration and emigration, demographers compute the *crude net migration rate*—the net number of migrants (total

SOCIAL PROBLEMS

IN GLOBAL PERSPECTIVE

BOX 15.1

Challenges and Opportunities Presented by Worldwide Migration

These countries in Europe will face the wall. They either bring in migrants, or they are going to decline in size. The model that the United States has—and Canada and Australia—is increasingly becoming attractive to some of the thinkers in those countries.

—*Joseph Chamie, director of the United Nations population division (Crossette, 2000:WK1)*

For years, many nations have strictly limited immigration. The United States has its own history of passing restrictive immigration laws, and recent anti-immigration sentiment has been seen in states such as California, where some residents have sought to pass legislation limiting immigrants' access to education, health care, and other public services. However, anti-immigrant sentiment does not bode well for a number of nations

in the future. According to the United Nations, because of the inequality between the rich and the poor in the world, numerous countries can expect large migrations. More than 900,000 Turkish "guest workers" have moved to Germany and the Scandinavian countries to work; nearly 3 million Mexicans live in the United States, and more than 1 million immigrants work in Saudi Arabia (Kane, 1995; U.S. Bureau of the Census, 1998). Migrants follow the flow of jobs, and in countries with severely shrunken labor forces and increasing ranks of older retirees, immigrants may be part of the solution to population concerns rather than part of the "problem" as they have been perceived in the past.

Today, many European countries (as well as the United States, Canada, and Japan) are faced with populations that will have more older people and fewer babies than ever before. If these nations want to maintain the social services and economic structures that many residents have become accustomed to, it will be necessary for them to "lower their borders"

---

in-migrants minus total out-migrants) per 1,000 people in a population in a given year. Currently, the net migration rate in the United States is about 2.4 per 1,000 population, which means that between two and three more people per 1,000 population enter this country than leave it each year (based on U.S. Bureau of the Census, 1998).

Many nations face the challenges and opportunities offered by the migration of people worldwide (see Box 15.1).

 ## The Impact of Population Growth

What is the effect of population growth on a society? Population growth affects *population composition*—the biological and social characteristics of a population, including such attributes as age, sex, race, marital status, education, occupation, income, and size of household. In the United States, for exam-

ple, the age distribution of the population is associated with the demand for community resources such as elementary and secondary schools, libraries, health care and recreational facilities, employment opportunities, and age-appropriate housing.

What are the effects of rapid population growth on individuals? According to Population Action International's *Human Suffering Index* (HSI), the countries that have the highest rates of growth also have the most human suffering. For example, twenty of the twenty-seven countries listed in the "extreme human suffering" category are in Africa, the fastest-growing region in the world (*Human Suffering Index*, 1992). The HSI also shows that while many people in poverty-stricken regions die from hunger and malnutrition each year, people in the most high-income nations spend billions of dollars annually on diet products and exercise gear because they think they are overfed and overweight.

and accept a change in the racial and ethnic composition of their populations (Crossette, 2000). According to some demographers, Italy will have to add about 9 million immigrants by 2025, at a rate of about 300,000 a year, to maintain its population at its 1995 level; Germany will need to import an additional 14 million people, or 500,000 a year; and France will need to add 2 million. Overall, the European Union will need to allow the immigration of about 35 million people to maintain the population at the level of the 1990s (Crossette, 2000). By comparison, the United States admitted almost 800,000 legal immigrants in 1997 (U.S. Bureau of the Census, 1998).

As the pressure from overpopulation builds in some nations, and the United States, Canada, and some European countries have increasingly "aging" populations, demographers believe that the flow of migrant workers will increase dramatically around the world. Many challenges remain, however.

Policies and programs to overcome hurdles like language barriers are scant in much of Europe because cultural homogeneity has been deeply valued, citizenship has often been defined ethnically or linguistically, and the naturalization process that has made Americans out of millions of foreigners does not exist. (Crossette, 2000:WK4)

In some European nations, cultural homogeneity has led to anti-immigration sentiment and hate crimes perpetrated against people based on perceptions about their racial group, ethnicity, or nationality. In Scandinavia and central and eastern Europe, skinhead violence has erupted on various occasions against non-Europeans.

While some nations continue to look to the past to determine what should be done about immigration in the future, spokespersons for organizations such as the United Nations believe that political leaders and citizens must acknowledge that their countries face either a declining population or a future that is built by immigrants (Crossette, 2000). What other issues are important to consider regarding global migration?

What are the consequences of global population growth? Not all social analysts agree on the answer to this question. As you will discover in the sections that follow, some analysts warn that the earth is a finite system that cannot support its rapidly growing population. Others believe that capitalism—if freed from government intervention—could develop innovative solutions to such problems as hunger and pollution. Still others argue that capitalism is part of the problem, not part of the solution.

THE MALTHUSIAN PERSPECTIVE

Rapid population growth and overpopulation are not new problems. Causes and solutions have been debated for nearly two centuries. In 1798, for example, Thomas Malthus, an English clergyman and economist, published *An Essay on Population*. Malthus (1965/1798) argued that the global population, if left unchecked, would exceed the available food supply. The population would increase in a geometric (exponential) progression (2, 4, 8, 16, . . .), but the food supply would increase only by an arithmetic progression (1, 2, 3, 4, . . .). Thus, the population would surpass the food supply, ending population growth and perhaps eliminating the world population (Weeks, 1998). Disaster, according to Malthus, could be averted only by positive checks (e.g., famine, disease, and war) or preventive checks (e.g., sexual abstinence before marriage and postponement of marriage for as long as possible) to limit people's fertility.

THE NEO-MALTHUSIAN PERSPECTIVE

Today, *neo-Malthusians* (or "new Malthusians") speak of the "population explosion" and "population bomb" to emphasize the urgent need to reduce global population growth. Among the best known neo-Malthusians are biologists Paul Ehrlich and Anne H.

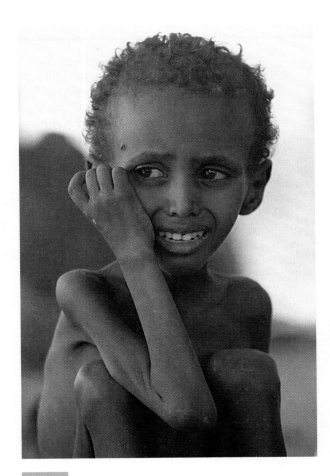

Starving children in nations such as Somalia raise important questions about Malthusian and neo-Malthusian perspectives. Is world hunger primarily a consequence of overpopulation or are other political and economic factors also important?

Ehrlich, who believe that world population growth is following the exponential growth pattern that Malthus described (Ehrlich and Ehrlich, 1991:15):

> Exponential growth occurs in populations because children . . . remain in the population and themselves have children. A key feature of exponential growth is that it often seems to start slow and finish fast. A classic example . . . is the pond weed that doubles each day . . . to cover the entire pond in thirty days. The question is,

how much of the pond will be covered in twenty-nine days? The answer, of course, is that just half of the pond will be covered in twenty-nine days. The weed will then double once more and cover the entire pond the next day. As this example indicates, exponential growth contains the potential for big surprises.

To neo-Malthusians, the earth is a dying planet with too many people in relation to the available food supply. Overpopulation and rapid population growth exacerbate global environmental problems ranging from global warming and rainforest destruction to famine and epidemics such as AIDS.

DEMOGRAPHIC TRANSITION THEORY

According to *demographic transition theory*, societies move from high birth and death rates to relatively low birth and death rates as a result of technological development. The demographic transition takes place in four stages. The *preindustrial stage* is characterized by little population growth: High birth rates are offset by high death rates. This period is followed by the *transitional* or *early industrial stage*, which is characterized by significant population growth as the birth rate remains high but the death rate declines because of new technologies that improve health, sanitation, and nutrition. Today, large parts of Africa, Asia, and Latin America are in this second stage. The third stage is *advanced industrialization and urbanization*: The birth rate declines as people control their fertility with various forms of contraception, and the death rate declines as medicine and other health care technologies control acute and chronic diseases. Finally, in the *postindustrial stage*, the population grows very slowly, if at all. In this stage, a decreasing birth rate is coupled with a stable death rate.

Proponents of demographic transition theory believe that technology can overcome the dire predictions of Malthus and the neo-Malthusians. Critics point out that not all nations go through all the stages or in the manner outlined. They think that demographic transition theory explains development in Western societies but not necessarily in others. As an example, they cite China, which is in the process of significantly reducing its birth rate but only because of the government's mandated one-child-per-family policy, not because of technological advances or urbanization (Weeks, 1998).

World Hunger

Food shortages, chronic hunger, and malnutrition are the consequences of rapid population growth, particularly in middle-income nations. Approximately 800 million people in middle-income nations experience continuous hunger or *chronic malnourishment*—inadequate food to provide the minimum energy necessary for doing light work over a period of time (FAO,

1995). Chronic malnutrition contributes to childhood health problems such as anemia (a blood condition that produces weakness and a lack of energy and can result in child mortality or impaired mental functioning), stunting (impaired physical growth or development), and being underweight (United Nations, 1995). In pregnant women, malnutrition increases the risk of anemia, infection, birth complications, and lack of breast milk (see Figure 15.1). In contrast,

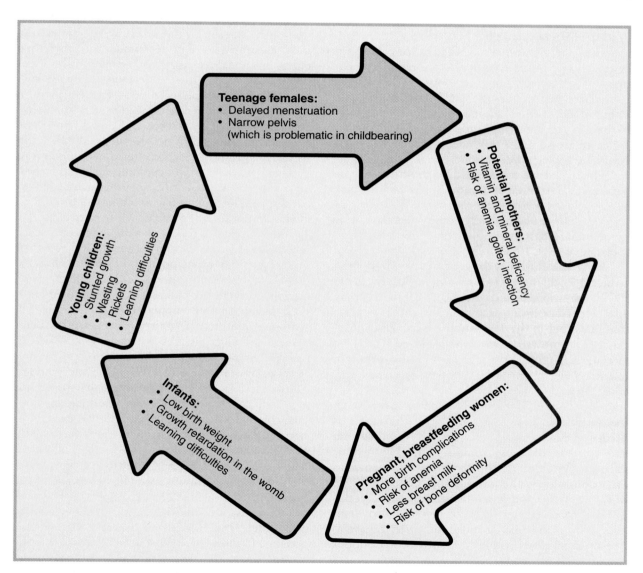

Teenage females:
• Delayed menstruation
• Narrow pelvis (which is problematic in childbearing)

Potential mothers:
• Vitamin and mineral deficiency
• Risk of anemia, goiter, infection

Young children:
• Stunted growth
• Wasting
• Rickets
• Learning difficulties

Infants:
• Low birth weight
• Growth retardation in the womb
• Learning difficulties

Pregnant, breastfeeding women:
• More birth complications
• Risk of anemia
• Less breast milk
• Risk of bone deformity

FIGURE 15.1   *The Circle of Malnutrition*
Source: Based on United Nations, 1995.

improvements in nutrition significantly reduce health risks and the spread of some communicable illnesses (Hauchler and Kennedy, 1994).

What efforts are being made to reduce global food shortages and world hunger? Organizations such as the United Nations, the World Health Organization, and the International Red Cross have programs in place, but the most far-reaching initiatives are known as the green revolution and the biotechnological revolution.

THE GREEN REVOLUTION

The *green revolution* refers to dramatic increases in agricultural production that have been made possible by high-yield "miracle" crops. In the 1940s, researchers at the International Maize and Wheat Improvement Center started the green revolution by developing high-yield varieties of wheat, which increased world grain production. The new dwarf-type wheat, which produces more stalks, has dramatically increased the wheat yield in countries, such as India and Pakistan, since the 1960s. Researchers have also developed a high-yield dwarf rice with twice as many grains per plant, greatly improving the rice output in India, Pakistan, the Philippines, Indonesia, and Vietnam (Weeks, 1998).

How successful has the green revolution been in reducing world hunger? During the 1970s, the green revolution helped to increase the global food supply at a somewhat faster pace than the global population grew, but in the 1980s and 1990s, agricultural production slowed considerably. Also, while the new miracle crops have increased food production in Latin America and Asia, they have not really benefited Africa (Kennedy, 1993).

They have not for several reasons. For one thing, the fertilizers, pesticides, and irrigation systems needed to produce them are very costly and beyond the budgets of most middle- and low-income nations. Furthermore, the fertilizers and pesticides often constitute health hazards and become a source of surface water and groundwater pollution (Weeks, 1998). Moreover, for the green revolution to eliminate hunger and malnutrition, the social organization of life in many middle- and low-income nations would have to change significantly. People would have to adopt the Western methods of farming on which the green revolution was built, and they would have to be willing to produce a single crop in

very high volume. But reliance on a single crop can lead to nutritional deficiencies if other varieties of food are not available. Even with these drawbacks, however, the green revolution continues. Researchers recently developed high-yield sorghum, yams, and other crops that can be grown successfully in the nations of Africa where some of the greatest food shortages exist (Weeks, 1998).

THE BIOTECHNOLOGICAL REVOLUTION

A second approach to reducing global food shortages, known as the *biotechnological revolution*, encompasses any technique for improving plants or animals or using microorganisms in innovative ways. Using growth hormone to increase milk output in cows is one technique. Scientists are also exploring ways to genetically alter the reproductive cells of fish, poultry, sheep, and pigs to speed up conventional breeding times (Kennedy, 1993). Scientists have already genetically altered microorganisms in several ways. Soon, for example, it should be possible to spray frost-sensitive plants, such as strawberries, with a strain of bacteria that will protect the plants against up to 95 percent of frost damage.

Some scientists believe that the biotechnological revolution can close the gap between worldwide food production and rapid population growth, but the new technology is not without problems. First, giving growth hormones to animals can make their meat unfit for human consumption. Hogs that get growth hormones are prone to gastric ulcers, arthritis, dermatitis, and other diseases (Kennedy, 1993). Second, the cost of biotechnological innovations is beyond the budgets of most middle- and low-income nations. Third, the new biotechnologies are developed for use with conventional (Western) farming methods (Hauchler and Kennedy, 1994). Fourth, genetic erosion (by breeding or gene manipulation) may eventually make the people of the world reliant on only a few varieties of plants and animals for their entire food supply and thus vulnerable to famine as the result of a single pest or disease. Finally, environmental accidents, such as the unintentional release of genetically manipulated microorganisms, pose a potential hazard.

Increasing the food supply is one way of coping with a rapidly growing world population, but hardly the only way. Some people believe that we can forestall the problem by controlling fertility.

CONTROLLING FERTILITY

The global population increase in the twentieth century has been unprecedented, and an additional three billion young people will soon enter their reproductive years (United Nations, 1995). Although demographers know that limiting fertility is the best way to slow down population growth, they also know that the issue is fraught with controversy. Consider the three preconditions that demographer Ansley Coale (1973) believes are necessary before there can be a sustained decline in a society's fertility:

 People must accept calculated choice as a valid element in marital fertility. If people believe a supernatural power controls human reproduction, it is unlikely that they will risk offending that deity by trying to limit fertility. On the other hand, the more worldly-wise people are, the more likely they are to believe they have the right to control reproduction.

Some *analysts believe that China's one-child policy has further devalued female infants. What long-term effects might such a policy have on the sex ratio (number of males in relation to number of females) in that country? Could this influence the number of females and males available for marriage and parenting in the future?*

 People must see advantages to reduced fertility. People must have some reason to want to limit fertility. Otherwise, natural attraction will lead to unprotected sexual intercourse and perhaps numerous children.

 People must know about and master effective techniques of birth control. The means for limiting family size must be available, and people must know how to use them successfully.

Although Coale believes that all three preconditions must be met to limit fertility effectively, most government policies focus only on the third: family planning measures (Weeks, 1998).

Family Planning

Family planning programs provide birth control information, contraceptive devices, sometimes sterilization and abortion procedures, and health services. The earliest programs were based on the assumption that women have large families because they do not know how to prevent pregnancy or they lack access to birth control devices. Though we know today that other issues are involved, most programs are still based on this assumption. They do little, for example, to influence a couple's desire to have children and appear not to realize that in some middle- and low-income nations, women are not free to make their own decisions about reproduction. There is overwhelming evidence that women want only the number of children that they can care for adequately (United Nations, 1995). In fact, an estimated 120 million women want to postpone the next birth or avoid further childbearing altogether (Westoff, 1995). At the same time, however, many of these women are socialized to accept the ideal of the perfect mother, so motherhood confers social status and a sense of personal achievement. Children are considered a gift and a blessing, providing women with affection that they might not otherwise receive and securing the mother's position in the kinship group and the larger society (O'Connell, 1994).

Critics of family planning programs argue that most policies are developed by political leaders in high-income nations who are motivated by race and class issues rather than by a genuine concern about world hunger or overpopulation. They say that high-income nations—such as England, France, and the

United States—encourage births among middle- and upper-income white women in their own countries but advocate depopulation policies in low-income regions such as sub-Saharan Africa, where most residents are people of color (O'Connell, 1994). For example, the French government is promoting larger families because of a rapidly aging population, a low fertility rate, and a national concern that the country is losing its identity because of high immigration rates (Weeks, 1998).

 ## Zero Population Growth

With *zero population growth,* **there is a totally stable population, one that neither grows nor decreases from year to year because births, deaths, and migration are in perfect balance** (Weeks, 1998). For example, the population growth rate would be zero if a nation had no immigration or emigration and the birth rate and the death rate were the same (Ehrlich and Ehrlich, 1991).

The United States is nearing zero population growth because of several factors: (1) A high proportion of women and men in the labor force find satisfaction and rewards outside of family life; (2) birth control is inexpensive and readily available; (3) the trend is toward later marriage (see Chapter 11); (4) the cost of raising a child from birth to adulthood is rising rapidly; and (5) schools and public service campaigns make teenagers more aware of how to control fertility (United Nations, 1995). Near-zero population growth is one characteristic of the U.S. population; another is a rapidly changing population.

IMMIGRATION AND ITS CONSEQUENCES

High rates of immigration are changing the composition of the U.S. population. Today, approximately 20 million people—or 8 percent of the total U.S. population—came here from other nations. In fact, the proportion of U.S. immigrants is at its highest point since the early 1940s, when people born in other countries accounted for 9 percent of the population. In 1944, immigration accounted for 30 percent of that year's increase in the U.S. population and contributed to the growth of large urban centers such as New York, Los Angeles, and Miami. On a

global basis, immigration and internal migration are causing urban populations to grow faster than the total population (see Map 15.1). Because most cities do not have the capacity to deal with existing residents, much less significant increases in the number of those residents, especially those with limited education and economic wherewithal, immigration and internal migration often lead to patterns of urban squalor and high levels of stress in daily living.

What are the consequences of today's high rate of immigration to the United States as a whole? Not all social analysts agree on the answer to this question. Some believe that immigrants cost U.S. taxpayers billions of dollars each year (see Huddle, 1993), although the cost varies widely from state to state. One study estimated that households in California pay about $1,200 a year in state and local taxes to cover services such as education, welfare, public health, and police protection for immigrants, whereas New Jersey residents pay about $230 a year for immigrant services (Serrin, 1997). But a study conducted by the National Academy of Sciences found that immigration also produces substantial economic benefits for the United States (Pear, 1997a). In fact, immigrants may contribute as much as $10 billion a year to the economic output of this country. This same study pointed out that low-skilled, U.S.-born workers can lose jobs because of competition from immigrant workers (Pear, 1997a). Economist James P. Smith sums up this way (Pear, 1997a:1, 15):

> It's true that some Americans are now paying more taxes because of immigration, and native-born Americans without a high school education have seen their wages fall slightly because of the competition sparked by lower-skilled, newly arrived immigrants. But the vast majority of Americans are enjoying a healthier economy as a result of the increased supply of labor and lower prices that result from immigration.

The National Academy of Sciences study also found that, despite a widespread belief to the contrary, African Americans are not universally hurt by immigration or competition with immigrants. It appears that only in big cities where many recent immigrants have settled, such as New York and Los Angeles, are African Americans likely to lose jobs directly because of immigrants (Pear, 1997a).

MAP 15.1

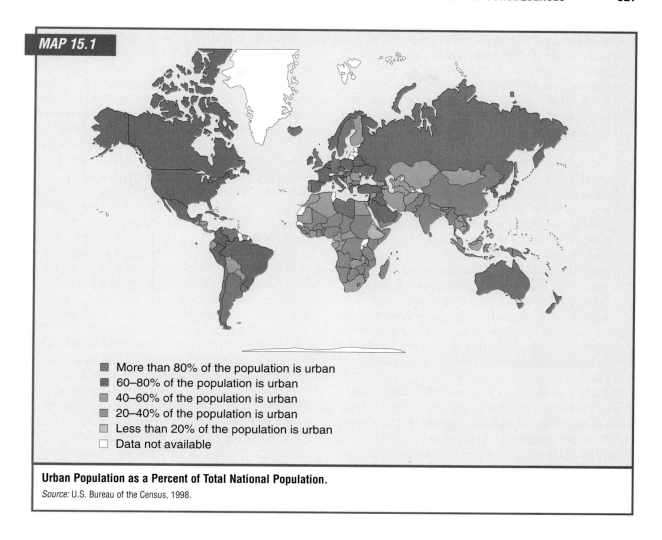

■ More than 80% of the population is urban
■ 60–80% of the population is urban
■ 40–60% of the population is urban
■ 20–40% of the population is urban
□ Less than 20% of the population is urban
□ Data not available

Urban Population as a Percent of Total National Population.

Source: U.S. Bureau of the Census, 1998.

Some other findings from the National Academy of Sciences's report provide important insights (Pear, 1997a:1, 15):

▲ If immigration to the United States continues at the present rate, it will account for nearly two-thirds of the expected population growth in the next fifty years.

▲ The wage gap between immigrants and U.S.-born workers will grow wider because many recent immigrants are arriving from poorer nations where the average levels of education, wages, and skills are far below those of the United States.

▲ Immigration has contributed to an increase in the number of high school dropouts in the United States, and this increase has lowered the wages of high school dropouts by about 5 percent.

One more consequence of immigration needs to be examined: immigrant-bashing. It is not a new phenomenon, but the recent influx of immigrants seems to have provided more opportunities for such behavior. Here is what a representative of an immigration rights organization found when she spent a day with some high school students (Duran, 1997:A7):

The students were predominantly white and upper-middle-class. I went in hoping to have an informed discussion about this divisive issue [immigration]. Instead, I glimpsed how entrenched immigrant-bashing is in the United States. . . . Some students said you can always tell illegal aliens by the way they look. How do they look? The students described Mexicans, ignoring that immigrants come from all parts of the globe, and that Mexican immigrants are only a fraction of the total. . . . I tried a different tack. I talked about people in Mexico who were starving, who needed to find work or join their families. Their need is so great that they endure desperate conditions on the journey. . . . I told of a woman who drowned attempting to swim the crossing [from Mexico] with her baby. Her last act was to hand over her baby to a companion, saving its life. The response was dismaying, "Why didn't they just use a boat?" a student asked. "If they're so stupid that they can't use a boat, what do they expect?" The class erupted into laughter. . . . As I continue to promote immigrant rights, my job will be to open those closed [hearts and minds], and to remind people that their fate is connected to the fate of others, including immigrants.

Most population-related policies in the United States focus on immigration, particularly undocumented workers or illegal immigrants. But stemming the flow of immigrants appears to be a virtually impossible task for any one nation, as does alleviating the problem of environmental degradation.

POPULATION AND THE ENVIRONMENT

Although it is popularly believed that most environmental problems arise from rapid growth in middle- and low-income nations, this isn't the case. Many scientists believe that high-income nations present a much greater threat to the earth's ecosystems (Ehrlich and Ehrlich, 1991). An *ecosystem* is "all the populations of plants and animal species that live and interact in a given area at a particular time, as well as the chemical and physical factors that make up the nonliving environment" (Cable and Cable, 1995:124). Thus an ocean is an ecosystem; a tropical rainforest is an ecosystem; and on a much smaller scale, a house on a lot is an ecosystem. When all of the earth's ecosystems are put together, they make up the *biosphere*.

Ecosystems do not have an infinite ability to support population growth or environmental depletion or destruction. In fact, some scientists believe that many of the world's ecosystems have already exceeded their *carrying capacity*—the maximum population that an ecosystem can support without eventually being degraded or destroyed (Cable and Cable, 1995). According to biologists Paul Ehrlich and Anne H. Ehrlich (1991), a baby born in the United States will have twice the destructive impact on the earth's ecosystems and services as a baby born in Sweden; 140 times the impact of a baby born in Bangladesh or Kenya; and 280 times the impact of a baby born in Chad, Rwanda, Haiti, or Nepal. How did the Ehrlichs reach such a conclusion? They developed a formula for determining the impact that human beings have on their environment: $I = P \times A \times T$, or Impact = Population × Affluence × Technology. Thus the size of the population, its level of affluence, and the technology available in the society are major contributing factors to *environmental degradation—disruptions to the environment that have negative consequences for ecosystems* (Cable and Cable, 1995). Environmental degradation involves both removing natural resources from the environment and adding to environmental problems through pollution.

In the United States, environmental degradation increases as people try to maintain the high levels of wealth and material comfort to which they have become accustomed. They consume the earth's resources and pollute its environment with automobiles, airplanes, speedboats, computers, television sets and VCRs, year-round air conditioning and heating, and other amenities that are far beyond the grasp of most of the world's people. Although these products are made possible by high levels of industrial production and economic growth, economic growth often depletes and destroys the environment.

▲ Economic Growth and Environmental Degradation

During most of the twentieth century, economic growth in the United States was based on increased output in the manufacturing sector. The environment is affected at all phases of the manufacturing process, from mining and transportation to manufacturing and waste disposal. As you may recall from Chapter 13, industrial production involves extracting raw materials—natural resources—from

"I'm rather fortunate. I have no parents, so Medicare is no problem, and I have no children, so the environment is no problem."

the environment, usually through mining. Mining depletes mineral resources and fossil fuel reserves—coal, oil, and natural gas. Mining also disturbs ecosystems, particularly surface mining, which strips bare the land, destroying natural vegetation and wildlife habitats. Other problems typically follow, including erosion of the land by wind and water and runoff of acids, silt, and toxic substances into nearby surface water and groundwater, which leads to the pollution of rivers and streams with toxic compounds that kill fish and other aquatic life (Cable and Cable, 1995).

The environmental impact of mining doesn't stop when the raw materials have been mined. Now the raw materials must be transported to a plant or factory, where workers will transform them into manufactured products. Transporting requires the use of energy—particularly the burning of fossil fuels—which contributes to air pollution because motor vehicles produce carbon monoxide, nitrogen oxides, and photochemical pollutants. Each of these pollutants is associated with various illnesses, including heart and respiratory disease and cancer. The manufacturing process further depletes fossil fuels and contributes to air pollution. People who work in or live near facilities that pollute the environment are often harmed by the manufacturing process, because of the solid or toxic wastes.

Many analysts believe that we cannot continue this pattern of environmental degradation. Future economic development—in the United States and globally—will require drastic changes in the structure of industry, especially in the energy, transportation, chemical, and agricultural sectors of the economy

(Hauchler and Kennedy, 1994). If we don't make changes, environmental degradation constitutes a major threat to the well-being of all human beings and ecosystems on the earth. Let's look now at some specific kinds of environmental degradation: air pollution; problems with water, soil, and forests; and solid, toxic, and nuclear waste.

 ## Air Pollution

Nature performs many *ecosystem services*—valuable, practical functions that help to preserve ecosystems. For example, if the atmosphere is not overburdened, it can maintain a proper balance between carbon dioxide and oxygen, as well as provide ozone for protection against ultraviolet radiation (see Table 15.1). However, air pollution interferes with many ecosystem services. The carbon dioxide that pollutes the air we breathe keeps the sun's heat from radiating back into space, thereby causing the earth to heat up (the greenhouse effect, discussed in the next section). Other air pollutants deplete the upper atmosphere ozone that shields the earth from ultraviolet radiation. The ozone layer, located thirty miles above our planet's surface, protects us from the sun's ultraviolet rays (Petersen, 1994). Ozone depletion can kill

the organic life that produces food and oxygen and thus make life unsustainable.

The drastic increase in air pollution during the twentieth century has placed an undue burden on the atmosphere's ecosystem services (Stevens, 1997). Beginning with the Industrial Revolution in the late nineteenth and early twentieth centuries, more and more pollutants have been emitted into the atmosphere by households, industries, and automobile traffic. The result is constantly increasing amounts of carbon dioxide, carbon monoxide, nitrogen oxide, and sulfur oxide, as well as heavy metals such as lead, zinc, and copper in our air (Hauchler and Kennedy, 1994). Today, 85 percent of the air pollution in urban areas can be attributed to the internal combustion engine used in automobiles and other vehicles (U.S. Bureau of the Census, 1998). Although laws have reduced the amount of pollution from automobiles and industries in the United States, more than 40 percent of the population resides in areas where air pollutants still exceed acceptable levels (Hauchler and Kennedy, 1994).

Air pollution affects all life and ecosystems on the planet. Air pollution in the form of acid rain destroys forests, streams and lakes, and other ecosystems. *Acid rain* is rainfall containing large concentrations of sulfuric and nitric acids (primarily from the burning of

TABLE 15.1 WHAT THE NATURAL WORLD DOES FOR US (IF WE DON'T MESS IT UP TOO MUCH)

Food production	Produces fish, game, and crops—even without our help.
Raw materials	Produces (without our help) the raw materials from which humans create things.
Genetic resources	On its own, creates the ability for crops, vegetation, and animals to survive.
Pollination	Without our help, plants and animals naturally reproduce.
Biological control	Somehow, most species of plants and animals survive for millions of years without our help.
Climate regulation	Unless we mess it up, nature has created an ozone layer that protects all plant and animal life from the sun's ultraviolet radiation.
Water regulation	If we don't mess with it, the world's water supply keeps reproducing and distributing itself.
Gas regulation	If we don't mess it up too badly, nature keeps carbon dioxide and oxygen in balance—a balance necessary for life.
Recreation	Just think of the wonderful sights and recreation that nature has created.

Source: Stevens, 1997.

| Air pollution is a pressing problem in many nations, but nowhere more so than in Mexico City, where daylight hours often look like this photo. How is air pollution related to people's health and life expectancy?

fuel and car and truck exhausts). In Germany, for example, acid rain is believed to have damaged more than half the trees—up to 80 percent in some regions (Hauchler and Kennedy, 1994). Efforts to reduce acid rain in the United States have been blocked by the automobile industry; companies that mine, haul, and sell high-sulfur coal; and coal miners. Fortunately, new industries are less dependent on burning coal than are older factories in the industrial Northeast and Midwest states (Petersen, 1994).

In the past, air pollution in middle- and low-income nations was attributed primarily to the fight for survival and economic development, whereas most air pollution in high-income nations was attributed to relatively luxurious lifestyles. However, distinctions between air pollution in high-income and middle- and low-income nations are growing weaker, even though the United States and other Western industrial nations account for about 68 percent of the carbon monoxide in the atmosphere (World Resources Institute, 1992). Automobile ownership, once considered a luxury, is rising rapidly in urban centers in middle-income nations such as Mexico, Brazil, Taiwan, Indonesia, and China (Bradsher, 1997). In 1997, for example,

São Paulo, Brazil, had approximately 4.5 million cars on its streets—more than twice the 2.1 million cars in New York City, which has about the same population (Bradsher, 1997). Mexico City, known as the smog capital of the world, has only thirty-seven days a year when the air quality measures as "satisfactory" (Walker, 1994). Affluent Mexican residents buy bottled oxygen at the drug store; the less affluent buy quick shots of oxygen at street-corner kiosks (Cleeland, 1991). Cities such as Bombay, Lagos, Shanghai, and Jakarta have also seen a significant increase in the number of automobiles, bringing a corresponding rise in air pollution and traffic problems (Bradsher, 1997).

But there are some hopeful signs that we are curbing fossil fuel pollution. In the United States, antipollution laws have brought about changes in how automobiles are made and the fuels they consume. Cars are now equipped with catalytic converters and other antipollution devices, and leaded gasoline (a major offender) has been phased out. However, while some middle-income nations are requiring antipollution devices on new vehicles, many leaded gas-burning cars—often used cars from the United States—are still a significant source of air pollution.

Industrial air pollution has been reduced in some regions of the United States, but pollution controls are often expensive, and many corporations try to find ways to avoid making costly plant conversions. Some move their plants to middle- and low-income nations that have less stringent environmental regulations; others try to avoid antipollution guidelines through government waivers, sometimes known as pollution credits. These credits were created by the federal Clean Air Act of 1990 to reward state agencies and companies that kept their emissions below federal governmental limits. Recently, however, New York State used its accumulated credits to lure heavily polluting corporations to the state. Essentially, then, the pollution credits that were earned by the state for reducing its own pollution emissions would allow these corporations to pollute in return for moving to the state and paying New York taxes (Hernandez, 1997). Environmental activists ask why the state should subsidize polluters in the name of economic development and at the expense of people's health and the environment (Hernandez, 1997).

THE GREENHOUSE EFFECT
Emissions from traffic and industry not only add to general air pollution but also contribute to

the *greenhouse effect*—an environmental condition caused by excessive quantities of carbon dioxide, water vapor, methane, and nitrous oxide in the atmosphere. When carbon dioxide molecules build up in the earth's atmosphere, they act like the glass roof of a greenhouse, allowing sunlight to reach the earth's surface but preventing the escape of solar infrared radiation (heat) back into space. The heat that cannot escape is reflected, causing the earth's surface temperature to rise (Weiner, 1990). Some scientists believe that the earth will have a temperature increase of as much as five degrees over the next hundred years. In fact, if current rates of emission into the atmosphere remain unchanged, temperature increases might eventually bring about catastrophic consequences.

One consequence could be significant changes in weather patterns and climate. Changes in weather patterns could bring increased evaporation, creating new deserts and decreasing regional water reserves. Changes in air circulation and climatic conditions could result in more frequent hurricanes, flooding, tidal waves, and droughts. Vegetation zones could shift, and forests in the northern hemisphere might die off.

Not all scientists believe that the greenhouse effect exists or that its effects will be this disastrous (Hauchler and Kennedy, 1994). However, studies show a marked retreat of glaciers and the beginning of a shift in vegetation, and one possible cause is the greenhouse effect (Hauchler and Kennedy, 1994).

To reduce greenhouse gases, political and economic leaders in high-income nations want middle- and low-income nations to lower their birth rates so that the total number of people contributing to the problem does not rise. But leaders in these nations think that high-income nations should institute stringent restrictions on consumption and pollution in their own countries and use some of their resources to help other countries with economic development. Then, they say, it may be possible to significantly reduce their birth rates (Hauchler and Kennedy, 1994).

DEPLETION OF THE OZONE LAYER

There is some indication that the ozone layer of the atmosphere has been endangered by air pollution. In 1992, a hole the size of North America was reported in the ozone layer over Antarctica, and scientists have concluded that the ozone layer has been thinning out at a rate of 6 percent a year in the 1990s (Hauchler and Kennedy, 1994). Ozone is vital to life on earth because it is the only gas in the atmosphere that can absorb the sun's dangerous ultraviolet radiation. A thinning ozone layer increases risk of skin cancer, damages marine life, and lowers crop yields. It is important to note that the ozone shrinkage that scientists are currently measuring is the result of emissions in the early 1980s. Thus, the emissions we produce today will exert their destructive effects in the future (Hauchler and Kennedy, 1994). Although past damage cannot be undone, many countries are now phasing out products that contain chemicals that damage the ozone layer, hoping to control damage to this delicate ecosystem in the future.

Problems with Water, Soil, and Forests

Water, soil, and forests (vegetation) are interdependent crucial resources that face increasing degradation or destruction because of pollution. As a result of climate changes, waste, pollution, and rapid depletion, the earth's drinking water is endangered and its fertile land is being lost.

WATER SHORTAGES AND POLLUTION

Water depletion and pollution are serious problems in the United States. The western United States already suffers from chronic water scarcity, and other regions are periodically affected by drought and other weather-related conditions. However, these problems are not limited to the United States. Although approximately 70 percent of the earth's surface is covered by water, most water is not drinkable: 97 percent is saltwater, 2 percent is in ice caps and glaciers, and most of the remaining 1 percent is so far underground that it is beyond human reach (Petersen, 1994). The primary sources of water for use and consumption are rainfall, streams, lakes, rivers, and aquifers (accessible underground water supplies).

Because of the current rate of world population growth and existing climatic conditions, water scarcity is increasing throughout the world. It is estimated that today many countries have only half as much water available per person as was available in 1975. If the greenhouse effect brings about changes in the climate, as many as twenty-one countries in Africa may experience serious water shortages that

In our delicate ecosystem, water pollution has a disastrous effect on all forms of life—not just on human life. What measures might we implement to reduce water pollution like this?

will be further exacerbated by the growing problem of water pollution (Hauchler and Kennedy, 1994).

Where does the water go? The largest amount (about 70 percent) is used for crop irrigation; in some African and Asian countries, as much as 85 percent of the available water is used in agriculture. The second largest use of water is in industry (23 to 25 percent). Industrial use of water depends on the level of development in a country and the structure of its economy. For example, high-income nations use as much as 60 percent of their water for industry, whereas a middle- or low-income nation may use less than 10 percent. A mere 8 percent of all available water is used for domestic or private household use. Affluent people in high-income nations use far more water (up to 1,000 quarts per person per day) than do families living in African villages, where water must often be carried several miles (about 2 to 5 quarts is the physical minimum). Medical analysts believe that about 80 percent of all illnesses in developing nations are partly due to insufficient water supplies (Petersen, 1994).

Water pollution seriously diminishes the available supply of water. Water may be polluted in a variety of ways. Most often, though, the cause is unpurified or insufficiently treated sewage from households and

industry discharged into groundwater or surface water or pesticides and mineral fertilizers leached from farmland (Hauchler and Kennedy, 1994). The pollutants range from nitrates and phosphates to metals, salts, and pathogenic microorganisms.

The paper-manufacturing industry is a major water polluter. Dioxin and other chlorinated organic compounds used in manufacturing paper products are emitted into the streams below paper mills. People can become seriously ill from drinking the polluted water or eating contaminated fish. Environmental activists believe that paper mills should be required to convert to totally closed systems in which there are no chemical discharges into nearby water. Converting is costly, but a few paper mills are leading the way in the United States. Mills in Canada and Europe are required to use closed systems (Cushman, 1997). But not all water pollution comes from industry. Agriculture, especially as practiced by transnational corporations that are engaged in agribusiness, also pollutes water. Fertilizers and pesticides containing hazardous toxic chemicals that seriously impair water quality are used extensively and often leach into water supplies.

SOIL DEPLETION AND DESERTIFICATION

About 11 percent of the earth's surface is used for growing crops, 32 percent is forest, and 24 percent is used to graze animals. Each year, however, many acres of usable land are lost through erosion and contamination. *Deforestation*—excessive removal of trees—usually results in serious erosion. Since the 1992 Earth Summit in Rio de Janeiro, high-income nations have made an effort to protect forests. Unfortunately, prior industrialization in the United States and other high-income nations has already taken a serious toll on forests, and the pattern is continuing in some middle- and low-income nations as they become more industrialized. In the United States, logging in the national forest system, especially in the Pacific Northwest, is an issue. Environmentalists say that logging increases landslides, floods, and changes in rivers and streams, which devastate fish stocks (Goldberg, 1997). Furthermore, when road building, which is necessary to get to the trees in the forest, is combined with cutting all the timber in an area (clear-cutting), the damage is even greater. More water flows down slopes, and when roads wash out, rocks and soil fall onto lower slopes and into streambeds (Goldberg, 1997).

SOCIAL PROBLEMS

AND SOCIAL POLICY   **BOX 15.2**

What to Do with Waste?
NIMBY (Not in My Back Yard!)

I'm very proud to be here today as we realize a dream and help fulfill a promise to the people of Staten Island. For too long, the Fresh Kills Landfill has weighed on the people of Staten Island. . . . All [of New York City's] residential waste—13,000 tons per day—has come to this landfill on the west coast of this island. . . . Today we take a major step toward our goal. . . . Instead of coming to Fresh Kills, this waste will be transported to a landfill in Waverly, Virginia.

—*New York City Mayor Rudolph W. Giuliani's
"Fresh Kills Exportation Announcement," on
July 1, 1997 (City of New York, 1997)*

For nearly fifty years, Fresh Kills on Staten Island served as a landfill; in 1991, however, New York City began using it as the city's only repository of residential solid waste. By the late 1990s, covering four square miles and reaching depths of more than 100 feet, Fresh Kills had gained the distinction of being the world's largest landfill. Several years ago, it was estimated that the landfill contained 2.9 billion cubic feet of trash, including 100 million tons of newspaper, paint cans, potato peels, cigarette butts, chicken bones, dryer lint, and an occasional corpse (Hawken, 1997).

Although the New York City Department of Sanitation's solution of awarding a contract to a landfill in Waverly, Virginia, may have reduced the problems of New York, has it contributed to the problems of people in Virginia? The contract went into effect in 1997, and perhaps it is too early to tell. However, environmentalists and others remind us that many people use the phrase "Not in my back yard" (NIMBY) to describe their feelings about having the burden of other people's trash piled on them or of air pollution or other forms of envi-

---

Today, many regions are losing an increasing amount of useable land as a result of *desertification*—**the process by which usable land is turned into desert because of overgrazing, harmful agricultural practices, or deforestation.** It is estimated that desertification destroys as many as 15 million acres of land a year. An additional 50 million acres of crop and pasture land become inefficient each year because of excessive application of herbicides and pesticides, insufficient crop rotation, and intensified agricultural production (United Nations Environmental Program, 1992).

Although desertification takes place in both high-income and middle- and low-income nations, its effects are particularly devastating in middle- and low-income nations. When a country is already hard hit by rapid population growth, virtually any loss of land or crops is potentially devastating to large numbers of people (United Nations Environmental Program, 1992). The United Nations and other international organizations have therefore tried to make protection of the environment an integral part of all economic development policy. However, environmental protection specialists say that to translate policy into action, conservation programs must be supported by the people and the major sources of the problem must also be addressed: overpopulation and poverty (United Nations Environmental Program, 1992).

 Solid, Toxic, and Nuclear Wastes

Even with a rapidly growing world population and ongoing economic development in industrialized nations, the planet might be able to sustain life for a long time if it weren't for all the solid and toxic chemical waste that is dumped into the environment.

SOLID WASTE

In the United States and some other high-income nations, people consume a vast array of products

ronmental degradation affecting them where they live.

Since social policies, including legislative and administrative decisions regarding such things as where waste will be discarded, are often made on a city-by-city or state-by-state basis, many decisions may be based on the immediate "good" of a specific group of people rather than looking at the larger picture of where and how problems may be solved. Discussions about moving nuclear waste across the country on trains or "planting" it in an area such as the Texas panhandle inevitably arise when states begin to wonder how to dispose of these wastes.

What other solutions might exist for reducing the amount of garbage that we generate? In the early 1990s, Germany passed the Ordinance on the Avoidance of Packaging Waste in response to its own shrinking landfill space (Montavalli, 1997). The policy placed on companies that make packages the responsibility for taking them back. As a result,

smaller and fewer packages are made in Germany. Toothpaste tubes, for example, are shaped like flat caps, and each tube has a tiny green dot, meaning that it's in compliance with Germany's packaging law (Montavalli, 1997). Recently, other European countries, as well as Japan and Canada, have passed similar packaging laws.

Efforts to pass such laws in the United States have met strenuous opposition from most companies that use packaging to sell their products. Because, for many transnational corporations, maintaining profits in light of increasing global economic competition is a more compelling consideration than environmental concerns, voluntary action has been taken by only a few companies, such as DuPont, Xerox, and Duracell.

How should the United States tackle its waste problem? Is it enough to simply move waste from place to place? What long-range planning will be necessary if we are to have a safe and comfortable environment in the future?

and—in these *disposable societies*—throw away huge quantities of paper, plastic, metal, and other materials. The typical North American creates over 1,500 pounds of municipal solid waste per year, compared to slightly more than 700 pounds produced by the average western European (Petersen, 1994). *Solid waste* is any and all unwanted and discarded materials that are not liquids or gases, including sewage solids. For example, each year people in the United States throw away:

▲ 16 billion disposable diapers
▲ 2 billion razors and razor blades
▲ 220 million tires
▲ more glass and aluminum than existed in the entire world before World War II (Petersen, 1994:107)

One partial solution is *recycling*—reusing resources that would otherwise be discarded. While there has been an increase in recycling, some cities have found

they are running out of landfill space and consequently have been moving their garbage to other regions as a temporary solution (see Box 15.2).

TOXIC WASTE

At the same time that technology has brought about improvements in the quality and length of life, it has created the potential for new disasters. One source of a potential disaster is *toxic waste*, the hazardous chemical by-products of industrial processes. Perhaps the most widely known U.S. case of toxic waste is Love Canal. In the late 1970s, residents of Niagara Falls, New York, learned that their children were attending a school that had been built on top of a toxic landfill (Gibbs, 1982). After large numbers of children became ill and the smell and appearance of the chemicals permeated the entire area, many mobilized against Hooker Chemical Company, which had dumped tons of chemicals there (Gibbs, 1982). Eventually, the federal government bought many of the houses, moved the residents out, and removed as much of the toxic waste as possible. Today, families again live in the area, but they have a highly visible neighbor: a forty-acre grassy landfill, thirty-feet high at the center, with an eight-foot-high chain-link fence surrounding it. The landfill contains 21,000 tons of toxic chemical waste and the remains of 239 contaminated houses (Hoffman, 1994).

Today, the U.S. government regulates the disposal of toxic wastes, but some hazardous wastes are not covered by regulations, and some corporations avoid the regulations by locating their factories in other countries (see Chapters 2 and 15). In addition, there is often nowhere to safely dispose of the chemicals. Many people take a "not in my backyard" attitude toward toxic chemical waste dumps (Dunlap, 1992; Freudenberg and Steinsapir, 1992).

What is it like to discover that your neighborhood is being polluted by toxic waste? A resident of the East Swallow Road neighborhood in Fort Collins, Colorado, describes the uncertainty and worry caused by pools of petroleum leaking out of a service station's underground tanks (Erikson, 1994:115):

> [Y]ou just sort of live your life on hold. I'm always saying, "God, will it ever end so we can get on with our lives?" You can't really make any plans, you just sort of live your life in limbo. Sometimes it's almost unbearable. It's like you really don't live, you just sort of exist, and you wait and you wait and you wait for it to end. But it doesn't, so you just struggle through each day and you worry. You know, it's really, really a pretty sad way to have to live.

NUCLEAR WASTE

Nuclear, or radioactive, wastes are the most dangerous of all toxic wastes. Radioactive waste comes primarily from manufacturers of nuclear weapons and nuclear power plants, although small amounts of waste are by-products of certain medical procedures. Weapons-manufacturing plants in Washington, South Carolina, and Colorado store huge amounts of radioactive waste and chemicals in underground tanks. Inspectors have found some of the older tanks leak and others are empty. When tanks leak, they contaminate groundwater and thousands of cubic feet of soil (Petersen, 1994).

Nuclear waste remains deadly for prolonged periods of time. For example, uranium waste from nuclear power plants (an estimated 50,000 tons by the early 2000s) will remain dangerously radioactive

for the next 10,000 years, and plutonium waste for the next 240,000 years (Petersen, 1994).

TECHNOLOGICAL DISASTERS

Technological disasters, such as the 1986 meltdown and radiation leak at the Chernobyl nuclear power plant in the Ukraine, have increased global awareness of the problems associated with radioactive waste. However, despite the disaster, the former Soviet Union was still using nineteen similar reactors in 1994 (Petersen, 1994), giving evidence to sociologist Kai Erikson's remarks. According to Erikson (1991:15), the world faces a new species of trouble today:

> [Environmental problems] contaminate rather than merely damage . . . they pollute, befoul, taint, rather than just create wreckage . . . they penetrate human tissue indirectly rather than just wound the surfaces by assaults of a more straightforward kind. . . . And the evidence is growing that they scare human beings in new and special ways, that they elicit an uncanny fear in us.

The chaos that Erikson (1994:141) describes is the result of *technological disasters*—"meaning everything that can go wrong when systems fail, humans err, designs prove faulty, engines misfire, and so on." Chernobyl and Love Canal were technological disasters, as were radiation leakage at the Three Mile Island nuclear power plant in Pennsylvania in 1979 and the leakage of lethal gases at the pesticide plant in Bhopal, India, in 1984. In the worst-case scenario, technological disasters kill tens of thousands of people; in the best-case scenario, they place tremendous stress on the world's ecosystems and greatly diminish the quality of life for everyone.

SOCIOLOGICAL PERSPECTIVES ON POPULATION AND THE ENVIRONMENT

As sociologists have examined how human behavior affects population and environmental problems, the subdiscipline of environmental sociology has emerged. According to Cable and Cable (1995:5), *"environmental sociology* examines people's beliefs about their environment, their behavior toward it, and the ways in which the structure of society influences them and contributes to the persistent abuse of the environment." Like all sociologists, environmental sociologists—as well as demographers—approach their study from one or another perspective.

 ## The Functionalist Perspective

Some functionalists focus on the relationship between social structure, technological change, and environmental problems. On the one hand, they say, technological innovation serves important functions in society. For example, automation and mass production have made a wide array of goods—from automobiles and computers to McDonald's burgers—available to many people. On the other hand, technological innovation has latent dysfunctions; automation and mass production, for example, create air pollution, overuse and depletion of natural resources, and excessive solid waste. From this point of view, some environmental problems are the price a society pays for technological progress. If this is true, the best way to alleviate the problem is to develop new technologies. This is what happened, some functionalists note, when the catalytic converter and other antipollution devices were developed for automobiles.

Other functionalists take a neo-Malthusian perspective and believe that to reduce food shortages and environmental problems, population must be controlled. In other words, the more people there are alive, the greater are the overuse of finite resources and degradation of soil, water, and land.

No matter which view functionalist environmental sociologists take, they believe that solutions to overpopulation and environmental degradation lie in social institutions such as education and the government. Educators can encourage population control by teaching people about the limits to agriculture and the difficulty of feeding rapidly increasing populations. Government leaders and international organizations such as the United Nations can cooperate to find far-reaching and innovative solutions and develop understandings about more equitable use of the world's resources (Ehrlich and Ehrlich, 1991).

 ## The Conflict Perspective

Analysts using a conflict framework believe that population and environmental problems have less to do with overpopulation and shortages of resources than they have to do with power differentials in societies and in the larger global economy. For

example, early conflict theorists, such as Karl Marx and Friedrich Engels (1976/1848), did not think that the food supply was threatened by overpopulation because agricultural technology (even in their era) could meet the food needs of the growing world population if it were not for poverty. According to Marx and Engels (1976/1848), poverty exists because workers are exploited by capitalists. They argued, for example, that poverty existed in England because the capitalists skimmed off some of the workers' wages as profits. Thus, the labor of the working classes was used by capitalists to earn profits, which, in turn, were used to purchase machinery that could replace the workers rather than supply food. From this classical Marxist point of view, population growth is encouraged by capitalists who use unemployed workers (the industrial reserve army) to keep other workers from demanding higher wages or better working conditions.

According to contemporary conflict theorists, corporations and the government are the two main power institutions in society. As a result, when economic decisions made by members of the capitalist class and elite political leaders lead to environmental problems, the costs are externalized, or passed along to the people (Cable and Cable, 1995:13):

> [The externalization of environmental costs of production] . . . means that the costs of production's negative impact on the environment (for example, the expense of cleaning polluted water to make it suitable for drinking) are not included in the price of the product. The company neither pays for the privilege of polluting the water nor cleans it; it saves the cost of proper waste disposal and makes environmentally conscious competition impossible. Not even the consumer of the product pays the environmental costs of production directly. Rather, the public at large essentially subsidizes the company, by either paying for the cleanup of the environment or enduring degraded environmental quality.

Although most conflict approaches to studying the environment focus on the relationship between members of the capitalist class and political elites, there is also an approach known as *ecofeminism*—the belief that patriarchy is a root cause of environmental problems. According to ecofeminists, patriarchy results in not only the domination of women by men but also the belief that nature is to be possessed and dominated rather than treated as a partner (Ortner, 1974; Merchant, 1983, 1992; Mies and Shiva, 1993).

Another conflict approach uses an *environmental justice framework*—examining how race and class intersect in the struggle for scarce environmental resources. Of particular interest to these theorists is *environmental racism*—**the belief that a disproportionate number of hazardous facilities are placed in areas populated primarily by poor people and people of color** (Bullard and Wright, 1992). Hazardous facilities include waste disposal and treatment plants and chemical plants (Schneider, 1993). A 1987 study by the Commission for Racial Justice concluded, "Race was the most potent variable in predicting the location of uncontrolled (abandoned) and commercial toxic waste sites in the United States" (Bullard and Wright, 1992:41). For example, the Carver Terrace housing subdivision in Texarkana, Texas, which is composed of 100 African American households, was built over an area that had been previously contaminated by a creosote wood treatment facility (Capek, 1993). The federal government eventually bought out some of the homeowners and relocated the subdivision, but not until a number of years after it was determined that toxins in the neighborhood had caused the deaths of twenty-six people and the illnesses of many others (Capek, 1993).

 The Interactionist Perspective

Since interactionists take a microlevel approach, viewing society as the sum of all people's interactions, they look at environmental problems in terms of individuals. Specifically, they think environmental problems are exacerbated by people's subjective assessment of reality. They point out that children learn core values that are considered important in the United States through socialization, but some of these values can be detrimental to the environment. Consider the following widely held beliefs (Cable and Cable, 1995:11–12):

▲ *A free market system provides the greatest good for the greatest number of people:* Economic decision making works best in private hands.
▲ *The natural world is inexhaustible:* There will always be more natural resources.
▲ *Faith in technology:* Any challenge can be met through technology.

▲ *The growth ethic:* Growth equals progress; bigger is better.
▲ *Materialism:* Success can be measured in terms of consumption.
▲ *Individualism:* Individual rights and personal achievement are most important.
▲ *An anthropocentric worldview:* Human beings are at the center of the world, and humans are superior to other species. Standing *apart from* nature rather than recognizing that we are *part of* nature, we attempt to conquer and subdue the environment.

It may be, however, that as people become aware of the effects of environmental degradation, concern for the environment will emerge as a core value in the United States. According to sociologist Alan Scott (1990), quality-of-life issues, such as concern for the environment, have become an impetus for new social movements. It may be, too, that concern will spread in the twenty-first century, resulting in global environmental movements.

POPULATION AND THE ENVIRONMENT IN THE TWENTY-FIRST CENTURY

The problems that we have discussed in this chapter present some of the greatest challenges that humans face in the twenty-first century. Global overpopulation and environmental depletion and devastation have irreversible consequences, and actions taken—or not taken—today will be with us far into the future. Futurists believe that we must use a wide-angle lens to examine population and environmental concerns (Peterson, 1994). We must see the world and our role in it in a much different way than we did in the past. We must understand that environmental issues are *security* issues—as much so as a terrorist threat or a missile or bomb (Peterson, 1994). Once we understand that, we will think of environmental problems in a completely different light. For example, to eliminate the global threats posed by overpopulation and environmental degradation, all societies can make the following changes (based on Petersen, 1994:109):

▲ Reduce the use of energy.

▲ Shift from fossil fuels to solar-based energy systems or other energy-efficient systems such as water power, wind power, or geothermal energy.

▲ Develop new transportation networks and city designs that reduce automobile use.

▲ Work for redistribution of land and wealth so that the poor in all nations can make a positive contribution.

▲ Push for equality between women and men in all nations, emphasizing literacy training, educational opportunities, and health care (including reproduction and contraception information) for women.

▲ Effect a rapid transition to smaller families.

▲ Cooperate internationally to reduce the consumption of resources by the wealthy nations and bring higher living standards to poorer nations.

Are these changes likely to occur? Probably not if people in high- and middle-income nations adhere to their current belief systems. Some social analysts think that it will take a threatening event—a drastic change in the earth's weather patterns or a sudden increase in natural disasters—to capture the attention of enough of the earth's people and to convince political leaders that a serious change in direction is required if the planet is to continue to support human life (Petersen, 1994). We can only hope that people will not wait until it's too late.

SUMMARY

➡ *What is the global population and why is population growth a problem?*

The world's population was more than 6 billion in 1999; it doubled in the last fifty years and if this trend continues, will double again in the next fifty years. The concern is whether the earth's resources can support this rapid population growth.

➡ *What are the primary factors that affect population growth?*

Three factors affect population growth: fertility, the actual number of children born to an individual or a population; mortality, the number of deaths that occur in a specific population; and migration, the movement of people from one geographic area to another for the purpose of changing residency.

➡ *How does population growth affect a society?*

Population growth affects population composition, the biological and social characteristics of a population, including such attributes as age, sex, race, marital status, education, occupation, income, and size of household. In the United States, for example, the age distribution of the population affects the need for schools, employment opportunities, health care, and age-appropriate housing.

➡ *What are the major theoretical perspectives on overpopulation?*

According to the Malthusian perspective, population expands geometrically while the food supply increases arithmetically; disaster can be averted through positive checks (e.g., famine, disease, war) or preventive checks (e.g., sexual abstinence, delayed marriage). The neo-Malthusians believe that the earth is a ticking bomb because population problems exacerbate environmental problems. The third perspective is more hopeful. According to demographic transition theory, societies move from high birth and death rates to low birth and death rates as a result of technological development. However, critics say that demographic transition theory applies chiefly to Western societies.

➡ *What solutions do we have to world hunger?*

Two of the most far-reaching initiatives are the green revolution (the growing of high-yield "miracle" crops) and the biotechnological revolution, which involves "improving" plants or animals or using microorganisms in innovative ways. However, some social analysts believe that the solution is not to produce more food but to control fertility.

➤ *How is immigration changing the population composition of the United States?*

Today, the proportion of U.S. immigrants in the population is the highest it has been since 1940. If immigration continues at the present rate, it will account for two-thirds of the expected population growth in the next fifty years. (The United States is otherwise almost at zero population growth—a stable population.) Immigration leads to higher taxes, but it also brings substantial economic benefits.

➤ *What is environmental degradation and what are its causes?*

Environmental degradation is caused by disruptions to the environment that have negative consequences for ecosystems. Human beings, particularly as they pursue economic development and growth, cause environmental degradation.

➤ *What is the major source of air pollution and what are its effects?*

The major source is fossil fuel pollution, especially from vehicles but somewhat from industry. One of the most serious consequences of air pollution is the greenhouse effect, an environmental condition caused by excessive quantities of carbon dioxide, water vapor, methane, and nitrous oxide in the atmosphere leading to global warming. Another is depletion of the ozone layer, the part of the earth's atmosphere that absorbs dangerous ultraviolet radiation from the sun.

➤ *What water, soil, and forest problems do we face?*

Water scarcity is increasing on a global basis, and water pollution further diminishes the available water supply. One of the major water polluters in the United States is the paper-manufacturing industry. About 15 million acres of soil are lost each year to desertification (the process by which usable land is turned into desert because of overgrazing, harmful agricultural practices) and deforestation (excessive removal of trees). Desertification is greatest in middle- and low-income nations.

➤ *Why are solid, toxic, and nuclear wastes a problem?*

High-income nations are running out of space for the amount of solid waste produced by their "disposable societies." Toxic waste (hazardous chemical by-products of industry) causes death and disease if it is not disposed of properly. Nuclear, or radioactive, waste is a problem because of the length of time it remains deadly.

➤ *What is the functionalist perspective on population and the environment?*

On the subject of environment, functionalists say that the latent dysfunctions of technology cause problems but that new technologies can solve these problems. Most functionalists take a neo-Malthusian perspective on population but believe that social institutions, especially education and the government, can cooperate to solve population and environmental problems.

➤ *What is the conflict perspective on population and the environment?*

In the classical Marxist view, there would be enough food for all people if poverty were alleviated, and poverty exists because capitalists skim workers' wages for profits. Contemporary conflict theorists believe that the two main power institutions in society—corporations and the government—make economic decisions that result in environmental problems. An approach known as ecofeminism says that patriarchy is a root cause of environmental problems: Nature is viewed as something to be possessed and dominated.

➤ *What is the interactionist perspective on population and environment?*

Interactionists see population and environment problems in microlevel—individual—terms. Through socialization, children learn core values that are often detrimental to the environment. However, there is some indication that concern for the environment is becoming a core value in the United States.

KEY TERMS

acid rain, pp. 330–331
demographic transition theory,
   p. 322
demography, p. 318
desertification, p. 334

environmental degradation,
   p. 328
environmental racism, p. 338
fertility, p. 318
greenhouse effect, p. 332

migration, p. 319
mortality, p. 318
population composition, p. 320
zero population growth, p. 326

QUESTIONS FOR CRITICAL THINKING

1. Which perspective on population growth do you favor—neo-Malthusian or demographic transition theory—and why?

2. Reread the excerpt on pp. 327–328 describing immigrant-bashing and develop an action plan for opening the "closed hearts and minds" of these high school students.

3. If you had to focus on a single aspect of environmental degradation—air pollution; water, soil, or forest problems; solid, toxic, or nuclear waste disposal—which would it be and why? What would you do to make people aware of the seriousness of the problem? What new solutions could you propose?

Chapter Sixteen

Urban Problems

The Number 6 [subway] train from Manhattan to the South Bronx makes nine stops in the 18-minute ride between East 59th Street [the Upper East Side] and Brook Avenue. When you enter the train, you are in the seventh richest congressional district in the nation. When you leave, you are in the poorest. . . . In 1991, the median household income of the [Brook Avenue] area . . . was $7,600. . . . The houses in which these children live, two-thirds of which are owned by the City of New York, are often as squalid as the houses of the poorest children I have visited in rural Mississippi, but there is none of the greenness and the healing sweetness of the Mississippi countryside outside their windows, which are often barred and bolted as protection against thieves. Some of these houses are freezing in the winter. In dangerously cold weather, the city sometimes distributes electric blankets and space heaters to its tenants. . . . In humid summer weather, roaches crawl on virtually every surface of the houses in which many of the children live. Rats emerge from holes in bedroom walls, terrorizing the infants in their cribs. In the streets outside, the restlessness and anger that are present in all seasons frequently intensify under the stress of heat. . . . If there is a deadlier place in the United States, I don't know where it is.

—Social analyst Jonathan Kozol describes life in one part of New York City
(Kozol, 1995:3–5)

"[Upper Fifth Avenue is] . . . the closest thing to heaven. When I close my eyes I can hear the seals [in Central Park] honking for their food in the children's zoo and the horses' hoofs as the carriages pass under my window. 'Where am I?' I think. It's wonderful. . . ." "The Metropolitan Museum is my children's best babysitter. We lived here so the children would be near the museum and the park. My children grew up knowing every animal in the zoo by name."

—Two women describing life on Upper Fifth Avenue in New York City
(Moonan, 1989:199)

an these people be describing life in the same city? Yes, most definitely. People living in the same city have very divergent experiences because of their positions in the social structure and particularly as their position is affected by race, class, gender, and age. Although the rich and the poor may live near one another in many cities, they are worlds apart in lifestyles and life chances. As the two examples on the preceding page indicate, African American children living in poverty in the South Bronx do not have the same opportunities as affluent white children who live on Upper Fifth Avenue in Manhattan. Differences in lifestyle and life chances can be attributed partly to the fact that most U.S. cities are enclaves of geographic, socioeconomic, and racial-ethnic isolation (Higley, 1995).

In this chapter, we examine some of the most pressing urban problems in the United States and other nations. Many social problems discussed in this book—including the wide gap between the rich and the poor, racial and ethnic strife, inadequate educational opportunities, and homelessness—are found in rural areas, but, of course, they are much more pronounced in densely populated urban areas. For example, crime rates typically are higher in urban areas, and schools tend to be dilapidated. City governments also seem to face fiscal crises periodically, and inadequate resources lead to drastic reductions in such vital services as public sanitation and police and fire protection. As a framework for examining urban problems today, let's briefly look at the changes in U.S. cities that have led to these problems.

CHANGES IN U.S. CITIES

Urban problems in the United States are closely associated with the profound socioeconomic, political, and spatial changes that have taken place since the Industrial Revolution. Two hundred years ago, most people (about 94 out of 100) lived in sparsely populated rural areas, where they farmed. Early in the twenty-first century, about 78 percent of the U.S. population lives in urban areas, and many of these people live in cities that did not exist two hundred years ago (U.S. Bureau of the Census, 1998).

▲ Early Urban Growth and Social Problems

Industrialization and urbanization bring about profound changes in societies and frequently spawn new social problems, such as housing shortages, overcrowding, unsanitary living and working conditions, environmental pollution, and crime (see Chapter 1). By definition, a city involves population density. According to sociologists, a *city* is a relatively dense and permanent settlement of people who secure their livelihood primarily through non-agricultural activities (Weeks, 1998). Although cities existed long before the Industrial Revolution, the birth of the factory system brought about rapid *urbanization,* which we defined in Chapter 1 as the process by which an increasing proportion of a population lives in cities rather than in rural areas. For example, the population of New York City swelled by 500 percent between 1870 and 1910 as rural dwellers and immigrants from Ireland, Italy, Germany, Poland, and other nations arrived in massive numbers, seeking jobs in factories and offices.

Early cities were a composite of commercial, residential, and manufacturing activities located in close proximity. But even then, rapidly growing cities such as New York had a few blocks (e.g., Upper Fifth Avenue) of houses where the wealthy lived (Palen, 1995). These residences were located near the center of the city, and their addresses were considered a sign of social and economic success (Baltzell, 1958; Birmingham, 1967). With the introduction of horse-drawn streetcar lines in the 1850s and electric streetcars in the 1880s, people were able to move more easily from place to place within the core city and to commute between the core city and outlying suburban areas. As a result, many middle-class families moved out of the central areas (Palen, 1995).

City leaders established municipal governments for building and repairing streets, fire protection, crime control, sewage disposal, lighting, and other general needs. In the late nineteenth and early in the twentieth century, improved transportation and new technologies for supplying water and disposing of waste enabled cities to grow even faster. However, municipal governments had trouble keeping pace with the negative side effects of "progress," including urban slums, traffic congestion, and high crime rates. Despite these problems, people continued to move to northeastern and midwestern cities in unprecedented numbers, looking for jobs, educational opportunities, and such new amenities as big department stores, parks, libraries, and theaters.

 ## Contemporary Urban Growth

The growth of suburbs and outlying areas forever changed the nature of city life in this country. Suburban areas existed immediately adjacent to many central cities as early as the nineteenth century, but in the 1920s, these communities began to grow in earnest because of the automobile. They were referred to as "bedroom communities" because most of the residents were there on nights and weekends but went into the central city for jobs, entertainment, and major shopping. During the 1930s, about 17 million people lived in suburban areas (Palen, 1995). With the exception of a few cities—for example, New York and Chicago—that built subways or other forms of mass transit, most suburban dwellers drove to work each day, establishing a pattern that would result, decades later, in traffic congestion and air pollution, problems that have drastically worsened in the past two decades (Palen, 1995).

Between the end of World War II (1945) and 1970, suburbanization brought about a dramatic shift in the distribution of the U.S. population. During the war, construction of apartments and single-family dwellings had halted as industry produced war-related goods. When the war ended, many veterans returned home, married, and had children (the "baby boom"

generation). Consequently, in the late 1940s, as many as 6 million families were unable to find housing; many had to live with relatives or friends until they could find a place of their own (Palen, 1995).

To reduce the housing shortage, the federal government subsidized what became a mass exodus from the central city to outlying suburbs. Congress passed the Housing Act of 1949, which gave incentives to builders to develop affordable housing. In addition, federal agencies such as the Veterans Administration (VA) and the Federal Housing Authority (FHA) established lenient lending policies so that war veterans could qualify to buy homes for their families (Palen, 1995). Other factors also contributed to the postwar suburban boom, including the availability of inexpensive land, low-cost mass construction methods for building tract houses, new federally financed freeway systems, inexpensive gasoline, racial tension in central cities, and consumers' pent-up demands for single-family homes on individually owned lots (Jackson, 1985). The most widely known, and perhaps the most successful, suburban developer of this era was Abraham Levitt and Sons, the company that developed Levittown (on Long Island, New York). Levittown was the first large-scale, mass-produced housing development in this country (see Map 16.1). Eventually, more than 17,000 single-family residences—occupied by more than 82,000 people—were located in Levittown. Sometimes referred to as "cracker boxes" because of their simple, square construction, Levitt houses were typically two-bedroom, one-bath

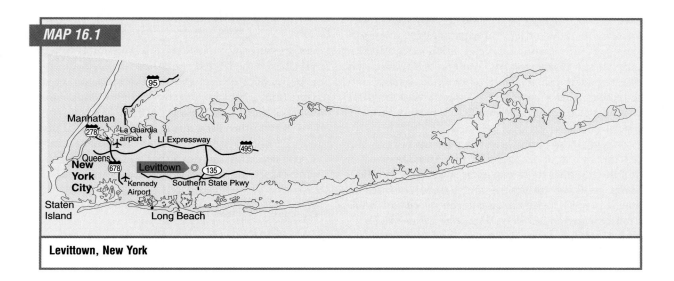

Levittown, New York

Cape Cod–style homes built on concrete slabs. Driveways were unpaved, and each home had its own small lawn with a couple of small bushes (Nieves, 1995).

Although early suburbanization provided many families with affordable housing, good schools and parks, and other amenities not found in the central city, the shift away from central cities set up an economic and racial division of interests between cities and suburbs that remains in place even today (Flanagan, 1995). Although many people in the suburbs still rely on the central city for employment, entertainment, or other services, they pay taxes to their local governments and school districts. As a result, suburban police and fire departments, schools, libraries, and recreational facilities are usually well funded and well staffed, with up-to-date facilities. Suburbs also have newer infrastructures (such as roads, sewers, and water treatment plants) and money to maintain them. In contrast, many central cities have aging, dilapidated schools and lack funds for essential government services (see Chapter 12). According to national estimates, for example, fewer than 40 percent of the African American students who attend school in predominantly minority central city districts have access to computers at school while nearly 60 percent of white schoolchildren in suburban schools do (Gardy, 1995).

Since 1970, cities in the South, Southwest, and West have been considered postindustrial cities because their economic production largely consists of information-processing or service jobs (Orum, 1995). Whereas cities in the Northeast and Midwest grew up around heavy manufacturing, the newer Sunbelt cities have grown through light industry (e.g., computer software manufacturing), information-processing services (e.g., airline and hotel reservation services), educational complexes, medical centers, convention and entertainment centers, and retail trade centers and shopping malls (Sawers and Tabb, 1984). In these postindustrial cities, most families do not live near the central business district.

Today, edge cities are springing up beyond the central cities and existing suburbs. An *edge city* is a **middle- to upper-middle-class area that has complete living, working, shopping, and leisure activities so that it is not dependent on the central city or other suburbs** (Garreau, 1991). The Massachusetts Turnpike Corridor, west of Boston, and the Perimeter Area, north of Atlanta, are examples of edge cities. Edge cities begin as residential areas, then retail establishments and office parks move into the adjacent area, creating an unincorporated edge city. Automobiles are the primary source of transportation in many edge cities, and pedestrian traffic is discouraged—and even dangerous—because streets are laid out to facilitate high-volume automobile traffic, not walkers or bicyclists. Edge cities may not have a governing body, so they drain taxes from central cities and older suburbs. Many businesses and industries move their physical plants—and tax dollars—to these areas because land is cheaper, workers are better educated, and utility rates and property taxes are lower than those in the city. As a result, many jobs move away from poor, minority workers in central cities, creating structural employment.

Over time, large-scale metropolitan growth produces a *megalopolis*—**a continuous concentration of two or more cities and their suburbs that have grown until they form an interconnected urban area.** The East Coast, for example, is a megalopolis, with Boston, Providence, Hartford, and their suburbs merging into New York City and its suburbs, which in turn, merge southward into Newark, Philadelphia, Baltimore, and Washington, D.C., and their suburbs. It is almost impossible to tell where one metropolitan area ends and another begins. When metropolitan areas merge into a megalopolis, there are big population changes that can bring about or exacerbate social problems and inequalities based on race, class, and gender.

URBAN PROBLEMS IN THE UNITED STATES

Even the most optimistic of observers tends to agree that cities in the United States have problems brought on by years of neglect and deterioration. As we saw in previous chapters, poverty, crime, racism, homelessness, inadequate public school systems, alcoholism and other drug abuse, and other social problems are most visible and acute in urban settings. Intertwined with and exacerbating these problems in many older central cities are periodic fiscal crises.

Fiscal Crisis in Cities

Not all U.S. cities are in a state of fiscal crisis and decline, but over the past three decades, there have been some that have teetered on the brink of bankruptcy. New York City was on the edge of financial collapse in 1975 until the federal government provided an elaborate bailout plan; Cleveland went into financial default in 1978. When federal aid to cities was slashed during the recession of the early 1980s, some state governments provided additional monies to cities, but most did not have the means to do so (Clark and Walter, 1994). As a result, the governments of Detroit, Boston, and New York had to drastically reduce services; they closed some public hospitals and other facilities, laid off employees, significantly cut public transit, and all but stopped maintaining the cities' infrastructures.

Finding a solution to the fiscal crises of the 1980s was a real dilemma, and the situation hasn't gotten much better. As middle- and upper-income people have moved to the suburbs, retail businesses and corporations have followed them or moved their operations to other countries. The shrinking central cities have been left with greatly reduced sources of revenue, and municipal governments can't very well increase taxes when their taxes are already much higher than those in the more affluent suburbs or in Sunbelt cities such as Las Vegas, Phoenix, and Arlington and Austin, Texas (Moore and Stansel, 1992). Many of the residents who remain in central cities are poor, unemployed, or older people living on fixed incomes. These individuals cannot pay additional taxes but still need city services such as hospitals, police and fire departments, and public transportation.

Joblessness and declining wages among central city residents further diminish the tax base in many cities and create tremendous social dislocation. To understand the extent of job loss and its impact on many cities, consider this description by sociologist William J. Wilson (1996:34–35) of the predominantly African American community of North Lawndale in central Chicago:

> After more than a quarter century of continuous deterioration, North Lawndale resembles a war zone. . . . Two large factories anchored the economy of this West Side neighborhood in its good days—the Hawthorne plant of Western Electric, which employed over 43,000 workers and an International Harvester plant with 14,000 workers. The world headquarters for Sears, Roebuck and Company was located there, providing another 10,000 jobs. The neighborhood also had a Copenhagen snuff plant, a Sunbeam fac-

tory, and a Zenith factory, a Dell Farm food market, an Alden's catalog store, and a U.S. Post Office bulk station. But conditions rapidly changed. Harvester closed its doors in the late 1960s. Sears moved most of its offices to the Loop in downtown Chicago in 1973; a catalogue distribution center with a workforce of 3,000 initially remained in the neighborhood but was relocated outside the state of Illinois in 1987. The Hawthorne plant gradually phased out its operations and finally shut down in 1984. The departure of the big plants triggered the demise or exodus of the smaller stores, the banks, and other businesses that relied on the wages paid by the large employers. . . . In 1986, North Lawndale, with a population of over 66,000, had only one bank and one supermarket; but it was also home to forty-eight state lottery agencies, fifty currency exchanges, and ninety-nine licensed liquor stores and bars.

Because of deindustrialization and plant closings similar examples can be given for Detroit and Flint, Michigan, among other cities (see Dandaneau, 1996).

The fiscal crisis of cities is extremely visible in the decaying infrastructure. For example, downtown Chicago suffered more than $1 billion in damage and lost revenues in the 1990s when an old water main burst and flooded office buildings, department stores, and other retail businesses. In many cities, roads are scarred with potholes, and sections of highways have fallen in. Railroad overpasses are buckled, and 40 percent of all bridges in the United States today are rated structurally deficient or functionally obsolete by the Department of Transportation (Eitzen and Baca Zinn, 1994). Given the acute shortage of funds, these problems will not be solved any time soon. Many cities have also experienced natural disasters such as floods, brushfires, earthquakes, hurricanes, or tornados—all of which add to the cities' financial burdens by creating new infrastructure problems at the same time that relief must be provided for the hardest-hit residents.

To what extent are cities' financial problems brought on by suburbanites? On the one hand, city governments bear the economic burden for the municipal services (e.g., street maintenance, fire and police departments) and amenities (e.g., parks and other recreational facilities) that are used by suburban residents. On the other hand, suburban dwellers

Signe Wilkinson, CARTOONISTS & WRITERS SYNDICATE/cartoonweb.com

frequently believe that they do their fair share to finance necessary services. Consider this recent editorial in which the writer states that although he and his family live in a suburban community outside the taxing authority of the city of Austin, they contribute significantly to the central city's sales tax, which helps to pay for the city's transit system (Barry, 1997:A13).

> You hear a lot of demonizing of suburban dwellers. . . . We use the city streets but don't pay for them; we work in town but pay property taxes to some other entity. . . . Of all the suburban-bashing mantras, the one that irks me most is the one that says we don't pay taxes. . . . We're still paying Austin taxes, and we still support Austin businesses. . . . Practically everything we buy, we buy in Austin. My sport utility vehicle and [my wife's] car were bought at Austin dealerships. . . . Although there's a grocery store two minutes from the house, we still do much of our grocery shopping in Austin. I eat at least five meals a week at Austin restaurants. . . . We gas up from Austin dealer's pumps. We buy clothes at Austin clothiers. We shop at Austin malls. My barber is in Austin, as is [my wife's] beauty shop

of choice. . . . Ninety percent of the [metropolitan transit authority] sales tax may be collected in Austin, but a lot of it is collected from people like us. . . . Austin is a city in a region, not a fortress. We're friends, neighbors and coworkers, not barbarians at the gate.

According to this point of view, cities benefit from suburban residents more than critics think. Still, the federal government programs that subsidized private housing and contributed to the mass exodus to the suburbs after World War II, combined with years of government neglect, have greatly intensified urban problems. Moreover, the financial crises that we've seen so far in the Northeast and Midwest are expected to spread to Sunbelt cities early in the twenty-first century (Lazare, 1991).

 ## The Crisis in Health Care

The growing problems in health care are most evident in the nation's largest cities. While hospitals and other medical facilities are subject to cutbacks and closings because of economic problems, poor people who live in central cities are more likely to become ill or injured than are people in more affluent suburbs.

Poverty is associated with many medical problems, including certain diseases (such as tuberculosis) and problems associated with inadequate nutrition and lack of preventive care (many children are not immunized against the basic childhood diseases). Moreover, drug-related problems and HIV/AIDS place tremendous financial burdens on already underfunded community clinics, hospitals, and other medical facilities. According to the National Centers for Disease Control and Prevention in Atlanta, both the number of AIDS patients and the costs of caring for AIDS patients are highest in central cities (Eitzen and Baca Zinn, 1994).

Because lack of funding has caused many community clinics and publicly financed hospitals to close, finding affordable health care is a major problem for city residents. Essential services have been cut back in many metropolitan hospitals. Furthermore, as managed care plans and large hospital chains have taken over the ownership of privately funded hospitals, some private hospitals now claim that they cannot afford to provide uncompensated care, and some refuse to admit uninsured patients except in life-threatening circumstances. As a result, although public hospitals cannot legally deny care to an individual, a patient may have to wait hours (sometimes even days) to see a physician or other medical personnel, who must deal with one life-and-death medical emergency after another. Today, many poor people use emergency rooms for all medical services because they do not have—and cannot afford to pay—a private physician. Consequently, the cost of providing medical services is driven higher at a time when public hospitals have greatly diminished resources. The growing homeless population in major urban areas has simply added to the cost of providing health care.

 Housing Problems

Many regions in the United States lack affordable housing for low-income individuals and families (see Chapter 2). Over the last ten years, there has been a significant increase in homelessness, especially among families with children. Each year, we are made aware of the plight of homeless people through extensive media coverage during the Thanksgiving to Christmas holiday season. During the rest of the year, many people view the homeless with less compassion (see Box 16.1).

THE HOUSING SHORTAGE

As city neighborhoods have become blighted and houses have been abandoned, the U.S. housing shortage has grown worse. While it may seem surprising that landlords will abandon rental property that they own, single-room-occupancy (SRO) hotels and inexpensive apartments for lower-income residents sometimes become so great an economic liability that landlords simply abandon the properties. Landlords are most likely to give up their property when they find themselves caught between increasing property taxes, demands from the city to maintain or upgrade the property to comply with safety standards or building codes, and tenants who demand services but do not pay their rent or severely damage the units.

Often, landlords have let the properties become substandard through years of neglect, as one journalist describes (Golden, 1992:27):

> Many SRO tenants . . . had long lost whatever human connections they might have had, and amid the brutal life of the hotel their mental and emotional condition deteriorated through sheer fear and isolation. These hotels were dirty, cold, depressing, and dangerous. The way landlords made a profit from the low rents charged was by not maintaining the buildings. Toilets and faucets did not work; heat was often nonexistent; locks were insecure; and the shared bathrooms in the hallways were particularly dangerous because men tried to break in while women were in the shower.

Abandoned buildings increase fear and isolation in the residents of adjoining properties. The empty buildings often become hiding places for drug dealers or fugitives, and some are dangerous places for children to play. In some cities, however, *urban squatters*—people who occupy land or property without any legal title to it—have moved into abandoned apartment buildings and fixed them up. As people take up unofficial residence in the buildings, they create a sense of community by watching out for each other's possessions. However, most of these projects have been short-lived. Developers who recognize potential in the area demand that the buildings be razed to make way for new hotels and office towers.

In recent years, some cities have instituted programs to provide low-cost owner-occupied housing,

Homelessness and the Holidays

The charity of the holiday season is traditional—and welcome. The problem is that so much is seasonal. . . . Come January, when people go back to their normal routines, the hunger and homelessness recognized in the holiday season will remain. It would be nice if most of the spirit of giving remained, too.

—*From a* Los Angeles Times *editorial, December 25, 1988*

Not only does charity toward the homeless wax and wane during the year, so does media coverage. At Thanksgiving, the nightly news teams show up with camera crews at city soup kitchens and interview volunteers serving turkey and trimmings to people still wearing their overcoats. A month later, around Christmastime, the press appears at homeless shelters to interview "Jimmy G." and "Sherry P.," and their stories are all the more poignant because, by now, in many parts of the country, the weather is pretty raw.

Research shows that the media, especially newspapers, give steady, fairly minimal coverage to the homeless until late fall (around Thanksgiving), when the amount increases. Coverage peaks in December (at Christmas), and then in January again diminishes until it returns to its standard plateau in April (Bunis, Yancik, and Snow, 1996; Snow and Anderson, 1991). Why does this happen?

For one thing, homeless people are human interest stories for the holiday season. For another thing, people are in a giving mood during the holidays, so if the media make us aware of the plight of the homeless, we are likely to help. One billboard poster, for example, showed a drawing of Jesus above the head, "How can you worship a homeless man on Sunday and ignore one on Monday?"

It is true that an important function of the media is to make the public aware of social problems. Sociologists, though, dig deeper. Why

do the media increase coverage at *this* time of year—during the holidays? Part of the explanation may come from sociologist Lewis A. Coser, who says "we have only so much emotional energy and yet we live in a world filled with inhumanity and suffering" (1969:104). Thus, sympathy for the afflicted in a society fluctuates over time. Otherwise, we would be emotionally overwhelmed.

Another reason comes from Emile Durkheim and points to the holidays as the time that most people express sympathy for the homeless: Holidays are times of ritual, opportunities to affirm shared values. But, of course, the values that are affirmed by any particular holiday ritual derive from the culture. In the United States, where individualism is highly valued but people believe, at the same time, that they are responsive to social problems, the holidays function to reassert community solidarity by redistributing goods in the community (Barnett, 1954).

Along these same lines, Thomas J. Scheff (1977:71–73), sees sympathy as a catharsis (emotional release) for guilt:

Insofar as Americans have imbibed this heady drink of socially induced ambition, they tend to ignore or slight the precepts of brotherhood, kindness, and cooperation in favor of those related to attaining individual success. However, many persons experience a sharp conflict of values because, though the ideals of brotherhood and kindness are relegated to a secondary place, they retain their normative quality. Therefore, widespread feelings of guilt develop into this clash of divergent social norms and furnish some of the motivation for Christmas charity (Bunis, Yancik, and Snow, 1996).

What have you observed in the media's coverage of social problems and particularly homelessness? Does "charity as catharsis" make sense to you?

but some social analysts believe that these programs promote the interests of the housing industry and protect property values more than they actually help people to acquire housing (Flanagan, 1995). One of the best-known federal government housing initiatives, the urban homesteading program, has been fraught with problems. The program was designed to allow low-income families to purchase—for a nominal fee—abandoned properties. In return, the purchasers had to agree to live in the property and make improvements to it for a period of time, after which the property could be sold. Unfortunately, it appears that the government did not provide sufficient housing units in a given area to meet the demand and offset the urban deterioration (Flanagan, 1995). In addition, the Federal Housing Administration (FHA) flooded central city neighborhoods with federally insured loans that were attractive to lenders and real estate agents, who often arranged for families to purchase homes that they were then unable to maintain when repairs became necessary. As a result, massive foreclosures occurred, causing people to lose their homes, bringing about further deterioration of central city neighborhoods (Squires, 1994).

Although the Department of Housing and Urban Development (HUD) continues to explore ways to provide affordable housing for low-income and poverty-level people, its efforts have not been successful. Federal housing policy continues to reinforce the patterns and practices of private housing industries, as sociologist Gregory D. Squires (1994: 51) explains:

> Working through their trade associations like the National Association of Homebuilders, the National Association of Realtors, the Associated General Contractors, the American Bankers Association, the U.S. League of Savings Institutions, and many others, housing-related industries have for over fifty years secured federal housing policies that focus on the provision of low-interest loans, mortgage interest subsidies, rent supplements, and other market-based inducements. Lobbyists have successfully kept public housing to a minimum in the United States (approximately 3% of all housing), labeling it as "socialistic" and, therefore, un-American. Again, it is the winners in the competitive market that have been the primary beneficiaries of housing policy.

The federal government's involvement in housing has been criticized on several fronts. Some critics believe that federal housing aid, which is supposed to provide decent housing for the poor, has done a better job of providing housing for more affluent people. Begun in the 1950s, federally funded urban renewal projects were supposed to replace housing units in slums with better-quality, affordable housing for the poor. However, some analysts say that once the slums were cleared, more expensive housing or commercial properties were built (Jacobs, 1961). Moreover, they say, sometimes the worst, most dilapidated housing units were not chosen for redevelopment because they were not in strategic locations for economic development. Because the power of *eminent domain* gives governmental officials the authority to condemn certain properties, individual owners' wishes regarding their property were not always taken into consideration (Flanagan, 1995). The most successful recent initiatives for replacing substandard housing and building lower-cost housing for poor and lower-income families have come from community groups and volunteer organizations. One of the best known of these is Habitat for Humanity, which has received extensive

In an effort to replace substandard housing and build lower-cost housing for poor and lower-income families, groups such as Habitat for Humanity continually build houses in communities across the country. Would you be willing to volunteer to build low-income housing for others like these Washington, D.C., volunteers are doing?

press coverage because of former President Jimmy Carter's participation.

A second major criticism of federal housing initiatives has been directed at public housing. Most federal and state housing projects have been huge, high-rise constructions that have intensified many problems and created new ones. Perhaps the Pruitt-Igoe project in St. Louis is the all-time bad example of public housing projects. Built as a monolithic high-rise, the building immediately had structural problems, high rates of crime, inadequate maintenance, and poor management. Pruitt-Igoe received media attention and was the subject of sociological research, but finding a solution to the building's many problems was virtually impossible, and it was demolished in the 1970s.

Most urban sociologists agree that public housing works best when it is situated in less densely populated areas with a small number of families in any one housing project. In Charleston, South Carolina, for example, one public housing project is located in a neighborhood of historic residences that tourists visit on horse-drawn carriage tours. Tour guides even point to the housing unit as a sign that their community has overcome housing segregation. But when some communities place federally funded housing projects in neighborhoods of middle-income apartments and housing, adjoining property owners object, fearing that the value of their property and their personal safety will be diminished.

Since the 1970s, some middle- and upper-middle-class families have reentered central city areas and gentrified properties. **Gentrification is the process by which people renovate or restore properties in central cities.** Centrally located, naturally attractive areas are the most likely candidates for gentrification (Palen and London, 1984). Some people view gentrification as the way to revitalize the central city. Others think that it further depletes the stock of affordable housing for the poor and pushes low-income people out of an area where they had previously lived (Palen and London, 1984; Flanagan, 1995). The worst outcome of the housing shortage has been a significant increase in the number of homeless people in the United States.

HOMELESSNESS

Accurate data about the actual number of homeless people in the United States is unavailable. The total is probably somewhere between the Bureau of the Census's figure of roughly 250,000 and the 3 million estimated by advocates for the homeless (Mathews, 1992). It is extremely difficult to count the num-

ber of homeless people because most avoid interviews with census takers and social scientists. Each year, however, the U.S. Conference of Mayors conducts a survey on urban homelessness, and some consistent patterns have emerged. Among the homeless, people of color are overrepresented; African Americans make up the largest part of the homeless population (about 50 percent), when compared to whites (33 percent), Latinas/os (11 percent), Native Americans (3 percent), and Asian Americans (1 percent) (U.S. Conference of Mayors, 1995). Families and children are the fastest-growing segment of the homeless population in both urban and rural areas of this country. Today, infants, preschoolers, school-age children, and their parents account for almost half of the homeless (Vissing, 1996).

Many people think that "the homeless" are all alike, but homeless people come from all walks of life and include Vietnam war veterans; people with mental illnesses, physical disabilities, or AIDS; the elderly; runaway children and teenagers; alcoholics and other substance abusers; recent immigrants; and families with young children (Torrey, 1988; Snow and Anderson, 1993; Vissing, 1996). According to social scientists, studies that focus exclusively on personal problems of the homeless, such as mental illness or substance abuse, may result in *specialism*—the assumption that individual characteristics of poor people cause their homeless condition and that, therefore, the only way to alleviate homelessness is to cure the individual's personal problems (Wagner, 1993). This approach downplays the significance of structural factors such as the unavailability of low-income housing and of mental health care, which are the most important determinants of homelessness. According to sociologists Marta Elliott and Lauren J. Krivo (1991:128), any solution to the problem of homelessness must take into account these two structural factors:

[A]ttempts to lower levels of homelessness in U.S. metropolitan areas must address the structural conditions which underlie this phenomenon. More specifically, mental health care services for the indigent mentally ill must be made more available to those who are or would become homeless without them. Furthermore, the structure of the housing market must be altered in order to have the greatest effects on reducing homelessness. This means that more low-cost rental housing needs to be made available to reach the most marginal and disadvantaged members of society. Such a restructuring of the housing market is unquestionably one of the primary means by which people will avoid or overcome homelessness. Without this basic resource of cheap housing in an area, some individuals fall out of the housing market completely, a problem exacerbated by an economic environment with proportionately higher numbers of unskilled jobs. Stable well-paid employment must replace this segment of the economy to reduce current levels of homelessness.

 Racial and Ethnic Segregation

Problems in housing are closely intertwined with racial and ethnic segregation in the United States. Despite passage of the Federal Fair Housing Act in 1968, segregation of African Americans and whites in major metropolitan areas declined only slightly since 1970. According to sociologists Douglas S. Massey and Nancy A. Denton (1992), no other racial or ethnic group in the history of this country has ever experienced the sustained high levels of residential segregation that African Americans have experienced in central cities. Moreover, residential segregation not only affects living conditions, but is also associated with other problems (Massey and Denton, 1992:2):

> Residential segregation is not a neutral fact; it systematically undermines the social and economic well-being of blacks in the United States. Because of racial segregation, a significant share of black America is condemned to experience a social environment where poverty and joblessness are the norm, where a majority of children are born out of wedlock, where most families are on welfare, where educational failure prevails, and where social and physical deterioration abound. Through prolonged exposure to such an environment, black chances for social and economic success are drastically reduced.

Although African Americans may have experienced the longest and most harmful effects of housing segregation in the United States, other groups have also suffered from housing discrimination (Santiago and Wilder, 1991; Menchaca, 1995; Santiago and Galster, 1995). A number of studies have documented a history of restrictive covenants that have prohibited Mexican Americans from living in white (Anglo) areas. Frequently these covenants were supported by racial harassment and violence (see Menchaca, 1995). In some cases, local custom has dictated residential segregation patterns that continue into the present. In one recent study of Mexican American segregation, one woman recalls that Twelfth Street was the dividing line between the white (Anglo) American and Mexican American neighborhoods in Santa Paula, California (Menchaca, 1995:27):

> *La calle doce* was the main division. The ranchers owned the homes in the northeast, and that was for the people whose parents worked in agriculture—which would be the lemon or the orange. . . . If you worked for them in the packing house or picking lemons, that's where you would live. . . . They used to tell us, You live in that side and we live in this side. . . . The rednecks used to tell us that.

Vestiges of similar patterns of residential segregation based on race or ethnicity remain in many cities. In Austin, Texas, the historic geographic and political divide between Mexican Americans and white (Anglo) Americans is an interstate highway. In other communities, the divide is a river or some other geographic or social boundary that is well known to local residents, whether or not they acknowledge its existence. Although there is less overt discrimination, and courts have ruled that racial and ethnic restrictive covenants on property are unenforceable, housing segregation continues through custom.

Some analysts argue that residence is a personal choice and that people voluntarily segregate themselves on the basis of who they want to live near. But many people are involuntarily segregated because of certain attributes—such as race, religion, age, or disability—that others devalue. Some landlords, homeowners, and white realtors perpetuate residential segregation through a discriminatory practice known as *steering*—guiding people of color to different neighborhoods than those shown to their white counterparts. Banks sometimes engage in a discriminatory (and illegal) practice known as *redlining*—refusing loans to people of color for properties in certain areas. The behavior of neighbors can also perpetuate residential segregation (see Feagin and Sikes, 1994; Squires, 1994).

Unequal property taxation is another kind of residential segregation problem. In a study of suburban property taxes, social scientist Andrew A. Beveridge found that African American homeowners are taxed more than white homeowners on comparable homes in 58 percent of the suburbs and 30 percent of the cities (cited in Schemo, 1994). This may happen because African Americans are more likely to move to suburbs with declining tax bases because they have limited finances or are steered there by real estate agents or because white flight occurs as African American homeowners move in. Since houses are often reassessed when they're sold, newcomers face a heavier tax burden than longer-term residents, whose taxes may not go up for some period of time or until they sell their own houses (Schemo, 1994).

The continual influx of immigrants into urban areas is changing the population composition in many of the nation's largest cities, including Los Angeles, Houston, Miami, Chicago, and New York. For example, Monterey Park, California, which is about a ten-minute drive east of Los Angeles during non-rush-hour traffic, has been slowly transformed from a white (Anglo) community in the 1960s to a predominantly Asian community. Indeed, within the Asian community, younger Chinese newcomers are replacing older U.S.-born Japanese Americans as the largest group (Horton, 1995).

The 1990 Census showed that for the first time, minorities had experienced a higher percentage of growth in the nation's suburbs than in its central cities. However, only 27 percent of all African Americans live in suburbs (U.S. Bureau of the Census, 1998). Overall, 41 percent of central city residents are African Americans and other people of color, although all minority groups combined constitute only 27.3 percent of the nation's population. As more African Americans have moved to the suburbs, some social analysts have suggested that we now have greater residential integration and minority social mobility in this country. This may be true for middle-class African Americans who have moved to suburbs near Atlanta, Dallas, or Washington, D.C., but it is certainly not true for all African Americans, as urban sociologist William G. Flanagan (1995:271) explains:

Increases in the black suburban population cannot be taken to represent either dramatic improvements in residential integration or minority social mobility. In general analysts agree that suburban blacks are found dispropor-

tionately in areas that share many features with poorer central city locations: low income, poor-quality older housing, and strained municipal finances. . . . Black residential areas tend to be suburban only in a technical, locational sense. That is, they are "sub-urban," located adjacent to, but not in, central city areas. For their residents these areas represent neither the political nor economic liberation from the problems of the city that the white suburbs do. The black suburban movement is overwhelmingly to suburbs that are already inhabited by blacks, locations from which whites are moving away.

Despite an increased minority presence, most suburbs are predominantly white, and many upper-middle-class and upper-class suburbs remain virtually all white. For example, only 5 percent of the population in northern Fulton County (adjoining Atlanta, Georgia) is African American. In Plano (adjoining Dallas, Texas), nearly nine out of ten students in the public schools are white, whereas the majority of students in the Dallas Independent School District are African American, Latina/o, or Asian and Pacific American (Roberts, 1993). Suburban Latinas/os are highly concentrated in eight metropolitan areas in California, Texas, and Florida. By far the largest such racial-ethnic concentration is found in the Los Angeles–Long Beach metropolitan area, with more than 1.7 million Latinas/os. Like other groups, affluent Latinas/os live in affluent suburbs, while poorer Latinas/os remain segregated in less desirable central city areas (Palen, 1995).

In the suburbs, people of color (especially African Americans) often become resegregated (see Feagin and Sikes, 1994). Chicago, for example, remains one of the most segregated metropolitan areas in the country in spite of its fair-housing ordinance. Most of the African Americans who have fled the high crime of Chicago's South Side live in nearby suburbs such as Country Club Hill and Chicago Heights; suburban Asian Americans are most likely to live in Skokie and Naperville; and suburban Latinos/as live in Maywood, Hillside, and Bellwood (De Witt, 1994).

What will be the future of racial and ethnic relations in the cities and suburbs of this country? Sociologist John Horton is optimistic and uses Monterey Park as an example of a community that has moved gradually and peacefully toward a culture of diversity (Horton, 1995:225):

Although the pressure to be American without "foreign" influence is increasing in California, in places like Monterey Park, where the world has already imploded, an Anglo or Eurocentric American identity is giving way to greater openness. The transformation happens unconsciously and on an incremental basis through compromise and accommodation in the pragmatic process of getting things done. It is also undertaken consciously at public events and festivals where diversity and patriotism come together, using a formula that varies with the ethnicity and politics of those who plan the events. . . . The results may be small and seemingly trivial, but in an era of virulent nationalism and ethnic genocide, these local experiments in multiculturalism are advances to be celebrated.

Still, we must acknowledge that some dominant group members, especially those in the upper classes, strive to perpetuate their position at the top of the societal pyramid not only by living in certain areas of the city, but also by isolating themselves from the "Other"—the poor and many minority group members (see Baltzell, 1958; Birmingham, 1967; Domhoff, 1983). Thus, in the United States at the beginning of the twenty-first century, racial segregation remains interlocked with class-based residential segregation (Santiago and Galster, 1995), as the vignettes at the beginning of the chapter show.

PROBLEMS IN GLOBAL CITIES

Although people have lived in cities for thousands of years, the time is rapidly approaching when more people worldwide will live in or near a city than live in a rural area. In 1900, only one person out of ten lived in a city; by 2005, one person out of two will live in a city (Crossette, 1996c). Moreover, two-thirds of the world's expected population of 8 to 9 billion people will live in cities by 2025 (Crossette, 1996c). Of all the middle- and low-income regions, Latin America is becoming the most urbanized: Four megacities—Mexico City (20 million), Buenos Aires (12 million), Lima (7 million), and Santiago (5 million)—already contain more than half of the region's population and continue to grow rapidly. By 2010, Rio de Janeiro and São Paulo are expected to have a combined population of about 40 million people living in a 350-mile-long megalopolis (Petersen, 1994). By 2015, no U.S. city will be among the ten most populous in the world (see Table 16.1).

Rapid global population growth is producing a wide variety of urban problems, including overcrowding, environmental pollution, and the disappearance of farmland. In fact, many cities in middle- and low-income nations are quickly reaching the point at which food, housing, and basic public services are available to only a limited segment of the population (Crossette, 1996c). With urban populations growing

TABLE 16.1 POPULATIONS OF THE WORLD'S TEN LARGEST CITIES

(IN MILLIONS, ESTIMATED)

1996		2015	
Tokyo, Japan	26.8	Tokyo, Japan	28.7
São Paulo, Brazil	16.4	Bombay, India	27.4
New York City, U.S.A.	16.3	Lagos, Nigeria	24.4
Mexico City, Mexico	15.6	Shanghai, China	23.4
Bombay, India	15.1	Jakarta, Indonesia	21.2
Shanghai, China	15.1	São Paulo, Brazil	20.8
Los Angeles, U.S.A.	12.4	Karachi, Pakistan	20.6
Beijing, China	12.4	Beijing, China	19.4
Calcutta, India	11.7	Dhaka, Bangladesh	19.0
Seoul, South Korea	11.6	Mexico City, Mexico	18.8

Source: New York Times, 1996c.

Overcrowded living conditions are a way of life for people residing in this area of Bombay. How will rapid population growth in the future affect urban areas in global cities?

at a rate of 170,000 people a day, cities such as Cairo, Lagos, Dhaka, Beijing, and São Paulo are likely to soon have acute water shortages; Mexico City is already experiencing a chronic water shortage (*New York Times*, 1996b).

Natural increases in population (higher birth rates than death rates) account for two-thirds of new urban growth, and rural-to-urban migration accounts for the rest. Some people move from rural areas to urban areas because they have been displaced from their land. Others move because they are looking for a better life. No matter what the reason, migration has caused rapid growth in cities in sub-Saharan Africa, India, Algeria, and Egypt. At the same time that the population is growing rapidly, the amount of farmland available for growing crops to feed people is decreasing. In Egypt, for example, land that was previously used for growing crops is now used for petroleum refineries, food-processing plants, and other factories (Kaplan, 1996). Some analysts believe that the United Nations should encourage governments to concentrate on rural development; otherwise, acute food shortages brought about by unchecked rural-to-urban migration may lead to riots (Kaplan, 1996).

As global urbanization has increased over the past three decades, differences in urban areas based on economic development at the national level have become apparent. According to sociologist Immanuel Wallerstein (1984), nations occupy one of three positions in the global economy: core, semiperipheral, and peripheral. **Core nations are dominant capitalist centers characterized by high levels of industrialization and urbanization.** The United States, Japan, and Germany, among others, are core nations. Some cities in core nations are referred to as *global cities*—interconnected urban areas that are centers of political, economic, and cultural activity. New York, Tokyo, and London are generally considered the largest global cities. They are also considered postindustrial cities because their economic base has shifted largely from heavy manufacturing to information technologies and services such as accounting, marketing, finance, mergers and acquisitions, telecommunications, and other highly specialized fields (Friedmann, 1995). Global cities are the sites of new and innovative product development and marketing, and they often are the "command posts" for the world economy (Sassen, 1995). But economic prosperity is not shared equally by all people in the core nation global cities. Growing numbers of poor people work in low-wage service sector jobs or in assembly production, in which they are paid by the item (piecework) for what they produce but they have no employment benefits or job security. Sometimes the living conditions of these workers more closely resemble the living conditions of workers in semiperipheral nations than those of middle-class workers in their own country.

Most African countries and many countries in South America and the Caribbean are *peripheral nations*—nations that depend on core nations for capital, have little or no industrialization (other than what may be brought in by core nations), and have uneven patterns of urbanization. According to Wallerstein (1984), the wealthy in peripheral nations support the exploitation of poor workers by core nation capitalists in return for maintaining their own wealth and position. Poverty is thus perpetuated, and the problems worsen because of the unprecedented population growth in these countries.

Between the core and the peripheral nations are the *semiperipheral nations*, which are more developed than peripheral nations but less developed than core nations. Only two global cities are located in semiperipheral nations: São Paulo, Brazil, the center of the Brazilian economy, and Singapore, the economic center for a multicountry region in Southeast Asia (Friedmann, 1995). Like peripheral nations, semiperipheral nations—such as India, Iran, and Mexico—are confronted with unprecedented population growth. In addition, a steady flow of rural migrants to large cities is creating enormous urban problems. Semiperipheral nations exploit peripheral nations, just as the core nations exploit both the semiperipheral and the peripheral nations.

According to Wallerstein, it is very difficult—if not impossible—for peripheral and semiperipheral nations to ever occupy anything but their marginal positions in the classlike structure of the world economy because of their exploitation by the core nations (Wallerstein, 1984). Capital investment by core nations results in uneven economic growth, and in the process, the disparity between the rich and the poor in the major cities increases. Such economic disparity and urban growth is obvious at the U.S.–Mexican border, where transnational corporations have built *maquiladora plants*—factories where goods are assembled by low-wage workers to keep production costs down—on the Mexican side. The demand for workers in these plants has caused thousands of people to move from the rural areas of Mexico to urban areas along the border in hope of earning higher wages. The influx has pushed already overcrowded cities far beyond their capacity. Because their wages are low and affordable housing is nonexistent, many people live in central city slums or at the edge of cities in *shantytowns*, where houses are made from discarded materials. Squatters are the most rapidly growing segment of the population in many Mexican cities (Flanagan, 1995).

Social analysts are just beginning to develop comprehensive perspectives on the position of cities in the contemporary world economy, and not all analysts agree with Wallerstein's hierarchy (1984). However, most scholars acknowledge that nations throughout the world are influenced by a relatively small number of cities (e.g., New York) and transnational corporations that have brought about a shift from an international to a more global economy (see Knox and Taylor, 1995; Wilson, 1997). In middle- and low-income nations, all social problems are "incubated and magnified in cities" (Crossette, 1996c:A3).

SOCIOLOGICAL PERSPECTIVES ON URBAN PROBLEMS

Throughout the twentieth century, sociologists have analyzed urban problems to determine the causes and consequences of rapid industrialization and urbanization on people's daily lives and the structure of society. The conclusions they reach about the underlying problems and possible solutions depend on the framework they apply.

 ### The Functionalist Perspective

In examining urban problems, most functionalists focus on three processes that have contributed to social disorganization and the disruption of social institutions. First, mass migration from rural areas to urban areas during the Industrial Revolution contributed to social disorganization by weakening personal ties in the family, religion, education, and other institutions. Second, large-scale immigration in the late nineteenth and early twentieth centuries was more than most cities could absorb, and many individuals were never fully assimilated into the cultural mainstream. With larger numbers of strangers living close together in central cities, symptoms of social disorganization, such as high rates of crime, mental illness, and suicide, grew more pronounced. According to Emile Durkheim (1933/1893), urban life changes people's relationships. Rural areas are characterized by *mechanical solidarity*—**social bonds based on shared religious beliefs and a simple division of labor**—but these bonds are changed with urbanization. Urban areas are characterized by *organic solidarity*—**social bonds based on interdependence and an elaborate division of labor (specialization).** Although Durkheim was optimistic that urbanization could be positive, he also thought that some things were lost in the process. Third, mass suburbanization created additional social disorganization, and most central cities have been unable to reach an equilibrium since the mass exodus to the suburbs following World War II. According to urban ecologist Amos Hawley (1950, 1981), new technologies, such as commuter railways and automobiles, have led to the decentralization of city life and the movement of industry from the central city to the suburbs, with disastrous results for some people. Although urbanization, mass immigration, and

SOCIAL PROBLEMS
AND SOCIAL POLICY

BOX 16.2

Urban Empowerment Zones: A New Initiative

For three generations, an enormous Cadillac factory stretched across eight blocks on the southwest side of the Motor City, providing a path to the middle class for tens of thousands of workers. It closed a decade ago, becoming a vast, derelict monument to the decay of a great manufacturing center. The surrounding neighborhood deteriorated almost as fast as the weeds grew up around the factory. The only high-paying job nearby was drug-dealing.

But [recently] the inner city where the factory is situated—an endless sprawl of blocks so bleak that rundown houses can sell for less than used cars—has been a magnet for business.

—*"Before" and "after" in the Detroit urban empowerment zone (Meredith, 1997:C1)*

The United States has never had a national urban development policy, and many urban sociologists believe that we have suffered for it with "a chronically underemployed and underhoused inner-city population" (Flanagan, 1995:345). Instead, our urban policy has been program after program in response to economic shifts. Sometimes that approach has worked. During the Great Depression of the 1930s when many people lost their homes, the Roosevelt administration responded with New Deal policies that created work.

Recently, continuing the program-by-program approach, the federal government developed a new initiative for rural areas, based on urban empowerment zones. In 1994, six areas were designated urban empowerment zones: Atlanta, Baltimore, Chicago, New York, Philadelphia, Camden (NJ), and Detroit. Since then, other federal empowerment zones have been added, including twenty that were designated as urban empowerment zones in 1999 (Kent, 1999). Cities receive development grants and businesses get tax breaks.

One of the oldest empowerment zones is an 18.4-square-mile area of Detroit, Michigan. This area has experienced economic distress due to high rates of unemployment, a weak economy, and a shortage in affordable housing for years. Like other urban areas designated as empowerment zones, Detroit has received federal grants and tax-exempt bonding authority to finance revitalization, housing, and job creation programs. Corporations play a large part in the revitalization process: public/private partnerships rebuild neighborhoods and commercial areas. In Detroit, for example, the automobile industry, including General Motors and Daimler-Chrysler, have pledged billions of dollars to the enterprise zone, and Detroit Edison has coordinated the efforts for the eighty nonprofit programs that are involved in bringing about change in the zone (Detroit Edison, 1999).

Now, the federal government has implemented rural empowerment zones and enterprise communities. To learn more about these areas, visit this Web site: www.ezec.gov. To learn how various cities seek out business partnerships for their enterprise zones, search Yahoo.com or other Internet search engines. For example, visit the Santa Ana, California, Web site: www.ci.santa-ana.ca.us/departments/cda/empowerment/tax_incentives.html.

What are the benefits of urban enterprise zones? What problems are associated with this approach to reducing unemployment, homelessness, and other pressing urban problems?

(*Note:* Web addresses often change. Those given here were accurate at the time of publication.)

suburbanization have had functional consequences—including U.S. citizenship, job opportunities, and home ownership—for many people, they have also created problems, particularly for people who are left behind in rapidly declining central cities and people who experienced discrimination.

How do functionalists suggest that urban problems may be reduced? To alleviate the fiscal crisis facing many cities and level the inequality in services provided in cities and suburbs, sociologist Anthony M. Orum (1995) suggests establishing metropolitan or regional governments. Problems such as water supply, pollution, and traffic congestion, which are not confined to one geographic area, could be dealt with more effectively through metropolitan or regional planning. However, as Orum acknowledges, it is unlikely that officials of cities and suburban municipalities will willingly give up some of their power, and people living in the more affluent suburbs are unlikely to be willing to take on the problems of central cities.

Another option for alleviating urban problems is expanding the urban tax base by creating urban enterprise zones. Cities could offer tax incentives for industries to open plants in central cities and provide job training for workers, so a match could be made between jobs and workers. Critics of enterprise zones argue that business tax incentives alone won't improve conditions in central cities (see Cozic, 1993). Some U.S. cities are finding that another program—urban empowerment zones—can be a catalyst for jobs and development in areas of high unemployment (see Box 16.2).

 The Conflict Perspective

Conflict analysts do not believe that cities grow or decline by chance. Members of the capitalist class and political elites make far-reaching decisions about land use and urban development that benefit some people at the expense of others (Castells, 1977; Feagin and Parker, 1990). According to conflict theorists, the upper classes have successfully maintained class-based and sometimes racially based segregation through political control and legal strategies such as municipal incorporation, defensive annexation, restrictive covenants, and zoning regulations (Feagin and Parker, 1990; Higley, 1995). But where do these

practices leave everyone else? Karl Marx suggested that cities are the arenas in which the intertwined processes of class conflict and capital accumulation take place; class consciousness and worker revolt were more likely to develop when workers were concentrated in urban areas (Flanagan, 1995).

Contemporary conflict theorists Joe R. Feagin and Robert Parker (1990) speak of a *political economy model*, believing that both economic *and* political factors affect patterns of urban growth and decline. Urban growth, they say, is influenced by capital investment decisions, power and resource inequality, class and class conflict, and government subsidy programs. Members of the capitalist class choose corporate locations, decide on sites for shopping centers and factories, and spread the population that can afford to purchase homes into sprawling suburbs located exactly where the capitalists think they should be located (Feagin and Parker, 1990). In this view, a few hundred financial institutions and developers finance and construct most major and many smaller urban development projects, including skyscrapers, shopping malls, and suburban housing projects. These decision makers can make housing more affordable or totally unaffordable for many people. Ultimately, their motivation rests not in benefiting the community, but rather in making a profit, and the cities they produce reflect this mindset (Feagin and Parker, 1990).

The concept of *uneven development*—the tendency of some neighborhoods, cities, or regions to grow and prosper while others stagnate and decline—is a by-product of the political economy model of urban development (Perry and Watkins, 1977). Conflict theorists argue that uneven development reflects inequalities of wealth and power in society. Uneven development not only affects areas in decline but also produces external costs that are paid by the entire community. Among these costs are increased pollution, traffic congestion, and rising rates of crime and violence. According to sociologist Mark Gottdiener (1985:214), these costs are "intrinsic to the very core of capitalism, and those who profit the most from development are not called upon to remedy its side effects." One advantage of the political economy framework is that it can be used to study cities in middle- and low-income nations as well as high-income nations (see Jaffee, 1990; Knox and Taylor, 1995; Wilson, 1997).

Demonstrators outside the Los Angeles police headquarters helped fuel one of many fires that ensued in the civil unrest following the acquittal of police officers charged in the brutal attack on Rodney King, an African American in police custody. How are issues of race, class, and gender inequality intertwined with concerns about political unrest in the United States?

Short of major changes in the political economy, most analysts who take a conflict perspective believe that urban problems can be reduced only through political activism and organized resistance to oppressive conditions. Some believe that central cities are powder kegs of urban unrest that periodically threaten to explode because of massive job loss and economic hardship, racial tensions, allegations of police brutality, controversial court cases, and similar issues. These analysts cite the Los Angeles civil unrest of 1992 as an example of what happens when people are cut off from mainstream social and economic institutions and have little, if any, hope of providing for themselves and their families. Although in the years since 1992, most of South Central Los Angeles has been physically restored, many of the old tensions remain. According to scholar Michael Dear, the 1992 violence proved that Los Angeles "didn't learn the lessons of the Watts riots

[in the 1960s] too well, because the same basic underlying structural tensions which we experienced in the region hadn't been addressed. It really took another economic downturn to bring them to the fore again" (cited in Purdum, 1997:16).

▲ The Interactionist Perspective

Interactionists examine urban problems from the standpoint of people's *experience* of urban life and how they subjectively define the reality of city living. How does city life affect the people who live in a city? According to early German sociologist Georg Simmel (1950), urban life is so highly stimulating that people have no choice but to become somewhat insensitive to events and individuals around them. Urban residents generally avoid emotional involvement with one another and try to ignore the events—including violence and crime—that take place nearby. They are wary of other people, looking at others as strangers; some people act reserved to cloak deeper feelings of distrust or dislike toward others. At the same time, Simmel thought that urban living could be liberating because it gives people opportunities for individualism and autonomy (Flanagan, 1995).

On the basis of Simmel's observations of social relations in the city, early University of Chicago sociologist Louis Wirth (1938) suggested that urbanism is a "way of life" that increases the incidence of both social and personality disorders in individuals. *Urbanism* refers to the distinctive social and psychological patterns of life that are typically found in the city. According to Wirth, the size, density, and heterogeneity of urban populations result in an elaborate division of labor and in spatial segregation of people by race/ethnicity, social class, religion, and/or lifestyle. The division of labor and spatial segregation produce feelings of alienation, powerlessness, and loneliness.

In contrast to Wirth's gloomy analysis of urban life, sociologist Herbert Gans (1982/1962) believed that not everyone experiences the city in the same way. On the basis of research in the West End of Boston in the late 1950s, Gans concluded that many residents develop strong loyalties and a sense of community in central city areas that outsiders often view negatively. According to Gans, personal behavior is shaped by the type of neighborhood a person lives in within the larger urban area. For example, *cosmopolites*—students, artists, writers, musicians, entertainers, and professionals—view the city as a place where they can be close to cultural facilities and people with whom they share common interests. *Unmarried people and childless couples* live in the city because they want to be close to work and entertainment. *Ethnic villagers* live in ethnically segregated neighborhoods because they feel most comfortable within their own group. The *deprived* and the *trapped* live in the city because they believe they have no other alternatives. Gans concluded that the city is a pleasure and a challenge for some urban dwellers and an urban nightmare for others.

According to interactionists, the deprived and the trapped contribute to a social construction of reality that stereotypes city dwellers as poor, down-and-out, and sometimes dangerous, whereas many city dwellers are not this way at all. Because movies, television shows, and, particularly, extensive media coverage of crime or racial unrest in the nation's largest metropolitan areas present a very negative image of cities, an antiurban bias remains strong among many nonurban dwellers.

To reduce problems of loneliness and alienation in city life, some interactionists propose that people who live in large metropolitan areas develop subcultural ties to help them feel a sense of community and identity. A *subculture* **is a group of people who share a distinctive set of cultural beliefs and behaviors that set them apart from the larger society.** Joining an interest group—from bowling with friends from the office to volunteering in a literacy program—is one way of feeling connected. Ethnic neighborhoods are an example of subcultures; some are tightly knit, whereas others have little influence on residents' daily lives. Interactionists note that members of subcultures, especially those based on race, ethnicity, or religion, sometimes come into conflict with each other. These conflicts can result in verbal exchanges, hate crimes, or other physical violence, or they can cause the individuals to withdraw almost entirely from the larger community and become more intensely involved with the subculture.

URBAN PROBLEMS IN THE TWENTY-FIRST CENTURY

In a best-case scenario, the United States would convert to regional governments to provide water, wastewater (sewage), transportation, schools, parks, hospitals, and other public services. In this scenario, revenues would be shared among central cities, affluent suburbs, and edge cities, since everyone would benefit from the improved quality of life. Admittedly, this may be an overly optimistic scenario. Still, if we are unable to do anything about urbanization at the macrolevel, we can at least exercise some degree of control over our communities and our own lives. There is increasing impetus to take control because one thing is certain: As the world population continues to grow in the twenty-first century, race-, class-, and age-related demographics will change globally, and these demographic changes will intensify urban problems and affect us all.

SUMMARY

➡ *How did urbanization come about?*

Urbanization—the process by which an increasing proportion of a population lives in cities rather than rural areas—began with industrialization. Before the Industrial Revolution, most people lived in sparsely populated rural areas, where they farmed. Industrialization led to the growth of cities, and urbanization brought about profound changes in societies and spawned new social problems such as housing shortages, overcrowding, unsanitary conditions, environmental pollution, and crime.

➡ *How did mass suburbanization occur and what were the results?*

Mass suburbanization began with government efforts to correct the housing shortage that followed World War II. The Housing Act of 1949 gave incentives to builders to develop affordable housing, while government agencies made it possible for returning veterans to qualify for home mortgages. Other factors included the availability of inexpensive land, low-cost mass construction methods, new federally financed highway systems, inexpensive gasoline, racial tension in central cities, and consumers' pent-up demands for single-family homes on individually owned lots. Mass suburbanization brought about a dramatic shift in the distribution of the U.S. population and set up an ongoing economic and racial division of interests between cities and suburbs.

➤ *Why are many cities in fiscal crisis?*

Large numbers of middle- and upper-income people have moved out of the central cities to the suburbs, and more recently, many retail businesses and corporations have also moved to the suburbs or moved their operations abroad. The shrinking central cities have been left with greatly reduced sources of revenue. Many of the remaining central city residents are poor, unemployed, or older people living on fixed incomes who cannot afford to pay higher taxes. At the same time, city governments must still provide city services for them. Moreover, suburbanites who regularly use city services do not pay taxes to the city to keep up these services.

➤ *Why is health care a crisis in U.S. cities?*

Health care is a problem in big cities because hospitals and other medical facilities are subject to cutbacks and closings when cities face economic problems. Also, people in impoverished sections of central cities are more likely to become ill or injured because poverty is associated with many medical problems. Drug-related problems and HIV/AIDS put an added burden on facilities. All of these problems are exacerbated when managed care plans and large hospital chains take over urban hospitals and streamline services to turn a profit.

➤ *Why is there a housing shortage in the United States and what is being done about it?*

When city agencies demand that a landlord comply with safety standards and building codes, many landlords abandon their buildings rather than make the investment. A bigger reason, however, is that the United States has yet to find a way to provide safe, livable, low-income housing. The urban homesteading program, for example, has been criticized for promoting the interests of the building industry instead of actually helping people to get good housing. Federal housing projects have characteristically been monolithic high-rises that intensify many problems and create new ones. One of the most successful initiatives for creating affordable housing is the volunteer organization Habitat for Humanity.

➤ *How great a problem is homelessness? Are there any solutions?*

Accurate data on the actual number of the homeless are extremely difficult to get because homeless people avoid interviews with census takers and social researchers. The U.S. Conference of Mayors surveys show that people of color are overrepresented in the homeless population, and the fastest-growing segment of the homeless population is families and children. Most experts agree that any long-term, successful solution to homelessness must take structural factors into account, especially low-income housing and mental health care.

➤ *Why does residential segregation exist even if it is illegal?*

In some cases, housing segregation continues through custom. Sometimes landlords, homeowners, and white realtors perpetuate residential segregation through steering—guiding people of color to different neighborhoods than those shown to their white counterparts. Unequal property taxation is another kind of residential segregation problem.

➤ *What are the major problems in global cities?*

By 2005, one out of every two people in the world will live in a city. Increasing population accounts for two-thirds of the new urban growth, and rural-to-urban migration accounts for the rest. Rapid urban growth brings a wide variety of problems, including overcrowding, environmental pollution, and the disappearance of farmland. The exploitation of semiperipheral nations by core nations and of peripheral nations by both semiperipheral and core nations serves to increase the urban problems in these nations. Core nations are dominant capitalist centers characterized by high levels of industrialization and urbanization. Peripheral nations depend on core nations for capital, have little or no industrialization (other than what is brought in by core nations), and have uneven patterns of urbanization. Semiperipheral nations are more developed than peripheral nations but less developed than core nations.

➡ *What are the functionalist and conflict perspectives on urban problems?*

Functionalists believe that today's urban problems are the result of mass migration from rural areas during the Industrial Revolution, large-scale immigration in the late nineteenth and early twentieth centuries, and mass suburbanization. One solution is to create metropolitan governments. Conflict theorists believe that cities grow or decline according to decisions made by capitalists and the political elite. In other words, theorists use a political economy model. Urban problems can be reduced through political activism and organized resistance to oppressive conditions.

➡ *What is the interactionist perspective on urban problems?*

Interactionists look at how people subjectively experience urban life. According to German sociologist Georg Simmel, urban life is so stimulating that people have no choice but to become somewhat insensitive to people and events around them. On the other hand, urban living gives people opportunities for individualism and autonomy. Sociologist Louis Wirth expanded on Simmel's ideas, saying that urbanism produces feelings of alienation and powerlessness. Herbert Gans concluded from his research that city life is a pleasure for some and a nightmare for others. The way to avoid alienation is to develop subcultural ties.

KEY TERMS

core nations, p. 356
edge city, p. 346
gentrification, p. 352
mechanical solidarity, p. 357

megalopolis, p. 346
organic solidarity, p. 357
peripheral nations, p. 356

semiperipheral nations,
  pp. 356–357
subculture, p. 361

QUESTIONS FOR CRITICAL THINKING

1. Where do you live—in the core central city, an edge city, a suburb, a megalopolis? What examples from your everyday life can you give that relate to the problems described in this chapter? Which sociological perspective do you think best explains the urban problems you observe?

2. The government has so far failed to provide adequate low-income and poverty-level housing. What new initiatives can you suggest?

3. Why do you think families with children are the fastest-growing segment of the homeless population in both urban and rural areas of this country? What can be done about the problem?

Chapter
Seventeen

Global Social Problems
War and Terrorism

It's hard to judge a generation by its statistics. . . . But there's at least one statistic that resonates: more of us are taking a full five years to get through college. Most of the country's parents look at this as a sort of slacker ritual. . . . But there's another way to regard that extra year: as a peace dividend. A generation ago, in the midst of the Vietnam War, the idea of a year off from college was dangerously ridiculous. Leaving school meant a one-way ticket to Saigon. Two generations ago it was Korea. Three generations ago, war-torn Europe or the inferno of the Pacific. My generation has had the blessing of growing up in peaceful times, and it has made all the difference. . . . It is premature (also probably unlucky) to call Generation X the peace generation, but the evidence is mounting. No generation in American history has had less traffic with war or its brutally congruent demands for sacrifice and faith. And because we haven't had to fight, we've been free from the conformist pressures of a nation at war. We've found our own, unique identity as a generation that thinks and does at it pleases. . . . But this peaceful outlook has brought with it a mouthful of unanswerably hard questions. Is an innocence of war a blessing or curse? Will our naiveté make us dangerously curious about the tools of violent power? Or is this the start of a thousand years of peace, secured by a certainty that what we have now is forever worth having?

▲ —*Author Joshua Cooper Ramo describes life in the absence of war for "Generation Xers."*
(Ramo, 1997:69)

Thankfully, as Ramo describes, a whole generation has grown up in the United States without having to have war and preparedness for war a part of their lives. They see the United States as a peaceful country, even though some social analysts believe that history shows us to be one of the most war-prone nations in the world (Fussell, 1992; Maas, 1996). With the collapse of the former Soviet Union and the end of the Cold War between the United States and the former Soviet bloc in the 1980s, prospects for world peace were bright. But today, there is conflict in the Congo (the former Zaïre), Rwanda, Serbia, and Bosnia, as well as Indonesia, Cameroon, the Central African Republic, Cyprus, and Russia. There are also state-versus-state conflicts in China and North Korea, and the threat of a global nuclear arsenal that could destroy all life on this planet (Daley, 1997).

The twentieth century saw the development of advanced technologies that provided new potential for wars that could be far more deadly than those in the past. These technologies are still with us. Long-range, hypersonic munitions that strike from the air have made it unnecessary to send aircraft into the theater of war (Friedman and Friedman, 1996). Moreover, the stockpile of nuclear weapons from the arms race between the former Soviet Union and the West has vastly increased the potential for waging war on a massive scale. But with the capability of war comes resistance to war, as social critic Barbara Ehrenreich (1997:239) has said: "If the twentieth century brought the steady advance of war and war-related enterprises, it also brought the beginnings of organized resistance to war. . . . in the situation where everyone is expected to participate in one way or another, and where anyone can become a victim whether they participate or not, opposition could at last develop to the institution of war itself." In this chapter, we examine war, terrorism, resistance to war and terrorism, and prospects for peace.

WAR AS A SOCIAL PROBLEM

What is war? Most people think of war as armed conflict between two countries or two factions within a country, such as the North and the South in the U.S. Civil War. But social scientists define war more broadly, including not only declared wars between nations or parties but also undeclared wars, civil and guerrilla wars, covert operations, and some forms of terrorism (Wright, 1964). To social scientists, *general warfare* refers to violent armed conflict between nations, whereas *regional warfare* refers to conflict between rival factions located within a specific geographic area. Social scientists also say that societies that are prepared at all times for war possess a **war system**—components of social institutions (e.g., the economy, government, and education) and cultural beliefs and practices that promote the development of warriors, weapons, and war as a normal part of the society and its foreign policy (Cancian and Gibson, 1990).

How, then, do social scientists define *peace*? Sociologists Francesca M. Cancian and James William Gibson (1990) believe that peace is a less clearly defined concept than war. Cancian and Gibson note that people generally agree that peace is highly desirable, but they often have different ideas of what constitutes peace. Some equate peace with harmonious relations in a world where there is no bloodshed between groups; but sometimes nations equate peace with prevailing in battle (Gibson and Cancian, 1990). Despite the problems associated with distinguishing between war and peace, we can conclude that both consist of actions and beliefs held by people like ourselves and that these actions and beliefs have serious consequences for individuals, groups, and nations.

▲ The Nature of War

First and foremost, war is an institution that involves *violence*—behavior intended to bring pain, physical injury, and/or psychological stress to people or to harm or destroy property (Sullivan, 1997). As we have seen, violence is a component of many social problems, particularly violent crime and domestic violence. Both of these forms of *interpersonal violence* typically involve a relatively small number of people who are responding to a particular situation or pursuing their own personal goals. In contrast, war is a form of **collective violence** that **involves organized violence by people seeking to promote their cause or resist social policies or practices that they consider oppressive** (Sullivan, 1997).

Except for media coverage and for those who go into combat or are friends or relatives of those who go, war is only a concept to most people in the United

TABLE 17.1 U.S. ARMED FORCES PERSONNEL CASUALTIES IN WARS

War	Battle Deaths (in thousands)	Wounds, Not Mortal (in thousands)
Spanish-American War	*	2
World War I	53	204
World War II	292	671
Korean conflict	34	103
Vietnam conflict	47	153

*Fewer than 500 total.

Source: U.S. Bureau of the Census, 1998.

More than 50 million people (17 million combatants and 35 million civilians) lost their lives. During World War II, U.S. casualties alone totaled almost 300,000 and more than 600,000 were wounded (see Table 17.1).

The consequences of all these wars, however, pale when compared to the consequences of an all-out nuclear war. The devastation would be beyond description. Although the development of nuclear weapons may have contributed to peace among the major world powers since the late 1940s, we can see the potentially destructive effects of nuclear war in the U.S. attacks on Hiroshima and Nagasaki, Japan. In an effort to end World War II, a U.S. aircraft dropped a 1.5-kiloton atomic bomb on Hiroshima, killing 130,000 people either instantly or over the next few months as a result of the deadly radiation that rained on the city (Erikson, 1994). Today, some nuclear warheads held by governments throughout the world are more than 4,000 times as powerful as the bombs that were dropped on Japan. In fact, scientists estimate that a nuclear war would kill more than 160 million people outright and that more than 1 billion people would die in the first few hours as a result of radiation poisoning, environmental contamination and destruction, and massive social unrest (Friedman and Friedman, 1996).

Even though an international treaty bans underground nuclear tests, nations may still be developing and stockpiling nuclear weapons. In 1997, the U.S. government became concerned that China was purchasing U.S.-made supercomputers to design lighter, more efficient nuclear warheads that could be put on missiles capable of reaching the United States (Gerth, 1997). These high-performance supercomputers, which operate at ten times the speed of the fastest personal computer available and can process huge amounts of data, would allow China to do very small underground nuclear weapons tests that outsiders would be unable to detect. U.S. government officials and military experts disagree over whether or not selling such technology to other nations, especially those not considered allies of the U.S. government, should be strictly monitored or even banned (Gerth, 1997).

Today, military strategy calls for deploying bombs and long-range missiles to eliminate the enemy's weapon production plants and supply centers. Because these plants are located in major cities, civilians are more likely to be killed than they were in the past. And whereas Europe was the primary battleground for most wars from 1500 through World War II, middle- and low-income nations with their growing populations are now the primary sites.

The trend toward more civilian casualties that began in World War II has continued in subsequent wars, including the Vietnam War and the Gulf War (Ehrenreich, 1997). Some analysts believe that civilians accounted for 75 percent of all war-related deaths in the 1980s and nearly 90 percent in the 1990s (Renner, 1993). Other social analysts disagree. In their recent book *The Future of War* (1996), George Friedman and Meredith Friedman argue that the use of precision-guided munitions ("smart weapons") in Desert Storm (another name for the Gulf War) made it possible for the United States to strike particular parts of particular buildings without striking noncombatants, hence keeping the civilian death count low. However, a demographer employed by the U.S. Bureau of the Census has calculated that 40,000 Iraqi soldiers were killed during the war but more than 80,000 Iraqi civilians, mostly women and children, were killed in air strikes—13,000 in precision bombing and 70,000 as a result of disease associated with the systematic destruction of water purification and sewage treatment systems in their country (Colhoun, 1992). Moreover, many hospitals were damaged or destroyed. In some cases, when nearby power plants were hit, hospitals could no longer operate basic equipment or provide emergency medical care to people injured by bombs (Burleigh, 1991).

In the United States, one immediate consequence of the Gulf War was a national festivity, which analyst

Barbara Ehrenreich (1997:223) believes was manipulated by television coverage of the war:

> Flags appeared everywhere, along with bumper stickers, T-shirts, and buttons urging Americans to SUPPORT OUR TROOPS. As if flags were not a sufficient proof of loyalty, they were joined by yellow ribbons. . . . In my town the Boy Scouts affixed yellow ribbons to every tree and bush lining the main street, and similar outbreaks of nationalistic fetishism occurred all over the country. Sports teams and public employees insisted on the right to wear American-flag patches on their uniforms; dissenters (and those deemed to look like Iraqis) were in some cases attacked or threatened with attack.

Patriotism, then, even when temporary, is another consequence of war. In this way, war is functional because it provides an external enemy for people to hate. During the Gulf War, this enemy was Iraqi leader Saddam Hussein (Ehrenreich, 1997). A dysfunctional aspect of war, however, is that the enemy is dehumanized—that is, seen as an object to obliterate rather than as another human being. Also, according to sociologist Tamotsu Shibutani (1970), prolonged conflicts such as wars tend to be turned into a struggle between good and evil; one's own side is, of course, righteous and just, while the other side has no redeeming social or moral value.

In 1997, more than 2 million U.S. veterans were receiving compensation from the government for injuries they sustained in war-related activities; about 156,000 of these veterans were totally disabled (U.S. Bureau of the Census, 1998). However, not all injuries sustained in wars are physical. We have no accurate count of the soldiers and civilians—of all nations involved—who experience psychological trauma that affects them the remainder of their lives. Consider, for example, the psychological effects of war on Vietnam War veteran Rod Kane, who was asked by a nurse whether he was having trouble with his concentration (Hynes, 1997:219–220):

> "Trouble with concentration?" I stare at her defensively. I forgot her name already. "Not necessarily. I concentrate on the war, or drinking . . . but I'm not here because of my concentration problems, or my memory. I will say that if I've had trouble with anything since Nam, it's been

sleeping. . . . One reason I drink so much, so I could pass out and not have to worry about nightmares. Of course, after a while, all the booze in the world couldn't keep them down . . . I mean, there are booby-trap nightmares that speak for themselves. Instant replay nightmares where, asleep or awake, I play the same scene over and over again. There are nightmares that combine Viet Nam action with stateside stuff. . . . Do I have to get into all this right away?"

Kane was diagnosed with a disorder known as post-traumatic stress disorder (PTSD). Symptoms include difficulty sleeping and concentrating; anxiety; and recurring flashbacks or nightmares, many of which are triggered by loud, sudden noises such as thunder, automobiles backfiring, or other things that sound like gunshots or explosions. When some stimulus triggers a flashback, the individual reexperiences the horror of some deeply traumatic wartime event. Some medical specialists link high rates of drug abuse and suicide among Vietnam War veterans with PTSD. According to one congressional study, more than 475,000 of the 3.5 million Vietnam veterans have severe symptoms of PTSD, and another 350,000 have moderate symptoms (Witteman, 1991).

While we cannot put a price tag on loss of life, physical disability, or psychological trauma associated with war, we know that the direct economic costs of war are astronomical. Consider, for example, the cost of forty F-117A stealth fighters deployed with laser-guided bombs during the Gulf War—over 4 billion dollars. These fighters, which are capable of penetrating enemy air defenses without being seen by radar or infrared or acoustical sensors, destroyed critical Iraqi air defense command posts and communication centers (Friedman and Friedman, 1996). We have no way of knowing the exact dollar amount of the property damage inflicted on Iraqi buildings, power plants, and communications centers, but we do know that the cost for the F-117A stealth fighters is only a minuscule part of our nation's approximately 250-billion-dollar annual defense budget. To put defense and war-related expenditures in perspective, twenty years ago, one analyst calculated that a single aircraft carrier would build 12,000 high schools and the cost of developing one new bomber would pay the annual salaries of 250,000 teachers to staff the schools (de Silva, 1980).

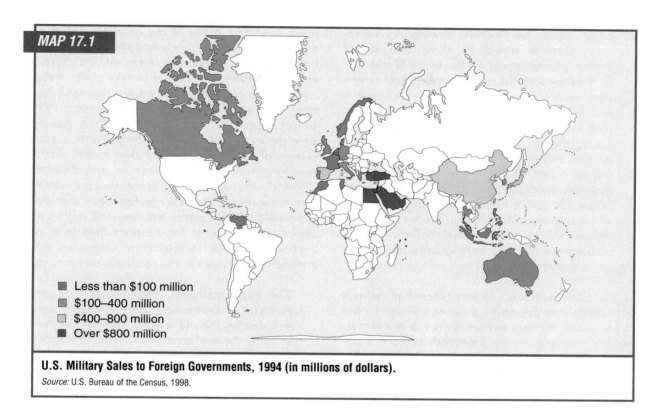

MAP 17.1

■ Less than $100 million
■ $100–400 million
□ $400–800 million
■ Over $800 million

U.S. Military Sales to Foreign Governments, 1994 (in millions of dollars).
Source: U.S. Bureau of the Census, 1998.

Today, more middle- and low-income nations are involved in defense buildups than in the past. Map 17.1 shows the nations that purchase military equipment and supplies from this country. In 1995, the nations of the world spent about 689 billion dollars on their military (U.S. Bureau of the Census, 1998). About 15 percent of the total amount was spent by middle- and low-income nations. In the United States, even in a time of peace, 16 cents of every dollar of taxpayers' money goes to defense, compared to 3 cents for education (Bagby, 1997).

MILITARY TECHNOLOGY AND WAR

War is conducted on the basis of the technology that is available in given societies at a specific point in time. However, wars are not necessarily won or lost on the basis of military technology alone. In the Vietnam War, for example, many factors contributed to the inability of the United States to declare a victory. Among these factors were conflicting ideologies and war strategies set forth by gov-

ernment officials and the fact that U.S. troops could not distinguish the Viet Cong ("the enemy") from the South Vietnamese ("the ally") (Hynes, 1997).

The most significant military technology is referred to as the *weapons system*, **which comprises a weapons platform (e.g., a ship, aircraft, or tank), a weapon (e.g. a gun, missile, or torpedo), and the means of command and communication** (Kaldor, 1981). The importance of the weapons system is pointed out by Friedman and Friedman (1996:25): "The rise and fall of strategically significant weapons systems is the history of the rise and fall of nations and epochs. **The *strategically significant weapon* is the one that brings force to bear in such a way that it decisively erodes the war-making capability of the enemy**" [bold in original]. According to Friedman and Friedman (1996:25–26), the use of strategically significant weapons determines the "winners" and "losers" in war:

[L]et us assume that the greatest threat presented by the enemy is the ability to move weapons platforms around quickly, and that by destroying his petrochemical production facilities we could impede his mobility. Strategically significant weapons would be those that would destroy petrochemical plants. So, in World War II, bombers with the range to reach these targets were such weapons. In Vietnam, the enemy's war-making ability could not be decisively crippled by the same sort of long-range bombers. There, the strategic weapon was North Vietnamese infantry, able to move stealthily and impose a rate of attrition on American troops that was politically unacceptable to the United States. The failure to recognize strategically decisive weapons is catastrophic. The Soviet Union's illusion that intercontinental ballistic missiles and swarms of tanks were strategically decisive led it to disaster.

In other words, though factors other than military technology may determine a nation's ability to win or lose a war, military technology is a dominant factor. For example, in the fourteenth century, Europeans used a simple new technology—black powder, an explosive made from charcoal, sulfur, and saltpeter—to overwhelm larger armies. Black powder could destroy the enemy's walls and other fortifications. When it was discovered that black powder could be exploded at the base of a metal tube and propel a projectile to a target, the gun became the basis of European and Western military power. Gunpowder made it possible for a small number of troops to overwhelm a much larger army that had only nonexplosive weapons (Friedman and Friedman, 1996).

Although black powder weapons remained the primary type of weaponry for many years, the platform that was used for carrying the weapons changed over time. With the development of such weapons platforms as coal-powered ships, petroleum-driven ships, and railroad locomotives, it became possible to move explosive-based technology virtually anywhere to destroy enemy forces. From the early 1900s to the end of World War II, the battleship, the tank, and the bomber were the primary weapons platforms. Today, the battleship has been replaced by the aircraft carrier, but the tank and the bomber continue to be important sources of weapons transportation (Friedman and Friedman, 1996).

As the U.S. military sought to enhance traditional weapons platforms to deal with enemy threats, new precision-guided munitions were devel-

oped, rendering many of the older ideologies and technologies obsolete, including the concept of the battlefield. No longer do foot soldiers have to engage in skirmishes for war to take place; missiles can be fired from sites located ten thousand miles from the target (Friedman and Friedman, 1996). Unfortunately, the same technology that makes possible the expanded battlefield brings with it a new system of intelligence that makes global warfare possible. According to Friedman and Friedman (1996:37–38), sensors, guidance systems, satellite communications, and other technologies that make it possible to hit a target ten thousand miles away also make it possible for weapons fired from one continent to guide themselves to targets on other continents very quickly and relatively inexpensively:

The hyperintelligent, hypersonic, long-range projectile is almost here. Born of the air age, it will destroy the old way of making war, while securing the new geopolitical system for generations. Where guns were inaccurate, these projectiles are extraordinarily precise. Where guns must travel to within miles of a target before firing, precision munitions can devastate an enemy from any distance. Where gun/petrochemical technology requires total commitment of resources and mass production, precision munitions require technical skill. The new weaponry places inherent limits on war, both in terms of scope and in terms of damage to unintended targets. The age of total war is at an end and a more limited type of war is at hand. . . . [A]s the new weapons culture [has] slowly emerged, the United States has been at war with itself over the nature of its military power and the principles that ought to guide that power. At its core, this has been a struggle to define the proper place of technology—and of technologies—in American military doctrine. More precisely, it has been an agonizing search for a doctrine that could define and control the overwhelming claims that technology makes on all aspects of American life—a search for principles of waging war that transcend mere weaponry.

Although the high-technology weaponry that is used in warfare has received widespread media coverage, less attention has been paid to the potential significance of poison gas manufacturing and the use of chemical and biological toxic agents by international and domestic terrorists (Vetter and Perlstein, 1991).

GLOBAL TERRORISM

Terrorism **is the use of calculated, unlawful physical force or threats of violence against a government, organization, or individual to gain some political, religious, economic, or social objective.** Terrorist tactics include bombing, kidnapping, hostage taking, hijacking, assassination, and extortion (Vetter and Perlstein, 1991). Although terrorists sometimes attack government officials and members of the military, they more often target civilians as a way of pressuring the government.

As collective violence, terrorism shares certain commonalities with war. Both terrorism and war are major threats to world stability and domestic safety. Terrorism and war also extract a massive toll on individuals and societies by producing rampant fear, widespread loss of human life, and extensive destruction of property.

One form of terrorism—political terrorism—is actually considered a form of unconventional warfare. *Political terrorism* uses intimidation, coercion, threats of harm, and other violent attempts to bring about a significant change in or overthrow an existing government. There are three types of political terrorism: revolutionary terrorism, repressive terrorism, and state-sponsored terrorism.

Revolutionary terrorism **refers to acts of violence against civilians that are carried out by internal enemies of the government who want to bring about political change.** Some groups believe that if they perpetrate enough random terrorist acts, they will achieve a political goal. In Lebanon and Jordan, for example, members of revolutionary movements engage in terrorist activities such as car bombings and assassinations of leading officials. On occasion, they also are the victims of such actions. For example, a car bomb in 1994 killed one of the officials of the Party of God, a militant Shiite group battling Israeli troops in southern Lebanon. At the time of the killing, the Party of God was suspected in the kidnappings of U.S. citizens (including a newspaper correspondent) who were living in Lebanon (*New York Times,* 1994a). In Jordan, members of a militant Muslim movement were accused of bombing

two theaters that showed adult films and attempting to bomb a supermarket that sold alcohol; pornography and alcohol are forbidden by Islam and thus represent decadent Western values that the Muslim movement adamantly opposes (*New York Times,* 1994c). In 1995, the Aum Shinri Kyo (Japanese for "sublime truth") religious sect allegedly set off a nerve gas attack in a Tokyo subway, killing ten people, making thousands more ill, and raising the specter of a new and even deadlier form of terrorism (WuDunn, 1995b). In some circumstances, revolutionary terrorists receive economic help from other governments that support their objectives (Vetter and Perlstein, 1991).

Unlike revolutionary terrorism, *repressive terrorism* **is conducted by a government against its own citizens for the purpose of protecting an existing political order.** Repressive terrorism has taken place in many countries around the world, including Haiti, the People's Republic of China, and Cambodia, where the Pol Pot regime killed more than 1 million people in the four years between 1975 and 1979. In 1975, for example, Cambodia's Khmer Rouge, a Communist faction, forced the evacuation of all city

War and terrorism keep some people's lives in a constant state of turmoil. Can you imagine what life must be like for this Chechen refugee who is shown here holding her baby as she returns home to Chechnya in the aftermath of Russian forces pounding Grozny, the Chechen capital, in an effort to crush Islamic militants?

dwellers to the countryside, where many died of disease or starvation. Teachers, civil servants, Buddhist monks, and other "enemies of the revolution" were killed in mass executions (Mydans, 1997). According to a recent book, *Children of Cambodia's Killing Fields* by Teeda Butt Mam (1997), everyone was a potential victim: the rebellious, the kind-hearted, the brave, the clever, the individuals, the people who wore glasses, the literate, the popular, the complainers, the lazy, those with talent, those who had trouble getting along with others, those with soft hands (Mam, 1997; cited in Mydans, 1997:5). After a Vietnamese invasion in 1979, the Khmer Rouge were driven into the mountains and jungles, where they tried to regain power through guerrilla warfare (Mydans, 1997).

In the third type of political terrorism, *state-sponsored terrorism,* **a government provides financial resources, weapons, and training for terrorists who conduct their activities in other nations.** In Libya, for example, Colonel Muammar Qaddafi has provided money and training for terrorist groups such as the Arab National Youth Organization, which was responsible for skyjacking a Lufthansa airplane over Turkey and forcing the Bonn government to free the surviving members of Black September. Black September is the terrorist group responsible for killing Israeli Olympic athletes in the 1970s (Parry, 1976). Other countries that have been charged with using terrorism as a form of surrogate warfare include Iran, Syria, Yugoslavia, Bulgaria, Israel, and the United States (Vetter and Perlstein, 1991). The United States conducted surrogate warfare when it supported the Contras, who waged war against the Sandinista government of Nicaragua, until the Sandinistas were defeated in a 1990 election (Vetter and Perlstein, 1991).

How widespread is terrorism? In 1995, terrorist attacks killed 311 people worldwide, one of the highest terrorist death tolls recorded (Weiner, 1997). Nearly 200 of the deaths are attributed to the Tamil Tigers, a separatist group in Sri Lanka. In 1996, there were 296 international terrorist incidents; however, most of the attacks did not kill anyone. Once again, the most deadly attack was carried out by the Tamil Tigers of Sri Lanka, who bombed a section of downtown Colombo (the capital), killing 90 people, and blew up a commuter train, killing 70 people (Weiner, 1997). Today, Iran, Iraq, Libya, North Korea, the Sudan, Syria, and Cuba are on the U.S. State Department's list of nations that are suspected of engaging in state-sponsored terrorism. According to the State Department report, however, no terrorist attack anywhere in the world during 1995 or 1996 equaled the April 1995 explosion in Oklahoma City. In fact, domestic terrorism is a greater problem in most nations—including the United States—than international terrorism is (Weiner, 1997).

DOMESTIC TERRORISM IN THE UNITED STATES

Domestic terrorism is sometimes referred to as "home-grown terrorism" by the media because the perpetrator is usually a resident of the country in which the incident occurs or has other strong ties to the country, such as relatives or acquaintances who live there. Like international terrorism, domestic terrorism typically is used to reach some political goal.

The worst act of domestic terrorism in the United States took place in 1995 when a bomb destroyed the Alfred P. Murrah Federal Building in Oklahoma City, taking 168 lives and injuring 850

Human faces tell an important and often forgotten story about the effects of domestic terrorism on the survivors of horrendous events such as the bombing of the federal building in Oklahoma City.

other people. The horror of this act—and its similarities to war—are brought home in this statement from police officer Jerry Flowers: "I saw a body in a blanket. When I opened up the blanket, there was a five-year-old boy. His face was gone" (cited in Collins, 1997:28). A Denver jury found Timothy McVeigh guilty of bombing the federal building and sentenced him to death on charges ranging from conspiracy to use a weapon of mass destruction to the murder of eight federal law-enforcement agents (Thomas, 1997). At present, McVeigh is appealing his sentence, a process that takes years.

Many who survived the bomb blast lost limbs or their vision or hearing or incurred other physical or psychological scars that will remain with them throughout their lives. One victim, Cliff Cagle, whose face was mangled by the bomb, testified in the McVeigh trial, saying "I lost my job, my honor, and my grandsons have to see me like this!" (cited in Collins, 1997:28). While the relatives and friends of those who died in the bomb blast realize that executing McVeigh will not bring back their loved ones (Bragg, 1997), McVeigh's death sentence helps some of them to cope with their losses. Survivors must find a way to cope, as Bud Welch, a father whose daughter Julie-Marie was a Spanish interpreter in the federal building, knows (Welch, 1997:36):

I now go to the fence [surrounding the memorial where the Murrah building once stood] about twice a week. . . . This place has a lot of meaning for me, especially the elm tree in the parking lot. We call it the Survivor Tree. Julie always liked to park her little red Grand Am on the east side of that tree, in the shade. Now it's the only living thing left in this place. When I go there, sometimes I lean against the trunk, close my eyes, listen to the leaves and think about the way it used to be. Then I go down to the fence, and strangers will sometimes ask me questions: "Where was the front door of the building?" or "Where was the truck [loaded with explosives] parked?" Then I tell them who I am, and they share their deepest thoughts with me. That's a very positive thing—to touch and see and talk and visit. And to continue to tell the story of who my Julie-Marie was.

The Oklahoma City bombing may be the worst case of domestic terrorism to occur in this country, but it is not the only recent case. In 1993, the World Trade Center in New York City was the target of a bombing

allegedly carried out by some followers of Sheik Omar Abdel Rahman. Six people were killed, more than a thousand were injured, and business at the Trade Center was disrupted for an extended period of time. Companies that stored important data on desktop computer systems spent weeks trying to recreate valuable records that were lost in the bombing, since—unlike mainframe computers—desktop computers often are not backed up regularly (Holusha, 1993).

The longest series of terrorists acts in the United States was carried out by the "Unabomber," later identified as Theodore Kaczynski. Between 1978 and 1995, Kaczynski allegedly mailed sixteen bombs that caused three deaths and twenty-two injuries. Primary targets for the self-described anarchist's bombs were business executives and university researchers. Kaczynski also allegedly threatened to blow up an airliner flying out of Los Angeles International Airport but did not follow through (Weiner, 1995). In a letter to the *New York Times,* the Unabomber stated that the terrorist group FC was conducting terrorist actions "to promote social instability in industrial society" (cited in Weiner, 1995:A1). But in a 35,000-word manifesto posted on the Internet, he gave a different reason, speaking of how difficult it is for some people to fit into society (cited in McFadden, 1996:12):

The moral code of our society is so demanding that no one can think, feel and act in a completely moral way. For example, we are not supposed to hate anyone, yet almost everyone hates somebody at some time or other, whether he admits it to himself or not. In order to avoid feelings of guilt, they continually have to deceive themselves about their own motives and find moral explanations for feelings and actions that in reality have a nonmoral origin. We use the term oversocialized to describe such people. Oversocialization can lead to low self-esteem, a sense of powerlessness, defeatism, guilt, etc. If a particular child is especially susceptible to such feelings, he ends by feeling ashamed of HIMSELF. . . .

The oversocialized person is kept on a psychological leash and spends his life running on rails society has laid down for him. In many oversocialized people this results in a sense of constraint and powerlessness that can be a severe hardship. We suggest that oversocialization is among the most serious cruelties that human beings inflict on one another.

SOCIAL PROBLEMS

BOX 17.2

Media and Terrorism: What Is the Line between Information and Fear?

We have said a hundred times or more that when modern revolutionaries carry out actions, what is important is not solely these actions themselves but also the propagandistic effect they are able to achieve. Hence we preach not only action in and for itself, but also action as propaganda.

—John Most, American anarchist, in 1880 (Laqueur, 1978:105, quoted in Vetter and Perlstein, 1991)

Even though news traveled slowly in 1880, John Most understood the importance of publicizing terrorist acts. Today, terrorists are equally aware of the importance of the media to accomplish their goals, especially since coverage is often live by satellite. At the same time, terrorism is news, and the public wants information. The media, then, play a pivitol role.

How do they do it? Do they provide objective, complete, noninflammatory coverage of terrorist events and potential terrorism?

Today, the U.S. media focus closely on four forms of terrorism that are believed to offer the greatest potential threat to U.S. citizens:

1. *Foreign sponsored terrorism on U.S. soil.* Extensive media coverage was given, for example, to the possibility of terrorist acts during millennium celebrations on December 31, 1999. The arrest of Ahmed Ressam when he crossed the border between Canada and the United States with bomb-making materials and appeared to be headed to a millennium celebration in Seattle, Washington, was reported throughout the country. During this time, the media were vigilant—and to some people's way of thinking, overzealous—regarding coverage of potential terrorism and other hazards.

2. *Domestic terrorism.* The media also focus on the concerns that the FBI and other federal investigative agencies have regarding domes-

Apparently having similar feelings about his own life, Kaczynski moved to the Montana wilderness, where he lived in a one-room wooden cabin until he was arrested. We will never know whether Kaczynski would have been apprehended if his brother hadn't notified authorities of his whereabouts in hopes of preventing more lives from being lost (Johnston and Scott, 1996).

In recent years, great potential for domestic terrorism has arisen in the form of militias opposed to the U.S. government. In 1996, an eighty-one-day standoff between the Montana Freemen and the Federal Bureau of Investigation was resolved peacefully. However, events leading up to that event were very violent. There was, first, the 1992 siege of white separatist Randy Weaver's farmhouse in Ruby Ridge, Idaho; Weaver's wife and son were killed by federal agents during the siege. There was also the 1993 standoff between armed Branch Davidian cult mem-

bers and U.S. agents near Waco, Texas, and a subsequent fire that killed eighty cult members. Militia members consider both events to be evidence that the U.S. government is determined to take away their freedom. Most militia groups view the Brady Bill, which established a mandatory waiting period for handgun purchases, as another form of government oppression.

Some militias are part of the far-right Patriot movement, which also includes white supremacists, neo-Nazis, and skinheads. Rejecting all state and federal laws and all constitutional amendments except the Bill of Rights, the Patriot movement has established "common-law courts" in as many as forty states. They base their authority on selected passages of English common law, the Bible, U.S. case law, and the Constitution (Janofsky, 1996). Groups such as the Militia of Montana have threatened violence against court officials. For example, when municipal

tic groups that could engage in acts of terrorism for political and religious reasons. People are advised that likely targets might include government facilities and different components of the infrastructure such as water plants, power stations, and pipelines.

3. *International terrorism that might affect U.S. citizens who are residing or traveling in other countries.* At the end of the twentieth century, the U.S. Department of State and media outlets worldwide issued travel advisories for U.S. citizens abroad for fear that some terrorist group might attack on December 31 or in the days immediately before or after the beginning of the new millennium. More recent travel advisories can be accessed through the State Department's Web site (http://www.state.gov).

4. *Information terrorism—the destruction of computer systems and/or records.* According to media sources and the Terrorism Research Center, information terrorism ranges from outright intrusions and denial-of-service attacks to remote code injection for future exploitation. Although terrorist-sponsored hackers are less likely, criminal

hackers often take advantage of situations such as the widely reported Y2K computer glitch, which appears to have been exaggerated or resolved before it could take place.

Of course, all of us want to be well informed by the media and federal authorities when our lives or homes may be in danger of terrorists; however, we also want to live from day to day without fearing for our lives unnecessarily. What is the happy medium? This question will remain a concern as new information technologies make it possible for news—whether fact or fiction—to reach us instantaneously and without filters from persons who may be more in the know than we are about possible threats.

If you would like to learn more about terrorism, information warfare, and other issues related to low-intensity political violence, access the Terrorism Research Center (http://www.terrorism.com) or the State Department Web site mentioned before.

(*Note:* Web addresses often change. Those given here were accurate at the time of publication.)

judge Martha A. Bethel summoned a Freeman who had not paid three parking tickets, she was "charged" with treason by the group and received numerous threats of kidnapping and death. According to Bethel (1995:A13), "This has been a living nightmare. As judges, we all expect to deal with disgruntled people who refuse to take responsibility for their actions. But who in their right mind would choose to serve their community when the community becomes defenseless in the face of such terrorism." As isolated as such threats may appear, experts believe that this kind of antigovernment militia ideology is what provoked the Oklahoma City bombing. If they are right, Timothy McVeigh and others like him may become martyrs for militia members, some of whom already believe that the government carried out the Oklahoma City bombing so that it could justify a crackdown on freedom in this country (*New York Times*, 1997e).

How can we stop domestic terrorism? According to some social analysts, acts of domestic terrorism will continue in this country as long as such behavior remains unchecked. They believe it is unlikely that Congress will tighten U.S. policies on terrorism because some members lack expertise on terrorism and others are sympathetic to some militias or organizations such as the National Rifle Association, which holds views on gun control and individual liberty similar to those of the militias (Dreyfuss, 1996; *New York Times*, 1997e). Moreover, should any action be taken, shortwave radio broadcasts and the Internet provide militia members with a communication network through which they can call for offensive action against the government (Noble, 1995). Although some members of militias shun media coverage, others—along with many domestic and international terrorists—realize the importance of the media to their goals (see Box 17.2).

EXPLANATIONS OF WAR AND TERRORISM

What causes collective violence such as war and terrorism? Can war and acts of terrorism be reduced? Despite centuries of war and terrorism, we still know little about the origins of violence or how to reduce such acts (Turpin and Kurtz, 1997). In Chapter 9, we discussed biological, psychological, and sociological explanations for violence. We will now examine these approaches as they relate to war and terrorism.

 ## Biological Perspectives

Analysts who use a biological framework for explaining war and terrorism emphasize that people inherit a tendency (or predisposition) toward aggressive behavior, which may culminate in warfare or terrorist acts. Contemporary policy makers who trace violent behavior to chemical or physical abnormalities such as a brain lesion, brain dysfunction, endocrine disorder, hormonal imbalance, or other genetic factors are taking such an approach (Turpin and Kurtz, 1997).

Do human beings have biological predispositions toward aggressive behavior? How do analysts using a biological perspective differ in their answers to this question as compared to those using a sociological perspective?

Perhaps the most widely known advocate for biological explanations of war and terrorism is anthropologist Konrad Lorenz (1966:261), who stated, "To the humble seeker of biological truth there cannot be the slightest doubt that human militant enthusiasm evolved out of a communal defense response of our prehuman ancestors." According to Lorenz, just as our hominid ancestors confronted and repelled predatory animals, we have an almost instinctive desire to protect ourselves from our perceived enemies. Therefore people engage in terrorism or fight wars when stimuli trigger their predisposition toward aggression. Lorenz believes that although the predisposition toward violence was functional at one time because it ensured survival of the most "fit," this instinct is a problem in contemporary societies. Philosopher William James suggested that the kind of courage and altruism people bring to war could better be directed toward some more worthy enterprise (cited in Ehrenreich, 1997).

Some scholars have sought to identify genetic influences on violence and warfare. Among the earliest was sociobiologist Edward O. Wilson (1975), who believed that aggressive tendencies are part of human nature but that people can learn not to engage in violent behavior. More recently, anthropologists Richard Wrangham and Dale Peterson, who study aggression in animals and humans, published their findings in *Demonic Males: Apes and the Origins of Human Violence* (1996). According to Wrangham and Peterson, both human and nonhuman animals, such as chimpanzees, have the inherent capacity to commit premeditated assaults. Premeditated violence is used by humans (especially males) and lower animals to intimidate enemies, beat them up, and destroy their ability to bring future challenges. Wrangham and Peterson believe that female chimps and humans are less apt to murder or take part in war. Women were deliberately excluded from participating in war-related activities in fifty-eight of the sixty-seven human societies that Wrangham and Peterson studied (Wheeler, 1997). But this brings up another question: Do women not participate in war by choice, or are they categorically excluded by social norms and customs? More research is needed to answer this and other questions about a biological origin for warfare and terrorism. Thus far, no scientific evidence conclusively demonstrates than humans are innately violent or that biological factors are more important than social factors in producing violent behavior (Turpin and Kurtz, 1997).

Psychological Perspectives

Psychologists have provided significant insights into violence, but they do not focus on collective violence in the form of war and terrorism. In fact, most psychological explanations emphasize individualistic sources of violence, resulting from such causes as abnormal psychological development. For example, Sigmund Freud contended that violent behavior occurs when the three aspects of the human personality come into conflict with one another. If the individual's id (unconscious drives and instincts) conflicts with the superego (internalized social values), and the ego (the mediator between the id and superego) is unable to resolve the conflict, violent behavior may ensue, particularly if the individual has an overdeveloped id, which contains the aggressive drive, or an underdeveloped superego (Turpin and Kurtz, 1997).

Contemporary social psychologists generally believe that both individual and cultural factors must be considered in explaining why people go to war or engage in terrorism. Some social psychologists focus primarily on the processes by which cultural influences make some individuals, but not others, behave violently. From these studies, they conclude that it is easier to harm enemies when they have been depersonalized (Milgram, 1974). People also are more likely to behave violently when they are placed in positions in which they have a great deal of power and authority over others (Haney, Banks, and Zimbardo, 1984).

An interesting insight into the psychological processes that are involved in violence comes from the work of Robert Jay Lifton (1997), who studied violence inflicted by Nazi doctors at Auschwitz. According to Lifton, these doctors—who had previously been committed to saving lives—were able to commit horrible atrocities because of the psychological principle of *doubling*—"the division of the self into two functioning wholes, so that a part-self acts as an entire self" (Lifton, 1997:30). Through the process of doubling, the doctors could embrace evil without restraint, remorse, or guilt and, at the same time, be loving parents and normal members of society. According to Lifton (1997), not only can doubling save the life of a soldier in combat who is confronted with the enemy, but it also can contribute to extreme wartime brutalities and the embracing of evil.

If social psychologists are correct in believing that individual personality factors contribute to war and terrorism, then how can such behavior be reduced? The answer is to emphasize social and cultural factors that head off violence and deadly conflict. In other words, societies should deemphasize violence and encourage peaceful behavior in daily life. However, social critic Barbara Ehrenreich (1977:76) believes that our impulse to make war resides in a deep ancestral memory of our role as prey and that we live in a society that still glorifies such impulses:

> Why . . . would human beings want to reenact . . . the terror of predation? Probably for the same reason that "civilized" people today pay to see movies in which their fellow humans are stalked and devoured by flesh-eating ghouls, vampires, and extraterrestrial monsters. Nothing gets our attention like the prospect of being ripped apart, sucked dry, and transformed into another creature's meal.

Although she concedes that people enjoy such fictional encounters because they are "fun," Ehrenreich also thinks that today's films and television programming pose interesting questions about why many people enjoy watching acts of violence and terrorism.

Ehrenreich's analysis brings up a larger question: Why are many people relatively positive about war, and why do they seemingly condone the violence associated with war? According to sociologists Jennifer Turpin and Lester R. Kurtz (1997:1), many people are deeply ambivalent about war because they believe that the only way to fight violence is with more violence:

> Since most people believe they can be secure only by repelling violence with violence, they simultaneously deplore and condone it. The use of violence is considered taboo almost universally in modern society except under certain conditions. It is widely abhorred yet widely used to promote social control in settings ranging from the household to the global socioeconomic order. Because of that ambivalence, elaborate social mechanisms have been institutionalized to distinguish between legitimate and illegitimate violence. Not only are individuals threatened by violence, but so are whole societies, and now—in the nuclear age—the species itself. Ironically, the very structures supposedly created to provide security against violence instead threaten everyone.

Sociological Explanations

Sociological explanations for war and terrorism use a functionalist, conflict, or interactionist perspective. We'll look at all three, starting with the functionalist.

THE FUNCTIONALIST PERSPECTIVE

Some functionalist explanations focus on the relationship between social disorganization and warfare or terrorism. According to these explanations, disorganization in social institutions, for example, the government, contributes to overall political instability. Militia members believe that the U.S. government no longer serves the purpose for which it was intended, namely, to protect the individual's rights and freedom. In their eyes, the U.S. government has become dysfunctional, and they engage in acts of terrorism to undermine the government so that it will change radically or be abolished.

Other functionalists focus on the functions that war serves. Looked at from this perspective, war can settle disputes between nations. However, in the age of nuclear weaponry, many nations seek other means to deal with their disagreements. Among these means are *economic sanctions*, cutting off all trade. Thus, the United States has imposed economic sanctions, rather than engaging in war or military action, against countries engaging in terrorism, environmental violations, abuse of workers' rights, regional strife, drug trafficking, human and political rights abuses, and nuclear proliferation (Myers, 1997). However, some political analysts argue that the United States is cutting off its nose to spite its face when it imposes economic sanctions against other governments: Economic sanctions are dysfunctional for another social institution—the economy. Also, even though the United States has used sanctions against other nations from its earliest days, corporations are concerned that the sanctions deny them access to the world's markets and the profits in those markets (Myers, 1997).

Some functionalists believe that we will always have wars because of other important functions that they serve in societies. First, war demonstrates that one nation or group has power over another. Historically, conquering forces acquire the "spoils of war," including more territory and material possessions. Second, war functions as a means of punishment in much the same manner that the U.S. government uses sanctions to force other nations to comply with our viewpoint on certain issues. Third, war is a way to disseminate ideologies, usually political or reli-

gious. For example, under the slogan "making the world safe for democracy," the United States has fought its largest wars in defense of a democratic form of government (Crossette, 1997). According to sociologist Seymour Martin Lipset, "We are a revolutionary country with a revolutionary tradition. We want everyone to be democrats" (cited in Crossette, 1997:E3). But not all democracies are friends of the United States. Larry Diamond, a scholar who has examined new democracies in other nations, explains (cited in Crossette, 1997:E3):

> Political freedom has deteriorated in several of the longest-surviving democracies of the developing world, including India, Sri Lanka, Colombia, and Venezuela. . . . It isn't enough to have elections. . . . Democracy is not something that is simply present or absent. It's not like a light switch that you flip on or off. It emerges in different fragments in different sequences in different countries and in different historical periods.

Finally, many functionalists point out the economic function of war. War benefits society because it stimulates the economy through increased war-related production and provides jobs for civilians who otherwise might not be able to find employment. In 1994, for example, the United States sold more than 10.3 billion dollars in military equipment and supplies to other countries (refer back to Map 17.1 on page 371). Conflict analysts also see an economic side to war, but they are not so optimistic.

THE CONFLICT AND INTERACTIONIST PERSPECTIVES

Conflict theorists view war from the standpoint of how militarism and aggressive preparedness for war contribute to the economic well-being of some, but not all, people in a society. According to sociologist Cynthia Enloe (1987:527), people who consider capitalism the moving force behind the military's influence "believe that government officials enhance the status, resources, and authority of the military in order to protect the interests of private enterprises at home and overseas." In other words, the origins of war can be traced to corporate boardrooms, not to the U.S. government's war room. Those who view war from this standpoint note that workers come to rely on military spending for jobs. Labor unions, for example, support defense spending because it provides well-paid, stable employment for union members.

A second conflict explanation focuses on the role of the nation and its inclination toward coercion in response to perceived threats. From this perspective, nations inevitably use force to ensure compliance within their societies and to protect themselves from outside attacks.

A third conflict explanation is based on patriarchy and the relationship between militarism and masculinity. Across cultures and over time, the military has been a male institution, and the "meanings attached to masculinity appear to be so firmly linked to compliance with military roles that it is often impossible to disentangle the two" (Enloe, 1987:531).

Interactionists would call this last perspective the *social construction of masculinity*. That is, certain assumptions, teachings, and expectations that serve as the standard for appropriate male behavior—in this case, values of dominance, power, aggression, and violence—are created and recreated presumably through gender socialization, particularly in military training. Historically, the development of manhood and male superiority has been linked to militarism and combat—the ultimate test of a man's masculinity (Enloe, 1987; Cock, 1994).

WAR AND TERRORISM IN THE TWENTY-FIRST CENTURY

What will happen during the twenty-first century? How will nations deal with the proliferation of arms and nuclear weapons? Will some of the missiles and warheads fall into the hands of terrorists? What should be done with the masses of nuclear waste being produced? No easy answers are forthcoming, as Ehrenreich explains (1997:239):

War . . . is a more formidable adversary than it has ever been. . . . war has dug itself into economic systems, where it offers a livelihood to millions. . . . It has lodged in our souls as a kind of religion, a quick tonic for political malaise and a bracing antidote to the moral torpor of consumerist, market-driven cultures. In addition, our incestuous fixation on combat with our own kind has left us ill-prepared to face many of the larger perils of the situation in which we find ourselves: the possibility of drastic climatic changes, the depletion of natural resources, the

relentless predations of the microbial world. The wealth that flows ceaselessly to the project of war is wealth lost, for the most part, to the battle against these threats.

But Ehrenreich, like most other social analysts, is not totally pessimistic about the future. She believes that human resistance to war can provide a means to spare this nation and the world from future calamities. According to Ehrenreich, the antiwar movements of the late twentieth century show that "the passions we bring to war can be brought just as well to the struggle *against* war." But, she notes, people must be willing to educate, inspire, and rally others to the cause. Like other forms of warfare, the people fighting for peace must be willing to continue the struggle even when the odds seem hopeless. Ehrenreich's point is supported by sociologists James William Gibson and Francesca M. Cancian (1990:9), who believe that making peace can be more difficult than making war:

[M]aking peace requires democratic relationships: soldiers who refuse to fight in a war they do not support; citizens who claim the right to participate in making decisions instead of accepting rule by elites who make decisions in secret; newspaper reporters, magazine editors, movie makers, and others in the mass media who question the necessity of casting another nation as an "enemy" and instead look for ways to communicate with other human beings who are potentially our friends.

Why do we end our discussion of social problems with war and terrorism? They are the ultimate category of social problems. When class, race, ethnicity, or any of the other dominant/subordinate categories discussed in this book escalate to a level of "doing something about it" regardless of the consequences, terrorism or war may be the result. Redressing inequality is an admirable goal, but perhaps the goal should be the one stated by Tim O'Brien, who wrote about his tour of duty in Vietnam (quoted in Hynes, 1997:283–284):

I would wish this book could take the form of a plea for everlasting peace, a plea from one who knows, from one who's been there and come back, an old soldier looking back at a dying war. . . . That would be good. It would be fine to integrate it all to persuade my younger brother and perhaps some others to say "No" to wars and other battles.

The international society—the community of all the nations of the world—must work to alleviate inequalities and create a better—peaceful—world for future generations. What role will you and I play during the twenty-first century? Will we be part of the problem or part of the solution? The answer is up to us.

SUMMARY

➤ *How do social scientists define war?*

Social scientists define war broadly. The term *war* includes armed conflict between two countries, undeclared wars, civil and guerrilla wars, covert operations, and some forms of terrorism. War is a form of collective violence that involves organized violence by people seeking to promote their cause or resist social policies or practices that they consider oppressive.

➤ *What are the consequences of war?*

The most direct effect of war is loss of human life. In World War I and before, it was mostly military personnel who lost their lives, but in World War II and thereafter, war was waged against civilians. If a nuclear war took place, the devastation would be beyond description. Other consequences for both military personnel and civilians are physical and psychological damage, including post-traumatic stress syndrome. Finally, the economic costs of war and war preparedness are astronomical.

➤ *How important is military technology to winning a war?*

Military technology is a dominant factor, as military history shows. In the fourteenth century, smaller European and Western armies defeated bigger armies by using the newly discovered black powder. Today, precision-guided munitions render old technologies obsolete and global warfare possible. But wars can be won on the basis of factors other than military technology, too, as the U.S. experience in Vietnam shows.

➤ *What is terrorism?*

Terrorism is the use of calculated unlawful physical force or threats of violence against a government, organization, or individual to gain some political, religious, economic, or social objective. Tactics include bombing, kidnapping, hostage taking, hijacking, assassination, and extortion.

➤ *What are the three types of political terrorism?*

Revolutionary terrorism involves acts of violence against civilians that are carried out by internal enemies of the government who want to bring about political change. Repressive terrorism is conducted by a government against its own citizens for the purpose of protecting an existing political order. In state-sponsored terrorism, a government provides financial resources, weapons, and training for terrorists who conduct their activities in other nations.

➤ *How extensive is domestic terrorism in the United States and what can be done about it?*

The Oklahoma City bombing in 1995 was the worst act of domestic terrorism in our country's history but not the only recent act (there were also the World Trade Center bombing and the Unabomber's terrorist activities). The major current threat of domestic terrorism comes from militia groups and the far-right Patriot movement, both of which reject the U.S. government. According to experts, one of the major obstacles to stopping domestic terrorism is the sympathy that some members of Congress have toward some militias and organizations such as the National Rifle Association that hold views on gun control similar to those of militias.

➤ *What are the biological perspectives on war and terrorism?*

Some biological proponents say that humans, especially males, are innately violent, but there is no conclusive scientific evidence to support this view or the view that biological factors are more important than social factors.

What are the psychological perspectives on war and terrorism?

Most strictly psychological perspectives focus on individualistic sources of violence, but social psychologists take both individual and cultural factors into account. Their research findings show that it is easier to harm enemies when they are depersonalized and that people are more likely to act violently when they are in positions of power. Some individuals can commit horrible atrocities without feeling guilt through the process of doubling. Social psychologists say that, to reduce war and terrorism, society must emphasize peace, not glorify violent impulses.

 What is the functionalist perspective on war and terrorism?

Some functionalists focus on the relationship between social disorganization and warfare or terrorism. Examining the growth of militias, they note that disorganization in social institutions contributes to overall political instability. Other functionalists say that war serves certain functions: War settles disputes; demonstrates that one nation or group has power over another; punishes; is one way to disseminate religious and political ideologies; and, finally, stimulates the economy.

➡ *What are the conflict and interactionist perspectives on war and terrorism?*

Some conflict theorists say that militarism and preparedness for war contribute to the economic well-being of some—not all—people. Another conflict perspective says that nations inevitably use force to ensure compliance within their society and to protect themselves from outside attacks. A third conflict perspective is based in patriarchy: Across cultures and over time, the military has been a male institution; it is almost impossible to untangle masculinity from militarism. Interactionists call this last perspective the *social construction of masculinity*—the connection between manhood and militarism is historically created and recreated through gender socialization.

KEY TERMS

collective violence, p. 366
repressive terrorism, p. 373
revolutionary terrorism, p. 373

state-sponsored terrorism, p. 374
strategically significant weapon, p. 371

terrorism, p. 373
war system, p. 366
weapons system, p. 371

QUESTIONS FOR CRITICAL THINKING

1. In World War II and every war since, more civilians than military personnel have died. Given the military technology available, how can we safeguard civilians?
2. How do you perceive the problem of domestic terrorism in the United States? Do you think militias pose a growing threat? What solutions can you suggest?
3. Consider the question posed in the last paragraph of this chapter: What can you yourself do to make the world a better—peaceful—place in the twenty-first century?

Chapter Eighteen

Can Social Problems Be Solved?

The _____ Hotel here is a favorite watering hole of the well-heeled and is known for its fantastic views of the city. . . . Just across the street in _____ Park, homeless people, more concentrated here than in most parts of the city, spend the day sipping from half-empty juice boxes and picking through the garbage discarded by children using the playground. . . . The gap between rich and poor . . . is widening, spurred by economic and social change.

▲ (Strom, 2000:A1)

Does this scenario describe New York City? San Francisco? Another large urban center in the United States? No, this is a reporter's description of what's going on in Tokyo, Japan, as the twenty-first century begins. Although the similarity of patterns associated with such social problems as homelessness in the United States and Japan leaves us concerned about their persistence, we are also hopeful that we may be able to find ways across cities, states, and nations to reduce or alleviate some of these problems in the twenty-first century. However, as social analysts have said, solving social problems is a far more complex undertaking than simply identifying them and pinpointing their social locations:

> Identifying social problems and calling for action are quite different matters from actually designing and implementing programs to solve them. Calling attention to the problem, for example, can often be accomplished relatively quickly and easily. Trying to actually carry out a solution, by contrast, involves innumerable obstacles, delays, and frustrations, and demands immense dedication and perseverance. (Weinberg, Rubington, and Hammersmith, 1981:6)

Perhaps the first obstacle that we face in trying to solve social problems is the difference between ideal solutions and practical solutions. As sociologists Martin S. Weinberg, Earl Rubington, and Sue Kiefer Hammersmith (1981:6) have stated, "There is usually considerable conflict between what the *ideal* solution would be and what a *workable* solution might be." Sometimes, for example, the ideal solution to a problem entails prohibitive costs. Sometimes there is no agreement about what the problem *is* and what efforts should be made to reduce or eliminate it. After all, the people and organizations involved in the problem-defining stage of a social problem generally are not the same people and organizations involved in the problem-solving stage of a social problem. Social problems are often identified and defined by political or social activists, journalists, social scientists, and religious leaders. In contrast, the problem-solving stage usually involves elected officials and/or people working in agencies and governmental bureaucracies. Moreover, sometimes a proposed solution to a problem only gives rise to a whole new set of problems (Weinberg, Rubington, and Hammersmith, 1981). In this chapter, we will review microlevel, midrange, and macrolevel approaches for dealing with social problems and pose a pressing question: What can you and others of your generation do to reduce social problems?

A REVIEW OF MAJOR SOCIAL THEORIES ON SOCIAL PROBLEMS

The underlying theoretical assumptions that we hold regarding social problems often have a profound influence on what we feel may be the best solution for a specific problem. Do we believe society is based on stability or conflict? Is conflict good for society or bad for society? According to the functionalist perspective, a society is a stable, orderly system that is composed of a number of interrelated parts, each of which performs a function that contributes to the overall stability of the society. From the functionalist perspective, social problems arise when social institutions do not fulfill the functions they are supposed to or when dysfunctions (undesirable consequences of an activity or social process that inhibit a society's ability to adapt or adjust) occur. Dysfunctions create social disorganization, which in turn causes a breakdown in the traditional values and norms that serve as social control mechanisms. As shown in Table 18.1, the social disorganization approach of functionalists traces the causes of social problems to any social change that leaves existing rules inadequate for current conditions. In societies undergoing social change—for example, high rates of immigration, rapid changes in technology, and increasingly complex patterns of social life—social disorganization produces stress at the individual level and inefficiency and confusion at the institutional and societal levels (Weinberg, Rubington, and Ham-

mersmith, 1981). Thus, the functionalist approach to reducing social problems has as central factors the prevention of rapid social changes, the maintenance of the status quo, and the restoration of order.

In contrast, the conflict perspective assumes that conflict is natural and inevitable in society. Value conflict approaches focus on conflict between the values held by members of divergent groups. These approaches also highlight the ways in which cultural, economic, and social diversity may contribute to misunderstandings and problems. According to Marxist, or critical-conflict, theorists, groups are engaged in a continuous struggle for control of scarce resources. As a result of the unjust use of political, economic, or social power, certain groups of people are privileged while others are disadvantaged. Thus, for critical-conflict theorists, social problems arise out of major contradictions that are inherent in the ways in which societies are organized. When this approach is used, the root causes of social problems—patriarchy, capitalism, and massive spending on the U.S. military-industrial complex at the expense of human services, for example—must be radically altered or eliminated altogether. Focusing on the political economy, one critical-conflict approach states that the capitalist economy, which is now global, maintains and reinforces domination and subordination in social relations. This approach also examines how political leaders may put their own interests ahead of any common good that might exist (Feagin and Feagin, 1997). Clearly, any solutions to social problems proposed by this approach would require radical changes in society and thus are not always viewed positively in societies in which economic prosperity based on individual attributes rather than collective activities is considered a mark of personal and social achievement. Other conflict theorists also view the interlocking nature of race, class, and gender as systems of domination and subordination as central to social problems. Thus their solutions for reducing or eliminating social problems that are embedded in racial and ethnic relations, class relationships, and gender inequalities also require dramatic changes in society.

Operating at the microlevel, the interactionist perspective focuses on how people act toward one another and make sense of their daily lives. From this perspective, society is the sum of the interactions of individuals and groups. Thus interactionists often study social problems by analyzing the process whereby a behavior is defined as a social problem and how individuals and groups then come to

TABLE 18.1 PERCEIVED PROBLEMS AND POSSIBLE SOLUTIONS

Perspective	Causes	Possible Solutions
FUNCTIONALIST:		
Social disorganization	Social change; inadequacy of existing social rules	Development and implementation of social rules that are explicit, workable, and consistent
CONFLICT:		
Value conflict	Conflict between different groups' values; economic, social, and cultural diversity	Group action involving confrontation of opponents and working for lasting changes in policy or legislation
Critical conflict (Marxist)	Relations of domination and subordination are reinforced by the global capitalist economy and political leaders who put other priorities ahead of the good of the people	Changing the nature of society, particularly inequalities that grow more pronounced as the wealthy grow richer and the poor worldwide become increasingly impoverished
INTERACTIONIST:		
Deviant behavior	Inappropriate socialization within primary groups	Resocialize or rehabilitate people so that they will conform
Labeling	How people label behavior, how they respond to it, and the consequences of their responses	Changing the definitions through discriminalization; limit labeling

Source: Based on Weinberg, Rubington, and Hammersmith, 1981; Feagin and Feagin, 1997.

engage in activities that a significant number of people view as major social concerns. Interactionist theories of deviance note that inadequate socialization or interacting with the "wrong" people may contribute to deviant behavior and crime. Similarly, interactionists who use the labeling framework for their analysis of social problems study how people label behavior, how they respond to people engaged in such behavior, and the consequences of their responses (Weinberg, Rubington, and Hammersmith, 1981).

Each of these sociological perspectives suggests ways in which social problems may be reduced. In doing so, they produce divergent views on social changes that might reduce or eliminate social problems.

SOCIAL CHANGE AND REDUCING SOCIAL PROBLEMS

It should be clear from what has been said in the preceding section that the concept of social change is important to our discussion of reducing social problems. *Social change* is the alteration, modification, or transformation of public policy, culture, or social institutions over time (Kendall, 2000). Notice that this definition states that social change occurs "over time." Thus social change has temporal dimensions. Some efforts to deal with social problems are *short-term* strategies, whereas others are *middle-term* remedies, and still others constitute *long-term* efforts to alleviate the root causes of a social problem. In other words, efforts to alleviate individual unemployment or reduce unemployment rates in a community have a different temporal dimension than efforts to change the political economy in such a manner that high levels of employment and greater wage equity are brought about throughout a nation or nations. Clearly, efforts to alleviate individual unemployment are a short-term solution to the problem of unemployment, while efforts to reduce unemployment in a community or to change the entire political economy are middle-term and long-term solutions. Sometimes discussions of social change sound idealistic or utopian because they are middle-term or long-term strategies that attempt to target the root causes of a social problem. For many social problems, however, a combination of strategies is required to reduce social problems.

MICROLEVEL ATTEMPTS TO SOLVE SOCIAL PROBLEMS

In Chapter 1 we described sociologist C. Wright Mills's (1959) belief that we should apply the sociological imagination to gain a better understanding of social problems. According to Mills, sociological imagination is the ability to see the relationship between individual experiences and the larger society. For Mills, social problems cannot not be solved at the individual level because they are more than personal troubles or private problems. However, sometimes social institutions cannot deal with a problem effectively and political and business leaders are unwilling, or unable, to allocate the resources necessary to reduce a problem. In these situations, we have no choice but to try to deal with the problem in our own way.

◢ Seeking Individual Solutions to Personal Problems

Microlevel solutions to social problems focus on how individuals operate within small groups to try to remedy a problem that affects them, their family, or friends. Usually when individuals have personal problems, they turn to their *primary groups*, small, less specialized groups in which members engage in face-to-face, emotion-based interactions over an extended period of time (Kendall, 2000). Primary

groups include one's family, close friends, and other peers with whom one routinely shares the more personal experiences in life.

How can participation in primary groups help us to reduce personal problems? According to sociologists, members of our primary groups usually support us even when others do not. For example, some analysts believe that we have many more people who are without a domicile (technically homeless) than current statistics suggest, but whenever possible, these people live with relatives or friends, many of whom may already live in overcrowded and sometimes substandard housing. Most people who seek individualized solutions to personal troubles believe the situation will be temporary. However, if the problem is widespread or embedded in the larger society, it may stretch out for months or years without resolution. At best, individualized efforts to reduce a problem are short-term measures that some critics refer to as a "Band-Aid approach" to a problem because these efforts do not eliminate the causes of the problem.

Microlevel attempts to solve social problems often focus on how individuals operating within small groups can try to remedy a problem that affects them. An example is how people use their extended families as a source of economic, social, and spiritual support in "tough times." Here, several generations of one family live under the same roof in an effort to minimize housing expenses.

Some microlevel approaches to reducing social problems focus on how individuals can do something about the problems they face. For example, a person who is unemployed or among the "working poor" because of low wages, seasonal employment, or other factors may be urged to get more education or training and work experience in order to find a "better" job and have the opportunity for upward mobility. Individuals who appear to have eliminated problems in their own lives through such efforts are applauded for their determination, and they are often used (sometimes unwillingly or unknowingly) as examples that others are supposed to follow.

Limitations of the Microlevel Solutions Approach

While certainly individuals must be responsible for their own behavior, and they must make decisions that help solve their own problems, there are serious limitations to the assumption that social problems can be solved one person at a time. When we focus on individualistic solutions to reducing social problems, we are not taking into account the fact that secondary groups and societal institutions play a significant part in creating, maintaining, and exacerbating many social problems. *Secondary groups are larger, more specialized groups in which members engage in impersonal, goal-oriented relationships for a limited period of time* (Kendall, 2000). Without the involvement of these large-scale organizations, which include government agencies and transnational corporations, it is virtually impossible to reduce large-scale social problems. Consider, for example, the problem of air pollution. According to scholars Mike Budd, Steve Craig, and Clay Steinman (1999:169-170):

Sport utility vehicles, for example, pollute the air and add to global warming far more than the cars they displaced on the nation's roads. Indeed, if a legal loophole did not consider them "light trucks" instead of cars, the environmental damage they cause would keep them off the road altogether. Light trucks, which also include pickup trucks and minivans, are the fastest-growing source of global warming gasses in the country, contributing nearly twice as much per vehicle as cars, according to a study by the Environmental Protection Agency.

Thus while I can stay inside all the time so that I do not inhale polluted air, this individual solution does not solve the problem of air pollution and does not address the role of others (vehicle manufacturers, gasoline producers, and consumers, among others) in the creation of air pollution. In other words, personal choices alone cannot do much to reduce many national and global problems. Even if one person decides to give up a sport utility vehicle or to stay inside all day when cities have smog alert warning days, the environment continues to be contaminated and the air quality for future generations comes more and more into question. On the other hand, suppose a group of people banded together in a grassroots effort to deal with a social problem: What effect might their efforts have on reducing or eliminating it?

MID-RANGE ATTEMPTS TO SOLVE SOCIAL PROBLEMS

Mid-range solutions to social problems focus on how secondary groups and formal organizations can deal with problems or assist individuals in overcoming problems such as drug addiction or domestic violence. Some groups help people cope with their own problems, and some groups attempt to bring about community change.

Groups That Help People Cope with Their Problems

Most mid-range solutions to social problems are based on two assumptions: (1) some social problems can best be reduced by reaching one person at a time, and (2) prevention and intervention are most effective at the personal and community levels. Groups that attempt to reduce a social problem by helping individuals cope with it, or eliminate it from their own lives, are commonplace in our society (see Table 18.2). Among the best known are Alcoholics Anonymous (AA) and Narcotics Anonymous (NA); however, a wide range of "self-help" organizations exist in most communities. Typically, self-help groups bring together individuals who have experienced the same problem and have the same goal: Quitting the behavior that has caused the problem, which can be anything from abuse of alcohol, tobacco, and other drugs

TABLE 18.2   SELECTED SELF-HELP GROUPS

Those with Web Sites and Local Support Groups	Those with Local Support Groups
Alcoholics Anonymous www.alcoholics-anonymous.org	Alzheimer's Support Group
Al-Anon and Alateen www.al-anon-alateen.org	Breast Cancer Support Group
Breast Cancer On-line Support pages.prodigy.net/reply/asap/bc	Bereavement Support Group
Children of Lesbians and Gays Everywhere www.colage.org	Bulimia, Anorexia Self-Help
Cocaine Anonymous www.ca.org	Co-Dependents Anonymous
Gamblers Anonymous www.gamblersanonymous.org	Diabetes Support Group
Narcotics Anonymous www.na.org	Grief Support Group
National Coalition for the Homeless nch.air.net	Parents Anonymous
Overeaters Anonymous www.overeatersanonymous.org	Parents Without Partners
Sex Addicts Anonymous www.sexaa.org	Suddenly Single
Step-Family Association of America www.stepfam.org	Veterans Outreach Program
United Fathers of America www.ufa.org	

Note: Web addresses often change. Those given here were accurate at the time of publication.

to overeating, gambling, and chronic worrying. Volunteers who have had similar problems (and believe they are on the road to overcoming them) act as role models for newer members. For example, AA and NA are operated by alcoholics and/or other substance abusers who try to provide new members with the support they need to overcome alcohol addiction or drug dependency. According to some analysts, AA is a subculture with distinct rules and values that alcoholics learn through their face-to-face encounters with other AA members (Maxwell, 1981). Social interaction is viewed as central for individual success in the programs. Confessing one's behavioral problems to others in an organizational setting is believed to have therapeutic value to those who are seeking help. Like other mid-range approaches, organizations such as

AA and NA may bring changes in the individual's life; however, they usually do not systematically address the structural factors (such as unemployment, work-related stress, and aggressive advertising campaigns) that may contribute to the problems. For example, AA typically does not lobby for more stringent laws pertaining to drunk driving or the sale and consumption of alcoholic beverages. As a result, larger societal intervention is necessary to reduce the problems that contribute to individual behavior.

 Grassroots Groups That Work for Community-Based Change

Some grassroots organizations focus on bringing about a change that may reduce or eliminate a social

problem in a specific community or region. *Grassroots groups* **are organizations started by ordinary people who work in concert to change a perceived wrong in their neighborhood, city, state, or nation.** Using this approach, people learn how to empower themselves against local and state government officials, corporate executives, and media figures who determine what constitutes the news in their area:

> By their nature, grassroots groups emerge to challenge individuals, corporations, government agencies, academia, or a combination of these when people discover they share a grievance. In their search for redress, they have encountered unresponsive, negative public agencies, self-serving private businesses, or recalcitrant individuals and groups. The answer for them is to select specific issues and find like-minded others. (Adams, 1991:9)

A central concern of those who attempt to reduce a social problem through grassroots groups is the extent to which other people are apathetic about the problem. Some analysts suggest that, even when people are aware of problems, they do not think that they can do anything to change them or they do not know how to work with other people to alleviate them:

> The biggest problem facing Americans is not those issues that bombard us daily, from homelessness and failing schools to environmental devastation and the federal deficit. Underlying each is a deeper crisis. Some see that deeper problem in the form of obstacles that block problem solving: the tightening concentration of wealth, the influence of money in politics, discrimination, and bureaucratic rigidity, to name a few. These are powerful barriers. But for us the crisis is deeper still. The crisis is that *we as a people don't know how to come together to solve these problems*. We lack the capacities to address the issues or remove the obstacles that stand in the way of public deliberation. Too many Americans feel powerless. (Lappé and Du Bois, 1994:9)

According to social analysts, more community dialogue is needed on social issues, and more people need to become involved in grassroots social movements. **A** *social movement* **is an organized group that acts col-**

Mid-range attempts to solve social problems typically focus on how secondary groups and formal organizations deal with problems or seek to assist individuals in overcoming problems. An example is this grassroots social movement whose members are protesting the placement of a low-level radioactive dumping site in their neighborhood.

lectively to promote or resist change through collective action (Goldberg, 1991). Because social movements when they begin are not institutionalized and are outside the political mainstream, they empower outsiders by offering them an opportunity to have their voices heard (Kendall, 2000). For example, when residents near Love Canal, located in Niagara Falls, New York, came to believe that toxic chemicals were damaging the health of their children, they banded together to bring about change in government regulations concerning the disposal of toxic wastes. Indeed, Love Canal was the birthplace of the environmental movement against dumping toxic waste. Social movements, such as Mothers Against Drunk Driving (MADD), Earth First!, People for the Ethical Treatment of Animals (PETA), and the National Federation of Parents for Drug Free Youth, began as community-based grassroots efforts. Over time, many mid-range organizations evolve into national organizations; however, their organization and focus often change in the process (Adams, 1991). Table 18.3 provides examples of activist organizations that seek to reduce specific social problems in communities.

TABLE 18.3   SELECTED ORGANIZATIONS THAT SEEK TO REDUCE A SOCIAL PROBLEM

Category	Organization	Web Site Address
ENVIRONMENT:	Earth First	www.efmedia.org
	Sierra Club	www.sierraclub.org
	Student Environmental Action Coalition	www.seac.org
DRIVING WHILE DRINKING:	Mothers Against Drunk Driving	www3.madd.org/dml/window.cfm
WAGES AND WORKING CONDITIONS:	Industrial Workers of the World	iww.org
NEIGHBORHOODS AND POVERTY:	Jobs and Opportunities to Improve Neighborhoods	libertynet.org/nol/join.html
	National Low Income Housing Coalition	www.nlihc.org
	National Neighborhood Coalition	www.comminfoexch.org/nnc
VIOLENCE AND WAR:	Food Not Bombs	www.webcom.com/~peace/PEACTREE/stuff/stuff/HOMEPAGE.html
	The Nonviolence Web	www.nonviolence.org

Note: Web addresses often change. Those given here were accurate at the time of publication.

Grassroots organizations and other local structures are crucial to national social movements because national social movements must recruit members and gain the economic resources that are necessary for nationwide or global social activism. Numerous sociological studies have shown that the local level constitutes a necessary microfoundation for larger scale social movement activism. According to social movement scholar Steve M. Buechler (2000:149):

[S]ome forms of activism not only require such microfoundations but also thematize local structures themselves as the sources of grievances, the site of resistance, or the goal of change. By consciously identifying local structures as the appropriate areas of contention, such movements comprise a distinct subset of the larger family of movements that all rely on microfoundations but do not all thematize local structures in this way.

To understand how grassroots organizations aid national social movements, consider the problem of environmental degradation. Leaders of national environmental organizations often participate in local or regional rallies, protests, and letter-writing or e-mail campaigns, particularly when politicians are making decisions that environmentalists believe will have a negative effect on the environment. By working with local and regional activists and seeking to influence local and regional power structures—city councils, statewide planning commissions, and legislatures—national organizations assert the need for their existence and attempt to garner additional supporters and revenue for their efforts nationwide or around the globe. By intertwining local, regional, and national organizational structures, these groups create a powerful voice for social change regarding some issue.

Limitations of the Mid-Level Solutions Approach

Although local efforts to reduce social problems affecting individuals and collectivities in a specific city or region bring about many improvements, they typically lack the sustained capacity to produce the larger, systemic changes, at national or international levels, that are necessary to actually reduce or eliminate the problem. For example, New York City's Coalition for the Homeless recently challenged the city's attempt to impose work requirements at its homeless shelters. While this effort certainly helped some of the city's homeless people, it did not address

SOCIAL PROBLEMS

AND SOCIAL POLICY   **BOX 18.1**

"If You Don't Work, You Don't Sleep"

As things stand today [in New York City], when you hear a panhandler on the subway complaining that he has no place to go for the night, you can tell yourself that he's a con man. When you walk by someone sleeping outside a church, you know that he could be sleeping in a bed provided unconditionally by taxpayers. If the homeless lose their right to shelter, the rest of us may gain the right to feel guilty.

—*Journalist John Tierney (2000:A11) describing how some people may feel if a mandatory work policy is implemented at New York City's homeless shelters*

Although we do not know precisely how many people are homeless in the United States, homelessness is one of the most troubling problems to emerge in recent years. In an effort to deal with this problem, most cities have established shelters where the homeless may go for a bed at night. Although some shelters have required that people work during the day in order to stay at the shelter at night, a recent attempt by the City of New York to make this a requirement in all shelters has been met by sustained opposition and court challenges by the Coalition for the Homeless. According to spokespersons for the coalition, one of the major problems with the proposed policy is the threat of eviction that hangs over people who are unable to find a job.

Advocates of the work policy believe that it is "immoral" for the public to subsidize people's self-destructive behavior, particularly when the people are able-bodied individuals who should be able to work (Tierney, 2000). Advocates ask: "If your son or brother became homeless, wouldn't you want him to learn to become self-sufficient? Wouldn't you want him to learn that his right to shelter comes with a responsibility?" (Tierney, 2000:A11). Those opposed to the mandatory work policy ask: "What if someone is wrongly evicted from a shelter? The mentally ill are supposed to be exempt, but what if their illness hasn't been diagnosed? What if someone gets confused by red tape?" (Tierney, 2000:A11).

An alternative proposal to evicting people from shelters and sending them back to the streets involves sending such individuals to "less richly serviced shelters." This means that individuals are given the worst possible accommodations, such as "drop-in centers" where they sleep in chairs, as an incentive to get a job so that they can move to a better shelter and eventually not be dependent on the shelters for housing accommodations.

New York City is not alone in its efforts to deal with homelessness and those individuals and families who experience the problem. Do you know the shelter policies for the homeless in your city? Is there a fair way to resolve classic battles such as this over individuals' rights versus their responsibilities?

---

the structural factors in the political economy, such as job loss and lack of affordable housing, that contribute to homelessness. Thus, the problems associated with homelessness remain intact (see Box 18.1).

Many people involved in mid-range organizations see themselves as local activists. Some display bumper stickers saying, "Think globally, act locally"

(Shaw, 1999). Many activists believe that, in the absence of any sustained national agenda, national problems such as child poverty, low wages, and lack of affordable housing can be reduced by community-based organizations; but some analysts believe that local activists must demand large-scale political and economic support to bring about necessary changes.

According to Randy Shaw (1999:2–3), the director of the Tenderloin Housing Clinic in San Francisco, California, and the founder of Housing America, a national mobilization campaign to increase federal housing funds:

> America's corporate and political elite has succeeded in controlling the national agenda because citizen activists and organizations are not fully participating in the struggles shaping national political life. As the constituencies central to reclaiming American's progressive ideas bypass national fights to pursue local issues, their adversaries have faced surprisingly little opposition in dismantling federal programs achieved by six decades of national grassroots struggle. Citizen activities and organizations have steadfastly maintained their local focus even as national policy making drastically cut the resources flowing to communities. From 1979 to 1997, for example, federal aid to local communities for job training, housing, mass transit, environmental protection, and economic development fell by almost one trillion real dollars.

As this statement suggests, those working in grassroots organizations may be fighting a losing battle because the loss of federal aid can only diminish their future efforts. Accordingly, some grassroots activists have changed their motto to "think locally and act globally" (Brecher and Costello, 1998), and now work at the macrolevel, attempting to educate national leaders and corporate executives about the part that governments and transnational corporations must play if social problems are to be reduced or solved.

MACROLEVEL ATTEMPTS TO SOLVE SOCIAL PROBLEMS

Macrolevel solutions to social problems focus on how large-scale social institutions such as the government and the media may be persuaded to become involved in remedying social problems. Sometimes individuals who view themselves as individually powerless bind together in organizations to make demands on those who make decisions at the national or global level. As one social analyst explains:

Most individuals are largely powerless in the face of economic forces beyond their control. But because millions of other people are affected in the same way, they have a chance to influence their conditions through collective action. To do so, people must grasp that the common interest is also their own personal interest. This happens whenever individuals join a movement, a union, a party, or any organization pursuing a common goal. It happens when people push for a social objective—say universal health care or human rights—which benefits them by benefiting all those similarly situated. It underlies the development of an environmental movement which seeks to preserve the environment on which all depend (Brecher and Costello, 1998:107).

For example, when U.S. workers organize to support the rights of workers in low-income nations and are able to bring about changes that keep them from having to compete with these workers, they not only help workers abroad, they also help themselves (Brecher and Costello, 1998).

▲ Working through Special Interest Groups for Political Change

At the national level, those seeking macrolevel solutions to social problems may become members of a *special interest group*—a political coalition composed of individuals or groups sharing a specific interest they wish to protect or advance with the help of the political system (Greenberg and Page, 1993). Examples of special interest groups include the AFL-CIO and public interest or citizens groups such as the American Conservative Union or Zero Population Growth (Kendall, 2000).

Through special interest groups, which are sometimes called *pressure groups* or *lobbies,* people seek to remedy social problems by exerting pressure on political leaders. These groups may be categorized on the basis of three factors:

1. *Issues.* Some groups focus on *single issues,* such as abortion, gun control, or school prayer; others focus on *multiple issues,* such as equal access to education, employment, and health care (Ash, 1972; Gamson, 1990).
2. *View of the present system of wealth and power.* Some groups make *radical demands* that would

involve the end of patriarchy, capitalism, governmental bureaucracy, or other existing power structures; others do not attack the legitimacy of the present system of wealth and power but insist on specific social reforms (Ash, 1972; Gamson, 1990).

3. *Beliefs about elites.* Some groups want to *influence* elites or incorporate movement leaders into the elite; others want to *replace* existing elites with persons whom they believe share their own interests and concerns (Ash, 1972; Gamson, 1990).

In recent decades, many special interest groups have been single-issue groups that focus on electing and supporting politicians who support their views. There may be more than one single-interest group working to reduce or eliminate a specific social problem. Usually, however, these groups do not agree on the nature and extent of the problem or on proposed solutions for the problem. For this reason, competing single-interest groups aggressively place their demands in front of elected officials and bureaucratic policy makers (see Chapter 13).

▲ Working through National Social Movements to Reduce Problems

Collective behavior and national social movements are significant ways in which people seek to resolve social problems. **Collective behavior is voluntary, often spontaneous, activity that is engaged in by a large number of people and typically violates dominant group norms and values** (Kendall, 2000). Public demonstrations and riots are examples of collective behavior. Since the civil rights movement in the 1960s, one popular form of public demonstration has been *civil disobedience*—**nonviolent action that seeks to change a policy or law by refusing to comply with it** (Kendall, 2000). People often use civil disobedience in the form of sit-ins, marches, boycotts, and strikes to bring about change. When people refuse to abide by a policy or law and challenge authorities to do something about it, they are demanding social change with some sense of urgency.

Groups that engage in activities that they hope will achieve specific political goals are sometimes referred to as *protest crowds.* For example, Cuban American demonstrators blocked access to the Port of Miami and snarled rush-hour traffic in Miami,

Collective behavior is a powerful form of social protest against perceived injustices. In early 2000, numerous protests were staged in Miami and other cities over the proposed return of Elián González, a six-year-old Cuban boy, to his father in Cuba. Why do sociologists refer to this form of protest as emancipatory politics rather than life politics?

Florida, angering motorists, and leading to the arrest of more than 100 people, in protest of (and in hopes of changing) the Clinton administration's decision to return Elián González, a six-year-old Cuban boy, to his father in Cuba. Elián arrived in the United States after an ill-fated boat trip from Cuba during which his mother, her boyfriend, and nine others drowned. Immigration officials ruled that federal and international laws compelled them to honor a request by the boy's father in Cuba to return Elián to him (Alvarez, 2000). It was the Cuban American Foundation that organized protesters in hopes of getting the decision overturned. Organizations such as this are usually said to be engaged in *emancipatory politics* as opposed to *life politics.*

Emancipatory politics involves "liberating people from adverse constraints on their life chances through the reduction or elimination of exploitation, inequality, and oppression, and through the promotion of justice, equality, and participation" (Buechler, 2000:150). Demands that Elián not be sent back to Cuba were a form of emancipatory politics because advocates perceived life under Fidel Castro's political regime in Cuba as an adverse constraint on the boy's life chances (Alvarez, 2000).

Unlike emancipatory politics, *life politics* involves lifestyles, particularly those issues and social problems pertaining to the self, sexuality, reproduction, and the human body. The women's movement is an example of the life politics approach, which is often expressed as the "personal is political" (Buechler, 2000:150). However, life politics also reaches outward to look at global concerns, such as ecological survival and nuclear devastation (Buechler, 2000).

What types of national and international social movements may be used to reduce social problems? National social movements may be divided into five major categories: reform, revolutionary, religious, alternative, and resistance movements. *Reform movements* seek to improve society by changing some specific aspect of the social structure. Environmental groups and disability rights groups are examples of groups that seek to change (reform) some specific aspect of the social structure. Reform movements typically seek to bring about change by working within

Religious movements are one kind of national social movement. Religious movements, such as the Promise Keepers (shown here), seek to renovate or renew people through "inner change." What are the strengths of this approach in bringing about personal change and reducing social problems? What are the limitations?

the existing organizational structures of society, whereas *revolutionary movements* seek to bring about a total change in society. Examples of revolutionary movements include utopian groups and radical terrorist groups that use fear tactics to intimidate and gain—at least briefly—concessions from those with whom they disagree ideologically. Some radical terrorists kill many people in their pursuit of a society that more closely conforms to their worldview.

Religious movements (also referred to as expressive movements) seek to renovate or renew people through inner change. Because these groups emphasize inner change, religious movements are often linked to local and regional organizations that seek to bring about changes in the individual's life. National religious movements often attempt to persuade political officials to enact laws that will reduce or eliminate what they perceive to be a social problem. For example, some national religious movements view abortion as a social problem and thus lobby for a ban on abortions. In contrast, *alternative movements* seek limited change in some aspects of people's behavior. Currently, alternative movements include a variety of so-called New Age movements that emphasize such things as the development of a new national spiritual consciousness.

Finally, *resistance movements* seek to prevent change or to undo change that has already occurred. In public debates over social policies, most social movements advocating change face resistance from reactive movements, which hold opposing viewpoints and want social policy to reflect their own beliefs and values. Examples of resistance movements include groups opposing domestic partnership initiatives for gay or lesbian couples; anti-abortion groups such as "Operation Rescue," which seek to close abortion clinics and make abortion illegal; and anti-immigrant groups seeking to close U.S. borders to outsiders or place harsher demands on immigrant workers.

Can national activism and social movements bring about the changes that are necessary to reduce social problems? Some analysts believe that certain social problems can be reduced through sustained efforts by organizations committed to change. According to social activist Randy Shaw (1999), efforts by Public Interest Research Groups and the Sierra Club, the nation's two largest grassroots environmental groups, have stimulated a new national environmental activism that is having an effect. Wanting to strengthen the Clean Air Act of 1967, these two organizations engaged in affirmative national environmental activism, mobilizing people who were previously disconnected from national environmental debates (Shaw, 1999). As a result, a strong working relationship developed between grassroots activists at the local level and the leaders of the national movement. In the past, national groups had believed that their national leaders knew what was best for the environmental movement and had relied solely on their leadership's relationship with lawmakers to bring about change (Shaw, 1999). However, this belief changed as activists sought to strengthen the Clean Air Act:

> The Clean Air Act standards became a battle over framing the issue. If the public saw the new standards as a health issue environmentalists would prevail. Industry would win if, as in the health care debate [of the 1990s], it could define its campaign as trying to stop Big Government from hampering the private sector's ability to improve people's lives. The campaign would revisit the philosophical battleground where corporate America had increasingly prevailed in the past decade. Whether environmentalists' new emphasis on national grassroots mobilizing would change this would soon be seen. (Shaw, 1999:157)

Eventually, supporters declared that the clean air campaign had been a success and vowed that they would continue to demand changes that they believed would benefit the environment and improve the quality of life (Shaw, 1999).

What about global activism? Once again, we turn to the environmental movement for an example. According to Jared Diamond, a physiology professor and director of World Wildlife Fund, some transnational corporations are becoming aware that they have a responsibility for the environment. Diamond (2000) believes that a new attitude has taken hold of corporations such as Chevron and Home Depot, both of which now claim to realize that it is better to have a clean operation than to have costly industrial disasters. Of course, consumers have also demanded that corporations become more accountable for their actions: "Behind this trend lies consumers' growing awareness of the risks that environmental problems

pose for the health, economies, and political stability of their own world and their children's world" (Diamond, 2000:A31). For example, growing consumer awareness has led some companies that buy and retail forest products to no longer sell wood products from environmentally sensitive areas of the world and instead give preference to certified wood—that is, lumber that has been derived from forests where guidelines for environmentally sound logging practices have been met (Diamond, 2000).

According to some analysts, what is needed is "globalization from below" (Brecher and Costello, 1998). In other words, people cannot rely on corporations to solve environmental problems. Indeed, it is necessary to develop a human agenda that will offset the corporate agenda that has produced many of the problems in the first place. Social activists Jeremy Brecher and Tim Costello (1998) suggest these criteria for any proposed human agenda:

- It should improve the lives of the great majority of the world's people over the long run.
- It should correspond to widely held common interests and should integrate the interests of people around the world.
- It should provide handles for action at a variety of levels.
- It should include elements that can be at least partially implemented independently but that are compatible or mutually reinforcing.
- It should make it easier, not harder, to solve noneconomic problems such as protection of the environment and reduction of war.
- It should grow organically out of social movements and coalitions that have developed in response to the needs of diverse peoples.

Based on these guidelines, the only way that a major global social problem, such as environmental degradation or world poverty, can be reduced is through a drastic redirection of our energies, as Brecher and Costello (1998:184) explain:

> The energies now directed to the race to the bottom need to be redirected to the rebuilding of the global economy on a humanly and environmentally sound basis. Such an approach requires limits to growth—in some spheres, sharp reductions—in the material demands that human

society places on the environment. It requires reduced energy and resource use; less toxic production and products; shorter individual work-time; and less production for war. But it requires vast growth in education, health care, human caring, recycling, rebuilding an ecologically sound production and consumption system, and time available for self-development, community life, and democratic participation.

Do you believe such human cooperation is possible? Will it be possible for a new generation of political leaders to separate *politics* from *policy* and focus on discovering the best courses of action for the country and the world? Where do ideas regarding possible social policies come from? Some of the ideas and policies of tomorrow are being developed today in public policy organizations and think tanks (see Table 18.4). If, as some analysts believe, these think tanks are increasingly setting the U.S. government's agenda, how much do we know about these groups, their spokespersons, and the causes they advocate?

Perhaps gaining more information about the current state of U.S. and global affairs is the first step toward individual efforts to be part of the solution rather than part of the problem in the future. Can the media, particularly the Internet, be part of our education or is the media part of the problem (see Box 18.2 on page 400)?

▲ Limitations of the Macrolevel Solution Approach

As C. Wright Mills stated, social problems by definition cannot be resolved without organizational initiatives that bring about social change. Thus macrolevel approaches are necessary for reducing or eliminating many social problems. However, some analysts believe that macrolevel approaches may overemphasize structural barriers in society and give people the impression that these barriers are insurmountable walls that preclude social change. Macrolevel approaches may also deemphasize the importance of individual responsibility. Reducing the availability of illegal drugs, for example, does not resolve the problem of the individual drug abuser who still needs a means to eliminate the problem in her or his

personal life. Similarly, macrolevel approaches usually do not allow for the possibility of positive communication and the kind of *human cooperation* that transcends national boundaries (Brecher and Costello, 1998). Experience, however, has shown us that positive communication and global cooperation are possible.

At the beginning of the twenty-first century, journalist Thomas L. Friedman (2000b:A23) used the events surrounding the turn of the century as an example of how human beings can transcend threats of terrorism, fear of computer failures, and the general apprehension associated with a change from one century to the next:

> Best of all, the Y2K computer bug didn't lead to a global meltdown—not because it was a false alarm, but because countries and companies got informed early and mobilized to defeat it, each in [their] own way. "We leveraged the resources of the whole planet to smash an incredibly powerful problem," said one IBM exec. Who knows, maybe it will inspire us to do the same for the environment, for poverty, for AIDS. Why not?

A similar idea was suggested by sociologist Immanuel Wallerstein, a former president of the International Sociological Association:

> We live in an imperfect world, one that will always be imperfect and therefore always harbor injustice. But we are far from helpless before this reality. We can make the world less unjust; we can make it more beautiful; we can increase our cognition of it. We need but to construct it, and in order to construct it we need but to reason with each other and struggle to obtain from each other the special knowledge that each of us has been able to seize. We can labor in the vineyards and bring forth fruit, if only we try. (Wallerstein, 1999:250)

As we conclude this book and our time together, won't you join with social scientists and others who seek to face up to one of the greatest challenges of the twenty-first century: bringing peace, justice, and greater social equality to all the world's people?

TABLE 18.4 EXAMPLES OF PUBLIC POLICY ORGANIZATIONS AND THINK TANKS

Action Institute for the Study of Religion and Liberty	Family Research Council
Adam Smith Institute	Fight Internet Taxes!
The AFL-CIO	Frontiers of Freedom Institute
Alliance for America	Galen Institute
American Civil Liberties Union	Goldwater Institute
American Conservative Union	Heartland Institute
American Enterprise Institute	Heritage Foundation
The American Institute for Full Employment	Hoover Institute
Americans for a Balanced Budget	Hudson Institute
Americans for Democratic Action	Independence Institute
Americans for Hope, Growth and Opportunity	Institute for Civic Values
Americans for Tax Reform	Institute for Economic Analysis, Inc.
Amnesty International	Institute for First Amendment Studies
Atlas Economic Research Foundation	Institute for Global Communications
Brookings Institution	Institute for Justice
Campaign for America's Future	Institute for Policy Innovation
The Carter Center	Leadership Institute
Cascade Policy Institute	League of Conservative Voters
Cato Institute	League of Women Voters
Center of the American Experiment	Ludwig von Mises Institute
Center for Defense Information	Madison Institute
Center for Equal Opportunity	Manhattan Institute
Center for Individual Rights	National Organization for Women
Center for Law and Social Policy	National Rifle Association
Center for Policy Alternatives	OMB Watch
Center to Prevent Handgun Violence	People for the American Way
Center for Public Integrity	Pioneer Institute for Public Policy Research
Center for Responsive Politics	Planned Parenthood
Century Foundation	Progress and Freedom Foundation
Children's Defense Fund	Project for Defense Alternatives
Christian Coalition	Public Citizen
Citizens Against Government Waste	RAND Corporation
Citizens for an Alternative Tax System	Reason Foundation
Citizens for Tax Justice	Tax Reform NOW!
Clare Boothe Luce Policy Institute	Union of Concerned Scientists
Claremont Institute	U.S. Term Limits
Discovery Institute	Worldwatch Institute
Economic Policy Institute	Young America's Foundation
Empower America	

SOCIAL PROBLEMS

IN THE MEDIA

BOX 18.2

Mobilizing for Change through the Echo Effect

Jeff Cohen, executive director of the media watchdog group Fairness and Accuracy in Reporting (FAIR), was speaking on the radio about journalism's "echo effect." This phrase refers to a story appearing in one news outlet that then reaches a far broader audience as it is discussed, featured, and "echoed" through other media sources. Cohen noted that news stories of interest to conservatives readily enter the national public debate by echoing through such sources as radio talk shows, televised discussions by Beltway pundits, and the writings of syndicated columnists. By contrast, a front-page exposé or newspaper series on corporate wrongdoing or a similar story that advances a progressive agenda is unlikely to be echoed; such stories then quickly pass from public consciousness.

—Activist Randy Shaw (1999:252) discussing his frustration with how little play certain kinds of social problems get in the media, particularly when activists cannot count on the "echo effect" working for their concerns

According to Shaw (1999), most national campaigns for social and economic justice require continuing media coverage by mainstream reporters and alternative media sources. However, Shaw believes that the media are, at best, a limited source for mobilizing people because today, (1) fewer people closely follow national news than in the past; and (2) those who do follow the news may get their information from a wide variety of sources, including network programming, cable news shows, radio, and the Internet. Among the people it is most important to mobilize are students and people under the age of thirty; however, individuals in these categories are increasingly hard to reach through traditional media sources.

Why are the mainstream media usually reluctant to carry information about some social problems? Shaw (1999:253) believes that the media have a vested interest in news decisions: "Media dependent on advertising dollars cannot afford to use their news and editorial bureaus to build campaigns in favor of policies that their advertisers likely oppose." Some national activists have worked with public relations firms to get out the word on their cause and to create the desired echo effect. Shaw gives the example of Thuygen

SUMMARY

➡ *Why is it difficult to reduce or eliminate social problems?*

According to social scientists, reducing or solving social problems is more complex than simply identifying such problems and pinpointing their

social locations because many obstacles, delays, and frustrations confront those who attempt to bring about social changes that may alleviate the problems. Solving a problem may entail prohibitive costs and may only give rise to a whole new set of problems.

Nguyen's 1997 report on Nike's abusive labor practices in Vietnam:

> There had been little publicity about such abuses until Thuygen Nguyen visited the Vietnam plants and wrote a shocking report for his group, Vietnam Labor Watch. Thuygen sent a press release about his report throughout the national media but received no response. He then contacted Global Exchange, which put . . . Communication Works to work. Communication Works took Nguyen's previously ignored report of Nike's Vietnam labor abuses and created a packed New York City press conference that brought widespread national media coverage. The Vietnam Labor Watch findings subsequently echoed through editorial columns, sports pages, and a series of strips in *Doonesbury*. Media stories about the anti-Nike campaign invariably cite Nguyen's report and the story is likely to echo for years after its release. Yet without the intervention of Communication Works Nguyen's pathbreaking report would likely have remained unknown. (Shaw, 1999:265)

Will the Internet open up new possibilities for activists to get information to those they would like to mobilize? Clearly, given the number of Web sites now open, a large number of individuals and organizations believe that this may be the case. Many sites serve as national mobilizing vehicles for groups seeking avenues to foster social change. Through news groups, bulletin boards, and other vehicles, people are able to learn from each other and share information about social problems. They are also able to join in collective action or encourage others to take some specific action. However, a 1998 nationwide survey found that only 7 percent of all Internet users had tried contacting an elected official on line or expressed an opinion on a political survey (Shaw, 1999). Although this percentage has increased somewhat in recent years, it is still a very low proportion of users. Perhaps those who consider themselves part of the mainstream have little interest in bringing about social change. It is also possible that younger activists who do not read newspapers also do not follow news on line. Shaw (1999:287) concludes that, for whatever reason, "the prospect of the Internet becoming the voice of new broad-based national movements . . . remains to be realized."

Do you follow the news about social issues? If so, do you get your information primarily from television, radio, the Internet, or other sources? Based on the information you receive from various media sources, are you motivated to participate in organizations that endeavor to bring about social change?

➤ *What is the primary focus of functionalist, conflict, and interactionist approaches to solving social problems?*

From the functionalist perspective, social problems arise when social institutions do not fulfill the functions they are supposed to or when dysfunctions occur; therefore, social institutions need to be made more effective and social change needs to be managed carefully. According to critical-conflict theorists, social problems arise out of the major contradictions inherent in the way societies are organized (particularly such factors as patriarchy and capitalism). Consequently, attempting to solve social problems requires major changes in the political economy. Interactionists focus on how certain behavior comes to be defined as a social problem and why some individuals and groups engage in that behavior. To reduce problems entails more adequate socialization of people as well as a better under-standing of how labeling affects people's behavior.

➤ *What is social change and why is it important in reducing social problems?*

Social change refers to the alternation, modifica-tion, or transformation of public policy, culture, or social institutions over time. Social change is impor-tant in reducing social problems because a combina-tion of strategies, some previously untried, are usu-ally required to reduce major social problems.

➤ *What are microlevel solutions to social prob-lems? What are the limitations of this approach?*

Microlevel solutions to social problems focus on how individuals operate within small groups to try to remedy a problem that affects them, their fam-ily, or friends. Most people turn to their primary groups to help them deal with a problem. However, solving social problems one person at a time does not take into account the fact that secondary groups and societal institutions play a significant part in creating, maintaining, and exacerbating many social problems.

➤ *What are mid-range attempts to deal with social problems? What are the limitations of this approach?*

Mid-range attempts to deal with social prob-lems focus on how secondary groups and formal organizations deal with problems or seek to assist individuals in overcoming problems such as addic-tion to drugs or alcohol. Grassroots groups often work to change a perceived wrong in their neigh-borhood, city, state, or nation. Although local efforts to reduce problems affecting individuals and collectivities in a specific city or region have brought about many improvements in the social life of indi-viduals and small groups, they usually lack the sus-tained capacity to produce the larger systemic changes needed at the national or international lev-els to reduce or eliminate the problems.

➤ *What are macrolevel attempts to deal with social problems? What are the limitations of this approach?*

Macrolevel solutions to social problems focus on how large-scale social institutions such as the govern-ment and the media may become involved in remedy-ing social problems. Some people work through social movements, others through special interest groups, and still others through various forms of collective behavior. While macrolevel approaches are necessary for reducing or eliminating many social problems, some analysts believe that these approaches may over-emphasize structural barriers in society and give peo-ple the impression that these barriers constitute insur-mountable walls that preclude social change. Macro-level approaches may also deemphasize the impor-tance of individual responsibility.

➤ *What are three key factors that can be used to differentiate special interest groups?*

The three factors by which special interest groups may be categorized are: (1) issues (single issue versus multiple demands); (2) view of the pres-ent system of wealth and power (positive versus neg-ative); and (3) beliefs about elites (whether to try to influence elites or seek to replace them).

➤ *What is collective behavior? How does civil dis-obedience occur?*

Collective behavior is voluntary, often sponta-neous activity that is engaged in by a large number of people and typically violates dominant group norms and values. As a form of collective behavior, civil disobedience refers to nonviolent action that seeks to change a policy or law by refusing to com-ply with it.

➤ *How does emancipatory politics differ from life politics?*

Emancipatory politics involves the liberation of people from adverse conditions by reducing or elim-inating exploitation, inequality, and oppression, or through the promotion of justice, equality, and par-ticipation. In contrast, life politics involves lifestyles, particularly those issues and social problems per-taining to the self, sexuality, reproduction, and the human body. Life politics also reaches outward to look at global concerns such as ecological survival and nuclear devastation.

➤ *What are the key characteristics of the five major categories of national social movements?*

National social movements are divided into five major categories: reform, revolutionary, religious, alternative, and resistance movements. Reform movements seek to improve society by changing some specific aspect of the social structure. Revolutionary movements seek to bring about a total change in society. Religious movements seek to renovate or renew people through "inner change." Alternative movements seek limited change in some aspects of people's behavior and currently include a variety of so-called New Age movements. Resistance movements seek to prevent change or undo change that has already occurred.

➡ *What is a human agenda? What might be the major criteria for such an agenda?*

According to some analysts, we need to develop a human agenda that focuses on the needs of people and offsets the corporate agenda that is currently taking precedence over other issues and concerns. Social activists Jeremy Brecher and Tim Costello suggest that any proposed human agenda should: (1) improve the lives of the great majority of the world's people; (2) correspond to widely held common interests as well as integrate the interests of people worldwide; (3) provide handles for action at a variety of levels; (4) include elements that can be implemented independently, at least in part, but that are compatible or mutually reinforcing; (5) make it easier to solve noneconomic problems such as environmental protection; and (6) grow out of social movements and coalitions that have developed in response to the needs of diverse peoples.

KEY TERMS

civil disobedience, p. 395
collective behavior, p. 395
grassroots groups, p. 391

primary groups, p. 388
secondary groups, p. 389
social change, p. 387

social movement, p. 391
special interest group, p. 394

QUESTIONS FOR CRITICAL THINKING

1. What is most useful about applying a sociological perspective to the study of social problems? What is least useful about a sociological approach? How can you contribute to a better understanding of the causes, effects, and possible solutions to social problems?

2. Do you believe that corporations can be trusted to do the right thing when it comes to reducing or eliminating existing social problems? Is good corporate citizenship a possibility in the global economy today? Why or why not?

3. Suppose that you were given the economic resources and political clout to reduce a major social problem. Which problem would you choose? What steps would you take to alleviate this problem? How would you measure your success or failure in reducing or eliminating the problem?

Glossary

absolute poverty a condition that exists when people do not have the means to secure the most basic necessities of life.

acid rain rainfall containing large concentrations of sulfuric and nitric acids (primarily from the burning of fuel and car and truck exhausts).

acquaintance rape forcible sexual activity that meets the legal definition of rape and involves people who first meet in a social setting.

acute diseases illnesses that strike suddenly and cause dramatic incapacitation and sometimes death.

ageism prejudice and discrimination against people on the basis of age.

amalgamation (the melting pot model) a process in which the cultural attributes of diverse racial-ethnic groups are blended together to form a new society incorporating the unique contributions of each group.

Anglo-conformity model a pattern of assimilation whereby members of subordinate racial-ethnic groups are expected to conform to the culture of the dominant (white) Anglo-Saxon population.

anti-Semitism prejudice and discriminatory behavior directed at Jews.

assimilation the process by which members of subordinate racial and ethnic groups become absorbed into the dominant culture.

blaming the victim a practice used by people who view a social problem as emanating from within the individual who exhibits the problem.

blended family a family that consists of a husband and wife, children from previous marriages, and children (if any) from the new marriage.

capitalism an economic system characterized by private ownership of the means of production, from which personal profits can be derived through market competition and without government intervention.

chronic diseases illnesses that are long-term or lifelong and that develop gradually or are present from birth.

civil disobedience nonviolent action that seeks to change a policy or law by refusing to comply with it.

class system a system of social inequality based on the ownership and control of resources and on the type of work people do.

codependency a reciprocal relationship between the alcoholic and one or more nonalcoholics who unwittingly aid and abet the alcoholic's excessive drinking and resulting behavior.

cohabitation two adults living together in a sexual relationship without being legally married.

collective behavior voluntary, often spontaneous, activity that is engaged in by a large number of people and typically violates dominant group norms and values.

collective violence organized violence by people seeking to promote their cause or resist social policies or practices that they consider oppressive.

comparable worth the belief that wages ought to reflect the worth of a job, not the gender or race of the worker.

conflict perspective a framework for viewing society that is based on the assumption that groups in society are engaged in a continuous power struggle for control of scarce resources.

contingent work part-time work, temporary work, and subcontracted work that offers advantages to employers but can be detrimental to workers' welfare.

core nations dominant capitalist centers characterized by high levels of industrialization and urbanization.

corporate crime illegal acts committed by corporate employees on behalf of the corporation and with its support.

crime a behavior that violates criminal law and is punishable by a fine, a jail term, or other negative sanctions.

criminal justice system the network of organizations, including the policy, courts, jails, and prisons, involved in law enforcement and the administration of justice.

cultural capital social assets, such as values, beliefs, attitudes, and competencies in language and culture, that are learned at home and required for success and social advancement.

deindustrialization the process by which capital is diverted from investment in basic industries (in the form of economic resources, plants, and equipment) to business practices such as mergers and acquisitions and foreign investment.

deinstitutionalization the practice of discharging patients from mental hospitals into the community.

democracy a political system in which the people hold the ruling power either directly or through elected representatives.

demographic transition theory the process by which some societies move from high birth and death rates to relatively low birth and death rates as a result of technological development.

demography the study of the size, composition, and distribution of populations.

dependency ratio the number of workers necessary to support people under age fifteen and over age sixty-three.

desertification the process by which usable land is turned into desert because of overgrazing, harmful agricultural practices, or deforestation.

deviance a behavior, belief, or condition that violates social norms.

differential association theory the belief that individuals have a greater tendency to deviate from societal norms when they frequently associate with people who tend toward deviance rather than conformity.

disability a restricted or total lack of ability to perform certain activities as a result of physical limitations or the interplay of these limitations, social responses, and the social environment.

discrimination actions or practices of dominant group members (or their representatives) that have a harmful impact on members of subordinate groups.

domestic partnership a household partnership in which an unmarried couple lives together in a committed, sexually intimate relationship and is granted the same rights and benefits accorded to a heterosexual couple.

drug any substance—other than food or water—that, when taken into the body, alters its functioning in some way.

drug addiction (or drug dependency) a psychological and/or physiological need for a drug to maintain a sense of well-being and avoid withdrawal symptoms.

drug subculture a group of people whose attitudes, beliefs, and behaviors pertaining to drug use differ significantly from those of most people in the larger society.

dual-earner marriages marriages in which both spouses are in the labor force.

edge city an area of middle- to upper-middle-class residences with complete working, shopping, and leisure activities so that it is not dependent on the central city or other suburbs.

education the social institution responsible for transmitting knowledge, skills, and cultural values in a formally organized structure.

elite model a view of society in which power in political systems is concentrated in the hands of a small group, whereas the masses are relatively powerless.

environmental degradation disruptions to the environment that have negative consequences for ecosystems.

environmental racism the belief that a disproportionate number of hazardous facilities are placed in areas populated primarily by poor people and people of color.

environmental tobacco smoke the smoke in the air as a result of other people's tobacco smoking.

erotica materials that depict consensual sexual activities that are sought by and pleasurable to all parties involved.

ethnic group a category of people who are distinguished, by others or by themselves, as inferior or superior, primarily on the basis of cultural or nationality characteristics.

ethnic pluralism the coexistence of diverse racial-ethnic groups with separate identities and cultures within a society.

ethnocentrism the assumption that one's own group and way of life are superior to all others.

extended family a family unit composed of relatives in addition to parents and children, all of whom live in the same household.

families relationships in which people live together with commitment, form an economic unit and care for any young, and consider the group critical to their identity.

family of orientation the family into which a person is born and in which early socialization takes place.

family of procreation the family that a person forms by having or adopting children.

felony a serious crime, such as murder, rape, or aggravated assault, that is punishable by more than a year's imprisonment or even death.

feminization of poverty the trend whereby women are disproportionately represented among individuals living in poverty.

fertility the number of children born to an individual or a population.

fetal alcohol syndrome (FAS) a condition characterized by mental retardation and craniofacial malformations that may affect the child of an alcoholic mother.

field research the study of social life in its natural setting: observing and interviewing people where they live, work, and play.

forcible rape the act of forcing sexual intercourse on an adult of legal age against her or his will.

framing the manner in which news content and its accompanying visual images are linked together to create certain audience perceptions and give specific impressions to viewers and readers.

functionalist perspective a framework for viewing society as a stable, orderly system composed of a number of interrelated parts, each of which performs a function that contributes to the overall stability of society.

functionally illiterate being unable to read and/or write at the skill level necessary for carrying out everyday tasks.

gender culturally and socially constructed differences between females and males that are based on meanings, beliefs, and practices that a group or society associates with "femininity" or "masculinity."

gender bias a situation in which favoritism is shown toward one gender.

gender gap the difference between a candidate's number of votes from women and men.

gendered division of labor the process whereby productive tasks are separated on the basis on gender.

gendered racism the interactive effect of racism and sexism in exploiting women of color.

genocide the deliberate, systematic killing of an entire people or nation.

gentrification the process by which people renovate or restore properties in central cities.

glass ceiling the invisible institutional barrier constructed by male management that prevents women from reaching top positions in major corporations and other large-scale organizations.

government a formal organization that has legal and political authority to regulate relationships among people in a society and between the society and others outside its borders.

grassroots groups organizations started by ordinary people who work in concert to change a perceived wrong in their neighborhood, city, state, or nation.

greenhouse effect an environmental condition caused by excessive quantities of carbon dioxide, water vapor, methane, and nitrous oxide in the atmosphere.

hate crime a physical attack against a person because of assumptions regarding his or her racial group, ethnicity, religion, disability, sexual orientation, national origin, or ancestry.

health maintenance organization (HMO) an organization that provides, for a fixed monthly fee, total health care with an emphasis on prevention to avoid costly treatment later.

hegemony theory the view that the media are instruments of social control and are used by members of the ruling classes to create "false consciousness" in the working classes.

hidden curriculum how certain cultural values and attitudes, such as conformity and obedience to authority, are transmitted through implied demands in the everyday rules and routines of schools.

high-income nations countries with highly industrialized economies; technologically advanced industrial, administrative, and service occupations; and relatively high levels of national and per capita (per person) income.

homophobia excessive fear or intolerance of homosexuality.

hospices organizations that provide a homelike facility or home-based care (or both) for people who are terminally ill.

illegitimate opportunity structures circumstances that allow people to acquire through illegitimate activities what they cannot achieve legitimately.

income the economic gain derived from wages, salaries, income transfers (governmental aid such as Temporary Aid to Needy Families, known as TANF), or ownership of property.

individual discrimination one-on-one acts by members of the dominant group that harm members of the subordinate group or their property.

industrialization the process by which societies are transformed from a dependence on agriculture and handmade products to an emphasis on manufacturing and related industries.

infant mortality rate the number of deaths of infants under one year of age per 1,000 live births in a given year.

institutional discrimination the day-to-day practices of organizations and institutions that have a harmful impact on members of subordinate groups.

interactionist perspective a framework that views society as the sum of the interactions of individuals and groups.

internal colonialism a process that occurs when members of a racial-ethnic group are conquered or colonized and forcibly placed under the economic and political control of the dominant group.

juvenile delinquency a violation of law or the commission of a status offense by a young person under a specific age.

kinship a social network of people based on common ancestry, marriage, or adoption.

labeling theory the proposition that delinquents and criminals are those people who have been successfully labeled as such by others.

latent functions hidden, unstated, and sometimes unintended consequences of activities in an organization or institution.

life chances the extent to which individuals have access to important societal resources such as food, clothing, shelter, education, and health care.

life expectancy an estimate of the average lifetime of people born in a specific year.

lifestyle–routine activity approach the belief that the patterns and timing of people's daily movements and activities as they go about obtaining the necessities of life—such as food, shelter, companionship, and entertainment—are the keys to understanding violent personal crimes and other types of crime in our society.

low-income nations primarily agrarian countries with little industrialization and low levels of national and personal income.

macrolevel analysis focuses on social processes occurring at the societal level, especially in large-scale organizations and major social institutions such as politics, government, and the economy.

majority (or dominant) group a group that is advantaged and has superior resources and rights in a society.

managed care any system of cost containment that closely monitors and controls health care providers' decisions about medical procedures, diagnostic tests, and other services that should be provided to patients.

manifest functions open, stated, and intended goals or consequences of activities within an organization or institution.

mass murder the killing of four or more people at one time and in one place by the same person.

master status the most significant status a person possesses because it largely determines how individuals view themselves and how they are treated by others.

mechanical solidarity social bonds based on shared religious beliefs and a simple division of labor.

media concentration the tendency of the media industries to cluster together in groups with the goal of enhancing profitability.

media industries major businesses that own or own interests in radio and television production and broadcasting; motion pictures, movie theaters, and music companies; newspaper, periodical (magazine) and book publishing; and Internet services and content providers that influence people and cultures worldwide.

medical-industrial complex a term that encompasses both local physicians and hospitals as well as global health-related industries such as the pharmaceutical and medical supply companies that deliver health care today.

megalopolis a continuous concentration of two or more cities and their suburbs that have grown until they form an interconnected urban area.

melting pot *see* **amalgamation.**

microlevel analysis focuses on small-group relations and social interaction among individuals.

middle-income nations countries undergoing transformation from agrarian to industrial economies.

migration the movement of people from one geographic area to another for the purpose of changing residency.

military-industrial complex the interdependence of the military establishment and private military contractors.

minority (or subordinate) group a group whose members, because of physical or cultural characteristics, are disadvantaged and subjected to unequal treatment by the dominant group and regard themselves as objects of collective discrimination.

misdemeanor a relatively minor crime that is punishable by a fine or less than a year in jail.

mixed economy an economic system that combines elements of both capitalism (a market economy) and socialism (a command economy).

monogamy a marriage between one woman and one man.

monopoly a situation that exists when a single firm controls an industry and accounts for all sales in a specific market.

mortality the number of deaths that occur in a specific population.

murder the unlawful, intentional killing of one person by another.

norms established rules of behavior or standards of conduct.

nuclear family a family unit composed of one or two parents and their dependent children who live apart from other relatives.

obscenity the legal term for pornographic materials that are offensive by generally accepted standards of decency.

occupational (white-collar) crime illegal activities committed by people in the course of their employment or normal business activity.

oligopoly a situation in which a small number of companies or suppliers control an entire industry or service.

organic solidarity social bonds based on interdependence and an elaborate division of labor (specialization).

organized crime a business operation that supplies illegal goods and services for profit.

patriarchy a hierarchical system of social organization in which cultural, political, and economic structures are controlled by men.

peripheral nations nations that depend on core nations for capital, have little or no industrialization (other than what may be brought in by core nations), and have uneven patterns of urbanization.

permanent government the top-tier civil service bureaucrats who have a strong power base and play a major role in developing and implementing government policies and procedures.

perspective an overall approach or viewpoint toward some subject.

pink-collar occupations relatively low-paying, nonmanual, semiskilled positions that are held primarily by women.

plea bargaining a process in a criminal trial whereby the prosecution negotiates a reduced sentence in exchange for a guilty plea.

pluralist model the view that power is widely dispersed throughout many competing interest groups in our political system.

political action committees (PACs) special-interest groups that fund campaigns to help elect (or defeat) candidates based on their positions on specific issues.

politics the social institution through which power is acquired and exercised by some people and groups.

population composition the biological and social characteristics of a population, including such attributes as age, sex, race, marital status, education, occupation, income, and size of household.

pornography the graphic depiction of sexual behavior though pictures and/or words—including by electronic or other data retrieval systems—in a manner that is intended to be sexually arousing.

poverty rate the proportion of the population whose income falls below the government's official poverty line—the level of income below which a family of a given size is considered to be poor.

power the ability of people to achieve their goals despite opposition from others.

power elite rulers of the United States, which at the top is composed of business leaders, the executive branch of the federal government, and the military (especially the "top brass" at the Pentagon).

prejudice a negative attitude based on faulty generalizations about members of selected racial and ethnic groups.

prestige the respect, esteem, or regard accorded to an individual or group by others.

primary deviance the initial act of rule breaking.

primary groups small, less specialized groups in which members engage in face-to-face, emotion-based interactions over an extended period of time.

primary prevention programs that seek to prevent drug problems before they begin.

primary sector production the extraction of raw materials and natural resources from the environment.

property crime the taking of money or property from another without force, the threat of force, or the destruction of property.

prostitution the sale of sexual services (of oneself or another) for money or goods and without emotional attachment.

punishment any action designed to deprive a person of things of value (including liberty) because of an offense the person is thought to have committed.

racial group a category of people who have been singled out, by others or themselves, sometimes as inferior or superior, on the basis of subjectively selected physical characteristics such as skin color, hair texture, and eye shape.

racism a set of attitudes, beliefs, and practices used to justify the superior treatment of one racial or ethnic group and the inferior treatment of another racial or ethnic group.

relative poverty a condition that exists when people may be able to afford basic necessities, such as food, clothing, and shelter, but cannot maintain an average standard of living in comparison to that of other members of their society or group.

repressive terrorism terrorism conducted by a government against its own citizens for the purpose of protecting an existing political order.

revolutionary terrorism acts of violence against civilians that are carried out by internal enemies of the government who want to bring about political change.

scapegoat a person or group that is blamed for some problem causing frustration and is therefore subjected to hostility or aggression by others.

second shift the domestic work that many employed women perform at home after completing their work day on the job.

secondary analysis of existing data a research design in which investigators analyze data that originally were collected by others for some other purpose.

secondary deviance the process that occurs when a person who has been labeled a deviant accepts that new identity and continues the deviant behavior.

secondary groups larger, more specialized groups in which members engage in impersonal, goal-oriented relationships for a limited period of time.

secondary sector production the processing of raw materials (from the primary sector) into finished products.

segregation the spatial and social separation of categories of people by race/ethnicity, class, gender, religion, or other social characteristics.

self-fulfilling prophecy the process by which an unsubstantiated belief or prediction results in behavior that makes the original false belief come true.

semiperipheral nations nations that are more developed than peripheral nations but less developed than core nations.

serial murder the killing of three or more people over more than a month by the same person.

sex the biological differences between females and males.

sexism the subordination of one sex, usually female, based on the assumed superiority of the other sex.

sexual harassment unwanted sexual advances, requests for sexual favors, or other verbal or physical conduct of a sexual nature.

sexual orientation a preference for emotional-sexual relationships with individuals of the same sex (homosexuality), the opposite sex (heterosexuality), or both (bisexuality).

sexuality sexual attraction and intimate relationships with others.

situational approach the belief that violence results from a specific interaction process, termed a "situational transaction."

social bond theory the proposition that criminal behavior is most likely to occur when a person's ties to society are weakened or broken.

social change the alteration, modification, or transformation of public policy, culture, or social institutions over time.

social control the systematic practices developed by social groups to encourage conformity and discourage deviance.

social disorganization the conditions in society that undermine the ability of traditional social institutions to govern human behavior.

social gerontology the study of the social (nonphysical) aspects of aging.

social learning theory a theory that is based on the assumption that people are likely to act out the behavior they see in role models and media sources.

social movement an organized group that acts collectively to promote or resist change through collective action.

social problem a social condition (such as poverty) or a pattern of behavior (such as substance abuse) that people believe warrants public concern and collective action to bring about change.

social stratification the hierarchical arrangement of large social groups on the basis of their control over basic resources.

socialism an economic system characterized by public ownership of the means of production, the pursuit of collective goals, and centralized decision making.

society a large social grouping that shares the same geographical territory and is subject to the same political authority and dominant cultural expectations.

sociological imagination the ability to see the relationship between individual experiences and the larger society.

sociology the academic and scholarly discipline that engages in systematic study of human society and social interactions.

special interest group a political coalition composed of individuals or groups sharing a specific interest they wish to protect or advance with the help of the political system.

state-sponsored terrorism political terrorism resulting from a government providing financial resources, weapons, and training for terrorists who conduct their activities in other nations.

statutory rape the act of having sexual intercourse with a person who is under the legal age of consent as established by state law.

stereotypes overgeneralizations about the appearance, behavior, or other characteristics of all members of a group.

strain theory the proposition that people feel strain when they are exposed to cultural goals that they cannot reach because they do not have access to culturally approved means of achieving those goals.

strategically significant weapon one that brings force to bear in such a way that it decisively erodes the war-making capability of the enemy.

subculture a group of people who share a distinctive set of cultural beliefs and behaviors that set them apart from the larger society.

subculture of violence hypothesis the hypothesis that violence is part of the normative expectations governing everyday behavior among young males in the lower classes.

survey research a poll in which researchers ask respondents a series of questions about a specific topic and record their responses.

terrorism the use of calculated, unlawful physical force or threats of violence against a government, organization, or individual to gain some political, religious, economic, or social objective.

tertiary sector production providing services rather than goods as the primary source of livelihood.

theory a set of logically related statements that attempt to describe, explain, or predict social events.

theory of limited effects a theory that states that the media have a minimal effect on the attitudes and perceptions of individuals.

theory of racial formation a theory that states that the government substantially defines racial and ethnic relations.

tolerance a condition that occurs when larger doses of a drug are required over time to produce the same physical or psychological effect that was originally achieved by a smaller dose.

total institution a place where people are isolated from the rest of society for a period of time and come under the complete control of the officials who run the institution.

tracking assigning students to specific courses and educational programs on the basis of their test scores, previous grades, or both.

transnational corporation a large-scale business organization that is headquartered in one country but operates in many countries, which has the legal power (separate from individual owners or shareholders) to enter into contracts, buy and sell property, and engage in other business activity.

urbanization the process by which an increasing proportion of a population lives in cities rather than in rural areas.

values collective ideas about what is right or wrong, good or bad, and desirable or undesirable in a specific society.

victimless crime a crime that many people believe has no real victim because it involves willing participants in an economic exchange.

violence the use of physical force to cause pain, injury, or death to another, or damage to another's property.

violent crime actions involving force or the threat of force against others.

wage gap the disparity between women's and men's earnings.

war system components of social institutions (e.g., the economy, government, and education) and cultural beliefs and practices that promote the development of warriors, weapons, and war as a normal part of the society and its foreign policy.

wealth the value of all economic assets, including income, personal property, and income-producing property.

weapons system military technology comprised of a weapons platform (e.g., a ship, aircraft, or tank), a weapon (e.g., a gun, missile, or torpedo), and the means of command and communication.

welfare state a program under which the government takes responsibility for specific categories of citizens by offering them certain services and benefits, such as employment, housing, health, education, or guaranteed income.

withdrawal a variety of physical and/or psychological symptoms that habitual drug users experience when they discontinue drug use.

zero population growth a situation in which a population is totally stable, one that neither grows nor decreases from year to year because births, deaths, and migration are in perfect balance.

References

aaionline. 1999. "Trade, Investment, and Economic Development: Overview." Retrieved January 1, 2000. Online: http://www.aaionline.org/tied/tied_current. html.

AAUW Educational Foundation. 1992. *The AAUW Report: How Schools Shortchange Girls.* Developed by the Wellesley College Center for Research on Women. Washington, DC: American Association of University Women Educational Foundation.

Abraham, Laurie Kaye. 1993. *Mama Might Be Better Off Dead: The Failure of Health Care in Urban America.* Chicago: University of Chicago Press.

Acuna, Rodolfo. 1984. *A Community under Siege: A Chronicle of Chicanos in East of the Los Angeles River, 1945–1975.* Los Angeles: Chicano Studies Research Center, University of California at Los Angeles.

Adams, Devon. 1999. "Mourn for the Killers, Too." *Newsweek* (August 23):41.

Adams, Karen L., and Norma C. Ware. 1995. "Sexism and the English Language: The Linguistic Implications of Being a Woman." In Jo Freeman (Ed.), *Women: A Feminist Perspective* (5th ed.). Mountain View, CA: Mayfield Publishing, pp. 331–346.

Adams, Tom. 1991. *Grass Roots: How Ordinary People Are Changing America.* New York: Citadel Press.

Aday, David P., Jr. 1990. *Social Control at the Margins: Toward a General Understanding of Deviance.* Belmont, CA: Wadsworth.

Adorno, Theodor W., Else Frenkel-Brunswick, Daniel J. Levinson, and R. Nevitt Sanford. 1950. *The Authoritarian Personality.* New York: Harper & Row.

Akers, Ronald L. 1992. *Drugs, Alcohol, and Society: Social Structure, Process, and Policy.* Belmont, CA: Wadsworth.

Albert, Steven M., and Maria G. Cattell. 1994. *Old Age in Global Perspective: Cross-Cultural and Cross-National Views.* New York: G.K. Hall.

Albrecht, Gary L. 1992. *The Disability Business: Rehabilitation in America.* Newbury Park, CA: Sage.

Alexander, Karl L., Doris Entwisle, and Maxine Thompson. 1987. "School Performance, Status Relations, and the Structure of Sentiment: Bringing the Teacher Back In." *American Sociological Review,* 52:665–682.

Allen, Robert L. 1974. *Reluctant Reformers.* Washington, DC: Howard University Press.

Allport, Gordon. 1958. *The Nature of Prejudice* (abridged ed.). New York: Doubleday/Anchor.

Almaguer, Tomás. 1995. "Chicano Men: A Cartography of Homosexual Identity and Behavior." In Michael S. Kimmel and Michael A. Messner (Eds.), *Men's Lives* (3rd ed.). Boston: Allyn and Bacon, pp. 418–431.

Alston, Maude H., Sharon H. Rankin, and Carol A. Harris. 1995. "Suicide in African American Elderly." *Journal of Black Studies,* 26(1):31–35.

Altman, Lawrence K. 1996a. "AIDS Meeting: Signs of Hope and Obstacles." *New York Times* (July 7):A1.

Altman, Lawrence K. 1996b. "India Quickly Leads in H.I.V. Cases, AIDS Meeting Hears." *New York Times* (July 8): A8.

Altman, Lawrence K. 1996c. "U.N. Reports 3 Million New H.I.V. Cases Worldwide for '96." *New York Times* (November 28):A6.

Alvarez, Lizette. 2000. "Irate Cuban-Americans Paralyze Miami: Hundreds Disrupt Traffic and Commerce to Protest Boy's Return." *New York Times* (January 7):A13.

Alwin, Duane, Philip Converse, and Steven Martin. 1985. "Living Arrangements and Social Integration." *Journal of Marriage and the Family,* 47:319–334.

American Association of University Women. 1992. *The AAUW Report: How Schools Short-Change Girls.* Washington, DC: The AAUW Educational Foundation and National Educational Association.

American Psychiatric Association. 1994. *Diagnostic and Statistical Manual of Mental Disorders IV.* Washington, DC: American Psychiatric Association.

Amott, Teresa, and Julie Matthaei. 1991. *Race, Gender, and Work: A Multicultural Economic History of Women in the United States.* Boston: South End Press.

Anders, George. 1996. *Health against Wealth: HMOs and the Breakdown of Medical Trust.* Boston: Houghton Mifflin.

Andersen, Margaret L., and Patricia Hill Collins (Eds.). 1995. *Race, Class, and Gender: An Anthology* (2nd ed.). Belmont, CA: Wadsworth.

Anderson, Elijah. 1990. *Streetwise: Race, Class, and Change in an Urban Community.* Chicago: University of Chicago Press.

Andrews, Alice C., and James W. Fonseca. 1995. *The Atlas of American Society.* New York: New York University Press.

Angel, Ronald J., and Jacqueline L. Angel. 1993. *Painful Inheritance: Health and the New Generation of Fatherless Families.* Madison, WI: University of Wisconsin Press.

Angier, Natalie. 1990. "New Antidepressant Is Acclaimed but Not Perfect." *New York Times* (March 29):B9.

Angier, Natalie. 1993. "Report Suggests Homosexuality Is Linked to Genes." *New York Times* (July 16):A1, C18.

Angier, Natalie. 1995. "If You're Really Ancient, You May Be Better Off: The Rise of the 'Oldest Old.'" *New York Times* (June 11):E1.

Anyon, Jean. 1980. "Social Class and the Hidden Curriculum of Work." *Journal of Education*, 162:67–92.

Apple, Michael W. 1982. *Education and Power: Reproduction and Contradiction in Education*. London: Routledge & Kegan Paul.

Applebome, Peter. 1995a. "For the Ultimate Safe School, Official Eyes Turn to Dallas." *New York Times* (September 20):A1, B8.

Applebome, Peter. 1995b. "Record Cost Cited to Fix or Rebuild Nation's Schools." *New York Times* (December 26): A1, A11.

Applebome, Peter. 1996a. "Dilapidated Schools Are Busting at Frayed Seams." *New York Times* (August 25):8.

Applebome, Peter. 1996b. "Education Summit Calls for Tough Standards to Be Set by States and Local School Districts." *New York Times* (March 27):B7.

Applebome, Peter. 1996c. "Grading For-Profit Schools: So Far, So Good." *New York Times* (June 26):A1, A13.

Applebome, Peter. 1996d. "Building Better Schools: One Size Doesn't Fit." *New York Times* (December 18):E4.

Applebome, Peter. 1997. "Mixed Results for Public School Proponents." *New York Times* (April 16):A17.

Arenson, Karen W. 1997a. "62 Top Colleges Endorse Bias in Admissions." *New York Times* (April 24):A17.

Arenson, Karen W. 1997b. "Standard for Equivalency Degree Is Raised." *New York Times* (April 9):A18.

Arnold, Regina A. 1990. "Processes of Victimization and Criminalization of Black Women." *Social Justice*, 17(3): 153–166.

Ash, Roberta. 1972. *Social Movements in America*. Chicago: Markham.

Association of American Medical Colleges. 1999. *Medical School Admission Requirements, 2000–2001, United States and Canada*. Washington, DC: Association of American Medical Colleges.

Atchley, Robert C. 2000. *Social Forces and Aging: An Introduction to Social Gerontology* (9th ed.). Belmont, CA: Wadsworth.

Atlas, James. 1995. "Here's the Future. Look Familiar?" *New York Times* (December 31):EI, E5.

Aulette, Judy Root. 1994. *Changing Families*. Belmont, CA: Wadsworth.

Austin American-Statesman. 1995. "Abuse of Elderly Is Increasing, Report Says" (May 2):A6.

Austin American-Statesman. 1997a. "Indonesia's Riady Family Wants into U.S. Banking" (April 27):A30.

Austin American-Statesman. 1997b. "Nation Needs Readers" (April 21):A6.

Axinn, William G., and Arland Thornton. 1992. "The Relationship between Cohabitation and Divorce: Selectivity or Casual Influence?" *Demography*, 29(3):357–374.

Bachman, Ronet. 1992. *Death and Violence on the Reservation: Homicide, Family Violence, and Suicide in American Indian Populations*. New York: Auburn House.

Bagby, Meredith (Ed.). 1997. *Annual Report of the United States of America 1997*. New York: McGraw-Hill.

Bailey, J. Michael, and D. S. Benishay. 1993. "Familial Aggregation of Female Sexual Orientation." *American Journal of Psychiatry*, 150 (February):272–277.

Bailey, J. Michael, and Richard C. Pillard. 1991. "A Genetic Study of Male Sexual Orientation." *Archives of General Psychiatry*, 48 (December):1089–1098.

Baldwin, James. 1963. *The Fire Next Time*. New York: Dial Press.

Ballantine, Jeanne H. 1997. *The Sociology of Education: A Systematic Analysis* (4th ed.). Englewood Cliffs, NJ: Prentice-Hall.

Baltzell, E. Digby. 1958. *Philadelphia Gentlemen: The Making of a National Upper Class*. New York: Free Press.

Bandura, Albert. 1973. *Aggression: A Social Learning Analysis*. Englewood Cliffs, NJ: Prentice-Hall.

Bandura, Albert, and R. H. Walters. 1977. *Social Learning Theory*. Englewood Cliffs, NJ: Prentice Hall.

Bane, Mary Jo. 1986. "Household Composition and Poverty: Which Comes First?" In Sheldon H. Danziger and Daniel H. Weinberg (Eds.), *Fighting Poverty: What Works and What Doesn't*. Cambridge, MA: Harvard University Press.

Bane, Mary Jo, and David T. Ellwood. 1994. *Welfare Realities: From Rhetoric to Reform*. Cambridge, MA: Harvard University Press.

Banta, Bob. 1996. "Hyde Hopes to Be Example to Drivers." *Austin American-Statesman* (September 27):A1, A11.

Barber, Benjamin R. 1996. *Jihad vs. McWorld: How Globalism and Tribalism Are Reshaping the World*. New York: Ballantine Books.

Barlett, Donald L., and James B. Steele. 1996. *America: Who Stole the Dream?* Kansas City, KS: Andrews and McMeel.

Barlow, Hugh D. 1996. *Introduction to Criminology* (7th ed.). New York: HarperCollins.

Barnett, James H. 1954. *The American Christmas: A Study in National Culture*. New York: Macmillan.

Baron, Harold M. 1969. "The Web of Urban Racism." In Louis L. Knowles and Kenneth Prewitt (Eds.), *Institutional Racism in America*. Englewood Cliffs, NJ: Prentice-Hall, pp. 134–176.

Barrett, Morris. 1999. "Another Gay Hate Killing Raises Troubling Questions." *Time* (March 5). Retrieved October 30, 1999. Online: http://www.time.com.

Barrows, Sydney Biddle, with William Novak. 1986. *Mayflower Madam: The Secret Life of Sydney Biddle Barrows*. New York: Ivy Books.

Barry, Kathleen. 1995. *The Prostitution of Sexuality*. New York: New York University Press.

Barry, Tom. 1997. "'Burb-arians Pay Share of Austin's Sales Tax." *Austin American-Statesman* (May 27):A13.

Barzansky, Barbara, Harry S. Jonas, and Sylvia I. Etzel. 1999. "Educational Programs in U.S. Medical Schools: 1998–1999, *Journal of the American Medical Association*, 282: 840–846.

Basow, Susan A. 1992. *Gender Stereotypes and Roles* (3rd ed.). Pacific Grove, CA: Brooks/Cole.

Bassi, Laurie J., and Amy B. Chasanov. 1996. "Women and the Unemployment Insurance System." In Cynthia Costello and Barbara Kivimae Krimgold (Eds.) for the Women's Research and Education Institute, *The American Woman 1996–97: Women and Work*. New York: W.W. Norton, pp. 104-126.

Bauerlein, Monika. 1995. "The Borderless Bordello." *Utne Reader* (November–December):30–32.

Bawer, Bruce. 1994. *A Place at the Table: The Gay Individual in American Society*. New York: Touchstone.

Becker, Gary S. 1964. *Human Capital*. New York: Columbia University Press.

Becker, Howard S. 1963. *Outsiders: Studies in the Sociology of Deviance*. New York: Free Press.

Beeghley, Leonard. 1989. *The Structure of Social Stratification in the United States*. Boston: Allyn and Bacon.

Belkin, Lisa. 1999. "Parents Blaming Parents." *New York Times Magazine* (October 31):60–67, 78, 94, 100.

Belknap, Joanne. 1996. *The Invisible Woman: Gender, Crime, and Justice*. Belmont, CA: Wadsworth.

Bell, Daniel. 1973. *The Coming of Post-Industrial Society: A Venture in Social Forecasting*. New York: Basic Books.

Belluck, Pam. 1995. "Educators Divided on Immigrant Schools." *New York Times* (March 26):13.

Belluck, Pam. 1997. "A Woman's Killer Is Likely to Be Her Partner, a Study Finds." *New York Times* (March 31):A12.

Belsky, Janet. 1990. *The Psychology of Aging: Theory, Research, and Interventions* (2nd ed.). Pacific Grove, CA: Brooks/Cole.

Bennett, Niel G., Ann Klimas Blanc, and David E. Bloom. 1988. "Commitment and the Modern Union: Assessing the Link between Premarital Cohabitation and Subsequent Marital Stability." *American Sociological Review,* 53:127–138.

Benokraitis, Nijole V. 1993. *Marriage and Families: Changes, Choices, and Constraints*. Englewood Cliffs, NJ: Prentice-Hall.

Benokraitis, Nijole V., and Joe R. Feagin. 1995. *Modern Sexism: Blatant, Subtle, and Covert Discrimination*. Englewood Cliffs, NJ: Prentice-Hall.

Berg, John C. 1994. *Unequal Struggle: Class, Gender, Race, and Power in the U.S. Congress*. Boulder, CO: Westview.

Berger, Peter. 1963. *Invitation to Sociology: A Humanistic Perspective*. New York: Anchor.

Berger, Peter, and Hansfried Kellner. 1964. "Marriage and the Construction of Reality." *Diogenes*, 46:1–32.

Berger, Peter, and Thomas Luckmann. 1967. *The Social Construction of Reality: A Treatise in the Sociology of Knowledge*. Garden City, NY: Anchor Books.

Berger, Ronald J., Patricia Searles, and Charles E. Cottle. 1991. *Feminism and Pornography*. Westport, CT: Praeger.

Bergmann, Barbara R. 1986. *The Economic Emergence of Women*. New York: Basic Books.

Berke, Richard L. 1996. "Is Age-Bashing Any Way to Beat Bob Dole?" *New York Times* (May 5):E1, E6.

Bernard, Jessie. 1982. *The Future of Marriage*. New Haven, CT: Yale University Press.

Bertram, Eva, Morris Blachman, Kenneth Sharpe, and Peter Andreas. 1996. *Drug War Politics: The Price of Denial*. Berkeley, CA: University of California Press.

Best, Joel. 1999. *Random Violence: How We Talk about New Crimes and New Victims*. Berkeley, CA: University of California Press.

Bethel, Martha A. 1995. "Terror in Montana." *New York Times* (July 20):A13.

Beutler, Ivan F., Wesley R. Burr, Kathleen S. Bahr, and Donald A. Herrin. 1989. "The Family Realm: Theoretical Contributions for Understanding Its Uniqueness." *Journal of Marriage and the Family*, 51:805–815.

Biagi, Shirley. 1998. *Media Impact: An Introduction to Mass Media* (3rd. ed.). Belmont, CA: Wadsworth.

Bieber, Irving, and the Society of Medical Psychoanalysts. 1962. *Homosexuality: A Psychoanalytic Study*. New York: Basic Books.

Birmingham, Stephen. 1967. *The Right Places*. Boston: Little, Brown.

Blauner, Robert. 1972. *Racial Oppression in America*. New York: Harper & Row.

Blount, Jeb. 1996. "Saltwater Spirituals and Deeper Blues." *Houston Chronicle* (February 25):24A.

Bluestone, Barry, and Bennett Harrison. 1982. *The Deindustrialization of America: Plant Closings, Community Abandonment, and the Dismantling of Basic Industry*. New York: Basic Books.

Boller, Gregory. 1997. "Sugar Daddies." *Mother Jones* (May–June):45.

Bonacich, Edna. 1972. "A Theory of Ethnic Antagonism: The Split Labor Market." *American Sociological Review*, 37:547–549.

Bonacich, Edna. 1976. "Advanced Capitalism and Black White Relations in the United States: A Split Labor Market Interpretation." *American Sociological Review*, 41:34–51.

Bonger, Willem. 1969. *Criminality and Economic Conditions* (abridged ed.). Bloomington, IN: Indiana University Press (orig. published in 1916).

Bonnin, Julie. 1997. "Knockout Drugs." *Austin American-Statesman* (February 2):E1, E12.

Botvin, Gilbert, and Stephanie Tortu. 1988. "Preventing Adolescent Substance Abuse through Life Skills Training." In Richard M. Price, Emory L. Cowen, Raymond P. Lorion, and Julia Ramos-McKay (Eds.), *Fourteen Ounces of Prevention: A Casebook for Practitioners*. Washington, DC: American Psychological Association, pp. 98–110.

Bourdieu, Pierre, and Jean-Claude Passeron. 1990. *Reproduction in Education, Society, and Culture*. Newbury Park, CA: Sage.

Bourdon, Karen H., Donald S. Rae, Ben Z. Locke, William E. Narrow, and Darrel A. Regier. 1992. "Estimating the Prevalence of Mental Disorders in U.S. Adults from the Epidemiological Catchment Area Survey." *Public Health Reports*, 107:663–668.

Bourgeois, Philippe. 1995. *In Search of Respect: Selling Crack in el Barrio*. New York: Cambridge University Press.

Bowers, William J. 1984. *Legal Homicide: Death as Punishment in America, 1864–1982*. Boston: Northeastern University Press.

Bowles, Samuel, and Herbert Gintis. 1976. *Schooling in Capitalist America: Education and the Contradictions of Economic Life*. New York: Basic Books.

Bradsher, Keith. 1997. "In the Biggest, Booming Cities, a Car Population Problem." *New York Times* (May 11):E4.

Bragg, Rick. 1997. "Many Find Satisfaction, but Few Find Any Joy." *New York Times* (June 14):8.

Brecher, Jeremy, and Tim Costello. 1998. *Global Village or Global Pillage: Economic Reconstruction From the Bottom Up* (2nd ed.). Cambridge, MA: South End Press.

Brill's Content. 2000. "Big Media Road Map" (January): 99–102.

Brinton, Mary C. 1988. "The Social-Institutional Bases of Gender Stratification: Japan as an Illustrative Case." *American Journal of Sociology*, 94(2):300–334.

Brinton, Mary C. 1989. "Gender Stratification in Contemporary Japan." *American Sociological Review*, 54:549–564.

Brody, Jane E. 1996. "Good Habits Outweigh Genes as Key to a Healthy Old Age." *New York Times* (February 28): B9.

Brooks, A. Phillips. 1997. "UT Minority Applicants Drop Sharply." *Austin American-Statesman* (February 27):B1, B7.

Brooks, A. Phillips, and Jeff South. 1996. "In Town after Town, Minorities Fill Programs." *Austin American-Statesman* (December 1):A1, A14.

Brooks, J. Michael, and Kendal L. Broad (Ed.). 1997. *Instructor's Resource Manual on Social Problems*. Washington, DC: American Sociological Association.

Brown, Phil. 1985. *The Transfer of Care: Psychiatric Deinstitutionalization and Its Aftermath*. Boston: Routledge & Kegan Paul.

Browne, Jan, and Victor Minichiello. 1995. "The Social Meanings behind Male Sex Work: Implications for Sexual Interactions." *British Journal of Sociology*, 46(4):598–623.

Browne, Jan, and Kirk R. Williams. 1987. "Gender Specific Effects on Patterns of Homicide Perpetration." Presented to the American Psychological Association (cited in Barlow, 1996).

Bruni, Frank. 1996. "Gay Couples Cheer Adoption Ruling, Saying It Lets Law Reflect Reality." *New York Times* (November 5):16.

Budd, Mike, Steve Craig, and Clay Steinman. 1999. *Consuming Environments: Television and Commercial Culture*. New Brunswick, NJ: Rutgers University Press.

Buechler, Steven M. 2000. *Social Movements in Advanced Capitalism: The Political Economy and Cultural Construction of Social Activism*. New York: Oxford University Press.

Bullard, Robert D., and Beverly H. Wright. 1992. "The Quest for Environmental Equity: Mobilizing the African-American Community for Social Change." In Riley E. Dunlap and Angela G. Mertig (Eds.), *American Environmentalism: The U.S. Environmental Movement, 1970–1990*. New York: Taylor & Francis, pp. 39–50.

Bullough, Vern, and Bonnie Bullough. 1987. *Women and Prostitution: A Social History*. Buffalo, NY: Prometheus.

Bumpass, Larry, James E. Sweet, and Teresa Castro Martin. 1990. "Changing Patterns of Remarriage." *Journal of Marriage and the Family*, 52:747–756.

Bunis, William K., Angela Yancik, and David Snow. 1996. "The Cultural Patterning of Sympathy toward the Homeless and Other Victims of Misfortune." *Social Problems* (November):387–402.

Burleigh, Nina. 1991. "Watching Children Starve to Death." *Time* (June 10):56–58.

Burnham, M. Audrey, Richard L. Hough, Marvin Karno, Javier I. Escobar, and Cynthia A. Telles. 1987. "Acculturation and Lifetime Prevalence of Psychiatric Disorders among Mexican Americans in Los Angeles." *Journal of Health and Social Behavior*, 28:89–102.

Burns, John F. 1996. "Denial and Taboo Blinding India to the Horror of Its AIDS Scourge." *New York Times* (September 22):A1.

Busch, Ruth C. 1990. *Family Systems: Comparative Study of the Family*. New York: P. Lang.

Busfield, Joan. 1996. *Men, Women and Madness: Understanding Gender and Mental Disorder*. Houndmills, Basingstoke, Hampshire, England: MacMillan Press.

Butler, Robert N. 1969. "Ageism: Another Form of Bigotry." *The Gerontologist*, 9:243–246.

Butler, Sandra, and Barbara Rosenblum. 1991. *Cancer in Two Voices*. San Francisco: Spinsters.

Butterfield, Fox. 1996. "Crimes of Violence among Juveniles Decline Slightly." *New York Times* (August 9):A1, A9.

Butterfield, Fox. 1997. "Serious Crime Decreased for Fifth Year in a Row." *New York Times* (January 5):8.

Bynum, Jack E., and William E. Thompson. 1996. *Juvenile Delinquency: A Sociological Approach*. Boston: Allyn and Bacon.

Cable, Sherry, and Charles Cable. 1995. *Environmental Problems, Grassroots Solutions: The Politics of Grassroots Environmental Conflict*. New York: St. Martin's Press.

Camp, Camille G., and George M. Camp. 1994. *The Corrections Yearbook, 1994*. Washington, DC: U.S. Department of Justice, Bureau of Justice Statistics.

Canadian Youth Rights Association (CYRA). 1998. "Media Ageism." Retrieved November 11, 1999. Online: http://www.cyra.org/media/shtml.

Cancian, Francesca M. 1990. "The Feminization of Love." In C. Carlson (Ed.), *Perspectives on the Family: History, Class, and Feminism*. Belmont, CA: Wadsworth, pp. 171–185.

Cancian, Francesca M., and James William Gibson. 1990. *Making War, Making Peace: The Social Foundations of Violent Conflict*. Belmont, CA: Wadsworth.

Cannon, Margaret. 1995. *The Invisible Empire: Racism in Canada*. Toronto: Random House of Canada.

Capek, Stella M. 1993. "The 'Environmental Justice' Frame: A Conceptual Discussion and an Application." *Social Problems*, 40:5–24.

Cargan, Leonard, and Matthew Melko. 1982. *Singles: Myths and Realities*. Newbury Park, CA: Sage.

Carmichael, Stokely, and Charles V. Hamilton. 1967. *Black Power: The Politics of Liberation in America*. New York: Vintage.

Carrier, James G. 1986. *Social Class and the Construction of Inequality in American Education*. New York: Greenwood Press.

Cass, Vivien C. 1984. "Homosexual Identity Formation: Testing a Theoretical Model." *Journal of Sex Research,* 20: 143–167.

Castells, Manuel. 1977. *The Urban Question*. London: Edward Arnold.

Catalano, Ralph A., and William McConnell. 1996. "A Time-Series Test of the Quarantine Theory of Involuntary Commitment." *Journal of Health and Social Behavior,* 37: 381–387.

Cavender, Gray. 1995. "Alternative Approaches: Labeling and Critical Perspectives." In Joseph F. Sheley (Ed.), *Criminology: A Contemporary Handbook* (2nd ed.). Belmont, CA: Wadsworth, pp. 349–367.

Chambliss, William J. 1988. *Exploring Criminology*. New York: Macmillan.

Chan, Sucheng (Ed.). 1991. *Entry Denied: Exclusion and the Chinese Community in America, 1882–1943*. Philadelphia: Temple University Press.

Chase-Lansdale, P. Lindsay, Jeanne Brooks-Gunn, and Roberta L. Palkoff. 1992. "Research and Programs for Adolescent Mothers: Missing Links and Future Promises." *Family Relations*, 40(4):396–403.

Chavez, Leo R. and Rebecca Martinez. 1996. "Mexican Immigration in the 1980s and Beyond: Implications for Chicanas/os." In David R. Maciel and Isidro D. Ortiz (Eds.), *Chicanas/Chicanos at the Crossroads: Social Economic, and Political Change*. Tucson, AZ: University of Arizona Press, pp. 25–41.

Chavez, Linda. 1991. *Out of the Barrio: Toward a New Politics of Hispanic Assimilation*. New York: Basic Books.

Chen, Hsiang-shui. 1992. *Chinatown No More: Taiwan Immigrants in Contemporary New York*. Ithaca: Cornell University Press.

Cherlin, Andrew J. 1992. *Marriage, Divorce, and Remarriage* (rev. and enlarged ed.). Cambridge, MA: Harvard University Press.

Chermak, Steven M. 1995. *Victims in the News: Crime and the American News Media*. Boulder, CO: Westview.

Chilcoat, Howard D., and Naomi Breslau. 1996. "Alcohol Disorders in Young Adulthood: Effects of Transitions into Adult Roles." *Journal of Health and Social Behavior,* 37(4):339–349.

Children's Defense Fund. 1995. *The State of America's Children Yearbook 1995*. Washington, DC: Children's Defense Fund.

Children's Defense Fund. 1999. *The State of America's Children Yearbook 1999*. Boston: Beacon Press.

Children's Express. 1993. "Voices from the Future: Our Children Tell Us about Violence in America." Edited by Susan Goodwillie. New York: Crown.

Chin, Rockwell. 1999. "Long Struggle for Justice." *ABA Journal* (November):66–67.

Chronicle of Higher Education. 1999. "Attitudes and Characteristics of Freshman, Fall 1998." Almanac Issue (August 27):28.

Chudacoff, Howard P. 1989. *How Old Are You? Age Consciousness in American Culture*. Princeton, NJ: Princeton University Press.

Churchill, Ward. 1992. *Fantasies of the Master Race*. Monroe, ME: Common Courage Press.

Churchill, Ward. 1994. *Indians Are Us? Culture and Genocide in Native North America*. Monroe, ME: Common Courage Press.

City of Austin. 1996. Internal communication from Information Systems Department (October 23).

City of New York. 1997. "Mayor Rudolph W. Giuliani Fresh Kills Exportation Announcement." Retrieved January 1, 2000. Online: http://www.ci.nyc.ny.us/html/om/html/freshkls.html.

Clark, Cal, and Oliver Walter. 1994. "Cuts, Cultures, and City Limits in Reagan's New Federalism." In Terry Nichols Clark (Ed.), *Urban Innovation: Creative Strategies for Turbulent Times*. Thousand Oaks, CA: Sage, pp. 169–196.

Cleary, Paul D. 1987. "Gender Differences in Stress-Related Disorders." In Rosalind C. Barnett, Lois Biener, and Grace K. Baruch (Eds.), *Gender and Stress*. New York: Free Press, pp. 39–72.

Cleeland, N. 1991. "Gasping in Smoggy Mexico City Oxygen Kiosk May Prove Helpful." *San Diego Union* (March 9). (Cited in Michael P. Soroka and George J. Bryjak. 1995. *Social Problems: A World at Risk*. Boston: Allyn and Bacon, p. 116.)

Clinard, Marshall B., and R. F. Meier. 1989. *Sociology of Deviant Behavior* (7th ed.). Fort Worth, TX: Holt, Rinehart and Winston.

Clines, Francis X. 1997. "'Soft' Money Source Proves Hard to Find." *New York Times* (July 31):A9.

Cloward, Richard A., and Lloyd E. Ohlin. 1960. *Delinquency and Opportunity: A Theory of Delinquent Gangs*. New York: Free Press.

Coale, Ansley. 1973. "The Demographic Transition." Proceedings of the International Population Conference, Liege. Vol. 1, pp. 53–72. (Cited in Weeks, 1992.)

Cock, Jacklyn. 1994. "Women and the Military: Implications for Demilitarization in the 1990s in South Africa. *Gender and Society*, 8(2):152–169.

Codina, G. Edward, and Frank F. Montalvo. 1994. "Chicano Phenotype and Depression." *Hispanic Journal of Behavioral Sciences*, 16 (August):296–307.

Cohen, Adam. 1999a. "A Life for a Life." *Time* (March 8). Retrieved October 30, 1999. Online: http://www.time.com.

Cohen, Adam. 1999b. "Who Should Still Be on Welfare?" *Time* (August 16):24–28.

Cohen, Lawrence E., and Marcus Felson. 1979. "Social Change and Crime Rate Trends: A Routine Activity Approach." *American Sociological Review,* 44:588–608.

Cohn, Jonathan. 1997. "Reform School." *Mother Jones* (May–June): 62.

Coleman, Eli. 1981/2. "Developmental Stages of the Coming Out Process." *Journal of Homosexuality,* 7:31–43.

Coleman, James S. 1966. *Equality of Educational Opportunity.* Washington, DC: U.S. Government Printing Office.

Coleman, James W. 1995. "Respectable Crime." In Joseph F. Sheley (Ed.), *Criminology: A Contemporary Handbook* (2nd ed.). Belmont, CA: Wadsworth, pp. 249–269.

Coles, Gerald. 1987. *The Learning Mystique: A Critical Look at "Learning Disabilities."* New York: Pantheon.

Colhoun, J. 1992. "Census Fails to Quash Report on Iraqi Deaths." *The Guardian* (April 22):5.

Collins, James. 1997. "Day of Reckoning." *Time* (June 16): 27–29.

Collins, Patricia Hill. 1990. *Black Feminist Thought: Knowledge, Consciousness, and the Politics of Entitlement.* London: HarperCollins Academic.

Collins, Patricia Hill. 1991. *Black Feminist Thought: Knowledge, Consciousness, and the Politics of Empowerment.* New York: Routledge.

Collins, Patricia Hill. 1995. "Symposium: On West and Fenstermaker's 'Doing Difference.'" *Gender and Society,* 9(4) (August):491–494.

Collins, Randall. 1979. *The Credential Society: An Historical Sociology of Education.* New York: Academic Press.

Coltrane, Scott. 1989. "Household Labor and the Routine Production of Gender." *Social Problems,* 36:473–490.

Community Childhood Hunger Identification Project. 1995. *A Survey of Childhood Hunger in the United States.* Washington, DC: Food Research and Action Committee (July).

Comstock, Gary David. 1991. *Violence against Lesbians and Gay Men.* New York: Columbia University Press.

Conant, Marcus. 1997. "This Is Smart Medicine." *Newsweek* (February 3):26.

Congressional Budget Office. 1999. "The Economic and Budget Outlook: An Update." Retrieved December 24, 1999. Online: http://www.cbo.gov/showdoc.cfm?index=1386& sequence=0&from=7.

Conley, Frances K. 1998. *Walking Out on the Boys.* New York: Farrar, Straus and Giroux.

Connell, Christopher. 1995. "Birth Rate for Unmarried Women Surges." *Austin American-Statesman* (June 7):A18.

Corelli, Rae. 1995. "A Tolerant Nation's Hidden Shame." *Maclean's* (August 14):38–43.

Corr, Charles A., Clyde M. Nabe, and Donna M. Corr. 1994. *Death and Dying, Life and Living.* Pacific Grove, CA: Brooks/Cole.

Cosby, Ennis. 1997. "Teaching from the Heart." *New York Times* (January 26):E13.

Cose, Ellis. 1993. *The Rage of a Privileged Class.* New York: HarperCollins.

Coser, Lewis A. 1969. "The Visibility of Evil." *Journal of Social Issues,* 25:101–109. In Bunis, William K., Angela Yancik, and David Snow. 1996. "The Cultural Patterning of Sympathy toward the Homeless and Other Victims of Misfortune." *Social Problems* (November):387–402.

Costello, Cynthia, Anne J. Stone, and Betty Dooley. 1996. "A Perspective on America's Working Women." In Cynthia

Costello and Barbara Kivimae Krimgold (Eds.) for the Women's Research and Education Institute, *The American Woman 1996–97: Women and Work.* New York: W.W. Norton, pp. 23–32.

Cottle, Charles E., Patricia Searles, Ronald J. Berger, and Beth Ann Pierce. 1989. "Conflicting Ideologies and the Politics of Pornography." *Gender and Society,* 3:303–333.

Coverman, Shelley. 1989. "Women's Work Is Never Done: The Division of Domestic Labor." In Jo Freeman (Ed.), *Women: A Feminist Perspective* (4th ed.). Mountain View, CA: Mayfield, pp. 356–368.

Cowan, Gloria, C. Lee, D. Levy, and D. Snyder. 1988. "Domination and Inequality in X-Rated Videocassettes." *Psychology of Women Quarterly,* 12:299–311.

Cowan, Gloria, and Margaret O'Brien. 1990. "Gender and Survival vs. Death in Slasher Films: A Content Analysis." *Sex Roles,* 23:187–196.

Cowgill, Donald O. 1986. *Aging around the World.* Belmont, CA: Wadsworth.

Cowley, Geoffrey. 1997. "Can Marijuana Be Medicine?" *Newsweek* (February 3):22–27.

Cox, Oliver C. 1948. *Caste, Class, and Race.* Garden City, NY: Doubleday.

Cozic, Charles P. (Ed.). 1993. *America's Cities: Opposing Viewpoints.* San Diego: Greenhaven Press.

Crossette, Barbara. 1996a. "Agency Sees Risk in Drug to Temper Child Behavior: Worldwide Survey Cites Overuse of Ritalin." *New York Times* (February 29):A7.

Crossette, Barbara. 1996b. "U.N. Survey Finds World Rich-Poor Gap Widening." *New York Times* (July 15):A3.

Crossette, Barbara. 1996c. "Hope, and Pragmatism, for U.S. Cities Conference." *New York Times* (June 3):A3.

Crossette, Barbara. 1997. "Democracies Love Peace, Don't They?" *New York Times* (June 1):E3.

Crossette, Barbara. 2000. "Europe Stares at a Future Built by Immigrants." *New York Times* (January 2):WK1, 4.

Cullen, Dave. 1999. "The Reluctant Activist." *Salon.com* (October 15):1–4. Retrieved November 15, 1999. Online: http://www.salon.com/news/feature/1999/10/15/laramie/index.html.

Cumming, Elaine C., and William E. Henry. 1961. *Growing Old: The Process of Disengagement.* New York: Basic Books.

Curatolo, Peter W., and David Robertson. 1983. "The Health Consequences of Caffeine." *Annals of Internal Medicine,* 98:641–653. (Cited in Levinthal, 1996.)

Curran, James, Michael Gurevitch, and Janet Woollacott. 1982. "The Study of the Media: Theoretical Approaches." In Michael Gurevitch, Tony Bennett, James Curran, and Janet Woollacott (Eds.). *Culture, Society and the Media.* London: Methuen, pp. 5–35.

Cushman, John H., Jr. 1997. "E.P.A. Seeks Cut, Not End, to Pollution by Paper Mills." *New York Times* (May 21):A10.

Dahl, Robert A. 1961. *Who Governs?* New Haven, CT: Yale University Press.

Daley, Suzanne. 1997. "Zaïre's Fall Jolts Neighboring Angola's Frail Peace." *New York Times* (June 8):3.

Daly, Kathleen, and Meda Chesney-Lind. 1988. "Feminism and Criminology." *Justice Quarterly*, 5:497–533.

Dandaneau, Steven P. 1996. *A Town Abandoned: Flint, Michigan, Confronts Deindustrialization*. Albany, NY: State University of New York Press.

Danziger, Sheldon, and Peter Gottschalk. 1995. *America Unequal*. Cambridge, MA: Harvard University Press.

Davidson, Julia O'Connell. 1996. "Sex Tourism in Cuba." *Race and Class*, 38(1):39–49.

Davis, F. James. 1991. *Who Is Black? One Nation's Definition*. University Park, PA: Pennsylvania State University Press.

Davis, Kingsley. 1937. "The Sociology of Prostitution." *American Sociological Review*, 2:744–755.

Davis, Kingsley, and Amyra Grossbard-Shechtman (Eds.). 1985. *Contemporary Marriage: Comparative Perspectives on a Changing Institution*. New York: Russell Sage Foundation.

Davis, Nancy J., and Robert V. Robinson. 1988. "Class Identification of Men and Women in the 1970s and 1980s." *American Sociological Review*, 53(February):103–112.

Dawes, Amy. 1995. "Latinos Keep Pounding on Network Doors." *Austin American-Statesman* (October 22):4.

Deans, Bob. 1995. "Women in Japan Still Face Family vs. Career Conflict." *Austin American-Statesman* (September 3):E4.

De Castro, Steven. 1994. "Identity in Action: A Filipino American's Perspective." In Karin Aguilar-San Juan (Ed.), *The State of Asian America: Activism and Resistance in the 1990s*. Boston: South End Press, pp. 295–320.

DePasquale, Katherine M. 1999. "The Effects of Prostitution." Retrieved December 3, 1999. Online: http://www.feminista.com/v1n5/depasquale.html.

de Silva, Rex. 1980. "Developing the Third World." *World Press Review* (May):48.

Detroit Edison. 1999. "Detroit's Empowerment Zone Working Together to Make It Work." Retrieved January 3, 2000. Online: http://www.detroitedison.com/business/busdev/ezone.html.

Devereaux, Anna. 1987. "Diary of a Prostitute." *Cosmopolitan* (October 1987):164, 166.

DeWitt, Karen. 1992. "The Nation's Schools Learn a 4th R: Resegregation." *New York Times* (January 19):A5.

DeWitt, Karen. 1994. "Wave of Suburban Growth Is Being Fed by Minorities." *New York Times* (August 15):A1, A12.

Dews, Peter B. 1984. "Behavioral Effects of Caffeine." In Peter B. Dews (Ed.), *Caffeine: Perspectives from Recent Research*. Berlin: Springer-Verlag, pp. 86–103. (Cited in Levinthal, 1996.)

Diamond, Jared. 2000. "The Greening of Corporate America." *New York Times* (January 8):A31.

Diamond, Timothy. 1992. *Making Gray Gold: Narratives of Nursing Home Care*. Chicago: University of Chicago Press.

Dietz, P. 1986. "Mass, Serial and Sensational Homicide." *Bulletin of the New England Medical Society*, 62:477–491.

DiFranza, Joseph R., and Robert A. Lew. 1995. "Effect of Maternal Cigarette Smoking on Pregnancy Complications and Sudden Infant Death Syndrome." *The Journal of Family Practice*, 40:385–394.

DiPietro, Ben. 1999. "Hawaii Rules Against Gay Marriages." *Austin American-Statesman* (December 11):A4.

dmnweb. 1999. "*The Dallas Morning News*: Media Kit." Retrieved December 24, 1999. Online: http://dmweb.dallasnews.com/mediakit/newspaper/company/belolist.htm.

Dobrzynski, Judith H. 1996a. "Study Finds Few Women in 5 Highest Company Jobs." *New York Times* (October 16):C3.

Dobrzynski, Judith H. 1996b. "When Directors Play Musical Chairs." *New York Times* (November 17):F1, F8, F9.

Dollard, John, Neal E. Miller, Leonard W. Doob, O. H. Mowrer, and Robert R. Sears. 1939. *Frustration and Aggression*. New Haven, CT: Yale University Press.

Domhoff, G. William. 1978. *The Powers That Be: Processes of Ruling Class Domination in America*. New York: Random House.

Domhoff, G. William. 1983. *Who Rules America Now?* New York: Touchstone.

Domhoff, G. William. 1990. *The Power Elite and the State: How Policy Is Made in America*. New York: Aldine De Gruyter.

Donziger, Steven R. (Ed.). 1996. *The Real War on Crime: The Report of the National Criminal Justice Commission*. New York: HarperPerennial.

Doss, Yvette. 1996. "Network TV: Latinos Need Not Apply." *Frontera Magazine* (Issue 2: n.d.). Retrieved November 11, 1999. Online: http://www.frontramag.com.

Doyle, James A. 1995. *The Male Experience* (3rd ed.). Madison, WI: Brown and Benchmark.

Dreyfuss, Robert. 1996. "Good Morning, Gun Lobby!" *Mother Jones* (July–August):38–47.

D'Souza, Dinesh. 1999. "The Billionaire Next Door." *Forbes* (October 11):50–62.

Du Phuoc Long, Patrick (with Laura Ricard). 1996. *The Dream Shattered: Vietnamese Gangs in America*. Boston: Northeastern University Press.

Dull, Diana, and Candace West. 1991. "Accounting for Cosmetic Surgery: The Accomplishments of Gender." *Social Problems*, 38(1):54–70.

Duncan, David F. 1991. "Violence and Degradation as Themes in 'Adult' Videos." *Psychology Reports*, 69(1):239–240.

Dunlap, David W. 1995. "Court Upholds Anti-Homosexual Initiative." *New York Times* (May 14):10.

Dunlap, David W. 1996. "Role of Openly Gay Episcopalians Causes a Rift in the Church." *New York Times* (March 21):A8.

Dunlap, Riley E. 1992. "Trends in Public Opinion toward Environmental Issues: 1965–1990." In Riley E. Dunlap and Angela G. Mertig (Eds.), *American Environmentalism: The U.S. Environmental Movement, 1970–1990*. New York: Taylor & Francis, pp. 89–113.

Dunn, Ashley. 1995. "Cram Schools: Immigrants' Tools for Success." *New York Times* (January 28):1, 9.

Duran, Lisa. 1997. "Ignorance about Immigrants." *Austin American-Statesman* (May 19):A7.

Durkheim, Emile. [1915] 1965. *The Elementary Forms of the Religious Life*, translated by J.W. Swain. New York: The Free Press. In Bunis, William K., Angela Yancik, and David Snow. 1996. "The Cultural Patterning of Sympathy toward the Homeless and Other Victims of Misfortune." *Social Problems* (November):387–402.

Durkheim, Emile. 1933. *Division of Labor in Society*. Trans. George Simpson. New York: Free Press (orig. published in 1893).

Durkheim, Emile. 1964. *The Rules of Sociological Method*. Trans. Sarah A. Solovay and John H. Mueller. New York: Free Press (orig. published in 1895).

Duster, Troy. 1995. "Symposium: The Bell Curve." *Contemporary Sociology: A Journal of Reviews*, 24(2):158–161.

Dworkin, Andrea. 1988. *Letters to a War Zone*. New York: Dutton/New America Library.

Dye, Thomas R. 2000. *The Irony of Democracy: An Uncommon Introduction to American Politics* (millennium ed.). Ft. Worth, TX: Harcourt College.

Dynes, Wayne R. (Ed.). 1990. *Encyclopedia of Homosexuality*. New York: Garland.

Eaton, William W. 1980. "A Formal Theory of Selection for Schizophrenia." *American Journal of Sociology*, 86:149–158.

The Ecologist. 1993. *Whose Common Future? Reclaiming the Commons*. Philadelphia: New Society Publishers.

The Economist. 1995. "Size of the Internet" (April 15):102.

Eder, Donna. 1985. "The Cycle of Popularity: Interpersonal Relations among Female Adolescents." *Sociology of Education*, 58(July):154–165.

Eder, Donna, and Stephen Parker. 1987. "The Cultural Production and Reproduction of Gender: The Effect of Extracurricular Activities on Peer Group Culture." *Sociology of Education*, 60:200–213.

Ehrenreich, Barbara. 1997. *Blood Rites: Origins and History of the Passions of War*. New York: Metropolitan Books.

Ehrlich, Paul R., and Anne H. Ehrlich. 1991. *The Population Explosion*. New York: Touchstone/Simon & Schuster.

Eitzen, D. Stanley, and Maxine Baca Zinn. 1994. *Social Problems* (6th ed.). Boston: Allyn and Bacon.

Elliott, Marta, and Lauren J. Krivo. 1991. "Structural Determinants of Homelessness in the United States." *Social Problems*, 38(1):113–131.

Elliott, Michael. 1999. "The New Radicals." *Newsweek* (December 13):36–39.

Engelhardt, H. Tristan, Jr. 1996. *Foundations of Bioethics*. New York: Oxford University Press.

Engels, Friedrich. 1972. *The Origins of the Family, Private Property, and the State*. (Ed. Eleanor Burke Leacock). New York: International.

Enloe, Cynthia H. 1987. "Feminists Thinking about War, Militarism, and Peace." In Beth Hess and Myra Marx Ferree (Eds.), *Analyzing Gender: A Handbook of Social Science Research*. Newbury Park, CA: Sage, pp. 526–547.

Epstein, Cynthia Fuchs. 1988. *Deceptive Distinctions: Sex, Gender, and the Social Order*. New Haven, CT: Yale University Press.

Epstein, Cynthia Fuchs. 1993. *Women in Law* (3rd ed.). Urbana, IL: University of Illinois Press.

Erikson, Kai T. 1962. "Notes on the Sociology of Deviance." *Social Problems*, 9:307–314.

Erikson, Kai T. 1991. "A New Species of Trouble." In Stephen Robert Crouch and J. Stephen Kroll-Smith (Eds.), *Communities at Risk: Collective Responses to Technological Hazards*. New York: Peter Land, pp. 11–29.

Erikson, Kai T. 1994. *A New Species of Trouble: Explorations in Disaster, Trauma, and Community*. New York: Norton.

Espiritu, Yen Le. 1995. *Filipino American Lives*. Philadelphia: Temple University Press.

Essed, Philomena. 1991. *Understanding Everyday Racism*. Newbury Park, CA: Sage.

Factbook on Global Sexual Exploitation. 1999. "United States of America: Facts on Trafficking and Prostitution." Retrieved December 3, 1999. Online: http://www.uri.edu/artsci/wms/hughes/catw/usa.htm.

Fagot, Beverly I. 1984. "Teacher and Peer Reactions to Boys' and Girls' Play Styles." *Sex Roles*, 11:691–702.

Fairstein, Linda A. 1995. *Sexual Violence: Our War against Rape*. New York: Berkley.

Faludi, Susan. 1991. *Backlash: The Undeclared War against American Women*. New York: Crown.

FAO. 1995. *FAO Yearbook 1995*. Rome, Italy: Food and Agricultural Organization of the United Nations.

Farnsworth, Clyde H. 1993. "Soaring Costs for Health Care Touch Off Service Cuts and Fees." *New York Times* (November 14):HD9.

Farrey, Tom. 1999. "Images from Sports Carry Racial Weight." *ESPN Sports*. Retrieved August 15, 1999. Online: http://espn.go.com/gen/features/race/farrey.html.

Feagin, Joe R. 1975. *Subordinating the Poor: Welfare and American Beliefs*. Englewood Cliffs, NJ: Prentice-Hall.

Feagin, Joe R., and Clairece Booher Feagin. 1997. *Social Problems: A Critical-Conflict Perspective* (5th ed.). Upper Saddle River, NJ: Prentice-Hall.

Feagin, Joe R., and Clairece Booher Feagin. 1999. *Racial and Ethnic Relations* (6th ed.). Upper Saddle River, NJ: Prentice-Hall.

Feagin, Joe R., and Robert Parker. 1990. *Building American Cities: The Urban Real Estate Game* (2nd ed.). Englewood Cliffs, NJ: Prentice-Hall.

Feagin, Joe R., and Melvin P. Sikes. 1994. *Living with Racism: The Black Middle-Class Experience*. Boston: Beacon Press.

Feagin, Joe R., and Hernán Vera. 1995. *White Racism: The Basics*. New York: Routledge.

Fedders, Charlotte, and Laura Elliott. 1987. *Shattered Dreams*. New York: Dell.

Federal Bureau of Investigation (FBI). 1999. *Crime in the United States, 1998*. Washington, DC: U.S. Government Printing Office.

Federal Election Commission. 1999. "Top 50 PACs—Contributions to Candidates, 1997–98." Retrieved December 24, 1999. Online: http://www.fec.gov/press/paccnt98.htm.

Federman, Joel. 1998. "Introduction." *National Television Violence Study*, vol. 3. Thousand Oaks, CA: Sage.

Fenstermacher, Gary D. 1994. "The Absence of Democratic and Educational Ideals from Contemporary Educational Reform Initiatives." The Elam Lecture, presented to the

Educational Press Association of America. Chicago, June 10.

Fernandez, Joseph M. 1991. "Bringing Hate Crime into Focus." *Harvard Civil Rights–Civil Liberties Law Review,* 26(1):261–293.

Findlen, Barbara. 1995. "Is Marriage the Answer? Domestic Partnership Activists Don't Think So." *Ms.* (May–June): 86–91.

Fine, Gary Alan. 1987. *With the Boys: Little League Baseball and Preadolescent Culture.* Chicago: University of Chicago Press.

Fine, Michelle. 1991. *Framing Dropouts: Notes on the Politics of an Urban Public High School.* Albany, NY: State University Press of New York.

Fineman, Howard. 1997. "Who Needs Washington?" *Newsweek* (January 27):50–52.

Finkelhor, David. 1984. *Child Abuse: New Theory and Research.* New York: Free Press.

Finkelhor, David, and Kersti Yllo. 1985. *License to Rape: Sexual Abuse of Wives.* New York: Free Press.

Firestone, Shulamith. 1970. *The Dialectic of Sex.* New York: Morrow.

Fishbein, Diana H., and Susan E. Pease. 1996. *The Dynamics of Drug Abuse.* Boston: Allyn and Bacon.

Fisher, Ian. 1995. "Tobacco Funds Go to Black Officials." *New York Times* (November 19):21.

Fisher, Lawrence M. 1996. "Health on Line: Doctor Is In, and His Disk Is Full." *New York Times* (June 14):C1, C8.

Flanagan, William G. 1995. *Urban Sociology: Images and Structure* (2nd ed.). Boston: Allyn and Bacon.

Flexner, Abraham. 1910. *Medical Education in the United States and Canada.* New York: Carnegie Foundation.

Foner, Philip S., and Daniel Rosenberg (Eds.). 1993. *Racism, Dissent, and Asian Americans from 1850 to Present.* Westport, CT: Greenwood Press.

Forbes. 1999. "The Forbes 400." (October 11):Entire edition.

Foreman, Judy. 1993. "Older Adults May Face Obstacles on Job." *San Antonio Express-News* (December 15):B7.

Foreman, Judy. 1996. "Caring for Parents Long-Distance Is a Baby Boomer's Nightmare." *Austin American-Statesman* (November 3):E1, E14.

Fox, Mary Frank. 1995. "Women and Higher Education: Gender Differences in the Status of Students and Scholars." In Jo Freeman (Ed.), *Women: A Feminist Perspective* (5th ed.). Mountain View, CA: Mayfield, pp. 220–237.

Fox Network. 1999. "The PJ's Message Board." Fox TV Network. Retrieved July 11, 1999. Online: http://www.foxnet.com/pjs/track1.htm.

Frankenberg, Ruth. 1993. *White Women, Race Matters: The Social Construction of Whiteness.* Minneapolis: University of Minnesota Press.

Franklin, John Hope. 1980. *From Slavery to Freedom* (3rd ed.). New York: Knopf.

French, Dolores, with Linda Lee. 1988. *Working: My Life as a Prostitute.* New York: E.P. Dutton.

Freudenberg, Nicholas, and Carl Steinsapir. 1992. "Not in Our Backyards: The Grassroots Environmental Movement." In Riley E. Dunlap and Angela G. Mertig (Eds.), *American*

Environmentalism: The U.S. Environmental Movement, 1970–1990. New York: Taylor & Francis, pp. 27–37.

Freund, Matthew, Nancy Lee, and Terri Leonard. 1991. "Sexual Behavior of Clients with Street Prostitutes in Camden, New Jersey." *Journal of Sex Research,* 28(4) (November): 579–591.

Friedan, Betty. 1993. *The Fountain of Age.* New York: Simon & Schuster.

Friedman, George, and Meredith Friedman. 1996. *The Future of War: Power, Technology, and American World Dominance in the 21st Century.* New York: Crown.

Friedman, Thomas L. 2000a. "Boston E-Party." *New York Times* (January 1):A31.

Friedman, Thomas L. 2000b. "The Spirit of Y2K." *New York Times* (January 7):A23.

Friedmann, John. 1995. "The World City Hypothesis." In Paul L. Knox and Peter J. Taylor (Eds.), *World Cities in a World-System.* Cambridge, England: Cambridge University Press, pp. 317–331.

Friedrichs, David O. 1996. *Trusted Criminals: White Collar Crime in Contemporary Society.* Belmont, CA: Wadsworth.

Friend, Tim. 1996. "Teens and Drugs: Today's Youth Just Don't See the Dangers." *USA Today* (August 21):1A, 2A.

Fullilove, Mindy Thompson, E. Anne Lown, and Robert E. Fullilove. 1992. "Crack 'Hos and Skeezers: Traumatic Experiences of Women Crack Users." *Journal of Sex Research,* 29(2):275–288.

Funderburg, Lise. 1994. *Black, White, Other: Biracial Americans Talk about Race and Identity.* New York: William Morrow.

Fussell, Paul. 1992. *Wartime: Understanding and Behavior in the Second World War.* New York: Oxford University Press.

Gabriel, Trip. 1995a. "A New Generation Seems Ready to Give Bisexuality a Place in the Spectrum." *New York Times* (June 12):C10.

Gabriel, Trip. 1995b. "Some On-Line Discoveries Give Gay Youths a Path to Themselves." *New York Times* (July 2): 1, 9.

Gabriel, Trip. 1996. "High-Tech Pregnancies Test Hope's Limit." *New York Times* (January 7):1, 10–11.

Gailey, Christine Ward. 1987. "Evolutionary Perspectives on Gender Hierarchy." In Beth B. Hess and Myra Marx Ferree (Eds.), *Analyzing Gender: A Handbook of Social Science Research.* Newbury Park, CA: Sage, pp. 32–67.

Galbraith, John Kenneth. 1985. *The New Industrial State* (4th ed.). Boston: Houghton Mifflin.

Gamson, Joshua. 1994. *Claims to Fame: Celebrity in Contemporary America.* Berkeley, CA: University of California Press.

Gamson, William. 1990. *The Strategy of Social Protest* (2nd ed.). Belmont, CA: Wadsworth.

Gans, Herbert. 1982. *The Urban Villagers: Group and Class in the Life of Italian Americans* (updated and expanded ed.; orig. published in 1962). New York: Free Press.

Gardner, Carol Brooks. 1995. *Passing By: Gender and Public Harassment.* Berkeley, CA: University of California Press.

Gardner, Tracey A. 1994. "Racism in Pornography and the Women's Movement." In Alison M. Jaggar (Ed.), *Living with Contradictions: Controversies in Feminist Social Ethics*. Boulder, CO: Westview, pp. 171–176.

Gardy, Alison. 1995. "Forging Links between Inner Cities and the Internet." *New York Times* (March 12):F10.

Garfinkel, Irwin, and Sara S. McLanahan. 1986. *Single Mothers and Their Children: A New American Dilemma*. Washington, DC: Urban Institute Press.

Garreau, Joel. 1991. *Edge City: Life on the New Frontier*. New York: Doubleday.

Gatz, Margaret (Ed.). 1995. *Emerging Issues in Mental Health and Aging*. Washington, DC: American Psychological Association.

Gawin, F. H., and E. H. Ellinwood, Jr. 1988. Cocaine and Other Stimulants: Actions, Abuse, and Treatment. *New England Journal of Medicine*, 318:1173–1182.

Gelfand, Donald E. 1994. *Aging and Ethnicity: Knowledge and Services*. New York: Springer.

Gentry, Cynthia. 1995. "Crime Control through Drug Control." In Joseph F. Sheley (Ed.), *Criminology: A Contemporary Handbook* (2nd ed.). Belmont, CA: Wadsworth, pp. 477–493.

Gerbner, George, 1995. "Television Violence: The Power and the Peril." In Gail Dines and Jean M. Humez (Eds.), *Gender, Face, and Class in Media: A Text-Reader*. Thousand Oaks, CA: Sage, pp. 547–557.

Gerson, Kathleen. 1993. *No Man's Land: Men's Changing Commitments to Family and Work*. New York: Basic Books.

Gerstel, Naomi, and Harriet Engel Gross. 1995. "Gender and Families in the United States: The Reality of Economic Dependence." In Jo Freeman (Ed.), *Women: A Feminist Perspective* (5th ed.). Mountain View, CA: Mayfield, pp. 92–127.

Gerth, Jeff. 1997. "China Buying U.S. Computers, Raising Arms Fears." *New York Times* (June 10):A1, A8.

Gessen, Masha. 1993. "Lesbians and Breast Cancer." *The Advocate* (February 9):22–23.

Gibbs, Lois Marie, as told to Murray Levine. 1982. *Love Canal: My Story*. Albany, NY: State University of New York Press.

Gibbs, Nancy. 1994. "Home Sweet School." *Time* (October 31):62–63.

Gibbs, Nancy. 1996. "Cause Celeb: Two High-Profile Entertainers Are Props in a Worldwide Debate over Sweatshops and the Use of Child Labor." *Time* (June 17):28–30.

Gibson, James William, and Francesca M. Cancian. 1990. "Is War Inevitable?" In Francesca M. Cancian and James William Gibson (Eds.), *Making War, Making Peace: The Social Foundations of Violent Conflict*. Belmont, CA: Wadsworth, pp. 1–10.

Gil, Vincent E., Marco S. Wang, Allen F. Anderson, Guo Matthew Lin, and Zongjian Oliver Wu. 1996. "Prostitutes, Prostitution and STD/HIV Transmission in Mainland China." *Social Science and Medicine*, 42(1):141–153.

Gilbert, Richard J. 1986. *Caffeine: The Most Popular Stimulant*. New York: Chelsea House.

Gilder, George. 1981. *Wealth and Poverty*. New York: Basic Books.

Giobbe, Evelina. 1993. "Surviving Commercial Sexual Exploitation." In Diana E. H. Russell (Ed.), *Making Violence Sexy: Feminist Views on Pornography*. New York: Teachers College Press, pp. 37–41.

Giobbe, Evelina. 1994. "Confronting the Liberal Lies about Prostitution." In Alison M. Jaggar (Ed.), *Living with Contradictions: Controversies in Feminist Social Ethics*. Boulder, CO: Westview, pp. 120–136.

Gladwell, Malcolm. 1997. "Damaged: Why Do Some People Turn into Violent Criminals?" *The New Yorker* (February 24–March 3):132–147.

Glaser, Barney, and Anselm Strauss. 1968. *Time for Dying*. Chicago: Aldine.

Glass Ceiling Commission. 1995. *Good for Business: Making Full Use of the Nation's Human Capital*. Washington, DC: Glass Ceiling Commission.

Gleick, Elizabeth. 1995. "Segregation Anxiety." *Time* (April 24):63.

Gleick, Elizabeth. 1996. "The Children's Crusade." *Time* (June 3):30–35.

Glick, Paul C., and Sung-Ling Lin. 1986. "More Young Adults Are Living with Their Parents: Who Are They?" *Journal of Marriage and the Family*, 48:107–112.

Goffman, Erving. 1961. *Asylums: Essays on the Social Situation of Mental Patients and Other Inmates*. Chicago: Aldine.

Golay, Michael, and Carl Rollyson. 1996. *Where America Stands: 1996*. New York: John Wiley.

Gold, Rachel Benson, and Cory L. Richards. 1994. "Securing American Women's Reproductive Health." In Cynthia Costello and Anne J. Stone (Eds.), *The American Woman, 1994–1995*. New York: W.W. Norton, pp. 197–222.

Goldberg, Carey, 1996. "A Victory for Same-Sex Parenting, at Least." *New York Times* (December 5):A20.

Goldberg, Carey. 1997. "Quiet Roads Bringing Thundering Protests." *New York Times* (May 23):A8.

Goldberg, Robert A. 1991. *Grassroots Resistance: Social Movements in Twentieth Century America*. Belmont, CA: Wadsworth.

Golden, Stephanie. 1992. *The Women Outside: Meanings and Myths of Homelessness*. Berkeley, CA: University of California Press.

Goode, Erich. 1989. *Drugs in American Society* (3rd ed.). New York: McGraw-Hill.

Goode, Erich. 1996. "Deviance, Norms, and Social Reaction." In Erich Goode (Ed.), *Social Deviance*. Boston: Allyn and Bacon, pp. 36–40.

Goode, William J. 1976. "Family Disorganization." In Robert K. Merton and Robert Nisbet (Eds.), *Contemporary Social Problems* (4th ed). New York: Harcourt Brace Jovanovich, pp. 511–554.

Goode, William J. 1982. "Why Men Resist." In Barrie Thorne with Marilyn Yalom (Eds.), *Rethinking the Family: Some Feminist Questions*. New York: Longman, pp. 131–150.

Goodman, Emily Jane. 1999. "Seducers, Harassers, and Wimps in Black Robes." *New York Times* (December 19):AR47, 51.

Goodman, Peter S. 1996. "The High Cost of Sneakers." *Austin American-Statesman* (July 7):F1, F6.

Gordon, David M. 1996. *Fat and Mean: The Corporate Squeeze of Working Americans and the Myth of Managerial "Downsizing."* New York: Martin Kessler Books/ The Free Press.

Gordon, Milton M. 1964. *Assimilation in American Life: The Role of Race, Religion, and National Origins.* New York: Oxford University Press.

Gottdiener, Mark. 1985. *The Social Production of Urban Space.* Austin, TX: University of Texas Press.

Gover, Tzivia. 1996a. "Fighting for Our Children." *The Advocate* (November 26):22–30.

Gover, Tzivia. 1996b. "Occupational Hazards." *The Advocate* (November 26):36–38.

Gover, Tzivia. 1996c. "The Other Mothers." *The Advocate* (November 26):31.

Graham, Lawrence Otis. 1995. "It's No Longer the Back of the Bus, but . . . " *New York Times* (May 21):F13.

Grasmuck, Sherri, and Patricia R. Pessar. 1991. *Between Two Islands: Dominican International Migration.* Berkeley, CA: University of California Press.

Gray, Herman. 1995. *Watching Race: Television and the Struggle for "Blackness."* Minneapolis: University of Minnesota Press.

Gray, Paul. 1996. "Gagging the Doctors." *Time* (January 8):50.

Green, Donald E. 1977. *The Politics of Indian Removal: Creek Government and Society in Crisis.* Lincoln, NE: University of Nebraska Press.

Greenberg, Edward S., and Benjamin I. Page. 1993. *The Struggle for Democracy.* New York: HarperCollins.

Greene, Vernon L., and J. I. Ondrich. 1990. "Risk Factors for Nursing Home Admissions and Exits." *Journal of Gerontology,* 45:S250–S258.

Greenhouse, Steven. 1999. "After Seattle, Labor Unions Point to Sustained Fight on Free Trade." *New York Times* (December 6):A1, A26.

Grobe, Jeanine (Ed.). 1995. *Beyond Bedlam: Contemporary Women Psychiatric Survivors Speak Out.* Chicago: Third Side Press.

Gross, Jane. 1994. "Simpson Case Is Galvanizing U.S. about Domestic Abuse." *New York Times* (July 4):1, 9.

Gross, Jane. 1997. "More AIDS Is Seen in People over 50." *New York Times* (March 16):23.

Gross, Leonard. 1983. *How Much Is Too Much: The Effects of Social Drinking.* New York: Random House.

Gup, Ted. 1996. "The Mother Jones 400." *Mother Jones* (March–April):39–59, 74–77.

Hacker, Andrew. 1995. *Two Nations: Black and White, Separate, Hostile, Unequal* (rev. ed.). New York: Ballantine Books.

Haddock, Vicki. 1999. "Study: Kids Are Hooked on Media." *Austin American-Statesman* (November 21):A32.

Hall, Roberta M., with Bernice R. Sandler. 1982. *The Classroom Climate: A Chilly One for Women?* Washington, DC: Association of American Colleges, Project on the Status and Education of Women.

Hall, Roberta M. 1984. *Out of the Classroom: A Chilly Campus Climate for Women.* Washington, DC: Association of American Colleges, Project on the Status and Education of Women.

Hamilton, James T. 1998. *Channeling Violence: The Economic Market for Violent Television Programming.* Princeton, NJ: Princeton University Press.

Hamper, Ben. 1991. *Rivethead: Tales from the Assembly Line.* New York: Warner Books.

Haney, Craig, Curtis Banks, and Philip Zimbardo. 1984. "A Study of Prisoners and Guards in a Simulated Prison." In E. Aronson (Ed.), *Readings about the Social Animal.* New York: W.H. Freeman.

Haney, Walter. 1993. "Testing and Minorities." In Lois Weis and Michelle Fine (Eds.), *Beyond Silenced Voices: Class, Race, and Gender in United States Schools.* Albany, NY: State University of New York Press, pp. 45–73.

Hansell, Saul. 1996. "Identity Crisis: When a Criminal's Got Your Number." *New York Times* (June 16):E1, E5.

Hansell, Saul. 2000. "America Online Agrees to Buy Time Warner for $165 Billion; Media Deal Is Richest Merger." *New York Times* (January 11):A1, C11.

Hardy, Eric S. 1996. "Annual Report on American Industry." *Forbes* (January 1):76–79.

Harlow, C. W. 1991. *Female Victims of Violent Crime.* Washington, DC: U.S. Department of Justice, Bureau of Justice Statistics.

Harper's Magazine. 2000. "The Searchable Soul: Privacy in the Age of Information Technology" (January):57–68.

Harrington Meyer, Madonna. 1990. "Family Status and Poverty among Older Women: The Gendered Distribution of Retirement Income in the United States." *Social Problems,* 37:551–563.

Harrington Meyer, Madonna. 1994. "Gender, Race, and the Distribution of Social Assistance: Medicaid Use among the Frail Elderly." *Gender and Society,* 8(1):8–28.

Hartley, Nina. 1994. "Confessions of a Feminist Porno Star." In Alison M. Jaggar (Ed.), *Living with Contradictions: Controversies in Feminist Social Ethics.* Boulder, CO: Westview, pp. 176–178.

Hartmann, Heidi. 1976. "Capitalism, Patriarchy, and Job Segregation by Sex." *Signs: Journal of Women in Culture and Society,* 1(Spring):137–169.

Hartmann, Heidi. 1981. "The Family as the Locus of Gender, Class, and Political Struggle: The Example of Housework." *Signs,* 6:366–394.

Harvard Medicare Project. 1986. "Special Report: The Future of Medicare." *New England Journal of Medicine,* 314:722–728.

Hauchler, Ingomar, and Paul M. Kennedy (Eds.). 1994. *Global Trends: The World Almanac of Development and Peace.* New York: Continuum.

Hauser, Robert M. 1995. "Symposium: The Bell Curve." *Contemporary Sociology: A Journal of Reviews,* 24(2):149–153.

Havighurst, Robert J., Bernice L. Neugarten, and Sheldon S. Tobin. 1968. "Disengagement and Patterns of Aging." In Bernice L. Neugarten (Ed.), *Middle Age and Aging.* Chicago: University of Chicago Press, pp. 161–172.

Hawken, Paul. 1997. "Resource Waste." *Mother Jones* (March–April):40–53.

Hawley, Amos. 1950. *Human Ecology*. New York: Ronald Press.

Hawley, Amos. 1981. *Urban Society* (2nd ed.). New York: Wiley.

Hays, Constance L. 1995a. "If the Hair Is Gray, Con Artists See Green: The Elderly Are Prime Targets." *New York Times* (May 21):F1, F5.

Hays, Constance L. 1995b. "Increasing Shift Work Challenges Child Care." *New York Times* (June 8):B5.

Heilbrunn, Leslie. 2000. "Mind Control?" *Brill's Content* (January):105–109.

Hendriks, Aart, Rob Tielman, and Evert van der Veen. 1993. *The Third Pink Book: A Global View of Lesbian and Gay Liberation and Oppression*. Buffalo, NY: Prometheus.

Henry, William A., III. 1990. "Beyond the Melting Pot." *Time* (April 9):28–35.

Herbert, Bob. 1995. "Not a Living Wage." *New York Times* (October 9):A11.

Herd, D. 1988. "Drinking by Black and White Women: Results from a National Survey." *Social Problems*, 35(5): 493–520.

Herek, Gregory M. 1995. "Psychological Heterosexism and Anti-Gay Violence: The Social Psychology of Bigotry and Bashing." In Michael S. Kimmel and Michael A. Messner (Eds.), *Men's Lives* (3rd ed.). Boston: Allyn and Bacon, pp. 341–353.

Hernandez, Raymond. 1997. "New York Offers Pollution Permits to Lure Companies." *New York Times* (May 19): A1, B8.

Herrnstein, Richard J., and Charles Murray. 1994. *The Bell Curve: Intelligence and Class Structure in American Life*. New York: Free Press.

Herz, Diane E., and Barbara H. Wootton. 1996. "Women in the Workforce: An Overview." In Cynthia Costello and Barbara Kivimae Krimgold (Eds.) for the Women's Research and Education Institute, *The American Woman 1996–97: Women and Work*. New York: W.W. Norton, pp. 44–78.

Higginbotham, Elizabeth. 1994. "Black Professional Women: Job Ceilings and Employment Sectors." In Maxine Baca Zinn and Bonnie Thornton Dill (Eds.), *Women of Color in U.S. Society*. Philadelphia: Temple University Press, pp. 113–131.

Higley, Stephen Richard. 1995. *Privilege, Power and Place: The Geography of the American Upper Class*. Lanham, MD: Rowman & Littlefield.

Hilden, Patricia Penn. 1995. *When Nickels Were Indians: An Urban, Mixed-Blood Story*. Washington, DC: Smithsonian Institution Press.

Hills, Stuart L. 1971. *Crime, Power, and Morality*. Scranton, PA: Chandler.

Hilsenrath, Jon. 1996. "In China, a Taste of Buy-Me TV." *New York Times* (November 17):F1.

Himmelstein, David U., and Steffie Woolhandler. 1994. *The National Health Program Book: A Source Guide for Advocates*. Monroe, ME: Common Courage.

Hirschi, Travis. 1969. *Causes of Delinquency*. Berkeley, CA: University of California Press.

Hirschi, Travis, and Michael J. Hindelang. 1977. "Intelligence and Delinquency: A Revisionist Review." *American Sociological Review*, 42:571–586.

Hoberman, John. 1997. *Darwin's Athletes: How Sport Has Damaged Black America and Preserved the Myth of Race*. Boston: Houghton Mifflin.

Hochschild, Arlie Russell, with Ann Machung. 1989. *The Second Shift: Working Parents and the Revolution at Home*. New York: Viking/Penguin.

Hodson, Randy, and Teresa A. Sullivan. 1995. *The Social Organization of Work* (2nd ed.). Belmont, CA: Wadsworth.

Hoffman, Andrew J. 1994. "Love Canal Lives." *E Magazine* (November–December):19–22.

Hoffman, Jan. 1997. "Crime and Punishment: Shame Gains Popularity." *New York Times* (January 16):A1, A11.

Holmes, Ronald M. 1983. *The Sex Offender and the Criminal Justice System*. Springfield, IL: Charles C. Thomas.

Holmes, Robert M. 1988. *Serial Murder*. Beverly Hills, CA: Sage.

Holmes, Robert M., and Stephen T. Holmes. 1993. *Murder in America*. Newbury Park, CA: Sage.

Holmes, Steven A. 1996a. "1996 Cost of Teen Pregnancy Is Put at $7 Billion." *New York Times* (June 13):A11.

Holmes, Steven A. 1996b. "Children of Working Poor Are Up Sharply, Study Says." *New York Times* (June 4):C19.

Holmes, Steven A. 1996c. "Education Gap Between Races Closes." *New York Times* (September 6):A8.

Holt, John C. 1964. *How Children Fail*. New York: Dell.

Holusha, John. 1993. "The Painful Lessons of Disruption." *New York Times* (March 17):C1, C5.

Hooker, Evelyn. 1957. "The Adjustment of the Male Overt Homosexual." *Journal of Projective Techniques*, 21:18–31.

Hooker, Evelyn. 1958. "Male Homosexuality and the Rorschach." *Journal of Projective Techniques*, 22:33–54.

Hooyman, Nancy R., and H. Asuman Kiyak. 1996. *Social Gerontology: A Multidisciplinary Perspective*. Boston: Allyn and Bacon.

Hopkins, Evans D. 1997. "Lockdown: Life Inside Is Getting Harder." *The New Yorker* (February 24/March 3):66–71.

Horowitz, Allan V. 1982. *Social Control of Mental Illness*. New York: Academic.

Horton, John. 1995. *The Politics of Diversity: Immigration, Resistance, and Change in Monterey Park, California*. Philadelphia: Temple University Press.

Hostetler, A. J. 1995. "Joe Camel Blamed for Rise in Teen Smoking." *Austin American-Statesman* (July 21):A2.

Hounsell, Cindy. 1996. "Women and Pensions: A Policy Agenda." In Cynthia Costello and Barbara Kivimae Krimgold (Eds.) for the Women's Research and Education Institute, *The American Woman 1996–97: Women and Work*. New York: W.W. Norton, pp. 166–173.

Houseknecht, Sharon, Suzanne Vaughn, and Anne Macke. 1984. "Marital Disruption among Professional Women: The Timing of Career and Family Events." *Social Problems*, 31(1):273–284.

Huddle, Donald. 1993. *The Net National Cost of Immigration*. Washington, DC: Carrying Capacity Network.

Human Suffering Index. 1992. Washington, DC: Population Crisis Committee (now Population Action International).

Huston, Aletha C. 1985. "The Development of Sex Typing: Themes from Recent Research." *Developmental Review*, 5:2–17.

Hutchison, Ray, and Charles Kyle. 1993. "Hispanic Street Gangs in Chicago's Public Schools." In Scott Cummings and Daniel J. Monti (Eds.), *Gangs: The Origins and Impact of Contemporary Youth Gangs in the United States*. Albany, NY: State University of New York Press, pp. 113–136.

Hynes, Samuel. 1997. *The Soldiers' Tale: Bearing Witness to Modern War*. New York: Allen Lane/Penguin.

Ignico, Arlene A., and Barbara J. Mead. 1990. "Children's Perceptions of Gender-Appropriate Physical Activities." *Perceptual and Motor Skills*, 71:1275–1281.

Ihinger-Tallman, Marilyn, and Kay Pasley. 1987. *Remarriage*. Newbury Park, CA: Sage.

Inciardi, James A., Ruth Horowitz, and Anne E. Pottieger. 1993a. *Street Kids, Street Drugs, Street Crime: An Examination of Drug Use and Serious Delinquency in Miami*. Belmont, CA: Wadsworth.

Inciardi, James, Dorothy Lockwood, and Anne E. Pottieger. 1993b. *Women and Crack-Cocaine*. New York: Macmillan.

Jack, Dana Crowley. 1993. *Silencing the Self: Women and Depression*. New York: HarperPerennial.

Jackson, Kenneth T. 1985. *Crabgrass Frontier: The Suburbanization of the United States*. New York: Oxford University Press.

Jacobs, Jane. 1961. *The Death and Life of Great American Cities*. New York: Random House.

Jaffee, David. 1990. *Levels of Socio-economic Development Theory*. Westport, CT: Praeger.

JAMA: The Journal of the American Medical Association. 1996. "Health Care Needs of Gay Men and Lesbians in the United States" (May 1):1354–1360.

James, William H., and Stephen L. Johnson. 1996. *Doin' Drugs: Patterns of African American Addiction*. Austin, TX: University of Texas Press.

Jameson, Sam. 1993. "Sailor on Gay Killing: 'I Would Do It Again.'" *Austin American-Statesman* (May 26):A6.

Jankowski, Martín Sánchez. 1991. *Islands in the Street: Gangs and American Urban Society*. Berkeley, CA: University of California Press.

Janofsky, Michael. 1996. "Home-Grown Courts Spring Up as Judicial Arm of the Far Right." *New York Times* (April 17):A1, A13.

Janofsky, Michael. 1997. "Old Friends, Once Felons, Regroup to Fight Crime." *New York Times* (March 10):A1, A10.

Jarrett, Robin L. 1997. "Living Poor: Family Life among Single Parent, African-American Women." In Diana Kendall (Ed.), *Race, Class, and Gender in a Diverse Society: A Text-Reader*. Boston: Allyn and Bacon, pp. 344–365.

Jayson, Sharon. 1997. "Case of Channel One." *Austin American-Statesman* (January 22):B1, B6.

Jencks, Christopher, Marshall Smith, Henry Acland, Mary J. Bane, David Cohen, Herbert Gintis, Barbara Heyns, and Stephan Michelson. 1972. *Inequality: A Reassessment of the Effect of Family and Schooling in America*. New York: Basic Books.

Jenik, Adriene. 1999. "What Is Paper Tiger Anyway?" Retrieved January 1, 2000. Online: http://www.papertiger.org/whatis.html.

Jensen, Robert. 1999. "Editorial: Corporate Power Is the Central Issue." *Austin American-Statesman* (December 10):A18.

Jeter, Jon. 2000. "AIDS in Africa: A Bitter Harvest." *Austin American-Statesman* (January 2):H1, H6.

Johnson, Bruce D., Paul J. Goldstein, Edward Preble, James Schmeidler, Douglas S. Lipton, Barry Spunt, and Thomas Miller. 1985. *Taking Care of Business: The Economics of Crime by Heroin Abusers*. Lexington, MA: Lexington Books.

Johnston, David, and Janny Scott. 1996. "The Tortured Genius of Theodore Kaczynski." *New York Times* (May 26):1, 15.

Johnston, Lloyd D., Patrick M. O'Malley, and Jerald G. Bachman. 1994. *National Survey Results on Drug Use from the Monitoring the Future Study, 1975–1993*, Vol. 1. Rockville, MD: National Institute on Drug Abuse.

Jolin, Annette. 1994. "On the Backs of Working Prostitutes: Feminist Theory and Prostitution Policy." *Crime and Delinquency*, 40(1):69–83.

Jones, M. Gail, and Jack Wheatley. 1990. "Gender Differences in Teacher-Student Interactions in Science Classrooms." *Journal of Research in Science Teaching*, 27(9): 861–874.

Jung, John. 1994. *Under the Influence: Alcohol and Human Behavior*. Pacific Grove, CA: Brooks/Cole.

Kalb, Claudia. 1999. "No Green Light Yet: A Long-Awaited Report Supports Medical Marijuana Use. So Now What?" *Newsweek* (March 29):35.

Kaldor, Mary. 1981. *The Baroque Arsenal*. New York: Hill and Wang.

Kalish, Richard A. 1985. *Death, Grief, and Caring Relationships* (2nd ed.). Monterey, CA: Brooks/Cole.

Kalish, Richard A., and D. K. Reynolds. 1981. *Death and Ethnicity: A Psychocultural Study*. Farmingdale, NY: Baywood.

Kaminer, Wendy. 1990. *A Fearful Freedom: Women's Flight from Equality*. Reading, MA: Addison-Wesley.

Kane, Hal. 1995. "Leaving Home." *Transaction: Social Science and Modern Society* (May–June):16–25.

Kantrowitz, Barbara. 1993. "Live Wires." *Newsweek* (September 6):42–48.

Kaplan, David A. 1993. "Dumber Than We Thought." *Newsweek* (September 20):44–45.

Kaplan, Robert D. 1996. "Cities of Despair." *New York Times* (June 6):A19.

Karmen, Andrew A. 1995. "Crime Victims." In Joseph F. Sheley (Ed.), *Criminology: A Contemporary Handbook* (2nd ed.). Belmont, CA: Wadsworth, pp. 145–164.

Kasindorf, Jeanie. 1988. "Hustling: Working Girl." *New York Times* (April 18):56.

Katz, Janet, and William J. Chambliss. 1995. In Joseph F. She-ley (Ed.), *Criminology: A Contemporary Handbook* (2nd ed.). Belmont, CA: Wadsworth, pp. 275–303.

Katz, Michael B. 1989. *The Undeserving Poor: From the War on Poverty to the War on Welfare.* New York: Pantheon Books.

Kayal, Philip M. 1993. *Bearing Witness: Gay Men's Health Crisis and the Politics of AIDS.* Boulder, CO: Westview.

Kaysen, Susanna. 1993. *Girl, Interrupted.* New York: Vintage.

Kelso, William A. 1994. *Poverty and the Underclass: Changing Perceptions of the Poor in America.* New York: New York University Press.

Kemp, Alice Abel. 1994. *Women's Work: Degraded and Devalued.* Englewood Cliffs, NJ: Prentice-Hall.

Kempadoo, Kamala, and Jo Doezema (Eds.). 1998. *Global Sex Workers: Rights, Resistance, and Redefinition.* New York: Routledge.

Kempe, C. Henry, F. Silverman, B. Steele, W. Droegemueller, and H. Silver. 1962. "The Battered-Child Syndrome." *Journal of the American Medical Association,* 181:17–24.

Kempe, Ruth S., and C. Henry Kempe. 1978. *Child Abuse.* Cambridge, MA: Harvard University Press.

Kendall, Diana. 2000. *Sociology in Our Times: The Essentials* (2nd ed.). Belmont, CA: Wadsworth.

Kennedy, Paul. 1993. *Preparing for the Twenty-First Century.* New York: Random House.

Kent, Bill. 1999. "In Brief: Four Cumberland County Towns Named as Enterprise Zone." *New York Times* (January 17):A15.

Kessler, Ronald C. 1994. "Lifetime and 12-Month Prevalence of DSM-III-R Psychiatric Disorders in the United States: Results of the National Comorbidity Survey." *JAMA, The Journal of the American Medical Association,* 271 (March 2):654D.

Kessler-Harris, Alice. 1990. *A Woman's Wage: Historical Meanings and Social Consequences.* Lexington, KY: University Press of Kentucky.

Kidron, Michael, and Ronald Segal. 1995. *The State of the World Atlas.* New York: Penguin.

Kiel, Douglas P., David T. Felson, Marian T. Hanna, Jennifer J. Anderson, and Peter W. F. Wilson. 1990. "Caffeine and the Risk of Hip Fracture: The Framington Study." *American Journal of Epidemiology,* 132:675–684.

Kilborn, Peter T. 1993. "Voices of the People: Struggle, Hope and Fear." *New York Times* (November 14):4A1, 4A14.

Kilborn, Peter T. 1996. "With Welfare Overhaul Now Law, States Grapple with the Consequences." *New York Times* (August 23):A1, A10.

Kilbourne, Jean. 1999. *Deadly Persuasion: Why Women and Girls Must Fight the Addictive Power of Advertising.* New York: Free Press.

Kim, Elaine H., and Eui-Young Yu. 1996. *East to America: Korean American Life Stories.* New York: New Press.

Kimmel, Michael S. 1987. "The Contemporary 'Crisis' in Masculinity in Historical Perspective." In Harry Brod (Ed.), *The Making of Masculinities.* Boston: Allen and Unwin, pp. 121–153.

Kimmel, Michael S. (Ed.). 1990. *Men Confront Pornography.* New York: Crown Books.

King, Leslie, and Madonna Harrington Meyer. 1997. "The Politics of Reproductive Benefits: U.S. Insurance Coverage of Contraceptive and Infertility Treatments." *Gender and Society,* 11(1):8–30.

Kipnis, Laura. 1996. *Bound and Gagged: Pornography and the Politics of Fantasy in America.* New York: Grove Press.

Kitano, Harry H. L., and Roger Daniels. 1995. *Asian Americans: Emerging Minorities* (2nd ed.). Englewood Cliffs, NJ: Prentice-Hall.

Kivel, Paul. 1996. *Uprooting Racism: How White People Can Work for Racial Justice.* Philadelphia: New Society Publishers.

Klockars, Carl B. 1979. "The Contemporary Crises of Marxist Criminology." *Criminology,* 16:477–515.

Klonoff, Elizabeth A. 1997. *Preventing Misdiagnosis of Women: A Guide to Physical Disorders That Have Psychiatric Symptoms.* Thousand Oaks, CA: Sage.

Kluger, Richard. 1996. *Ashes to Ashes: America's Hundred-Year Cigarette War, the Public Health and the Unabashed Triumph of Philip Morris.* New York: Alfred A. Knopf.

Knapp, Caroline. 1996. *Drinking: A Love Story.* New York: Dial.

Knox, Paul L., and Peter J. Taylor (Eds.). 1995. *World Cities in a World-System.* Cambridge, England: Cambridge University Press.

Knudsen, Dean D. 1992. *Child Maltreatment: Emerging Perspectives.* Dix Hills, NY: General Hall.

Kolata, Gina. 1995. "New Picture of Who Will Get AIDS Is Crammed with Addicts." *New York Times* (February 28): A16.

Kolata, Gina. 1996a. "Experts Are at Odds on How Best to Tackle Rise in Teen-Agers' Drug Use." *New York Times* (September 18):A17.

Kolata, Gina. 1996b. "New Era of Robust Elderly Belies the Fears of Scientists." *New York Times* (February 27):A1, B10.

Kolata, Gina. 1996c. "On Fringes of Health Care, Untested Therapies Thrive." *New York Times* (June 17):A1, C11.

Kosmin, Barry A., and Seymour P. Lachman. 1993. *One Nation under God: Religion in Contemporary American Society.* New York: Crown Trade Paperbacks.

Kozol, Jonathan. 1986. *Illiterate America.* New York: Plume/Penguin.

Kozol, Jonathan. 1991. *Savage Inequalities: Children in America's Schools.* New York: HarperPerennial.

Kozol, Jonathan. 1995. *Amazing Grace: The Lives of Children and the Conscience of a Nation.* New York: Crown.

Kramer, Peter D. 1993. *Listening to Prozac.* New York: Viking.

Kristof, Nicholas D. 1996a. "Aging World, New Wrinkles." *New York Times* (September 22):E1, E5.

Kristof, Nicholas D. 1996b. "Asian Childhoods Sacrificed to Prosperity's Lust." *New York Times* (April 14):1, 6.

Krohn, Marvin. 1995. "Control and Deterrence Theories of Criminality." In Joseph F. Sheley (Ed.), *Criminology: A Contemporary Handbook* (2nd ed.). Belmont, CA: Wadsworth, pp. 329–347.

Kübler-Ross, Elisabeth. 1969. *On Death and Dying*. New York: Macmillan.

Kurz, Demie. 1989. "Social Science Perspectives on Wife Abuse: Current Debates and Future Directions." *Gender and Society*, 3(4):489–505.

Kurz, Demie. 1995. *For Richer, for Poorer: Mothers Confront Divorce*. New York: Routledge.

Lamanna, Marianne, and Agnes Riedmann. 1994. *Marriages and Families: Making Choices and Facing Change* (5th ed.). Belmont, CA: Wadsworth.

Landers, Peter. 1996. "Women in Japan Covet Flight Positions." *Austin American-Statesman* (April 28):G5.

Langelan, Martha J. 1993. *Back Off! How to Confront and Stop Sexual Harassment and Harassers*. New York: Fireside/Simon & Schuster.

Lantos, T. 1992. "The Silence of the Kids: Children at Risk in the Workplace." *Labor Law Journal*, 43:67–70.

Lappé, Frances Moore, and Paul Martin Du Bois. 1994. *The Quickening of America: Rebuilding Our Nation, Remaking Our Lives*. San Francisco: Jossey-Bass.

Laqueur, W. 1978. *The Terrorism Reader: A Historical Anthology*. New York: New American Library.

Lasswell, Harold D. 1969. "The Structure and Function of Communication in Society." In Wilbur Schramm (Ed.), *Mass Communications*. Urbana, IL: University of Illinois Press, pp. 103–130.

Lauber, Almon W. 1913. *Indian Slavery in Colonial Times within the Present Limits of the United States*. New York: Columbia University Press.

Lauderback, David, and Dan Waldorf. 1993. "Whatever Happened to ICE: The Latest Drug Scare." *Journal of Drug Issues*, 23:597–613.

Lauer, Robert H. 1995. *Social Problems and the Quality of Life* (6th ed.). Madison, WI: Brown.

Lauer, Robert H., and Jeannette C. Lauer. 1991. "The Long-Term Relational Consequences of Problematic Family Backgrounds." *Family Relations*, 40:286–290.

Laurence, Leslie, and Beth Weinhouse. 1994. *Outrageous Practices: The Alarming Truth About How Medicine Mistreats Women*. New York: Fawcett Columbine.

Lawrence, Mike. 1996. "Prisoners of Another Reality." *The Mission*, 23 (Spring). San Antonio, TX: The University of Texas Health Science Center at San Antonio.

Lazare, Daniel. 1991. "Urbacide!" *The Village Voice* (December 10). Reprinted in Charles P. Cozic (Ed.), *America's Cities: Opposing Viewpoints*. San Diego: Greenhaven Press, 1993, pp. 17–24.

Lazare, Daniel. 1999. "Your Constitution Is Killing You (Right to Bear Arms)." *Harper's Magazine* (October):57.

Leaper, Campbell. 1994. *Childhood Gender Segregation: Causes and Consequences*. San Francisco: Jossey-Bass.

Leary, Warren E. 1996. "Even When Covered by Insurance, Black and Poor People Receive Less Health Care." *New York Times* (September 12):A10.

Lee, D. J., and Kyriakos S. Markides. 1990. "Activity and Mortality among Aged Persons over an Eight Year Period." *Journal of Gerontology*, 45:S39–S42.

Lee, Felicia R. 1996. "Infertile Couples Forge Ties within Society of Their Own." *New York Times* (January 9):A1, A7.

Lefrançois, Guy R. 1999. *The Lifespan* (6th ed.). Belmont, CA: Wadsworth.

Lehmann, Jennifer M. 1994. *Durkheim and Women*. Lincoln, NE: University of Nebraska Press.

Lehne, Gregory K. 1995. "Homophobia among Men: Supporting and Defining the Male Role." In Michael S. Kimmel and Michael A. Messner (Eds.), *Men's Lives* (3rd ed.). Boston: Allyn and Bacon, pp. 325–336.

Leinen, Stephen. 1993. *Gay Cops*. New Brunswick, NJ: Rutgers University Press.

Leland, John. 1995. "Bisexuality." *Newsweek* (July 17):44–50.

Lemert, Edwin. 1951. *Social Pathology*. New York: McGraw-Hill.

Leong, Russell (Ed.). 1996. *Asian American Sexualities: Dimensions of the Gay and Lesbian Experience*. New York: Routledge.

Leong, Wai-Teng. 1991. "The Pornography 'Problem': Disciplining Women and Young Girls." *Media, Culture, and Society*, 13:91–117.

Lerman, Hannah. 1996. *Pigeonholing Women's Misery: A History and Critical Analysis of the Psychodiagnosis of Women in the Twentieth Century*. New York: Basic Books.

Lester, David. 1992. *Why People Kill Themselves: A 1990s Summary of Research Findings of Suicidal Behavior* (3rd ed.). Springfield, IL: Thomas.

LeVay, Simon, and Dean H. Hamer. 1994. "Evidence for a Biological Influence in Male Homosexuality." *Scientific American* (May):45–49.

Lever, Janet. 1978. "Sex Differences in the Complexity of Children's Play and Games." *American Sociological Review*, 43:471–483.

Levin, Jack, and Jack McDevitt. 1993. *Hate Crimes: The Rising Tide of Bigotry and Bloodshed*. New York: Plenum.

Levin, William C. 1988. "Age Stereotyping: College Student Evaluations." *Research on Aging*, 10(1):134–148.

Levine, Peter. 1992. *Ellis Island to Ebbets Field: Sport and the American Jewish Experience*. New York: Oxford University Press.

Levinthal, Charles F. 1996. *Drugs, Behavior, and Modern Society*. Boston: Allyn and Bacon.

Lewin, Tamar. 1995. "The Decay of Families Is Global, Study Says." *New York Times* (May 30):A5.

Lewis, Neil A. 1995. "Administration Won't Join Attack on Gay Rights Ban." *New York Times* (June 9):A11.

Lewis, Oscar. 1966. *La Vida: A Puerto Rican Family in the Culture of Poverty—San Juan and New York*. New York: Random House.

Liebow, Elliot. 1993. *Tell Them Who I Am: The Lives of Homeless Women*. New York: Free Press.

Lifton, Robert Jay. 1997. "Doubling: The Faustian Bargain." In Jennifer Turpin and Lester R. Kurtz (Eds.), *The Web of Violence: From Interpersonal to Global*. Urbana and Chicago: University of Illinois, pp. 31–44.

Lindblom, Charles. 1977. *Politics and Markets*. New York: Basic Books.

Lindsey, Linda L. 1994. *Gender Roles: A Sociological Perspective* (2nd ed.). Englewood Cliffs, NJ: Prentice-Hall.

Link, Bruce G., and Bruce P. Dohrenwend. 1989. "The Epidemiology of Mental Disorders." In Howard E. Freeman and Sol Levine (Eds.), *Handbook of Medical Sociology* (4th ed.). Englewood Cliffs, NJ: Prentice-Hall, pp. 102–127.

Lips, Hilary M. 1993. *Sex and Gender: An Introduction* (2nd ed.). Mountain View, CA: Mayfield.

Loeb, Paul Rogat. 1994. *Generation at the Crossroads: Apathy and Action on the American Campus*. New Brunswick, NJ: Rutgers University Press.

London, Kathryn A. 1991. "Advance Data Number 194: Cohabitation, Marriage, Marital Dissolution, and Remarriage: United States 1988." U.S. Department of Health and Human Services. Vital and Health Statistics of the National Center, January 4.

London, Kathryn A., and Barbara Foley Wilson. 1988. "Divorce." *American Demographics*, 10(10):23–26.

Lorber, Judith. 1994. *Paradoxes of Gender*. New Haven, CT: Yale University Press.

Lorenz, Konrad. 1966. *On Aggression*. New York: Bantam.

Los Angeles Times. 1988. "If Only the Spirit of Giving Could Continue" (December 25).

Lottes, Ilsa. 1993. "Reactions to Pornography on a College Campus: For or Against?" *Sex Roles: A Journal of Research*, 29(1–2):69–90.

Loury, Glenn C. 1997. "Integration Has Had Its Day." *New York Times* (April 23):A21.

Luckenbill, David F. 1977. "Criminal Homicide as a Situated Transaction." *Social Problems*, 25:176–186.

Luker, Kristin. 1996. *Dubious Conceptions: The Politics of Teenage Pregnancy*. Cambridge, MA: Harvard University Press.

Lundy, Katherine Coleman. 1995. *Sidewalk Talk: A Naturalistic Study of Street Kids*. New York: Garland Publishing.

Maas, Peter. 1996. *Love Thy Neighbor: A Story of War*. New York: Vintage.

Maccoby, Eleanor E., and Carol Nagy Jacklin. 1987. "Gender Segregation in Childhood." *Advances in Child Development and Behavior*, 20:239–287.

MacCorquodale, Patricia, and Gary Jensen. 1993. "Women in the Law: Partners or Tokens?" *Gender and Society*, 7(4): 582–593.

MacDonald, Kevin, and Ross D. Parke. 1986. "Parental-Child Physical Play: The Effects of Sex and Age of Children and Parents." *Sex Roles*, 15:367–378.

Macdonald, Scott. 1995. "The Role of Drugs in Workplace Injuries: Is Drug Testing Appropriate?" *Journal of Drug Issues*, 25(4):703–723.

MacFarquhar, Neil. 1996. "The Internet Goes to School, and Educators Debate." *New York Times* (March 7):C3.

MacKinnon, Catharine. 1987. *Feminism Unmodified: Discourses on Life and Law*. Cambridge, MA: Harvard University Press.

MacLeod, Jay. 1995. *Ain't No Makin' It: Aspirations and Attainment in a Low-Income Neighborhood*. Boulder, CO: Westview Press.

Macy, Marianne. 1996. *Working Sex: An Odyssey into Our Cultural Underworld*. New York: Carroll & Graf.

MADD. 1999. "Rating the States 2000 Report Card." Mothers Against Drunk Driving and the GuideOne Foundation. Retrieved December 4, 1999. Online: http:www.madd.org.

Madden, Patricia A., and Joel W. Grube. 1994. "The Frequency and Nature of Alcohol and Tobacco Advertising in Televised Sports, 1990 through 1992." *The American Journal of Public Health*, 84(2):297–300.

Males, Mike. 1994. "Bashing Youth: Media Myths about Teenagers." *Extra!* (March/April). Retrieved November 11, 1999. Online: http://www.fair.org/extra/9403/bashing-youth.html.

Malinowski, Bronislaw. 1964. "The Principle of Legitimacy: Parenthood, the Basis of Social Structure." In Rose Laub Coser (Ed.), *The Family: Its Structure and Functions*. New York: St Martin's Press.

Malthus, Thomas R. 1965. *An Essay on Population*. New York: Augustus Kelley, Bookseller (orig. published in 1798).

Mam, Teeda Butt. 1997. *Children of Cambodia's Killing Fields*. New Haven, CT: Yale University Press.

Mandel, Ruth B. 1981. *In the Running: The New Woman Candidate*. New Haven, CT: Ticknor & Fields.

Mann, Coramae Richey. 1993. *Unequal Justice: A Question of Color*. Bloomington, IN: Indiana University Press.

Mann, Patricia S. 1994. *Micro-Politics: Agency in a Post-Feminist Era*. Minneapolis: University of Minnesota Press.

Marable, Manning. 1995. *Beyond Black and White: Transforming African-American Politics*. New York: Verso.

Marcus, Eric. 1992. *Making History: The Struggle for Gay and Lesbian Equal Rights*. New York: HarperCollins.

Marger, Martin N. 1994. *Race and Ethnic Relations: American and Global Perspectives*. Belmont, CA: Wadsworth.

Marine, William M., and Tracy Jack. 1994. "Analysis of Toxology Reports from the 1992 Census of Fatal Occupational Injuries." *Compensation and Working Conditions*, 46(10):1–7.

Marquart, James W., Sheldon Ekland-Olson, and Jonathan R. Sorensen. 1994. *The Rope, the Chair, and the Needle*. Austin, TX: University of Texas Press.

Marshall, Gordon. 1998. *A Dictionary of Sociology* (2nd ed.). New York: Oxford University Press.

Marshall, Victor W. 1980. *Last Chapters: A Sociology of Aging and Dying*. Monterey, CA: Brooks/Cole.

Marshall, Victor W., and Judith Levy. 1990. "Aging and Dying." In Robert H. Binstock and Linda George (Eds.), *Handbook of Aging and the Social Sciences* (3rd ed). New York: Academic Press.

Martin, Carol L. 1989. "Children's Use of Gender-Related Information in Making Social Judgments." *Developmental Psychology*, 25:80–88.

Martin, Laura. 1992. *A Life without Fear*. Nashville, TN: Rutledge Hill Press.

Martin, Teresa Castro, and Larry L. Bumpass. 1989. "Recent Trends in Marital Disruption." *Demography*, 26:37–51.

Marx, Karl, and Friedrich Engels. 1971. "The Communist Manifesto." [orig. published in 1847]. In Dirk Struik (Ed.), *The Birth of the Communist Manifesto*. New York: International.

Marx, Karl, and Friedrich Engels. 1976. *The Communist Manifesto*. New York: Pantheon (orig. published in 1848).

Massey, Douglas S., and Nancy A. Denton. 1992. *American Apartheid: Segregation and the Making of the Underclass*. Cambridge, MA: Harvard University Press.

Massey, James L., and Marvin D. Krohn. 1986. "A Longitudinal Examination of an Integrated Social Process Model of Deviant Behavior." *Social Forces*, 65:106–134.

Mastrofski, Stephen D. 1995. "The Police." In Joseph F. Sheley (Ed.), *Criminology: A Contemporary Handbook* (2nd ed.). Belmont, CA: Wadsworth, pp. 373–405.

Mathews, Jay. 1992. "Rethinking Homeless Myths." *Newsweek* (April 6):29.

Mathis, Nancy. 1996. "Clinton Urges Student Uniforms." *Houston Chronicle* (February 25):6A.

Matthewsplace.com. 1999. "Dennis Shepard's Statement to the Court" (November 4). Retrieved November 15, 1999. Online: http://www.matthewsplace.com/dennis2.htm.

Maxwell, Milton A. 1981. "Alcoholics Anonymous." In Martin S. Weinberg, Earl Rubington, and Sue Kiefer Hammersmith (Eds.), *The Solution of Social Problems: Five Perspectives* (2nd ed.). New York: Oxford University Press, pp. 152–156.

Mayall, Alice, and Diana E. H. Russell. 1993. "Racism in Pornography." In Diana E. H. Russell (Ed.), *Making Violence Sexy: Feminist Views on Pornography*. New York: Teachers College Press, pp. 167–177.

Maynard, Joyce. 1994. "To Tell the Truth." In Jay David (Ed.), *The Family Secret: An Anthology*. New York: William Morrow, pp. 79–85.

McCaffrey, Barry R. 1997. "We're on a Perilous Path." *Newsweek* (February 3):27.

McCall, Nathan. 1994. *Makes Me Wanna Holler: A Young Black Man in America*. New York: Random House.

McChesney, Robert W. 1999. *Rich Media, Poor Democracy: Communication Politics in Dubious Times*. Urbana, IL: University of Illinois Press.

McDonnell, Janet A. 1991. *The Dispossession of the American Indian, 1887–1934*. Bloomington, IN: Indiana University Press.

McElvogue, Louise. 1997. "Making a Killing Out of Nature." *Television Business International* (November):52.

McFadden, Robert D. 1996. "From a Child of Promise to the Unabomb Suspect." *New York Times* (May 26):1, 12–15.

McIntosh, Peggy. 1995. "White Privilege and Male Privilege: A Personal Account of Coming to See Correspondences through Work in Women's Studies." In Margaret A. Andersen and Patricia Hill Collins (Eds.), *Race, Class, and Gender: An Anthology*. Belmont, CA: Wadsworth, pp. 76–87.

McKinlay, John B. 1994. "A Case for Refocusing Upstream: The Political Economy of Illness." In Peter Conrad and Rochelle Kern (Eds.), *The Sociology of Health and Illness*. New York: St. Martin's, pp. 509–530.

McLanahan, Sara, and Gary D. Sandefur. 1994. *Growing Up with a Single Parent: What Hurts, What Helps*. Cambridge, MA: Harvard University Press.

McLarin, Kimberly J. 1994. "A New Jersey Town Is Troubled by Racial Imbalance between Classrooms: Would End to Tracking Harm Quality?" *New York Times* (August 11):A12.

McLean, Mora. 1999. "The 'Africa Story' in American News." *Foreign Policy* (Fall):6.

McNamara, Robert P. 1994. *The Times Square Hustler: Male Prostitution in New York City*. Westport, CT: Praeger.

McWilliams, Carey. 1968. *North from Mexico: The Spanish-Speaking People of the United States*. Westport, CT: Greenwood (orig. published in 1948).

McWilliams, Peter. 1996. *Ain't Nobody's Business If You Do: The Absurdity of Consensual Crimes in Our Free Country*. Los Angeles: Prelude Press.

Mead, Margaret. 1966. "Marriage in Two Steps." *Redbook*, 127:48–49, 85–86.

Mead, Rebecca. 1994. "Playing It Straight: In and out of the Closet." *New York* (June 20):40–46.

Mechanic, David, and David A. Rochefort. 1990. "Deinstitutionalization: An Appraisal of Reform." *Annual Review of Sociology*, 16:301–350.

Meckler, Laura. 1999. "Study: Under Welfare Reform, Some of the Poor Get Poorer." *Austin American-Statesman* (August 22):A11.

Meers, Erik Ashok. 1996. "Murder, He Wrote." *The Advocate* (March 5):49–52.

Meisler, Andy. 1995. "The World According to Channel One." *New York Times* (January 8):4A.

Melendez, Edgardo. 1993. "Colonialism, Citizenship, and Contemporary Statehood." In Edwin Melendez and Edgardo Melendez (Eds.), *Colonial Dilemma: Critical Perspectives on Contemporary Puerto Rico*. Boston: South End Press, pp. 41–52.

Menchaca, Martha. 1995. *The Mexican Outsiders: A Community History of Marginalization and Discrimination in California*. Austin, TX: University of Texas Press.

Mendoza, Manuel. 1995. "Minority Actors Scarce on TV." *Austin American-Statesman* (June 12):B12.

Merchant, Carolyn. 1983. *The Death of Nature: Women, Ecology, and the Scientific Revolution*. San Francisco: Harper and Row.

Merchant, Carolyn. 1992. *Radical Ecology: The Search for a Livable World*. New York: Routledge.

Mercy, James A., and Linda E. Saltzman. 1989. "Fatal Violence among Spouses in the United States, 1976–1985." *The American Journal of Public Health*, 79:595–599.

Meredith, Robyn. 1997. "Motown Enters the Zone." *New York Times* (April 11):C1.

Merton, Robert. 1938. "Social Structure and Anomie." *American Sociological Review*, 3(6):672–682.

Merton, Robert King. 1968. *Social Theory and Social Structure* (enlarged ed.). New York: Free Press.

Messer, Ellen, and Kathryn E. May. 1994. *Back Rooms: Voices from the Illegal Abortion Era*. Buffalo, NY: Prometheus.

Michael, Robert T., John H. Gagnon, Edward O. Laumann, and Gina Kolata. 1994. *Sex in America: A Definitive Survey*. New York: Warner Books.

Michigan Department of Education. 1990. *The Influence of Gender Role Socialization on Student Perceptions.* Lansing, MI: Michigan Department of Education, Office of Sex Equity in Education.

Mickelson, Roslyn Arlin, and Stephen Samuel Smith. 1995. "Education and the Struggle Against Race, Class, and Gender Inequality." In Margaret L. Andersen and Patricia Hill Collins (Eds.), *Race, Class, and Gender* (2nd ed.). Belmont, CA: Wadsworth, pp. 289–304.

Mies, Maria, and Vandana Shiva. 1993. *Ecofeminism.* Atlantic Highlands, NJ: Zed Books.

Milgram, Stanley. 1974. *Obedience to Authority.* New York: Harper & Row.

Milkman, Harvey, and Stanley Sunderwirth. 1987. *Craving for Ecstasy: The Consciousness and Chemistry of Escape.* Lexington, MA: Heath.

Miller, Casey, and Kate Swift. 1991. *Words and Women: New Language in New Times* (updated). New York: Harper-Collins.

Miller, Eleanor M. 1986. *Street Woman.* Philadelphia: Temple University Press.

Miller, Michael W. 1994. "Quality Stuff: Firm Is Peddling Cocaine, and Deals Are Legit." *Wall Street Journal* (October 17):A1, A14.

Miller, Patricia G. 1993. *The Worst of Times.* New York: HarperCollins.

Mills, C. Wright. 1959a. *The Power Elite.* Fair Lawn, NJ: Oxford University Press.

Mills, C. Wright. 1959b. *The Sociological Imagination.* London: Oxford University Press.

Mills, C. Wright. 1976. *The Causes of World War Three.* Westport, CT: Greenwood Press.

Minow, Newton N., and Craig L. LaMay. 1999. "Changing the Way We Think." In Robert M. Baird, William E. Loges, and Stuart E. Rosenbaum (Eds.), *The Media and Morality.* Amherst, NY: Promethus Books, pp. 309–330.

Mintz, Beth, and Michael Schwartz. 1985. *The Power Structure of American Business.* Chicago: University of Chicago Press.

Mirowsky, John. 1996. "Age and the Gender Gap in Depression." *Journal of Health and Social Behavior,* 37 (December):362–380.

Mirowsky, John, and Catherine E. Ross. 1980. "Minority Status, Ethnic Culture, and Distress: A Comparison of Blacks, Whites, Mexicans, and Mexican Americans." *American Journal of Sociology,* 86:479–495.

Mohawk, John. 1992. "Looking for Columbus: Thoughts on the Past, Present, and Future of Humanity." In M. Annette Jaimes (Ed.), *The State of Native America: Genocide, Colonization, and Resistance.* Boston: South End Press, pp. 439–444.

Monahan, John. 1992. "Mental Disorder and Violent Behavior: Perceptions and Evidence." *American Psychologist,* 47: 511–521.

Montavalli, Jim. 1997. "The Producer Pays." *E Magazine* (May–April):36–41.

Moonan, W. L. 1989. "At Home on Fifth." *Town and Country Magazine* (September):199–207.

Moore, Joan W. (with Harry Pachon). 1976. *Mexican Americans* (2nd ed.). Englewood Cliffs, NJ: Prentice-Hall.

Moore, Stephen, and Dean Stansel. 1992. "The Myth of America's Under-Funded Cities." *Cato Policy Analysis* (December). (Reprinted in Charles P. Cozic (Ed.), *America's Cities: Opposing Viewpoints.* San Diego: Greenhaven Press, 1993, pp. 25–32.)

Morales, Ed. 1996. "The Last Blackface." *Si Magazine* (Summer 1996):44–47, 85.

Morgan, S. Philip, Diane N. Lye, and Gretchen A. Condran. 1988. "Sons, Daughters, and the Risk of Marital Disruption." *American Journal of Sociology,* 94(1):110–129.

Morris, Betsy. 1997. "Is Your Family Wrecking Your Career (and Vice Versa)?" *Fortune* (March 17):71–90.

Mosher, Steven W. 1994. *A Mother's Ordeal: One Woman's Fight against China's One-Child Policy.* New York: Harper Perennial.

Mowbray, Carol T., Sandra E. Herman, and Kelly L. Hazel. 1992. "Gender and Serious Mental Illness." *Psychology of Women Quarterly,* 16(March):107–127.

Murphy-Milano, Susan. 1996. *Defending Our Lives: Getting Away from Domestic Violence and Staying Safe.* New York: Anchor.

Muto, Sheila. 1995. "Student Uniforms Pay Off, One School District Says." *New York Times* (September 20):B6.

Mydans, Seth. 1997. "Brutal End for an Architect of Cambodian Brutality." *New York Times* (June 14):5.

Myers, Daniel J., and Kimberly B. Dugan. 1996. "Sexism in Graduate School Classrooms: Consequences for Students and Faculty." *Gender and Society,* 10(3):330–350.

Myers, Steven Lee. 1997. "Converting the Dollar into a Bludgeon." *New York Times* (April 20):E5.

Myerson, Allen R. 1996. "A Double Standard in Health Coverage." *New York Times* (March 17):F1, F13.

Nagourney, Adam. 1996. "Affirmed by the Supreme Court." *New York Times* (May 26):E4.

Nath, Pamela S., John G. Borkowski, Thomas L. Whitman, and Cynthia J. Schellenbach. 1991. "Understanding Adolescent Parenting: The Dimensions and Functions of Social Support." *Family Relations,* 40:411–420.

National Council on Crime and Delinquency. 1969. *The Infiltration into Legitimate Business by Organized Crime.* Washington, DC: National Council on Crime and Delinquency

National Television Violence Study. 1998. "Executive Summary," *National Television Violence Study,* vol. 3. Retrieved October 31, 1999. Online: http://www.ccsp.ucsb.edu/execsum.pdf.

National Victim Center. 1992. *Rape in America: A Report to the Nation.* Arlington, VA/Charleston, SC: National Victim Center.

National Victims Resource Center. 1991. *Juvenile Prostitution: Fact Sheet.* Rockville, MD: Victims Resource Center.

Nava, Michael, and Robert Dawidoff. 1994. *Created Equal: Why Gay Rights Matter to America.* New York: St. Martin's Press.

Navarrette, Ruben, Jr. 1997. "A Darker Shade of Crimson." In Diana Kendall (Ed.), *Race, Class, and Gender in a*

Diverse Society. Boston: Allyn and Bacon, pp. 274–279. (Reprinted from Ruben Navarette, Jr., *A Darker Shade of Crimson*. New York: Bantam, 1993.)

Navarro, Mireya. 1996. "Marijuana Farms Are Flourishing Indoors, Producing a More Potent Drug." *New York Times* (November 24):13.

NBC.com/Will&Grace. 1999. "Will & Grace." Retrieved November 25, 1999. Online: http://www.nbc.com/will&grace.

Nechas, Eileen, and Denise Foley. 1994. *Unequal Treatment: What You Don't Know about How Women Are Mistreated by the Medical Community*. New York: Simon & Schuster.

Neckerman, Kathryn M., and Joleen Kirschenman. 1991. "Hiring Strategies, Racial Bias, and Inner-City Workers." In Diana Kendall (Ed.), *Race, Class, and Gender in a Diverse Society*. Boston: Allyn and Bacon, pp. 388–404.

Neergaard, Lauran. 1996. "FDA Prepares to Regulate Medical Info on the Internet." *Austin American-Statesman* (October 20):A7.

Neuman, Elena. 1992. "Cancer: The Issue Feminists Forgot." *Insight* (February 24):7–11, 32–43.

New York Times. 1993. "Despite 6-Year U.S. Campaign, Pornography Industry Thrives" (July 4):10.

New York Times. 1994a. "Car Bomb Kills 3 in Beirut; Arabs Accuse Israel" (December 22):A5.

New York Times. 1994b. "Educating Elderly on AIDS" (August 9):A8.

New York Times. 1994c. "Jordan Dooms 11 Militants" (December 22):A5.

New York Times. 1995. "Malnutrition Hits Many Elderly" (July 3):A7.

New York Times. 1996a. "Aging World, New Wrinkles" (September 22):E1.

New York Times. 1996b. "The Megacity Summit" (April 8):A14.

New York Times. 1996c. "Where the Drugs Come From" (March 2):5.

New York Times. 1997a. [Advertisement] "On the Importance of Diversity in University Admissions" (April 24):A17.

New York Times. 1997b. "A New Study of Day Care Shows Benefit of Attention" (April 5):A10.

New York Times. 1997c. "Public's Assessment of Presidents and Problems" (January 20):A10.

New York Times. 1997d. "Sugar's Sweet Deal" (April 27):E14.

New York Times. 1997e. "The Militia Threat" (June 14):18.

New York Times. 1999a. "Editorial: The Collapse in Seattle" (December 6):A28.

New York Times. 1999b. "What's the Problem?" (August 1):WK4.

Newsweek. 1999a. "An Editorial: Guns in America: What Must Be Done" (August 23):23–25.

Newsweek. 1999b. "The Gun War Comes Home" (August 23):26–32.

Nicklin, Julie L. 1996. "Elementary Partnership." *Chronicle of Higher Education* (July 5):A13.

Niebuhr, Gustav. 1996. "Bishop Who Ordained Gay Deacon Is Accused of Heresy." *New York Times* (Februrary 28):A8.

Nieves, Evelyn. 1995. "Wanted in Levittown: One Little Box, with Ticky Tacky Intact." *New York Times* (November 3):A12.

Noble, Kenneth B. 1995. "U.S. Studies Wave of Violence in Nevada." *New York Times* (December 22):A10.

Norman, Michael. 1993. "One Cop, Eight Square Blocks." *New York Times Magazine* (December 12):62–90, 96.

Oakes, Jeannie. 1985. *Keeping Track: How Schools Structure Inequality*. New Haven, CT: Yale University Press.

O'Connell, Helen. 1994. *Women and the Family*. Prepared for the UN-NGO Group on Women and Development. Atlantic Highlands, NJ: Zed Books.

O'Connor, Mike. 1996. "Muslim Widows in Bosnia Try to Rebuild Lives without Men." *New York Times* (July 13):A4.

O'Hare, William P., and Margaret Usdansky. 1992. "What the 1990 Census Tells Us about Segregation in 25 Large Metros." *Population Today*, 20(9). Washington, DC: Population Reference Bureau.

O'Leary, Devin D. 1998. "Will & Grace." *Weekly Alibi* (November 16). Retrieved November 25, 1999. Online: http://www.weeklywire.com/filmvault/alibi/w/willgrace1.html.

Oliver, Melvin L., and Thomas M. Shapiro. 1995. *Black Wealth/White Wealth: A New Perspective on Racial Inequality*. New York: Routledge.

Olzak, Susan, Suzanne Shanahan, and Elizabeth H. McEneaney. 1996. "Poverty, Segregation, and Race Riots: 1960 to 1993." *American Sociological Review*, 61(August):590–613.

Omi, Michael, and Howard Winant. 1994. *Racial Formation in the United States: From the 1960s to the 1990s* (2nd ed.). New York: Routledge.

Orenstein, Peggy (in association with the American Association of University Women). 1994. *School Girls: Young Women, Self-Esteem, and the Confidence Gap*. New York: Anchor/Doubleday.

Orenstein, Peggy. 1996. "For Too Many Schoolgirls, Sexual Harassment Is Real." *Austin American-Statesman* (October 4):A15.

Ortner, Sherry B. 1974. "Is Female to Male as Nature Is to Culture?" In Michelle Rosaldo and Louise Lamphere (Eds.), *Women, Culture, and Society*. Stanford, CA: Stanford University Press.

Orum, Anthony M. 1995. *City-Building in America*. Boulder, CO: Westview.

Otis, Leah. 1985. *Prostitution in Medieval Society*. Chicago: University of Chicago Press.

Oxendine, Joseph B. 1995. *American Indian Sports Heritage*. Lincoln, NE: University of Nebraska Press (orig. published in 1988).

Padilla, Felix M. 1993. *The Gang as an American Enterprise*. New Brunswick, NJ: Rutgers University Press.

Palen, J. John. 1995. *The Suburbs*. New York: McGraw-Hill.

Palen, J. John, and Bruce London. 1984. *Gentrification, Displacement, and Neighborhood Revitalization*. Albany, NY: State University of New York Press.

Parenti, Michael. 1988. *Democracy for the Few* (5th ed.). New York: St. Martin's Press.

Parenti, Michael. 1998. *America Besieged*. San Francisco: City Lights Books.

Parker, Keith D., Greg Weaver, and Thomas Calhoun. 1995. "Predictors of Alcohol and Drug Use: A Multi-ethnic Comparison." *Journal of Social Psychology,* 135(5):581–591.

Parker, Robert Nash. 1989. "Poverty, Subculture of Violence, and Type of Homicide." *Social Forces,* 67:983–1007.

Parker, Robert Nash. 1995. "Violent Crime." In Joseph F. Sheley (Ed.), *Criminology: A Contemporary Handbook* (2nd ed.). Belmont, CA: Wadsworth, pp. 169–185.

Parry, A. 1976. *Terrorism: From Robespierre to Arafat*. New York: Vanguard Press.

Parsons, Talcott. 1951. *The Social System*. New York: Free Press.

Parsons, Talcott. 1955. "The American Family: Its Relations to Personality and to the Social Structure." In Talcott Parsons and Robert F. Bales (Eds.), *Family, Socialization, and Interaction Process*. Glencoe, IL: Free Press, pp. 3–33.

Pateman, Carole. 1994. "What's Wrong with Prostitution?" In Alison M. Jaggar (Ed.), *Living with Contradictions: Controversies in Feminist Social Ethics*. Boulder, CO: Westview, pp. 127–132.

Paton, Dean. 1999. "War of Words: Virtual Media versus Mainstream Press." *Christian Science Monitor* (December 3). Retrieved December 3, 1999. Online: http://www.cs monitor.com/durable/1999/12/03/fp3s1-csm.shtml.

Patterson, Charlotte J. 1992. "Children of Lesbian and Gay Parents." *Child Development,* 63:1025–1042.

Patterson, James, and Peter Kim. 1991. *The Day America Told the Truth*. Englewood Cliffs, NJ: Prentice-Hall.

Patterson, Martha Priddy. 1996. "Women's Employment Patterns, Pension Coverage, and Retirement Planning." In Cynthia Costello and Barbara Kivimae Krimgold (Eds.) for the Women's Research and Education Institute, *The American Woman 1996–97: Women and Work*. New York: W.W. Norton, pp. 148–165.

Pear, Robert, 1994. "Health Advisers See Peril in Plan to Cut Medicare." *New York Times* (August 31):A1, A10.

Pear, Robert. 1996. "Health Costs Pose Problems for Millions, a Study Finds." *New York Times* (October 23):A14.

Pear, Robert. 1997a. "Academy's Report Says Immigration Benefits the U.S." *New York Times* (May 18):1, 15.

Pear, Robert. 1997b. "H.M.O.'s Limiting Medicare Appeals, U.S. Inquiry Finds." *New York Times* (March 18):A1, A11.

Pearce, Diana M. 1978. *The Feminization of Poverty: Women, Work, and Welfare*. Chicago: University of Illinois Press.

Pedersen-Pietersen, Laura. 1997. "You're Sober at Last. Now Prove It to the Boss." *New York Times* (January 12):F10.

Perdue, William Dan. 1993. *Systemic Crisis: Problems in Society, Politics, and World Order*. Fort Worth, TX: Harcourt Brace Jovanovich.

Perrucci, Robert, and Earl Wysong. 1999. *The New Class Society*. Lanham, MD: Rowman & Littlefield.

Perry, David C., and Alfred J. Watkins (Eds.). 1977. *The Rise of the Sunbelt Cities*. Beverly Hills, CA: Sage.

Perry-Jenkins, Maureen, and Ann C. Crouter. 1990. "Men's Provider Role Attitudes: Implications for Household Work and Marital Satisfaction." *Journal of Family Issues,* 11:136–156.

Petersen, John L. 1994. *The Road to 2015: Profiles of the Future*. Corte Madera, CA: Waite Group Press.

Peterson, V. Spike, and Anne Sisson Runyan. 1993. *Global Gender Issues*. Boulder, CO: Westview Press.

Petras, James F. 1983. *Capitalist and Socialist Crises in the Late Twentieth Century*. Totowa, NJ: Rowman and Allenheld.

Pettigrew, Thomas. 1981. "The Mental Health Impact." In Benjamin Bowser and Raymond G. Hunt (Eds.), *Impacts of Racism on White Americans*. Beverly Hills, CA: Sage, p. 117.

Phillips, Kevin. 1995. *Arrogant Capital: Washington, Wall Street, and the Frustration of American Politics*. Boston: Little, Brown.

Phillips, Peter. 1999. *Censored 1999: The News That Didn't Make the News*. New York: Seven Stories Press.

Pierce, Jennifer L. 1995. *Gender Trials: Emotional Lives in Contemporary Law Firms*. Berkeley, CA: University of California Press.

Pizzo, Steve, M. Fricker, and P. Muolo. 1991. *Insider Job: The Looting of America's Savings and Loans*. New York: HarperPerennial.

Polakow, Valerie. 1993. *Lives on the Edge: Single Mothers and Their Children in the Other America*. Chicago: University of Chicago Press.

Pollack, Andrew. 1996a. "Barbie's Journey in Japan." *New York Times* (December 22):E3.

Pollack, Andrew. 1996b. "Square Pegs Stay Home from Japan's Schools." *New York Times* (September 15):A4.

Poniewozik, James. 1999. "The Vast Whiteland." *Time* (June 26). Retrieved November 11, 1999. Online: http://www.time.com.

Ponse, Barbara. 1978. *Identities in the Lesbian World: The Social Construction of Self*. Westport, CT: Greenwood Press.

Popenoe, David. 1988. *Disturbing the Nest: Family Change and Decline in Modern Societies*. New York: Aldine de Gruyter.

Popenoe, David. 1995. "The American Family Crisis." *National Forum: The Phi Kappa Phi Journal,* 73(Summer 1995):15–19.

Popenoe, David. 1996. *Life without Father: Compelling New Evidence That Fatherhood and Marriage Are Indispensable for the Good of Children and Society*. New York: Martin Kessler/Free Press.

Portes, Alejandro, and Dag MacLeod. 1996. "Educational Progress of Children of Immigrants: The Roles of Class, Ethnicity, and School Context." *Sociology of Education,* 69(4):255–276.

Potterat, John J., Donald E. Woodhouse, John B. Muth, and Stephen Q. Muth. 1990. "Estimating the Prevalence and Career Longevity of Prostitute Women." *Journal of Sex Research,* 27(May):233–243.

Preston, Jennifer. 1996. "Hospitals Look on Charity Care as Unaffordable Option of Past." *New York Times* (April 14): 1, 15.

Pride, Mike. 1999. "Out Here: Missing Voices." *Brill's Content* (August). Retrieved November 17, 1999. Online: http://www.brillscontent.com/columns/outhere_0899.html.

Purdum, Todd S. 1997. "Legacy of Riots in Los Angeles: Fears and Hope." *New York Times* (April 27):1, 16.

Purdum, Todd S. 1999. "Few Clues to Gunman's Rage in Hawaii Killings." *New York Times* (November 4):A14.

Purvis, Andrew. 1996. "The Global Epidemic: AIDS Is Tightening Its Grip on the Developing World." *Time* (December 30):76–78.

Quadagno, Jill, and Catherine Fobes. 1995. "The Welfare State and the Cultural Reproduction of Gender." *Social Problems,* 42(2):171–190.

Raffalli, Mary. 1994. "Why So Few Women Physicists?" *New York Times Supplement* (January):Sect. 4A, 26–28.

Ramo, Joshua Cooper. 1997. "Peace is an Xcellent Adventure." *Time* (June 9):69.

Rank, Mark Robert. 1994. *Living on the Edge: The Realities of Welfare in America.* New York: Columbia University Press.

Rankin, Robert P., and Jerry S. Maneker. 1985. "The Duration of Marriage in a Divorcing Population: The Impact of Children." *Journal of Marriage and the Family,* 47(February):43–52.

Raphael, Ray. 1988. *The Men From the Boys: Rites of Passage in Male America.* Lincoln, NE: University of Nebraska Press.

Rather, Dan. 1999. *Deadlines and Datelines.* New York: William Morrow.

Rawlings, Steve W. 1995. "Households and Families." *Population Profile of the United States: 1995.* Washington, DC: U.S. Department of Commerce, Bureau of the Census.

Rawls, John. 1971. *A Theory of Justice.* Cambridge, MA: Harvard University Press.

Reckless, Walter C. 1967. *The Crime Problem.* New York: Meredith.

Reid, Sue Titus. 1987. *Criminal Justice.* St. Paul, MN: West.

Reiss, I. L. 1986. *Journey into Sexuality: An Exploratory Voyage.* Englewood Cliffs, NJ: Prentice-Hall.

Relman, Arnold S. 1992. "Self-Referral—What's at Stake?" *New England Journal of Medicine,* 327 (November 19):1522–1524.

Renner, Michael. 1993. *Critical Juncture: The Future of Peacekeeping.* Washington, DC: Worldwatch Institute.

Renzetti, Claire M., and Daniel J. Curran. 1995. *Women, Men, and Society* (3rd ed.). Boston: Allyn and Bacon.

Reskin, Barbara F., and Heidi Hartmann. 1986. *Women's Work, Men's Work: Sex Segregation on the Job.* Washington, DC: National Academy Press.

Reskin, Barbara F., and Irene Padavic. 1994. *Women and Men at Work.* Thousand Oaks, CA: Pine Forge.

Reynolds, Helen. 1986. *The Economics of Prostitution.* Springfield, IL: Charles C. Thomas.

Richardson, Laurel. 1993. "Inequalities of Power, Property, and Prestige." In Virginia Cyrus (Ed.), *Experiencing Race, Class, and Gender in the United States.* Mountain View, CA: Mayfield, pp. 229–236.

Rimer, Sara. 1999. "Principal Tells of His Anguish, Guilt, and Hope." *New York Times* (April 26):A1, A17.

Risman, Barbara J. 1987. "Intimate Relationships from a Microstructural Perspective: Men Who Mother." *Gender and Society,* 1:6–32.

Ritzer, George. 1995. *Expressing America: A Critique of the Global Credit Card Society.* Thousand Oaks, CA: Pine Forge.

Roane, Kit R. 1996. "In Bosnia, Paint and Plumbing Alone Cannot Heal." *New York Times International* (May 5): A4.

Roberts, Nickie. 1992. *Whores in History: Prostitution in Western Society.* London: HarperCollins.

Roberts, Sam. 1993. *Who We Are: A Portrait of America Based on the Latest U.S. Census.* New York: Times Books.

Rogers, Deborah D. 1995. "Daze of Our Lives: The Soap Opera as Feminine Text." In Gail Dines and Jean M. Humez (Eds.), *Gender, Race and Class in Media: A Text-Reader.* Thousand Oaks, CA: Sage, pp. 325–331.

Rogg, E. 1974. *The Assimilation of Cuban Exiles: The Role of Community and Class.* New York: Aberdeen.

Romero, Mary. 1992. *Maid in the U.S.A.* New York: Routledge.

Romo, Harriett D., and Toni Falbo. 1996. *Latino High School Graduation.* Austin, TX: University of Texas Press.

Roos, Patricia A., and Barbara F. Reskin. 1992. "Occupational Desegregation in the 1970s: Integration and Economic Equity?" *Sociological Perspectives,* 35:69.

Ropers, Richard H. 1991. *Persistent Poverty: The American Dream Turned Nightmare.* New York: Plenum.

Rose, Arnold. 1951. *The Roots of Prejudice.* Paris: UNESCO.

Rosenbaum, David E. 1996. "In Political Money Game, the Year of Big Loopholes." *New York Times* (December 26): A1, A10.

Rosenberg, Janet, Harry Perlstadt, and William Phillips. 1993. "Now That We Are Here: Discrimination, Disparagement and Harassment at Work and the Experience of Women Lawyers." *Gender and Society,* 7(3):415–433.

Rosenthal, Elisabeth. 1993. "The Inner City: Lack of Doctors for the Poor Is Obstacle to Health Plans." *New York Times* (November 14):HD6.

Rosenthal, Elisabeth. 1997. "The H.M.O. Catch: When Healthier Isn't Cheaper." *New York Times* (March 16):E1, E4.

Rosenwein, Rifka. 2000. "Why Media Mergers Matter." *Brill's Content* (January):93–95.

Rosser, Sue V. 1994. *Women's Health—Missing from U.S. Medicine.* Bloomington, IN: Indiana University Press.

Rossi, Peter H. 1989. *Down and Out in America: The Origins of Homelessness.* Chicago: University of Chicago Press.

Rothchild, John. 1995. "Wealth: Static Wages, Except for the Rich." *Time* (January 30):60–61.

Rothman, Robert A. 1993. *Inequality and Stratification: Class, Color, and Gender* (2nd ed.). Englewood Cliffs, NJ: Prentice-Hall.

Rubin, Lillian B. 1976. *Worlds of Pain: Life in the Working-Class Family.* New York: Basic Books.

Rubin, Lillian B. 1994. *Families on the Fault Line.* New York: HarperCollins.

Rubington, Earl, and Martin S. Weinberg (Eds.). 1996. *Deviance: The Interactionist Perspective* (6th ed.). Boston: Allyn and Bacon.

Ruggles, Patricia. 1990. *Drawing the Line: Alternative Policy Measures and Their Implications for Public Policy.* Washington, DC: Urban Institute Press.

Ruggles, Patricia. 1992. "Measuring Poverty." *Focus,* 14(1):1–5.

Russell, Diana E. H. 1993. "Introduction." In Diana E. H. Russell (Ed.), *Making Violence Sexy: Feminist Views on Pornography.* New York: Teachers College Press, pp. 1–20.

Ryan, William. 1976. *Blaming the Victim* (rev. ed.). New York: Vintage.

Sachs, Aaron. 1994. "The Last Commodity: Child Prostitution in the Developing World." *World Watch,* 7(4) (July–August):24–31.

Sadker, Myra, and David Sadker. 1994. *Failing at Fairness: How America's Schools Cheat Girls.* New York: Scribner.

Safilios-Rothschild, Constantina. 1969. "Family Sociology or Wives' Family Sociology? A Cross-Cultural Examination of Decision-Making." *Journal of Marriage and the Family,* 31(2):290–301.

Sale, Kirkpatrick. 1990. *The Conquest of Paradise.* New York: Knopf.

Sampson, Robert J. 1986. "Effects of Socioeconomic Context on Official Reactions to Juvenile Delinquency." *American Sociological Review,* 51(December):876–885.

Sanday, Peggy Reeves. 1996. *A Woman Scorned: Acquaintance Rape on Trial.* New York: Doubleday.

Sanger, David E. 1999. "Global Economy Dances to Political Tune." *New York Times* (December 20):C21.

Sanger, David E. 2000. "In Leading Nations, a Population Bust?" *New York Times* (January 1):YNE8.

Santiago, Anna M., and George Galster. 1995. "Puerto Rican Segregation in the United States: Cause or Consequence of Economic Status?" *Social Problems,* 42:361–389.

Santiago, Anna M., and Margaret G. Wilder. 1991. "Residential Segregation and Links to Minority Poverty: The Case of Latinos in the United States." *Social Problems,* 38:701–723.

Sapon-Shevin, Mara. 1993. "Gifted Education and the Protection of Privilege: Breaking the Silence, Opening the Discourse." In Lois Weis and Michelle Fine (Eds.), *Beyond Silenced Voices: Class, Race, and Gender in United States Schools.* Albany, NY: State University of New York Press, pp. 25–44.

Sassen, Saskia. 1995. "On Concentration and Centrality in the Global City." In Paul L. Knox and Peter J. Taylor (Eds.), *World Cities in a World-System.* Cambridge, England: Cambridge University Press, pp. 63–75.

Sawers, Larry, and William K. Tabb (Eds.). 1984. *Sunbelt/ Snowbelt: Urban Development and Regional Restructuring.* New York: Oxford University Press.

Scarr, Sandra. 1995. "The Two Worlds of Child Care." *National Forum: The Phi Kappa Phi Journal,* 75(3):39–41.

Scheff, Thomas J. 1977. "The Distancing of Emotion in Ritual." *Current Anthropology,* 18:483–505. In Bunis, William K., Angela Yancik, and David Snow. 1996. "The Cultural Patterning of Sympathy toward the Homeless and Other Victims of Misfortune." *Social Problems* (November): 387–402.

Schemo, Diana Jean. 1994. "Suburban Taxes Are Higher for Blacks, Analysis Shows." *New York Times* (August 17):A1, A16.

Schickler, Rob. 1999. "Society's Reaction to Killings Getting Predictable." *Baylor Lariat* (November 4):2.

Schiller, Herbert I. 1996. *Information Inequality: The Deepening Social Crisis in America.* New York: Routledge.

Schneider, Keith. 1993. "The Regulatory Thickets of Environmental Racism." *New York Times* (December 19):E5.

Schreuder, Cindy. 1996. "What Kindergartners Can Teach Us about Living in a Multicultural World." *Austin American-Statesman* (July 7):F1, F5.

Schrof, Joanne M. 1993. "The Gender Machine." *U.S. News and World Report* (August 2):42–44.

Schur, Edwin M. 1965. *Crimes without Victims: Deviant Behavior and Public Policy.* Englewood Cliffs, NJ: Prentice-Hall.

Scott, Alan. 1990. *Ideology and the New Social Movements.* Boston: Unwin & Hyman.

Scott, Denise Benoit. 1996. "Shattering the Instrumental-Expressive Myth: The Power of Women's Networks in Corporate-Government Affairs." *Gender and Society,* 10(3):232–247.

Searight, H. Russell, and Priscilla R. Searight. 1988. "The Homeless Mentally Ill: Overview, Policy Implications, and Adult Foster Care as a Neglected Resource." *Adult Foster Care Journal,* 2:235–259.

Seavor, Jim. 1996. "Closing the Books on Homophobia." *Austin American-Statesman* (November 24):E11.

Seelye, Katharine Q. 1997a. "Future U.S.: Grayer and More Hispanic." *New York Times* (March 27):A18.

Seelye, Katharine Q. 1997b. "Trickle of Television Liquor Ads Releases Torrent of Regulatory Uncertainty." *New York Times* (January 12):8.

Segal, Lynn. 1990. "Pornography and Violence: What the 'Experts' Really Say." *Feminist Review,* 36:29–41.

Seidman, Steven A. 1992. "An Investigation of Sex-Role Stereotyping in Music Videos." *Journal of Broadcasting & Electronic Media* (Spring):212.

Seligman, Martin E. P. 1975. *Helplessness: On Depression, Development and Death.* San Francisco: Freeman.

Serrill, Michael S. 1992. "Struggling to Be Themselves." *Time* (November 9):52–54.

Serrin, Judith. 1997. "Immigration Helps Economy, Analysis Shows." *Austin American-Statesman* (May 18):A7.

Shah, Sonia. 1994. "Presenting the Blue Goddess: Toward a National Pan-Asian Feminist Agenda." In Karin Aguilar-San Juan (Ed.), *The State of Asian America: Activism and Resistance in the 1990s.* Boston: South End Press, pp. 147–158.

Shannon, Kelley. 1996. "Allocations, Segregation Hurt Latinos' Schooling." *Austin American-Statesman* (September 13):A11.

Shaw, Randy. 1999. *Reclaiming America: Nike, Clean Air, and the New National Activism.* Berkeley, CA: University of California Press.

Shea, Christopher. 1996. "A Scholar Links Sexual Orientation to Gender Roles in Childhood." *Chronicle of Higher Education* (November 22):A11, A12.

Shedler, J., and J. Block. 1990. "Adolescent Drug Users and Psychological Health." *American Psychologist,* 45:612–630.

Sheff, David. 1995. "If It's Tuesday, It Must Be Dad's House." *New York Times Magazine* (March 26):64–65.

Sheldon, William H. 1949. *Varieties of Delinquent Youth: An Introduction to Constitutional Psychiatry.* New York: Harper.

Sheley, Joseph F. (Ed.). 1995. *Criminology* (2nd ed.) Belmont, CA: Wadsworth.

Shelton, Beth Ann. 1992. *Women, Men and Time: Gender Differences in Paid Work, Housework and Leisure.* Westport, CT: Greenwood.

Shenon, Philip. 1996a. "AIDS Epidemic, Late to Arrive, Now Explodes in Populous Asia." *New York Times* (January 21):A1.

Shenon, Philip. 1996b. "Jet Makers Preparing Bids for a Rich Pentagon Prize." *New York Times* (March 12):A1, C4.

Shenon, Philip. 1996c. "When 'Don't Ask, Don't Tell' Means Do Ask and Do Tell All." *New York Times* (March 3):E7.

Sher, Kenneth J. 1991. *Children of Alcoholics: A Critical Appraisal of Theory and Research.* Chicago: University of Chicago Press.

Shibutani, Tamotsu. 1970. "On the Personification of Adversaries." In Tamotsu Shibutani (Ed.), *Human Nature and Collective Behavior.* Englewood Cliffs, NJ: Prentice-Hall, pp. 223–233.

Shilts, Randy. 1988. *And the Band Played On: Politics, People, and the AIDS Epidemic.* New York: Penguin.

Shilts, Randy. 1993. *Conduct Unbecoming: Lesbians and Gays in the U.S. Military, Vietnam to the Persian Gulf.* New York: St. Martin's Press.

Shweder, Richard A. 1997. "It's Called Poor Health for a Reason." *New York Times* (March 9):E5.

Sidel, Ruth. 1996. *Keeping Women and Children Last: America's War on the Poor.* New York: Penguin.

Simmel, Georg. 1950. *The Sociology of Georg Simmel.* Trans. Kurt Wolff. Glencoe, IL: Free Press (orig. written in 1902–1917).

Simon, Brenda M. 1999. *"United States v. Hilton."* *Berkeley Technology Law Journal* 14:385–403.

Simon, David R. 1996. *Elite Deviance* (5th ed.) Boston: Allyn and Bacon.

Singer, Bennett L., and David Deschamps. 1994. *Gay and Lesbian Stats.* New York: New Press.

Sivard, Ruth L. 1991. *World Military and Social Expenditures—1991.* Washington, DC: World Priorities.

Sivard, Ruth L. 1993. *World Military and Social Expenditures—1993.* Washington, DC: World Priorities.

Skolnick, Arlene. 1991. *Embattled Paradise: The American Family in an Age of Uncertainty.* New York: HarperCollins.

Skolnick, Jerome H. 1975. *Justice without Trial* (2nd ed.). New York: Wiley.

Sleeter, Christine E. 1996. "White Silence, White Solidarity." In Noel Ignatiev and John Garvey (Eds.), *Race Traitor.* New York: Routledge, pp. 257–265.

Smith, Alexander B., and Harriet Pollack. 1994. "Deviance as Crime, Sin, and Poor Taste." In Patricia A. Adler and Peter Adler (Eds.), *Constructions of Deviance: Social Power, Context, and Interaction.* Belmont, CA: Wadsworth.

Smith, M. Dwayne. 1995. "The Death Penalty in America." In Joseph F. Sheley (Ed.), *Criminology: A Contemporary Handbook* (2nd ed.). Belmont, CA: Wadsworth, pp. 557–572.

Smolowe, Jill. 1996. "The Stalled Revolution." *Time* (May 6):63.

Snell, Cudore L. 1995. *Young Men in the Street: Help-Seeking Behavior of Young Male Prostitutes.* Westport, CT: Praeger.

Snitow, Ann Barr. 1994. "Mass Market Romance: Pornography for Women Is Different." In Alison M. Jaggar (Ed.), *Living with Contradictions: Controversies in Feminist Social Ethics.* Boulder, CO: Westview, pp. 181–188.

Snow, David A., and Leon Anderson. 1991. "Researching the Homeless: The Characteristic Features and Virtues of the Case Study." In Joe R. Feagin, Anthony M. Orum, and Gideon Sjoberg (Eds.), *A Case for the Case Study.* Chapel Hill: University of North Carolina Press, pp. 148–173.

Snow, David A., and Leon Anderson. 1993. *Down on Their Luck: A Study of Homeless Street People.* Berkeley, CA: University of California Press.

Snyder, Benson R. 1971. *The Hidden Curriculum.* New York: Knopf.

Soble, Alan. 1986. "Pornography in Capitalism: Powerlessness." In Alan Soble, *Pornography: Marxism, Feminism and the Future of Sexuality.* New Haven, CT: Yale University Press, pp. 78–84.

Spanier, Graham, and Paul Glick. 1981. "Marital Instability in the U.S.: Some Correlates and Recent Changes." *Family Relations,* 30(July):329–338.

Squires, Gregory D. 1994. *Capital and Communities in Black and White: The Intersections of Race, Class, and Uneven Development.* Albany, NY: State University of New York Press.

Stanko, Elizabeth. 1990. *Everyday Violence: How Women and Men Experience Sexual and Physical Danger.* London: HarperCollins.

Stanley, Alessandra. 1995. "Russian Mothers, from All Walks, Walk Alone." *New York Times* (October 21):A1.

Stanley, Alessandra. 1996. "Dec. 25 in Russia: The Adoration of the Monetary." *The New York Times International* (December 24):A4.

Stanley, Julia P. 1972. "Paradigmatic Woman: The Prostitute." Paper presented at South Atlantic Modern Language Association, Jacksonville, FL, cited in Jessie Bernard, *The Female World.* New York: Free Press, 1981.

Staples, Robert. 1994. *The Black Family: Essays and Studies* (5th ed.). Belmont, CA: Wadsworth.

Stares, Paul B. 1996. *Global Habit: The Drug Problem in a Borderless World.* Washington, DC: Brookings Institution.

Starr, Paul. 1982. *The Social Transformation of American Medicine.* New York: Basic Books.

Stead, Deborah. 1997. "Corporations, Classrooms, and Commercialism." *New York Times Education Supplement* (January 5):30–33.

Steering Committee of the Physicians' Health Study Group. 1989. "Final Report on the Aspirin Component of the Ongoing Physician's Health Study." *New England Journal of Medicine*, 321:129–135.

Stefanac, Suzanne. 1993. "Sex and the New Media." *New Media* (April):38–45.

Steffensmeier, Darrell, and Emilie Allan. 1995. "Criminal Behavior: Gender and Age." In Joseph F. Sheley (Ed.), *Criminology: A Contemporary Handbook* (2nd ed.). Belmont, CA: Wadsworth, pp. 83–143.

Stein, Peter J. 1976. *Single*. Englewood Cliffs, NJ: Prentice-Hall.

Stein, Peter J. (Ed.). 1981. *Single Life: Unmarried Adults in Social Context*. New York: St. Martin's Press.

Steingart, R. M., M. Packer, P. Hamm, and others. 1991. "Sex Differences in the Management of Coronary Artery Disease." *New England Journal of Medicine*, 325:226–230.

Stern, Christopher. 1998. "Researchers Shocked to Find—TV Violence." *Variety* (April 20–26):24.

Sterngold, James. 1993. "Killer Gets Life as Navy Says He Hunted Down Gay Sailor." *New York Times* (May 28):A1, A11.

Stevens, Patricia E. 1992. "Lesbian Health Care Research: A Review of the Literature from 1970 to 1990." *Health Care for Women International*, 13.

Stevens, William K. 1997. "How Much Is Nature Worth? For You, $33 Trillion." *New York Times* (May 20):B7, B9.

Stevenson, Richard W. 1997. "Clinton and Congress in Accord on Budget, Except for Tax Cuts." *New York Times* (May 2):A1, A12.

Stewart, Charles T., Jr. 1995. *Healthy, Wealthy, or Wise? Issues in American Health Care Policy*. Armonk, NY: M.E. Sharpe.

Stock, Robert W. 1995. "Balancing the Needs and Risks of Older Drivers." *New York Times* (July 13):B5.

Stolberg, Sheryl Gay. 1997a. "Breaks for Mental Illness: Just What the Government Ordered." *New York Times* (May 4):E1, E5.

Stolberg, Sheryl Gay. 1997b. "Wary of Big Steps, U.S. Isn't Moving to Curb Tobacco." *New York Times* (May 2): A1, A16.

Stoll, Clifford. 1996. "Invest in Humanware." *New York Times* (May 19):E15.

Stoller, Robert J. 1991. *Porn: Myths for the Twentieth Century*. New Haven, CT: Yale University Press.

Story, Paula. 1997. "L.A. Police Assess Robbers' Greater Firepower." *Austin American-Statesman* (March 2):A5.

Straus, Murray A., Richard J. Gelles, and Suzanne K. Steinmetz. 1980. *Behind Closed Doors: Violence in the American Family*. New York: Anchor.

Strom, Stephanie. 2000. "Tradition of Equality Fading in New Japan." *New York Times* (January 4):A1, A6.

Substance Abuse and Mental Health Services Administration. 1996. *National Household Survey on Drug Abuse: Population Estimates 1995*. Rockville, MD: U.S. Department of Health and Human Services.

Sugarmann, Josh. 1999. "Laws That Can't Stop a Bullet." *New York Times* (November 4):A27.

Sullivan, Maureen. 1996. "Rozzie and Harriet? Gender and Family Patterns of Lesbian Coparents." *Gender and Society*, 10(6):747–767.

Sullivan, Teresa A., Elizabeth Warren, and Jay Lawrence Westbrook. 1989. *As We Forgive Our Debtors: Bankruptcy and Consumer Credit in America*. New York: Oxford University Press.

Sullivan, Thomas J. 1997. *Introduction to Social Problems* (4th ed.). Boston: Allyn and Bacon.

Sutherland, Edwin H. 1939. *Principles of Criminology*. Philadelphia: Lippincott.

Sutherland, Edwin H. 1949. *White Collar Crime*. New York: Dryden.

Takagi, Dana Y. 1992. *The Retreat from Race: Asian-American Admissions and Racial Politics*. New Brunswick, NJ: Rutgers.

Takaki, Ronald. 1993. *A Different Mirror: A History of Multicultural America*. Boston: Little, Brown.

Tannen, Deborah. 1990. *You Just Don't Understand: Women and Men in Conversation*. New York: William Morrow.

Tannen, Deborah. 1994. *Gender and Discourse*. New York: Oxford University Press.

Tatara, Toshio, and Lisa B. Kuzmeskus. 1996. "Domestic Elder Abuse Information Series #1, Types and Number of Domestic Elder Abuse Cases." Retrieved December 4, 1999. Online: http://www.gwjapan.com/NCEA/basic/pl.html.

Taylor, J., and B. Jackson. 1990. "Factors Affecting Alcohol Consumption in Black Women." *International Journal of the Addictions*, 25(12):1415–1427.

Taylor, Verta, and Nicole C. Raeburn. 1995. "Identity Politics as High-Risk Activism: Career Consequences for Lesbian, Gay, and Bisexual Sociologists." *Social Problems*, 42(2):252–273.

Terkel, Studs. 1996. *Coming of Age: The Story of Our Century by Those Who've Lived It*. New York: St. Martin's Griffin.

Texas Lawyer. 1997. "A.G.'s Opinions: *Hopwood*/Scholarship Programs/Equal Protection" (February 17):24–25.

Theriault, Reg. 1995. *How to Tell When You're Tired: A Brief Examination of Work*. New York: W.W. Norton.

Thomas, Cal. 1996. "Overrule Same-Sex Marriage." *Austin American-Statesman* (December 6):A15.

Thomas, Gale E. 1995. "Conclusion: Healthy Communities as a Basis for Healthy Race and Ethnic Relations." In Gail E. Thomas (Ed.), *Race and Ethnicity in America: Meeting the Challenge in the 21st Century*. Bristol, PA: Taylor & Francis, pp. 335–342.

Thomas, Jo. 1997. "McVeigh Jury Decides on Sentence of Death in Oklahoma Bombing." *New York Times* (June 14):1, 8.

Thompson, Mark. 1999. "Why Do People Have to Push Me Like That?" *Time* (December 13):56–57.

Thomson, Elizabeth, and Ugo Colella. 1992. "Cohabitation and Marital Stability: Quality or Commitment?" *Journal of Marriage and the Family*, 54:259–267.

Thorne, Barrie. 1995. "Girls and Boys Together . . . But Mostly Apart: Gender Arrangements in Elementary School." In

Michael S. Kimmel and Michael A. Messner (Eds.), *Men's Lives* (3rd ed.). Boston: Allyn and Bacon, pp. 61–73.

Thornton, Arland. 1989. "Changing Attitudes toward Family Issues in the United States." *Journal of Marriage and the Family*, 51 (November):873–893.

Thornton, Michael C., Linda M. Chatters, Robert Joseph Taylor, and Walter R. Allen. 1990. "Sociodemographic and Environmental Correlates of Racial Socialization by Black Parents." *Child Development*, 61:401–409.

Thornton, Russell. 1984. "Cherokee Population Losses during the Trail of Tears: A New Perspective and a New Estimate." *Ethnohistory*, 31:289–300.

Thornton, Russell. 1987. *American Indian Holocaust and Survival*. Norman: University of Oklahoma Press.

Tienda, Marta, and Haya Stier. 1996. "Generating Labor Market Inequality: Employment Opportunities and the Accumulation of Disadvantage." *Social Problems*, 43(2): 147–165.

Tierney, John. 1994. "Porn, the Low-Slung Engine of Progress." *New York Times* (January 9):H1, H18.

Tierney, John. 2000. "Left and Right, Analyzing the Down and Out, Switch Ideological Hats." *New York Times* (January 8):A11.

Time. 1996. "A Journey of 10,000 Miles Begins with the Shoes." *Time* (June 17):78.

Tme. 1999a. "Canada 2005: The Changing Tapestry" (May 31). Retrieved November 13, 1999. Online: http://www.time.com.

Time. 1999b. "Here's My Marijuana Card, Officer: In the Capital of Legal Pot, You Don't Need Much of an Excuse" (May 3):7.

Time. 1999c. "A Week in the Life of a High School" (October 25). Retrieved November 11, 1999. Online: http://www.time.com.

Toner, Robin. 1993. "People without Health Insurance." *New York Times* (November 14):HD16.

Toner, Robin. 1995. "No Free Rides: Generational Push Has Not Come to Shove." *New York Times* (December 31): E1, E4.

Toner, Robin, and Robert Pear. 1995. "Medicare, Turning 30, Won't Be What It Was." *New York Times* (July 23):1, 12.

Torrey, E. Fuller. 1988. *Nowhere to Go: The Tragic Odyssey of the Homeless Mentally Ill*. New York: Harper and Row.

Tower, Cynthia Crosson. 1996. *Child Abuse and Neglect* (3rd ed.). Boston: Allyn and Bacon.

Travis, John. 1995. "X Chromosome Again Linked to Homosexuality." *Science News*, 148 (November 4):295.

Trice, Harrison M., and Paul Michael Roman. 1970. "Delabeling, Relabeling, and Alcoholics Anonymous." *Social Problems*, 17(4):538–546.

Tumulty, Karen. 1996. "Why Subsidies Survive." *Time* (March 25):46–47.

Turk, Austin T. 1966. "Conflict and Criminality." *American Sociological Review*, 31:338–352.

Turk, Austin T. 1971. *Criminality and Legal Order*. Chicago: Rand McNally.

Turner, Richard. 1999. "All Carnage, All the Time." *Newsweek* (August 23):45.

Turpin, Jennifer, and Lester R. Kurtz. 1997. "Introduction: Violence The Micro/Macro Link." In Jennifer Turpin and Lester R. Kurtz (Eds.), *The Web of Violence: From Interpersonal to Global*. Urbana and Chicago: University of Illinois, pp. 1–27.

Tyson, Eric K. 1993. "Credit Crackdown: Control Your Spending Before It Controls You." *San Francisco Examiner* (November 28):E1. (Cited in Ritzer, 1995.)

Uchitelle, Louis. 1995. "Retirement's Worried Face: For Many, the Crisis Is Now." *New York Times* (July 30):F1, F4.

United Nations. 1995. *The World's Women 1995: Trends and Statistics*. New York: United Nations.

United Nations Development Programme. 1999. *Human Development Report: 1999*. New York: Oxford University Press.

United Nations Environmental Program. 1992. *Status of Desertification and Implementation of the United Nations Plan of Action to Combat Desertification*. Nairobi, Egypt: United Nations.

U.S. Bureau of the Census. 1998. *Statistical Abstract of the United States, 1998* (118th ed.). Washington, DC: U.S. Government Printing Office.

U.S. Bureau of the Census. 1999a. "Money Income in the United States: 1998." Retrieved November 17, 1999. Online: http://www.census.gov/hhes/www.income1998.html.

U.S. Bureau of the Census. 1999b. "Poverty in the United States: 1998." Retrieved November 17, 1999. Online: http://www.census.gov/hhes/www/povty98.html.

U.S. Bureau of Labor Statistics. 1995. *Current Population Survey*. Washington, DC: U.S. Government Printing Office, January.

U.S. Bureau of Labor Statistics, 1999. *Current Population Survey*. "Highlights of Women's Earnings in 1998." Retrieved November 28, 1999. Online:http://www.bls.gov/cpswom98.htm.

U.S. Conference of Mayors. 1995. *A Status Report on Hunger and Homelessness in America's Cities*. Washington, DC: United States Conference of Mayors.

U.S. Department of State. 1996. *International Narcotics Control Strategy Report*. Washington, DC: U.S. Department of State.

U.S. House of Representatives, Committee on Ways and Means. 1994. *1994 Green Book*. Washington, DC: U.S. Government Printing Office.

Urschel, Joe. 1996. "How Girls Get Scared Away from Computers." *USA Today* (June 26):1D–2D.

Valdez, Avelardo. 1993. "Persistent Poverty, Crime, and Drugs: U.S.-Mexican Border Region." In Joan Moore and Raquel Pinderhughes (Eds.), *In the Barrios: Latinos and the Underclass Debate*. New York: Russell Sage Foundation, pp. 173–194.

Vanneman, Reeve, and Lynn Weber Cannon. 1987. *The American Perception of Class*. Philadelphia: Temple University Press.

Vetter, Harold J., and Gary R. Perlstein. 1991. *Perspectives on Terrorism*. Pacific Grove, CA: Brooks/Cole.

Vissing, Yvonne M. 1996. *Out of Sight, out of Mind: Homeless Children and Families in Small-Town America.* Lexington, KY: University Press of Kentucky.

Vito, Gennaro F., and Ronald M. Holmes. 1994. *Criminology: Theory, Research and Policy.* Belmont, CA: Wadsworth.

Viviano, Frank. 1995. "The New Mafia Order." *Mother Jones* (May–June):45–55.

Wagner, David. 1993. *Checkerboard Square: Culture and Resistance in a Homeless Community.* Boulder, CO: Westview.

Wald, Matthew L. 1996a. "A Fading Drumbeat against Drunken Driving." *New York Times* (December 15):E5.

Wald, Matthew L. 1996b. "Group Says Alcohol-Related Traffic Deaths Are Rising." *New York Times* (November 27):A11.

Walker, S. L. 1994. "Critics Fume at Mayor of World Smog Capital. *San Diego Union-Tribune* (April 22). (Cited in Michael P. Soroka and George J. Bryjak, *Social Problems: A World at Risk.* 1995. Boston: Allyn and Bacon, p. 115.)

Wallerstein, Immanuel. 1984. *The Politics of the World Economy.* Cambridge, England: Cambridge University Press.

Wallerstein, Immanuel. 1999. *The End of the World as We Know It: Social Science for the Twenty-First Century.* Minneapolis: University of Minnesota Press.

Wallerstein, Judith, and Sandra Blakeslee. 1989. *Second Chances: Men, Women and Children a Decade after Divorce.* New York: Ticknor & Field.

Wallis, Claudia. 1994. "A Class of Their Own." *Time* (October 31):53–61.

Warr, Mark. 1995. "Public Perceptions of Crime and Punishment." In Joseph F. Sheley (Ed.), *Criminology: A Contemporary Handbook* (2nd ed.). Belmont, CA: Wadsworth, pp. 15–31.

Warshaw, Robin. 1994. *I Never Called It Rape.* New York: HarperPerennial.

Wartella, Ellen. 1995. "The Commercialization of Youth: Channel One in Context." *Phi Delta Kappan,* 76 (February):448–451.

Waters, Malcolm. 1995. *Globalization.* New York: Routledge.

Watson, Roy E. L., and Peter W. DeMeo. 1987. "Premarital Cohabitation Versus Traditional Courtship and Subsequent Marital Adjustment: A Replication and a Follow-Up." *Family Relations,* 36:193–197.

Weeks, John R. 1998. *Population: An Introduction to Concepts and Issues* (7th ed.). Belmont, CA: Wadsworth.

Weinberg, Martin S., and Colin Williams. 1975. *Male Homosexuals.* New York: Penguin.

Weinberg, Martin S., Earl Rubington, and Sue Kiefer Hammersmith. 1981. *The Solution of Social Problems: Five Perspectives* (2nd ed.). New York: Oxford University Press.

Weinberg, Martin S., Colin J. Williams, and Douglas W. Pryor. 1994. *Dual Attraction: Understanding Bisexuality.* New York: Oxford University Press.

Weiner, Jonathan. 1990. *The Next One Hundred Years: Shaping the Fate of Our Living Earth.* New York: Bantam.

Weiner, Tim. 1994. "The Men in the Gray Federal Bureaucracy." *New York Times* (April 10):E4.

Weiner, Tim. 1995. "Serial Bomber Threatens Blast aboard a Los Angeles Airliner." *New York Times* (June 29):A1, A6.

Weiner, Tim. 1997. "Terrorism's Worldwide Toll Was High in 1996, U.S. Report Says." *New York Times* (May 1):A10.

Weisner, Thomas S., Helen Garnier, and James Loucky. 1994. "Domestic Tasks, Gender Egalitarian Values, and Children's Gender Typing in Conventional and Nonconventional Families." *Sex Roles,* 30:23–54.

Weiss, Leslie. 1996. "Tightening the Beltway." *Mother Jones* (March–April):57.

Weiten, Wayne, and Margaret A. Lloyd. 1994. *Psychology Applied to Modern Life: Adjustment in the 90s.* Pacific Grove, CA: Brooks/Cole.

Weitz, Rose. 1996. *The Sociology of Health, Illness, and Health Care: A Critical Approach.* Belmont, CA: Wadsworth.

Weitzman, Lenore J. 1985. *The Divorce Revolution.* New York: Free Press.

Welch, Bud. 1997. "A Father's Urge to Forgive." *Time* (June 16):36.

Wellman, David T. 1993. *Portraits of White Racism* (2nd ed.). New York: Cambridge University Press.

Westoff, Charles F. 1995. "International Population Policy." *Society* (May–June):11–15.

Wheeler, David L. 1997. "The Animal Origins of Male Violence." *Chronicle of Higher Education* (March 28): A15–A16.

Wilkie, Jane Riblett. 1993. "Changes in U.S. Men's Attitudes toward the Family Provider Role, 1972–1989." *Gender and Society,* 7(2):261–279.

Williams, Christine L. 1995. *Still a Man's World: Men Who Do Women's Work.* Berkeley, CA: University of California Press.

Williams, David R., David T. Takeuchi, and Russell K. Adair. 1992. "Socioeconomic Status and Psychiatric Disorders among Blacks and Whites." *Social Forces,* 71:179–195.

Williams, Gregory Howard. 1996. *Life on the Color Line: The True Story of a White Boy Who Discovered He Was Black.* New York: Plume/Penguin.

Williams, Richard G. 1997. "Once a Doctor, Now a 'Provider.'" *Austin American-Statesman* (March 19):A19.

Williams, Robin M., Jr. 1970. *American Society: A Sociological Interpretation* (3rd ed.). New York: Knopf.

Williamson, Robert C., Alice Duffy Rinehart, and Thomas O. Blank. 1992. *Early Retirement: Promises and Pitfalls.* New York: Plenum Press.

Willis, Ellen. 1981. *Beginning to See the Light.* New York: Alfred Knopf.

Willis, Ellen. 1983. "Feminism, Moralism, and Pornography." In Ann Snitow, Christine Stansell, and Sharon Thompson (Eds.), *Powers of Desire: The Politics of Sexuality.* New York: Monthly Review Press, pp. 460–466.

Wilson, David (Ed.). 1997. "Globalization and the Changing U.S. City." *The Annals of the American Academy of Political and Social Science,* 551(May). Special Issue. Thousand Oaks, CA: Sage.

Wilson, Edward O. 1975. *Sociobiology: A New Synthesis.* Cambridge, MA: Harvard University Press.

Wilson, Patricia A. 1992. *Exports and Local Development: Mexico's New Maquiladoras.* Austin, TX: University of Texas Press.

Wilson, William Julius. 1996. *When Work Disappears: The World of the New Urban Poor.* New York: Knopf.

Wirth, Louis. 1938. "Urbanism as a Way of Life." *American Journal of Sociology,* 40:1–24.

Wirth, Louis. 1945. "The Problem of Minority Groups." In Ralph Linton (Ed.), *The Science of Man in the World Crisis.* New York: Columbia University Press, p. 38.

Witteman, P. 1991. "Lost in America." *Time* (February 11):76-77.

Wolf, Robin. 1996. *Marriages and Families in a Diverse Society.* New York: HarperCollins.

Wolfgang, Marvin E., and Franco Ferracuti. 1967. *The Subculture of Violence: Towards an Integrated Theory in Criminology.* Beverly Hills, CA: Sage.

Women's International Network. 1995. "Sex Trade Flourishing in Japan." *WIN News* 21(1) (Winter):42.

Women's Research and Education Institute. 1994. *The American Woman 1994–95: Women and Health.* Edited by Cynthia Costello and Anne J. Stone. New York: W.W. Norton.

Women's Research and Education Institute. 1996. *The American Woman 1996–97: Women and Work.* Edited by Cynthia Costello and Barbara Kivimae Krimgold. New York: W.W. Norton.

Women's Sports Foundation. 1989. *The Women's Sports Foundation Report, Minorities in Sports: The Effect of Varsity Sports Participation on the Social, Educational, and Career Mobility of Minority Students.* New York: Women's Sports Foundation.

Woods, James D., with Jay H. Lucas. 1993. *The Corporate Closet: The Professional Lives of Gay Men in America.* New York: Free Press.

Woodward, Bob. 1997. "Chinese Officials Linked to Influence-Buying Plan." *Austin American-Statesman* (April 27):A3.

Woog, Dan. 1995. *School's Out: The Impact of Gay and Lesbian Issues on America's Schools.* Boston: Alyson Publications.

World Bank. 1995. *World Development Report: 1995.* New York: Oxford University Press.

World Health Organization. 1946. *Constitution of the World Health Organization.* New York: World Health Organization Interim Commission.

World Resources Institute. 1992. *World Resources 1992–93.* New York: Oxford.

Wrangham, Richard, and Dale Peterson. 1996. *Demonic Males: Apes and the Origins of Human Violence.* New York: Houghton Mifflin.

Wren, Christopher. 1996a. "Clinton Declares That Columbia Has Failed to Curb Drug Trade." *New York Times* (March 2):1, 5.

Wren, Christopher. 1996b. "Teen-Agers Find Drugs Easy to Obtain and Warnings Easy to Ignore." *New York Times* (October 10):A12.

Wright, Erik Olin. 1979. *Class Structure and Income Determination.* New York: Academic Press.

Wright, Erik Olin. 1985. *Class.* London: Verso.

Wright, Erik Olin. 1997. *Class Counts: Comparative Studies in Class Analysis.* Cambridge, England: Cambridge University Press.

Wright, Erik Olin, Karen Shire, Shu-Ling Hwang, Maureen Dolan, and Janeen Baxter. 1992. "The Non-Effects of Class on the Gender Division of Labor in the Home: A Comparative Study of Sweden and the U.S." *Gender and Society,* 6(2):252–282.

Wright, Quincy. 1964. *A Study of War.* Chicago: University of Chicago Press.

Wright, Richard T., and Scott Decker. 1994. *Burglars on the Job: Streetlife and Residential Break-ins.* Boston: Northeastern University Press.

WuDunn, Sheryl. 1995a. "In Japan, Still Getting Tea and No Sympathy." *New York Times* (August 27):E3.

WuDunn, Sheryl. 1995b. "Japanese Cult: A Strong Lure and a Danger to Challenge." *New York Times* (March 24):A1.

WuDunn, Sheryl. 1995c. "Japanese Women Fight Servility." *New York Times* (July 9):6.

WuDunn, Sheryl. 1996. "In Japan, Even Toddlers Feel the Pressure to Excel." *New York Times* (January 23):A3.

Young, J. H. 1961. *The Toadstool Millionaires: A Social History of Patent Medicine in America before Federal Regulation.* Princeton, NJ: Princeton University Press.

Young, Jeffrey. 1996. "Spies Like Us." *Forbes ASAP* (June 3): 71–76.

Young, Michael Dunlap. 1994. *The Rise of the Meritocracy.* New Brunswick, NJ: Transaction.

Zate, Maria. 1996. "Hispanics Struggle for Corporate Stature." *Austin American-Statesman* (August 11):H1, H3.

Zelizer, Viviana. 1985. *Pricing the Priceless Child: The Changing Social Value of Children.* New Haven, CT: Yale University Press.

Name Index

Reskin, Barbara F., 70, 71, 73, 75, 77, 81
Ressam, Ahmed, 376
Reuther, Victor, 103
Reuther, Walter, 103
Reynolds, D. K., 93
Reynolds, Helen, 133
Riady, James, 285
Ricard, Laura, 57
Richards, Cory L., 237, 239
Richardson, Laurel, 80
Riedmann, Agnes, 226, 232, 242
Rimer, Sara, 1
Rinehart, Alice Duffy, 100
Risman, Barbara J., 235
Ritzer, George, 278, 279, 281, 293
Roane, Kit R., 368
Roberts, Nickie, 129
Roberts, Sam, 354
Robertson, David, 157
Robinson, Robert V., 15
Rochefort, David A., 209
Rockefeller, John D., 278
Rogers, Deborah D., 70
Rogg, E., 54
Rollyson, Carl, 103, 285
Roman, Paul Michael, 169
Romo, Harriett D., 258, 260
Roos, Patricia A., 75
Ropers, Richard H., 29, 32
Rose, Arnold, 58
Rosenbaum, David E., 283
Rosenberg, Daniel, 56
Rosenberg, Janet, 76
Rosenblum, Barbara, 201, 202
Rosenthal, Elisabeth, 214, 217
Rosenwein, Rifka, 299
Ross, Catherine E., 211
Rosser, Sue V., 217, 218, 238
Rossi, Peter H., 33
Rothchild, John, 29
Rothman, Robert A., 21
Rubin, Lillian B., 232, 246
Rubington, Earl, 128, 385, 386, 387
Ruggles, Patricia, 30
Ruis, José Luis, 48
Runyan, Anne Sisson, 65, 78, 82
Russell, Diana E. H., 137, 138, 140, 141, 143
Ryan, William, 36

Sachs, Aaron, 131
Sadker, David, 68, 69
Sadker, Myra, 68, 69
Safilios-Rothschild, Constantina, 232
Sale, Kirkpatrick, 50
Saltzman, Linda E., 245
Sampson, Robert J., 192
Sanday, Peggy Reeves, 179, 180
Sandefur, Gary D., 235
Sandler, Bernice R., 69

Sanger, David E., 318
Santiago, Anna M., 353, 355
Sapon-Shevin, Mara, 257
Sassen, Saskia, 356
Sawers, Larry, 346
Scarr, Sandra, 246
Schatzkamer, Scott, 296
Scheff, Thomas J., 350
Schellenbach, Cynthia J., 241
Schemo, Diana Jean, 354
Schickler, Rob, 16
Schiller, Herbert I., 301
Schmeidler, James, 162
Schneider, Keith, 338
Schreuder, Cindy, 59
Schrof, Joanne M., 261
Schur, Edwin M., 119
Schwartz, Michael, 280
Scott, Alan, 338
Scott, Denise Benoit, 79
Scott, Janny, 162
Searight, H. Russell, 210
Searight, Priscilla R., 210
Searles, Patricia, 142
Sears, Robert R., 46, 188
Seelye, Katharine Q., 152, 235
Segal, Lynn, 142, 143
Segal, Ronald, 22
Seidman, Steven A., 70
Seligman, Martin E. P., 212
Senturia, Ben, 286
Serrill, Michael S., 51
Serrin, Judith, 326
Shah, Sonia, 55
Shanahan, Suzanne, 47
Shannon, Kelley, 260
Shapard, Virginia, 82
Shapiro, Thomas M., 25
Sharpe, Kenneth, 157, 168
Shaw, Randy, 393, 394, 396–397, 400, 401
Shea, Christopher, 119
Shedler, J., 164
Sheff, David, 236
Sheindlin, Judy, 308
Sheldon, William H., 187
Sheley, Joseph F., 192
Shelton, Beth Ann, 77
Shenon, Philip, 116, 206, 288
Shepard, Dennis, 107, 116
Shepard, Judy, 117
Shepard, Matthew, 6, 9, 107, 108, 116, 117, 181
Sher, Kenneth J., 154
Shibutani, Tamotsu, 370
Shilts, Randy, 115, 122
Shire, Karen, 235
Shiva, Vandana, 338
Shoels, Michael, 1
Shweder, Richard A., 219
Sidel, Ruth, 36

Sikes, Melvin P., 5, 52, 211, 353, 354
Silver, H., 243
Silverman, F., 243
Simmel, Georg, 12, 360, 363
Simon, Brenda M., 140
Simon, David R., 183
Simpson, Nicole Brown, 245
Simpson, O. J., 245
Singer, Bennett L., 113, 118
Sivard, Ruth L., 368
Skolnick, Arlene, 228
Skolnick, Jerome H., 193
Sleeter, Christine E., 46, 47
Smith, Alexander B., 128
Smith, M. Dwayne, 196
Smith, Marshall, 33
Smith, Stephen Samuel, 261
Smolowe, Jill, 246
Snell, Cudore L., 129, 133
Snitow, Ann Barr, 138
Snow, David A., 350, 352
Snyder, Benson R., 253
Snyder, D., 139
Soble, Alan, 140
Sorensen, Jonathan R., 196
South, Jeff, 256, 259
Spanier, Graham, 242
Spielberg, Steven, 300
Spunt, Barry, 162
Squires, Gregory D., 45, 351, 353
St. James, Margo, 136
Stanko, Elizabeth, 177
Stanley, Alessandra, 228, 278
Stanley, Julia P., 78
Stansel, Dean, 247
Staples, Robert, 233
Stares, Paul B., 166
Starr, Paul, 212
Stead, Deborah, 265
Steele, B., 243
Steele, James B., 286, 290
Stefanac, Suzanne, 143
Steffensmeier, Darrell, 185, 186
Stein, Peter J., 232
Steingart, R. M., 217
Steinman, Clay, 297, 299, 300, 303, 389
Steinmetz, Suzanne K., 244
Steinsapir, Carl, 336
Stern, Christopher, 304
Stevens, Patricia E., 114
Stevens, William K., 330
Stevenson, Richard W., 289
Stewart, Charles T., Jr, 202, 219
Stier, Haya, 52
Stock, Robert W., 86
Stolberg, Sheryl Gay, 220, 287
Stoll, Clifford, 269
Stoller, Robert J., 138
Stone, Anne J. Stone, 72
Story, Paula, 193

Subject Index

Note: Italicized letters *f, m,* and *t* following page numbers indicate figures, maps, and tables, respectively.

Social construction of reality, 13
Social control, 128
Social disorganization, 8, 357, 380, 386
Social drift framework, 212
Social gerontology, 86
Social learning theory, 309
Social life, 18
Social mobility, 21
Social movements, 391, 392, 395
Social problem(s), 18, 386–402
    activities, 386–387
    alternative movements, 396
    behavior, 395, 402
    conflict perspective, 18, 386, 401
    critical-conflict perspective, 18
    definition of, 4
    functionalist perspective, 18, 386, 401
    future of, 399
    global perspective, 24
    influence, 395
    and information technology, 16–17
    interactionist perspective, 18, 386–387, 401
    intervention, 389
    issues, 3–4, 394
    limitations, 389, 392–393, 399
    macrolevel attempts, 394–399, 402
    and the media, 6, 399
    in the media, 48, 400–401
    microlevel attempts, 388–389, 402
    mid-range attempts, 389–394, 402
    middle-term strategies, 387
    new look, 1–19
    organizations, 392t
    perceptions of, 4t
    personal, 388–389
    policy, 399
    prevention, 389
    protests, 395
    short-term strategies, 387
    and social policies, 393
    solutions, 384–403, 387t
    strategies, 387–388
    theories, 386–387
    in the twenty-first century, 399
Social protection, 195
Social-psychological perspective, 46
Social Security, 96, 98, 101, 102, 103
Social Security Administration, 30
Social stratification, 23–25, 38
Social stress framework, 211
Socialism, 276
Socialist feminists, 80, 81
Socializing agents, 65–71, 81
Socially determined prejudice, 108
Society, 4
Socioeconomic status, 211

Sociological examination, 6
Sociological Imagination, The, 6
Sociological perspectives, 7–13
    on drug abuse, 164–166
    on drug addiction, 170
    on economies, 292–293
    on education, 252–257
    on environmental crisis, 336–338
    on families, 247
    on health care, 218–221, 222
    on the media, 309–311
    on politics, 336–338
    on terrorism, 380–381
    on urban problems, 357–361
    on war, 380–381
Sociological research methods, 18
Sociology, 4
Soft money loophole, 283, 286
Soil depletion, 333–334, 340
Solid waste, 334–335, 340
Somatotype theory, 187
Spanish-American War, 54, 55
Special interest groups, 285–287, 394, 395, 402
Split-labor market theory, 47–48
Spouse abuse, 244–245
Squatters, 349
Standardized tests, 256
State-sponsored terrorism, 374
Statutory rape, 179
Steering, 353
Stereotypes
    African Americans, 51
    Asian and Pacific Americans, 55
    definition of, 44
    elderly, 86
    ethnic, 306–307, 314
    gender, 65, 66, 70, 307–309, 313, 314
    homosexuality, 109
    Latinos/as, 54
    in the media, 306–309, 314
    Native Americans, 50
    racial, 306–307, 314
Stimulants, 158, 160–161, 170
Strain theory, 189
Strategically significant weapon, 371
Streetwalkers, 132–133
Student loans, 263
Subcontracting, 276
Subculture, 361
Subculture of violence hypothesis, 8, 9, 190
Subjective awareness, 5–6
Subjective component, 148–149
Subordinate groups, 43, 48
Suburbanites, 347–348
Suburbanization, 345, 361
Suburbs, 345

Suicide, 94, 95
Survey research, 14
Synergy, 299
System of checks and balances, 282

Talented students, 256
TANF. See Temporary Aid to Needy Families
Tax base, 347, 359
Teachers, 72, 269
Technological disasters, 336
Technology, 16–17, 297, 312, 366, 371–373
Teenagers
    and drugs, 158
    pregnancy, 240m, 241–242, 248
    reporting on, 90–91
    and tobacco, 155
Television, 297–299, 300, 306–309, 310
    studying violence in programming, 16–17
Temporary Aid to Needy Families (TANF), 25–26, 34–35
Terrorism, 373–383
    aggressive behavior, 378
    biological perspectives, 378, 382
    conflict perspective, 380–381, 383
    deaths, 374
    definition of, 373
    domestic, 374–377, 382
    explanations, 378–381
    functionalist perspective, 380, 383
    future of, 381–382
    global, 373–374
    interactionist perspective, 380–381, 383
    in the media, 376–377
    political, 373, 382
    psychological perspectives, 379, 382–383
    repressive, 373
    revolutionary, 373
    similarities to war, 373
    sociological explanations, 380–381
    state-sponsored, 374
    stopping, 377
    in the twenty-first century, 381–382
    in the United States, 374–377
Tertiary sector production, 275
THC (tetrahydrocannabinol), 158
Theory, 7
Theory of limited effects, 309
Theory of racial formation, 49–50
Think tanks, 398t, 399
Tobacco, 148, 154–155, 170
    cardiovascular problems, 154
    college students and, 151f

PHOTO CREDITS